ROUTLEDGE HANDBOOK OF LAW AND THE COVID-19 PANDEMIC

The COVID-19 pandemic not only ravaged human bodies but also had profound and possibly enduring effects on the health of political and legal systems, economies and societies. Almost overnight, governments imposed the severest restrictions in modern times on rights and freedoms, elections, parliaments and courts. Legal and political institutions struggled to adapt, creating a catalyst for democratic decline and catastrophic increases in poverty and inequality.

This handbook analyses the global pandemic response through five themes: governance and democracy; human rights; the rule of law; science, public trust and decision making; and states of emergency and exception. Containing 12 thematic commentaries and 25 chapters on countries of diverse size, wealth and experience of COVID-19, it represents the combined effort of more than 50 contributors, including leading scholars and rising voices in the fields of constitutional, international, public health, human rights and comparative law, as well as political science, and science and technology studies.

Taking stock after the onset of global emergency, this book provides essential analysis for politicians, policy-makers, jurists, civil society organisations, academics, students and practitioners at both national and international level on the best, and most concerning, practices adopted in response to COVID-19 – and key insights into how states and multilateral institutions should reform, adapt and prepare for future emergencies.

Joelle Grogan is Senior Lecturer in Law, School of Law, Middlesex University, London, UK, and Research Fellow, CEU Democracy Institute, Budapest, Hungary.

Alice Donald is Associate Professor of Human Rights Law, School of Law, Middlesex University, London, UK.

"This book provides an exceptional comparative account of how institutions of constitutional democracies can either act as bulwarks or be threatened in emergency times. The COVID-19 pandemic will leave an enduring mark on the world's constitutional history and this volume provides intriguing critical readings of the facts and governmental responses related to it."

Judge Luís Roberto Barroso*, Justice of the Supreme Federal Court of Brazil*

"This excellent collection of essays both addresses and transcends the legal issues raised by responses to the pandemic, both within particular countries and globally. The health care crisis pushed other concerns to the margins of our political radar and the legal mechanisms adopted have not received the attention that trends in response to 9/11 did. Since the pandemic affected the exercise of political and legal power in ways that may have long term consequences for democracy, populism, authoritarianism and the role of scientific knowledge in our policy decisions, this book is an invaluable interdisciplinary resource."

David Dyzenhaus*, University Professor of Law and Philosophy and Albert Abel Chair, University of Toronto*

"Grogan and Donald's edited volume makes a spectacular contribution to ongoing discussions regarding COVID-19 and the law. Contributions from leading thinkers provide fresh theoretical insights and empirical observations regarding the pandemic's impacts on who exercises power and how, which should be read by everyone concerned with the rule of law in a post-COVID-19 future."

Alicia Ely Yamin*, Senior Fellow on Global Health and Rights, Petrie-Flom Center for Health Law Policy, Biotechnology and Bioethics, Harvard Law School*

ROUTLEDGE HANDBOOK OF LAW AND THE COVID-19 PANDEMIC

Edited by Joelle Grogan and Alice Donald

Routledge
Taylor & Francis Group
LONDON AND NEW YORK

Cover image: Joelle Grogan

First published 2022
by Routledge
2 Park Square, Milton Park, Abingdon, Oxon OX14 4RN

and by Routledge
605 Third Avenue, New York, NY 10158

Routledge is an imprint of the Taylor & Francis Group, an informa business

British Library Cataloguing-in-Publication Data
A catalogue record for this book is available from the British Library

Library of Congress Cataloging-in-Publication Data
Names: Grogan, Joelle, 1988- editor. | Donald, Alice, editor.
Title: Routledge handbook of law and the COVID-19 pandemic / edited by Joelle Grogan and Alice Donald.
Description: Abingdon, Oxon ; New York, NY : Routledge, 2022. | Series: Routledge handbooks in law | Includes bibliographical references and index. |
Identifiers: LCCN 2021056224 | ISBN 9781032078854 (hardback) | ISBN 9781032078878 (paperback) | ISBN 9781003211952 (ebook)
Subjects: LCSH: COVID-19 (Disease)--Law and legislation.
Classification: LCC K3575.C68 R68 2022 | DDC 344.04/362414--dc23/eng/20220202
LC record available at https://lccn.loc.gov/2021056224

ISBN: 978-1-032-07885-4 (hbk)
ISBN: 978-1-032-07887-8 (pbk)
ISBN: 978-1-003-21195-2 (ebk)

DOI: 10.4324/9781003211952

Typeset in Bembo
by Deanta Global Publishing Services, Chennai, India

To the researchers throughout the world, working in pandemic isolation but in global community for the betterment of our collective future.

CONTENTS

CONTRIBUTORS

Rasha Al Saba is Head of the Middle East and North Africa Department, Minority Rights Group International, London, UK.

Maria Ela L Atienza is Professor of Political Science, University of the Philippines Diliman, Quezon City, Philippines.

Ratna Rueban Balasubramaniam is Associate Professor of Law and Legal Studies, Carleton University, Ottawa, Canada.

Marie-Laure Basilien-Gainche is Professor of Law and a member of the International, European and Comparative Law Research Center, University Jean Moulin Lyon 3, France.

Julinda Beqiraj is Maurice Wohl Senior Research Fellow in European Law, Bingham Centre for the Rule of Law, British Institute of International and Comparative Law, London, UK.

Denis Bikesha is Dean, School of Law, University of Rwanda, Kigali, Rwanda.

Thomas Bustamante is Professor of Jurisprudence, Federal University of Minas Gerais, Brazil.

Başak Çalı is Co-Director, Centre for Fundamental Rights, and Professor of International Law, Hertie School, Berlin, Germany.

Iain Cameron is Professor in Public International Law, Uppsala University, Sweden.

Wen-Chen Chang is Professor at National Taiwan University College of Law and Joint Appointment Professor of National Yang Ming Chiao Tung University School of Law, Taipei, Taiwan.

Shirin Chua is Research Associate, Centre for Asian Legal Studies, National University of Singapore, Singapore.

Anna Jonsson Cornell is Professor in Comparative Constitutional Law, Uppsala University, Sweden.

Stéphanie Dagron is Professor of Law, Faculty of Law, Faculty of Medicine and Global Studies Institute, University of Geneva, Switzerland.

Tom Gerald Daly is Deputy Director, School of Government, University of Melbourne, and Director, COVID-DEM Pandemic & Global Democracy Tracker database (www.covid-dem-tracker.org) Australia.

Marzieh Tofighi Darian is SJD candidate (Doctor of Juridical Science), Harvard Law School, Cambridge, Massachusetts, US.

Jacques deLisle is Stephen A Cozen Professor of Law and Professor of Political Science and Director, Center for the Study of Contemporary China, University of Pennsylvania, US.

Alice Donald is Associate Professor of Human Rights Law, School of Law, Middlesex University, London, UK.

Ahmed Ellaboudy is Fellow, Rule of Law for Development Program, Loyola University Chicago, Rome, Italy.

Cassandra Emmons is Postdoctoral Fellow, Research Cluster on Regions in a Multipolar World, Weatherhead Center for International Affairs, Harvard University, Cambridge, Massachusetts, US

Julián Gaviria-Mira is Assistant Professor, School of Law of Universidad EAFIT, Medellín, Colombia.

Samrawit Gougsa is Head of Communications, Minority Rights Group International, London, UK.

Mark A Graber is Regents Professor of Law, Carey School of Law, University of Maryland, Baltimore, US.

Hans Petter Graver is Professor, Institute of Private Law, University of Oslo, Norway.

Chiara Graziani is Postdoctoral Researcher in Comparative Public Law, University of Milan-Bicocca, Italy, and Academic Fellow, Bocconi University, Milan, Italy.

Joelle Grogan is Senior Lecturer in Law, School of Law, Middlesex University, London, UK, and Research Fellow, CEU Democracy Institute, Budapest, Hungary.

Stephen Hilgartner is Professor of Science and Technology Studies, Cornell University, Ithaca, New York, US.

Esteban Hoyos-Ceballos is Dean of the School of Law of Universidad EAFIT, Medellín, Colombia.

Tara Imalingat is an advocate and human rights lawyer, Kenya Legal and Ethical Issues Network on HIV and AIDS (KELIN), Nairobi, Kenya.

Sheila Jasanoff is Pforzheimer Professor of Science and Technology Studies, John F Kennedy School of Government, Harvard University, Cambridge, Massachusetts, US.

Dean R Knight is Associate Professor, Faculty of Law and New Zealand Centre for Public Law, Victoria University of Wellington, New Zealand.

Kriszta Kovács is Marie Skłodowska-Curie Fellow, WZB Center for Global Constitutionalism, Berlin, Germany, and Associate Professor, ELTE University Faculty of Social Sciences.

Melodie Labuschaigne is Professor in Medical Law and Ethics, Department of Jurisprudence, School of Law, University of South Africa, Pretoria, South Africa.

Philip Leach is Professor of Human Rights Law and Director of the European Human Rights Advocacy Centre (EHRAC), Middlesex University, London, UK.

Rawin Leelapatana is Lecturer, Faculty of Law, Chulalongkorn University, Bangkok, Thailand.

Chun-Yuan Lin is Associate Professor of Chung Yuan Christian University School of Law, Department of Financial and Economic Law, Taoyuan City, Taiwan.

Allan Maleche is an advocate and human rights lawyer, Kenya Legal and Ethical Issues Network on HIV and AIDS (KELIN), Nairobi, Kenya.

Anna Katharina Mangold is Professor of European Law, Europa-Universität Flensburg, Germany.

Emílio Peluso Neder Meyer is Professor of Constitutional Law, Federal University of Minas Gerais, Brazil.

Allan T Moore is Senior Lecturer in Criminology, University of West London, UK.

Jaclyn L Neo is Associate Professor of Law and Director of the Centre for Asian Legal Studies, National University of Singapore, Singapore.

Michael O'Flaherty is Director, the Fundamental Rights Agency of the European Union.

Thulasi K Raj is a lawyer of the Indian Supreme Court and Equality Fellow, Centre for Law and Policy Research, Bangalore, India.

Marco Rizzi is Senior Lecturer, University of Western Australia Law School, Perth, Australia.

Martin Scheinin is British Academy Global Professor, University of Oxford, UK, and a part-time professor, European University Institute, Florence, Italy.

Shen Kui is Professor at Law and Executive Director of Center for Constitutional and Administrative Law, Peking University, China.

Jerome Amir Singh is Director, Scientific Advisory Group on Emergencies (SAGE), Academy of Science of South Africa (ASSAf), South Africa; Adjunct Professor of Clinical Public Health, Dalla Lana School of Public Health, University of Toronto, Canada; and Honorary Research Fellow, Howard College School of Law, University of KwaZulu-Natal, Durban, South Africa.

Ciara Staunton is Senior Researcher, Institute for Biomedicine, Eurac Research, Italy (and a former Senior Lecturer, Middlesex University, London, UK).

Shaheera Syed is Programme Officer, Democracy Reporting International, Islamabad, Pakistan.

Nadia Tariq-Ali is Senior Programme Officer, Democracy Reporting International, Islamabad, Pakistan.

Khemthong Tonsakulrungruang is Lecturer, Chulalongkorn University, Bangkok, Thailand.

Tamara Tulich is Associate Professor, University of Western Australia Law School, Perth, Australia.

Emre Turkut is Postdoctoral Researcher, Centre for Fundamental Rights, Hertie School, Berlin, Germany.

Arianna Vedaschi is Full Professor of Comparative Public Law, Bocconi University, Milan, Italy.

Nerima Were is an advocate and human rights lawyer, Kenya Legal and Ethical Issues Network on HIV and AIDS (KELIN) and University of Nairobi, Kenya.

FOREWORD

The COVID-19 pandemic has critically challenged the capacities of political, legal, health and social systems to respond to emergency situations. The pandemic dramatically exposed and heightened deeply embedded social and economic inequalities. Its impact on commitment to human rights has been extensive, with some states using the contagion as a pretext for severe incursions into rights and freedoms. Economic dislocation has overwhelmed already weak social welfare systems.

The crisis has profoundly changed assumptions about the functions of national and multilateral institutions, governance during emergency, and the role of the law. It is within this context that editors Joelle Grogan and Alice Donald have presented this handbook on *Law and the COVID-19 Pandemic.*

The volume brings together researchers from across the world to examine the impact of the pandemic on national and global governance systems, bringing forward important questions relating to the protection of human rights, the meaning of democracy in crisis and how to uphold the value of the rule of law. The 25 states examined range from high- to low-income countries, have divergent experiences of previous emergencies, and sit at various points on the political spectrum. Taken together, and supplemented by 12 illuminating thematic commentaries, the volume offers important insights into the diversity of experience in how governments, parliaments, courts and civil society have acted, or failed to act, in the face of this unprecedented crisis. The value of the volume lies not only in the rich accounts of experience at national and local level within, but also in elucidating transversal themes and common promising and bad practice. We learn, for example, that states everywhere have been equally vulnerable to the virus in terms of both health and institutional outcomes, and that building public trust and tackling disinformation are of cardinal importance in combatting disease.

The editors and the 51 other contributors bring to their accounts of the crisis the perspective of scholars, lawyers and practitioners. Their collective insights offer a compelling record of the first 18 months of the COVID-19 pandemic, and a guide to action for ensuring that democratic values, human rights and the rule of law are among the building blocks of recovery.

As the world emerges unevenly and uncertainly from the COVID-19 pandemic, it is to be hoped that this volume finds a wide audience among politicians, policy-makers, jurists, civil society organisations, academics, students and practitioners at national, regional and international levels.

Professor Michael O'Flaherty
Director, the Fundamental Rights Agency of the European Union (writing in a personal capacity)
September 2021

PREFACE

As we write in the second summer of the COVID-19 pandemic, the scale of human suffering continues to be revealed in statistics that defy imagination: a cumulative total of more than 220,000,000 confirmed cases worldwide and over 4,575,000 confirmed deaths.[1,2] As this book goes to press, while some states are loosening restrictions and daring to talk of life "after the pandemic", others are reeling from new waves of infection and (re)imposing some of the severest restrictions on rights and freedoms in modern times. Vaccination offers the surest route out of the contagion, yet immunisation rates globally remain grossly unequal: the head of the World Health Organisation lamented in May 2021 that 75% of all vaccines had been administered in just ten countries,[3] and to date, less than 3% of people in low-income states have received at least one dose, compared to almost 60% in high-income states.[4]

The virus has not only ravaged human bodies but has also had profound and potentially enduring effects on political and legal systems, economies and societies. Governing under extended de facto or de jure emergency regimes, executives have commonly operated relatively free of legislative or judicial oversight. Lockdowns, curfews, closure of educational institutions and businesses, suspension of parliaments and courts, restrictions on seeing loved ones or gathering for the purposes of worship, commemoration or protest: most of the world's popu-

1 All websites accessed on 7 September 2021.

2 World Health Organisation Coronavirus (COVID-19) Dashboard <https://covid19.who.int>.

3 World Health Organisation, 'Director-General's Opening Remarks at the World Health Assembly – 24 May 2021' <https://www.who.int/director-general/speeches/detail/director-general-s-opening-remarks-at-the-world-health-assembly---24-may-2021>.

4 United Nations Development Programme, COVID-19 Data Futures Platform, Global Dashboard for Vaccine Equity <https://data.undp.org/vaccine-equity/>.

lation have experienced some or all of these measures, sometimes for extended or indefinite periods. Remarkable sums have been spent on emergency social welfare support, but not enough (or in the right ways) to prevent catastrophic increases in poverty and inequality. This burden has fallen heaviest on the lives and livelihoods of those already living precariously or facing exclusion and discrimination.

This volume shines a light on the impact of COVID-19 on governance and democracy, human rights and the rule of law. It represents the combined effort of 53 individual contributors across the world, including leading scholars and practitioners and rising voices in the fields of constitutional, international, public health, human rights and comparative law, as well as political science, and science and technology studies. Our aim was to provide authoritative analysis on the best, and most concerning, practices adopted in response to COVID-19. The result is a volume that conveys the urgency and fast-moving nature of the pandemic and its repercussions for law and governance, while also reflecting ahead on how states and multilateral institutions should reform, adapt and prepare for future emergencies.

The book is organised into five parts covering transversal themes: governance and democracy; human rights; the rule of law; science, public trust and decision-making; and states of emergency and exception. Each part begins with an overview signposting the themes and countries it covers. Altogether, the book analyses 25 countries: Australia, Brazil, China, Colombia, Egypt, Finland, France, Germany, Hungary, India, Iran, Kenya, Malaysia, New Zealand, Pakistan, the Philippines, Rwanda, Singapore, South Africa, Sweden, Taiwan, Thailand, Turkey, the United Kingdom and the United States. These states were selected for the diversity they represent in terms of geography, population size and density, income levels, forms of governance, legal traditions, experience (or not) of previous pandemics and COVID-19 infection and mortality rates. Framing and contextualising the country analyses are 12 thematic commentaries, which explore, inter alia, the impact of the pandemic on the state of global democracy, human rights and the rule of law; the geopolitics of vaccine manufacture, distribution and access; the changing roles of science and data in decision-making; the significance of public trust; the (mis)use of emergency powers; and the protection of minorities and marginalised populations.

Recognising the urgency of the project and the need for informed and expert analysis to counter destructive narratives, our contributors, and we as editors, have worked at speed to produce chapters in weeks rather than the months or years normally reserved for academic publishing; the book will have taken just over one year from inception to publication. We are immensely grateful to the authors for their patience with our unusually punishing schedule and for the exceptional quality of their analysis, made more remarkable by the fact that they were, in effect, analysing a 'moving target' of such magnitude and import, while themselves living with the pressures and anxieties of the pandemic.

A head start was provided by the fact that the majority of chapters are based on analysis from two online symposia convened by Joelle Grogan: in April–May

2020, the 'COVID-19 and States of Emergency' symposium,[5] and a year later, one of similar breadth and ambition entitled 'Power and the COVID-19 Pandemic'.[6] These were hosted by the great team at the *Verfassungsblog* led by Max Steinbeis, with editing by Sinthiou Buszewski, Evin Dalkilic and Eva Neumann, and supported by the Horizon-2020 RECONNECT project and Democracy Reporting International under the re:constitution program supported by Stiftung Mercator. In these online series, over 100 contributors drawn from academia, civil society, NGOs, the judiciary and legal practice from more than 65 countries reflected on how their legal and political systems had adapted to the pandemic, analysing the legal measures and use of powers which has exerted such profound impact on the majority of the world's population.

While across the world, people were isolated and locked down, it is a testament to the generosity and adaptability of the global academic and research community that such collaboration was possible. Such a wide range of representation could not have been achieved without the invisible support of a network of academics, NGOs, human rights advocates, judges and legal professionals who reached out to become involved with the symposia and/or this volume, or connected us with in-country experts. We express our deepest gratitude to this global community.

The life of editors can be made exponentially easier with good research assistance, and for us it was a joy to work with Felicitas Benziger and Maaike de Ridder. If it is appropriate to put a reference in a preface, then we would warmly encourage you to offer them a research position.

Warm thanks are due to Alison Kirk at Routledge for her enthusiastic support for the book from the start, and her wise and patient advice throughout. We are also grateful to Emmy Summers and Anna Gallagher at Routledge, and Stephanie Derbyshire at Deanta Global, for their assistance with the production of the book.

Joelle and Alice would each like to put on record that it has been a delight and privilege to work with each other, especially when the final weeks of manuscript preparation permitted a long-awaited reunion at our office in Middlesex University, our collegiate and much-missed academic home.

We are grateful to our families, friends and colleagues who have supported us throughout the pandemic and during the intense weeks of manuscript preparation – some at close quarters and some, sadly but unavoidably, from a distance.

Joelle would like to thank her husband Tom Oliver for his humour, support and provision of countless cups of decaffeinated drinks, as well as her parents Bernadette Buckley and Al Grogan who, while long-separated by the borders of pandemic restrictions, nevertheless provided a boundless source of encouragement and love.

5 'COVID-19 and States of Emergency' symposium <https://verfassungsblog.de/introduction-list-of-country-reports/>.

6 'Power and the COVID-19 Pandemic' symposium <https://verfassungsblog.de/power-and-the-covid-19-pandemic/>.

Alice would like to thank her partner David Salisbury Jones, her children Nathan and Ruby Rogers, her parents Trevor and Diana Donald, and her brother and sister-in-law, Paul Donald and Fiona Roberts, for their love and support.

We leave the last word to welcome Joelle's son, Seán, whose own arrival coincided with the delivery of this book.

Joelle Grogan and Alice Donald
London, September 2021

PART I

Governance and Democracy

Overview

Democracy was in global retreat even before COVID-19, and the pandemic shrunk and fractured the global map of democracies still further. The burgeoning of authoritarian governance, actively hollowing out liberal-democratic institutions and eschewing expertise, was turbo-charged by the pandemic, as many governments seized the chance to evade the scrutiny of legislatures, courts, independent media and popular mobilisation. Yet the rollback of democracy and good governance has not been relentless, as Part I of this volume attests. The two thematic commentaries, and five chapters analysing New Zealand, China, the United Kingdom, the United States and Singapore, identify grounds to despair, certainly, but also opportunities for a rejuvenation of democratic governance.

In the first commentary, Tom Gerald Daly offers an ambitious global appraisal of institutional and geo-political responses to the pandemic. He detects no single fault-line between supposedly efficient autocracies and democracies hampered from taking decisive action by the need to respect constitutional norms. Nor is there a sharp distinction between the success of the pandemic response in countries in the Global South or Global North, or in younger and older democracies. Rather, Daly detects multiple fault-lines based on states' capacity, the presence or absence of effective and rational governance, and levels of public trust in authority. If the pandemic was a 'tipping point' towards autocracy and 'anti-truth' politics, Daly nevertheless sees grounds for optimism. He points to electoral innovation, hybrid parliaments and an explosion of grassroots activism as providing opportunities to rethink, regenerate and reclaim democracy, both at the national level and in geopolitical alliances and institutions.

Jerome Amir Singh maintains the focus on global governance in his commentary on COVID-19 vaccine manufacture, procurement, disbursement, access and uptake. He identifies four structural factors that vitiate individual autonomy

DOI: 10.4324/9781003211952-1

to access vaccines at the grassroots level: geopolitics; corporate self-interest and sovereign fiscal constraints; sovereignty and governance; and protectionism and nationalism. As long as vaccines remain an "intellectual property battleground" and "geopolitical currency", Singh argues, states will continue to flout their obligation to guarantee the right to the highest attainable standard of health.

In the first country-based analysis, Dean R Knight charts **New Zealand**'s success at stamping out transmission of COVID-19 through hard and swift lockdowns, border control and other public health measures, while simultaneously forestalling economic dislocation and preserving – and even enhancing – democratic accountability. Knight proffers a 'relational' or 'dialogic' conception of accountability. This seeks to understand how the government publicly accounted for its aggressive elimination strategy and use of emergency powers, and how it was "interrogated" by Parliament, the courts, the media and civil society. Knight concludes that the executive's use of power was subject to meaningful checks, and documents how lessons were learned and applied from this virtuous cycle of dialogue.

China's response to the exceptional challenge of COVID-19 was, unsurprisingly, devoid of such democratic constraints, and, indeed, was not 'exceptional' in the sense that it reflected endemic features of Chinese law and governance. Jacques deLisle and Shen Kui venture that the initial, fatally delayed and dysfunctional response to the pandemic exposed the conflicting and ambiguous allocations of authority and accountability along fragmented functional (vertical) and geographic (horizontal) lines within China's vast and multi-layered governance system, resulting in decisions made in bureaucratic 'silos'. Later in the pandemic, the centralised state mustered its formidable capacity to mobilise resources and shape and constrain citizens' behaviour, creating a narrative of 'success' that looks set to stifle any calls for transformative reform to prevent or prepare for future pandemics.

Although on a less monumental scale, fragmentation was also a feature of the **United Kingdom**'s response to the pandemic, not only in the early stages but throughout. Joelle Grogan analyses how COVID-19 exposed fractures in the constitutional settlement of power between government, Parliament and the devolved legislatures. Largely unchecked executive dominance; stop-gap and U-turn policy-making; severe and not always rationally and transparently justified restrictions; and blurred distinctions between law, guidance and advice were all lamentable features of the UK's response. They amounted to an *absence* of governance – and the "(un) governed" UK as a consequence experienced one of the highest per capita mortality rates in Western Europe.

The fatal repercussions of executive action – and inaction – were starkly evident, too, in the **United States** under President Trump. Mark A Graber characterises Trump as uninterested in science – or in governing. The populist attack on evidence-based politics and constitutional democracy in the US resulted in a policy too often based on ideology, partisanship and wishful or fantastical thinking rather than on scientific consensus. Institutions that might have blunted the populist challenge had been captured before the pandemic or were captured during it, notably the Supreme Court. The election of President Biden restored rationality and kickstarted vaccine distribution. But, Graber argues, the health of America's body politic remains in peril from partisan battles over voting rights, among other issues.

The resilience of **Singapore**'s political and legal institutions was tested during the pandemic, especially as it held elections in July 2020. Shirin Chua and Jaclyn L Neo suggest that Singapore escaped the global trend towards democratic regression, as the government rejected the path of unchecked emergency powers and the pandemic presented opportunities for democratic consolidation. These took the form of greater institutionalisation of opposition politics; the deepening of a "shared epistemic articulation" of constitutional democratic workings; and stronger civil society engagement with the state. Chua and Neo urge vigilance, however: democratic gains may be fragile and Singapore's low-wage migrant workforce continues to live precariously and under disproportionate restrictions. If the pandemic is to catalyse true democratic renewal, they argue, the most marginalised must share the fruits and everyone must "[interrogate] what it means to live together and what we owe to one another".

1

THE PANDEMIC AND THE FUTURE OF GLOBAL DEMOCRACY

Tom Gerald Daly

1. Introduction[1]

If global democracy were a patient, it was already ailing when the United Nations declared a global health emergency in January 2020. Democracy assessment organisations had been registering a 15-year trend of declines in the quality and persistence of liberal democracy worldwide; defined here as a political system comprising at minimum elections, core democratic rights and meaningful constraints on government.[2] Democracies were struggling to address the diffuse but intensifying challenges of hyper-polarisation, political fragmentation, yawning economic inequality, disengaged and distrustful electorates, a distorted and fractured information landscape hollowing out the shared epistemic basis and trust fundamental to democratic society, and most acutely, the proliferation of neo-authoritarian governments actively dismantling liberal-democratic systems or at least challenging their liberal components; especially counter-majoritarian constraints such as independent courts.[3] They were also facing a re-shaped geo-political environment with the rapid rise of China as an authoritarian superpower, and the increasing employment of 'sharp power' against liberal democracies by illiberal governments.[4] That

1 All websites accessed on 24 June 2021.

2 See e.g. V-Dem Institute, *Democracy Report 2021: Autocratization Turns Viral* (10 March 2021); and Freedom House, *Freedom in the World 2021: Democracy under Siege* (3 March 2021).

3 See Tom Gerald Daly, 'Democratic Decay: Conceptualising an Emerging Research Field' (2019) 11(1) Hague Journal on the Rule of Law 9.

4 Larry Diamond, *Ill Winds: Saving Democracy from Russian Rage, Chinese Ambition, and American Complacency* (Penguin Press 2019).

DOI: 10.4324/9781003211952-2

said, counter-trends of democratic innovation and reinvention were also gathering momentum, epitomised by the spread of citizens' assemblies.[5]

The pandemic's impact on global democracy might now be viewed as a burgeoning cross-disciplinary sub-field of its own.[6] This chapter, drawing on contributions to the *Verfassungsblog* symposia in 2020 and 2021,[7] seeks to reflect on the future of global democracy and capture key trends and developments in institutional and geo-political responses through three questions: has COVID-19 helped to rehabilitate liberal democracy's reputation as a political system by revealing effectiveness in crisis? Has the pandemic crystallised a dramatic redrawing of the democratic atlas? Does the hardening of global tensions between China and competitor states during the crisis risk an unhelpful reframing of global democracy as merely an 'anti-China club'?

Section 2 outlines the immediate impact of governmental crisis responses from January to May 2020. Section 3 assesses government responses and the broader democratic impact from the longer view of 2021. Section 4 identifies key positive trends, while section 5 addresses the risk of seeing the 'free world' as merely a counter to authoritarian Chinese power. The driving argument is that while negative trends are dominant, positive trends and developments offer many reasons for hope.

2. Immediate Impact: January–May 2020

From the outset, unlike undemocratic states like China or the UAE, which have a freer hand to suppress the virus by any means necessary, democratic states were faced with the twin challenges of addressing the virus effectively and remaining compliant with the democratic constitutional framework and *desiderata*, including respect for the rule of law.

The global pandemic evidently had an immediate and dramatic impact on democratic systems and practices worldwide. An unprecedented number of states – by April 2020 over half of the world – simultaneously declared a state of emer-

5 See Stephen Elstub and Oliver Escobar, 'Defining and Typologising Democratic Innovations' in Stephen Elstub and Oliver Escobar (eds), *Handbook of Democratic Innovation and Governance* (Edward Elgar 2019).

6 See, for instance, the over 3,000 items curated on COVID-DEM (www.covid-dem-tracker.org), including a range of books, e.g. Miguel Poiares Maduro and Paul W Kahn (eds), *Democracy in Times of Pandemic: Different Futures Imagined* (Cambridge University Press 2020); David Seedhouse, *The Case for Democracy in the COVID-19 Pandemic* (SAGE Publications 2020); Stefan Kirchner (ed), *Governing the Crisis: Law, Human Rights and COVID-19* (Lit Verlag 2021); Linda Hantrais and Marie-Thérèse Letablier, *Comparing and Contrasting the Impact of the COVID-19 Pandemic in the European Union* (Taylor & Francis 2020); and Matteo Bonotti, *Recovering Civility during Covid-19* (Springer 2021).

7 Tom Gerald Daly, 'Democracy and the Global Emergency – Shared Experiences, Starkly Uneven Impacts' (*Verfassungsblog*, 15 May 2020) <https://verfassungsblog.de/democracy-and-the-global-emergency-shared-experiences-starkly-uneven-impacts/>; and 'Democracy and the Global Pandemic' (*Verfassungsblog*, 1 May 2021) <https://verfassungsblog.de/democracy-and-the-global-pandemic/>.

gency (e.g. Australia,[8] France[9] and Mexico) or introduced emergency measures without a formal emergency declaration (e.g. Ireland, Japan and Poland).[10] Over 50 states postponed elections, often with little certainty as to when and how they would be held.[11] Concerns about global 'pandemic backsliding' were voiced but not yet fully substantiated.[12]

As we were still in the throes of COVID-19's first impact, authoritarian states and their cheerleaders were crowing about their superior virus responses and denigrating democracies as decadent failures.[13] Yet, far from being a monolithic category, democracies – the healthy, ailing and critically ill – were adopting divergent responses. Country reports in the 2020 *Verfassungsblog* symposium revealed clear commonalities. Governments assumed sweeping powers and citizens had to submit to rights restrictions, 'stay at home' orders, expanded police powers and surveillance apps, often without anything close to an acceptable level of democratic scrutiny as parliaments and the media were hobbled by the lockdown.[14] In April 2020, it was estimated that suspensions or restrictions of parliament across just 18 countries affected some two billion people.[15]

Yet beyond these commonalities, by May 2020 it was clear that the effect of the COVID-19 response on the democratic system was starkly uneven across democracies worldwide, due to the different democratic 'starting point' of each state as the pandemic hit. Four broad categories of government response can be discerned:

Effective Rationalists: Some democratic governments effectively addressed the pandemic through rational fact-based policy, acted within the constraints of the law, and placed clear limitations on emergency actions to preserve maximal democratic functioning. In New Zealand, for instance, parliamentary committees continued and an Epidemic Response committee was established to scrutinise government action.[16] South Korea flattened the curve primarily

8 See Rizzi and Tulich, chapter 37.

9 See Basilien-Gainche, chapter 35.

10 Joelle Grogan, 'States of Emergency: Analysing Global Use of Emergency Powers in Response to COVID-19' (2020) 4 European Journal of Law Reform 338, 342.

11 See International Institute for Democracy and Electoral Assistance (IDEA), 'Global Overview of COVID-19: Impact on Elections' (last updated: 1 June 2021) <https://www.idea.int/news-media/multimedia-reports/global-overview-covid-19-impact-elections>.

12 See e.g. the initial report: V-Dem Institute Pandemic Backsliding project, *Pandemic Backsliding: Does Covid-19 Put Democracy at Risk?* (4 May 2020) <https://www.v-dem.net/media/filer_public/52/eb/52eb913a-b1ad-4e55-9b4b-3710ff70d1bf/pb_23.pdf>.

13 Edward Lucas, Jake Morris and Corina Rebegea, *Information Bedlam: Russian and Chinese Information Operations During Covid-19* (Center for European Policy Analysis, 15 March 2021).

14 See Ittai Bar-Siman-Tov, 'Covid-19 Meets Politics: the Novel Coronavirus as a Novel Challenge for Legislatures' (2020) 8(1–2) The Theory and Practice of Legislation 11; and International Press Institute, 'WPFD 2020: COVID-19 Accelerating a Global Decline in Media Freedom' (1 May 2020).

15 Ittai Bar-Siman-Tov (n 14) 12.

16 Dean Knight, 'Lockdown Bubbles through Layers of Law, Discretion and Nudges – New Zealand' (*Verfassungsblog*, 7 April 2020) <https://verfassungsblog.de/covid-19-in-new-zealand

through contact tracing and successfully held national elections on 15 April – the first country to do so.[17] These states benefited from their starting position of high-quality democratic governance, high state capacity and the economic ability to assist individuals negatively affected by emergency measures.

Constrained Rationalists: Other governments also adopted a broadly rational and law-abiding approach but were in a starkly different position due to limited state capacity. In May 2020 Staunton and Labuschaigne offered that South Africa was facing a 'state of disaster' due to emergency measures preventing access to food, water and even basic hygiene.[18] The state was also less equipped to address the economic fall-out of the lockdown, with uncertain implications for its fragile young democracy.

Autocratic Opportunists: In the third camp, in states where clear trends of democratic decay had been proceeding apace for years, governments seemingly recognised the reality of the threat but pounced on the crisis to further consolidate and expand their power. Hungary is the poster child, with the parliament acting quickly to empower the prime minister to rule by decree, setting no time-limit for the emergency, and arming the government with a law criminalising "publication of false or distorted facts".[19]

Fantasists: The final category includes governments whose immediate response was impeded and distorted by partial or full denial of the facts presented by experts, and engagement in conspiracy theories (e.g. that the pandemic was a Chinese bio-weapon).[20] The Trump administration's 'pandemic denial' rapidly turned the US into a global outbreak hotspot, encouraged inaction at federal and state levels – an odd case of 'executive underreach' – and endlessly undermined any concerted action taken.[21] Similarly, as Meyer and Bustamante assert, Brazil's President Bolsonaro persistently refused to act on the basis that "politics comes before truth".[22] Both are extreme examples of what Sophia Rosenfeld calls "antitruth governance", based on "indifference to the bound-

-lockdown-bubbles-through-layers-of-law-discretion-and-nudges/>. For general discussion, see Knight, chapter 3.

17 Antonio Spinelli, 'Managing Elections under the COVID-19 Pandemic: The Republic of Korea's Crucial Test' (2020) International IDEA Technical Paper 2/2020 <https://www.idea.int/publications/catalogue/managing-elections-under-covid-19-pandemic-republic-korea-crucial-test>.

18 Ciara Staunton and Melodie Labuschaigne, 'COVID-19 in South Africa: A Year in Review' (*Verfassungsblog*, 11 March 2021) <https://verfassungsblog.de/covid-19-in-south-africa-a-year-in-review/>. See also Labuschaigne and Staunton, chapter 28.

19 Kriszta Kovács, 'Hungary's Orbánistan: A Complete Arsenal of Emergency Powers' (*Verfassungsblog*, 6 April 2020) <https://verfassungsblog.de/hungarys-orbanistan-a-complete-arsenal-of-emergency-powers/>. See also Kovács, chapter 21.

20 Monica Stephens, 'A Geospatial Infodemic: Mapping Twitter Conspiracy Theories of COVID-19' (2020) 10(2) Dialogues in Human Geography 276.

21 See e.g. Kim Lane Scheppele and David Pozen, 'Executive Overreach and Underreach in the Pandemic' in Maduro and Kahn (eds), *Democracy in Times of Pandemic* (n 6).

22 Emilio Peluso Neder Meyer and Thomas Bustamante, 'Authoritarianism Without Emergency Powers: Brazil Under COVID-19' (*Verfassungsblog*, 8 April 2020) <https://verfassungsblog.de

aries between truth and falsehood" and an aversion to objective institutional expertise.[23]

In many states, the pandemic simply laid bare the true nature of the political system. Where commitment to good governance and the rule of law endures, it was reflected in the action taken. Where democratic government has not led to hoped-for prosperity and security, or has unwound previous economic and state supports, this was exposed in desolate detail. Where democratic rot had set in, COVID-19 rendered it more visible. In Poland, for instance, the presidential elections scheduled for 10 May 2020 were postponed in a highly unorthodox process: the announcement was made, not by the government or the election commission, but by the true power in the state, Jarosław Kaczyński (alongside his coalition partner Jarosław Gowin), leader of the ruling party and *eminence grise* but officially a mere backbencher in parliament.[24] This marked a damning confirmation of how democratic power has been wrenched from its constitutional locus since the Law and Justice (PiS) government won power in 2015 and is now exercised in an openly undemocratic manner.

3. The Longer View

By the time the second *Verfassungsblog* symposium was nearing its conclusion in May 2021 we had a much richer evidence base for assessing the pandemic's impact on democracy worldwide. Early indications that the pandemic appeared to reveal no single fault-line between supposedly efficient autocracies and sluggish democracies[25] is now supported by systematic analysis, including a COVID-19 Performance Index launched in January 2021, which finds: "No single political system has, at this point, stood out as being significantly or consistently more effective at managing the health crisis."[26] This might not amount to wholesale rehabilitation of liberal democracy as a political system but it at least seriously undermines autocracies' longstanding claims of inherently superior effectiveness. Nor is there a simple division between the Global South and Global North, or between younger and older democracies. Instead, we see multiple fault-lines based

/authoritarianism-without-emergency-powers-brazil-under-covid-19/>. See also Bustamante and Meyer, chapter 18.

23 Chapter 1, 'The Problem of Democratic Truth' in Sophia Rosenfeld, *Democracy and Truth: A Short History* (University of Pennsylvania Press 2018) 12.

24 Jan Cienski and Zosia Wanat, 'In Poland, Schrödinger's Election' (*Politico*, 5 August 2020) <https://www.politico.com/news/2020/05/08/in-poland-schrodingers-election-244482>.

25 See Rachel Kleinfeld, 'Do Authoritarian or Democratic Countries Handle Pandemics Better?' (Carnegie Endowment for International Peace, 31 March 2020) <https://carnegieendowment.org/2020/03/31/do-authoritarian-or-democratic-countries-handle-pandemics-better-pub-81404>.

26 Lowy Institute, Covid Performance Index <https://interactives.lowyinstitute.org/features/covid-performance>.

on state capacity, effective government, governance based on observable fact and citizen trust in government.

The pandemic does appear to have helped re-shape the democratic atlas and reshuffled democratic reputations. From October 2020 to March 2021, a slew of reports from leading democracy assessment bodies, presenting the first fuller assessments of COVID-19's impact, depict a shrinking democratic atlas that is more fragmented than it has been for decades after a steep decline in every world region. Using different criteria and datasets, the V-Dem Institute, Freedom House, Economist Intelligence Unit and International IDEA generally concur that the pandemic has "exacerbated the global decline in freedom",[27] although the V-Dem Institute suggests its "direct effects on global levels of liberal democracy were limited in 2020".[28]

Given widespread pre-existing democratic decay, even if the COVID-19 crisis only nudged states further down the wrong path it seems to have produced a global tipping point, epitomised by multiple reports de-listing India as a genuine democracy: it is now deemed an 'electoral autocracy' (V-Dem Institute) or 'partly free' (Freedom House).[29] V-Dem now ranks US democracy below its much younger Argentine and Mongolian counterparts.[30] Poland, once a star entrant to the EU's putative club of democracies, is billed as the world's "top 'autocratizing' state".[31] Some democracies, like Taiwan, have seen their reputations burnished – pipping Japan to Asia's top slot.[32] Immediate fears for further global decline centred on the 'ratchet' effect; the continuation or normalisation of emergency measures beyond the needs of the crisis.[33] Across political systems, the impact has been asymmetric: many democracies have shown resilience, with declines concentrated in hybrid and authoritarian states.[34]

In the democratic camp, taking the four broad categories in Part I, it is clear that no pandemic response was unproblematic. Effective rationalists like Australia were lauded for achieving 'COVID zero' and some return to normality. Critics of the political system's dysfunction were surprised by the capacity of a new intergovernmental body, the National Cabinet, to coordinate executives of different party colours across the federation, cutting through the hyper-partisan status quo to achieve consensus on nationwide action[35] – a blunt contrast to the chaotic tussles in the

27 Freedom House (n 2) 10.

28 V-Dem Institute (n 2) 13.

29 See V-Dem Institute (n 2) 20–21; and Freedom House (n 2) 26.

30 See country scores at <https://freedomhouse.org/countries/freedom-world/scores>.

31 V-Dem Institute (n 2) 19.

32 Grace Li, 'Taiwan Leapfrogs Japan and South Korea to Top Asia Democracy Table' (*Nikkei Asia*, 4 February 2021) <https://asia.nikkei.com/Politics/Taiwan-leapfrogs-Japan-and-South-Korea-to-top-Asia-democracy-table>.

33 Jan Petrov, 'The COVID-19 Emergency in the Age of Executive Aggrandizement: What Role for Legislative and Judicial Checks?' (2020) 8(1) The Theory and Practice of Legislation 71, 75.

34 International IDEA, *GSoD in Focus Special Brief: Taking Stock of Global Democratic Trends before and during the COVID-19 Pandemic* (December 2020).

35 See three policy briefs from the Melbourne School of Government: Tom Gerald Daly, *Prioritising Parliament: Roadmaps to Reviving Australia's Parliaments* (Governing During Crises Policy Brief

US throughout 2020 between federal and state governments over everything from the validity of state lockdowns to the purchase and retention of protective equipment.[36] Yet, democratic deficiencies in the pandemic response include the sidelining of parliaments across the federation due to a failure to explore alternative means for sitting (unlike, e.g., the UK and Canada, discussed below), excessive reliance on executive law-making with weak oversight, and insufficient transparency in the operation of new bodies such as National Cabinet and the National COVID-19 Commission.[37]

Constrained rationalists struggled. While South Africa's government cannot be labelled an 'autocratic opportunist', analysts suggest problematic tendencies toward stifling legitimate criticism of government policy and disabling oversight under the pressures of the highest number of cases in Africa.[38] Across both categories, pandemic responses often betrayed a wrong-headed view that command-and-control action through executive-led responses, rather than a broad-based institutional response, is the only viable way to address any crisis – especially a crisis of the scale and magnitude of this pandemic.

True autocratic opportunists continued to actively degrade the democratic system and disable accountability mechanisms during 2021 (e.g. in Bulgaria, Hungary and Indonesia). However, autocracy can just as easily produce drift and complacency. India, after initial success in its pandemic response, in April 2021 descended into a hell of record daily cases surpassing 350,000, collapsing health systems and a government reaction dominated by censoring criticism of its pandemic response.[39] This was not inevitable: the authoritarian turn and concentration of power in Prime Minister Modi's hands since 2014, combined with his domination of the policy-making process and distaste for dissent, meant that personal complacency produced government-wide complacency and a lack of preparation.[40]

Finally, fantasists took starkly divergent paths. In Brazil, President Bolsonaro's continuing denial of the crisis had led to over 470,000 deaths by June 2021.[41]

No.3, 1 August 2020) 3; Pritam Dey and Julian Murphy, *Accountable Lawmaking: Delegated Legislation & Parliamentary Oversight during the Pandemic* (Policy Brief No.9, 1 February 2021); and Cheryl Saunders, *A New Federalism: The Role and Future of the National Cabinet* (Policy Brief No.2, 2 July 2020).

36 See e.g. Scheppele and Pozen (n 21); and John Kincaid and J Wesley Leckrone, 'Federalism and the COVID-19 Crisis: Federalism and the COVID-19 Crisis in the United States of America' Forum of Federations (June 2020).

37 Marco Rizzi and Tamara Tulich, 'The Australian Response to COVID-19: A Year in Review' (*Verfassungsblog*, 22 February 2021) <https://verfassungsblog.de/the-australian-response-to-covid-19-a-year-in-review/>.

38 Staunton and Labuschaigne (n 18).

39 See Maximilian Beyer, Sangeeta Mahapatra and Matthias C Kettemann, 'Fighting Platforms and the People, not the Pandemic: #ResignModi and Disinformation Governance in India – an Update' (*Verfassungsblog*, 7 June 2021) <https://verfassungsblog.de/disinfo-censorship/>.

40 See Sanjay Ruparelia, '"Minimum Government, Maximum Governance": The Restructuring of Power in Modi's India' (2015) 38(4) South Asia: Journal of South Asian Studies 755.

41 WHO Coronavirus (COVID-19) Dashboard <https://covid19.who.int/>.

By contrast, the US abruptly changed tack once the Biden administration took office in January 2021, broadly landing in the effective rationalist camp, including meeting its target of 220 million vaccine doses administered in its first 100 days.[42] Without presenting the Biden administration as faultless, the US case reminds us just how much elections matter, political leadership matters, and effective, rational and responsive governance matter, although rehabilitation of US democracy's reputation remains a long-term challenge.

Democracies in all categories also faced an array of common challenges intensified by the pandemic. Far-right groups sought to grow their support by organising online marches and singling out minority communities in new ways; for instance, blaming Muslims for failing to comply with physical distancing. The mainstreaming of conspiracy theories accelerated in countries from the UK to the US during the crisis – including in Ireland, where the extreme right had made little political headway by European standards.[43] Governments worldwide, from Brazil to India, rushed to pass fake news laws or abuse existing laws (e.g. Singapore, Indonesia and Kenya), amplifying censorship of the opposition and media under the pretence of addressing pandemic misinformation.[44] More subtly, in Hungary the public broadcaster's news programme Híradó established an online "fake news monitor" on its website to ostensibly debunk false statements about the pandemic, but again the main targets were opposition politicians and articles critical of the government.[45]

At the geopolitical level, authoritarian governments expanded anti-democratic propaganda. In June 2020, a report from the European Commission concluded that Russia and China were the primary agents rolling out targeted disinformation campaigns "seeking to undermine democratic debate and exacerbate social polarisation, and improve their own image in the COVID-19 context".[46] The ascendant perception of an increasingly harsh international climate, and a hardening division between China and democratic states, was further fuelled by the Chinese government's frontal assault on Hong Kong's freedoms under cover of the pandemic,

42 'President Biden's First 100 Days as President Fact-Checked' (*BBC News*, 29 April 2021) <https://www.bbc.co.uk/news/56901183>.

43 See e.g. Seána Glennon, 'The Anti-Mask Movement and the Rise of the Right in Ireland: What Does It Mean for Our Democracy?' (*IACL-AIDC blog*, 7 January 2021) <https://blog-iacl-aidc.org/2021-posts/2021/1/12/the-anti-mask-movement-and-the-rise-of-the-right-in-ireland-what-does-it-mean-for-our-democracy>.

44 International Press Institute (IPI), 'Rush to Pass "Fake News" Laws during Covid-19 Intensifying Global Media Freedom Challenges' (22 October 2020) <https://ipi.media/rush-to-pass-fake-news-laws-during-covid-19-intensifying-global-media-freedom-challenges/>. For general discussion, see Chua and Neo, chapter 7; Imalingat Were and Malache, chapter 15.

45 Megan Cox, 'States of Emergency and Human Rights during a Pandemic: A Hungarian Case Study' (2020) 24(1) Human Rights Brief 32, 37–38.

46 European Commission, *Tackling COVID-19 Disinformation – Getting the Facts Right*, JOIN/2020/8 final (10 June 2020) <https://eur-lex.europa.eu/legal-content/EN/TXT/?uri=CELEX%3A52020JC0008>.

including a new national security law and measures to reshape its electoral and political system and effectively bar pro-democracy politicians from political contention.[47]

4. Positive Developments

That said, the pandemic also prompted impressive innovation and revealed resilience. Three examples are discussed here: electoral innovation, hybrid parliaments and grassroots activism.

Sweeping changes were made to the conduct of elections, with special voting arrangements such as early, postal and proxy voting becoming more common.[48] In South Korea, which was among the first countries to organise national parliamentary elections under pandemic conditions in April 2020, candidates made an unprecedented shift to the use of digital and online technology, primarily by sharing video messages on social media, using text messages and smartphone apps, and even embracing augmented reality technology in some cases – achieving the highest voter turnout since 1992 with 66% of eligible voters.[49] Globally, developments that have improved voter turnout and inclusiveness include a 60% increase in advance voting in New Zealand, drive-through voting in Czechia and the extension of absentee voting arrangements for specific groups to the entire public in US states such as Michigan.[50] The next question is whether and how these innovations will be retained or modified after the crisis ends, and whether some political forces will seek to reverse these reforms.

Hybrid parliaments present a further example of how government institutions have been transformed. Perhaps most striking is UK parliamentarians' willingness to re-think how the venerable Westminster Parliament operates. On 22 April 2020, the House of Commons made history when a new hybrid system mixing in-person and remote attendance was trialled for the first time. In mid-May the first votes were cast from across the country.[51] Observers reported interesting results, such as less booing and jeering during Prime Minister's Questions, greater focus on the substance of debates, MPs being able to spend more time in their constituencies and more contributions from female MPs.[52] This model was adopted in other states such as Canada and Australia. The organisers of citizens' assemblies, too,

47 See e.g. Tom Gerald Daly, *Elections During Crisis: Global Lessons from the Asia-Pacific* (Governing during Crises Policy Brief No.10, 17 March 2021) 7.

48 See Therese Pearce Laanela, 'Special Voting Arrangements: Between the Convenience of Voting and the Integrity of Elections' (International IDEA, 2 June 2021).

49 Daly (n 47) 5–6.

50 Laanela (n 48) 2.

51 Daly (n 35) 5.

52 Sarah Moulds, 'As the First "Remote" Sitting Starts in Canberra, Virtual Parliaments Should Be the New Norm, Not a COVID Bandaid' (*The Conversation*, 24 August 2020) <https://thecon-

learned how to make them work online, opening up greater possibilities for how these might operate in the future.[53]

Beyond formal state institutions, there has been an explosion of creativity at grassroots level. Activists managed to arrange visually striking physical protests compliant with social distancing regulations, including against the perceived assault on democracy in Israel.[54] In India, grassroots response to the 'silencing' of the federal Parliament included an online 'people's parliament' (Janta Parliament) organised by civil rights organisations during August 2020 as an alternative forum for deliberation about a range of issues such as health, economic and rights issues arising from the pandemic.[55] The creation of cooperative citizens' media organisations at local level in the UK aims to re-make local media.[56] The Global Civic Engagement Index has indicated an increase of 81% of people joining or signing online petitions – with a particularly significant increase in South Africa.[57] These initiatives have all provided powerful reminders that although democracy has been constrained under the pandemic, it has not been suspended – and in some respects, has found new energy.

For those critical of the dominant present iteration of democratic capitalism and preservationist narratives of merely protecting the democracies we have from the ravages of the pandemic, the crisis has presented a critical opportunity to more fully re-think how democratic government works, in a way that achieves better economic outcomes for all societal groups, inspired by how many state actors have shown remarkable flexibility and inventiveness contrary to the dominant neoliberal caricature of official inefficiency and inertia since the 1970s.[58] Most remarkable is the broader shift in thinking across government: as Maduro and Kahn offer, "nations are reconsidering the fundamentals of the social contract".[59]

---

versation.com/as-the-first-remote-sitting-starts-in-canberra-virtual-parliaments-should-be-the-new-norm-not-a-covid-bandaid-144737>.

53 Mel Stevens, 'Necessity Is the Mother of Invention: Taking Climate Assemblies Online' (*Involve UK*, 3 March 2021) <https://www.involve.org.uk/resources/blog/opinion/necessity-mother-invention-taking-climate-assemblies-online>.

54 See e.g. Thomas Carothers and David Wong, 'The Coronavirus Pandemic Is Reshaping Global Protest' (Carnegie Endowment for International Peace, 4 May 2020).

55 Aarefa Johari, 'Citizens Are Hosting Their Own Parliament to Hold Government Accountable during Covid-19 Crisis' (*Scroll.in*, 18 August 2020) <https://scroll.in/article/970638/citizens-are-hosting-their-own-parliament-to-hold-government-accountable-during-covid-19-crisis>.

56 See e.g. Nick Pearce, 'Recommendations from Newham for Deepening Local Democracy' (*Involve UK*, 16 July 2020) <https://www.involve.org.uk/resources/blog/opinion/recommendations-newham-deepening-local-democracy>.

57 'Introducing a Barometer of Digital Civic Engagement' (*Change.org*, 25 August 2020) <https://reports.changefoundation.org/pandemic-report-2020/introducing-a-barometer-of-digital-civic-engagement/>.

58 See e.g. Alfredo Saad-Filho, 'From COVID-19 to the End of Neoliberalism' (2020) 46(4–5) Critical Sociology 477.

59 Miguel Poiares Maduro and Paul W Kahn, 'Introduction: A New Beginning' in Maduro and Kahn (eds), *Democracy in Times of Pandemic* (n 6) 2.

5. The Free World: More Than an 'Anti-China Club'

As the positive innovations above indicate, the global picture is not universally bleak. It is also important to recall Scheppele's warning that assessment through indicators is always limited.[60] Standardised criteria cannot fully capture the tales of innovation, resilience and defiance that do not ping loudly enough on our radars. Moreover, assessment frameworks are descriptive but not predictive: they can paint a picture of the present but not of what is to come. Whether some states will rebound. Whether emergency measures will be unjustifiably extended. Whether a quiescent populace today might roil with protest tomorrow. Whether today's troubles will spur a concerted transnational democratic reaction. The qualitative assessments in this volume, and the material curated through the COVID-DEM database, help us to see the future with hope as well as fear. As Krizsta Kovács observes in her 2021 report on Hungary, citizen demands for freedom are being voiced across the world, including in Poland, Belarus, Russia and Myanmar.[61]

In this sense, the free world is not just a colour-coded political map but a global community of hope, a community of action and resolve. It links the defiant anti-coup protester in Yangon with the committed constitutionalist in Warsaw, the ousted professor in New Delhi[62] with democratic innovators in Santiago. It reminds us that freedom is ours to claim and reclaim, claim and reclaim, claim and reclaim – that the free world is also an imagined future we strive towards, one in which genuine, lived freedom, both political and material, is a shared reality. Thulasi K Raj urges the need to "reclaim" Indian democracy,[63] and that sentiment resonates internationally, with many autocrats and illiberal leaders, including Brazil's Bolsonaro and India's Modi, facing intensifying resistance due to their failures in addressing the pandemic.[64]

Yet, there can be a stark mismatch between domestic grassroots pushback and geopolitics. Take UK Prime Minister Boris Johnson's proposal for the establishment of a new D10 ('D' for democracy) inter-governmental body to group together the G7 states (Canada, France, Germany, Italy, Japan, the UK and the USA) with Australia, India and South Korea.[65] Is the inclusion of India simple denial or ignorance of reality, a reflection of hope – that India's authoritarian turn

60 Kim Lane Scheppele, 'The Rule of Law and the Frankenstate: Why Governance Checklists Do Not Work' (2013) 26(4) Governance 559.

61 Kriszta Kovács, 'Hungary and the Pandemic: A Pretext for Expanding Power' (*Verfassungsblog*, 11 March 2021) <https://verfassungsblog.de/hungary-and-the-pandemic-a-pretext-for-expanding-power/>.

62 Mukul Kesavan, 'Dhamma Descending' (*The Telegraph Online*, 28 March 2021) <https://www.telegraphindia.com/opinion/dhamma-descending-an-ashoka-for-our-times/cid/1810842>.

63 Thulasi K Raj, 'COVID-19 and the Crisis in Indian Democracy' (*Verfassungsblog*, 26 February 2021) <https://verfassungsblog.de/covid-19-and-the-crisis-in-indian-democracy/>. See also Raj, chapter 12.

64 See e.g. Beyer, Mahapatra and Kettemann (n 39).

65 V-Dem Institute (n 2) 36.

can be reversed – or *realpolitik*? In a world where loud voices insist on framing a new 'Cold War' between 'illiberal' powers and the 'free world', with US–China rivalry at its centre[66] (or conversely, urge the need to work effectively with autocratic states through a new 'concert of powers'[67]) geopolitical heft is increasingly prized more than democratic quality – not that the balance was ever decisively tilted toward the latter.

There must be a better way forward than adopting a logic of 'the enemy of my enemy is my friend' to justify a free pass for governments that hollow out their own democratic systems but help to contain Chinese power. Democratic governments would do well to follow the example of individuals worldwide, showing courage, resolve and ingenuity in the cause of freedom. Tarunabh Khaitan, for instance, has suggested that the Biden administration's plan to hold a global Summit of Democracy should include the main political opposition figures as well as governments, arguing that this would respect domestic democratic pluralism as well as strategically push autocratic leaders to publicly decide whether to accept such inclusion.[68]

6. Conclusion: Holding on to Hope

The immediate prognosis for global democracy can look grim. The pandemic has clearly intensified the pre-existing global democratic recession. Yet, there remain many heartening signs of vitality. Before COVID-19 hit, democracies worldwide appeared to be in a negative holding pattern, beset by multiple challenges but straitjacketed by paradigms that clouded the ability to see or craft any real solutions – at times narrowing our field of vision to merely the aim of recapturing some preferred status quo ante before the contemporary trend of democratic recession took hold. The COVID-19 crisis, by laying bare the stark deficiencies of even the most well-regarded democracies worldwide, more sharply revealing sources of resilience, and shifting our thinking on what reform options are possible has potentially broken this holding pattern, freeing governments, policymakers, scholars and citizens to more ambitiously re-engineer and re-imagine democracy to render it fit for the decades to come. While the pandemic's impact will continue to be starkly uneven from state to state, and there is no one silver bullet for democracy's many ills, different pieces of the potentially positive future so many of us hope for are being trialled and built, right now, in states and communities

66 See Hy Rothstein, 'Containing China' (Hoover Institution, 28 January 2021) <https://www.hoover.org/research/containing-china>.

67 Richard N Haass and Charles A Kupchan, 'The New Concert of Powers' (*Foreign Affairs*, 23 March 2021) <https://www.foreignaffairs.com/articles/world/2021-03-23/new-concert-powers>.

68 Tarunabh Khaitan, 'Who Should Attend a Global Democracy Summit?' (*Balkinization*, 5 April 2021) <https://balkin.blogspot.com/2021/04/who-should-attend-global-democracy.html>.

across the world. They are a practical manifestation of hope that the solutions to global democracy's challenges lie within democratic practice itself and may sow the seeds for widespread renewal of a political system that has repeatedly managed to reinvent itself to meet the challenges of the moment. As Arjun Appadurai puts it, hope is a "collectively mobilized resource": "democracy rests on a vision. And all visions require hope".[69]

69 Arjun Appadurai, 'Hope and Democracy' (2007) 19(1) Public Culture 29.

2

COVID-19 VACCINES AND GLOBAL GOVERNANCE

How Structural Factors Dictate Procurement and Vitiate Patient Autonomy

Jerome Amir Singh

1. Introduction[1]

Since SARS-COV-2, the causative agent of Coronavirus Disease 2019 (COVID-19), was first identified, reported global infections number in the hundreds of millions, and millions of individuals have succumbed to the disease.[2] To date, several COVID-19 candidate vaccines have been authorised by multiple drug regulatory agencies and are being deployed globally. To ensure that everyone enjoys the highest attainable standard of health and achieves the full realisation of their right to health, states are obliged to prevent and control epidemics.[3] Mass immunisation – characterised as delivering immunisations to a large number of people at one or more locations in a short interval of time – has proven to be a successful strategy for preventing the spread of many infectious diseases. Besides providing protection at the individual level, mass immunisation programmes also aim for vaccine-induced herd or population immunity – that is, immunising a large proportion of

1 All websites accessed on 29 July 2021.

2 This chapter is based on work as part of an Epidemic Ethics/WHO initiative which has been supported by FCDO/Wellcome Grant 214711/Z/18/Z. The funders had no role in study design, data collection and analysis, decision to publish, or preparation of the chapter. It draws on the following post by the author, 'COVID-19 Vaccines: How Structural Factors Can Vitiate Patient Autonomy and Dictate Vaccine Choice' (*Verfassungsblog*, 10 May 2021) <https://verfassungsblog.de/covid-19-vaccines-how-structural-factors-can-vitiate-patient-autonomy-and-dictate-vaccine-choice/>.

3 International Covenant on Economic, Social and Cultural Rights, Article 12(2)(c).

 DOI: 10.4324/9781003211952-3

the population to protect non-vaccinated, immunologically naïve, and immunocompromised individuals by reducing the percentage of vulnerable hosts to a level below the transmission threshold.[4] The attainment of vaccine-induced population immunity will depend on the procurement of effective vaccines and their widespread uptake. Vaccine uptake, in turn, depends on potential vaccine recipients exercising their right to health and autonomously embracing vaccination. However, while voluntariness lies at the heart of autonomous decision-making, several structural factors could vitiate self-determination.

This chapter begins by characterising structural factors and the notion of patient autonomy. Thereafter, the focus shifts to how four structural factors have impacted COVID-19 vaccine procurement and patient autonomy: geopolitics; corporate self-interest and sovereign fiscal constraints; sovereignty and governance; and protectionism and nationalism.

2. Structural Factors and Patient Autonomy

At the broadest level, structural factors are the political, economic, social and environmental conditions and institutions at national, regional and international levels that influence the overall environment in which individuals, families and communities are situated and which shape their beliefs, decisions and behaviours.[5] Geopolitics, conflicts, political systems, sovereignty, governance, respect for human rights and the rule of law count as examples of structural factors. In the field of health ethics, the principle of autonomy has been characterised as "self-rule that is free from both controlling interference by others and from limitations, such as inadequate understanding, that prevent meaningful choice".[6] The notion of autonomy is epitomised by the argument that "free people must be free to make bad decisions—and to enjoy the rewards or suffer the consequences".[7] The legal doctrine of informed consent upholds the principle of autonomy by requiring clinicians to inform mentally competent patients of all relevant therapeutic and prophylactic alternatives and to respect the patients' choices in that regard. While multiple COVID-19 candidate vaccines were granted emergency use designation in various settings, structural factors dictated their access at a grassroots level. As a result, patients were denied their autonomous right to access a vaccine of their choice.

4 Christie Aschwanden, 'The False Promise of Herd Immunity for COVID-19' (*Nature*, 21 October 2020) <https://www.nature.com/articles/d41586-020-02948-4>.

5 International Organisation on Migration, *Handbook on Protection and Assistance for Migrants Vulnerable to Violence, Exploitation and Abuse* (IOM 2019) <https://publications.iom.int/system/files/pdf/avm_handbook.pdf>.

6 Jukka Varelius, 'The Value of Autonomy in Medical Ethics' (2006) 9(3) Med Health Care Philos 377.

7 Christina Sandefur, 'Tear Up the Permission Slip: Medical Autonomy Is a Fundamental Right' (*Cato Unbound*, 19 July 2017) <https://www.cato-unbound.org/2017/07/19/christina-sandefur/tear-permission-slip-medical-autonomy-fundamental-human-right>.

2.1 How Geopolitics Dictates Vaccine Procurement and Impacts on Patient Autonomy

Geopolitical factors deprived hundreds of millions of people of their right to autonomy in regard to COVID-19 vaccine choice. Hamstrung by decades of United States (US) sanctions, Cuba strived for self-sufficiency in relation to vaccine production. Cuba accordingly did not import any COVID-19 vaccines through bilateral deals with foreign vaccine developers, nor did the country seek COVID-19 vaccines through the COVAX facility coordinated by the World Health Organisation (WHO), among others. Instead, Cuba began developing at least four homegrown COVID-19 vaccines and trialled the vaccines domestically, and in Iran and Venezuela.[8] However, the hardening of US sanctions during the Trump presidency made Cuban procurement of the raw ingredients necessary for vaccine production more difficult.[9] This means that Cubans were not just denied an opportunity to seek a foreign vaccine of their choice, but that geopolitics also impacted their access to potential domestic vaccines.Venezuela procured Russian COVID-19 vaccines because US sanctions against the country allegedly ruled out the procurement of certain vaccine candidates.[10] Similarly, while Iran's Supreme Leader barred the importation of vaccines from the US and the United Kingdom (UK)[11] because of mistrust of Western powers, Iranian politicians simultaneously urged the US to lift sanctions against Iran to enable the country to import COVID-19 vaccines.[12] While such sanctions formally exempted the importation of food, medicine and other humanitarian supplies, Iranian health workers and sanctions experts claimed that US sanctions resulted in lost oil revenue for the country and prevented the importation of pharmaceuticals and medical supplies,[13] including the raw materials and equipment needed to manufacture medicines domestically. Oil revenue losses due to sanctions left Iran with fewer financial resources to effectively tackle the COVID-19 pandemic. Iranian officials also claimed that foreign and multilateral

8 'Cuba Accelerating Vaccine Roll-out on Hospital Staff' (*France 24*, 29 March 2021) <https://www.france24.com/en/live-news/20210329-cuba-accelerating-vaccine-roll-out-on-hospital-staff>.

9 Talha Burki, 'Behind Cuba's Successful Pandemic Response' (2021) 21(4) Lancet Infectious Diseases 465.

10 'West Refused to Unfreeze Venezuelan Funds for Vaccine Purchase: President' (*Business Standard*, 5 January 2020) <https://www.business-standard.com/article/current-affairs/west-refused-to-unfreeze-venezuelan-funds-for-vaccine-purchase-president-121010400205_1.html>.

11 Patrick Wintour, 'Iran Bans Importation of Covid Vaccines from the US and UK' (*The Guardian*, 8 January 2020) <https://www.theguardian.com/world/2021/jan/08/untrustworthy-covid-vaccines-from-us-and-uk-banned-by-iran>.

12 'Iran Urges Biden to Lift Sanctions Affecting Medicines as it Fights COVID-19' (*Reuters*, 26 January 2021) <https://www.reuters.com/article/health-coronavirus-iran-int-idUSKBN29V1G2>.

13 Erin Cunningham, 'As Coronavirus Cases Explode in Iran, U.S. Sanctions Hinder Its Access to Drugs and Medical Equipment' (*The Washington Post*, 28 March 2020) <https://www.washingtonpost.com/world/middle_east/as-coronavirus-cases-explode-in-iran-us-sanctions-hinder-its-access-to-drugs-and-medical-equipment/2020/03/28/0656a196-6aba-11ea-b199-3a9799c54512_story.html>.

lending institutions were deterred or blocked[14] from concluding agreements with the country, including in relation to humanitarian initiatives. For instance, in March 2020, during Iran's first wave of COVID-19, the US blocked[15] Iran's request for an emergency US$5 billion International Monetary Fund (IMF) loan aimed at helping the country respond to the pandemic. In December 2020, Iran reported[16] that all methods by the country to transfer funds to secure vaccines through the COVAX facility for COVID-19 vaccines were unsuccessful because foreign assets had been frozen and monetary transfers involving Iran required permits from the US Treasury, by virtue of US sanctions. As a result, Iran procured Russian, Chinese and Indian vaccines and simultaneously trialled Cuban and homegrown candidate vaccines.[17] However, notwithstanding Iran's Supreme Leader barring the deployment of US and UK vaccines in the country, Iran received more than four million doses of AstraZeneca vaccines through the WHO's COVAX facility.[18]

National pride, geopolitical tensions and mistrust also potentially deprived people in some settings of their autonomous right to access a vaccine of their choice, including those developed by countries deemed to be 'rivals'. While there are documented cases of drug regulators restricting or permitting access to health interventions based on domestic politics and not on science, global geopolitics can also dictate access to healthcare interventions. US officials are unlikely to procure and deploy state-sponsored Chinese or Russian candidate vaccines because of mistrust and transparency concerns.[19] China and Russia only deployed their own respective domestically produced vaccines,[20] despite US and European vaccines demonstrating superior efficacy. China was accused of attempting to discredit Western vaccines[21] and indirectly pressuring foreign expats to take its vaccines by announcing in mid-March 2021 that the country would facilitate the processing

14 'US Hits Iran's Financial Sector with Fresh Round of Sanctions' (*Reuters*, 8 October 2020) <https://www.jpost.com/breaking-news/us-hits-irans-financial-sector-with-fresh-round-of-sanctions-645072>.

15 Maziar Motamedi, 'Iran's Top Banker Says US Blocking COVID-19 Vaccine Purchase' (*Al Jazeera*, 7 December 2020) <https://www.aljazeera.com/news/2020/12/7/iran-says-us-blocking-covid-19-vaccine-purchase>.

16 ibid.

17 Golnaz Esfandiari, 'Iran Talks Up Homegrown COVID-19 Vaccines In Show Of Self-Reliance' (*Radio Free Europe Radio Liberty*, 16 March 2021) <https://www.rferl.org/a/iran-homegrown-covid-19-vaccines-show-of-self-reliance/31154417.html>.

18 World Health Organisation, 'COVAX Interim Distribution Forecast as of 3 February 2021' (3 February 2021) <https://www.who.int/docs/default-source/coronaviruse/act-accelerator/covax/covax-interim-distribution-forecast.pdf?sfvrsn=7889475d_5>.

19 'US Raises Safety Issue in China, Russia Vaccines' (*The Straits Times*, 2 August 2020) <https://www.straitstimes.com/world/united-states/us-raises-safety-issue-in-china-russia-vaccines>.

20 UNICEF, 'COVID-19 Vaccine Market Dashboard' <https://app.powerbi.com/view?r=eyJrIjoiNmE0YjZiNzUtZjk2OS00ZTg4LThlMzMtNTRhNzE0NzA4YmZlIiwidCI6Ijc3NDEwMTk1LTE0ZTEtNGZiOC05MDRiLWFiMTg5MjAyMzY2NyIsImMiOjh9&pageName=ReportSectiona329b3eafd86059a947b>.

21 James Griffiths, 'China is Hitting Back at Criticism of Its Vaccines with a Dangerous Disinformation Campaign' (*CNN*, 19 January 2021) <https://edition.cnn.com/2021/01/19/china/china-vaccine-disinformation-intl-hnk/index.html>.

of visa applications only if applicants had been vaccinated with Chinese vaccines.[22] The European Union (EU) has since announced that it would only issue a 'vaccines passport' to individuals who had been vaccinated with vaccines approved by the European Medicine Agency.[23] This approach disqualifies most citizens of low- and middle-income countries who may have been immunised with equivalent vaccines produced outside of Europe and distributed by the COVAX initiative.

Geopolitical factors also dictated vaccine procurement and disbursement between countries that develop and manufacture vaccines, and those that do not. For example, Pakistan found itself in a challenging position because of historical tensions with India. In what could be viewed as national pride trumping national interest, Pakistan did not directly approach Indian vaccine manufacturers to procure COVID-19 vaccines,[24] despite India producing billions of vaccine doses for countries globally.[25] Ironically, Pakistan indirectly received millions of vaccine doses sourced from India[26] through the COVAX facility. Conversely, while India donated millions of doses of domestically produced vaccines to neighbouring countries and globally, as part of a goodwill 'vaccine diplomacy' effort to counter the influence of China, Pakistan was a notable omission in the list of regional beneficiaries.[27] Instead, China filled the philanthropy void by donating millions of doses of Chinese vaccines to Pakistan as part of the Chinese government's vaccine diplomacy efforts.[28] Pakistan was also separately procuring and deploying Chinese vaccines,[29] despite high levels of scepticism[30] amongst Pakistanis towards Chinese COVID-19 candidate vaccines.

22 Embassy of the People's Republic of China in the United States, 'Notice on Visa Facilitation for Applicants Inoculated with Chinese COVID-19 Vaccines' (15 March 2021) <http://www.china-embassy.org/eng/visas/t1861379.htm>.

23 Paul Adepoju and Elaine Ruth Fletcher, 'Most COVAX Vaccine Recipients Excluded from New EU COVID "Green Pass" – Thanks to Unapproved AstraZeneca Jab' (*Health Policy Watch*, 25 June 2021) <https://healthpolicy-watch.news/most-covax-vaccine-recipients-excluded/>.

24 'Pakistan Set to Get 45 Million India-made' (*The Times of India*, 10 March 2021) <http://timesofindia.indiatimes.com/articleshow/81422619.cms?utm_source=contentofinterest&utm_medium=text&utm_campaign=cppst>.

25 Shruti Menon, 'India Coronavirus: Can Its Vaccine Producers Meet Demand?' (*BBC News*, 14 April 2021) <https://www.bbc.com/news/world-asia-india-55571793#:~:text=India%20will%20produce%20850%20million,production%20has%20not%20yet%20started>.

26 World Health Organisation (n 18).

27 Rajesh Roy and Saeed Shah, 'India Starts Donating Covid-19 Vaccines to Neighboring Countries' (*The Wall Street Journal*, 21 January 2021) <https://www.wsj.com/articles/india-starts-covid-19-vaccine-drive-to-neighboring-countries-11611234933>.

28 Agence France Presse, 'China To Donate 500,000 Covid-19 Vaccines To Pakistan' (*Barrons*, 21 January 2021) <https://www.barrons.com/news/china-to-donate-500-000-covid-19-vaccines-to-pakistan-01611245404?tesla=y>.

29 Gibran Naiyyar Peshimam, 'Pakistan to Purchase 1.2 million COVID-19 Vaccine Doses from China's Sinopharm' (*Reuters*, 31 December 2020) <https://www.reuters.com/article/us-health-coronavirus-pakistan-vaccine/pakistan-to-purchase-1-2-million-covid-19-vaccine-doses-from-chinas-sinopharm-idUSKBN2950DQ?edition-redirect=in>.

30 Iain Marlow, Faseeh Mangi and Kari Soo Lindberg, '"I Won't Take It": China Struggles to Get the World to Trust Its Vaccines' (*Japan Times*, 29 December 2020) <https://www.japantimes.co.jp/news/2020/12/29/asia-pacific/china-coronavirus-vaccines-trust/>.

Taiwan offers another example of how geopolitical factors can impact vaccine procurement and patient autonomy. On the back of high levels of mistrust of Chinese vaccines amongst Taiwanese nationals,[31] the Taiwanese government indicated that it was prepared to help its diplomatic allies buy COVID-19 vaccines, conditional upon Taiwanese funding not being used to procure Chinese vaccines.[32] Concurrently, Taiwan accused China of trying to pressure the Paraguayan government into severing diplomatic ties with Taiwan in return for Paraguay receiving millions of vaccine doses from China.[33] Geopolitical factors also impacted the autonomy of Taiwanese nationals to access a COVID-19 vaccine of their choice. In March 2020, Biopharmaceutical New Technologies (BioNTech), a German biotechnology company, entered into collaborative agreements with Pfizer Inc., a US company, for the right to co-development and distribution of its mRNA-based COVID-19 vaccine, BNT162b2, in various parts of the world, including the US, Europe and Japan.[34] Concurrently, Shanghai Fosun Pharmaceutical (hereinafter Fosun), a Chinese company, entered into a separate agreement with BioNTech to co-develop and distribute the BNT162b2 vaccine in China.[35] After BNT162b2 demonstrated efficacy in November 2020 and multiple countries and the WHO granted BNT162b2 emergency use designation, Taiwan tried to procure BNT162b2 directly from Pfizer and BioNTech. However, these attempts were unsuccessful because Fosun asserted that the company's commercialisation and distribution agreement with BioNTech covered 'Greater China', which Fosun insisted applied to Taiwan, too.[36] As China claims Taiwan as its territory, the Taiwanese government blamed the Chinese government for hindering Taiwan's procurement efforts. However, Fosun denied that the Chinese government had intervened in the matter, maintaining that any sale of BNT162b2 to Taiwan would have to go through its distribution network. However, direct procurement by the Taiwanese government from a Chinese company is politically unpalatable as it would be tantamount to conceding that Taiwan was part of 'Greater China'. To overcome these geopolitical factors, and to facilitate COVID-19 vaccine access to

31 Wu Su-wei and William Hetherington, 'COVID-19: Majority Say No to Chinese Vaccines' (*Taipei Times*, 21 March 2021) <https://www.taipeitimes.com/News/front/archives/2021/03/21/2003754201>.

32 'Taiwan to Help Allies Buy Vaccines, But Not From China' (*Reuters*, 24 March 2021) <https://www.reuters.com/article/us-health-coronavirus-taiwan-idUSKBN2BG0H1>.

33 'Taiwan Accuses China of "Vaccine Diplomacy" in Paraguay' (*BBC News*, 7 April 2021) <https://www.bbc.com/news/world-asia-56661303>.

34 Pfizer, 'Pfizer and BioNTech Announce Further Details on Collaboration to Accelerate Global COVID-19 Vaccine Development' (9 April 2020) <https://www.pfizer.com/news/press-release/press-release-detail/pfizer-and-biontech-announce-further-details-collaboration>.

35 'BioNTech in China Alliance with Fosun over Coronavirus Vaccine Candidate' (*Reuters*, 16 March 2020) <https://www.reuters.com/article/biontech-fosunpharma-vaccine-collaborati/biontech-in-china-alliance-with-fosun-over-coronavirus-vaccine-candidate-idUSL8N2B90UW>.

36 Yang Sheng-ju, Chang Shu-ling and Frances Huang, 'Chinese Firm Asserts Right to Distribute BNT Vaccine to Taiwan: Report' (*Focus Taiwan*, 6 June 2021) <https://focustaiwan.tw/cross-strait/202106120015>.

its citizens amidst severe vaccine shortages in the country, Taiwan procured other candidate vaccines directly from developers and relied on donations of candidate vaccines from other countries.[37] To facilitate Taiwan's access to BNT162b2, two major Taiwanese corporates eventually purchased the vaccines directly from Fosun and donated the vaccines to the Taiwanese government.[38]

In arguably the ultimate display of vaccines being used as geopolitical currency, Israel allegedly secretly purchased Russian vaccines for the Syrian government, to facilitate the release of prisoners[39] held by the Syrian regime. While Syria's first tranche of vaccines through the COVAX facility were deployed in specific areas of the country and subject to independent monitoring by monitors deployed by WHO and the United Nations Children's Fund (UNICEF),[40] the alleged Israeli-sourced Russian vaccines were used by the Syrian regime to launch the government's COVID-19 vaccination campaign, leading to concerns that many individuals in government-controlled and rebel-held areas would be deprived of vaccines without international oversight.[41] In all the above situational contexts, geopolitics is dictating vaccine procurement and supply at the macro level and indirectly vitiating autonomy at the individual level.

2.2 How Corporate Self-interest and Sovereign Fiscal Constraints Dictate COVID-19 Vaccine Procurement at the Macro Level and Undermine Personal Autonomy at the Grassroots Level

As was the case with HIV, COVID-19 became an intellectual property battleground. On 2 October 2020, South Africa and India petitioned the Trade-Related Aspects of Intellectual Property Rights (TRIPS) Council at the World Trade Organisation (WTO) to waive certain provisions of the TRIPS Agreement for the prevention, containment and treatment of COVID-19, until the majority of the world's population had access to effective vaccines and developed immunity to COVID-19. Specifically, South Africa and India advocated for intellectual property waivers that would temporarily suspend certain vaccine technology patent

37 Shanghai Fosun Pharmaceutical, 'Fosun Pharma Announces the Supply of 10 Million Doses of mRNA-based COVID-19 Vaccine to Taiwan Region' (7 July 2021) <https://www.fosun-pharma.com/en/news/news-details-3858.html>.

38 'Taiwan Tech Giants Foxconn and TSMC to Buy 10m Covid Jabs' (*BBC News*, 12 July 2021) <https://www.bbc.com/news/business-57801031>.

39 Oliver Holmes, 'Israel: Use of Covid Vaccines in Prisoner Swap Deal Sparks Row' (*The Guardian*, 21 February 2021) <https://www.theguardian.com/world/2021/feb/21/israel-use-of-covid-vaccines-in-prisoner-swap-deal-sparks-row>.

40 World Health Organisation, 'The World Health Organization is Committed to Ensuring Fair Distribution of COVID-19 Vaccine to the Whole of Syria' (*Reliefweb*, 31 March 2021) <https://reliefweb.int/report/syrian-arab-republic/world-health-organization-committed-ensuring-fair-distribution-covid-19>.

41 Anchal Vohra, 'Syria Launches COVID Vaccine Drive as Israel Questions Swirl' (*Al Jazeera*, 17 March 2021) <https://www.aljazeera.com/news/2021/3/17/syria-launches-covid-vaccination-drive-amid-economic-challenges>.

monopoly protections during the COVID-19 pandemic, thus enabling countries with vaccine manufacturing capabilities to access a candidate's 'recipe' (including the active ingredients as well as other substances) and manufacturing protocols, to enable domestic companies to produce generic versions of the vaccines. Such measures are permitted under the TRIPS Agreement[42] and the Doha Declaration on the TRIPS Agreement and Public Health,[43] which affords countries the right to grant compulsory licenses, the freedom to determine the grounds upon which compulsory licences are granted, and the freedom to determine what constitutes a national emergency or other circumstances of extreme urgency. South Africa and India's initiative found strong support from the Director-General of the WHO, Tedros Adhanom Ghebreyesus, who argued: "If a temporary waiver to patents cannot be issued now, during these unprecedented times, when will be the right time?"[44] Despite the pharmaceutical industry arguing that temporary patent waivers would harm innovation and entrepreneurship and damage the industry, on 5 May 2021, the US government announced its support for waiving intellectual property protections for COVID-19 vaccines.[45] Patent waivers, however, will not translate to instantaneous vaccine access as there are practical challenges to scaling-up vaccine production related to manufacturing capabilities, technology transfer (the patent holder has to supply technical know-how, including on-site development and equipment installation activities and personnel), skills development, regulation and quality control.

The Director-General of the WTO, Ngozi Okonjo-Iweala, touted broadening COVID-19 vaccine access through technology transfers within the framework of multilateral rules through licensing agreements between patent holders and generics manufacturers.[46] However, technical transfers through licensing agreements also do not necessarily equate to timely downstream access to a vaccine. For instance, while the WHO supported a South African consortium's award of Africa's first COVID mRNA vaccine technology transfer hub to supply mRNA vaccines to African countries, the arrangement ultimately entailed South African vaccine manufacturers obtaining drug and biologics substances from facilities in Europe, and manufacturing finished doses in South Africa.[47] Such 'fill and finish'

42 World Trade Organisation, 'Compulsory Licensing of Pharmaceuticals and TRIPS' (undated) <https://www.wto.org/english/tratop_e/trips_e/public_health_faq_e.htm>.

43 World Trade Organisation, 'Declaration on the TRIPS Agreement and Public Health' (14 November 2001) <https://www.wto.org/english/thewto_e/minist_e/min01_e/mindecl_trips_e.htm>.

44 Tedros Adhanom Ghebreyesus on Twitter (3 March 2021). <https://mobile.twitter.com/drtedros/status/1367428637314670606?lang=en>.

45 Office of the United States Trade Representative, 'Statement from Ambassador Katherine Tai on the Covid-19 Trips Waiver' (5 May 2021) <https://ustr.gov/about-us/policy-offices/press-office/press-releases/2021/may/statement-ambassador-katherine-tai-covid-19-trips-waiver>.

46 World Trade Organisation, 'Statement of Director-General Elect Dr. Ngozi Okonjo-Iweala to the Special Session of the WTO General Council, 13 February 2021' (15 February 2021) <https://www.wto.org/english/news_e/news21_e/dgno_15feb21_e.pdf>.

47 'Pfizer and BioNTech Announce Collaboration With Biovac to Manufacture and Distribute COVID-19 Vaccine Doses Within Africa' (*Business Wire*, 21 July 2021) <https://www

arrangements amount to patent holders sharing ingredients, but not the recipe. If the party exporting the vaccine ingredients experiences supply constraints or the supplier country imposes export controls, the party contracted to do the 'fill and finish' would not be able to supply vaccines to target markets.

If a country does not issue compulsory licenses to enable domestic production of COVID-19 vaccines (assuming the country has the technical capability and the vaccine 'recipe' to do so), realising the right to health through vaccine access will largely be determined by donors; a country's ability to mass-produce foreign vaccines to meet local (and foreign) demand through voluntary licensing agreements (as was the case with India); developing homegrown vaccines by necessity (as was the case with some countries that are subject to economic sanctions, such as Cuba and Iran); and/or a country's financial capability to enter into bilateral and multilateral financing and procurement mechanisms to access the COVID-19 vaccine market. Such mechanisms can function at a global level, such as COVAX's Advance Market Commitments (AMCs); at a regional level, such as the European Commission's Advanced Market Agreements (AMAs) and the African Union's Advanced Procurement Commitments (APC); and/or at a bilateral level, which involves direct contracts between country authorities and vaccine developers/manufacturers, sometimes concurrent to procurement through AMAs, AMCs and APCs.

Current COVID-19 candidate vaccines differ widely in terms of cost per dose, which is an important factor in determining vaccine procurement. By 1 April 2021, of all vaccine doses administered globally, approximately 75% had gone to only 10 countries.[48] Moreover, while 83% of vaccines administered globally had been administered in high-income and upper-middle-income countries, only 0.1% of doses had been administered in low-income countries.[49] AMCs were touted as providing assurances of future demand and financing, thus serving as a 'pull' mechanism to incentivise manufacturers to invest in development and manufacturing of COVID-19 vaccines. It was argued that AMCs can also serve as 'push' funding, whereby public sector funds directly finance expanded vaccine manufacturing, securing critical raw materials and equipment, and transferring technology from developers to manufacturers. However, APAs can hold threats as countries risk getting locked into purchasing inferior or cost-ineffective products that could divert scarce resources from more optimal COVID-19 responses, including superior vaccines. Proponents of this view argued that if all or most available funding flows to the first market entrant, the second or third entrants may be boxed out of the market – even if their product is of better value or more efficacious. Such factors highlight how a country's lack of domestic/regional vaccine production

.businesswire.com/news/home/20210721005475/en/Pfizer-and-BioNTech-Announce-Collaboration-With-Biovac-to-Manufacture-and-Distribute-COVID-19-Vaccine-Doses-Within-Africa>.

48 Josh Holder, 'Tracking Coronavirus Vaccinations Around the World' (*The New York Times*, 21 July 2021) <https://www.nytimes.com/interactive/2021/world/covid-vaccinations-tracker.html>.

49 ibid.

capability, and its financial ability to enter AMCs and AMAs, can impact on vaccine access at the grassroots level.

2.3 How Sovereignty and Governance Impact upon COVID-19 Vaccine Procurement and Personal Autonomy

A variety of vaccine procurement modalities apply globally. Sovereignty – defined for the purpose of this chapter as the decision-making authority of a government or non-state entity – is crucial to vaccine procurement. In settings such as Brazil, all levels of government and the private sector were permitted to procure COVID-19 vaccines directly from developers and manufacturers.[50] In the Philippines, the private sector was permitted to purchase vaccines[51] for private sector employees, provided that half the supply was donated to the government. Private sector vaccine procurement raises critical issues, including who pays for the vaccine: government (if so, which level?), private sector employer, health insurer, donor or recipient? Moreover, who decides on prioritisation and the vaccination schedule for target populations – government, private sector or civil society? Can two or more parallel systems operate? Should pricing be regulated? India offers an example of a country where the private sector was permitted to independently procure COVID-19 vaccines,[52] but where pricing was capped at a quarter of the rate that vaccine manufacturers said they would sell to the private sector.[53] Some criticised the Indian government's decision to cap vaccine prices, arguing that market forces should determine pricing.[54] However, where people are willing to pay higher prices to be vaccinated (especially in settings where universal vaccination coverage applies), they could get vaccinated ahead of prioritisation frameworks established by policymakers. This leads to affluent people getting vaccinated before poor people and potentially accessing more effective vaccines that have not been procured by the government because of fiscal constraints. Some argued that allowing market forces to dictate pricing could also drive up prices, tempt manufacturers to prioritise higher-paying private sector purchasers and lead to an increase in fraud and black market activity. Kenya offers an example of a country where private sector procurement was suspended on fears that the country was at

50 Brazil Federal Law No. 14,124/2021 (10 March 2021).

51 'Philippines, Private Firms to Sign Vaccine Supply Deal with AstraZeneca' (*Reuters*, 26 November 2020) <https://www.reuters.com/article/us-health-coronavirus-philippines-vaccin-idUSKBN2860W7>.

52 Anonna Dutt, 'Covid-19: Private Vaccine Prices Capped at ₹250 a Shot' (*Hindustan Times*, 28 February 2021) <https://www.hindustantimes.com/health/covid19-private-vaccine-prices-capped-at-rs-250-a-shot-101614467531868.html>.

53 Vishnu Som, 'Oxford Vaccine At ₹ 1,000 if Centre Allows Us to Sell: Adar Poonawalla' (*NDTV*, 4 January 2021) <https://www.ndtv.com/india-news/serum-institute-s-vaccine-at-rs-1-000-a-shot-centre-to-give-it-for-free-2347308>.

54 Govindraj Ethiraj, 'Price Caps Limit Private Sector COVID-19 Vaccinations to Cities' (*Indiaspend*, 12 March 2021) <https://www.indiaspend.com/indiaspend-interviews/price-caps-limit-private-sector-covid-19-vaccinations-to-cities-734842>.

risk of counterfeit vaccines and price gouging.[55] Barring or dissuading a country's private sector from procuring vaccines could also have been motivated by fears that ineligible private sector clientele could 'queue-jump' over eligible individuals with fewer means. Such a situation played out in Pakistan, where private sector COVID-19 vaccine procurement was permitted. There, most private sales of COVID-19 vaccines took place in large cities, such as Karachi, and vaccines were largely inaccessible to poorer residents in more rural areas.[56] Such outcomes had major ethical and equity implications. In all such instances, sovereignty (central/state/provincial/local government/shared mandates/private sector) and governance (clinical guidance/prioritisation frameworks) impact equity and personal autonomy at the grassroots level.

The authority to procure vaccines, however, does not necessarily translate into time-sensitive access. Orders from the private sector are not prioritised by vaccine manufacturers.[57] Further, the cost per dose is significantly more expensive than public-sector procurement.[58] Given such factors, central procurement could arguably be advantageous as parallel negotiations between various levels of government and multiple private sector and civil society actors, could drive up prices amid already fierce international competition and supply constraints. South Africa offers an example of a highly inequitable setting where COVID-19 vaccine procurement was centralised, despite the country having a dual public sector and private sector health system. The South African government indicated that while the country's private sector could co-fund centralised vaccine procurement and also participate in vaccination drives as service providers, only the national/federal government could source, distribute and oversee the country's COVID-19 vaccine rollout. While such a strategy may hold the advantage of resource-pooling and facilitating economy of scale negotiations, the country's civil society, at least one provincial government, the private health sector and some actors in the corporate sector voiced their preference to independently and directly procure their own COVID-19 vaccines. The central government's stance on vaccine procurement led to accusations of monopolisation, nationalisation and threats of court action. In situations where vaccine procurement was centralised, individuals who are willing to be vaccinated may find themselves faced with no other option but to

55 Tom Odula, 'Kenya Stops The Private Importation of COVID-19 Vaccines' (*AP News*, 3 April 2021) <https://apnews.com/article/health-kenya-coronavirus-pandemic-africa-541094c0e7e8412f5c49885908bb2c92>.

56 Jessie Yeung and Sophia Saifi, 'Vaccines Sell Out in Pakistan as the Private Market Opens, Raising Concerns of Inequality' (*CNN*, 12 April 2021) <https://edition.cnn.com/2021/04/12/asia/pakistan-covid-private-vaccines-dst-intl-hnk/index.html>.

57 Bharat Manjesh, 'India Coronavirus Dispatch: Private Market to See a Long Wait for Vaccines' (*Business Standard*, 21 January 2021) <https://www.business-standard.com/article/current-affairs/india-coronavirus-dispatch-private-market-to-see-a-long-wait-for-vaccines-121012100677_1.html>.

58 Rupali Mukherjee, 'Private Hospitals, Companies May Get Vaccine by March: Serum CEO' (*The Times of India*, 4 January 2021) <http://timesofindia.indiatimes.com/articleshow/80088520.cms?utm_source=contentofinterest&utm_medium=text&utm_campaign=cppst>.

accept the vaccines that their central government procures (subject to the regulator's approval), regardless of personal preference or their financial ability to directly purchase a COVID-19 vaccine of their choice and/or their regional government's procurement preferences.

2.4 How Protectionism and Nationalism Can Dictate Vaccine Access and Impact on Autonomy at the Grassroots Level

Uneven distribution of vaccine manufacturing and financing capabilities yielded unequal access to COVID-19 vaccines. Severe supply chain constraints, even in affluent settings, such as the EU, where multiple COVID-19 candidate vaccines were deployed, is well documented. In such settings, individuals eligible for vaccination may face the possibility of not being vaccinated with a candidate vaccine of their choice because of supply constraints. In such instances, the individual faces the option of being vaccinated with an available vaccine they lack confidence in, or refusing vaccination and remaining at risk of COVID-19 infection until their preferred candidate vaccine becomes available. Such a situation played out in some EU countries[59] and India.[60] On the other hand, some authorities may only have procured a candidate vaccine that was mistrusted in their setting. In such instances, eligible but sceptical individuals face the option of acquiescing to vaccination with a product they mistrust, or declining vaccination and remaining indefinitely at risk of infection. Such a scenario played out in settings such as Russia.[61]

Some settings are demonstrating that self-interest trumps global health and the ethics principle of solidarity. The US, EU and India count amongst the world's largest producers of COVID-19 vaccines.[62] Severe COVID-19 vaccine supply constraints resulted in the EU[63] and India[64] imposing COVID-19 vaccine export restrictions, for self-serving reasons. Similarly, the US federal government used

59 Leila Abboud, Daniel Dombey, Silvia Sciorilli Borrelli and Guy Chazan, 'Europe's AstraZeneca Stockpile Mounts as Citizens Snub Jab' (*The Financial Times*, 27 February 2021) <https://www.ft.com/content/767fdd85-5329-479d-b565-4ec85d28b492>.

60 Manavi Kapur, 'India's Homegrown Vaccine Has an Uphill Climb to Gaining People's Trust' (*Quartz India*, 5 March 2021) <https://qz.com/india/1980334/is-bharat-biotechs-covaxin-safe-now-that-it-shows-81-percent-efficacy/>.

61 TRT World, 'Russian Distrust of Sputnik V Hurts Vaccine Rollout' (*TRT World*, 9 March 2021) <https://www.trtworld.com/magazine/russian-distrust-of-sputnik-v-hurts-vaccine-rollout-44860>.

62 Airfinity, 'COVID-19 Vaccine Production Summit' (*Airfinity*, 8 March 2021) <https://www.ifpma.org/wp-content/uploads/2021/03/Airfinity_global_summit_master_final.pdf>.

63 European Commission, 'Commission Extends Transparency and Authorisation Mechanism for Exports of COVID-19 Vaccines' (11 March 2021) <https://ec.europa.eu/commission/presscorner/detail/en/ip_21_1121>.

64 Krishna N Das, 'Exclusive: India Delays Big Exports of AstraZeneca Shot, as Infections Surge' (*Reuters*, 24 March 2021) <https://www.reuters.com/article/health-coronavirus-india-vaccine-exclusi-idUSKBN2BG27D>.

the country's Defense Production Act (DPA)[65] to spur domestic COVID-19 vaccine production. The DPA gives the US President powers to allocate "materials, services, and facilities" and award contracts that take priority over any other contract to "promote the national defence". In the context of the COVID-19 pandemic, the DPA was used to 'defend' the country against the COVID-19 pandemic. The DPA can also be used to prevent companies from exporting certain goods, to ensure their availability within the US. As a result, the US President had to approve the export of COVID-19 vaccines and vaccine-related raw materials. By 1 March 2021, the US had not exported any COVID-19 vaccines produced in the country.[66] While the US subsequently lifted its ban on vaccine exports to enable key allies to gain access to US-made COVID-19 vaccines that were not being locally deployed, by 20 April 2021, the US had still not lifted its export ban of raw materials necessary to produce COVID-19 vaccines.[67] Such prohibitions had a paralysing impact on vaccine production. For example, the BioNTech/Pfizer vaccine contained 280 ingredients sourced from 19 countries.[68] As a consequence of such export bans, COVAX suppliers, including those in India, could experience major production constraints that could have global implications. In all such instances, protectionism, self-interest and vaccine nationalism could frustrate the realisation of the right to health and will dictate vaccine availability and choice at the individual level.

3. Conclusion

Financial self-interest, fiscal considerations, geopolitics, sovereignty, governance, protectionism and nationalism are currently dictating COVID-19 vaccine procurement at the macro level. Such structural factors indirectly vitiate autonomy at the grassroots level and run counter to the ideal that individuals should have access to the highest attainable standard of health.

65 Sydney Lupkin, 'Defense Production Act Speeds Up Vaccine Production' (*NPR*, 13 March 2021) <https://www.npr.org/sections/health-shots/2021/03/13/976531488/defense-production-act-speeds-up-vaccine-production#:~:text=Ethics-,Defense%20Production%20Act%20Hastens%20COVID%2D19%20Vaccine%20Production%20%3A%20Shots%20%2D,the%20country%20against%20the%20coronavirus>.

66 Niall McCarthy, 'America First? Covid-19 Production & Exports' (*Statista*, 31 March 2021) <https://www.statista.com/chart/24555/vaccine-doses-produced-and-exported/>.

67 'No US Confirmation of Lifting Ban on Vaccines Raw Material Exports' (*The Times of India*, 20 April 2021) <https://timesofindia.indiatimes.com/world/us/no-us-confirmation-of-lifting-ban-on-vaccine-raw-material-exports/articleshow/82158105.cms>.

68 Thomas B Cueni, 'Challenges and Solutions to Scaling-up COVID-19 Vaccine Manufacturing Capacity' (International Federation of Pharmaceutical Manufacturers and Associations, 29 April 2021) <https://www.ifpma.org/global-health-matters/challenges-and-solutions-to-scaling-up-covid-19-vaccine-manufacturing-capacity/>.

3

ACCOUNTABILITY THROUGH DIALOGUE

New Zealand's Experience during the First Year of the COVID-19 Pandemic

Dean R Knight

1. Introduction[1]

New Zealand has been fêted as one of the exemplars of success during the COVID-19 pandemic. Its ability, during the first year or so of the pandemic, to stamp out the virus and protect against its ills is well known. As of July 2021, the country has managed to keep the number of diagnosed cases at just under 2,500 and the number of deaths to 26.

Most of those diagnosed cases were caught at the border and less than a quarter of cases arose from community transmission. After a swift and aggressive lockdown in the early stages of the pandemic, the country was blessed with long virus-free periods, allowing day-to-day life to largely continue with minimal restriction.[2]

Without question, the government's response in New Zealand is a study in the wonders of modern government, given the magnitude of the threat, the different dimensions of community wellbeing at stake and the different parts of government involved in the response. Public health guidance, clinical health care, economic support and stimulus, social welfare and support, border security and surveillance. The list goes on. The response to the pandemic was no simple task and engaged all facets of the government apparatus.

But at what (civic) cost? A perennial concern in times of crisis and emergency is loss of accountability. The need for a swift and potent response often leads to deployment of enormous and discretionary executive powers absent the usual

1 All websites accessed 30 July 2021.

2 This chapter draws on Dean R Knight, 'New Zealand: Rendering Account During the COVID-19 Pandemic' (*Verfassungsblog*, 19 April 2021) <https://verfassungsblog.de/new-zealand-rendering-account-during-the-covid-19-pandemic/>.

DOI: 10.4324/9781003211952-4

checks and balances. Did resort to emergency power and crisis management in New Zealand lead to the erosion of governmental accountability and dilution of the usual checks and balances that mitigate the exercise of state power?

Curiously, no, I suggest. Accountability was generally preserved, if not enhanced, during the height of the pandemic in New Zealand over the first year or so. While trying to achieve the best outcomes for communities in these relatively unfamiliar emergency settings, the government was expected to honour the usual civic expectations: constitutionality, legality, legitimacy, fairness – and kindness. The government was still expected to explain its actions and be judged against these standards – whether favourably or unfavourably.

It is that phenomenon of rendering account, in a time of crisis, that this chapter focuses on. The various forms of accountability the government was exposed to during the pandemic are be identified and assessed. In doing so, I adopt a relational or dialogical conception of accountability, which looks at conversations where the government renders account, is interrogated, its response is appraised and consequences may follow.[3] This study of those conversations is organised around three dimensions: the first two familiar typologies of accountability – democratic and constitutional – and the third less so – learning.

2. Strategy: Elimination Through Going Hard and Going Early

New Zealand's strategy during this early period, ultimately based around elimination, has been well catalogued (although it was not a strategy without challenges).[4] Much of the success in stamping out the virus is attributed to the government's 'go hard, go early' response. An aggressive nationwide lockdown of seven weeks from late March to mid-May 2020 broke the chain of community transmission. A border fortress was constructed, with mandatory state-managed quarantine for 14 days on entry. Within this nationwide bubble, the country was fortunate to have long virus-free periods, interspersed with small outbreaks arising from border breaches. That is to be expected under the elimination strategy, which contemplated a sophisticated form of 'whack-a-mole' if the virus re-emerged. Short, sharp regional lockdowns, temporary elevation of other precautions, super-charged contact tracing and testing, and forensic examination of transmission were all used to dampen down any flare-ups.

3 Mark Bovens, 'Analysing and Assessing Accountability: A Conceptual Framework' (2007) 13 European Law Journal 447.

4 Michael Baker and others, 'New Zealand's Covid-19 Elimination Strategy' (2020) 213 Medical Journal of Australia 198; David Skegg, 'The Covid-19 Pandemic: Lessons For Our Future' (2021) 17(1) Policy Quarterly 3; Dean R Knight, 'Stamping out Covid-19 in New Zealand' (2021) Public Law 241; Dean Knight, 'New Zealand: Legal Responses to Covid-19' in Jeff King and Octavio Ferraz (eds), *The Oxford Compendium of National Legal Responses to Covid-19* (Oxford University Press 2021); John Hopkins, 'Smoke, Mirrors and Legal Uncertainty: the Rights and Wrongs of New Zealand's Covid-19 Response' in Stefan Kirchner (ed), *Governing the Crisis: Law, Human Rights and Covid-19* (Lit Verlag 2021); and Janet McLean and others, 'Legality in Times of Emergency: Assessing NZ's response to Covid-19' (2021) 51 Journal of the Royal Society of New Zealand S197.

New Zealand's success during this first year or so can probably be explained by a mix of factors. We can point to factors such as the late onset of the virus, early and aggressive lockdown, favourable geographical settings, effective leadership, coherent communication and community cooperation. But the significance of a good sprinkling of luck cannot be discounted either.

Stamping out the virus – first so in June 2020 and then again after flare-ups in August 2020 and February 2021 especially – also means there are at least two different stories to tell about New Zealand's response to the pandemic. The first – and the focus of this chapter, penned in the middle of 2021 – is the first year or so of the pandemic while the public health response was at its peak and regulatory settings were significantly elevated. The second captures the periods of calm where ordinary life largely returned, within the protective nationwide bubble, while the country awaited vaccination and promised reintegration with the rest of the world. It is suspected that there will be a different story to tell about accountability in subsequent stages of a pandemic, as diminishing fear, rising apathy and eerie normality take hold. But that is a story for another day.

3. Framework: Directive Executive Powers, Some Old, Some New

A multi-layered and evolving framework of emergency legal powers was used by the government to respond to the pandemic and to impose very severe restrictions.

The main legal tool used was the power to issue health orders and directions. At the outset of the pandemic, health orders were issued by the Director-General of Health under long-standing special powers in the Health Act 1956 to combat infectious diseases. Health orders were used to close premises, prohibit public congregation, require people to stay at home in their household bubbles and regulate incoming travel and border quarantine.[5] In mid-2020, a more nuanced and sophisticated legal regime, the COVID-19 Public Health Response Act 2020, was passed, transferring the primary power to make health orders (now COVID-19 orders) to a minister and wrapping the emergency directive powers with additional checks and balances and safeguards.[6] After the Act was passed, COVID-19 orders were the main vehicle for imposing all sorts of public health restrictions, such as regional lockdowns, a contact tracing regime, wearing of face-coverings in some situations, testing requirements, the border quarantine regime and so forth.[7] Notably, health and COVID-19 orders are instruments of executive government and secondary legislation. While powerful, they may be invalidated by the courts – if they are

5 See e.g. Ashley Bloomfield, 'Section 70(1)(m) Notice to Close Premises and Forbidding Congregation in Outdoor Places of Amusement or Recreation' (25 March 2020); Ashley Bloomfield, 'Section 70(1)(f) Notice to all Persons in New Zealand' (3 April 2020); Health Act (Covid-19 Alert Level 3) Order 2020 (24 April 2020).

6 For analysis of the bespoke legislation, see Claudia Geiringer, 'The Covid-19 Public Health Response Act 2020' [2020] New Zealand Law Journal 159; Janet McLean, 'Risk and Rule of Law' (2020) 16 Policy Quarterly 11; Knight, 'Stamping Out' (n 4).

7 See e.g. Covid-19 Public Health Response (Alert Level 2) Order 2020; Covid-19 Public Health Response (Alert Level Requirements) Order (No 8) 2021.

contrary to their empowering statute or unjustifiably limit protected rights under the New Zealand Bill of Rights Act 1990.[8]

More generic emergency directive powers were also available under the Civil Defence Emergency Management Act 2002, activated by a state of national emergency in place from late-March 2020 to mid-May 2020.[9] The Epidemic Preparedness Act 2006 triggered these emergency powers, through the declaration of an epidemic, a declaration that remains in force in the middle of 2021.[10] This declaration also enlivened dormant provisions throughout the statute book, alleviating administrative hurdles and unlocking a (barely used) 'Henry VIII' power to modify primary legislation by secondary legislation. At a community-wide level, health and COVID-19 orders reflected alert levels set by cabinet under an extra-legal alert level framework.[11] The system of four alert levels – exhorting the general nature of risk and commensurate restrictions – stood at the heart of an extremely powerful and effective communications strategy. On the ground, more surgical directive orders were also issued by health officials to particular people and communities, especially to manage small flare-ups after the virus occasionally broke through the border fortress.[12]

It is impossible to ignore the breadth and depth of the regulatory powers deployed during the pandemic by the executive – unprecedented in recent times. Add to this the enormous suite of social welfare and business support measures, such as a wage subsidy scheme, a redundancy scheme, increased and extended benefit payments, business cashflow support programmes and economic support.[13] All-in-all, an eye-watering amount of government spending during the pandemic.

4. Accountability: Democratic, Constitutional, Learning

Against that backdrop, we can turn to the question of accountability. In other words, to what extent was the government held to account for the decisions it made under the framework of emergency powers and other actions it took while managing the crisis? To answer this, we might think about accountability as a relational concept, as Bovens invites us to: [14]

8 Ross Carter, J McHerron and R Malone, *Subordinate Legislation in New Zealand* (Wellington, LexisNexis 2013); *Drew v Attorney-General* [2002] 1 NZLR 58 (CA); Covid-19 Public Health Response Act 2020, s 13(2).

9 PEG Henare, 'Declaration of State of National Emergency by Minister of Civil Defence' (*New Zealand Gazette*, 25 March 2020).

10 Jacinda Ardern, 'Epidemic Preparedness (Covid-19) Notice 2020' (*New Zealand Gazette*, 24 March 2020).

11 On government communication generally, see Dean R Knight, 'Government Expression and the Pandemic: Advising, Nudging, Urging, Commanding' (2020) 31 Public Law Review 391.

12 See e.g. Niki Stefanogiannis, 'Direction under s 70 of the Health Act 1956 [locations of interest in Wellington, New Zealand]' (25 June 2021).

13 Knight, 'National Responses' (n 4).

14 Mark Bovens, 'Analysing and Assessing Accountability: A Conceptual Framework' (2007) 13 European Law Journal 447. See also Mark Bovens, Thomas Schillemans and Paul 't Hart, 'Does

> Accountability is a relationship between an actor and forum in which an actor has an obligation to explain and to justify his or her conduct, the forum can pose questions and pass judgement, and the actor may face consequences.

Seen in this way, accountability is a series of dialogical conversations which appraise the government's actions.[15]

Those conversations were many and varied during the pandemic. Accountability conversations are also coloured by the standards against which the actor will be judged by the forum. Broadly speaking, some of those conversations take on a political hue, some are framed in legal terms and others focus on continuous improvement and efficacy – in other words, the democratic, constitutional and learning perspectives of accountability.[16]

4.1 Democratic

Democratic accountability, both formal and informal, was the most prominent means by which the New Zealand government's actions were judged.

Parliamentary proceedings were barely disrupted.[17] The House of Representatives only adjourned for just over a month during the nationwide level 4 lockdown in March and April 2020. When the House resumed its usual operations, interrogating the efficacy of the government's response dominated its proceedings – in parliamentary questions, general and specific debates, and debates on pandemic-related legislation. Resort to special logistical arrangements (reduced quorum, adjustments to proxy voting, physical distancing, etc) were not needed, other than for a couple of weeks in total.

The Epidemic Response Committee served as New Zealand's 'Parliament-in-miniature', while the House was adjourned and for a little time after.[18] Chaired

---

Public Accountability Work? An Assessment Tool' (2008) 86 Public Administration 225; Richard Mulgan, *Holding Power to Account: Accountability in Modern Democracies* (Palgrave Macmillan 2003); Mark D Javis and Paul G Thomas, 'The Limits of Accountability: What Can and Cannot Be Accomplished in the Dialectics of Accountability?' in Herman Bakvis and Mark D Jarvis (eds), *From New Public Management to New Political Governance* (McGill-Queen's University Press 2012).

15 Matthew SR Palmer and Dean R Knight, *The Constitution of New Zealand: A Contextual Analysis* (Hart Publishing 2020) ch 8.

16 Bovens (n 14).

17 See generally David Wilson, 'How the New Zealand Parliament Responded' in Study of Parliament Group, *Parliaments and the Pandemic* (2021) 187; Dean R Knight, 'Law-Making and Accountability in Responding to Covid-19: the Case of New Zealand' (Briefing paper, Melbourne Forum: Representation in Democracies During Emergencies, University of Melbourne, September 2020); Gabor Hellyer, 'Assessing Parliament's Response to the Covid-19 Pandemic' (2021) 17(1) Policy Quarterly 20.

18 Knight, 'Stamping Out' (n 4); Luke Harris, 'New Zealand Parliament: Setting up the Epidemic Response Committee to Scrutinize Response to Covid-19' (2020) 101 The Parliamentarian 112. I am grateful to Eddie Clark for coining this phrase in this context.

by the leader of the opposition and with an opposition majority, this specially constituted select committee was quite effective in interrogating ministers, officials and experts on all aspects of the government's response and played an important agenda-setting role in political discourse.

Other select committees kept up their work and oversight of government as well. Especially notable – and quietly effective – was the scrutiny of health and COVID-19 orders by the Regulations Review committee in accordance with their standard remit over secondary legislation.[19] So, too, the Finance and Expenditure Committee and its post-enactment inquiry into the operation of the COVID-19 Public Health Response Act 2020.[20] The inquiry was mandated, based on suggestions from scholars, after the draft legislation was rushed through without the usual select committee scrutiny and public consultation (the particular committee chosen for its cross-party expert membership, not its particular subject alignment). One disappointment with the latter process is that the committee's recommended tweaks to the legislation have not (as of the middle of 2021) been adopted.

After the initial height of the pandemic had passed, the scrutiny work of subject-based select committees continued but the diminishing sense of crisis sometimes saw partisan politics creep back in. For example, in early 2021, backbench government MPs were criticised for stonewalling the questioning of key officials – earning a rebuke from the Speaker.[21]

More broadly, the government rendered account directly to the community – *kanohi ki te kanohi* (face to face). Daily media briefings, watched religiously by a large swathe of the public, saw the government interrogated deeply about all aspects of the pandemic and response. Those briefings continued after the initial height of the pandemic passed and throughout 2021, although less frequently. The Prime Minister, Director-General and others supplemented official briefings with live updates on social media. Especially notable was an address by the Attorney-General, who took to Facebook Live to give a detailed explanation of the legal basis for the lockdown when question marks had been raised.[22] Despite occasional protestations that the government was evading responsibility or concern that briefings

19 See e.g. Regulations Review Committee, 'Briefing to Review Secondary Legislation Made in Response to Covid-19' (Four Interim Reports, May–August 2020); Regulations Review Committee, 'Final Report' (August 2020); Regulations Review Committee, 'Examination of Orders Made under Section 11 of the Covid-19 Public Health Response Act 2020' (September 2020); Regulations Review Committee, 'Examination of Covid-19 Orders' (December 2020; February 2021; March 202; May 2021).

20 Finance and Expenditure Committee, 'Inquiry into the Operation of the Covid-19 Public Health Response Act 2020' (July 2020).

21 Jane Patterson, 'Covid-19 Committee Carry-On Catches Labour Lacking' (*RNZ*, 15 April 2021) <https://www.rnz.co.nz/news/on-the-inside/440564/covid-19-committee-carry-on-catches-labour-lacking>.

22 David Parker, 'New Zealand's Covid-19 Response: Legal Underpinnings and Legal Privilege' (Facebook Live transcript *beehive.govt.nz*, 8 May 2020) <https://www.beehive.govt.nz/speech/new-zealand's-covid-19-response-legal-underpinnings-and-legal-privilege>.

were unduly stage-managed, the reality is that the pandemic supercharged a direct accountability conversation between government and public like never before.

Transparency was also super-charged on a systemic basis. A whole-of-government website – 'Unite Against COVID-19' – stocked information on every aspect of the pandemic and response.[23] All cabinet papers and minutes during the pandemic were released month-by-month, with only minor redactions (apparently unprecedented amongst comparable jurisdictions, although a now routine practice that preceded the pandemic).[24] Proactive disclosure of the machinations of executive government during the crisis sparked some remarkable accounts of government decision-making, as well as providing lines of enquiry for investigative journalism.[25]

Ultimately, the people's judgement was a positive one. During the lockdown, public opinion polls showed remarkable support for the government's action: for example, 92% of the public supported the decision to lock down the country.[26] And a general election – the ultimate political test – was held in October 2020 (slightly delayed due to a minor outbreak of the virus).[27] Understandably framed as the COVID-19 election, the government's track record in combating the virus was the hot topic on the hustings. Prime Minister Jacinda Ardern and her Labour Party were returned to power, increasing their support from 36.9% to 50% – the first time a single party has achieved an outright majority in over two decades of proportional representation. One of her minor coalition partners (NZ First) did not fare so well, missing out on re-election; another confidence-and-supply partner (Greens) also increased their support and re-joined Labour in government.

Overall, political discourse and dynamics continued throughout the pandemic, largely unabated. Democratic accountability was active and rich.

4.2 Constitutional

Constitutional accountability played a notable, but relatively infrequent, role during the first year or so of the pandemic. Most of the legal focus was directed at the legal authority for the nationwide lockdown.

In the main challenge, *Borrowdale v Director-General of Health*, the High Court rejected a claim that health orders mandating the nationwide lockdown were

23 New Zealand Government, 'Unite Against Covid-19' <www.covid19.govt.nz>.

24 New Zealand Government, 'Proactive Release' <www.covid19.govt.nz>; Cabinet Office, 'Proactive Release of Cabinet Material' CO(18)4 (23 October 2018).

25 See e.g. Matt Nippert, 'Inside Story of how NZ Fought Covid 19' (*New Zealand Herald*, 16 May 2020) <https://www.nzherald.co.nz/nz/covid-19-coronavirus-the-inside-story-of-how-new-zealand-fought-the-pandemic/STTJAT5X52BORXVEB26XXDM5ZE/>; Mark Daalder, 'The Month that Changed New Zealand' (*Newsroom*, 13 May 2020) <https://www.newsroom.co.nz/long-read-the-month-that-changed-new-zealand>.

26 Jenna Lynch, 'Overwhelming Number of Kiwis Back Government's Lockdown Decision' (*Newshub*, 18 May 2020).

27 Dean R Knight, 'New Zealand's 2020 General Election: Not an Ordinary Election, Not an Ordinary Time' (2021) Public Law 439. On the political dynamics associated with the delayed polling date, see Knight, 'Law-Making and Accountability' (n 17).

ultra vires but accepted that some early messages to stay at home lacked the necessary legal underpinning.[28] The nationwide lockdown was implemented through: (a) a health order closing premises, other than essential businesses, and prohibiting public congregation; and (b) another health order, issued nine days into the lockdown, formally requiring everyone in the country to isolate at home in their household bubbles, subject to narrow exceptions. The main argument in *Borrowdale* was about whether the power in s 70(1)(f) of the Health Act 1956 to "require persons … to be isolated [or] quarantined" could be used to require the entire country to stay at home. Was it a narrow individualised or targeted power, only to be used on a case-by-case basis to isolate or quarantine those infected or suspected of being infected? Or was it a broad power able to be used, as it was, universally over the entire community? The court accepted the latter interpretation was open, especially given the power's emergency purpose, context and history. Significantly, the court rejected an argument that statutory recognition of the principle of legality in s 6 of the Bill of Rights Act dictated a narrow, rights-consistent reading. But, while rights-demands did not narrow the gateway for accessing the emergency powers, the court rightly acknowledged that the *exercise* of those powers must be rights-consistent. And the court went on to observe that the lockdown was "a necessary, reasonable and proportionate response to the COVID-19 crisis at that time" (even though the point was not contested in the judicial review proceedings).[29] Other quibbles with the terms of the health orders were also dismissed.

The court, however, found that the government's messages to stay at home during the first nine days of lockdown – before the health order formally requiring isolation was issued – were unlawful. Urging people to stay at home in media briefings and speeches, the court ruled, limited their mobility rights under the Bill of Rights Act without the necessary legal mandate. In constitutional terms, the limitation on people's freedom of movement was not *prescribed by law*, as it needed to be if it was to operate as a justified limitation on protected rights (even though, in substantive terms, the limitation *was* justified). Central to this ruling was the crucial finding that the words of the Prime Minister, Director-General and police commissioner came with normative force; in other words, the messages were "replete with commands", "conveyed that there was a legal obligation on New Zealanders to comply", and were not merely advisory statements counselling

28 *Borrowdale v Director-General* [2020] NZHC 2090, [2020] 2 NZLR 864. For analysis, see also Marcelo B Rodriguez Ferrere, '*Borrowdale v Director-General of Health*: An Unlawful But Justified National Lockdown' (2020) 31 Public Law Review 234; Claudia Geiringer and Andrew Geddis, 'Judicial Deference and Emergency Power: A Perspective on *Borrowdale v Director-General*' (2020) 31 Public Law Review 376; Dean R Knight, 'Government Expression and the Pandemic' (2020) 31 Public Law Review 391; Hanna Wilberg, 'Interpreting Pandemic Powers: Qualifications to the Principle of Legality' (2020) 31 Public Law Review 370; Edward Willis, 'Borrowdale and Executive Power' (2020) New Zealand Law Journal 397; Knight, 'Stamping Out' (n 4); for an earlier unsuccessful *habeas corpus* challenge, see *Nottingham v Ardern* [2020] NZCA 144.

29 *Borrowdale* (n 28) [292].

voluntary compliance.[30] Only a declaration was issued and it is not expected that the finding had significant knock-on consequences; the police were not aggressively enforcing the lockdown in the early days and the handful of prosecutions appear to have been for breaches of other legally authentic requirements, not the generic stay-at-home message.

The *Borrowdale* case required the government to explain its theory of the legal underpinnings of the lockdown. A formal explanation of the legal authority for the public measures was demanded in the judicial review proceedings – an explanation subject to close forensic scrutiny against the usual rule of law standards. The government was successful in defending and justifying most of its actions; only a bit of the legal foundation in the early days proved fragile. Thus, the government was able to shrug off the partial adverse appraisal – forgivable action during the early hectic days of lockdown and unlawfulness long since remedied. Borrowdale appealed to the Court of Appeal and the same arguments were once again rehearsed when the appeal was heard in July 2021, over a year after the lockdown was lifted. At the time of writing, a decision on the appeal was still awaited.

A couple of other cases called on the government to explain refusals to grant compassionate exemptions to family members from stay-at-home restrictions to visit dying relatives.[31] The government's actions were criticised by the courts – both in terms of legality and basic fairness – and led to the government reviewing and improving its decision-making processes. Later, in 2021, the approval of the Pfizer vaccine was contested by judicial review.[32] The Minister of Health granted provisional consent for the Pfizer vaccine to be used to vaccinate all those over the age of 16. The Minister relied on a power in the Medicines Act 1981 allowing expedited approval of new medicines "on a restricted basis for the treatment of a limited number of patients" (albeit relying on the substantive evidence submitted for a parallel application for full approval).[33] An anti-vaccination group applied for interim orders stopping the vaccination roll-out because approval was not restricted to treatment of a limited number of patients. The High Court refused to grant interim orders; it acknowledged that, first, the provisional approval did not generate undue safety risks and, second, stopping the rollout would have caused adverse public health consequences and undermined the legitimacy of the vaccination campaign. However, Ellis J accepted that the anti-vaccination group had a point about the class restriction and it was reasonably arguable that approval for treatment on a wider basis was unlawful.

In a similar spirit, the Ombudsman also upheld a few complaints under its maladministration jurisdiction relating to pandemic measures. These included, for example, complaints about a failure to consult residents about the use of apartment

30 *Borrowdale* (n 28) [184].

31 *Christiansen v Director-General of Health* [2020] NZHC 887; *Hattie v Attorney-General* (CIV-2019-404-303),

32 *Nga Kaitiaki Tuku Iho Medical Action Society Inc v Minister of Health* [2021] NZHC 1107.

33 Medicines Act 1981, s 23.

hotels for managed isolation,[34] and cancellation of face-to-face access between a mother and son in state care.[35]

Overall, the lack of resort to the courts to contest the legality of the government's actions is not atypical. An appellate judge has previously noted that, as a small democracy, New Zealand tends to "only have an irregular supply of cases" and single judicial review cases "have a disproportionate impact".[36] That holds true in the case of legal challenges during the pandemic. And the absence of a multiplicity of legal challenges also perhaps says something about New Zealand's constitutional culture: a high degree of trust in government and an instinct to contest policy through political means.[37]

4.3 Learning

Learning accountability – systematic improvement through ongoing feedback loops – is tricky to quantify. But there is reason to believe this form of accountability was especially rich throughout the pandemic. The government's actions were often described as, to borrow a rugby term, a 'rolling maul': the response continually evolved and morphed – in the light of reflexive self-appraisal, external quibbles and suggestions, and improved appreciation of health risks and efficacy of precautions. Some of this change was no doubt also nudged along by the other forms of accountability, such as the political and the legal.

We can point to, as examples, several formal reviews, addressing matters such as contact tracing systems, personal protective equipment and the roll-out of border testing.[38] In early 2021, after the initial height of the pandemic had passed, a standing advisory body of experts was commissioned to scrutinise the response on an ongoing basis, partly prompted by a flare up from a border breach.[39] More subtle were conversations taking place beyond the public gaze between those affected by pandemic restrictions and ministers, MPs and officials; unquestionably, these active feedback loops played an important role in improving government actions. The list of essential businesses allowed to operate during the nationwide lockdown was

34 Ombudsman, 'Consultation on Health and Safety Plans for Managed Isolation Facility' (Case 530273) (13 October 2020).

35 Ombudsman, 'Cancellation of Access between Mother and Son due to Covid Alert Level 4 Lockdown' (Case 524040) (16 June 2020).

36 *Lab Tests Auckland Ltd v Auckland District Health Board* [2009] 1 NZLR 776, [396]–[397] (Hammond J).

37 Matthew SR Palmer, 'New Zealand Constitutional Culture' (2007) 22 New Zealand Universities Law Review 565; Palmer and Knight (n 15) ch 1.

38 Ayesha Verrall, *Rapid Audit of Contact Tracing for Covid-19 in New Zealand* (Ministry of Health, 20 April 2020); Controller and Auditor-General, *Management of personal protective equipment in response to Covid-19* (Ministry of Health, June 2020); Heather Simpson and others, *New Zealand Covid-19 Surveillance Plan and Testing Strategy* (Ministry of Health, September 2020).

39 Chris Hipkins, 'Independent Group to Oversee Continual Improvement in Covid-19 Response' (*Beehive.govt.nz*, 9 March 2021) <https://www.beehive.govt.nz/release/independent-group-oversee-continual-improvement-covid-19-response>.

often updated to reflect anomalies pointed out. Alert level rules were revised to address concerns raised by businesses, community groups and scholars. MPs were given a hotline to pursue problems raised by their constituents directly with mid-level departmental officials.

Overall, incremental improvement was common – prompted by reflexive experience and ongoing feedback.

5. Conclusion

This chapter started with the usual worry that emergency conditions risk eroding the accountability of government. Yet, it is striking – and perhaps curious – that accountability was not dodged or evaded in New Zealand during the first year or so of the pandemic. The government worked hard to render account about its actions. Throughout the pandemic, especially during periods of heightened risk and precaution, there remained many and varied opportunities for its response to be interrogated and judged. Sometimes the accountability conversations differed from usual times, especially as some novel forums eclipsed some traditional forums when the latter were not able to operate as normal. Beneath this rough sketch of the chorus of accountability, inevitably, there will be particular instances where accountability did not bite in the way that we might have hoped. But, in general terms, accountability was preserved – and perhaps enhanced – during the early period of this study; the jury remains out on whether the chorus of accountability has been maintained once the sense of crisis waned.

My suspicion is that the openness to responsibility during the height of the pandemic was crucial in fortifying the social licence for the extreme measures the government took. In other words, the government bred legitimacy for its response through its open attitude to accountability. This speaks to another aspect of constitutional culture in New Zealand – a sense of civic virtue that predates the pandemic but was rarefied throughout it.[40] The drivers of this willingness to publicly render account are yet to be fully untangled. One obvious driver is the sense that the previous (National) government was judged poorly for accountability failures following severe earthquakes in Canterbury.[41] Concerns were expressed that the government there tried to insulate its response to and (especially) recovery from the earthquake from the sunlight of accountability, shifting key decisions away from the political arena and to immunise them from legal challenge. But distilling the ingredients that fuelled this admirable type of civic virtue during the COVID-19 pandemic will take some time and further reflection.

Ultimately, the point made in this chapter is a simple one. The New Zealand experience shows the maintenance of accountability mechanisms during the pandemic. That is not to say the government's response was always judged favourably

40 Knight, 'Stamping Out' (n 4).

41 Hopkins, 'Smoke, Mirrors' (n 4); John Hopkins, 'Law, Luck and Lessons (Un)Learned: New Zealand Emergency Law from Canterbury to Covid-19' (2020) 31 Public Law Review 371.

in those conversations: some of the appraisal was positive, some was negative, and consequences flowed accordingly. But a substantive tally of appraisals is not the concern of this chapter; the concern is the survival of the culture and network of accountability during the time of crisis.

The larger task that follows from this sketch of the accountability conversations animated during the pandemic is a deeper dive into the efficacy of the particular mechanisms.[42] In other words, did the particular democratic mechanisms provide the expected popular control and induce government actors to act consistently with citizens' preferences? Did the particular constitutional mechanisms actually prevent abuse of power on the ground and avoid concentration of power in the few? Did the instances of learning in fact stimulate a consistent governmental focus in achieving socially desirable outcomes? There is reason to believe that to be the case with many of the different mechanisms, especially because, as we have seen, the civic conditions supported and maintained the rendering of account and judgement required for the realisation of those goals.

42 Bovens (n 3) 465.

4

CHINA AND COVID-19

An Archetypal Legal and Governmental Response to an Exceptional Challenge

Jacques deLisle and Shen Kui

1. Introduction[1]

Much remains to be learned about the emergence of the COVID-19 pandemic, and much is uncertain about changes China may undertake to address shortcomings revealed in the response to the novel coronavirus. Despite the extraordinary nature of the challenge and the reaction to it, the Chinese regime's approach – and the roles of law in it – have been consistent with long-evident patterns. The initial, brief but costly,[2] delay in responding to a deadly new contagion was consistent with problematic incentives generated by conflicting or ambiguous allocations of authority along functional and geographic lines and imposition of accountability along vertical and horizontal dimensions. The subsequent measures to contain the virus showed the system's capacity to mobilise vast resources and shape citizens' behaviour. Throughout, Chinese authorities acted largely free of legal constraints, including citizens' rights. Reforms to address vulnerabilities revealed in the crisis have been under consideration, but they are unlikely to be transformative. Laws and related mechanisms are, of course, only part of China's response to COVID-19, but they reflect features in China's system of law and governance that do much

1 All websites accessed on 29 July 2021.

2 One study asserts that a three-week earlier lockdown of Wuhan could have prevented 95% of the spread, and a one-week earlier lockdown could have prevented two-thirds. See e.g. Shengjie Lai and others, 'Effect of Non-Pharmaceutical Interventions for Containing the COVID-19 Outbreak in China' (2020) 585 (7825) Nature 410, 411 <https://www.nature.com/articles/s41586-020-2293-x.pdf>.

DOI: 10.4324/9781003211952-5

to explain the shortcomings, successes and character of China's handling of the pandemic and the prospects for reform.[3]

2. A Troubled Legal and Political Response: Systemic Weaknesses in Authority and Accountability

Although judging when serious measures should have been taken is difficult, ample reasons for concern predated by weeks the central authorities' late January 2020 decision to lock down the epicentre of Wuhan.[4] Cases likely began in the autumn of 2019 and the disease became known to Wuhan hospitals by early December, when a doctor's WeChat messages reporting multiple cases of a possibly contagious Severe Acute Respiratory Syndrome (SARS)-like illness were shared so widely that public security officials quashed their distribution.[5] At year's end, China's National Health Commission (NHC) and Centre for Disease Control (CDC) sent expert investigative teams to Wuhan, China informed the World Health Organisation's country office about a cluster of cases of "pneumonia of unknown etiology" and the Wuhan branch of the NHC issued warnings about an "unexplained pneumonia outbreak".[6] But it was not until 20 January that the leader of a third centrally dispatched delegation announced that the disease was communicable,[7] Xi Jinping publicly called on Chinese Communist Party (CCP) committees and governments at all levels to take effective action against the outbreak[8] and central public health

3 This chapter draws on Jacques deLisle and Shen Kui, 'Lessons from China's Response to COVID-19' (2020) 16 University of Pennsylvania Asian Law Review 66; 'China's Response to COVID-19' (2021) 73 Administrative Law Review 19.

4 Chris Buckley and Steven Lee Myers, 'As New Coronavirus Spread, China's Old Habits Delayed Fight' (*The New York Times*, 7 February 2020) <https://www.nytimes.com/2020/02/01/world/asia/china-coronavirus.html>; 杨海 [Yang Hai], '武汉早期疫情上报为何一度中断' [Why the Early Report of the Epidemic Situation in Wuhan Was Interrupted] 中国青年报 [*China Youth Daily*] (5 March 2020) <https://mp.weixin.qq.com/s/69pdSrjNH_4qN3RrQ-Yk0Q>.

5 'He Warned of Coronavirus. Here's What He Told Us Before He Died' (*The New York Times*, 7 February 2020) <https://www.nytimes.com/2020/02/07/world/asia/Li-Wenliang-china-coronavirus.html>; 龚菁琦 [Gong Jingqi], '发哨子的人' [The Whistleblower] 人物 [*People*] (10 March 2020) <https://tinyurl.com/sggfhq8>.

6 World Health Organisation, 'Novel Coronavirus (2019-nCoV) Situation Report – 1' (21 January 2020) <https://www.who.int/docs/default-source/coronaviruse/situation-reports/20200121-sitrep-1-2019-ncov.pdf>; 'NHC Take Positive Actions to Fight New Coronavirus' (20 January 2020) <http://en.nhc.gov.cn/2020-01/20/c_76000.htm>; 武汉市卫生健康委关于不明原因的病毒性肺炎情况通报 [Wuhan Municipal Health Commission Notice on Unexplained Viral Pneumonia Outbreak] (11 January 2020) <http://www.nhc.gov.cn/xcs/yqtb/202001/1beb46f061704372b7ca41ef3e682229.shtml>.

7 Emily Feng and Amy Cheng, 'They Call Him a Hero: Dr. Zhong is the Public Face of China's War against Coronavirus' (*NPR*, 2 April 2020) <https://www.npr.org/sections/goatsandsoda/2020/04/02/825957192/dr-zhong-is-the-supreme-commander-in-china-s-war-against-coronavirus>.

8 周楚卿 [Zhou Chuqing], '习近平对新型冠状病毒感染的肺炎疫情作出重要指示 强调要把人民群众生命安全和身体健康放在第一位 坚决遏制疫情蔓延势头 李克强作出批示' [Xi Jinping Issues Important Instruction on Novel Coronavirus Infectious Pneumonia Epidemic;

authorities declared that strict measures for Class A pathogens (the highest level under China's Infectious Disease Law) would apply.[9] On 23 January, the directive was issued locking down Wuhan, suspending travel, closing businesses and largely confining residents to their homes.[10] Level 1 emergencies (the highest in China's scale) were declared within days across the country.[11]

The troubled initial response reflects endemic and interrelated features of law and governance in China: *tiao-tiao/kuai-kuai*, fragmented governance and ambiguous mandates.[12] In China, authority and responsibility for a substantive area of regulation often are allocated in an overlapping manner along two axes: a function-based hierarchical bureaucracy reaching up to a ministry-level entity in the central government (*tiao* – a long, narrow stick) and the general-purpose geographic government at the same level (*kuai* – a block or clump). Sound rationales support both approaches in the context of potential pandemics and more generally. *Tiao*-style measures call for reporting through specialised, expert channels to inform central-level policy decisions on public health threats of national or global significance. Requirements for rapid reporting within a *tiao* can bypass delays associated with level-by-level decision-making in China's vast, multi-tiered system. *Kuai*-type rules recognise that effective handling of epidemics and other threats must rely on local officials to monitor developments, coordinate among front-line units across *tiao* lines, and mobilise state and societal assets. Assignments of responsibility, as well as authority, at a particular level of government can ameliorate shirking and 'passing the buck upward'.

The laws in place when the novel coronavirus outbreak began embodied both approaches. The Emergency Response Law, the Law on the Prevention and Treatment of Infectious Diseases ('Infectious Disease Law') and other laws include many *kuai* elements. They assign to the most local-level government (provincial, municipal or county) principal authority and responsibility for preparing for, detecting, declaring, informing and warning about, as well as responding to, public health emergencies, disease outbreaks and potential pandemics. They give subna-

Emphasis on People's Lives and Health as Top Priority; Resolutely Contain the Epidemic's Spread; Li Keqiang Issues Instructions] (*Xinhua*, 20 January 2020) <http://www.xinhuanet.com/politics/leaders/2020-01/20/c_1125486561.htm>.

9 中华人民共和国国家卫生健康委员会公告, 2020年第1号 [Announcement of the National Health Commission of the People's Republic of China, 2020 No 1] (20 January 2020) <http://www.nhc.gov.cn/jkj/s7916/202001/44a3b8245e8049d2837a4f27529cd386.shtml>.

10 武汉市新型冠状病毒感染的肺炎疫情防控指挥部通告（第1号）[Notice from the Wuhan Municipal Novel Coronavirus Infection Pneumonia Epidemic Prevention and Control Command Center (No 1)] (23 January 2020) <http://www.gov.cn/xinwen/2020-01/23/content_5471751.htm>.

11 'Updates on Coronavirus Outbreak (January 22–March 9)' (*Global Times*, 10 March 2020) <https://www.globaltimes.cn/content/1181093.shtml>; Emma Graham-Harrison and Lily Kuo, 'China's Coronavirus Lockdown Strategy: Brutal but Effective' (*The Guardian*, 19 March 2020) <https://www.theguardian.com/world/2020/mar/19/chinas-coronavirus-lockdown-strategy-brutal-but-effective>.

12 See generally Kenneth Lieberthal, *Governing China: From Revolution through Reform* (W.W. Norton, 2nd ed. 2004) 187.

tional governments authority to require and receive reports on disease outbreaks and potential epidemics from medical units and same-level branches of the public health bureaucracy, coordinate across public health and other units of the state at the relevant level, impose (with reports to, or approval from higher levels) drastic limits on economic and social activities (including quarantines and travel bans) and deploy extensive public and private resources.[13]

Tiao elements are prominent as well. The Emergency Response Law assigns departments (such as the NHC) under the State Council (China's council of ministers) responsibility for developing response plans, structures and criteria for declaring public health emergencies, deploying experts to assess possible emergencies and evaluating threats. Along with related regulations, it gives specific NHC-empowering rules priority over more general laws concerning public health emergencies and the NHC (and other central departments) broad authority to address public health emergencies that endanger the national economy.[14] The Infectious Disease Law and related regulations assign the NHC, the CDC and their subnational branches multiple roles in preventing, supervising and controlling infectious diseases, as well as monitoring, investigating, receiving reports from – and issuing warnings to – peer institutions, subordinate branches and the public about potential epidemics and public health emergencies.[15] The Direct Reporting System mandates near-real-time reporting of infectious diseases to higher-level authorities in the public health bureaucracy.[16]

Some of these provisions reflect reforms to redress problems seen in responding to SARS in 2002, including local-level concealment, and slow reporting to higher levels, of early indications of the outbreak; a lack of timely warnings to the public; inadequate mobilisation of resources to combat the epidemic; and balkanising responses by local officials that impeded coordinated responses.[17] As the initial handling of the COVID-19 outbreak shows, well-intentioned legal mechanisms that seek to reap the benefits of *tiao*- and *kuai*-style approaches may not succeed.[18] The

13 中华人民共和国突发事件应对法 [Emergency Response Law of the People's Republic of China] (2007); 中华人民共和国传染病防治法 [Law of the People's Republic of China on Prevention and Treatment of Infectious Diseases] (2013).

14 突发公共卫生事件应急条例 [Regulations on Responses to Public Health Emergencies] (2011).

15 Regulations on Responses (n 14); 突发公共卫生事件与传染病疫情监测信息报告管理办法 [Measures for the Administration of Information Reporting on Monitoring Public Health Emergencies and Epidemics of Infectious Diseases] (2006).

16 国务院关于传染病防治工作和传染病防治法实施情况的报告 [Report of the State Council on Work on Control and Prevention of Infectious Diseases and Implementation of the Law on Control and Prevention of Infectious Diseases] (28 August 2013) <http://www.npc.gov.cn/zgrdw/npc/xinwen/2013-08/28/content_1804522.htm>; Regulations on Responses (n 14); Measures for Information Reporting (n 15).

17 Jacques deLisle, 'SARS, Greater China, and the Pathologies of Globalization and Transition' (2003) 47 Orbis 587, 595–601.

18 Shen Kui, 'The Delayed Response in Wuhan Reveals Legal Holes' (*The Regulatory Review*, 20 April 2020) <https://www.theregreview.org/2020/04/20/delayed-response-wuhan-reveals-legal-holes>.

coexistence of *tiao* and *kuai* features – and the problematic relationship between them – that are commonplace in China's law and governance create conflicting or ambiguous imperatives for subnational-level officials and invite the dysfunction seen in the initial response to COVID-19. Officials with responsibility for public health at subnational levels (along with counterparts in other fields) must serve two masters: higher-level authorities in the functionally defined *tiao* and the multi-competent *kuai* of same-level government.

On the *kuai* side, a 'double or nothing' bet faces local officials encountering a problem of uncertain seriousness (including a novel contagion). The official can report to superiors (or allow subordinates in the local public health bureaucracy to do so) – as called for by policies and laws such as the Infectious Disease Law and the Direct Reporting System. This path may have few apparent upsides for the official because the threat may later be judged (correctly or not) to have been minor and reporting may be seen as 'crying wolf' (and needlessly inflicting economic costs or triggering public alarm) or as an attempt to shift responsibility. Alternatively, the official can try to ride out or resolve a not-yet-dire situation without higher level authorities or the public becoming aware. If information gets out (for example, through whistleblowers, such as the hospital doctors in Wuhan) or the problem proves much more consequential (as with COVID-19), the official may face graver consequences, both for the greater harm due to delay and for having violated reporting obligations.

These dynamics appear to have operated in Wuhan. Public security officials, accountable to the local government, silenced the doctors who raised alarm about the new illness on social media.[19] Hospital officials, answerable to the Wuhan Health Commission (WHC) and WHC officials appear to have directed, successfully, medical staff to withhold information indicating human-to-human transmission from the teams sent by central public health authorities.[20] According to some accounts, the CDC learned of the outbreak at the end of 2019 only from leaked online versions of two undisclosed emergency notices the WHC issued to local medical institutions.[21] For senior Wuhan officials, making timely public disclosure and taking aggressive control measures would have been especially fraught because such moves would have disrupted the high-profile annual sessions of the

19 Josh Rudolph, 'Translation: Li Wenliang's "Admonishment Notice",' (*China Digital Times*, 3 January 2020) <https://chinadigitaltimes.net/2020/02/translation-li-wenliangs-admonishment-notice/> .

20 俞琴 黎诗韵 [Yu Qin and Li Shiyun], '专访卫健委派武汉第二批专家:为何没发现人传人?' [Interview of Second Team of Experts Sent by NHC to Wuhan: Why Wasn't Inter-Personal Transmission Discovered?] 新浪网 [*Sina*] (26 February 2020) <https://news.sina.cn/gn/2020-02-26/detail-iimxxstf4577244.d.html?from=wap>; Dali L Yang, 'Wuhan Officials Tried to Cover Up Covid-19—And Sent It Careening Outward' (*The Washington Post*, 10 March 2020) <https://www.washingtonpost.com/politics/2020/03/10/wuhan-officials-tried-cover-up-covid-19-sent-it-careening-outward/>.

21 Yang (n 20); Michael D. Swaine, 'Chinese Crisis Decision Making—Managing the COVID-19 Pandemic, Part One: The Domestic Component' (2020) 64 China Leadership Monitor <https://www.prcleader.org/swaine>.

Wuhan Municipal and Hubei Provincial People's Congress and People's Political Consultative Conference in early and mid-January 2020 and the heavy travel season for the national lunar New Year's holiday that would begin on 24 January.[22] It soon became clear that Wuhan officials had lost their bet. Outside reports blamed local authorities' fear of giving bad news to superiors for the failure of the supposedly automatic reporting system.[23] By early February, Xi criticised failures by local party, government and public health officials in Wuhan, and sackings of the provincial and municipal party chiefs and many lower-level officials began.[24]

Tiao-related features also pose challenges, often through interactions with *kuai*-based elements in what is often called China's 'fragmented authoritarianism':[25] institutions (function-based/vertical and geography-based/horizontal) frequently act – often with underpinnings in legal and policy mandates – as discrete entities, pursuing independent interests and conflicting agendas, battling or bargaining to protect turf and influence policies. Members – and especially leaders – often identify strongly with their own units (*danwei*) and view counterparts in other bodies as outsiders. Such 'siloing' is, of course, a near-universal problem, but it is distinctive and highly salient in China, including in the initial response to COVID-19.

The public health/disease prevention and control bureaucratic system (*xitong*) is comparatively weak. In the formal hierarchy, the CDC is a *ting* – a sub-ministry-level entity under the NHC. The NHC is the equivalent of a ministry, headed by a director with the rank of minister (*buzhang*) – formally the peer of heads of more than two-dozen ministries and commissions and on a par with a provincial governor. The de facto stature of the public health *xitong* has been lower. Its leaders have not had the political prominence or super-ministerial ranks of heads of major ministries or commissions in higher-priority policy areas. It has been troubled and unstable, with the then-Ministry of Health severely criticised for SARS and the restructuring that produced the NHC occurring less than two years before COVID-19. Despite post-SARS reforms, responsibility for public health on the eve of COVID-19 remained

22 Kyle Jaros, 'China's Early COVID-19 Missteps Have an All-Too-Mundane Explanation' (*The Diplomat*, 9 April 2020) <https://thediplomat.com/2020/04/chinas-early-covid-19-struggles-have-an-all-too-mundane-explanation/>.

23 Steven Lee Myers, 'China Created a Fail-Safe System to Track Contagions. It Failed' (*The New York Times*, 17 April 2020) <https://www.nytimes.com/2020/03/29/world/asia/coronavirus-china.html>; Edward Wong and others, 'Local Officials in China Hid Coronavirus Danger from Beijing, U.S. Agencies Find' (*The New York Times*, 17 September 2020) <https://www.nytimes.com/2020/08/19/world/asia/china-coronavirus-beijing-trump.html>.

24 Qiang Lijing and others, 'China Penalizes Derelict Officials in Coronavirus Fight' (*Xinhua*, 5 February 2020) <http://www.xinhuanet.com/english/2020-02/05/c_138755872.htm>; 习近平 [Xi Jinping], '在中央政治局常委会会议研究应对新型冠状病毒肺炎疫情工作时的讲话' [Speech at the Politburo Standing Committee's meeting on novel coronavirus responses] 人民网 [*People.cn*] (16 February 2020) para 1, 2, 4 <http://cpc.people.com.cn/n1/2020/0216/c64094-31589177.html>.

25 See Kenneth G Lieberthal, 'The "Fragmented Authoritarianism Model" and Its Limitations' in Kenneth G Lieberthal and David M Lampton (eds) *Bureaucracy, Politics and Decision Making in Post-Mao China* (University of California Press 1992) 1–32.

spread across many government organs.[26] In Wuhan, a monitoring system that depended on cooperation among hospital administrators and numerous government units at various levels failed – "monumentally", in the judgment of one expert.[27] Internal documents cited the Hubei CDC's low capacity and morale, and the passivity of sub-provincial branches during the early days of COVID-19.[28] Senior public health officials and experts have long complained about the meagre powers and resources of the CDC and their field's low priority with leaders and the public.[29] The leader of the third expert team sent to Wuhan lamented the impediments encountered as revealing the CDC's "too low" position.[30] Prioritising the economy over public health concerns – a false dilemma and hardly unique to China – pervaded the response, with concerns about economic impacts likely deterring an early lockdown in Wuhan and Xi and the CCP's COVID-19-focused leading small group beginning to emphasise reopening the economy by spring 2020.[31]

Notwithstanding the pulls of 'dual rule' (with accountability running along both *tiao* and *kuai* lines), *kuai* often dominates *tiao*, especially where the relevant *tiao* is weak (as with the public health bureaucracy) and legal rules and policies assign key roles to both types of organs (as with the Infectious Disease Law and the Emergency Response Law). In the early reaction to COVID-19 in Wuhan, public health officials and hospital leaders who were part of, or accountable to, local authorities did not follow the Direct Reporting System (for weeks into the epidemic) and other requirements to convey information immediately to central authorities, and they obstructed the investigative teams dispatched by higher-level NHC and CDC authorities.[32] The legal framework was part of the problem. Post-SARS reforms had not raised the *tiao*-enhancing Direct Reporting System to the status of law, nor (at least in the view of critics) established clear thresholds and duties for designating and directly reporting not-previously-identified diseases (such as COVID-19, prior to the late January 2020 central directive mandating

26 See generally Alex Jingwei He, 'Manoeuvring Within a Fragmented Bureaucracy: Policy Entrepreneurship in China's Local Healthcare Reform' (2018) 236 China Quarterly 1088.

27 Dali L Yang, 'China's Early Warning System Didn't Work on Covid-19. Here's the Story' (*The Washington Post*, 24 February 2020) <https://www.washingtonpost.com/politics/2020/02/24/chinas-early-warning-system-didnt-work-covid-19-heres-story>.

28 Nick Paton Walsh, 'The Wuhan Files' (CNN, 1 December 2020) <https://www.cnn.com/2020/11/30/asia/wuhan-china-covid-intl/index.html?utm_medium=social&utm_source=twCNN&utm_content=2020-11-30T22:15:04> .

29 Lilia Wu and Evelyn Cheng, 'Virus Disclosure in China Was Delayed Because Disease Control Group Lacks Authority, Top Scientist Says' (*CNBC*, 28 February 2020) <https://www.cnbc.com/2020/02/28/chinas-cdc-lacks-authority-to-alert-public-on-virus-scientist-says.html>; 李立明 [Li Liming] and others, '疫情早期，疾病预防控制体系失声原因何在?' [At the Early Stage of Pandemic, Why Was the Disease Prevention and Control System Silent?], 知识分子 [*Intellectual*] (3 March 2020) <http://zhishifenzi.com/depth/depth/8392.html>.

30 魏芙蓉 [Wei Furong] and others, '武汉疫情初期，网络直报系统为何失灵? [Why Did the Direct Network Reporting System Fail at the Beginning of the Wuhan Epidemic?] (*Phoenix New Media*, 14 March 2020) <http://news.ifeng.com/c/7uqH6A5PWt7>; Yang (n 4).

31 State Council Information Office, 'Fighting Covid-19: China in Action' (June 2020) pt II.

32 Myers (n 23); Walsh (n 28); Wei (n 30).

Class A pathogen protocols), nor remade a system in which medical personnel reported on worrying outbreaks through their hospitals or local-level CDC branches, nor (as the leader of the second expert team to Wuhan complained) displaced the system of "territorial management" in addressing infectious disease outbreaks.[33]

Chinese officials in public health (and other mass harm-related regulatory fields) often operate with ambiguous mandates due to complex, overlapping roles that laws and policies assign to multiple entities and the absence of reliable meta-rules or formal procedures to reduce uncertainty or resolve conflicts among directives from different sources (even where rules have formally unequal stature). This phenomenon may explain a notorious incident from the early phase of COVID-19. The mayor of Wuhan – who also headed the city's COVID-19 control and prevention headquarters – asserted that he had delayed public release of information because, as a "local government" official, he could disclose only after receiving authorisation.[34] If sincere, this position adopts a plausible if problematic interpretation of relevant law: the Infectious Disease Law assigns the NHC authority to release information about possible outbreaks and epidemics and to authorise provincial-level branches to do so, arguably implying that a mere mayor could not be authorised; but the Emergency Response Law empowers local governments, such as the municipal government headed by Wuhan's mayor, to issue early warnings and information to the public about an imminent public health emergency – so long as such action is consistent with other law.[35] If disingenuous, the mayor's position demonstrates the potential to exploit regulatory ambiguity by adopting – even retroactively – a self-serving reading to avoid responsibility when losing the double-or-nothing bet on not promptly reporting the outbreak.

Such problems of rule-ambiguity are compounded by CCP rules, which coexist – and sometimes merge – with state laws and policies and can overshadow them. Party rules require reporting to higher levels on policy implementation and seeking instructions on "major matters", including serious disease outbreaks.[36] A COVID-19-focused notice from the CCP Central Committee exhorted party committees and members to take unspecified leadership roles in epidemic-response work by government entities.[37] As such measures reflect, the centralisa-

33 Edward Gu and Lantian Li, 'Crippled Community Governance and Suppressed Scientific/Professional Communities: A Critical Assessment of Failed Early Warning for the COVID-19 Outbreak in China' (2020) 5 Journal of Chinese Governance 160; Yang (n 4); Yu and Li (n 20); Wu and Cheng (n 29).

34 张雨亭 [Zhang Yuting], '武汉市长称无权公布疫情' [Mayor of Wuhan Claiming No Right to Make Public the Pandemic], 南方都市报 [*Sothern Metropolitan Daily*] (30 January 2020) <https://www.sohu.com/a/369630319_161795>.

35 Infectious Disease Law (n 13) arts. 19, 38; Emergency Response Law (n 13) art. 42–45; Regulations on Responses (n 14) art. 25; Measures for Information Reporting (n 15) art. 32.

36 'Regulations of the Communist Party of China on Requests for Instructions and Reports on Major Issues' (19 April 2019) <http://lnupd.com/english/article/shows/269>.

37 中共中央印发'关于加强党的领导、为打赢疫情防控阻击战提供坚强政治保证的通知' [Communist Party of China Central Committee issued the 'Notice on Strengthening the Party's

tion of authority has long been a principal means to redress fragmentation in law and governance. Centralisation, however, can exacerbate shirking by local officials (who are incentivised to await clarifying directives and who may see nonfeasance as the safer course when higher authorities are monitoring behaviour or revising mandates). It also can entail risks for regime leaders, as when retrospective declarations that Xi had been directing the COVID-19 response from early January drew scepticism about their veracity and questions about why the leadership had not acted sooner and more decisively.[38] Yet, capacity to centralise is also a strength of the system that helps account for successes in responding to COVID-19.

3. Coordinated Mobilisation Without Constraints: Systemic Strengths of State, Law and Politics

Although when central authorities comprehended the trouble in Wuhan is disputed,[39] once centrally mandated efforts to contain COVID-19 began, they were effective, as well as draconian. They reflected characteristic strengths of China's authoritarian state – including its use of law – in mobilising resources and controlling society. Tens of thousands of medical personnel and vast stores of equipment were deployed to Wuhan and rudimentary hospitals were built within two weeks after lockdown. Teams composed, or under the direction, of government staff were stationed in neighbourhoods and apartment blocks to perform health checks, provide daily necessities, impose isolation and quarantine, build physical barriers and conduct contact-tracing. Similar methods were used in other hotspots.[40] By early March 2020, authorities declared the initial outbreak "curbed".[41] During and after the first-wave response, old-style, labour-intensive and newer, high-tech methods were employed to monitor and control citizens. The familiar ubiquitous guards at building entrances implemented prohibitions on entry and exit and mandatory temperature checks. Residents' committees – long-established unofficial bodies under local party-state leadership – enforced restrictions on mobility, provided

Leadership and Providing a Strong Political Guarantee for Winning the War of Prevention and Control of the Epidemic'] (28 January 2020) <http://www.gov.cn/zhengce/2020-01/28/content_5472753.htm>.

38 Amy Qin, 'China's Leader, Under Fire, Says He Led Coronavirus Fight Early On' (*The New York Times*, 15 February 2020) <https://www.nytimes.com/2020/02/15/world/asia/xi-china-coronavirus.html>; Wong and others (n 23); Xi (n 24).

39 Swaine (n 21); 'What Did Xi Jinping Know About the Coronavirus, and When Did He Know It?' (*The Washington Post*, 19 February 2020) <https://www.washingtonpost.com/opinions/global-opinions/what-did-xi-jinping-know-about-the-coronavirus-and-when-did-he-know-it/2020/02/19/35482fe2-5340-11ea-b119-4faabac6674f_story.html>.

40 Gerry Shih, 'Locked Down in Beijing, I Watched China Beat Back the Coronavirus' (*The Washington Post*, 16 March 2020) <https://www.washingtonpost.com/world/asia_pacific/locked-down-in-beijing-i-watched-china-beat-back-the-coronavirus/2020/03/16/f839d686-6727-11ea-b199-3a9799c54512_story.html>; State Council Information Office (n 31) pts III.3–III.4.

41 Stephen McDonell, 'Coronavirus: China Says Disease 'Curbed' in Wuhan and Hubei' (BBC *News*, 10 March 2020) <https://www.bbc.com/news/world-asia-china-51813876>.

supplies to people under lockdown, and surveilled inhabitants' activities and health status. In urban areas, the 'grid system' (established in the 2010s for more fine-grained 'social management') was reinforced with personnel seconded from government offices to conduct monitoring, transmit directives and provide resources to residents. Prosecutors' offices urged citizens to report violations of containment rules.[42] After the lockdowns, state authorities deployed formidable assets to track, trace and limit the spread of cases. In cities, reliance on mobile phone-based apps for daily activities, pervasive networks of security cameras, and extensive use of facial recognition technology gave monitors potent tools.[43] Health status, reflected in on-phone QR codes, regulated access to public transit, and longer-distance travellers were tracked down after exposure to infected fellow passengers. Big data and artificial intelligence were employed to identify risks of outbreaks and mobility patterns to guide imposition or lifting of restrictions.[44] In later 2020 and 2021, localised outbreaks triggered rapid massive-scale testing and temporary lockdowns, and a swift and vast vaccination programme was launched.[45]

Although at times evaded or marginalised, legal rules were part of the large-scale, centre-driven response. Xi asserted the importance of pursuing pandemic prevention and control "according to law" and following "the path of the rule of law" and called for punishing official dereliction of duty and criminal activities that impeded responses to the epidemic or took advantage of the circumstances.[46] The State Council's White Paper recounting the first months of the response

42 'Community Grid System Helps China Fight Virus' (*Global Times*, 5 February 2020) <https://www.globaltimes.cn/content/1178528.shtml>; Emily Feng and Amy Cheng, 'Restrictions And Rewards: How China Is Locking Down Half A Billion Citizens' (NPR, 21 February 2020) <https://www.npr.org/sections/goatsandsoda/2020/02/21/806958341/restrictions-and-rewards-how-china-is-locking-down-half-a-billion-citizens>; Jeremy Page, 'China's Progress Against Coronavirus Used Draconian Tactics Not Deployed in the West' (*The Wall Street Journal*, 24 March 2020) <https://www.wsj.com/articles/the-west-is-misinterpreting-wuhans-coronavirus-progressand-drawing-the-wrong-lessons-11585074966>; Wang Wenwen, 'Neighborhood Committees are in the Vanguard of Virus Control' (*Global Times*, 31 March 2020) <https://www.globaltimes.cn/content/1184356.shtml>.

43 Yingzhi Yang and Julie Zhu, 'Coronavirus Brings China's Surveillance State out of the Shadows' (*Reuters*, 7 February 2020) <https://www.reuters.com/article/us-china-health-surveillance/coronavirus-brings-chinas-surveillance-state-out-of-the-shadows-idUSKBN2011HO>; 'To Curb Covid-19, China is Using its High-Tech Surveillance Tools' (*The Economist*, 29 February 2020) <https://www.economist.com/china/2020/02/29/to-curb-covid-19-china-is-using-its-high-tech-surveillance-tools>.

44 Rajib Shaw and others, 'Governance, Technology and Citizen Behavior in Pandemic: Lessons from COVID-19 in East Asia' (2020) 6 Progress in Disaster Science 1, 8.

45 Anna Fifield and Lyric Li, 'Beijing Goes into 'Wartime Mode' as Virus Emerges at Market' (*The Washington Post*, 13 June 2020) <https://www.washingtonpost.com/world/beijing-goes-into-wartime-mode-as-virus-emerges-at-market-in-chinese-capital/2020/06/13/65c5aac8-ad40-11ea-868b-93d63cd833b2_story.html>; 'The Latest: More Cases in Virus Cluster in Southern China' (*The Washington Post*, 2 June 2021) <www.washingtonpost.com/business/the-latest-oslo-virus-surge-linked-to-high-school-parties/2021/06/02/38969e94-c389-11eb-89a4-b7ae-22aa193e_story.html%3foutputType=amp>.

46 'Xi Stresses Law-based Infection Prevention, Control' (*Xinhua*, 5 February 2020) <http://www.xinhuanet.com/english/2020-02/05/c_138758782.htm>; 习近平 [Xi Jinping],

similarly emphasised law.[47] Reporting to higher-level authorities, conducting on-the-ground investigations, informing the public, imposing travel restrictions and quarantines, requisitioning and providing resources and shutting down suspected sources of the outbreak in animal markets were all measures that broadly tracked legal requirements and violations were criticised and sanctioned.[48] The response depended on coordinated exercises of already-in-place authority among many state organs, including the NHC, CDC and their local branches, public security organs, the Ministry of Transportation, local public transport agencies, the Ministry of Commerce (on supply issues), the Ministry of Information Technology (for big data and AI), the military (for hospital construction and medical services) and the Ministry of Education (for school closures and health screening), as well as many local governments and party committees. Such coordination has been a hallmark of China's crisis management and pervades legal frameworks for addressing potential pandemics – including the Emergency Response Law and the Infectious Disease Law, with their levels of emergencies and mandates for the State Council and lower-level governments to lead whole-of-government and whole-of society responses.[49]

The centralising response that surged in January 2020 also relied on high-level organisational fixes that had long been in the repertoire for addressing urgent governance challenges and were sometimes at least resonant with established law. For example, the NHC's announcement, under the direction of Premier Li Keqiang and the State Council, of the adoption of Class A pathogen-style restrictions for a SARS-like Class B disease was consistent with the Infectious Disease Law.[50] The State Council's establishment of a Joint Control and Prevention Mechanism (with a leadership role for the vice premier with responsibility for the NHC and a mandate to coordinate across 32 subject matter-based sectors) and the creation of analogous coordinating organs at lower levels were consistent with the Emergency Response Law and related regulations authorising "headquarters" and "command bodies" to respond to public health emergencies and serious disease outbreaks.[51]

'全面提高依法防控依法治理能力,健全国家公共卫生应急管理体系' [Comprehensively Improving Law-Based Epidemic Prevention and Control and the National Public Health Emergency Management System], 求是 [*Seek Truth*] (May 2020) <http://www.qstheory.cn/dukan/qs/2020-02/29/c_1125641632.htm>.

47 State Council Information Office (n 31) pt II.

48 See generally Emergency Response Law (n 13); Infectious Disease Law (n 13); State Council Information Office (n 31) pts. I.2–I.3.

49 See also Regulations on Responses (n 14); Jacques deLisle, 'States of Exception in an Exceptional State: Emergency Powers Law in China' in Victor V Ramraj and Arun K Thiruvengadam (eds), *Emergency Powers in Asia* (Cambridge University Press 2010) 342–390.

50 国家卫生健康委会同相关部门联防联控 全力应对新型冠状病毒感染的肺炎疫情 [National Health Commission of the People's Republic of China and Relevant Departments Joint Prevention and Control Mechanism: All-Out Efforts to Combat Novel coronavirus Epidemic] (21 January 2020) <http://www.nhc.gov.cn/yjb/s7860/202001/d9570f3a52614113ae0093df51509684.shtml>; Announcement of the National Health Commission (n 9).

51 Emergency Response Law (n 13) art. 8; Regulations on Responses (n 14) art. 3; State Council Information Office (n 31) pt II.1.

Also in the mix were legally informal but politically familiar methods, including: establishment of a CCP-centred "leading small group" [*lingdao xiaozu*] – a trademark move of the Xi era – to "work to counter the new coronavirus" and chaired by Premier Li;[52] reliance on "normative documents" [*guifanxing wenjian*] and "departmental work documents" [*bumen gongzuo wenjian*] lacking the force of law to authorise intrusive tracking and tracing procedures – an approach arguably inconsistent with the rule of law; and rhetoric evocative of the CCP's traditional "campaign" mode declaring a "people's war" against a "devil" virus that Xi's administration would "not let hide".[53]

Although in many respects successful, this repertoire prompted prudential and normative concerns. For example, informed observers warned that China's "at-all-costs and by-all-means approach" faced diminishing returns and criticised China's authoritarian methods.[54]

4. Rights and Liberties as (Non)Constraints

In combatting the pandemic, Chinese authorities have been relatively unconstrained by legal rights and rules and public pressure that have been significant elsewhere. Federalism and separation-of-powers-like principles have not constituted major obstacles. Although the initial crisis in Wuhan showed the perils of de facto decentralisation and bureaucratic siloing, China is – in constitutional principle – a unitary state where powers legitimately exercised by lower-level governments (or organs under the State Council) are delegated by the central state and can be reclaimed (or reallocated) at will, and China is – in practice – a polity where the central leadership can reassert control, at least in times of crisis or in pursuit of high-priority goals and especially amid Xi's broader recentralisation of power.[55] Although early handling of the outbreak reflected risks of fragmented and ambiguous regulatory powers and a weak public health bureaucracy, the party-state's discretion in coping with COVID-19 was not greatly limited by concerns about legal bases for particular rules, or institutions' actions or directives, or ad

52 Wen-Hsun Tsai and Wang Zhou, 'Integrated Fragmentation and the Role of Leading Small Groups in Chinese Politics' (2019) 82 China Journal 1, 1; Li Keqiang, 'Premier of the State Council Chairs a Meeting of the Central Committee's Leading Group on Responding to the Pneumonia Outbreak Caused by the Novel Coronavirus' (5 February 2020) <http://www.china-embassy.org/eng/zgyw/t1740693.htm>.

53 Xi (n 24); 'Notice on Strengthening the Party's Leadership' (n 37); Zeng Rong, 'Embassy Spokesperson's Letter to the Economist on its Unjustified Comments on China's Fight against the Novel Coronavirus Epidemic' (21 February 2020) <http://www.chinese-embassy.org.uk/eng/PressandMedia/t1748533.htm>.

54 Ian Johnson, 'How Did China Beat Its Covid Crisis?' (*The New York Review of Books*, 5 November 2020); Yanzhong Huang, 'The Myth of Authoritarian Superiority: China's Response to Covid-19 Revisited' (2021) 68 China Leadership Monitor <www.prcleader.org/yanzhong-huang>.

55 See e.g. Sangkuk Lee, 'An Institutional Analysis of Xi Jinping's Centralization of Power' (2017) 26 Journal of Contemporary China 325; Yuen Yuen Ang, 'When COVID-19 Meets Centralized, Personalized Power' (2020) 4 Nature Human Behavior 445.

hoc organisational innovations to coordinate responses or obligations imposed on citizens and non-state actors.

Individual liberties and legal rights did not impose significant limits. Chinese legal experts raised concerns about highly intrusive tracking, tracing and surveilling mandates that lacked clear legal foundations (based, as they were, partly on directives lacking the force of law), infringed privacy and threatened coercive measures.[56] In China, the proper balance between public interest (including public health) and privacy rights (including data privacy) has become a focus of legal and policy discourse[57] and a growing concern in society. Protections for data privacy and privacy rights (primarily from infringement by non-state actors) have been foci of recent law-making.[58] Some internet companies resisted providing information to public health officials fighting the epidemic,[59] and some local governments anonymised identities when issuing public warnings about sources of potential outbreaks. The more extreme methods adopted to contain the contagion elicited visible popular discontent.[60]

But, especially at the highest levels where the ambitious response to the pandemic was framed, such phenomena had limited impact. The regime's low tolerance for resistance and formidable tools for stifling opposition afford insulation from public preferences when choosing methods for tackling the pandemic. Actionable legal protections for civil liberties are weak. Judicial review is unavailable for many party and state policies that impose burdens or obligations on citizens. Chinese law thus offers no avenues for general legal challenges to mask requirements, shutdown orders, digital tracking and tracing or other centrally mandated measures to address the pandemic. A modest effort to sue local state actors in Wuhan for death caused by the mishandling of the outbreak made little headway.[61]

56 See 沈岿 [Shen Kui], '大疫之下善待每一个人的基本权利' [Protecting Everybody's Basic Rights Under a Great Epidemic] 博雅公法 [*Boya Public Law*] (17 February 2020) <https://mp.weixin.qq.com/s/FSqrvCo9SkEEfG1apkeE6A>; 童之伟 [Tong Zhiwei], '在法治轨道上化解公共卫生危机' [Resolve the Public Health Crisis on Tracks of the Rule of Law], 爱思想 [*Love Thought*] (2 March 2020) <http://www.aisixiang.com/data/120415.html>.

57 Shen Kui, 'The Stumbling Balance between Public Health and Privacy amid the Pandemic in China' (*Chinese Journal of Comparative Law*, 1 February 2021) <https://doi.org/10.1093/cjcl/cxaa035>.

58 中华人民共和国民法典 [Civil Code of the People's Republic of China], Bk. IV, ch. 6 (2020); 中华人民共和国个人信息保护法 [Personal Information Protection Law of the People's Republic of China] (2021).

59 Peter Hessler, 'How China Controlled the Coronavirus' (*The New Yorker*, 10 August 2020) <https://www.newyorker.com/magazine/2020/08/17/how-china-controlled-the-coronavirus>.

60 Anna Fifield, 'As Coronavirus Goes Global, China's Xi Asserts Victory on First Trip to Wuhan Since Outbreak' (*The Washington Post*, 20 March 2020) <https://www.washingtonpost.com/world/asia_pacific/chinas-xi-attempts-a-coronavirus-victory-lap-with-visit-to-wuhan/2020/03/10/ca585ddc-6281-11ea-8a8e-5c5336b32760_story.html>.

61 Joyce Huang, 'Relative of COVID-19 Victim in China Takes Legal Action Against Local Governments' (*Voice of America*, 12 June 2020) <https://www.voanews.com/east-asia-pacific/voa-news-china/relative-covid-19-victim-china-takes-legal-action-against-local>.

Despite recent trends, cultural norms of privacy are generally seen as weaker in China than in the West.[62] Some evidence suggests that many Chinese citizens saw some of the regime's methods as legitimate: accounts of public opinion claim the party-state's response received high marks;[63] and state-imposed measures that resembled some of China's saw high levels of compliance in liberal and democratic polities in East Asia that share aspects of China's culture and social norms, recent experience with pandemics and extensive government reach (but that lack some of China's enforcement tools).[64]

5. Legal (and Other) Reforms: Agendas and Prospects

Assessing the handling of the pandemic, the Chinese leadership, including Xi and the State Council, declared that legal reforms were needed.[65] Broadly echoing post-SARS moves, reform efforts focused on the Infectious Disease Law and reporting systems, expansion of the criminal prohibition of actions potentially spreading Class A pathogens and creation of a new Bureau for Disease Control and Prevention under the NHC (which promised to address more proactively, and respond better to, public health emergencies).[66] Such changes face the familiar problem that apparently well-intentioned and well-designed reforms may fall short in implementation. The logic and entrenchment of *kuai* and *tiao* remain formidable, and reform advocates tellingly made arguments on both sides of the

62 Bonnie S. McDougall, 'Privacy in Modern China' [2004] 2 History Compass 1, 5–6; Kenneth Neil Farrall, 'Global Privacy in Flux: Illuminating Privacy Across Cultures in China and the U.S.' (2008) 2 International Journal of Communications 993, 1005–15.

63 She Jingwei, 'China Gets Top Marks as Citizens Rank their Governments' Response to the COVID-19 Pandemic' (*CGTN*, 8 May 2020) <https://news.cgtn.com/news/2020-05-08/Survey-shows-China-s-response-to-COVID-19-gets-top-mark-among-public-Qk5KbpG78k/index.html>; Cary Wu, 'How Chinese Citizens View their Government's Coronavirus Response' (*The Conversation*, 4 June 2020) <https://theconversation.com/how-chinese-citizens-view-their-governments-coronavirus-response-139176>.

64 Andrew Sheng and Xiao Geng, 'How the East Asian Mind-Set Succeeded with the Coronavirus When Western Individualism Failed' (*Market Watch*, 30 August 2020) <https://www.marketwatch.com/story/how-the-east-asian-mind-set-succeeded-with-the-coronavirus-when-western-individualism-failed-11598561912>; Brian Y An and Shui-Yan Tang, 'Lessons from COVID-19 Responses in East Asia: Institutional Infrastructure and Enduring Policy Instruments' (2020) 50 American Review of Public Administration 790 <https://journals.sagepub.com/doi/full/10.1177/0275074020943707>; Jacques deLisle, 'When the Fever Breaks?: COVID-19, U.S.-China Relations, and East Asia' (2021) 65 Orbis 231, 252–256.

65 Xi (n 24); 'Xi Jinping Calls for Improving Epidemic Monitoring, Early Warning Capabilities' (*CGTN*, 25 May 2020) <https://news.cgtn.com/news/2020-05-24/Xi-Jinping-joins-panel-discussion-with-NPC-deputies-from-Hubei-QKQwiYvCO4/index.html>; State Council Information Office (n 31) pt II.

66 中华人民共和国刑法 [Criminal Law of the People's Republic of China] [2021 amendment] art. 330; 'China Inaugurates National Disease Control and Prevention Bureau' (*CGTN*, 13 May 2021) <https://news.cgtn.com/news/2021-05-13/China-inaugurates-national-disease-control-and-prevention-bureau-10eaOSmBMpW/index.html>.

chronic *tiao/kuai* dilemma in critiquing flaws in the infectious disease and emergency response laws and institutions exposed during the crisis.[67]

The reform agenda extended to the suspected source of COVID-19 in wildlife markets. The Infectious Disease Law and the Wild Animal Conservation Law drew criticism for being lax in controlling hunting, marketing and selling of wild animals, despite widespread recognition that human proximity to such animals risked pandemics.[68] Amid the outbreak, regulatory agencies, the National People's Congress Standing Committee and local governments issued emergency decisions imposing strict bans and sanctions on the wild animal trade, at least for the duration of the pandemic.[69] Soon thereafter, a change in the Animal Epidemic Prevention Law stiffened wild animal quarantine requirements and a new Biosecurity Law reprised relevant parts of the existing Infectious Disease Law.[70] But these were modest efforts and other once-fast-tracked amendments to key laws stalled and drew criticism for being too weak or leaving too many loopholes.[71] Laws limiting wildlife trade could prove especially hard to implement, given the myriad targeted entities, inevitable reliance on local-level enforcement and popularity of the proscribed activities.

Lab safety in China has become a matter of international concern as the view that the virus may have escaped from the Wuhan Institute of Virology regained traction in mid-2021 and concerns mounted – especially in the United States

67 王俊 [Wang Jun], '17年后疫情再袭，官方透露《传染病防治法》将再修' [17 years later, an epidemic strikes again; officials disclose that the 'Law on the Prevention and Control of Infectious Diseases' will be revised again] 新京报 [*Beijing News*] (25 March 2020) <http://www.bjnews.com.cn/news/2020/03/25/708946.html>.

68 James Gorman, 'China's Ban on Wildlife Trade a Big Step, but Has Loopholes, Conservationists Say' (*The New York Times*, 27 February 2020) <https://www.nytimes.com/2020/02/27/science/coronavirus-pangolin-wildlife-ban-china.html>.

69 市场监管总局等 [State Administration for Market Regulation and others] 关于禁止野生动物交易的公告 [Announcement on the Prohibition of Trading in Wild Animals] (26 January 2020) <http://www.gov.cn/zhengce/zhengceku/2020-01/26/content_5472280.htm>; 全国人民代表大会常务委员会关于全面禁止非法野生动物交易、革除滥食野生动物陋习、切实保障人民群众生命健康安全的决定 [Decision on Completely Prohibiting Illegal Trade in Wildlife, Eliminating the Bad Habit of Indiscriminately Eating Wild Animals, and Earnestly Ensuring the Life, Health, and Safety of the People].

70 中华人民共和国生物安全法 [Biosecurity Law of the People's Republic of China] (2020); Sun Bao Jun, 'New Animal Quarantine Law Significant Progress' (*China Daily*, 1 January 2021) <www.chinadaily.com.cn/a/202101/25/WS600e0590a31024ad0baa4b68.html>; 'China's Biosecurity Law Goes into Effect' (*People's Daily Online*, 16 April 2021) <http://en.people.cn/n3/2021/0416/c90000-9840082.html>.

71 William Yang, 'How Loopholes in China's Wildlife Protection Laws Risk New Virus Outbreaks' (*The Independent*, 1 February 2021) <www.independent.co.uk/stop-the-illegal-wildlife-trade/wildlife-trade-law-china-virus-outbreaks-b1794500.html>; James Gorman, 'China's Ban on Wildlife Trade a Big Step, but Has Loopholes, Conservationists Say' (*The New York Times*, 27 February 2020) <https://www.nytimes.com/2020/02/27/science/coronavirus-pangolin-wildlife-ban-china.htm>; Steven Lee Myers, 'China Vowed to Keep Wildlife Off the Menu, a Tough Promise to Keep' (*The New York Times*, 7 June 2020) <https://www.nytimes.com/2020/06/07/world/asia/china-coronavirus-wildlife-ban.html>.

– that WHO-led investigations into COVID-19's origins lacked adequate access and yielded inconclusive results.[72] Significant change in China's relevant regulatory regime is unlikely, however. Despite calls for stronger international legal requirements, the WHO will not become able to require great transparency from China (or other states). Although official sources touted the new Biosecurity Law's safety requirements,[73] the law does not set rules for public disclosure. The incentives to opacity by local officials and regulated entities seen in Wuhan hospitals would extend to dangerous leaks at sensitive labs. Potential reforms addressing these issues had become politically fraught after the accidental lab leak claim and the intentional leak/bioweapon conspiracy theories became conflated in China-condemning American political discourse and Chinese officials bristled at mounting criticism, suspicion and calls for transparency, especially from the US.[74]

Finally, reforms might empower mechanisms outside the CCP and China's administrative state to address potential pandemics. Building on modest provisions in existing law and drawing lessons from the costly early censoring of information about COVID-19, laws protecting or mandating disclosure (including by non-officials) to the public (possibly grounded in a more robust 'right to know') and permitting open discussion could reduce risks of delayed response to new pandemic threats and other emergencies.[75] Expanding the remedies promised under China's Administrative Litigation Law, suits by injured, abused or aggrieved citizens could bring at least retrospective accountability for flawed government responses to COVID-19 and similar threats, and thereby deter recurrence. Such legal change is unlikely, however. It would require wrenching change in a system where broad and vague rules prohibit and punish spreading rumours,[76] new and old media face

72 Jeremy Page and others, 'How the WHO's Hunt for Covid's Origins Stumbled in China' (*The Wall Street Journal*, 17 March 2021) <www.wsj.com/articles/who-china-hunt-covid-origins-11616004512?mod=article_inline>; Nandita Bose and Trevor Hunnicutt, 'Biden Orders Review of COVID Origins as Lab Leak Theory Debated' (*Reuters*, 26 May 2021) <www.reuters.com/business/healthcare-pharmaceuticals/biden-says-us-intelligence-community-divided-covid-origin-2021-05-26/>.

73 Liu Caiyu, 'New Law Fortifies China's Legal Shield on Biosecurity Labs against Future Infectious Diseases' (*Global Times*, 15 April 2021) <www.globaltimes.cn/page/202104/1221202.shtml>.

74 Katerina Ang and Adam Taylor, 'As U.S. Calls for Focus on Covid Origins, China Repeats Speculation about U.S. Military Base' (*The Washington Post*, 27 May 2021) <www.washingtonpost.com/world/2021/05/27/virus-china-fort-detrick/>; Yasmeen Abutaleb and Matt Viser, 'Trump and His Allies Try to Rewrite, Distort History of Pandemic While Casting Fauci as Public Enemy No. 1' (*The Washington Post*, 7 June 2021) <www.washingtonpost.com/politics/trump-fauci-wuhan-lan-leak/2021/06/05/8469f022-c55b-11eb-9a8d-f95d7724967c_story.html>.

75 Xiaoling Zhang, 'Breaking News, Media Coverage and "Citizen's Right to Know" in China' (2007) 16 Journal of Contemporary China 535; 沈岿 [Shen Kui], '论突发传染病信息发布的法律设置' [On the Legal Settings of the Information Release of Emergent Infectious Diseases], (2020) 4 当代法学 [Contemporary Law Review] 34–35; Dai Ruikai, 'Information Accessibility for Public Health Emergencies – a Case Study of Information Accessibility during the New Coronavirus Outbreak' (2021) 16 Frontiers of Law in China 58.

76 See generally Rogier Creemers, 'Cyber China: Upgrading Propaganda, Public Opinion Work and Social Management for the Twenty-First Century' (2017) 26 Journal of Contemporary China 85, 91–93.

close supervision and control and courts decline to adjudicate politically charged – and especially mass action-like – cases, whether on their own initiative or under directives from political authorities.

Unlike in many other countries, China's response to the exceptional circumstances of COVD-19 was consistent with fundamental features of law and governance. There are few signs of, and little reason to expect, transformative change in a system where the regime – along with many of the people whom it rules – have concluded that, for all its flaws, the system mostly (if belatedly) worked.

5

(UN)GOVERNING

The COVID-19 Response in the UK

Joelle Grogan

1. Introduction[1]

In its initial response, the UK government downplayed concerns arising from the spread of COVID-19: Prime Minister Boris Johnson suggested the country should "take it on the chin" and pursued a policy which introduced no significant measures beyond encouraging handwashing for 20 seconds,[2] leading to a widely held assumption that the UK would experiment with a 'herd immunity' strategy.[3] On 12 March 2020, the same day schools and businesses were shut in the Republic of Ireland and France, and three days after Italy was placed under a nationwide lockdown, the prime minister announced a move to a 'delay phase' and advised, though did not direct, over-70s to stay home, and travellers to avoid cruises. Large gatherings, such as the Cheltenham Festival attracting nearly 70,000 spectators, went ahead. On 19 March, following the rapid and exponential increase of infections, the government announced that there was "zero prospect"[4] of a lockdown in London which would place limits on people's movement. Four days later, on 23 March, the capital along with the rest of the UK entered lockdown, which extended to June 2020.

Following a short second national lockdown in November 2020 and despite rising rates of infection indicating the widely predicted 'second wave' already

1 All websites accessed 16 August 2021.

2 'Coronavirus: UK Moving Towards "Delay" Phase ofVirus Plan as Cases Hit 115' (*BBC News*, 5 March 2020) <https://www.bbc.co.uk/news/uk-51749352>.

3 Sarah Boseley, 'Herd Immunity: Will the UK's Coronavirus Strategy Work?' (*The Guardian*, 13 March 2020) <https://www.theguardian.com/world/2020/mar/13/herd-immunity-will-the-uks-coronavirus-strategy-work>.

4 Kate Proctor and Vikram Dodd, '"Zero Prospect" of London Lockdown Involving Movement Limits, Says No 10' (*The Guardian*, 19 March 2020) <https://www.theguardian.com/world/2020/mar/19/zero-prospect-of-london-lockdown-involving-movement-limits-says-no-10>.

DOI: 10.4324/9781003211952-6

impacting neighbouring European countries, Boris Johnson mocked the opposition for wanting to "cancel Christmas" by reintroducing lockdown restrictions.[5] Three days later on 19 December 2020, London and the south-east were locked down, followed on 7 January by the third national lockdown, which ended in July 2021. Since March 2020, the UK has spent a majority of time under some form of lockdown, which included closure of schools, universities and a majority of businesses deemed non-essential, prohibition of gatherings of more than two people outdoors from separate households, and the limitation of movement beyond the home.

In its response to COVID-19, UK governance has been characterised by political hyperbole from the Westminster executive coupled with a lax if not lackadaisical response, succeeded by sudden U-turn policymaking and severely restrictive measures. The hypertrophied executive dominance of action coupled with the lack of parliamentary oversight, as well as uncertainty as to the distinctions between law, guidance and advice, have plagued the COVID-19 response in the UK. Despite initial signs of coordination and cooperation across the four nations which constitute the UK, the Westminster government and the devolved legislatures of Northern Ireland, Scotland and Wales adopted at points diverging approaches to the management of the health crisis, leading to inconsistency and uncertainty across internal borders. This chapter examines these core issues of law and governance (section 2), parliamentary oversight (section 3), and devolution (section 4), as well as concerns for human rights and access to justice (section 4).

2. Governance and Law Underpinning the COVID-19 Response

While the government rhetorically "declared war" on the virus,[6] it did not, however, call upon 'state of emergency' provisions under the Civil Contingencies Act 2004. While providing for far more wide-reaching centralised executive powers, the Act also contains explicit provisions for judicial review and additional parliamentary oversight, as well as a 30-day sunset clause for regulations under its provisions. Where this Act was not relied upon, targeted legislation was instead needed to introduce the powers necessary to address the pandemic emergency, and to account for the fact that health is a devolved competence: the devolved legislatures of the UK (the Northern Irish Assembly, the Scottish Parliament and the Welsh Senedd) have legislative power to regulate the area. Described as a "manifestation of excessive executive dominance"[7] for its trifecta of wide del-

5 Jasmine Cameron-Chileshe, Andy Bounds and others, 'Johnson Defies Calls to "Cancel Christmas", Urging Small Gatherings' (*The Financial Times*, 16 December 2020) <https://www.ft.com/content/39325afc-90e0-40fd-92e3-69a03063ad76>.

6 Jonathan Ford, 'The New Wartime Economy in the Era of Coronavirus' (*The Financial Times*, 25 March 2020) <https://www.ft.com/content/5945c61a-6dc7-11ea-89df-41bea055720b>.

7 Jake Hinks, 'The Coronavirus Act 2020: An Example of "Excessive Executive Dominance"' (*UK Constitutional Law Blog*, 9 June 2020) <https://ukconstitutionallaw.org/2020/06/09/jake-hinks-the-coronavirus-act-2020-an-example-of-excessive-executive-dominance/>.

egated powers, Henry VIII powers (where government ministers can repeal or amend statutory law) and lack of parliamentary scrutiny, the Coronavirus Bill, at 359 pages, was published on 19 March 2020, and fast-tracked through Parliament with only one day of debate to receive royal assent four parliamentary days later on 25 March.

The Coronavirus Act 2020 provides for a myriad of measures including the reduction of certain administrative checks relating to the certification of deaths and the detention and treatment of mental health patients, as well as the introduction of a number of new offences. The Act notably did not give specific lockdown powers. The secretary of state for health had at that point already introduced lockdown through secondary legislation under the Public Health (Control of Disease) Act 1984, as amended in 2008 following the SARS outbreak. The Coronavirus Act did, however, extend powers to public authorities across the UK to quarantine those who have tested positive (or inconclusive) as well as to test those suspected of having the disease. Powers to restrict or close premises, as well as the power to prohibit any gatherings, were given to ministers in devolved executives where not pre-existing.

Notably from the question of privacy and surveillance, the Act (temporarily) amended the Investigatory Powers Act 2016 to allow for the appointment of judicial commissioners to issue arrest and surveillance warrants, as well as extending the time for retroactive approval of arrest warrants issued in urgent cases. Under the Act, too, the secretary of state could make regulations to extend the time that biometric samples (e.g. DNA and fingerprints) may be retained for national security. The Coronavirus Act 2020 was not excluded from the Human Rights Act 1998 (which gives legal effect to the European Convention on Human Rights (ECHR) in the UK), and so powers under it could be subject to review for compatibility with the ECHR.

The Act has a sunset clause (or an 'expiry date') of two years, with the option for parliament-approved six-month extensions beyond that point. This was initially met with strong opposition to such a long period. It can be contrasted with the Scottish equivalent, the Coronavirus (Scotland) Act 2020, which was drafted to include only a six-month sunset clause with the option for renewal by the Scottish Parliament. One concession accepted by government in the form of an amendment to the Coronavirus Act 2020 was a six-month parliamentary review in the form of a debate on the date of the expiry of the Act. This follows two-month status reports, and a debate on non-devolved matters in the Act in both Houses of Parliament after a year. A welcome aspect of the Coronavirus Act was its self-containment, serving as a model for other pandemic legislation in this regard. The Act's provisions could only be interpreted as relating to the COVID-19 pandemic. Upon expiry, its effects – even where it has modified other primary Acts – disappear. In distinction to concerns in other states as to permanent changes to the law following the introduction of emergency powers, the Coronavirus Act 2020 was not expected, or designed, to create permanent change. However, a majority and the most restrictive of statutory instruments governing UK pandemic management were adopted under the Public Health (Control of Disease) Act 1984 – not the Coronavirus Act – the *vires* of which was questioned by critics,[8] though the courts declined to review it.[9]

Between March 2020 and August 2021, over 480 statutory instruments were introduced with little or no parliamentary scrutiny as 71% were subject to the 'made negative' procedure whereby the regulation can be laid before Parliament *after* it has been signed into law by a minister.[10] Nearly 44% of these regulations came into effect *before* they were laid before parliament, in breach of parliamentary convention to allow for scrutiny or objection.[11] Such regulations have included powers delegated to police forces to enter private premises day or night, and to issue fines of up to £10,000 (approximately US$13,675 or €11,695) for breach of self-isolation rules – the latter rule coming into force within hours of being introduced.[12] Deeply concerning from the perspective of legality, at some points orders had no legislative underpinning: on 30 July 2020 the secretary of state for health announced a ban on different households meeting indoors from midnight, though this did not have legislative effect until 5 August.[13]

Nearly a quarter of COVID-19-related instruments were subject to the urgent procedure under the Public Health (Control of Disease) Act 1984, which was often not justified by reason of a lack of time. As highlighted by the Hansard Society, in one such instance, mandatory face coverings had been policy-trialled for weeks, before being introduced under the urgent procedure ostensibly due to the lack of time to properly consider such a measure.[14] The lack of oversight coupled with rapid introduction, amendment and revocation correlated with frequent errors in the regulations, and compounded concerns over legal uncertainty and potentially unlawful exercises of power. The International Travel Regulations were amended over 50 times before finally being revoked; the single replacement regulation began itself to be subject to a number of amendments within days. Such rapid change challenges the capacity of the public and public authorities, especially those charged with enforcement, to follow rules and to adapt.

8 Tom Hickman QC, Emma Dixon and Rachel Jones, 'Coronavirus and Civil Liberties in the UK' (2020) Judicial Review 151.

9 *R (Dolan) v Secretary of State for Health and Social Care* [2020] EWCA Civ 1605, [2021] 1 All ER 780.

10 Hansard Coronavirus Statutory Instruments Dashboard, <https://www.hansardsociety.org.uk/publications/data/coronavirus-statutory-instruments-dashboard>.

11 ibid.

12 The Health Protection (Coronavirus, Restrictions) (Self-Isolation) (England) Regulations 2020, SI 2020/1045.

13 Public Administration and Constitutional Affairs Committee, *Fourth Report – Parliamentary Scrutiny of the Government's Handling of Covid-19*, HC 377 (10 September 2020) <https://publications.parliament.uk/pa/cm5801/cmselect/cmpubadm/377/37703.htm#_idTextAnchor000>.

14 Ruth Fox, Meg Russell, Ronan Comacain and Joe Tomlinson, 'The Marginalisation of the House of Commons under Covid Has Been Shocking; A Year On, Parliament's Role Must Urgently Be Restored' (*Hansard Society*, 21 April 2021) <https://www.hansardsociety.org.uk/publications/briefings/the-marginalisation-of-the-house-of-commons-under-covid-has-been-shocking-a>.

A connected criticism of government action was the difficulty of distinguishing between government advice, guidance and the law.[15] Such uncertainty creates problematic issues for the rule of law, where police forces may interpret and enforce 'guidance-as-law', and in doing so unlawfully act beyond their powers. This was all the more heightened where the government announced measures in press conferences rather than in Parliament,[16] justified their decision-making in articles behind newspaper paywalls, and (at least rhetorically) adopted draconian penalties for breach of COVID-19 measures which may not have had a sound legal basis. For example, the Westminster government defended plans to jail any person found to have lied about their recent travel history for up to ten years (by scale comparison, causing death by dangerous driving holds a maximum sentence of five years), and stated that Parliament would not be given a vote on such a new offence.[17] Where consent could be evidenced to be more effective than coercion, and public trust in the decision-making of governments is key to the most effective responses to pandemic management,[18] modes of governance characterised by executive dominance, uncertainty, inconsistency, and occasionally even by senior government officials not abiding by *their own rules*,[19] only serves to undermine any collective social and good faith efforts to cope with crisis and emergency.

3. Parliamentary Oversight

Despite some of the highest expenditure of public funds and the most restrictive measures on personal liberty, commerce and education to be enforced within

15 See e.g. Joint Committee on Human Rights, *The Government's Response to COVID-19: Human Rights Implications*, HC 265 (September 2020) 21; and Lords Constitution Committee, *COVID-19 and the Use and Scrutiny of Emergency Powers*, HL Paper 15 (10 June 2021).

16 See e.g. Christopher Hope, 'Speaker Angered by Matt Hancock Locking Down his Constituency before Warning Parliament' (*The Telegraph*, 19 September 2021) <https://www.telegraph.co.uk/politics/2020/09/19/speaker-angered-bymatt-hancock-locking-constituency-warning/>; cf Pablo Grez, 'Protecting Parliament's Place in the Announcement of Covid-Related Policies: New Restrictions Announced in Scotland' (*COVID-19 Review Observatory*, 6 January 2021) <https://blog.bham.ac.uk/cvro/covid-19/protecting-parliaments-place-in-the-announcement-of-covid-related-policies-new-restrictions-announced-in-scotland/>.

17 'Covid-19: 10-year Jail Term for Travel Lies Defended' (*BBC News*, 10 February 2021) <https://www.bbc.co.uk/news/uk-56007798>. See also James Bevan, '10-year Prison Sentences for Breaching COVID-19 Entry Requirements into the United Kingdom? Governmental Decree is Undermining the Rule of Law' (*UK Constitutional Law Blog*, 24 February 2021) <https://ukconstitutionallaw.org/2021/02/24/james-bevan-10-year-prison-sentences-for-breaching-covid-19-entry-requirements-into-the-united-kingdom-governmental-decree-is-undermining-the-rule-of-law/>.

18 See Jasanoff and Hilgartner, chapter 23.

19 Rajeev Syal, Matthew Weaver and Peter Walker, 'Johnson's Defence of Cummings Sparks Anger from Allies and Opponents Alike' (*The Guardian*, 24 May 2020) <https://www.theguardian.com/politics/2020/may/24/boris-johnson-defence-dominic-cummings-anger-from-allies-and-opponents-alike>; George Parker, 'Matt Hancock Clings on as Pressure Mounts over Links to Adviser' (*The Financial Times*, 25 June 2021) <https://www.ft.com/content/a08d14f8-7b01-497e-a880-311365a727e4>.

peacetime, parliamentary oversight and scrutiny has been minimal, and its role has been marginalised.[20] Procedurally, limited effort was made to support virtual participation in parliamentary debates. An app-based voting system was quickly developed and then as quickly abandoned in favour of in-person and then proxy voting. The Leader of the House of Commons, Jacob Rees-Mogg, argued that virtual working was not a way of holding (his party's) government to account, unable to replace the "cut and thrust" of live debate.[21] This had the effect of excluding medically vulnerable members of Parliament or those unable to travel from participation outside a small number of events for just over 220 days during 2020.[22] Proxy voting gave only 18 people (primarily party whips) the votes of 595 members of parliament, which risked undermining the decision-making process where votes were essentially cast before any debate took place, or only along party lines. The Scottish Parliament and Welsh Senedd, by contrast, both adopted virtual sessions and voting without significant issue.[23]

Meaningful scrutiny is needed to ensure parliamentary sovereignty over the executive and the effective consideration of the proportionate, justified and intended use of powers. The promised regular reporting and debated six-month renewals to ameliorate the deficiency in parliamentary scrutiny which oversaw the arrival of the Coronavirus Act has been disappointing at best: the mandated bimonthly reports have "primarily been descriptive, with either no or only a short and fairly cosmetic discussion of rights and equality impacts".[24] By May 2021, the Act and measures taken under it had been subject to only five hours of parliamentary debate,[25] *including* the time taken to debate its renewal. Even where such debate existed, it did not extend to the Public Health (Control of Disease) Act 1984 upon which much of the pandemic response was based. This lack of oversight can be contrasted with that of the devolved legislature in Scotland whose approach was described as "impressive (though imperfect) political accountability characterised by openness and transparency by the government, cross-party collaboration, and energetic parliamentary committees performing high quality scrutiny", including the production of extensive two-monthly reports.[26]

20 Fox and others (n 14).

21 'Covid-19: MPs with Cancer "Excluded" from Cancer Debate' (*BBC News*, 13 March 2020) <https://www.bbc.co.uk/news/uk-politics-54925320>.

22 Fox and others (n 14).

23 Paul Evans, 'Parliaments and the Pandemic' (*The Constitution Unit Blog*, 5 March 2021) <https://constitution-unit.com/2021/03/05/parliaments-and-the-pandemic/>.

24 Fiona de Londras, 'Six-Monthly Votes on the Coronavirus Act 2020: A Meaningful Mode of Review?' (*UK Constitutional Law Blog*, 25 March 2021) <https://ukconstitutionallaw.org/2021/03/25/fiona-de-londras-six-monthly-votes-on-the-coronavirus-act-2020-a-meaningful-mode-of-review/>.

25 Fox and others (n 14).

26 Pablo G Hidalgo, Fiona de Londras and Daniella Lock, 'Parliamentary Scrutiny of Extending Emergency Measures in the Two Scottish Coronavirus Acts: On the Question of Timing' (*UK Constitutional law Blog*, 21 June 2021) <https://ukconstitutionallaw.org/2021/06/21/pablo-g

The UK Parliament exercises less oversight and control over public expenditure as compared with other analogous legislatures.[27] In response to the pandemic, there was a drastic increase in public spending through raised limits on contingency spending which does not require prior parliamentary approval (from 2% to 50% in 2020, and by a further 12% in 2021[28]). Concerns have been raised that the government will be able to spend up to £469 billion (approximately US$639 billion or €547 billion) in 2021–2022 without parliamentary scrutiny to determine whether there is adequate justification.[29] Such spending has amplified larger concerns related to political connections[30] in the securing of government contracts,[31] the "unacceptably high"[32] potential waste of taxpayer money in the procurement of personal protective equipment, and the "repeated failure to provide a full rationale for key decisions".[33]

Eighteen months with little parliamentary oversight or intervention was tantamount to "government by decree",[34] which was compounded by justified criticism of the opacity of decision-making processes, data and information access, and the lack of published rationalisation of measures.[35] That government is accountable to Parliament is a foundational constitutional principle. It is not only a point of law and to ensure the democratic legitimacy of executive action, but also has clear practical benefit: debate and scrutiny allow for the identification and remedy of contradiction and confusion.

4. Devolution and the COVID-19 Response

By way of brief introduction to the complex schema of devolution within the UK, the Westminster Parliament functions both as the UK Parliament and also legislates on matters solely related to England, while the scope of powers and

-hidalgo-fiona-de-londras-and-daniella-lock-parliamentary-scrutiny-of-extending-emergency-measures-in-the-two-scottish-coronavirus-acts-on-the-question-of-timing/>.

27 Allen Schick, 'Can National Legislatures Regain an Effective Voice in Budget Policy?' (2002) vol 1/3 OECD Journal on Budgeting.

28 Larry Honeysett and Philip Brien, *Research Briefing: Contingencies Fund (No.2) Bill* (House of Commons Library, 9 March 2021) <https://commonslibrary.parliament.uk/research-briefings/cbp-9155/>.

29 Fox and others (n 14).

30 National Audit Office, *Investigation into Government Procurement during the COVID-19 Pandemic*, HC 959 Session 2019–2021 (26 November 2020).

31 House of Commons Committee of Public Accounts, *Forty-Second Report COVID-19: Government Procurement and Supply of Personal Protective Equipment* HC 928 (10 February 2021).

32 House of Commons Committee of Public Accounts, *Thirteenth Report of Session 2021–22: Initial Lessons from the Government's Response to the COVID-19 Pandemic* HC 175 (19 July 2021).

33 ibid.

34 Keith D Ewing, 'Covid-19: Government by Decree' (2020) King's Law Journal 1. See Grogan and Beqiraj, chapter 16.

35 Public Administration and Constitutional Affairs Committee, *Eighth Report – Government Transparency and Accountability during Covid 19: The Data Underpinning Decisions* HC 803 (15 March 2021).

areas of competence vary between the devolved legislatures of Scotland, Wales and Northern Ireland. Health policy is one such area of devolved competence. In the initial response to the pandemic, there was indication that the Westminster and devolved governments would act in close coordination during the pandemic – for example, in the publication of the joint Coronavirus Action Plan in March 2020 and common regulations during the first lockdown in March 2020.[36] Indeed, in its framework and delegation of powers, the Coronavirus Act 2020 promoted a "culture of intergovernmental co-operation",[37] and legislative consent to the bill was given by the devolved legislatures on 24 March.

However, it appeared that such collective efforts at a coordinated approach quickly dissipated. The decision by the UK prime minister to ease the first lockdown in England in May 2020 was disowned by the devolved administrations, which also highlighted the lack of communication and efforts at UK-wide coordination by the UK government.[38] The Scottish first minister claimed she had only learned of the reduction of restrictive measures via an article in the *Sunday Telegraph*,[39] and the prime minister's 'address to the nation' announcing the changes failed to mention that they only applied to England.[40] From that point onwards, policies crucially and significantly diverged and operated on the basis of separately published and varying exit strategies for phased reduction of restrictions, as well as rules for the reintroduction of measures.[41]

While "divergence is not only acceptable but also necessary"[42] to allow for the positive benefits of local adaptation and legal autonomy, significant disparities create challenges. Adoption of different criteria for regulation (e.g. limiting the number of 'households' assembling in Scotland and Wales, but 'individuals' in England and Northern Ireland) fostered confusion. As national media is dominated by England and the Westminster Parliament, there was significant uncertainty for people as to what rules did (or did not) apply to them.[43] This was a

36 Department of Health and Social Care, *Coronavirus Action Plan: A Guide to What You Can Expect Across the UK* (3 March 2020) <https://www.gov.uk/government/publications/coronavirus-action-plan/coronavirus-action-plan-a-guide-to-what-you-can-expect-across-the-uk>.

37 Gareth P Evans, 'Devolution and COVID-19: Towards a "New Normal" in the Territorial Constitution?' (2021) Public Law 19–27, 21.

38 'Coronavirus: Welsh Government Not Told about "Stay Alert"—Drakeford' (*BBC News*, 15 May 2020) <https://www.bbc.co.uk/news/uk-politics-52677444>.

39 Rowena Mason and Haroon Siddique, 'Nicola Sturgeon Leads Chorus of Disapproval over Johnson's "Stay Alert" Message' (*The Guardian*, 10 May 2020) <https://www.theguardian.com/world/2020/may/10/nicola-sturgeon-leads-criticism-of-uks-new-stay-alert-coronavirus-lockdown-advice>.

40 Boris Johnson, 'Prime Minister's Statement on Coronavirus (Covid-19)' (10 May 2020) <www.gov.uk/government/speeches/pm-address-to-the-nation-on-coronavirus-10-may-2020>.

41 Jess Sargeant, *Co-ordination and Divergence: Devolution and Coronavirus* (Institute for Government, October 2020); and Akash Paun, 'Five Key Questions about Coronavirus and Devolution' (*The Constitution Unit Blog*, 31 March 2020) <https://constitution-unit.com/2020/05/31/five-key-questions-about-coronavirus-and-devolution/>.

42 ibid.

43 Stephen Cushion, Nikki Soo, Maria Kyriakidou and Marina Morani, 'Different Lockdown Rules in the Four Nations Are Confusing the Public' (*LSE Blog*, 22 May 2020) <https://blogs

particular challenge for those living and working across internal borders: in May 2020, the UK government encouraged a return to offices (in England) – which was challenging for those who lived in Wales where strict restrictions on distance permissibly travelled were still in place. The introduction of a 'three-tier' (and later 'four-tier') exit strategy in October 2020 for England[44] was distinct from the finer level of detail within the 'Level 0 to Level 4' framework subsequently adopted in Scotland.[45]

Northern Ireland's border with the Republic of Ireland highlighted immediate disparities between the responses of the UK and Irish governments to the pandemic. The latter adopted a cautious and restrictive approach to pandemic management, reacting earlier to the pandemic and continuing restrictive measures for longer. While it generated similar critiques of executive dominance north and south of the border,[46] it also at points correlated with lower infection and mortality rates in the Republic of Ireland, creating divergence in outcomes between the two states on the same island.[47]

As England removed nearly all COVID-19 measures on 19 July 2021, mask mandates and other restrictive measures were still in place in Scotland and Wales, while lockdown measures were still in place in Northern Ireland[48] – obligating public messaging on divergences when crossing internal borders, particularly where individuals could still be subject to fines for non-compliance. Variance between easing restrictions for businesses across the UK also created challenges to supply-chain management and competition. Cumulatively, while the UK government's decision to rely on ordinary health legislation in the management of the pandemic, rather than centralised emergency powers, enabled the delegation of powers, heightened levels of engagement with devolved legislatures and adaptation to local epidemiological conditions, its effectiveness was hampered by a lack of communication and information-sharing, and deficient efforts at UK-wide coordination and cooperation: a lasting failure where the virus has no borders.

.lse.ac.uk/covid19/2020/05/22/different-lockdown-rules-in-the-four-nations-are-confusing-the-public/>.

44 The Health Protection (Coronavirus, Restrictions) (All Tiers) (England) Regulations 2020.

45 Scottish Government, *Scotland's Strategic Framework* (October 2020) <www.gov.scot/binaries/content/documents/govscot/publications/strategy-plan/2020/10/covid-19-scotlands-strategic-framework/documents/covid-19-scotlands-strategic-framework/covid-19-scotlands-strategic-framework/govscot%3Adocument/covid-19-scotlands-strategic-framework.pdf>.

46 Oran Doyle, 'Pandemic Response as Accentuation of Existing Characteristics: Vague Requirements and Executive Dominance in Ireland' (*Verfassungsblog*, 17 March 2021) <https://verfassungsblog.de/pandemic-response-as-accentuation-of-existing-characteristics-vague-requirements-and-executive-dominance-in-ireland/>.

47 Eunan McConville, 'Covid-19: NI Has the Highest Infection Rate in the UK' (*BBC News*, 7 August 2021) <https://www.bbc.co.uk/news/world-europe-58124142>.

48 Sarah Barber, Jennifer Brown and Daniel Ferguson, *Coronavirus: Lockdown Laws* (House of Commons Library, 30 July 2021) <https://researchbriefings.files.parliament.uk/documents/CBP-8875/CBP-8875.pdf>.

5. Concerns for Human Rights and Access to Justice

Even where there has been little scrutiny to date, there are some safeguards: the 1984 Act requires measures introduced to be proportionate and compatible with ECHR rights. However, engagement with rights has been notably absent from both parliamentary debate and government action in consideration of the pandemic response. This is, at least in part, attributable to the prevalent "inhospitable political environment" for human rights but also the "scale, complexity, and polycentricity of the pandemic response",[49] which created a challenging situation for engaged political and legal debate over the questions of rights, limitations and proportionality. The lack of engagement was concerning, where, in line with global trends,[50] vulnerable groups and minority communities were the most negatively impacted by both the virus and the measures taken in response to it.

According to a Wellcome Trust report, BAME (Black, Asian and minority ethnic) communities were more concerned about the impact of the pandemic on their financial resources and mental and physical health; more likely to find governmental restrictions and public health information difficult to follow; and less likely to trust information from official sources.[51] This correlates with both vaccine hesitancy in BAME communities,[52] and also disproportionate rates of fines for breach of measures among these communities, in addition to among young people, men of all ethnicities and those from socially deprived areas.[53] The consequence of non-payment of fines is criminalisation, favouring those able to pay fines of between £200 (not wearing a mask) and £10,000 (organised gathering) to avoid court and a criminal record, but also creating a false incentive not to challenge what could (and may likely be) an incorrectly applied charge.

In April 2021, the Joint Committee on Human Rights (JCHR), a cross-parliamentary group, called for *all* fixed penalty notices (FPNs) – over 85,000 of which had been issued since March 2020 for breach of COVID-19 measures – to be reviewed, finding them to be "muddled, discriminatory and unfair" and subject to a process which "disproportionately hits the less well-off and criminalises the poor over the better off".[54] The report highlighted long-standing concerns with the design of the FPNs, including the validity of such penalties, the inadequacy of the review process, the size of penalties and criminalisation for non-payment. As there is no appeal process to an FPN, the only way to 'challenge' it is not to pay the fine and risk criminal prosecution. In one particularly damning finding, the JCHR

49 de Londras (n 24).

50 See Al Saba and Gougsa, chapter 32.

51 Sylvie Craig, Curtis Jessop and others, *Wellcome Monitor 2020: Covid-19 Study* (August 2020) <https://wellcome.org/reports/wellcome-monitor-2020-covid-19-study>.

52 See e.g. Mohammed S Razai, Tasnime Osama and others, 'Covid-19 Vaccine Hesitancy among Ethnic Minority Groups' (2021) BMJ 372.

53 Craig and others (n 51).

54 Joint Committee on Human Rights, *Fourteenth Report of Session 2019–21: The Government Response to Covid-19: Fixed Penalty Notices* HC 1364, HL Paper 272 (27 April 2021).

found that the offences introduced by the Coronavirus Act 2020 which related to (potentially) infectious people had been misunderstood and wrongly applied to the extent that *all* criminal charges under the Act were unsafe.[55]

With regard to access to justice during the COVID-19 health crisis, the Coronavirus Act 2020 made provision for the expansion of the availability of video links for criminal, civil, family and tribunal proceedings. However, paired with the equal but opposite concern of *not* holding proceedings leading to lengthy postponements, such provisions may not have provided sufficient support for vulnerable defendants, or those with no (or only limited) access to technology and the internet.[56] In terms of the review of COVID-19 regulations, the most significant decision was handed down by the Court of Appeal in refusing permission to bring a judicial review claim,[57] expressing significant deference to government decisions made on the basis of expert advice. Where judges could be challenged by, if not be averse to, evaluating and delivering judgments on scientific evidence and public health policy, it is all the more essential for Parliament to uphold its constitutional duty not only to protect rights, but also to give due scrutiny to the actions of government which impact on their exercise.

6. Conclusion

On 19 July 2021, nearly all COVID-19 measures were removed in England following the decision by the executive that the link "between infection and mortality"[58] had been broken by relatively high vaccination rates (61.33% of the population has been fully vaccinated as of 18 August 2021[59]). This was described as a "dangerous and unethical experiment"[60] which risked exposing mainly young and unvaccinated populations to the virus, creating a "fertile ground for the emergence of vaccine-resistant variants", further burdening the already strained healthcare system, and deepening endemic socio-economic inequalities through the disproportionate impact of the pandemic on disadvantaged communities.[61] Nevertheless, the decision shifted the burden of responsibility in managing a global health crisis – which was by no means over – to the individual and private sector. An enduring 'end' to the pandemic in the UK – at least from a regulatory perspective – is equally uncertain, as the experience of pandemic U-turn governance has evidenced.

55 ibid.

56 ibid.

57 *R (Dolan and others) v Secretary of State for Health and Social Care* [2020] EWCA Civ 1605.

58 Becky Morton, 'Covid: Boris Johnson Upbeat About Easing Lockdown in England on 19 July' (*BBC News*, 1 July 2021) <https://www.bbc.co.uk/news/uk-57681216>.

59 Johns Hopkins University, Coronavirus Resource Center, Mortality Analyses <https://coronavirus.jhu.edu/data/mortality>.

60 Deepti Gurdasani, John Drury and others, 'Mass Infection Is Not an Option: We Must Do More to Protect Our Young' (2021) 398 The Lancet 297.

61 ibid.

As of August 2021, the UK has suffered over 154,800 COVID-19-related deaths,[62] and over two million people may be suffering the effects of 'long COVID'.[63] The country has at the time of writing the third highest per capita mortality in Western Europe, and the 20th highest in the world.[64] In reflecting on what impact the COVID-19 pandemic has (so far) made on UK law and governance, it is difficult to separate the global health crisis from the other challenges (if not crises) that have faced UK governance, including those which pre-dated it: the country has yet to come to terms with the social and economic consequences of its withdrawal from the European Union (or Brexit) on 31 January 2020. Concerns for supply-chain disruption and food and product shortages often feature in media reports, and are variously blamed on the pandemic, but too often without necessary analysis of the underlying multiplicity of interrelated causes.

One essential point is that the pandemic presented a complex and multifaceted social, economic, financial and health crisis which required far more than stop-gap and last-minute legislating, with poor communication and strategising to the detriment of concerted action across internal borders and the exclusion of parliamentary accountability. The movement towards executive dominance is not new to the UK, and instead reflects a pre-existing trend within the enduring constitutional debate over the limits of executive power and the ultimate authority of Parliament. It is, however, accelerating. The pressures of pandemic management and the fissures of failure exposed call urgently for deeper scrutiny of preparation for pandemic response, crisis management, but also – and fundamentally – how government is *(un)governed*.

62 UK Government Coronavirus (COVID-19) in the UK Data Centre <https://coronavirus.data.gov.uk/details/deaths>.

63 Justine Alford, 'Over 2 Million Adults in England May Have Had Long COVID' (*Imperial REACT*, 24 June 2021) <https://www.imperial.ac.uk/news/224853/over-million-adults-england-have-long/>.

64 Johns Hopkins University, Coronavirus Resource Center <https://coronavirus.jhu.edu/data/mortality>.

6

COVID-19, THE UNITED STATES AND EVIDENCE-BASED POLITICS

Mark A Graber

1. Introduction[1]

The COVID-19 pandemic revealed the extent to which attacks on evidence-based politics are part and parcel of the right-wing populist challenge to constitutional democracy in the United States and elsewhere.[2] Right-wing populism in Europe and Latin America challenges constitutional commitments to the rule of law and basic liberal freedoms, as such strongmen as Recep Tayyip Erdoğan in Turkey, Victor Orbán in Hungary and Nicolás Maduro in Venezuela seize control of courts and persecute dissidents. Populist responses to the pandemic in the United States raise equally important questions about the constitutional commitments to science and reason that are as central to constitutional democracy as the rule of law.

Liberal constitutional democracy is a child of the Enlightenment. A central claim of Enlightenment thinkers was that truth was best pursued through reason and empirical investigation.[3] Liberal constitutional democracy was grounded in beliefs that ordinary citizens had sufficient capacity to use reason and evidence to reach sound conclusions on public policy, particularly when the sense of the public was refined through representation.[4] Liberal constitutional democracy as a

1 All websites accessed on 30 July 2021.

2 Mark A Graber, Sanford Levinson and Mark Tushnet, *Constitutional Democracy in Crisis?* (Oxford University Press 2018). See also Mark A Graber, 'COVID-19, the United States and Evidence-Based Politics' (*Verfassungsblog*, 14 April 2021) on which this chapter is based <https://verfassungsblog.de/covid-19-the-united-states-and-evidence-based-politics/>.

3 The classic expression of this view is John Stuart Mill, *On Liberty* (Dover Publications 2002/1859).

4 The classic expression of this view is Alexander Hamilton, James Madison and John Jay, *The Federalist Papers* (Clinton Rossiter ed, New American Library 1961).

 DOI: 10.4324/9781003211952-7

child of the Enlightenment, in short, was committed to an evidence-based politics, in which political decisions were grounded in empirical investigation rather than faith, authority, partisanship or wishful thinking.

The pandemic hit the United States when Donald Trump was president and Republicans controlled the upper house of the national legislature. The Republican Party before Trump assumed office had already been engaged in an unprecedented war against science.[5] Even before anyone became ill, Trump had already demonstrated an unprecedented disdain for facts, lying at rates never before achieved by a prominent American politician[6] and denying uncontested evidence of climate change. That past became prologue as Americans fell sick. Trump, supported by prominent Republicans in Congress, repeatedly misrepresented the threat the virus presented to public life. He disregarded the advice of leading public health officials, who were subsequently savaged by presidential allies in the House of Representatives and the Senate. Abandoning liberal constitutional commitments to an evidence-based politics, Trump and the Republican Party adopted policies and non-policies that left, as of May 2021, more than 600,000 Americans dead.

The populist attack on evidence-based politics in the United States resulted in a public policy too often based on ideology, partisanship and wishful thinking rather than on scientific consensus. Institutions that might have blunted the populist challenge to evidence-based politics in the United States had been captured before the pandemic or were captured during the pandemic. Hundreds of thousands of people may have died because President Trump was uninterested in science (or in governing). Most notably, while the Supreme Court initially placed more emphasis than the Trump administration on evidence-based public health concerns, ideology, partisanship and wishful thinking had a major say and increased influence on that tribunal's voting and religion jurisprudence after Justice Ruth Bader Ginsburg died and was replaced by Justice Amy Comey Barrett.

The year 2021 witnessed a partial restoration of evidence-based politics after Democrats regained the White House and control of Congress, in part on the basis of commitments to govern according to scientific consensus. The United States, which was once a global laggard in response to COVID-19, is now a global leader, criticised primarily for refusing to share vaccines with less developed and more needy nations. Nevertheless, Democrats control the government only by a razor-thin margin. The Republican Party maintains controls over the federal judiciary and members of that ostensibly minority coalition continue to demonstrate little interested in tempering their recent opposition to science as a foundation for policy-making during a pandemic.

5 Chris Mooney, *The Republican War on Science* (Basic Books 2005).

6 'In Four Years, President Trump Made 30,573 False or Misleading Claims' (*The Washington Post*, 24 January 2021) <https://www.washingtonpost.com/graphics/politics/trump-claims-database/>.

2. Polarisation, Populism and the Political Attack on Evidence-Based Politics

American politics was polarised long before the COVID-19 virus crossed the border.[7] The Republican Party, captured by right-wing populists, and the Democratic Party, that remained a more traditional centre-left coalition, bitterly fought for control over the national government and the 50 state governments. Science was one prominent site of struggle. Democrats insisted that public policy reflect scientific consensus on such diverse matters as the human responsibility for climate change and the wide range of normal expressions of human sexuality. Republicans increasingly sought to deny evidence and expertise, preferring wishful thinking on climate change and conservative religious doctrine on human sexuality. Voting rights were a particularly prominent site of partisan struggle.[8] Aided by the Supreme Court, Republicans in the states had adopted numerous policies ostensibly designed to prevent voting fraud, that empirical investigation revealed did not exist,[9] except when engaged in by Republicans,[10] and that in practice disenfranchised poor persons and persons of colour who typically voted for Democrats. Religion was a third site of partisan struggle. Republican judicial appointees on the federal courts repeatedly insisted that religious organisations be given exemptions from basic civil rights laws and that excluding religious organisations from variations benefits was unconstitutional.[11]

The collapse of Republican commitment to an evidence-based politics structured the American response to COVID-19. Supported by Republicans in the federal and state governments, Trump repeatedly belittled the expert consensus on the virus. He claimed the virus was easily containable, was no deadlier than the flu, that deaths would be few, that deaths had been overestimated and that masking and other preventions were unnecessary.[12] He even suggested bleach as a potential prophylactic measure, later claiming that he was only kidding. Trump's supporters believed him. Republicans in the states delayed before implementing measures recommended by health experts and abandoned those measures at any sign of recovery. Republican citizens flouted state mask mandates at every opportunity. Some Trump supporters even drank bleach. When public health experts in gov-

7 Nolan McCarthy, Keith T Poole and Howard Rosenthal, *Polarized America: The Dance of Ideology and Unequal Riches* (The MIT Press 2006).

8 Terri L Peretti, *Partisan Supremacy: How the GOP Enlisted Courts to Rig America's Election Rules* (University Press of Kansas 2020).

9 The Brennan Center for Justice, *The Myth of Voter Fraud* <https://www.brennancenter.org/issues/ensure-every-american-can-vote/vote-suppression/myth-voter-fraud>.

10 Leslie McCrae Dowless, 'Political Operative, Charged in North Carolina Congressional Race' (*PBS News House*, 27 February 2019) <https://www.nbcmiami.com/news/national-international/n-carolina-ballot-fraud-defendant-now-faces-federal-charges/2223060/>.

11 *Trinity Lutheran Church of Columbia, Inc., v Comer*, 582 U.S. ___(2017).

12 Christian Paz, 'All the President's Lies About the Coronavirus' (*The Atlantic*, 2 November 2020) <https://www.theatlantic.com/politics/archive/2020/11/trumps-lies-about-coronavirus/608647/>.

ernment questioned administration policies, they were fired or otherwise silenced. The result was a national government, a political party and a considerable portion of the public that spent most of the pandemic in denial.

3. COVID-19 and Government Powers in the United States

The Trump administration's disinterest in aggressively combating the pandemic inverted conventional wisdom on the consequences of crises for government structure. Conventional wisdom maintains that crises centralise power. Power flows from local governments to the national government. Within the national government, power flows from the legislature and judiciary to the executive. This poses substantial danger that "presidents and prime ministers may claim special powers that are then used to curb civil liberties, marginalize political opponents, and subvert the rule of law".[13] The opposite occurred in the United States. As Kim Lane Scheppele and David Pozen documented, President Trump engaged in novel forms of constitutional underreach. Rather than using the pandemic as an opportunity to increase national and executive power, the Trump administration allowed power to devolve to Congress and the states. Very few executive orders determined the course of American policymaking, even as members of Congress urged the President to invoke existing powers. "[T]he national executive's efforts to control the pandemic", Pozen and Scheppele assert, "have been disastrously insubstantial and insufficient".[14] More often, states made policy with very little national guidance or coordination. Some states imposed strict mask requirements that have not yet been lifted. Others imposed mask requirements only when local COVID-19 rates spiked dramatically, abandoning those restrictions at the first sign of a downward turn.

Executive underreach might be conceptualised as strictly a political failure. Scheppele and Pozen point out,

> As a matter of positive law, an underreaching executive *could* do much more to protect the population from an imminent threat to its health, safety, or welfare. As a matter of political morality, an underreaching executive *should* do more, given the severity of the threat and the rationale behind the executive's delegated or inherent power to confront it.[15]

This account implicitly relies on the Constitution of the United States as a "charter of negative liberties"[16] that often limits government action, but rarely mandates government action. Trump should have done more, and any decent, intelligent person would have done more, but the Constitution of the United States did not obligate Trump to do more.

13 David E Pozen and Kim Lane Scheppele, 'Executive Underreach, in Pandemics and Otherwise' (2020) 114 American Journal of International Law 608, 608.

14 ibid 608.

15 ibid 609.

16 *Bowers v DeVito*, 686 F. 2d 616, 618 (7th Cir. 1986).

On a different view, Trump's indifference to science raises questions at the core of the constitutional regime in the United States. Some questions go to constitutional law. Several prominent scholars insist that the Constitution does require government action in the public interest, even when such actions may not be compelled by the federal judiciary.[17] Trump, from this perspective, violated his constitutional oath to "preserve, protect and defend the Constitution of the United States", even though no federal court would issue an injunction compelling the president to behave as a president. Other questions go to the functioning of the constitutional regime. The Constitution of the United States was designed to ensure to the extent humanly feasible that government would be staffed with persons who have the capabilities and interest to respond appropriately to such events as a pandemic. Trump's failure from this perspective is another manifestation of the "constitutional rot" Jack Balkin maintains infects the American regime[18] and is the sort of policy failure that Stephen Griffin sees as undermining the basic trust needed to operate a constitutional democracy.[19]

4. COVID-19 and Individual Rights in the United States

The official response to the COVID-19 pandemic in the United States also raised questions about the conventional wisdom that emergencies provide occasion for shrinking individual rights. Many rights seemingly developed immunities to the virus long before most persons did. Many state courts delayed criminal trials or held criminal trials virtually, without significant constitutional objection. No local authority invoked COVID-19 as a means for preventing the mass protests that occurred after police with little or no justification killed innocent persons of colour in several American cities. When individual rights controversies broke out, responses reflected preexisting attitudes towards the rights and science, rather than any generalised desire to limit rights during an emergency. The one consistent element in conservative judicial decisions rejecting voting rights claims while expanding the rights of religious conservatives was disinterest in evidence-based politics or decision-making.

5. COVID-19 and Voting

Unlike the COVID-19 crisis, which was acute, voting rights struggles in the United States are chronic. Voting rights would have been front and centre in American constitutional politics had every American citizen enjoyed perfect health during the Trump presidency. Nevertheless, the pandemic heightened the stakes in exist-

17 Sotirios Barber, *Welfare and the Constitution* (Princeton University Press 2003).

18 Jack M Balkin, 'Constitutional Crisis and Constitutional Rot. Constitutional Democracy in Crisis?' (2018) Maryland Law Review 77, 13–28.

19 Stephen M Griffin, *Broken Trust: Dysfunctional Government and Constitutional Reform* (University Press of Kansas 2015).

ing voting rights controversies and created new opportunities for voter suppression. The same misrepresentations that structured Republican public health policy quickly became part of an electoral strategy designed to reduce Democratic turnout.

During the 21st century, Democrats and Republicans became more sharply divided on more issues than had occurred in American history,[20] but Democrats crept ahead in popular support. The Democratic candidate for president in 1992, 1996, 2000, 2008, 2012 and 2016 gained more popular votes than the Republican candidate. More voters supported Democratic candidates for Congress than Republican candidates for Congress. Republicans nevertheless managed to compete as at least equals from 1992 to 2020 because of both hardwired and (literally) gerrymandered Republican biases in the American electoral system. The Electoral College enabled Republicans George W Bush in 2000 and Donald Trump in 2016 to gain the presidency despite losing the popular vote. The constitutional commitment to state equality in the Senate enabled low population Wyoming, which consistently elected Republicans, to enjoy the same representation in the upper house of Congress as high population New York, which consistently elected Democrats. Gerrymandering in crucial states often enabled Republicans to win a majority of the seats in the House of Representatives, even when more Americans voted for the local Democratic candidate for Congress.[21] Conventional wisdom in this environment regarded voting turnout as the key to the 2020 national election. The higher the voting turnout, particularly among younger voters and voters of colour, the more likely a decisive victory for the Democratic candidate for president and Democrats running for Congress.

COVID-19, partisanship and commitments to evidence-based politics intensified struggles over voting rights during the 2020 election cycle. Most states under Democratic control, or states in which no threat existed to Republican control, took steps to prevent long lines on election day for both primary and general elections. They made absentee voting easier, in some cases, mailing ballots to all voters. They increased times and places for early voting. They recruited new poll workers for election day and took steps to make in-person voting safe. Other states, most notably, Wisconsin, Georgia, Pennsylvania and Texas baulked.[22] In almost all cases, states that rejected evidence-based voting policies were those in which Trump had won the popular vote in 2016 and had Republican-controlled state legislatures, but were thought to be possible Democratic pick-ups in 2020.

20 Geoffrey C Layman and Thomas M Carsey, 'Party Polarization and "Conflict Extension" in the American Electorate' (2002) 26 American Journal of Political Science 786, 789; Lawrence Baum and Neal Devins, *The Company They Keep: How Partisan Divisions Came to the Supreme Court* (Oxford University Press 2019).

21 See Michael S Kang, 'Hyperpartisan Gerrymandering' (2020) 61 Boston College Law Review 1379, 1424–1425.

22 For a survey of state voting rights policies during the 2020 national election, see Brennan Center for Justice, 'Voting Laws Roundup 2020' <https://www.brennancenter.org/our-work/research-reports/voting-laws-roundup-2020-0>.

Voting rights activists enjoyed some successes in state courts and lower federal courts when they challenged state failures to ensure persons could vote safely in the primary and national elections.[23] With important exceptions, however, the Supreme Court often insisted abstractions were more important than evidence-based politics. If, for obvious partisan reasons, state legislatures were not going to facilitate voting in national elections, the conservative majority of the Supreme Court maintained, federal courts should not intervene in ways that would enable people with the legal right to vote to be able in practice to cast a ballot.[24] If, for example, voters had good reason to fear that because of postal delays caused by the pandemic an absentee ballot requested in August might arrive after the election in November, that was just tough luck.

Broad agreement among the justices and legal commentators existed that state legislatures had the right to adjust voting rules in light of the pandemic. When state legislatures extended the time for absentee voting, expanded early voting sites, or otherwise took steps to prevent long lines on election day, those measures were acknowledged to be fully constitutional.[25] The Supreme Court, which under federal law has almost complete discretion over its docket, did not bother reviewing any of these cases. No justice even hinted that a constitutional problem existed with state legislation expanding opportunities to vote during the pandemic.

The Supreme Court gave the lower federal courts no similar leeway. The Supreme Court majority insisted that federal courts had no business changing the election rules shortly before an election. If the democratically elected state legislature did not think a rule change was necessary, federal courts should ordinarily abide by that decision. Justice Neil Gorsuch maintained

> Last-minute changes to longstanding election rules … invit[e] confusion and chaos and erod[e] public confidence in electoral outcomes. No one doubts that conducting a national election amid a pandemic poses serious challenges. But none of that means individual judges may improvise with their own election rules in place of those the people's representatives have adopted.[26]

The four more liberal justices on the court sharply disagreed. In their view, the right to vote trumped concerns about rule changes, particularly when state failures to respond to a public health crisis had no basis in evidence on the ground. Justice Elena Kagan accused the conservative majority of "refus[ing] to engage

23 *Pennsylvania Democratic Party v Boockvar*, (2020) 238 A. 3d 345.

24 See, e.g., *Andino v Middleton*, ___ U.S. ___ (2020) (Kavanaugh J concurring).

25 For examples of state legislation expanding voting opportunities, see The Brennan Center, 'Voting Laws Roundup, 2020' (4 February 2020) <https://www.brennancenter.org/our-work/research-reports/voting-laws-roundup-2020>.

26 *Democratic National Committee v Wisconsin State Legislature*, 411 S. Ct. 28, 30 (2020) (Gorsuch J concurring).

with" the undisputed evidence that "a veritable tsunami (in the form of a pandemic) has hit Wisconsin's election machinery and disrupted all its usual mail ballot operations".[27]

State courts were also given leeway, although by a more closely divided court. The Supreme Court of Pennsylvania allowed absentee votes to be counted even if they arrived after election day.[28] Whether by intention or by incompetence the US Postal Service, under the leadership of a person whose only qualification for the position seemed to be significant donations to the Trump campaign, had not been delivering the mail as efficiently. Pennsylvania judges insisted that these postal slowdowns should not prevent otherwise legal votes from being counted. The Supreme Court refused to intervene when requested to do so by the Republican Party. The crucial vote was cast by Chief Justice Roberts, who in other opinions indicated that the ban on interfering with election rules immediately before an election was for federal courts, but that state courts interpreting the state constitution were freer to change the rules. "[T]the Pennsylvania applications," he wrote, "implicated the authority of state courts to apply their own constitutions to election regulations", and did not "involve … federal intrusion on state lawmaking processes". Chief Justice Roberts concluded, "[d]ifferent bodies of law and different precedents govern these two situations".[29]

The replacement of Justice Ruth Bader Ginsburg by Justice Amy Comey Barrett in 2020 has so far not changed this very delicate balance. Justice Barrett, during her rushed confirmation hearings, refused to state whether and how she would rule on the election disputes that arose during the pandemic. When, however, Republicans after the 2020 election sought to overturn the Pennsylvania election in court on the ground that the state court had unduly interfered with the state legislature, Justice Barrett pointedly refused to join the more conservative justices on the Supreme Court who in dissent insisted that the court should adjudicate the matter.[30]

6. COVID-19, Public Health and Religious Freedom

Justice Barrett made a substantial difference in the course of Supreme Court policymaking on religious freedom. During the pandemic, most states adopted rules and regulations sharply limiting public gatherings. These rules typically differentiated between different institutions. Grocery stores could remain open under certain conditions. Movie theatres could be open only on more stringent conditions. Religious services typically were placed somewhere in between. They faced more stringent limits than grocery stores, but less stringent limits than movie theatres. Some religious denominations accepted these limits. Others protested, claiming

27 *Democratic National Committee v Wisconsin State Legislature*, at 44 (Kagan J dissenting).

28 *Pennsylvania Democratic Party v Boockvar*, 238 A. 3d 345 (Pa. 2020).

29 *Democratic National Committee v Wisconsin State Legislature*, at 28 (Roberts CJ concurring).

30 *Republican Party of Pennsylvania v Boockvar*, ___ S. Ct. ___ (2020).

either that states could not bar religious services at all or that the rules discriminated against religious services.

The Supreme Court while Justice Ginsburg lived deferred to state legislatures.[31] Such legislation, judicial opinions pointed out, was rooted in medical expertise. Grocery stores were not as much hotspots as churches. Persons shopping for groceries tend to be spend limited time inside, partly because grocery stores are not sites for the singing and chanting that routinely takes place in religious services. Evidence indicated that many outbreaks of COVID-19 were strongly associated with attendance at religious services.[32] The four most conservative justices dissented, insisting that the differences in stringency discriminated against religion.

Justice Barrett's appointment converted a 5–4 majority in favour of deference into a 5–4 majority in favour of religious freedom, or religious freedom as defined by the most conservative members of the Supreme Court. A commitment to evidence-based politics was at the root of the difference between the justices in the majority and minority. The conservatives in the majority speculated that some permitted activities might have been as risky as the religious activities that were prohibited. Justice Neil Gorsuch observed, "no one is barred from lingering in shopping malls, salons, or bus terminals"[33] without asking whether people in fact linger in these places and whether such lingering is statistically associated with COVID-19 outbreaks. Justice Kagan's call for evidence rather than speculation fell on deaf ears. In an opinion which detailed the medical testimony justifying the differential treatment of religious institutions, Justice Kagan declared,

> the Court displaces the judgments of experts about how to respond to a raging pandemic. The Court orders California to weaken its restrictions on public gatherings by making a special exception for worship services. The majority does so even though the State's policies treat worship just as favorably as secular activities (including political assemblies) that, according to medical evidence, pose the same risk of COVID transmission.[34]

As the pandemic wore on, the Supreme Court moved towards according religion a 'most favoured nation' status. Local restrictions on religion not placed on some other public gatherings were struck down, even when the same or more onerous restrictions were placed on other public gatherings.[35] Under this approach, government had to treat religion as favourably as any plausibly analogous secular activity when making public health policy and, presumably, any other activity. If there

31 *Calvary Chapel Dayton Valley v Sisolak*, 140 S. Ct., 2603 (2020).

32 Kerry Breen, 'Why are Places of Worship to Susceptible to COVID-19 Outbreaks?' (*Today*, 30 July 2020) <https://www.today.com/health/why-are-places-worship-so-susceptible-covid-19-outbreaks-t188095>.

33 *South Bay United Pentecostal Church v Newsom*, 141 S. Ct. 716, 719 (2021) (statement of Gorsuch J).

34 *South Bay United Pentecostal Church*, at 720 (Kagan J dissenting).

35 *Tandon v Newsom*, 141 S. Ct. 1294 (2021); *South Bay United Pentecostal Church*.

were no limits on people congregating on beaches but substantial limits on people going to the theatre, religious meetings had to be treated as analogous to beaches rather than the theatre, even when public health specialists suggested the theatre analogy was more appropriate. Justice Brett Kavanaugh, the leading proponent of this view maintains, "[u]nless the State provides a sufficient justification otherwise, it must place religious organizations in the favored or exempt category".[36]

The problems with this 'most favoured nation' status are numerous. Supreme Court precedent before the pandemic was increasingly being made in response to petitions asking for injunctions on lower federal or state court decisions. This is referred to as the "shadow docket".[37] The use of the shadow docket accelerated during the pandemic, particularly in cases involving claims of religious exemption. The result is that the court repeatedly discarded the advice of public health experts without full briefing or oral argument. Requiring communities to always "place religious organizations in the favored or exempt category" is likely to skew public policy dramatically towards support for religion. Suppose, for example, a community decided to sponsor a local opera company on the ground that they believe more opera will improve the cultural life of the residents. Must that community also give a local church choir the same funds on the ground that more religion will improve the cultural life of the residents? If they provide funds for a soccer stadium, must they provide the same funds for a mega-church?

7. The Past and Future of COVID-19 and Evidence-Based Politics

The main event in constitutional politics during the first year of the pandemic was the invasion of the Capitol by Trump supporters on 6 January 2021. The connections between that event and public health policy during the pandemic are unclear. On the one hand, Trump supporters were frustrated by legislative regulations requiring wearing masks in public (most protestors flouted that regulation), and limiting businesses and religious services. On the other hand, Trump was a notoriously sore loser who would have contemplated challenging the electoral result under any circumstances. So a fair case can be made that something like 6 January would have occurred in American politics even if COVID-19 had never occurred. In this vein, one might note that COVID-19 had surprisingly little impact on voting choices during the election. Voting choices tended to reflect preexisting partisanship rather than blame or credit for handling the pandemic.[38]

The insurrection nevertheless highlighted the continued weakening of evidence-based politics and the concomitant lack of respect for basic facts that played a major role in the pandemic and American political affairs. Basic facts about the

36 *Calvary Chapel Dayton Valley v Sisolak*, at 2612 (Kavanaugh J dissenting).

37 Stephen I Vladeck, 'The Solicitor General and the Shadow Docket' (2018) 133 Harvard Law Review 123.

38 Hannah Miao, 'Here's What Mattered Most to Voters in the 2020 Election, According to Exit Polls' (*CNBC*, 3 November 2020) <https://www.cnbc.com/2020/11/03/exit-polls-heres-what-mattered-most-to-voters-in-the-2020-election.html>.

world have played less and less of a role in American political life, even as the threats presented by expert assessment of those facts have multiplied. Nearly 20 years ago, the United States invaded Iraq in part because of fears about missiles that turned out not to exist. Still, at least some evidence suggested that Iraq was developing a more dangerous nuclear stockpile than proved to be the case, even as the Bush administration ignored the advice of most people who actually knew something about the Middle East. The Trump administration in crucial matters discarded evidence altogether. Trump smashed the lie barrier for political officials, making false claims and claims made on no evidence at unprecedented rates. His administration denied the climate changes that all environmentalists acknowledge are taking place, even as disagreements exist on the details. Trump claimed an election was stolen even as Republicans in office and in the courts could not find evidence of malfeasance. At least one aspect of Trump's practice was evidence-based. No evidence existed that Trump's lies and disregard for basic facts was politically costly. The 45% of the people who supported him insisted that while Trump exaggerated, he was far more to be trusted than the so-called experts who insisted that climate change was real, immigrants posed no threat to the economy and the election was not stolen.

Former Vice President Joe Biden's triumph in the 2020 presidential election and the return of the Senate to (bare) Democratic control increased the immediate impact of evidence-based politics on public policy in the United States, both with respect to COVID-19 and other matters. Unlike the Trump administration, the Biden administration developed a plan for distributing vaccines that was based on institutional capacity rather than wishful thinking and political advantage. At the time of writing, distribution appears to be taking place faster than expected. Divisions exist over the proper forms of relief, but the plans preferred by progressive Democrats, centrist Democrats and the most moderate of the very conservative Republicans are rooted in evidence about how the virus has affected individuals and the economy. To use a phrase coined to describe Hillary Clinton by 'never-Trumpers', if persons within the range from the democratic socialist Representative Alexandria Ocasio-Cortez of New York and to the conservative Republican Senator Rob Portman of Ohio are wrong, they are "wrong within the normal parameters"[39] of democratic politics.

Nevertheless, COVID-19 accelerated activities outside the parameters of normal democratic and evidence-based politics. Texas, Mississippi and other Republican-controlled states ended mask mandates even though experts agreed such policies would increase the spread of the virus and lead to more deaths.[40] Republicans in

39 Nick Gass, 'P.J. O'Rourke Hate-Endorses Hillary Clinton on NPR Quiz Show' (*Politico*, 9 May 2016) <https://www.politico.com/story/2016/05/pj-orourke-endorses-hillary-clinton-222954>.

40 For the most recent update on what states lifted mask mandates, see 'See Reopening Plans and Mask Mandates for All 50 States' (*The New York Times*, 1 June 2020) <https://www.nytimes.com/interactive/2020/us/states-reopen-map-coronavirus.html>. For experts on lifting mask mandates, see Sujata Gupta, Tina Hesman Saey and Erin Garcia de Jesus, 'The CDC's Changes to

state legislatures found ways of increasing minority control by gerrymandering and further restricting voting.[41] The Trump family vowed to return to politics, even as evidence continued to mount that they bore a greater resemblance to the crime families of motion pictures than to the Bush and Kennedy dynasties.[42] A superficial glimpse of COVID-19 numbers and the Biden administration may suggest the clouds were clearing during 2021,[43] but the better view may be the United States was in the eye of the storm.

Mask Guidelines Raised Questions. Here are 5 Answers' (*ScienceNews*, 24 May 2021) <https://www.sciencenews.org/article/cdc-mask-guideline-question-answer-coronavirus-covid-pandemic>.

41 Dave Montgomery and Nick Carasaniti, 'After Dramatic Walkout, a New Fight Looms Over Voting Rights in Texas' (*The New York Times*, 31 May 2021) <https://www.nytimes.com/2021/05/31/us/politics/texas-voting-bill-.html?action=click&module=Spotlight&pgtype=Homepage>.

42 Brett Bachman, 'Investigators Reportedly Approaching Trump Org. as if it were a Mafia family' (*Salon*, 30 May 2021) <https://www.salon.com/2021/05/30/prosecutors-reportedly-approaching-trump-org-investigation-as-if-it-were-a-mafia-family/>.

43 Centers for Disease Control and Prevention, 'COVID Data Tracker Weekly Review' (28 May 2021) <https://www.cdc.gov/coronavirus/2019-ncov/covid-data/covidview/index.html>.

7

DEMOCRACY IN THE TIME OF COVID-19

Pandemic Management, Public Trust and Democratic Consolidation in Singapore

Shirin Chua and Jaclyn L Neo

1. Introduction[1]

The COVID-19 pandemic appears to have exacerbated pre-existing trends[2] of global democratic decay.[3] The importance and currency of this inquiry can be seen in the numerous databases monitoring the impact of COVID-19 responses on democracy.[4] Of these, the V-Dem Institute, Freedom House, the Economist Intelligence Unit and International IDEA frameworks generally concur that global democratic regression has intensified as a result of COVID-19.[5] In particular, the biggest threat arose from executive aggrandisement, through emergency measures

1 All websites accessed on 21 July 2021.

2 Aurel Croissant and Jeffrey Haynes, 'Democratic Regression in Asia' (2021) 28(1) Democratization 1, 1–15; Natasha Lindstaedt, *Understanding Democratic Decay and Authoritarian Resurgence* (Bristol University Press 2021); Roberto S Foa and Yascha Mounk, 'The Signs of Deconsolidation' (2017) 28(1) Journal of Democracy 5.

3 Joelle Grogan, 'Power, Law and the COVID-19 Pandemic – Part I: The Year of Pandemic' (*Verfassungsblog*, 15 May 2021) <https://verfassungsblog.de/power-law-and-the-covid-19-pandemic-part-i-the-year-of-pandemic>; Lauri Rapeli and Inga Saikkonen, 'How Will the COVID-19 Pandemic Affect Democracy?' (2020) 7(2) Democratic Theory 25; Anna Lührmann and others, 'Does the Coronavirus Endanger Democracy in Europe? (*Carnegie Europe*, 23 June 2020) <https://carnegieeurope.eu/2020/06/23/does-coronavirus-endanger-democracy-in-europe-pub-82110>.

4 *See* COVID-DEM, 'Databases' <https://www.democratic-decay.org/databases>.

5 Tom G Daly, 'Democracy and the Global Pandemic: Reshuffled Reputations and the Future of the "Free World"' (*Verfassungsblog*, 1 May 2021) <https://verfassungsblog.de/democracy-and-the-global-pandemic/>. See also Daly, chapter 1 in this volume.

 DOI: 10.4324/9781003211952-8

and otherwise, catalysed by the urgent need to respond to a multi-faceted and fast-changing pandemic.[6]

Singapore similarly found its legal, political, economic and public health systems severely tested by COVID-19. However, Singapore's institutions generally proved resilient. Contrary to the global trend, it even seems that the pandemic threw up opportunities for democratic consolidation in Singapore as a result of increased citizen-state interactions during this time.

In making this claim, we are mindful that there are multiple competing conceptions of democratic consolidation. The 'classic' definition of a consolidated democracy is where democracy has become "the only game in town", as Linz and Stepan point out, namely when: (i) *behaviourally*, no significant national, social, economic, political or institutional actors spend significant resources attempting to achieve their objectives by creating a non-democratic regime; (ii) *attitudinally*, when the overwhelming majority of the people believe that any further political change must emerge from within the parameters of democratic procedures; and (iii) *constitutionally*, when all actors become habituated to the fact that political conflict within the state will be resolved according to established norms.[7] These may constitute what Ginsburg and Huq have referred to as the "shared epistemic foundation" required by democracy.[8]

A 'minimalist' or 'prospective' conception of democratic consolidation primarily associates consolidation with the durability of democracy.[9] Schedler observes that "consolidating democracy means reducing the probability of its breakdown to the point where [we] can feel reasonably confident that democracy will persist".[10] This has not been a real issue in Singapore; even while it has a dominant party system, there has never been any threat that elections would not be called within the constitutionally required limits. However, when it comes to identifying democratic consolidation in a more 'maximalist' or 'substantive' manner, associating it with a set of specific outcomes,[11] Singapore may not necessarily fit the bill. For example, Linz and Stepan propose that democracy is consolidated when conditions exist for the development of a free and lively civil society and a relatively autonomous political society; when all major political actors are subjected "to a rule of law that

6 Rapeli and Saikkonen (n 3) 28; Victor V Ramraj and Arun K Thiruvengadam, 'Pandemics and Emergency Powers in Asia' in Victor V Ramraj (ed) *COVID-19 in Asia: Law and Policy Contexts* (Oxford University Press 2020) 133, 139–140.

7 Juan J Linz and Alfred Stepan, 'Toward Consolidated Democracies' (1996) 7(2) Journal of Democracy 14, 15–16.

8 Tom Ginsburg and Aziz Z Huq, *How to Save a Constitutional Democracy* (University of Chicago Press 2018), 155.

9 Andreas Ufen, 'Political Party and Party System Institutionalization in Southeast Asia: Lessons for Democratic Consolidation in Indonesia, the Philippines and Thailand' (2008) 21(3) Pacific Review 327, 329–331; Milan Svolik, 'Which Democracies Will Last? Coups, Incumbent Takeovers and the Dynamic of Democratic Consolidation' (2015) 45(4) British Journal of Political Science 715, 715–716.

10 Andreas Schedler, 'What Is Democratic Consolidation?' (1998) 9(2) Journal of Democracy 91, 95.

11 Ufen (n 9) 329–331; Svolik (n 9) 715–716.

protects individual freedoms and associational life"; when there is a state bureaucracy that is usable by the new democratic government; and when there is an institutionalised economic society.[12]

Accordingly, this chapter analyses Singapore's response to COVID-19 as having presented opportunities for democratic consolidation primarily in the form of (i) the institutionalisation of opposition politics; (ii) the deepening of a shared epistemic articulation of constitutional democratic workings; and (iii) the development of stronger civil society engagement with the state.[13] This chapter's analysis is agnostic as to what stage or type of democracy characterised Singapore's system before the pandemic,[14] as well as what stage or type of democracy will be Singapore's 'final destination' based on the trends we discuss. In this, this contribution is aligned with Schedler, who argues that the 'normative horizons' of democratic consolidation vary depending on "where we stand" – in particular, whether the starting point is 'authoritarianism', 'electoral democracy', 'liberal democracy', or 'advanced democracy'.[15] This analysis thus diverges from Linz and Stephan insofar as they insist that consolidation does not apply to "liberalized nondemocratic regimes", "pseudo-democracies" or "hybrid democracies".[16] It is submitted here, that the major developments discussed below point towards an overall trend of democratic consolidation in Singapore, even while there are developments that may have led in different directions.

2. An Overview of Singapore's Legal and Political Response to COVID-19: Legislative Approach and Executive Power

Singapore did not declare a state of emergency in response to COVID-19. Instead, it relied on a 'legislative approach', using ordinary statutes to expand ministerial powers to manage the pandemic.[17]The key plank of this legislative approach is the COVID-19 (Temporary Measures) Act (CTMA) 2020.[18]

Presented, debated and passed within a day under provisions for expedited legislation, the provisions of the CTMA are wide-ranging. In the private law realm,

12 Linz and Stepan (n 7) 15–16.

13 This chapter builds on our earlier contribution: Shirin Chua and Jaclyn L Neo, 'COVID-19 as an Opportunity for Democratic Consolidation? Law, Politics, and Citizen-State Interactions in Singapore' (*Verfassungsblog*, 24 February 2021) <https://verfassungsblog.de/covid-19-as-an-opportunity-for-democratic-consolidation/>.

14 See Jaclyn L Neo and others, 'Singapore: The State of Liberal Democracy' in Richard Albert and others (eds), *The I·CONnect-Clough Center 2017 Global Review of Constitutional Law* (2018) 244; Kevin YL Tan, 'Is Singapore a Constitutional Authoritarian Regime? So What If It Is?' in Weitseng Chen and Hualing Fu (eds), *Authoritarian Legality in Asia: Formation, Development and Transition* (Cambridge University Press 2020).

15 Schedler (n 10) 92–94.

16 Linz and Stepan (n 7) 15.

17 Jaclyn L Neo and Darius Lee, 'Singapore's Legislative Approach to the COVID-19 Public Health "Emergency"' (*Verfassungsblog*, 18 April 2020) <https://verfassungsblog.de/singapores-legislative-approach-to-the-covid-19-public-health-emergency>; Chua and Neo (n 13).

18 COVID-19 Temporary Measures Act No 14 of 2020.

the CTMA introduced temporary measures granting relief to financially distressed individuals and businesses. In the public law realm, the CTMA granted broad ministerial powers to enact movement control orders if satisfied that COVID-19 constitutes a serious threat to public health and that such orders are "necessary or expedient".[19]

Under the CTMA, the Minister can issue orders – subject to criminal penalties – requiring people to not leave a specified place; restricting movement of or contact between people; requiring premises or facilities to be closed or be subject to limited access; restricting the time, manner or extent for the carrying out of any business, undertaking or work; and prohibiting or restricting the conduct of or participation in any event or gathering.[20] At the time of writing, a set of regulations promulgated under the CTMA (Control Order Regulations) continues to prescribe the vast majority of public health measures in response to COVID-19, and is amended as necessary.[21] This allowed Singapore to be nimble in updating these measures, which was efficacious in responding to a pandemic where circumstances evolved rapidly. However, it also placed significant power in the hands of a minister.

In opting for a legislative approach, Singapore may be said to have avoided the biggest threat to democracy that the pandemic has presented elsewhere, namely a state of emergency and its potential for abuse. In passing specialised legislation on COVID-19, Singapore also avoided another pitfall encountered elsewhere, namely the risk of the government exercising excessive discretion or overly broad powers when deploying pre-existing legislation for purposes for which it is ill-suited.[22] Nevertheless, executive aggrandisement at the expense of other democratic institutions can also occur in the absence of a formal state of emergency or under tailor-made legislation.[23] For this reason, the robustness of legislative and judicial oversight is critical to an analysis of whether Singapore's legislative approach represents a preservation of constitutional democracy or an emergency in all but name.

3. Legislative Scrutiny, Rule of Law and the Consolidation of Parliamentary Democracy

Parliament is not only an organ of democracy, but, in parliamentary democracies, also its most visible symbol. Its continued functioning is existential. As outlined by Bar-Simon-Tov, COVID-19 challenged this continued functioning because legislatures are fundamentally based on the assembly of many people; indeed, many constitutions impose mandatory quorum rules that require physical presence.[24]

19 ibid s 34(1).

20 ibid s 34(2).

21 See also Chua and Neo (n 13).

22 Ramraj and Thiruvengadam (n 6) 135 and 140.

23 ibid 138; Grogan (n 3).

24 Ittai Bar-Siman-Tov 'Covid-19 Meets Politics: the Novel Coronavirus as a Novel Challenge for Legislatures' (2020) 8 The Theory and Practice of Legislation 11, 14–17.

In this regard, it bears noting that the powers of the health minister under the CTMA are subject to legislative control. First, Parliament retains oversight of all control orders. All control orders and any amendments thereto must be presented to Parliament "as soon as possible". Parliament may annul any control order, amendment or any part thereof by passing a resolution.[25] Second, these powers are temporally limited by the CTMA. Any power to extend this period lies with Parliament – by amending the CTMA – and not the health minister alone.

However, the time limit originally prescribed by the CTMA – one year from its entry into force, ie expiring on 7 April 2021 – was twice as long as the six months' validity Singapore's Constitution grants to Proclamations of Emergency.[26] A subsequent amendment extended this to 8 April 2022.[27] While this did not necessarily represent executive aggrandisement, at the time of writing, it remains to be seen whether and to what extent Parliament extends this validity beyond 8 April 2022 – and, thus, whether the CTMA may ultimately, in substance, create "permanent changes to the legal system or … in the balance of powers".[28]

To ensure legislative oversight, the legislature must continue to function. In Singapore, there was no imposed or consequent hiatus on Parliament's work. In fact, Parliament amended the Constitution to create a mechanism for meetings to take place with members in different places but in contemporaneous communication if it was impossible, unsafe or inexpedient for Parliament to meet in one place.[29] Members of Parliament, including those in the opposition, voted unanimously for the amendments.[30] Singapore thus avoided the challenges that deadlocked legislative proceedings elsewhere.[31]

However, even while the legislative function continued, another key obstacle to robust legislative oversight in Westminster parliamentary systems may be the legislative-executive fusion of powers. In Singapore, this tends to be deepened by the dominance of the ruling People's Action Party in Parliament and in the Cabinet.[32] In fact, it may be argued that Singapore's choice not to invoke emergency powers was only possible in this context. At the time the CTMA was passed, there were only six opposition members, belonging to the same party, out of a total of 89 parliamentarians. In any case, all the elected opposition as well as non-elected members voted for the CTMA without proposing any amendments.[33] This

25 CTMA, ss 34(4)–(5).
26 Neo and Lee (n 17).
27 CTMA, s 1(7).
28 Grogan (n 3).
29 Constitution of the Republic of Singapore, 1999 Rev Ed, Art 64A.
30 Parliamentary Debates: Official Report, vol 94 (5 May 2020).
31 Bar-Siman-Tov (n 24) 15–16.
32 Lynette J Chua and Jack J G Lee, 'Governing through Contagion' in Victor V Ramraj (ed) *COVID-19 in Asia: Law and Policy Contexts* (Oxford University Press 2020) 115, 120.
33 Parliamentary Debates: Official Report, vol 94 (7 April 2020).

consensus as to the need for such pandemic management measures is indicative. Even though the opposition and non-elected parliamentarians do not have the numbers to stop laws from passing, their objections could serve as a barometer for the extent of community support. Opposition parliamentarians had, for instance, strongly objected to the passing of some controversial laws, such as the Protection from Online Falsehoods and Manipulation Act 2019 (POFMA).[34] They did not do so here.

In some countries where emergency proclamations delayed elections, incumbent governments claimed that public health trumped the calling of elections.[35] The calculus was reversed in Singapore. Without a fixed term Parliament, the incumbent government always has leeway over the timing of elections but must do so before Parliament's term expires. Somewhat ironically, though not entirely unstrategically, it was the incumbent that maintained the need to do so, whereas the opposition suggested delaying elections.[36] Fears were expressed that the pandemic would drive a 'flight of safety' towards the incumbent ruling party and cause an 'opposition wipeout'.[37]

Accordingly, Singapore organised general elections on 10 July 2020, nine months before Parliament's term expired. In calling the election, the prime minister specifically highlighted the need to seek a new mandate to respond to COVID-19 and its consequences.[38] The Parliamentary Elections (COVID-19 Special Arrangements) Act 2020 allowed political candidates, if ill, to file nomination papers electronically, and allowed voters subject to control orders to vote at facilities outside their electoral divisions.[39] These measures had limited temporal remit; "election" was defined in the Act as "an election … held on or before 14 April 2021".

Apart from unusually long queues at polling stations, leading to some unhappiness among voters and an apology from the Elections Department, the elections were largely uneventful, organised and safe. Political parties were able to employ

34 Tham Yuen-C, 'Parliament: Fake News Law Passed After 2 Days of Debate' (*The Straits Times*, 9 May 2019) <https://www.straitstimes.com/politics/parliament-fake-news-law-passed-after-2-days-of-debate>.

35 Toby James and Erik Asplund, *What Happens After Elections Are Postponed? Responses to Postponing Elections During COVID-19 Vary by Regime Type* (Institute for Democracy and Electoral Assistance, 2 September 2020) <https://www.idea.int/news-media/news/what-happens-after-elections-are-postponed-responses-postponing-elections-during>.

36 Chua and Neo (n 13).

37 Kevin YL Tan and Terence Lee, 'Introduction: The Shift Continues Amidst a Pandemic': Singapore's 2020 General Elections' in Kevin YL Tan and Terence Lee (eds), *Voting in a Time of Change: Singapore's 2020 General Election* (Ethos Books 2021) 14; see also Rapeli and Saikkonen (n 3) 26 (on the 'rally round the flag' effect).

38 Prime Minister's Office Singapore, 'Speech on General Election 2020 by PM Lee Hsien Loong' (23 June 2020).

39 Parliamentary Elections COVID-19 Special Arrangements Act No 21 of 2020.

social media and other online tools to campaign effectively.[40] There was no spike in COVID-19 infections following the election.[41]

The election results, however, caused ripples. The largest opposition party in Parliament, the Workers' Party, won ten seats, the highest number won by an opposition party in post-independence history.[42] This prompted the establishment of a formal office of the Leader of the Opposition, heralding an even more robust future role for the opposition.[43] There was some handwringing within the incumbent party, which won 61.2% of the vote – a solid victory by any global standard, but which represented a nearly 9% drop from its share in the last election and just slightly above its record low of 60.1% in 2011.[44]

In reflecting on the results, the prime minister-elect noted that COVID-19 had played a significant role.[45] At least one post-election study has suggested that the pandemic triggered and reinforced longstanding issues of concern to the electorate, including social inequality and the lack of inclusive political engagement.[46]

Singapore's 'COVID-elections' could be said to have facilitated substantive consolidation of parliamentary democracy in the following ways. Firstly, insofar as the institutionalisation of political parties and party systems is a feature of democratic consolidation,[47] the increased opposition presence in Parliament and the institutionalised Leader of the Opposition is important. The prohibition on physical rallies, previously the main form of political campaigning, led the government to provide for alternatives that may be difficult to roll back in subsequent elections. These alternatives were primarily on national television and online,[48] raising the possibility that 'internet elections' may have played a role in increasing the competitiveness of Singapore's party system.[49]

Secondly, the "shared epistemic foundation"[50] of constitutional democracy was amply reflected. Even in the heated contestation as to whether elections should be held, all actors framed their claims with reference to constitutional requirements and mechanisms. Opposition leaders spoke of the constitutionality of caretaker

40 Jaclyn Neo, 'Singapore: Efficient Government, but "No Blank Cheque"' (Melbourne Forum on Constitution-Building, September 2020) <https://law.unimelb.edu.au/__data/assets/pdf_file/0008/3475952/MF20-Web2-Singapore-Neo-FINAL.pdf>. See also Bridget Welsh, 'PAP's Pandemic Backfire: The Covid-19 Factor in Singapore's 2020 Polls' in Kevin YL Tan and Terence Lee (eds), *Voting in a Time of Change: Singapore's 2020 General Election* (Ethos Books 2021) 44.

41 Welsh (n 40) 44.

42 Chua and Neo (n 13).

43 ibid.

44 ibid.

45 Neo (n 40).

46 Welsh (n 40) 48–49.

47 Schedler (n 10) 100; E Sridharan, 'Theorizing Democratic Consolidation, Parties and Coalition' in E Sridharan, *Coalition Politics and Democratic Consolidation in Asia* (Oxford University Press 2013) 1, 4–5.

48 Neo (n 40).

49 ibid; see also Alvin Tan, 'GE2020: Not Quite a Digital Election?' in Kevin YL Tan and Terence Lee (eds), *Voting in a Time of Change: Singapore's 2020 General Election* (Ethos Books 2021).

50 Ginsburg and Huq (n 8) 155.

governments,[51] while the government stressed in retort the constitutional imperative of holding elections before Parliament's term expired.[52] For the first time, a constitutional challenge was filed against the calling of elections, on the basis that doing so in the middle of a pandemic was contrary to the right to vote.The urgent application was, however, dismissed *ex tempore* by Singapore's highest court.[53]

Thirdly, insofar as a vibrant civil society is a component of a consolidated democracy,[54] the elections appear to galvanise citizen engagement in political matters. For instance, the debates in Parliament as to constitutional amendments to allow the above-mentioned continuity arrangements revived the question of livestreaming parliamentary proceedings, hitherto a contested proposition, generally along party lines.[55] This appears to have led to the livestreaming of parliamentary proceedings for the first time, which garnered more than 80,000 views.[56] The rights of overseas voters were another issue which attracted civic debate and activism.[57]

4. Judicial Scrutiny and Access to Justice

The availability of judicial remedies against the state and its officials is an important component of the rule of law.[58] Some consider robust judicial review to be an essential feature of constitutionalism, albeit of the liberal form. Since Singapore did not invoke emergency powers, constitutional rights such as the freedom of movement, speech, assembly and association and religion remain in force. Courts may review the consistency of the CTMA and the Control Order Regulations (as well as any other legislative or executive action) on the basis of those rights and/or the usual administrative law rules, though it may be difficult to challenge the wide discretion accorded to the health minister to issue control orders, since the terms of the CTMA are broadly worded.[59]

As a matter of the rule of law, judicial oversight of government action can only be effectively exercised where parties can practicably access the courts. In this regard, Singapore's legislature and judiciary cooperated to ensure that access to the courts was not suspended. For the period during which the most restrictive public health measures were in place, the courts adjourned all hearings except for "essen-

51 Chua and Neo (n 13).

52 Prime Minister's Office Singapore (n 38).

53 *Daniel De Costa Augustin v Attorney-General* [2020] 2 SLR 621 (Court of Appeal).

54 Linz and Stepan (n 7) 17; Larry Diamond, *Developing Democracy: Toward Consolidation* (Johns Hopkins Press 1999), 65–67; see also Robert Dahl, *Democracy and its Critics* (Yale University Press 1989).

55 Parliamentary Debates: Official Report, vol 94 (7 April 2020).

56 Chua and Neo (n 13).

57 ibid.

58 Linz and Stepan (n 6); Ramraj and Thiruvengadam (n 6) 139.

59 Darius Lee, 'COVID-19 in Singapore: "Responsive Communitarianism" and the Legislative Approach to the "Most Serious Crisis" since Independence' (2020) Singapore Journal of Legal Studies 630, 643.

tial and urgent matters".[60] Applications for judicial review, including "in relation to implementation of COVID-19 measures", were expressly listed as "essential and urgent" before the Supreme Court.[61] The CTMA also provided for remote hearings, thus harnessing technology to strike a balance between public health concerns and the efficient administration of justice.

5. Human Rights and Civil Liberties – Trust, Legitimacy and Marginalised Groups

5.1 A Matter of Trust: Civil Liberties Without Rights Adjudication

Overall, there has not to date been widespread vocal opposition to the COVID-19 measures.[62] Apart from the above-mentioned constitutional challenge, there was no other effort to sue the government for such measures. This is consistent with Singapore's constitutional culture, where judicial review cases have been fairly limited and only recently started to become more frequent.[63] At the same time, it would be too simplistic to attribute this relative absence of opposition to 'authoritarianism'.[64] As Ramraj and Thiruvengadam argue, legal frameworks do not operate in a vacuum; rather, institutional resilience depends on the way in which a legal framework interacts with dynamics of expertise, public trust in institutions, and government responsiveness to feedback.[65]

To this end, Lee has argued that Singapore's COVID-19 response reflects a "responsive communitarian" model – characterised not just by shared values, norms and culture, but also by a high level of responsiveness.[66] This corresponds with the legitimacy of government in Singapore, which is largely based on its performance.[67] Such performance legitimacy requires a strong relationship of trust between the people and the government. The government accordingly took pains to cultivate this trust by providing regular updates publicly on the spread of COVID-19 and measures deployed, through multiple channels of communication, both online and offline.[68] Thus, despite the limits of competitive politics and judicial review in Singapore, there were efforts at ensuring a relatively open exchange of information and a highly responsive government.[69]

60 Supreme Court of the Republic of Singapore, Registrar's Circulars No 4 and No 5 of 2020 (5 April 2020 and 24 April 2020); State Courts of the Republic of Singapore, Registrar's Circulars No 8 and No 9 of 2020 (5 April 2020 and 24 April 2020).

61 ibid.

62 Chua and Neo (n 13).

63 Jaclyn Neo, 'Judging the Singapore Constitution' in Jaclyn Neo (ed) *Constitutional Interpretation in Singapore: Theory and Practice* (Routledge 2016) 3–4.

64 Neo and Lee (n 17).

65 Ramraj and Thiruvengadam (n 6) 141.

66 Lee (n 59) 646–647 and 663–664.

67 Chua and Neo (n 13).

68 ibid.

69 Lee (n 59) 658.

These complex dynamics of performance legitimacy and responsiveness are reflected in relation to the government's response to the public backlash regarding the use of contact tracing data. Residents had initially been reluctant to use an app called 'TraceTogether' for reasons including data privacy concerns.[70] The government then gave a public assurance that the data would only be used for COVID-19 contact tracing purposes.[71] Public outrage ensued when it was subsequently revealed that data collected by TraceTogether remains subject to the Criminal Procedure Code (and had, in fact, been used in investigations in one murder case), reflecting a sense of betrayal of trust. The relevant minister apologised publicly, acknowledging the oversight.[72] The government also sought to clarify that the data would only be used for "very serious offences" as a matter of police discretion,[73] but when this was not sufficient to assuage the public, the government introduced an expedited bill amending the CTMA to this effect.[74]

Citizen reaction to the government's use of POFMA also suggests the need for more nuanced approaches. POFMA is a pre-COVID-19 law that confers wide discretion on the executive to take various actions to correct falsehoods in the 'public interest'. At the time of passing the law, the government justified it on the basis of the need to preserve public trust in Singapore's democratic institutions[75] – in other words, to protect the "shared epistemic foundation" of a democracy. However, the use of POFMA during the 2020 elections may have undermined this trust. POFMA was significantly more intensely used during the elections than before. During the ten-day campaigning period, 17 correction directions were issued, compared to the 34 orders issued over the previous eight months.[76] Several correction directions were directed at claims about the government's COVID-19 management, of which several were by opposition politicians.[77] It is arguable that the seemingly zealous deployment of POFMA during the elections may have

70 Dewey Sim and Kimberley Lim, 'Coronavirus: Why Aren't Singapore Residents Using the TraceTogether Contact-tracing App?' (*South China Morning Post*, 18 May 2020) <https://www.scmp.com/week-asia/people/article/3084903/coronavirus-why-arent-singapore-residents-using-tracetogether>.

71 Dhany Osman, 'TraceTogether Data Can Be Used for Criminal Investigations: Desmond Tan' (*Yahoo! News*, 4 January 2021) <https://sg.news.yahoo.com/trace-together-data-criminal-investigations-desmond-tan-080806396.html?soc_src=community&soc_trk=tw>.

72 Kenny Chee, 'Vivian Balakrishnan Says He "Deeply Regrets" Mistake on TraceTogether Data' (*The Straits Times*, 2 February 2021) <https://www.straitstimes.com/singapore/vivian-balakrishnan-says-he-deeply-regrets-mistake-on-tracetogether-data-first-realised-it>.

73 H Bahrudin, 'Police Will Restrict Use of TraceTogether Data to "Very Serious Offences", says Shanmugam' (*The Straits Times*, 5 January 2021) <https://www.straitstimes.com/singapore/politics/parliament-police-will-restrict-use-of-tracetogether-data-to-very-serious>.

74 COVID-19 (Temporary Measures) (Amendment) Bill No 2/2021 (01 February 2021).

75 Howard Lee, 'POFMA – A Discursive Roadmap to an Election' in Kevin YL Tan and Terence Lee (eds), *Voting in a Time of Change: Singapore's 2020 General Election* (Ethos Books 2021) 161–182.

76 ibid.

77 ibid.

undermined public trust in the government's legitimacy as 'gatekeeper' of acceptable public discourse in Singapore.[78]

5.2 A World Apart: Low-Wage Migrant Workers

Globally, COVID-19 has thrust socio-economic inequality into the spotlight. In particular, populations in vulnerable circumstances are at the highest risk of contracting COVID-19 and are also the most negatively impacted by measures adopted in response to it.[79] In Singapore's context, besides those from lower socio-economic backgrounds whose jobs became precarious during lockdown measures, it is the approximately 350,000 low-wage migrant workers who have borne – and continue to bear – vastly disproportionate limits on their freedom of movement. This had initially been a response to the rapid spread of COVID-19, at the height of the pandemic between April and July 2020, in crowded dormitories where migrant workers mostly live.[80] As of December 2020, 47% of workers in dormitories had had COVID-19, as compared to a 0.25% rate among the rest of the population.[81]

Even though dormitory spread was contained, migrant workers remained subject to a much more onerous regime of movement control than the rest of the population. At the time of writing, workers in the construction sector are banned from taking public transport, even if they have been vaccinated and/or repeatedly tested negative during fortnightly swabs;[82] they are prohibited from leaving their dormitories for non-work purposes except as approved by the Controller of Manpower, where required by lawful authority to evacuate the dormitory or to seek medical treatment. Movement within their dormitories remains highly controlled. This prolonged confinement, among other factors, took a heavy toll on the mental health of migrant workers, leading to instances of self-harm and suicide.[83]

These differentiated measures bear out the exclusionary premise of Singapore's work permit regime, which normalises the physical sequestration of migrant workers from the rest of society.[84] They also mirror trends elsewhere in Southeast

78 ibid.

79 Grogan (n 3). See also Al Saba and Gougsa, chapter 32.

80 Chua and Neo (n 13).

81 ibid.

82 Building and Construction Authority of Singapore, 'COVID-Safe Worker Accommodation and Transport' <https://www1.bca.gov.sg/COVID-19/faqs/construction-sector/covid-safe-worker-accommodation-transport>; Ministry of Manpower, 'Employers To Ensure Workers Go Through Rostered Routine Testing (18 August 2020) <https://www.mom.gov.sg/newsroom/press-releases/2020/0818-employers-to-ensure-workers-go-through-rostered-routine-testing>.

83 Wong Pei Ting, 'Managing Migrant Workers' Mental Health a "Work in Progress", says MOH Official After Self-Harm Incidents' (*Today*, 6 August 2020) <https://www.todayonline.com/singapore/managing-migrant-workers-mental-health-dormitories-work-progress-says-moh-official-after?cid=h3_referral_inarticlelinks_03092019_todayonline>.

84 Jaclyn Neo, 'Riots and Rights: Law and Exclusion in Singapore's Migrant Worker Regime' (2015) 2 Asian Journal of Law and Society 137.

Asia of migrant workers increasingly experiencing their living premises as 'total' or 'disciplinary' institutions as a result of COVID-19.[85] In doing so, these measures rearticulate the "rule of colonial difference" inherited by Singapore in its technologies of pandemic management, merely producing new permutations in an independent sovereign Singapore.[86] Besides migrant workers in dormitories, the pandemic also exacerbated the long-existing vulnerabilities of other key communities, such as foreign domestic workers and migrant wives (usually from lower socio-economic backgrounds in developing countries in Asia) without independent residence rights in Singapore.[87]

6. Looking Forward

Whereas COVID-19 resulted in political upheaval and democratic backsliding in many countries, Singapore's legal and political institutions generally proved resilient. In its commitment to the continued functioning of the ordinary constitutional order, of Parliament, of access to the courts, and of constitutionally mandated elections – as well as in the promulgation of clear, accessible, non-retrospective laws and regulations as to the terms on which such functioning was to take place during the pandemic – Singapore arguably complied with formal rule of law requirements of legality and legal certainty.

Nevertheless, this democratic order is not to be taken for granted. Legal controls put in place during exceptional times could be normalised, creating what Dyzenhaus has famously termed the "permanence of the temporary".[88] Democratic controls and citizen engagement remain the most robust ways of resisting such normalisation, particularly in Singapore's political context. While a shared epistemic understanding of constitutional democracy was strongly articulated through this crisis, it is too early to conclude one way or another as to the likely longevity of the institutionalisation of key democratic elements (i.e. the numerically larger and more formalised presence of a parliamentary opposition and a more assertive civil society).

Finally, Singapore will need to do more to ensure that its most vulnerable communities do not disproportionately bear the burdens of the pandemic. The crisis should ultimately encourage Singapore to confront more fundamental questions as to the nature of democracy and the identity of its political community. More than one million foreigners live in Singapore, the vast majority of whom are low-

85 Helen Lansdowne and James Lawson, 'Southeast Asian Workers in a Just-in-Time Pandemic' in Victor V Ramraj (ed.) *COVID-19 in Asia: Law and Policy Contexts* (Oxford University Press 2020) 445, 455–456.

86 Chua and Lee (n 32) 129.

87 Chua and Neo (n 13).

88 David Dyzenhaus, 'The Permanence of the Temporary: Can Emergency Powers be Normalized?' in Ronald J Daniels and others (eds), *The Security of Freedom* (University of Toronto Press 2001). See also Chua and Lee (n 32) 121.

wage migrants, out of a total population of 5.69 million.[89] Many Singaporean families now include non-citizen members.[90] In the starkly interconnected world that globalisation has built, and that the COVID-19 pandemic threw into sharp relief, democracy requires interrogating what it means to live together and what we owe to one another, in a manner faithful to the dignity of the human person. Ultimately, we are only as strong as our most vulnerable.

89 Chua and Neo (n 13).

90 Association of Women for Action and Research, 'Migrant Wives in Distress' (*AWARE*, 1 June 2020) <https://www.aware.org.sg/wp-content/uploads/AWARE-Report-1-June-2020-Migrant-Wives-in-Distress.pdf>.

PART II

Human Rights

Overview

The COVID-19 pandemic laid bare and worsened the grotesque inequity in the realisation of human rights globally: lockdowns hit the poorest hardest, causing regression across a plethora of rights from health and education to free expression and the right to protest. By a similar token, international human rights law provides a framework by which to identify and confront this inequity. Part II examines how human rights fared during the pandemic, and how human rights law has been used to pursue accountability for the actions and omissions of states. It does so through three commentaries that explore the wide-ranging nature of states' obligations during a pandemic and five chapters that analyse states with varying levels of human rights compliance: Finland, India, Colombia, Thailand and Kenya.

For Alice Donald and Philip Leach, COVID-19 revealed the interdependence of rights, as states' pre-existing failure to realise economic and social rights, especially the right to health, hastened the spread of the virus, in turn creating the conditions for severe incursions into rights of all kinds. Another connecting thread in their commentary is the way in which the burden of the pandemic – and of state responses to it – fell heaviest on the lives and livelihoods of already marginalised communities. Rejecting the notion that human rights hinder decisive action to contain disease, Donald and Leach argue that human rights offer a means of transparently balancing competing priorities in the pressured and fast-moving context of decision-making during a health emergency.

Echoing these themes, Martin Scheinin's commentary presents the findings of a pilot study assessing the human rights performance of 17 states in their response to COVID-19 during the second half of 2020. The study encompasses economic, social and cultural rights; civil and political rights; equality rights; and the rule of law dimension of human rights such as the existence of effective remedies. It debunks the notion that compliance with human rights in a pandemic is a zero-

DOI: 10.4324/9781003211952-9

sum game, in which (say) the right to health must be traded off against civil liberties. On the contrary, Scheinin concludes that a strong human rights performance in respect of *any* category of human rights correlates with high compliance across *all* categories – a finding that held across different regions.

Stéphanie Dagron, whose commentary explores the (only recently acknowledged) linkages between health and human rights, concurs that a human rights-based approach enables states to respond to a pandemic with measures that are legal, necessary, proportionate and non-discriminatory. She ventures that human rights compliance benefits the protection of public health, and vice versa, and concludes with a call for international institutions such as the World Health Organisation to formulate more concrete guidance about states' obligations during a pandemic in order to support their preparedness for future emergencies.

Finland's relative success at containing COVID-19 without far-reaching restrictions upon human rights or economic dislocation, and while preserving the role of Parliament, is the focus of the first country-based chapter. Martin Scheinin provides an account of how Finland's pandemic response was underpinned by an ambitious catalogue of constitutional rights, coupled with strong public communications. At the same time, Scheinin argues that Finland's legislative response to the pandemic was piecemeal and inadequate, and requires thorough revision to prepare for future emergencies.

The response by the authorities in **India** to COVID-19, documented by Thulasi K Raj, presents a glaring contrast, being characterised by a lack of transparency; a heavy concentration of powers in the executive, with limited parliamentary or judicial scrutiny or involvement of state authorities; rampant suppression of civil liberties; and reckless management such as the holding of politically motivated 'superspreader' events. Raj concludes with an urgent plea for a revival of India's federal structure and ailing democratic institutions.

The assessment of **Colombia**'s institutional response to the pandemic by Julián Gaviria-Mira and Esteban Hoyos-Ceballos is scarcely more positive. Gaviria-Mira and Hoyos-Ceballos identify a pre-existing authoritarian drift in Colombia, accompanied by severe economic stress, leading to cycles of social unrest and repression which the pandemic only aggravated. Not only that, but supposedly independent watchdog bodies were hobbled by the appointment of presidential allies to run them. The authors urge parliamentarians and the courts to adopt a less supine approach and to use the tools the Colombian constitution provides to check executive aggrandisement and ensure public participation in decision-making.

Thailand exhibited a similarly centralised, authoritarian approach in its response to COVID-19 through the use of harsh emergency powers. Moreover, as discussed by Khemthong Tonsakulrungruang and Rawin Leelapatana, the Thai government's response was conditioned by its militarised mentality, ineffective bureaucracy and corrupt ties to corporate interests. Human rights, the authors argue, were considered irrelevant to decision-making; the result, notwithstanding Thailand's world class health services, was an avoidably high death toll and an economic convulsion with no social safety net, which led to deepening poverty and popular unrest. Compounding this mismanagement, vaccine procurement and rollout was chaotic. Thus, while promising to protect "health before rights", the Thai authorities effectively guaranteed neither.

Unchecked executive power and egregious abuses of rights are a dominant theme, too, in the analysis of **Kenya**'s response to COVID-19 by Tara Imalingat, Nerima Were and Allan Maleche. The authors document measures including the use of mandatory quarantine as a punishment for law-breaking, police brutality and forceful detention for non-payment of medical bills – practices based on executive-made rules of dubious legality (in the absence of a declared state of emergency) that were nevertheless rubber-stamped by Parliament. A renewal of Kenya's constitutional democracy, the authors conclude, is a pre-requisite for future pandemic preparedness.

8

HUMAN RIGHTS – THE ESSENTIAL FRAME OF REFERENCE IN RESPONSE TO THE COVID-19 PANDEMIC

Alice Donald and Philip Leach

1. Introduction[1]

The COVID-19 pandemic created a situation unparalleled in the post-1945 era, as all nations faced the same mortal threat simultaneously. The peril posed by the virus called for a universally recognised framework sufficiently expansive and flexible to address the complex and fast-moving policy landscape. International human rights law provides this framework.[2] This chapter argues that it is mistaken to conceive of COVID-19 – or future pandemics – principally as a threat whose eradication requires rights to be sacrificed. Nor do human rights hinder decisive action to contain the virus. Rather, human rights standards and principles offer a means of making a structured and transparent assessment of competing priorities in the heat of decision-making during a health emergency, and of ensuring both real-time and retrospective accountability for the actions and omissions of national authorities. Moreover, human rights, with their inherent concern for non-discrimination and the equal worth of every human being, render visible the structural injustices that determined the pandemic's disproportionate impact on certain sectors of the pop-

1 All websites accessed on 19 August 2021 unless otherwise stated.

2 This chapter draws on two posts by the authors: 'Human Rights and COVID-19: Forging Recovery After a Pandemic of Abuses?' (*Verfassungsblog*, 10 April 2021) <https://verfassungsblog.de/human-rights-and-covid-19-forging-recovery-after-a-pandemic-of-abuses/>; 'Human Rights – The Essential Frame of Reference in the Global Response to COVID-19' (*Verfassungsblog*, 12 May 2020) <https://verfassungsblog.de/human-rights-the-essential-frame-of-reference-in-the-global-response-to-covid-19/>.

DOI: 10.4324/9781003211952-10

ulation and demand action to redress them. Not only that, but rights-respecting responses which secure public trust[3] are likely to be more effective and sustainable in the longer-term than arbitrary or repressive ones.

At the same time, we should not misconstrue or overstate the contribution that human rights institutions, practitioners and scholars made during the pandemic: this is, for the most part, a story of unfulfilled potential. As Carver notes, there is no evidence that the voice of the human rights movement was "widely heard or … [influenced] policy where it matters" in the context of the pandemic.[4] Human rights experts were generally not among the epistemic communities, such as epidemiologists and economists, with a seat around national policy tables.[5] Only exceptionally did governments perform well in human rights terms,[6] among the states covered in this volume: Finland,[7] New Zealand[8] and Taiwan.[9] Far more pronounced were the dismal trends of authoritarianism, populism and "fragmentation and social inequalities within and between our societies".[10]

This chapter examines, in section 2, the relevance of human rights and the duty not to discriminate to the pandemic and synthesises trends in states' performance. Section 3 discusses states' human rights obligations during a pandemic, while section 4 explores routes to accountability for their actions and omissions in upholding human rights during and after the COVID-19 crisis. Section 5 considers the human rights issues connected to COVID-19 vaccines. Section 6 concludes by looking ahead to the application of human rights in the post-COVID-19 world and preparedness for future pandemics.

2. Why Are Human Rights and the Duty Not to Discriminate Relevant to the Pandemic?

International human rights law embraces two interdependent sets of entitlements – and corresponding obligations – that should underpin states' responses to a pandemic. Economic, social and cultural rights are concerned with human survival, development and flourishing, and include the rights to the highest attain-

3 Jasanoff and Hilgartner, chapter 23.
4 Richard Carver, 'Forum: Human Rights Practice in the Age of Pandemic' (2020) 12(2) Journal of Human Rights Practice 247, 248.
5 Martin Scheinin and Helga Molbæk-Steensig, 'Human-Rights Based Versus Populist Responses to the Pandemic' in Morten Kjaerum, Martha F Davis and Amanda Lyons (eds), *COVID-19 and Human Rights* (Routledge 2021) 21–22.
6 Scheinin, chapter 9.
7 Scheinin, chapter 11.
8 Knight, chapter 3.
9 Chang and Lin, chapter 25.
10 Alicia Ely Yamin, 'A Wake-Up Call in Our Upside-Down World: Three Starting-Points for Advancing Health Rights and Social Justice in a Post-Pandemic Future' (2020) 12(2) Journal of Human Rights Practice 260, 261.

able standard of health,[11] an adequate standard of living (including food, water and housing), social security and education. Civil and political rights exist, inter alia, to protect life, liberty, dignity, physical and psychological integrity and freedom to express ideas and beliefs without intrusion by an overbearing state or private entities. These rights are enshrined in the International Covenant on Economic, Social and Cultural Rights (ICESCR) and the International Covenant on Civil and Political Rights (ICCPR), both of which were adopted in 1966, as well as other UN and regional treaties and many national laws and constitutions. All are to be enjoyed without discrimination, and all give rise both to *negative* obligations on states to respect and not to violate rights and *positive* obligations to take protective or preventive steps to protect and fulfil rights.

The indivisibility and interdependence of all human rights – now an orthodoxy in human rights practice and scholarship – was laid bare by the COVID-19 pandemic. States' pre-existing failure to realise economic and social rights, especially the right to health, aggravated the spread of the virus, in turn creating the conditions for authoritarian power grabs and severe incursions into rights of all kinds. The United Nations Secretary-General, António Guterres, deplored the "vicious circle of violations" in which civic freedoms were attacked around the globe, and the parallel "infodemic" caused by invasive digital platforms and unchecked state surveillance.[12] According to Human Rights Watch, dozens of governments used the pandemic as a pretext to crush dissent and criminalise basic freedoms, silencing independent media, bloggers, lawyers, whistleblowers and opposition figures through physical attacks, dismissals, fines, closure orders, censorship, and arbitrary arrest, detention and prosecution.[13] Such abuses have been tracked and quantified in global human rights indices[14] and symposiums.[15] Chapters in this volume attest to rampant violations, such as intensive surveillance in China[16] and Iran;[17] indiscriminate bans on protest and criminalisation of dissent in Egypt,[18] Hungary,[19]

11 Dagron, chapter 10.

12 UN Office of the High Commissioner for Human Rights, 'Secretary-General Guterres Calls for a Global Reset, "to Recover Better, Guided by Human Rights"' (22 February 2021) <https://www.ohchr.org/EN/NewsEvents/Pages/DisplayNews.aspx?NewsID=26769>.

13 Human Rights Watch, 'Covid-19 Triggers Wave of Free Speech Abuse' (undated) <https://features.hrw.org/features/features/covid/index.html>.

14 See, especially, CIVICUS Monitor <https://findings2020.monitor.civicus.org/fr.html>; International Center for Not-for Profit Law, COVID-19 Civic Freedom Tracker <https://www.icnl.org/covid19tracker/>; International IDEA, Global Monitor of COVID-19's Impact on Democracy and Human Rights <https://www.idea.int/2020-annual-report/global-monitor-covid-19s-impact-democracy-and-human-rights>; University of Oxford / Blavatnik School of Government, COVID-19 Government Response Tracker <https://www.bsg.ox.ac.uk/research/research-projects/covid-19-government-response-tracker>.

15 See, for example, the 'Power and the COVID-19 Pandemic' symposium, hosted by the *Verfassungsblog* in 2021 <https://verfassungsblog.de/power-and-the-covid-19-pandemic/>.

16 deLisle and Shen, chapter 4.

17 Darian, chapter 29.

18 Ellaboudy, chapter 33.

19 Kovács, chapter 21.

India[20] and Thailand;[21] and extrajudicial killing of protestors in Colombia,[22] Kenya[23] and the Philippines (where curfew violators were also subject to humiliating punishment such as being held in dog-cages).[24]

Socio-economic rights were also imperilled. The World Bank found that the pandemic had led to 97 million more people falling into poverty in 2020, a historically unprecedented increase, which was projected to continue in low-income countries in 2021.[25] The UN Special Rapporteur on extreme poverty and human rights, Olivier De Schutter, argues that the world was ill-equipped to deal with the socio-economic impacts of COVID-19 because it never recovered from the austerity measures imposed after the global financial crisis of 2008–2011.[26] Dilapidated public health systems, precarious and undervalued work and rising inequality were among the fatal legacies of that period. Remarkable sums were channelled into emergency social protection measures worldwide during the pandemic – as of May 2021, US$2.9 trillion or 3% of global gross domestic product in 2021, according to the World Bank.[27] Yet, too many of these, De Schutter argues, were "maladapted, short-term, reactive, and inattentive to the realities of people in poverty".[28] In these unprecedented conditions, the Special Rapporteur calls for nothing less than the mobilisation of domestic resources and international solidarity to ensure that social security is seen neither as charity nor as an emergency response to crisis, but as "a set of permanent entitlements prescribed by domestic legislation, defining individuals as rights-holders and public authorities as duty-bearers".[29] Thus, what began as an unparalleled peacetime challenge became an ambitious agenda for a human rights-based recovery.

A similarly transformative response was demanded by the UN Special Rapporteur on violence against women, who expressed horror at the "pandemic of femicide and gender-based violence" caused by COVID-19.[30] As one indicator,

20 Raj, chapter 12.

21 Tonsakulrungruang and Leelapatana, chapter 14.

22 Gaviria-Mira and Hoyos-Ceballos, chapter 13.

23 Imalingat, Were and Maleche, chapter 15.

24 Atienza, chapter 36.

25 Daniel Gerszon Mahler and others, 'Updated Estimates of the Impact of COVID-19 on Global Poverty: Turning the Corner on the Pandemic in 2021?' (*World Bank Blogs*, 24 June 2021) <https://blogs.worldbank.org/opendata/updated-estimates-impact-covid-19-global-poverty-turning-corner-pandemic-2021>.

26 UN Special Rapporteur on extreme poverty and human rights, 'Looking Back to Look Ahead: A Rights-Based Approach to Social Protection in the Post-COVID-19 Economic Recovery' (11 September 2020) para 52 <https://www.ohchr.org/Documents/Issues/Poverty/covid19.pdf>.

27 Ugo Gentilini and others, 'Social Protection and Jobs Responses to COVID-19: A Real-Time Review of Country Measures' (World Bank, 14 May 2021) 14 <https://openknowledge.worldbank.org/bitstream/handle/10986/33635/Social-Protection-and-Jobs-Responses-to-COVID-19-A-Real-Time-Review-of-Country-Measures-May-14-2021.pdf?sequence=25&isAllowed=y>.

28 United Nations Special Rapporteur on extreme poverty and human rights (n 26) para 6.

29 ibid para 75.

30 UN Office of the High Commissioner for Human Rights, 'Urgent Action Needed to End Pandemic of Femicide and Violence Against Women, Says UN Expert' (23 November 2020)

calls to domestic abuse helplines increased five-fold in some countries as rates of reported intimate partner violence increased.[31] Restrictions on movement, economic insecurity, a decrease in police interventions and the closure of courts and emergency services emboldened perpetrators and aggravated the risks faced by women and girls. This "shadow pandemic",[32] resulting from a perfect storm of factors, itself exemplifies the interdependence of all human rights. Encouragingly, almost 150 states took proactive steps to prevent or respond to gender-based violence, yet the response remained uneven, not only in relation to gender-based violence but also other COVID-19 induced threats to gender equality, such as the unprecedented increase in unpaid care work, and the large-scale loss of women's jobs, incomes and livelihoods.[33]

The COVID-19 pandemic exposed other structural inequalities in the social determinants of health both within and between nations. This "unique ecology of sickness", as characterised by the World Health Organisation, provided the starkest possible illustration of the effects of indirect discrimination.[34] The pandemic fell heaviest on the lives and livelihoods of people in vulnerable circumstances. Minorities and indigenous peoples suffered disproportionate rates of infection, mortality and unemployment, and experienced discriminatory treatment in the form of repressive policing and inequitable access to vaccines,[35] compounded for indigenous peoples by a rolling back of social and environmental safeguards by states and private actors under the guise of COVID-19.[36] Refugees and internally displaced persons, homeless people and those living in informal settlements were unable to respect social distancing or hygiene measures.[37] People working precariously in the informal economy faced catastrophic declines in their incomes.[38] Disabled people were "excluded and deprioritised

<https://www.ohchr.org/EN/NewsEvents/Pages/DisplayNews.aspx?NewsID=26533&LangID=E>.

31 UN Women, 'Facts and Figures: Ending Violence Against Women' (updated as of March 2021) <https://www.unwomen.org/en/what-we-do/ending-violence-against-women/facts-and-figures>.

32 UN Women, 'COVID-19 Global Gender Response Tracker: Global Factsheet' (Version 2, 22 March 2021) 1 <https://www.undp.org/publications/covid-19-global-gender-response-tracker-fact-sheets>.

33 ibid.

34 World Health Organisation, 'Addressing Human Rights as Key to the COVID-19 Response' (21 April 2020) 1 <https://www.who.int/publications/i/item/addressing-human-rights-as-key-to-the-covid-19-response#.Xp9Sn4vjlQs.twitter>.

35 Al Saba and Gougsa, chapter 32; Singh, chapter 2.

36 Sofea Dil and others, *Rolling Back Social and Environmental Safeguards in the Time of COVID-19: The Dangers for Indigenous Peoples and for Tropical Forests* (Forest Peoples Programme 2021) <https://www.forestpeoples.org/sites/default/files/documents/Rolling%20Back%20Social%20and%20Environmental%20Safeguards%20-%20Global%20Report%20ENGLISH%20FINAL.pdf>.

37 Lorenzo Guadagno, *Migrants and the COVID-19 Pandemic: An Initial Analysis* (Migration Research Series N° 60, International Organization of Migration, 2021) 4.

38 International Labour Organisation, 'Impact of Lockdown on the Informal Economy' (*ILO Brief*, April 2020) <https://www.ilo.org/wcmsp5/groups/public/---ed_protect/---protrav/---travail/documents/briefingnote/wcms_743523.pdf>.

from international and national government planning".[39] Older people were not only more likely to suffer serious illness or death from COVID-19 but were also subject to age-based measures such as stricter restrictions on their movement and other rights than younger age groups.[40] The positive duties which result from a genuinely human rights-based approach require states to respond (in different ways, as necessary) to protect the lives and health (and other rights) of groups in vulnerable circumstances – as Portugal did, for example when it decided to treat all migrants as residents to give them full access to health and other public services during the pandemic.[41]

Human rights bodies also sounded the alarm about direct discrimination and stigma targeted at communities on the basis of, among other characteristics, their religion, nationality or ethnic origin; the UN Special Rapporteur on racism reserved special opprobrium for President Trump's reference to COVID-19 as a "Chinese" virus, which spawned attacks on people of Chinese or other East Asian descent.[42]

The connecting thread between these various forms of discrimination is clear: where states failed to pay explicit attention to the vulnerabilities faced by certain groups, or tolerated or encouraged stigmatising behaviour, this not only violated the human rights of those groups but also undermined the broader COVID-19 response and prolonged the danger to everyone.

3. What Are States' Obligations During a Pandemic?

For states to adopt a 'rights-respecting' policy, they must go beyond simply avoiding interference with human rights, and take protective or preventive steps which positively ensure that certain standards are met. Such a responsibility creates potentially far-reaching obligations during a pandemic, especially towards those who are worst affected. Take the right to life, a non-derogable right in peacetime: the state's obligation to protect life encompasses the *general* duty to establish and enforce the requisite legal and administrative framework to safeguard life; the *operational* duty to protect people from real and immediate risks to life that the state knows or ought to know about; and the duty to *investigate* potential breaches of the right to life, including those caused by the state's omission.[43] The Human Rights

39 Vera Kubenz and Dina Kiwan, *The Impact of the COVID-19 Pandemic on Disabled People in Low- and Middle-Income Countries: A Literature Review* (Global Research Challenges Fund / University of Birmingham 2021) 1 <https://disabilityundersiege.org/wp-content/uploads/2021/03/Impact-of-COVID-19-on-disabled-people-literature-review.pdf>.

40 Camilla Williamson and others, *Bearing the Brunt: The Impact of COVID-19 on Older People in Low- and Middle-Income Countries – Insights from 2020* (Help Age International 2021).

41 'Portugal to Treat Migrants as Residents During Coronavirus Crisis' (*Reuters*, 28 March 2020) <https://www.reuters.com/article/uk-health-coronavirus-portugal-idUKKBN21F0MC?edition-redirect=uk>.

42 UN Office of the High Commissioner for Human Rights, 'States Should Take Action Against COVID-19-Related Expressions of Xenophobia, says UN Expert' (23 March 2020) <https://www.ohchr.org/en/NewsEvents/Pages/DisplayNews.aspx?NewsID=25739&LangID=E>.

43 Human Rights Committee, General Comment No 36 (2018) on article 6 of the International Covenant on Civil and Political Rights, on the right to life, CCPR/C/GC/36, 30 October 2018.

Committee, which monitors the ICCPR, requires states to adopt "appropriate measures to address the general conditions in society that may give rise to direct threats to life", including life threatening diseases.[44] Such measures include disaster management and contingency planning to increase preparedness; guaranteeing access on a non-discriminatory basis to food, water, shelter, healthcare and sanitation; and bolstering emergency health services.

The right to life is directly engaged in respect of people in the custody or care of the state, such as in prisons, immigration centres, psychiatric institutions and other residential institutions, especially care homes for older people, where COVID-19 wreaked devastating impact (accounting for 41% of all COVID-19 deaths as of February 2021, according to one international survey).[45] Early in the pandemic, multiple UN agencies urged states to mitigate the heightened vulnerability of people in closed settings through release mechanisms and guaranteed access to healthcare,[46] and the closure of immigration detention facilities.[47] Yet, states' responses were mixed. In respect of immigration detention, some states, such as Spain and Canada, released all or most detainees at least temporarily, while others increased their detention of non-nationals on supposed public health grounds.[48] Meanwhile, it is estimated that less than 6% of the global prison population was released due to COVID-19,[49] while in some states even higher proportions of releases were not enough to reduce transmission in chronically overcrowded facilities. Elsewhere, releases were either offset or exceeded by detentions for COVID-19-related offences.[50] Women and children were often excluded from release schemes,[51] as were human rights defenders.[52] Prisoners were some-

44 ibid para 26.

45 Adelina Comas-Herrera and others, 'Mortality Associated with COVID-19 in Care Homes: International Evidence' (International Long Term Care Policy Network, 1 February 2021) 2 <https://ltccovid.org/wp-content/uploads/2021/02/LTC_COVID_19_international_report_January-1-February-1-1.pdf>.

46 World Health Organisation, 'UNODC, WHO, UNAIDS and OHCHR Joint Statement on COVID-19 in Prisons and other Closed Settings' (13 May 2020). <https://www.who.int/news/item/13-05-2020-unodc-who-unaids-and-ohchr-joint-statement-on-covid-19-in-prisons-and-other-closed-settings>.

47 UN Office of the High Commissioner for Human Rights, 'COVID-19 Exacerbates the Risk of Ill-Treatment and Torture Worldwide – UN Experts' (26 June 2020) <https://www.ohchr.org/en/NewsEvents/Pages/DisplayNews.aspx?NewsID=25995&LangID=e>.

48 Global Detention Project, 'Submission to the UN Special Rapporteur on the Human Rights of Migrants: The Impact of COVID-19' (15 June 2021) <https://www.globaldetentionproject.org/submission-to-the-un-special-rapporteur-on-the-human-rights-of-migrants-the-impact-of-covid-19-on-the-human-rights-of-migrants>.

49 Penal Reform International, *Global Prison Trends 2021* (May 2021) 12 <https://cdn.penalreform.org/wp-content/uploads/2021/05/Global-prison-trends-2021.pdf>.

50 ibid 13.

51 ibid 7.

52 Amnesty International, 'Virus-hit Prisons Still Full of Human Rights Defenders, as Attacks Continue' (6 August 2020) <https://www.amnesty.org/en/latest/news/2020/08/attacks-on-hrds-during-pandemic-report/>.

times omitted from official COVID-19 infection and mortality data, as happened in Thailand.[53] At the same time, human rights bodies reminded states that anti-COVID-19 measures must never result in inhuman or degrading treatment of people deprived of their liberty; for example, through excessive use of solitary confinement or visitation bans.[54]

Beyond closed settings, how far does the state's duty to protect the right to life during a pandemic extend? Certainly, as Stubbins Bates ventures, states' positive obligations may be triggered in the case of health and care workers required to work without adequate protective equipment, and instances where "systematic or structural dysfunction in hospital services" results in medically vulnerable patients being deprived of access to life-saving treatment.[55]

In respect of the right to health and other rights protected under ICESCR, additional obligations arise. Notably, states have a duty to devote their "maximum available resources" to combatting a pandemic, without imposing a further economic burden on marginalised groups.[56] States are also obliged to take immediate measures to protect the jobs, pensions and other social benefits of workers during the pandemic, and to mitigate its economic impacts.[57] Such measures included eviction bans enacted by some states to protect the right to adequate housing, although many were temporary, while in other states, such as Brazil, India and Kenya, mass forced evictions continued.[58] International assistance and cooperation are also enshrined in ICESCR, requiring states to share research, medical equipment and supplies, and best practices in combating the virus, with priority to be given to disadvantaged groups and fragile states.[59]

4. Accountability for Restrictions on Rights

When states take far-reaching steps to protect life and health during a pandemic, it almost invariably results in the restriction of other rights. However, while COVID-

53 Tonsakulrungruang and Leelapatana, chapter 14.

54 European Committee for the Prevention of Torture and Inhuman or Degrading Treatment or Punishment, 'Statement of Principles Relating to the Treatment of Persons Deprived of their Liberty in the Context of the Coronavirus Disease (Covid-19) Pandemic CPT/Inf(2020)13 (20 March 2020).

55 Elizabeth Stubbins-Bates, 'Article 2 ECHR's Positive Obligations – How Can Human Rights Law Inform the Protection of Health Care Personnel and Vulnerable Patients in the COVID-19 Pandemic?' (*Opinio Juris*, 1 April 2020) <http://opiniojuris.org/2020/04/01/covid-19-symposium-article-2-echrs-positive-obligations-how-can-human-rights-law-inform-the-protection-of-health-care-personnel-and-vulnerable-patients-in-the-covid-19-pandemic/>.

56 Committee on Economic, Social and Cultural Rights, 'Statement on the Coronavirus Disease (COVID-19) Pandemic and Economic, Social and Cultural Rights' E/C.12/2020/1 (17 April 2020) para 14.

57 ibid para 16.

58 World Economic Forum, 'Can We Prevent a Surge in Pandemic-Related Homelessness?' (21 August 2020) <https://www.weforum.org/agenda/2020/08/can-we-prevent-surge-covid19-pandemic-homelessness-eviction-poverty/>.

59 Committee on Economic, Social and Cultural Rights (n 56) para 19.

19 justified or even required exceptional emergency measures, it did not give carte blanche to states to take actions that are impermissible under international human rights law.[60] With respect to qualified rights that may be restricted or derogated from, such as the rights to privacy, freedom of assembly and freedom of movement, positive obligations to protect life and health only extend to measures that constitute legal, necessary and proportionate limitations on those rights—or, in the case of lawful derogation, measures that are strictly required by the exigencies of the emergency threatening the life of the nation.[61] Since scientific evidence is constantly changing, it follows that emergency measures must be time-limited and subject to continuous oversight and review, since a restriction that is necessary and proportionate today may not be tomorrow. All too often, when imposing lockdown measures, states failed to consider whether the public health aims could be met with less restrictive means, and reached too readily for criminalisation and enforcement by the police or military rather than measures underpinned by public trust and social solidarity.[62]

Civil society activism is critical to counteracting this trend, as "civil society actors initiate movements that hold governments accountable and push for change".[63] In Taiwan, a vibrant civil society, as a counterbalancing force to both local and central authority, achieved tangible gains in protecting privacy rights and promoting transparency.[64] By contrast, in Colombia, the social unrest that erupted before and during the pandemic led to an increased concentration of power, as the government eschewed the tools of public participation provided by the constitution.[65]

4.1 Accountability Through Parliaments

How have more formal accountability mechanisms fared through the course of the pandemic? This dynamic environment described above means that reasonable measures demanded by positive obligations to secure rights must remain responsive to the fluid circumstances, in terms of their necessity and proportionality. Such a scenario only serves to underline the need for rolling parliamentary oversight, and in particular the importance of real-time parliamentary scrutiny of COVID-19 measures for their compliance with human rights norms, because the pace of

60 Natasa Mavronicola, 'Positive Obligations in Crisis' (*Strasbourg Observers*, 7 April 2020) <https://strasbourgobservers.com/2020/04/07/positive-obligations-in-crisis/>.

61 Emmons, chapter 30.

62 Katharina Ó Cathaoir, 'Human Rights and Health in Times of Pandemics: Necessity and Proportionality' in Kjaerum, Davis and Lyons (eds) (n 5).

63 The Global Initiative for Economic, Social and Cultural Rights, 'The COVID-19 Pandemic and its Impact on Economic, Social and Cultural Rights - Opportunities and Avenues out of the Crisis' (April 2021) 9 <https://static1.squarespace.com/static/5a6e0958f6576ebde0e78c18/t/608a84944458802aa02cb0e9/1619690648689/2021-Pushing-Barriers-2-Will-the-pandemic-force-the-shift.pdf>.

64 Chang and Lin, chapter 25.

65 Gaviria-Mira and Hoyos-Ceballos, chapter 13.

judicial review proceedings often lags behind the rate of legislative or regulatory change.[66] All too often, parliamentary scrutiny of rights-restricting executive action was curtailed or bypassed by use of executive decrees, for example in Australia,[67] Colombia,[68] India[69] and Iran.[70] Parliament was suspended altogether in Malaysia.[71] However, elsewhere, there was evidence of better practice, such as regular parliamentary scrutiny of the extensions of the declaration of a 'state of alarm' in Spain[72] and of COVID-19-related restrictions in Finland[73] and New Zealand;[74] innovations such as live-streaming of parliamentary proceedings for the first time in Singapore;[75] and effective monitoring work by parliamentary committees in Scotland and Wales, illustrating the importance of human rights at the sub-national level.[76]

4.2 Judicial Oversight

In some jurisdictions, higher national courts intervened decisively to defend fundamental rights, although the picture is mixed. Among other notable decisions, the Supreme Court in Brazil upheld indigenous peoples' right to health by ordering the federal government to devise a plan to provide adequate health policies concerning the pandemic and supervising its application; and ordered the health ministry to resume publishing COVID-19 statistics as required by the right to information.[77] Insisting that the right to human dignity should prevail, the Bogota Administrative Court in Colombia overturned a decree ordering the stricter lockdown of the over 70s as being disproportionate, discriminatory and ineffective, although this was a lone decision among an otherwise passive judiciary.[78] Early in 2021, the Israeli Supreme Court issued a series of judgments which led to the suspension of the state's contact-tracing surveillance programme; suspended

66 See, for example, *R v Secretary of State for Health and Social Care and Secretary of State for Education ex parte Dolan and Others* [2020] EWCA Civ 1605 (challenge to regulations issued during the pandemic found to be academic, as the regulations had been repealed).
67 Rizzi and Tulich, chapter 37.
68 Gaviria-Mira and Hoyos-Ceballos, chapter 13.
69 Raj, chapter 12.
70 Darian, chapter 29.
71 Balasubramaniam, chapter 34.
72 Alicia Cebada Romero and Elvira Dominguez Redondo, 'Spain: One Pandemic and Two Versions of the State of Alarm' (*Verfassungsblog*, 22 February 2021) <https://verfassungsblog.de/spain-one-pandemic-and-two-versions-of-the-state-of-alarm/>.
73 Scheinin, chapter 11.
74 Knight, chapter 3.
75 Chua and Neo, chapter 7. For discussion of democratic (de)consolidation generally, see Daly, chapter 1.
76 Pablo Grez, 'Good Practice in COVID-19 Review: Lessons from Scotland and Wales' (University of Birmingham, 14 April 2021) <https://blog.bham.ac.uk/cvro/covid-19/good-practice-in-covid-19-review-lessons-from-scotland-and-wales/>.
77 Bustamante and Meyer, chapter 18.
78 Gaviria-Mira and Hoyos-Ceballos, chapter 13.

legislation permitting the transfer of personal data of non-vaccinated individuals; removed travel quotas on the number of Israeli nationals eligible to enter the country; and struck down regulations restricting public demonstrations (with the Chief Justice, Esther Hayut, noting the "extra importance that should be assigned to the ability to criticize the government in times of emergency").[79] Interestingly, for Shany, this last judgment represented a "teaching moment" in which the Supreme Court underscored the importance of the right to demonstrate and the fact that a serious justification is required for any restrictions on such a fundamental right.[80]

In another significant judgment, the Spanish Constitutional Court ruled that the state of alarm declared in March 2020 was unconstitutional since lockdown measures should have been imposed under a state of emergency requiring prior parliamentary approval, the narrow margin of 6–5 indicating the finely balanced nature of the debate.[81] Elsewhere, a local authority ban on visiting elderly care homes was overturned in Sweden.[82] In the United Kingdom, the High Court found that the use of former army barracks (Napier Barracks) to accommodate destitute asylum-seekers was unlawful and that the overcrowded dormitories failed to protect residents from COVID-19.[83] In Ukraine, the courts established that 90% of administrative cases for alleged breaches of quarantine regulations were baseless.[84]

But these were some of the relatively rare judicial decisions holding governments to account. In Australia, there were unsuccessful legal challenges, including in relation to restrictions on free movement;[85] in Greece, the highest administrative court, the Council of State, rejected an application to lift a blanket ban on rallies;[86] while in India, the overly deferential approach by the Supreme Court has also been condemned.[87]

Undue deference to executive action may see claims proceed to supranational courts, and at the time of writing this has started to happen. The European Court of Human Rights (ECtHR) found, for example, that Malta had inflicted degrad-

79 Yuval Shany, 'The Return to Balfour: Israel's Supreme Court Strikes Down Coronavirus Regulations Curbing the Right to Protest' (*Lawfare*, 13 April 2021) <https://www.lawfareblog.com/return-balfour-israels-supreme-court-strikes-down-coronavirus-regulations-curbing-right-protest>.

80 ibid.

81 José María Brunet, 'Spain's Top Court Rules that the Coronavirus State of Alarm was Unconstitutional' (*El País*, 14 July 2021) <https://english.elpais.com/spain/2021-07-14/spains-top-court-rules-that-the-coronavirus-state-of-alarm-was-unconstitutional.html>.

82 Cameron and Jonsson Cornell, chapter 19.

83 *NB & Ors v Secretary of State for the Home Department* [2021] EWHC 1489.

84 Roman Petrov and Bohdan Bernatskyi, 'Pandemic and Fragile Government: A Year of COVID-19 Fatigue and Disorder in Ukraine' (*Verfassungsblog*, 4 March 2021) <https://verfassungsblog.de/pandemic-and-fragile-government-a-year-of-covid-19-fatigue-and-disorder-in-ukraine/>.

85 Rizzi and Tulich, chapter 37.

86 George Karavokyris, 'Constitutionalism and COVID-19 in Greece: The Normality of Emergency' (*Verfassungsblog*, 25 February 2021) <https://verfassungsblog.de/constitutionalism-and-covid-19-in-greece-the-normality-of-emergency/>.

87 Raj, chapter 12.

ing treatment on a Nigerian man held in immigration detention, partly because his health had been unnecessarily endangered by being held with people under COVID-19 quarantine.[88] Potential applicants to the ECtHR contesting lockdown measures, however, will not take comfort from a decision concerning Romania, which held that restrictions on leaving one's home, including a night-time curfew, did not constitute a deprivation of liberty.[89] A series of pending applications brought by detainees complaining of various risks created by COVID-19 have been referred for replies to the governments of the United Kingdom, Greece, Malta and Romania, while cases communicated to Greece, Romania, Croatia and Switzerland concern restrictions arising from the pandemic that have allegedly breached the rights to freedom of religion, freedom of assembly and free movement.[90]

There is also potential for the application of urgent measures aimed at preventing irreparable harm (known as interim measures under the European Convention and in the UN system, and precautionary or provisional measures in the inter-American human rights system). For example, urgent orders have been sought to ensure that vulnerable people in detention are properly protected. The ECtHR received more than 350 interim measures requests related to COVID-19, mainly brought by people detained in prison or in reception or detention centres for asylum seekers and migrants, concerning France, Greece, Italy, Spain, Turkey and the United Kingdom.[91] Most of these applications were rejected, however, with just a few being granted that related to especially vulnerable people, including unaccompanied minors, people with serious medical conditions and pregnant women.

4.3 Scrutiny from Watchdogs

Beyond the courtroom, other accountability mechanisms, such as regulators, provide examples of effective review. A Commission of Inquiry established in Sweden exposed the lack of medically qualified staff at care homes for the elderly.[92] This view was corroborated by the Swedish Health and Social Care Inspectorate which suggested that some elderly patients had received palliative care, instead of hospital care. In the United Kingdom, the Care Quality Commission highlighted the blanket use of 'do not resuscitate' notices for care home residents which led to "potentially avoidable deaths".[93] In Spain, the Ombudsperson (*Defensor del Pueblo*) reviewed several hundred petitions challenging the constitutionality of the dec-

88 *Feilazoo v Malta* App no 6865/19 (ECtHR, 11 March 2021).

89 *Terheş v Romania* App no 49933/20 (ECtHR, 20 May 2021).

90 European Court of Human Rights, 'Factsheet: COVID-19 Health Crisis' (updated as of July 2021) <https://www.echr.coe.int/Documents/FS_Covid_ENG.pdf>.

91 ibid 6–7.

92 Cameron and Jonsson Cornell, chapter 19.

93 Clare Dyer, 'Some Care Home Residents May Have Died because of Blanket DNR Orders, says Regulator' (2020) British Medical Journal 371:m4733 <https://www.bmj.com/content/371/bmj.m4733>.

laration of the 'state of alarm'.[94] By contrast, where watchdog bodies have been 'captured' by the executive, as in Colombia, scrutiny of violations such as police brutality is blunted.[95]

5. Vaccines and Human Rights

The development of vaccines against COVID-19 has spawned numerous human rights questions. Indeed, the evident inequity between nations has been described by the UN Secretary General as the "latest moral outrage".[96] As of August 2021, almost 54% of people in high-income countries had received at least one dose of a COVID-19 vaccine, compared to just 1.6% in low-income countries.[97] Foreseeing this atrocious situation, the UN Committee on Economic, Social and Cultural Rights, which monitors ICESCR, had called on states to strengthen their international cooperation to guarantee universal and equitable access to vaccines.[98] In August 2021, the World Health Organisation called for a moratorium on coronavirus vaccine boosters, so that supplies could be focused on helping all countries vaccinate at least 10% of their populations.[99] Amidst concerns about the market power of 'big pharma', there have also been calls from the World Trade Organisation, states, UN bodies and unions to waive copyright on COVID-19 medical products.[100] Questions have arisen, too, about access to the vaccine *within* nations. In the United Kingdom, in a welcome rights-respecting measure, adults with learning disabilities were given priority access to vaccinations following evidence that they are far more likely to die from COVID-19 than the general population.[101] By contrast, in Pakistan, some three million stateless people and others on the social periphery are denied access to vaccines for want of the required identification documents.[102]

94 Cebada Romero and Dominguez Redondo (n 72).

95 Gaviria-Mira and Hoyos-Ceballos, chapter 13.

96 UN Office of the High Commissioner for Human Rights (n 12). See also Singh, chapter 2, for an explanation of rights and duties in respect of COVID-19 vaccines and medicines; and Brook K Baker, 'Campaigning for Both Innovation and Equitable Access to COVID-19 Medicines' in Kjaerum, David and Lyons (eds) (n 5).

97 United Nations Development Programme, COVID-19 Data Futures Platform, Global Dashboard for Vaccine Equity (updated as of 11 August 2021) <https://data.undp.org/vaccine-equity/>.

98 Committee on Economic, Social and Cultural Rights, 'Statement on Universal and Equitable Access to Vaccines for COVID-19/' E/C.12/2020/2 (27 November 2020).

99 World Health Organisation, 'WHO Director-General's Opening Remarks at the Media Briefing on COVID-19' (4 August 2021) <https://www.who.int/director-general/speeches/detail/who-director-general-s-opening-remarks-at-the-media-briefing-on-covid-4-august-2021>.

100 Public Services International, 'Waive WTO Copyrights on Covid-19 Medical Products!' (1 July 2021) <https://publicservices.international/campaigns/waive-wto-copyrights-on-covid-19-medical-products?id=11380&lang=en>.

101 Public Health England, 'JCVI Advises Inviting People on Learning Disability Register for Vaccine' (24 February 2021) <https://www.gov.uk/government/news/jcvi-advises-inviting-people-on-learning-disability-register-for-vaccine>.

102 Syed and Tariq-Ali, chapter 22.

The consequences of opting *not* to be vaccinated also raise human rights questions. The possible introduction of 'immunity certificates' in some countries – for example, as a condition of certain types of employment or to access services – led Privacy International to raise concerns about "exclusion and discrimination, the exploitation of people's data, surveillance of people, and mission creep".[103] Scheinin and Molbæk-Steensig reject the idea of immunity certificates outright on the basis that it would risk violating the rights to non-discrimination and to just and favourable conditions of work.[104] Guidance on this issue came from the first judgment of the ECtHR on compulsory childhood vaccinations, in which the Grand Chamber held that for the Czech Republic to fine parents who fail to vaccinate their children without good reason, and thereby deny their children access to nursery schools, does not breach their right to respect for private life, since the policy is a proportionate means of achieving the legitimate aim of protecting health and the rights of others.[105] It remains to be seen if a similarly wide margin of appreciation would be applied in any future challenge to compulsory vaccination of adults or children against COVID-19. Certainly, the judgment (and especially its discussion of proportionality[106]) offers useful guidance to states in designing vaccination regimes that meet human rights standards. Meanwhile, the Court rejected requests for interim measures to annul a Greek law which imposes compulsory vaccination of health professionals against COVID-19 as a condition for continuing to exercise their occupation, on the basis that they lay outside the scope of the urgent mechanism.[107]

6. Looking Ahead

In recent years, some politicians and commentators have decried the expansiveness of human rights laws, and complained about "mission creep"[108] by both national and regional courts. However, international human rights conventions were deliberately drafted as broadly framed sets of standards, which could be applied in any and every situation, including, as now, during an unforeseen pandemic. They need to have sufficient range and flexibility, so that they can be interpreted dynamically and applied to novel proposals and circumstances, such as the design of technology to counter infectious disease. In this sense, human rights offer a guide to

103 Privacy International, 'Immunity Passport' (undated) <https://privacyinternational.org/examples/immunity-passport>.

104 Scheinin and Molbæk-Steensig (n 5) 27–28.

105 *Vavřička and Others v the Czech Republic* App no 47621/13 (ECtHR Grand Chamber, 8 April 2021).

106 ibid [290]–[309].

107 European Court of Human Rights, 'Refusal of requests for interim measures in respect of the Greek law on compulsory vaccination of health-sector staff against Covid-19' ECHR 266 (2021) (9 September 2021).

108 Jonathan Sumption, 'Lecture 3: Human Rights and Wrongs', The Reith Lectures 2019: Law And The Decline Of Politics (4 June 2019) <http://downloads.bbc.co.uk/radio4/reith2019/Reith_2019_Sumption_lecture_3.pdf>.

action and a means of transparently balancing competing interests and priorities in the national context, without prescribing a blueprint for policy design during a pandemic. Measures that comply with human rights are, in turn, likely to be more effective in protecting life and health, than ones that restrict other rights disproportionately: for example, contact tracing apps and other "digital identity solutions" that rely on a critical mass of uptake will be hampered if people do not trust that their privacy will be protected from undue invasion.[109]

In our view, the scale of human suffering during the pandemic should be a catalyst for developing rights in a progressive direction; for example, the digitalisation of every area of life, from education to political participation, creates a strong basis for insisting that access to the internet should be recognised as a fundamental right.[110] COVID-19 also made "the most compelling argument there has ever been for universal and affordable access to health care".[111] Beyond that, there are opportunities to improve enjoyment of existing rights: take, for example, proposals to use technologies developed or applied under the pressure-cooker of the pandemic to improve access to justice,[112] or to build more resilient and inclusive education systems after "the largest disruption … in history" affecting the right to education of virtually all students in low- and middle-income states.[113] The pandemic also underscored the importance of vigorously protecting freedom of expression, since heavy-handed restrictions impede epidemiological control by silencing journalists, whistleblowers or legitimate dissent that exposes failings.

Accountability mechanisms of all kinds will be crucial role in upholding human rights in the months and years ahead. One imperative is to prevent illiberal measures becoming normalised without justification. Another is to ensure that national authorities are held accountable, through public inquiries or other means, for errors in the handling of the pandemic which caused large-scale avoidable deaths.[114] The framework for adequate investigations under the right to life developed by the ECtHR provides the benchmark for such inquiries in terms of their effectiveness, independence, timeliness and participation of survivors and bereaved families.[115]

109 Ana Beduschi, 'Rethinking Digital Identity for Post-COVID-19 Societies: Data Privacy and Human Rights Considerations' (2021) 3 Data and Policy e15.

110 Sonia Jorge, Eleanor Sarpong and Maiko Nakagaki, *Covid-19 Policy Brief: Internet Access & Affordability* (Alliance for Affordable Internet and Web Foundation 2020).

111 UN Office of the High Commissioner for Human Rights, 'COVID is "a Colossal Test of Leadership" Requiring Coordinated Action, High Commissioner tells Human Rights Council' (9 April 2020).

112 European Commission For The Efficiency Of Justice, 'Lessons Learnt And Challenges Faced By The Judiciary During And After The Covid-19 Pandemic' CEPEJ (2020)8rev (10 June 2020).

113 United Nations, *Policy Brief: Education During COVID-19 and Beyond* (August 2020) 2.

114 As has been promised in the United Kingdom to start in 2022; 'Covid Inquiry: What Is it and How Will it Work?' (*BBC News*, 12 May 2021) <https://www.bbc.co.uk/news/explainers-57085964>.

115 European Court of Human Rights, *Guide on Article 2 of the European Convention on Human Rights: Right to Life* (updated on 30 April 2021) Part IV <https://www.echr.coe.int/Documents/Guide_Art_2_ENG.pdf>.

Upholding the right to participation and strengthening forms of community engagement more broadly is foundational to future pandemic preparedness. As Ely Yamin argues, "the agency and engagement of individuals and communities are essential for effectively managing the spread of disease".[116] The voice of communities that have borne the brunt of the pandemic – and of governmental responses to it – must be at the forefront of advocacy for human rights and social justice. It is their experience that should "shape the social learning we will take from this horrific calamity".[117]

116 Ely Yamin (n 10) 263.
117 ibid 265.

9

ASSESSING HUMAN RIGHTS COMPLIANCE DURING COVID-19

Martin Scheinin

1. Introduction

This short contribution complements the excellent chapter by Alice Donald and Philip Leach.[1] It is based on earlier work[2] where we developed a structured model for the comprehensive and indicator-based assessment of the human rights conformity of strategies by governments (or other actors) in the fight against COVID-19. The model covers all categories of human rights and all types of state obligations that flow from them. It applies state-of-the-art methodology of structural, process and outcome indicators, and relies on marking by volunteers from a pool of recognised experts. This chapter presents the results from a pilot exercise of assessing the human rights compliance of 17 countries' responses to COVID-19 during the second half of 2020.

2. The Pilot Study (the Evidence)

Basing themselves on uniform instructions from this author,[3] country experts or teams of experts assigned marks on a scale from 0 to 10 for 12 aspects of human rights compliance. These 12 aspects, called *items*, were selected so as to be representative in respect of all main categories of human rights and all types of state obligations flowing from them. The items were clustered into four *baskets*, each representing

1 Donald and Leach, chapter 8.

2 Martin Scheinin and Helga Molbæk-Steensig, *Pandemics and Human Rights: Three Perspectives on Human Rights Assessment of Strategies Against COVID-19* (EUI Working Paper LAW 2021/1). A revised version of Chapter 1 has been published as 'Human-Rights-Based Versus Populist Responses to the Pandemic' in Morten Kjaerum, Martha F Davis and Amanda Lyons (eds), *COVID-19 and Human Rights* (Routledge 2021).

3 Scheinin and Molbæk-Steensig, *Pandemics and Human Rights* (n 2) Chapter 3 and Annex 1.

DOI: 10.4324/9781003211952-11

one of the main categories of human rights, namely: (1) economic, social and cultural rights, where compliance primarily was measured in respect of so-called positive human rights obligations; (2) civil and political rights, where attention shifts to restrictions that must have a legal basis, serve a legitimate aim and meet the tests of necessity and proportionality; (3) equality rights, including prohibitions against discrimination or arbitrariness as well as paying special attention to vulnerable groups whether for reasons of age, gender or disability; and, finally (4) the rule of law dimension of human rights, including but not limited to the use of emergency powers and the question of effective remedies for grievances during COVID-19.

Human rights obligations, and hence human rights assessments, focus on states and not directly on private actors. That said, the assessment put equal emphasis on states' obligations not only to *respect* human rights by not violating them but also to *protect* the human rights of their inhabitants against intrusions by third parties, including private actors, and to *fulfil* their obligations by facilitating the effective enjoyment of human rights in society.

For each item, a set of *indicators* was identified, relying on a framework of *structure*, *process* and *outcome* indicators.[4] Within each basket, the respective three items had predefined *weights* between 25% and 50%, reflecting their importance in assessing overall human rights compliance. The initial marks and the weighting produced percentage grades (0 to 100) for each basket. The overall outcome of the assessment was an average value of the four grades. However, only countries that received a minimum 50% grade for every one of the four baskets were assessed as human rights compliant. The right to life, measured through an outcome indicator based on COVID-19 deaths per million people, had the highest weight, 50% within Basket 1. Even a very high number of deaths would not alone cause a fail grade if the country received strong marks within the same basket (based on the provision of income support and securing the right to education). Italy provided an example of this.

Marking in Basket 2 (civil and political rights) was based on a test for permissible limitations, including the requirements of necessity and proportionality. Notably, if a country received a grade below 50% for any one of the four baskets after a weighted combination of its marks for the three items within it, this was treated as failing, not only under the basket in question but also in the overall assessment. Japan is a case in point: the average of its four grades was slightly above 50% but it nevertheless failed in overall assessment of human rights compliance because it failed under Basket 3 (equality rights) (Figure 9.1 and Table 9.1).

3. Discussion

The results from the pilot demonstrate clear variation in the assessments of some countries' performance in respect of different categories of human rights, reflect-

4 Office of the United Nations High Commissioner for Human Rights, *Human Rights Indicators: A Guide to Measurement and Implementation* (2012) < accessed https://www.ohchr.org/Documents/Publications/Human_rights_indicators_en.pdf>on 3 August 2021.

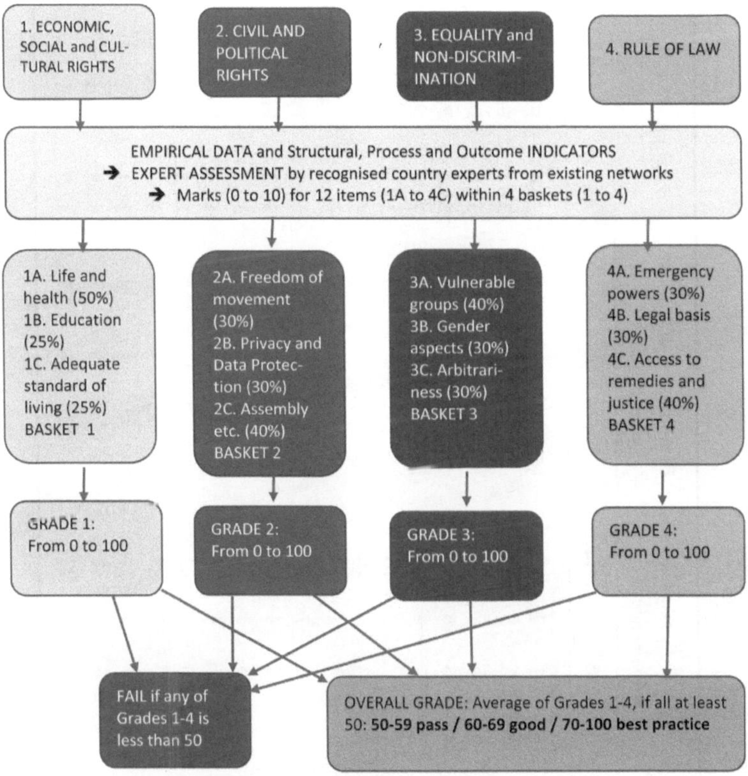

Figure 9.1 Presents the modular structure of the assessment model.

ing the idea of these countries having made a choice between, for instance, civil and political rights and economic and social rights. Turkey[5] allowed economic and social rights and equality to trump civil and political rights and the rule of law, while the United Kingdom,[6] Brazil[7] and Ukraine did almost the opposite, by prioritising traditional liberties over the health and welfare of their inhabitants. All these countries failed the assessment.

However, there were also many cases of very consistent marks across the four categories of human rights, demonstrating that compliance with human rights during COVID-19 has not been a zero-sum game, for instance between liberty and equality. Taiwan,[8] Finland,[9] Portugal, Denmark, Italy and Chile were the six countries that were assigned a passing grade throughout. Of these countries, the

5 See Çalı and Turkut, chapter 20.
6 See Grogan, chapter 5.
7 See Bustamante and Meyer, chapter 18.
8 See Chang and Lin, chapter 25.
9 See also Scheinin, chapter 11.

Table 9.1 Presents the results from the assessments of 17 pilot countries, across 12 substantive human rights issues clustered into four baskets that represent the main categories of human rights. For each country, the percentage grade for each basket resulting from the weighted marks for the three items within the basket, as well as the overall outcome as the average of the four grades and as 'pass or fail' are presented. Here, 'pass' requires at least a 50% grade for every one of the four baskets.

Country	*Basket 1: Economic, social, cultural rights*				*Basket 2: Civil and political rights*				*Basket 3: Equality and non-discrimination*				*Basket 4: Rule of law (procedural rights)*				*Overall Outcome*	
	1A	*1B*	*1C*	*Grade 1*	*2A*	*2B*	*2C*	*Grade 2*	*3A*	*3B*	*3C*	*Grade 3*	*4A*	*4B*	*4C*	*Grade 4*	*Average*	*Fail/ Pass*
Bangladesh	5	2	3	**37.5**	1	0	1	**7**	5	3	2	**35**	5	4	3	**39**	**29.6**	**Fail**
Brazil	0	3	2	**12.5**	5	5	6	**54**	2	5	5	**38**	2	6	5	**44**	**37.1**	**Fail**
Chile	5	5	5	**50**	5	7	5	**56**	5	5	7	**56**	5	6	6	**57**	**54.8**	**Pass**
Denmark	6	7	8	**67.5**	5	8	7	**67**	4	6	6	**52**	9	5	6	**66**	**63.1**	**Pass**
Finland	8	8	8	**80**	6	9	8	**77**	7	7	9	**76**	10	8	8	**86**	**79.8**	**Pass**
France	2	3	3	**25**	3	2	1	**19**	1	1	2	**13**	1	1	1	**10**	**16.8**	**Fail**
Hong Kong	6	7	-	**63.3**	8	7	0	**45**	4	3	5	**40**	5	7	6	**60**	**52.1**	**Fail**
Indonesia	5	6	5	**52.5**	6	1	3	**33**	4	3	4	**37**	5	3	3	**36**	**39.6**	**Fail**
Italy	6	6	6	**60**	6	7	6	**63**	5	6	7	**59**	6	6	6	**60**	**60.5**	**Pass**
Japan	5	5	5	**50**	5	7	5	**56**	5	5	4	**47**	5	5	5	**50**	**50.8**	**Fail**
N Macedonia	1	5	5	**30**	6	6	3	**48**	3	3	3	**30**	5	5	5	**50**	**39.5**	**Fail**
Philippines	3	6	5	**42.5**	4	5	5	**47**	4	-	4	**40**	4	4	-	**40**	**42.4**	**Fail**
Portugal	5	7	7	**60**	7	7	9	**78**	5	6	10	**68**	10	10	10	**100**	**76.5**	**Pass**
Taiwan	10	10	10	**100**	8	4	10	**76**	7	10	10	**88**	10	5	8	**77**	**85.3**	**Pass**
Turkey	6	5	4	**52.5**	0	2	0	**6**	4	1	4	**31**	0	0	2	**8**	**24.4**	**Fail**
Ukraine	3	6	4	**40**	5	5	8	**62**	3	6	4	**42**	3	2	3	**27**	**42.8**	**Fail**
UK	2	1	2	**17.5**	5	5	6	**54**	2	3	2	**23**	6	5	6	**57**	**37.9**	**Fail**

three first ones received excellent (or 'best practice') grades throughout (7 or more on a 10-point scale) and the three latter ones 'good' (Denmark and Italy) or 'pass' (Chile) grades.

For the overall pass or fail outcome, Basket 3 (equality rights) proved to be the most critical. Here, only six countries were assigned a passing grade. As none of them failed under any other basket, they were also the six countries that came through as human rights compliant overall. Even if an overall pass was to be determined on the basis of a simple average of the grades from the four baskets, only Japan and Hong Kong would be added to the top six that received a passing grade for every basket independently.

For each of the three other Baskets (1: economic and social rights, 2: civil and political rights, 4: rule of law), ten out of 17 countries received a passing grade, but not always the same ten. The top six countries listed above were, of course, always there, but the other four countries differed from basket to basket and included Japan (Baskets 1, 2 and 4), Hong Kong (Baskets 1 and 4), the United Kingdom (Baskets 2 and 4), Indonesia (Basket 1), Turkey (Basket 1), Ukraine (Basket 2), Brazil (Basket 2) and North Macedonia (Basket 4) (Table 9.2).

With the single exception of Denmark making it into the top-three for Basket 1, the three highest grades were always assigned to the same three countries, albeit in different order. Portugal and Taiwan alternated as number 1, while Finland was consistently number 2. This outcome supports the conclusion that strong human rights performance in respect of any category of human rights entails or requires general human rights compliance across all categories, demonstrating the principle of the interdependence and indivisibility of all human rights.

The geographical location of the ten countries that received the highest grades allows for some observations: while Taiwan, an island state, emerged in first place, the next Asian countries Hong Kong and Japan came, respectively, seventh and eighth. Between these three Asian countries came a cluster of four EU countries (second to fifth) and also the sole Latin American country that received a passing grade, Chile (sixth). These findings dismiss the perception that Asian countries would have fought the epidemic at a high cost to human rights, while the high death toll in the West has been unavoidable because of their respect for human rights. Finland and Denmark, with the lowest death rates in the EU, came through as highest-ranking Western countries for general human rights compliance.

The right to life, assessed by using as the indicator the COVID-19 death rate during the second half of 2020, weighed heavily in the assessment model (50% within Basket 1). Still, there were countries with a heavy death toll that otherwise received high grades: Portugal came third despite a surge of deaths towards the end of 2020, and Italy and Chile came fifth and sixth even with their heavy overall death tolls. Three of the top countries, Taiwan (first), Finland (second) and Denmark (fourth) nevertheless had comparatively low death rates within their region.

It is clear that the methodology applied has its limitations. As most country assessments were conducted by a single country expert, this may have affected some marks or grades due to positive or negative bias. All country experts were

Table 9.2 Presents the top three and bottom two country assessments for the four baskets, with the numerical grades rounded up or down along a 10-point scale.

Basket	1. Economic, social and cultural rights	2. Civil and political rights	3. Equality and non-discrimination	4. Rule of law
Top three	Taiwan 10	Portugal 8	Taiwan 9	Portugal 10
	Finland 8	Finland 8	Finland 8	Finland 9
	Denmark 7	Taiwan 8	Portugal 7	Taiwan 8
Bottom two	Brazil 1	Turkey 1	France 1	Turkey 1
	United Kingdom 2	Bangladesh 1	North Macedonia 2	France 1

recruited as volunteers from pre-existing expert networks working on human rights issues related to COVID-19. The project team conducted parallel assessments of two countries (Denmark and Finland), resulting in either very similar (Denmark) or virtually identical (Finland) results as those reported in Table 9.1. Another limitation of the methodology relates to drastic variations over time in both the COVID-19 epidemic and national policies. This risk was mitigated by instructing all country experts to assess the respective country's performance during the second half of 2020. Selecting a different period of time could in many cases produce a different outcome, which only reflects the sensitivity of the assessment model in respect of changes in circumstances, including in the strategies or policies of a country.

Despite these limitations, the pilot study demonstrated that a structured assessment of national strategies against COVID-19 as to human rights compliance, informed by concepts, categorisations and indicators developed in international human rights law, is possible and can produce significant results that will have added value for strategy, policy and governance. A structured assessment model that can be adapted to the specific characteristics of a particular pathogen or pandemic, can become an important dimension in building up global, regional and national health resilience. As the resulting grades will always relate to a specific period of time, conducting regular assessments would allow for the monitoring of the changing situation from a consistent human rights perspective and thereby support choosing a human rights compatible course.

10

GOING BEYOND THE RHETORIC

Taking Human Rights Seriously in the Post-COVID-19 World

Stéphanie Dagron

1. Introduction[1]

The COVID-19 pandemic has renewed and reinvigorated the international community's calls for the grounding of all actors' activities on human rights.[2] Around the world, this unprecedented crisis is being accompanied by discussions on both the protection of health and the protection of human rights which invariably end in the same way: with calls to take human rights more seriously. In April 2020, UN Secretary General (UNSG) António Guterres summarised the situation clearly: "The COVID-19 pandemic is a public health emergency—but it is far more. It is an economic crisis. A social crisis. And a human crisis that is fast becoming a human rights crisis."[3] The consequence of this diagnosis? That a human rights-based approach, a central UN strategy for achieving development outcomes for over a decade,[4] "can and must guide the COVID-19 response and recovery".[5]

1 All websites accessed on 7 July 2021.

2 This chapter draws on Stéphanie Dagron, 'Going Beyond the Rhetoric: Taking Human Rights Seriously in the Post-COVID-19 New Paradigm' (*Verfassungsblog*, 27 March 2021) <https://verfassungsblog.de/going-beyond-the-rhetoric-taking-human-rights-seriously-in-the-post-covid-19-new-paradigm/>.

3 Antonio Guterres, 'We Are All in This Together: Human Rights and COVID-19 Response and Recovery' (United Nations, 23 April 2020) <https://www.un.org/en/un-coronavirus-communications-team/we-are-all-together-human-rights-and-covid-19-response-and>.

4 United Nations Development Group, *The Human Rights Based Approach to Development Cooperation: Towards a Common Understanding Among UN Agencies* (September 2003) <https://unsdg.un.org/resources/human-rights-based-approach-development-cooperation-towards-common-understanding-among-un>.

5 Guterres (n 3).

DOI: 10.4324/9781003211952-12

This approach, relying on the principle of human dignity, strengthens the focus on marginalised and vulnerable groups as well as the capacities of rights-holders to make their claims; it also requires governments to meet their obligations by embedding the fundamental principles of participation, equality, non-discrimination, transparency and accountability into their practices. For the UNSG, this approach brings two advantages: it offers a response to the immediate crisis through emergency measures that are legal, proportionate, necessary and non-discriminatory; and it orientates the preparation of our societies for future (health) crises, the strengthening of economic and social rights, bolstering "resilience for the long haul".[6]

This chapter first analyses the various dimensions of the public health and human rights crisis, in order to identify, second, the breadth of the efforts that need to be made for a short- and long-term human rights-based response to COVID-19.

2. COVID-19: A Public Health and Human Rights Crisis

The UNSG's description of the COVID-19 pandemic as a human rights crisis needs to be deciphered in order to expose the extent of the links between public health – defined as "what we, as a society, do collectively, to assure the conditions for people to be healthy"[7] – and human rights. His characterisation refers to their interconnectedness: that while public health measures can have a negative impact on human rights, human rights violations can also negatively impact public health.

First, public health measures affect, and in some cases can violate, human rights. This is illustrated by the violations perpetuated all over the world by governments adopting disproportionate and discriminatory surveillance and control measures, ostensibly to protect populations and limit the spread of the virus but in practice also to solidify their power. For instance, governments have violated the rights of journalists and human rights defenders – as was the case in China[8] and Turkey,[9] according to Amnesty International. Generally, discrimination was prevalent against LGBTQ+ persons,[10] members of the Roma community (in relation to access to health and sanitation facilities or drinking water),[11] migrants and asylum

6 ibid.

7 Institute of Medicine (US) Committee for the Study of the Future of Public Health, 'The Future of Public Health' (National Academic Press 1988) 19.

8 Amnesty International, 'China: COVID-19 Journalist Tortured for Exposing Truth: Zhang Zhan' (10 December 2020) <https://www.amnesty.org/en/documents/asa17/3447/2020/en/>. See also deLisle and Kui, chapter 4.

9 Amnesty International, 'Turkey: Stifling Free Expression During the COVID-19 Pandemic' (16 June 2020) <https://www.amnesty.org/en/latest/campaigns/2020/06/turkey-stifling-free-expression-during-the-covid19-pandemic/>. See also Çalı and Turkut, chapter 20.

10 UNGA, 'Report of the Independent Expert on protection against violence and discrimination based on sexual orientation and gender identity, Victor Madrigal-Borloz, on violence and discrimination based on sexual orientation and gender identity during the coronavirus disease (COVID-19) pandemic', A/75/258 (28 July 2020).

11 Ed Holt, 'COVID-19 Lockdown of Roma Settlements in Slovakia' (2020) 20(6) The Lancet: Infectious Diseases <https://www.thelancet.com/journals/laninf/article/PIIS1473-3099(20)30381-9/fulltext>.

seekers (ill-treatment, stigmatisation and discrimination, denial of access to the asylum procedure)[12] and prisoners.[13] Such measures have been condemned by the United Nations High Commissioner for Human Rights, who reminded states in October 2020 that the pandemic was not an excuse for committing human rights violations.[14]

Second, human rights violations can negatively impact public health. The COVID-19 pandemic highlighted the deep and long-term socio-economic inequalities between countries and between individuals within countries. These disparities can be violations of human rights in and of themselves, but they have also led to the increased vulnerability to the virus of certain already vulnerable populations. As such, their existence undermines global efforts to control the propagation of the virus and to protect the whole community. Several analyses have shown the link between poverty and vulnerability to COVID-19. For instance, in the United States, where black American populations bore a disproportionate burden from the pandemic, analyses quickly established a connection with the historic economic and social inequalities, discrimination and racism suffered by those populations, which has hampered the realisation of their human rights to education, decent accommodation, access to health care, access to a social protection system and decent working conditions, among others.[15]

The link between COVID-19 and economic and social rights violations was also expressed by UN human rights experts such as Philip Alston, the Special Rapporteur on Extreme Poverty until 2020, who characterised the pandemic as "a crisis that disproportionately affects poor people, who are more likely to have health complications, live in crowded housing, lack the resources to stay at home for long periods, and work low-paid jobs that force them to choose between risking their health or losing their income".[16] The strong link established between poverty, the violation of socio-economic rights and negative health outcomes in the case of the COVID-19 is extremely worrying. Figures released by the World

12 OECD Policy Responses to Coronavirus (COVID-19), *What Is the Impact of the COVID-19 Pandemic on Immigrants and their Children?* (19 October 2020) <https://www.oecd.org/coronavirus/policy-responses/what-is-the-impact-of-the-covid-19-pandemic-on-immigrants-and-their-children-e7cbb7de/>.

13 Office of the United Nations High Commissioner for Human Rights (Human Rights Treaties Branch), *Compilation of Statements by Human Rights Treaty Bodies in the Context of COVID-19* (September 2020) <https://www.ohchr.org/Documents/HRBodies/TB/COVID19/External_TB_statements_COVID19.docx>.

14 Office of the United Nations High Commissioner for Human Rights, *Emergency Measures and COVID-19: Guidance* (27 April 2020) <https://www.ohchr.org/Documents/Events/EmergencyMeasures_COVID19.pdf>.

15 Oliver Laughland and Lauren Zanolli, 'Why is Coronavirus Taking Such a Deadly Toll on Black Americans?' (*The Guardian*, 25 April 2020) <https://www.theguardian.com/world/2020/apr/25/coronavirus-racial-disparities-african-americans>. See also Graber, chapter 6.

16 Office of the United Nations High Commissioner for Human Rights, '"Responses to COVID-19 are Failing People in Poverty Worldwide" – UN Human Rights Expert' (22 April 2020) <https://www.ohchr.org/EN/NewsEvents/Pages/DisplayNews.aspx?NewsID=25815>.

Bank in 2020 concerning the increase in extreme poverty caused by the pandemic indeed raise fears not only for the protection of the health of vulnerable populations, but also for states' capacities to effectively fight the pandemic while dealing with the rise in poverty.[17]

From the understanding that the public health and human rights crises are intimately intertwined follows a consequence, already developed in theory by the literature on health and human rights[18] and now asserted by the UNSG, that the promotion and protection of human rights benefits the promotion and protection of public health, and vice versa. As such, the response to the COVID-19 crisis should be based on a human rights-based approach to health, respectful of human rights generally, and of the right to health specifically. This conclusion was also framed as essential by Dr Tedros Adhanom Ghebreyesus, Director General of the World Health Organisation (WHO), who promoted a resolution to this effect at the World Health Assembly in May 2020.[19] The COVID-19 pandemic offers a unique opportunity to make the concrete links between health and human rights clear once and for all, and to develop guidance for states on how to take practical steps to protect human rights in the context of this and future health crises. Yet, the success of the implementation of a human rights-based approach is far from assured.

3. From Affirmation to Implementation: The Human Rights-Based Approach to Public Health after COVID-19

Two knowledge gaps exist that must be filled before a human rights-based approach can be fully implemented in public health. First, the impacts of either the violation or the promotion of human rights on physical and mental health are under-researched and under-analysed. There is thus little understanding of the principles that must be applied to limit human rights during global public health emergencies. Second, the lack of human rights-based guidance concerning states' longer-term preparations for future public health emergencies must also be addressed.

With regards to the first knowledge gap, efforts must be made to compensate for the lack of understanding about how health and human rights intersect, as well as the principles to be applied when limiting human rights during global public health emergencies. This research is essential to translate human rights into practical national measures. The knowledge gap is in part due to the fact that the links between health and human rights were neither expressly nor strongly affirmed until the end of the 20th century. Despite the acknowledgement of the right to health in the WHO's Constitution, it was only following the HIV/AIDS pan-

17 The World Bank, *Poverty and Shared Prosperity 2020: Reversals of Fortune* (2020) <https://www.worldbank.org/en/publication/poverty-and-shared-prosperity>.

18 Jonathan M Mann, 'Medicine and Public Health, Ethics and Human Rights' 1997 27(3) The Hastings Center Report 6.

19 World Health Assembly, 'COVID-19 Response' Doc. WHA73.1 (19 May 2020) <https://apps.who.int/gb/ebwha/pdf_files/WHA73/A73_R1-en.pdf>.

demic and the coalescence of a global pro-human rights civil society movement that a human rights-based approach to health emerged. As such, since 1996, in the field of HIV/AIDS, guidelines,[20] general comments of UN treaty bodies,[21] codes of practice[22] and declarations[23] have been adopted by UN institutions in charge respectively of the protection and promotion of human rights, social justice, public health or peace and security. However, and despite some early efforts to address women's specific health issues,[24] for instance, the human rights-based approach to health only began to be recognised in more recent global health strategies,[25] and in UN General Assembly resolutions adopted since 2018. These include resolutions on the fight against tuberculosis,[26] the prevention and control of non-contagious diseases,[27] and the fulfilment of universal health coverage for all.[28] Efforts by the same UN institutions must be made to combine all information on human rights protection and promotion relating to global health issues in order to fully explore the links between human rights and health and their potential impact on public health strategies.

A comparable situation can be found relating to knowledge about permissible limitations on human rights during public health crises; in practice, many difficulties are connected with the inadequacy of the existing rules in this area. The immediate response to COVID-19 has been characterised by an apparent reinforcement of social protection, a central economic and social human right, with the expansion of economic assistance and social security programmes around the world.[29] By contrast, the pandemic saw multiple limitations and derogations from

20 For example, Joint United Nations Programme on HIV/AIDS (UNAIDS), *International Guidelines on HIV/AIDS and Human Rights 2006: Consolidated Version* (Geneva, 2006).

21 For example, United Nations Committee on the Rights of the Child, General Comment No. 3 (2003) HIV/AIDS and the Rights of the Child CRC/GC/2003/3, 17 March 2003.

22 For example, International Labour Organisation, *An ILO Code of Practice on HIV/AIDS and the World of Work* (Geneva, June 2001).

23 For example, United Nations General Assembly (UNGA), 'Political Declaration on HIV and AIDS: Ending Inequalities and Getting on Track to End AIDS by 2030' Res 75/284 UN doc A/RES 75/284 (9 June 2021).

24 Office of the United Nations High Commissioner for Human Rights, *Human Rights-Based Approach to Reduce Preventable Maternal Morbidity and Mortality: Technical Guidance* (Geneva, undated).

25 World Health Organisation, *The End TB Strategy* (2015) <https://apps.who.int/iris/handle/10665/331326>.

26 UNGA, 'Political Declaration on the High-Level Meeting of the General Assembly on the Fight Against Tuberculosis: Resolution Adopted by the General Assembly' Res 73/3 UN Doc A/RES/73/3 (18 October 2018).

27 UNGA, 'Political Declaration of the Third High-Level Meeting of the General Assembly on the Prevention and Control of Non-Communicable Diseases' Res 73/2 UN Doc A/RES/73/2 (17 October 2018).

28 UNGA, 'Political Declaration of the High-Level Meeting on Universal Health Coverage' Res 74/2 UN doc A/RES/74/2 (18 October 2019).

29 Special Rapporteur on Extreme Poverty and Human Rights, *Looking Back to Look Ahead: A Rights-Based Approach to Social Protection in the Post-COVID-19 Economic Recovery* (11 September 2020) <https://www.ohchr.org/Documents/Issues/Poverty/covid19.pdf>.

civil and political rights. Under the International Covenant on Civil and Political Rights, states are authorised to impose limitations on most rights and liberties in public emergencies.[30] The Siracusa Principles specify the conditions for these limitations: they must be motivated by a legitimate aim, provided for by law, proportionate and evidence-based, of limited duration and subject to review against abusive applications.[31] Moreover, limitations must respect the principles of equality and non-discrimination and therefore particular attention must be attributed to the protection of vulnerable groups. These principles, however, designed to be applicable in each and all situations of national public emergency and to achieve "an effective implementation of the rule of law", have been extremely difficult to operationalise in the case of the COVID-19 crisis. While identifying violations may be straightforward in some cases – such as, for example, the imprisonment of journalists – determining whether particular health measures adopted by governments were proportionate and well designed to attain the objective pursued is far more challenging. These difficulties are not surprising due to scientific uncertainties concerning a new virus, its transmission, the measures to be adopted and the duration of the crisis. A consequence of this confusion is that the protection of human rights, such as freedom of movement, the right to privacy or freedom of religion, has been invoked or instrumentalised to delegitimise certain public health measures such as the obligation to wear a mask.[32] These difficulties must be rapidly addressed.

With regard to the second knowledge gap, efforts must be made to compensate for the lack of human rights-based guidance for states to prepare for future public health emergencies. The International Health Regulations (IHR),[33] which were adopted in 2005 and establish a legal framework to manage the collective defences in order to detect disease events and respond to public health risks and emergencies, do not impose on states precise obligations relating to the protection of human rights. Under the IHR, states must develop certain core capacities of surveillance and response throughout their territories and specific capacities at certain points of entry into their territory. But none of these capacities is directly designed to ensure, for instance, non-discriminatory access to healthcare services or goods for vulnerable populations, or participation in the development of public health measures by categories of the population most affected by these measures. Moreover, emphasis has been put on the technical preparation of states for future outbreaks and not on the human rights protection and socio-economic resilience of societies as illustrated by the Global Health Security Agenda (GHSA).[34] The

30 See Emmons, chapter 30.

31 Siracusa Principles on the Limitation and Derogation of Provisions in the International Covenant on Civil and Political Rights, Annex, UN Doc E/CN.4/1984/4 (1984).

32 Rahel Philipose, 'Covid-19: A Look at Anti-Mask Rallies Held Around the World Amid the Pandemic' (*The Indian Express*, 6 September 2020) <https://indianexpress.com/article/world/covid-19-a-look-at-anti-mask-rallies-held-around-the-world-amid-the-pandemic-6585722/>.

33 World Health Organisation, *International Health Regulations* (Third edition, 2005).

34 See website of the Global Health Security Agenda at <https://ghsagenda.org>.

GHSA, launched by 30 states and international organisations as a reaction to the 2014 West African Ebola crisis, indeed identifies key objectives (or key 'Action Packages') for the improvement of the international community's capacity to prevent and respond to public health emergencies. Yet, none of the 11 key objectives concerns human rights or the socio-economic preparation of states through, for example, the implementation of a universal health coverage system allowing access to health care for all. Moreover, much weight in the assessment of states' health security capacities is attributed to a reduced number of indicators only, such as human resources for health, infection control capacity (laboratories) and availability of equipment. The WHO's tool for monitoring and evaluating states' IHR core capacities, developed in collaboration with the GHSA, further emphasises the importance of technical capacities for preparedness.[35]

Proposals have already been formulated in favour of interpreting the IHR's core capacity obligations with regard to the human right to health.[36] Such proposals should be applauded and implemented as they offer concrete guidance to states. But they need to be developed further to address not only the need to strengthen healthcare systems and improve access to health services and medicinal products, but also to restructure societies in preparation for future crises of the intensity of COVID-19. The realisation of the right to health strongly depends on the realisation of other economic, social and cultural rights – such as the right to social protection and the right to enjoy the benefits of scientific progress. Combining attention on the protection and promotion of all these rights will undoubtedly facilitate a more rapid and sustainable recovery.

4. Conclusion

The COVID-19 pandemic should mark the beginning of a new era in which a human rights-based approach is not just recommended or seen as an aspiration, but is a legal obligation on states when developing immediate and long-term responses to public health crises. Where human rights were previously simply mentioned (alongside the Sustainable Development Goals, for instance), they should now form the basis for the construction of resilient societies in the post-COVID-19 area.

35 World Health Organisation, IHR Monitoring and Evaluation Framework (updated 2021) <https://extranet.who.int/sph/ihr-monitoring-evaluation>.

36 Brigit Toebes, Lisa Forman and Giulio Bartolini, 'Toward Human Rights-Consistent Responses to Health Emergencies: What Is the Overlap between Core Right to Health Obligations and Core International Health Regulation Capacities?' 2020 22(2) Health and Human Rights Journal 99.

11

FINLAND'S SUCCESS IN COMBATTING COVID-19

Mastery, Miracle or Mirage?

Martin Scheinin

1. Introduction[1]

Finland became one of the champions[2] of a response to COVID-19 that saw comparatively low numbers of cases and deaths,[3] coupled with only moderate adverse impact upon human rights or the economy, and the preservation of constitutional and democratic structures, including a major de jure and de facto role for Parliament. The question this chapter seeks to address is whether this outcome can be explained by wise decisions (mastery), or whether it has followed from mere coincidences (miracle) and therefore may fade away (mirage). The chapter builds upon the author's contributions to two *Verfassungsblog* symposia[4] and covers subsequent developments until late July 2021. It closes with a forecast into what could then be expected by the end of 2021.

1 All websites accessed on 5 August 2021 unless otherwise stated.

2 Bloomberg rankings as of 18 June 2021 <https://www.bloomberg.com/graphics/covid-resilience-ranking/>; Der Spiegel index as of 8 July 2021 (paywalled) <https://www.spiegel.de/ausland/corona-laendervergleich-wo-der-kampf-gegen-die-pandemie-gelingt-a-b253bbd9-fe9b-4d5e-9169-63b57d771216>.

3 Hannah Ritchie and others, 'Finland: Coronavirus Pandemic Country Profile' (Our World In Data, updated daily) <https://ourworldindata.org/coronavirus/country/finland?country=~FIN#citation>.

4 Martin Scheinin, 'The COVID-19 Emergency in Finland: Best Practice and Problems' (*Verfassungsblog*, 16 April 2020) <https://verfassungsblog.de/the-covid-19-emergency-in-finland-best-practice-and-problems>; 'Finland: Soft Measures, Respect for the Rule of Law, and Plenty of Good Luck: Overview of Legal and Political Response and Adaptation to COVID-19' (*Verfassungsblog*, 23 February 2021) <https://verfassungsblog.de/finland-soft-measures-respect-for-the-rule-of-law-and-plenty-of-good-luck>. See also chapter 9 in this volume.

 DOI: 10.4324/9781003211952-13

2. Overview of the Legal and Political Framework of Finland's Response to COVID-19

Finland has a modern Constitution with an ambitious catalogue of fundamental rights, resulting from a fundamental rights reform of 1995 and its consolidation as Chapter II of a new Constitution that entered into force in 2000.[5] The catalogue of constitutional rights, strongly influenced by international and European human rights law, includes all categories of human rights, recognising also their interdependence. From a human rights perspective, the main feature of Finland's response to COVID-19 has been that civil and political rights, economic, social and cultural rights, equality rights and the rule of law have received attention in the spirit of interdependence and indivisibility.

2.1 Emergency Powers and their Use

The Constitution includes an internationally inspired clause on derogations from fundamental rights when facing an emergency. The main elements of s 23 on temporary exceptions to fundamental rights can be broken down as follows: (a) such exceptions are not limited to situations of armed conflict but may be allowed also in other emergency situations defined by an Act of Parliament; (b) temporary exceptions can be issued directly by Parliament through a simple majority in the application of s 23 itself; (c) alternatively, should Parliament foresee and define certain categories of emergencies through an Act, it can delegate limited authority to activate exceptions from fundamental rights by government decree; (d) all exceptions must be compatible with Finland's international human rights obligations; and (e) Parliament shall be operative during a state of emergency but it may shift from full legislative procedure to exercising a power of *veto* in respect of emergency decrees.

What complicates the matter further is that the Emergency Powers Act[6] was *not* enacted on the basis of s 23 but through a traditional power of Parliament, maintained in s 73 of the Constitution, to enact *exceptions* to the Constitution through the qualified procedure required for amending the text of the Constitution. Section 23 of the Constitution provides a constitutional framework for eventual *new* emergency powers but the Emergency Powers Act provides a parallel source for emergency powers. During COVID-19, the Emergency Powers Act has been activated twice for a short duration, and some specific provisions have been adopted pursuant to s 23 of the Constitution.

The Emergency Powers Act defines a dangerous contagious illness as one of five emergency situations foreseen. There is a four-step sequence in the application of emergency powers under the Emergency Powers Act: (1) the cabinet, jointly with the President of the Republic, declares that Finland is faced with an

5 Act 731/1999. An English translation of the Constitution is available at <https://www.finlex.fi/fi/laki/kaannokset/1999/en19990731.pdf>.

6 Act 1552/2011.

emergency; (2) the cabinet issues a decree that defines which specific provisions of the Emergency Powers Act are activated, subject to review by Parliament; (3) the cabinet exercises the authority thereby created, by issuing decrees, again subject to review by Parliament; and finally (4) administrative authorities apply the decrees.

It must also be mentioned that some ordinary laws include emergency-type provisions. A case in point is the Communicable Diseases Act[7] that provides for declaring, through a decree issued by the cabinet, of a hazardous communicable disease, as was done also in the case of COVID-19. This triggers far-reaching powers such as mandatory testing, quarantine and even detention of individuals, as well as the closing of schools and other educational institutions, banning of public gatherings, etc. Even if normally such powers are decentralised, the cabinet has instructed regional state authorities for uniform nationwide application. During COVID-19, the Communicable Diseases Act was one cornerstone in Finland's response to the pandemic and also subject to many piecemeal temporary amendments.

2.2 Problems in the Application of Emergency Powers during the COVID-19 Pandemic: Unprepared, Undecided and Unprofessional

Much of Finland's response to the pandemic was based on legal measures other than formal emergency powers, namely on *recommendations* to the public and on measures under the Communicable Diseases Act. This reflects the principle of normalcy and is therefore commendable. For instance, physical distancing in everyday life was implemented through 'soft' recommendations to the public and employers, coupled with 'hard' unilateral decisions by public authorities about the moving of education online and physical closing of many public buildings such as libraries and museums.

Nevertheless, on 16 March 2020 the Emergency Powers Act was activated. Several emergency decrees were issued and subsequently upheld by Parliament. The provisions of the Emergency Powers Act that were triggered relate to health care and social services (ss 86–88), educational institutions (s 109), derogations from employees' rights concerning annual holidays, working hours and resignation (ss 93–94), enabling compulsory work for health care professionals (s 95 et seq), and restrictions upon freedom of movement (s 118).

In addition to these emergency decrees issued pursuant to the Emergency Powers Act, restaurants were closed down for two months, save for take-out orders, through a separate Act of Parliament enacted pursuant to s 23 of the Constitution, as an exception to the fundamental rights of property and free conduct of business.[8]

The application of the Emergency Powers Act in March–June 2020 and a brief and more limited repetition of the exercise in March–April 2021 revealed a number of shortcomings:

7 Act 1227/2016.
8 Act 153/2020.

There is no parliamentary scrutiny of declaring a state of emergency: even if Parliament reviews the exercise of emergency powers through decrees, it does not review the initial step when the cabinet, jointly with the President of the Republic, declares the existence of a situation of emergency. This became evident when both a health emergency and an economic emergency were declared but not a single decree was ever issued under the latter. By not resorting to any of the potentially available far-reaching powers that resemble a state-run wartime economy, the government itself proved that there was no economic emergency. It is nevertheless a design flaw of the Emergency Powers Act that such an emergency was declared but not reviewed.

The cabinet kept stumbling over the complicated structure of the Emergency Powers Act and the failure to synchronise it with s 23 of the Constitution. Parliament's Constitutional Law Committee urged the cabinet to follow the rulebook and to respect the separation between different types of emergency decrees under the Emergency Powers Act. The Committee also stated that the cabinet had triggered several provisions of the Emergency Powers Act prematurely.

Lack of expertise: the Government suffers from lack of adequate legal and constitutional expertise in crafting emergency decrees. This problem can be attributed to the senior lawyers and other civil servants advising the cabinet rather than to the ministers themselves. The decrees appeared amateurish, not only in the way indicated in the previous point, but also by not properly specifying the legal basis for each decree, and by failing to provide a proper assessment of compatibility with Finland's international human rights obligations. Neither does the commendable scrutiny by Parliament always utilise all available expertise. Professors of constitutional law are heard as external experts but issues related to international human rights treaties, economic, social and cultural rights or rights of vulnerable groups such as persons with disabilities were not adequately reflected when inviting experts.

Risk of neglecting international human rights obligations: during COVID-19, Finland applied the questionable view that its emergency decrees constituted limitations or exceptions to fundamental rights enshrined in the Constitution, but did not entail derogating from human rights treaties. In its review of emergency decrees, the Constitutional Law Committee reminded those who would *apply* the emergency decrees about the requirement to comply with international human rights but stopped short of addressing whether a decree might breach non-derogable human rights. For instance, the sealing off of the Uusimaa region, where one-third of the population lives, was decided as an exception to freedom of movement, under the justification of protecting the right to life of people living outside Uusimaa where the virus was less prevalent but where there also is less capacity for patients needing intensive care. The problem with the decree was that it failed to introduce protective measures *within* Uusimaa, so as to protect the elderly and other persons belonging to high-risk categories. Without such measures, sealing off Uusimaa might in a worst-case scenario have compromised the right to life of those people in the name of protecting the right to life of others.

These shortcomings allow for the conclusion that Finland was unprepared and unprofessional in its response to COVID-19 as an emergency. The Emergency Powers Act was proven not fit for purpose during a health emergency. The same can be said of the Communicable Diseases Act, which needed continuously to be complemented by new powers better suited for COVID-19 but often crafted in haste and unprofessionally.

A separate problem in the application of emergency powers followed from the lack of a coherent strategy to combat the epidemic. Due to its geographic location and other advantages, Finland might have followed the example of New Zealand, Australia, Iceland and many Asian states to suppress or eliminate the pandemic. Instead, the cabinet declared a 'hybrid' strategy that entailed mitigation rather than suppression of the virus.[9] Finland remained undecided as to its strategy, which in turn influenced which measures would be assessed as necessary and proportionate. Restrictions that would be necessary and proportionate to suppress the epidemic are unlikely to pass the necessity test if the target is mere mitigation, i.e. to flatten the curve. This became a key issue in March 2021, as will be demonstrated in section 3. Finland's hybrid strategy entailed emphasis on testing, tracing, (primarily voluntary) quarantine, working from home when possible, income support to people in quarantine, reduction of all travel across international borders and limitations on public gatherings. In comparative terms, measures related to masks, restaurants, public transport and 'non-public' (such as religious) gatherings remained very relaxed.

The central government's response can also be described as more communicative than regulatory. With an early declaration of a state of emergency in March 2020 and a rapid return to the state of normalcy, and with strong emphasis on recommendations, the population was made conscious of the severity of the threat but de jure left at liberty as to their everyday conduct.

2.3 Elements of Best Practice

Despite these problems, there are several best practice lessons that Finland may be able to provide in respect of emergency powers.

The principle of normalcy: Parliament was not suspended but very much involved in day-to-day management of the emergency, even if not always in the form of full legislative procedure.

Human rights clauses: both the emergency clause in the Constitution and the Emergency Powers Act contain explicit clauses that require compliance with international human rights obligations.

Sunset clauses: all emergency decrees are required to be of temporary nature, of a maximum six months and in practice during the COVID-19 epidemic

9 Government Resolution on a Plan for a Hybrid Strategy to Manage the COVID-19 Crisis 6 May 2020 <https://stm.fi/-/10616/valtioneuvoston-periaatepaatos-suunnitelmasta-koronakriisin-hallinnan-hybridistrategiaksi?languageId=en_US>.

much shorter, and to lapse automatically if not renewed by cabinet and Parliament.

Systematic and pluralistic review of constitutionality and fundamental-rights-conformity: the Chancellor of Justice screens the legality of every decree before it is decided by the cabinet. As part of parliamentary review, the standing Constitutional Law Committee scrutinises the constitutionality and fundamental rights conformity of every emergency decree. In so doing, the Committee hears external academic experts, typically professors of constitutional law whose legal opinions are made public. The decrees are also subject to real-time public scrutiny in traditional and social media.[10]

3. The Executive and its Powers in Response to Emergency

Finland is a unitary state with relatively autonomous municipalities and a more far-reaching regional autonomy of the Åland Islands with their own legislature.[11] The mainland territory of the country is allotted into the jurisdiction of six Regional State Administrative Agencies[12] which are organs of the central government. The law is unclear as to whether they are mere administrative arms of the cabinet or closer to semi-autonomous agencies that belong to the state administration but are not under the direct command and control of cabinet ministers. For instance, the important expert institution dealing with epidemics, the Finnish Institute for Health and Welfare,[13] is one such agency.

Measures against COVID-19 were primarily dealt with by the cabinet, including in respect of the triggering of the Emergency Powers Act (twice),[14] recommendations to the public, and the frequently amended regime at the country's territorial borders amounting to de facto closing the borders. The three most prominent ministries were the Prime Minister's Office, the Ministry for Social Affairs and Health, and the Ministry of the Interior.

Section 80 of the Constitution entails a strict requirement that matters affecting the rights and duties of individuals must be regulated through an Act of Parliament, which can delegate legislative power to the executive only to a limited degree. Chapter II of the Constitution, on fundamental rights, imposes strict requirements that restrictions must be enacted in the form of an Act of Parliament. Amendments to existing Acts of Parliament, of course, require the application of the full legislative procedure.

10 The Finnish-language blog *Perustuslakiblogi* (Constitution Blog) has a central role in the public debate and is followed, inter alia, by politicians and journalists: <https://perustuslakiblogi.wordpress.com>.

11 Act 1144 of 1991.

12 Act 896 of 2009.

13 Act 668 of 2008.

14 The Emergency Powers Act was applied between 17 March 2020 (Decree 124 of 2020) and 16 June 2020 (Decree 445 of 2020) and again between 11 March 2021 (Decree 186 of 2021) and 27 April 2021 (Decree 356 of 2021).

In contrast, the Emergency Powers Act does shift legislative power into the hands of the cabinet. That said, it is an important feature of the regime for emergencies that there is real-time constitutional and parliamentary scrutiny of emergency decrees issued. As a consequence, major dimensions of Finland's response to COVID-19 were decided by Parliament where the Constitutional Law Committee exercises continuous scrutiny over the constitutionality and human rights conformity both of legislative bills and of decrees issued under the Emergency Powers Act.

While the Emergency Powers Act had prime place in March–June 2020, later on the legislative response mainly focused on frequent piecemeal amendments to the Communicable Diseases Act, even if the Emergency Powers Act was again briefly triggered in March–April 2021. As the inadequacy of the toolbox provided by the Emergency Powers Act was by then understood, the cabinet on 25 March 2021 proposed the parallel enactment of a COVID-specific, temporary Act of Parliament pursuant to s 23 of the Constitution to provide a legal basis for foreseen restrictions, primarily of freedom of movement and when necessary derogating from constitutional rights.[15] Importantly, this Bill never passed. The Constitutional Law Committee held that the proposed powers were not necessary,[16] and the cabinet withdrew it.

While the case demonstrates the strength of parliamentary scrutiny, it is also another indication of how Finland's response to COVID-19 has been unprepared, undecided and unprofessional. Neither the Emergency Powers Act nor the frequently amended Communicable Diseases Act were, even after one year of COVID-19, fit for purpose. The country's response to the pandemic followed several parallel tracks, including now the rather novel approach of invoking the derogations power available under s 23 of the Constitution. But the bill suffered from unprofessional drafting and reflected how Finland remained undecided on its strategy against the epidemic: mitigation or suppression. Ultimately the project stumbled upon the many meanings of the word 'necessary': neither the bill nor the opinion by the Constitutional Law Committee were clear about whether the proposed powers were necessary to *use*, or necessary to *enact*, and whether necessity was to be assessed in the context of a state of emergency or as if times were normal. Notably, the Parliamentary Ombudsman was heard by the Committee as one of the external experts. Their expert opinion, manifestly with strong impact, was written applying the standard permissible limitations test and not the specific provision of s 23 of the Constitution.[17]

Where measures against COVID-19 were not handled through decrees issued under the Emergency Powers Act or through legislative bills, the role of the execu-

15 Government Bill 39/2021 for an Act on Restrictions upon Freedom of Movement and Interpersonal Contacts.

16 Opinion 12/2021 by the Constitutional Law Committee of Parliament (31 March 2021).

17 The expert opinions submitted to the Constitutional Law Committee are public. The submission in question is available at <https://www.eduskunta.fi/FI/vaski/JulkaisuMetatieto/Documents/EDK-2021-AK-362951.pdf>.

tive was much greater and parliamentary scrutiny quite limited. A case in point is Finland's restriction of all international travel, including intra-EU travel, which amounted to a de facto closure of borders, even until July 2021 without proper legal basis. By formally invoking its legitimate power temporarily to reintroduce measures of border control at the EU's internal borders,[18] Finland in fact extended the application of its provisions of internal law[19] concerning the *external* borders of the EU to *all* border crossings. It also introduced a combination of serially reissued or revised cabinet decisions, determined communication to the public, and systematic individual questioning by its border guards, to stop anything but indispensable travel.[20] Finland did not apply quarantine hotels or similar measures to discourage and control entry. Rather, it simply prevented most arrivals.[21] Paradoxically, this questionable aspect of Finland's measures against the pandemic may have been key to its success in keeping the numbers down throughout the epidemic. Regarding Finland as a model of rule of law and human rights compliance may not represent the whole truth.

4. The Effectiveness of Judicial and Legislative Scrutiny and Oversight

Courts generally adapted themselves to the situation by modifying their methods of work. The epidemic resulted in delays in court proceedings but not as severely as in many other countries. Administrative courts gradually started to decide cases directly related to COVID-19, such as restrictions imposed by institutions of care.[22]

The two main institutions for oversight of legality, the Chancellor of Justice (of the cabinet) and the (Parliamentary) Ombudsman received a large number of complaints related to responses to COVID-19. Both appeared to adopt a fairly soft approach of pointing out shortcomings and even mistakes but not finding illegality or instituting criminal prosecution, which would have been within their powers. On the issue of measures at Finland's territorial borders, mentioned in the preceding section as an area where the measures lacked proper legal basis, both oversight institutions criticised the cabinet and the Border Control Agency for ambiguous drafting of, and misleading communication on, decisions that had the appearance of legally binding regulations but that on closer analysis were recommendations.[23] In failing to address the absence of a proper legal basis for the measures, these deci-

18 Title III, Chapter II, of EU Regulation 2016/399 (Schengen Borders Code).

19 The Border Guard Act 578/2005.

20 Emilia Korkea-aho and Martin Scheinin, '"Could You, Would You, Should You?" Regulating Cross-Border Travel Through COVID-19 Soft Law in Finland' (2021) 12(1) European Journal of Risk Regulation 26 <https://doi.org/10.1017/err.2020.112>.

21 According to Government Bill 105/2021 (p 16), the number of all travellers arriving in Finland in the spring of 2021 was one tenth of the equivalent period in 2019.

22 Supreme Administrative Court 2021:1, ECLI:FI:KHO:2021:1.

23 Chancellor of Justice 1 October 2020, OKV/61/10/2020; Parliamentary Ombudsman 12 November 2020, EOAK/3257/2020.

sions can be read as reflecting an acceptance of extra-constitutional emergency powers, which would be very uncharacteristic for Finland.

5. Federal, Regional and Local Response and Coordination

While the response was primarily in the hands of the central government, and in particular the cabinet, the Communicable Diseases Act creates an important exception as it is largely based on a decentralised model where the role of Regional State Administrative Authorities, municipalities and specialist doctors is significant. Issues such as mandatory health screening, mandatory quarantine, contagion tracing, physical closing of educational institutions and banning or restricting public assemblies all primarily pertain to the parallel jurisdiction of the respective municipality and Regional State Administrative Authority. As the latter are nevertheless authorities of the state, they closely coordinated their actions and were also receptive to instructions from the cabinet.

Due to the central role of the Ministry of Social Affairs and Health in the national response and the decentralised model of the Communicable Diseases Act, one recurring theme in legislative responses considered has been efforts to make the powers and role of this ministry more prominent. In February 2021, Parliament, following its Constitutional Law Committee,[24] rejected an important amendment of the Act that would have brought into its scope powers to restructure and reorganise the provision of health and social services, powers that otherwise would only be available pursuant to the Emergency Powers Act but were now proposed to be exercised by the Ministry of Social Affairs and Health without the parliamentary scrutiny that would apply if the Emergency Powers Act was triggered. Had the Bill been adopted, it would have represented function creep through the insertion of delegated emergency powers into ordinary legislation, undoing the safeguards related to the actual use of the Emergency Powers Act.

6. Human Rights Considerations

In addition to a full catalogue of fundamental rights, the Constitution includes a comprehensive and therefore interdependence-based clause (s 22) on *positive obligations* in respect of both constitutional rights and international human rights. A pluralist system entails that fundamental rights scrutiny is built into the drafting of bills, parliamentary proceedings and the application of legislation or regulations. There is also a lively public debate on any legal reform with human rights implications.

During COVID-19, rights protections worked relatively well. Examples of strict upholding of the standards include the right to privacy (the COVID-19 app *Koronavilkku* which warns the user of exposure but is firewalled in respect of contact-tracing) and freedom of religion (exclusion of religious gatherings from

24 Opinion 44/2020.

the scope of restrictions upon assemblies). Confusion and failures to respect human rights did, however, result from ambiguously worded recommendations, including visiting rights at institutions of care. No proper legal basis was found or created for restrictions on cross-border movement which therefore remained dubious until July 2021.

Finland's choice of a hybrid strategy translated into reluctance to impose certain restrictions widely in use elsewhere. Wearing of face masks was dealt with mainly in the form of recommendations that lacked consistency. Restaurants were subjected to temporary restrictions through several amendments of the law but in substance those measures were relaxed compared to many other countries. These and some other cases of refraining from rapid action may be criticised as failures to meet the country's positive human rights obligations under the right to health and the right to life. The lack of a coherent approach also had the result that cultural and other events were subject to stricter restrictions than restaurants, and indirectly resulted in local elections that were scheduled for 18 April 2021 being postponed by two months.

7. Developments in 2021 and a Forecast

7.1 Twists and Turns

In January 2021, Finland was slow in its response to the emergence of more contagious variants of COVID-19. Instead of proceeding with legislative amendments that would have addressed the inadequacies of the Emergency Powers Act and the Communicable Diseases Act, the cabinet decided to rely on and update its hybrid strategy, continue its proactive communication and postpone legislative action to a time when the epidemic might pose a risk to the capacity of the hospitals.[25] Such a risk was forecast for April 2021.

Accordingly, the Emergency Powers Act was taken into use on 9 March, and on 25 March a separate government bill was presented to Parliament that was based on the emergency clause in s 23 of the Constitution and would have provided a legal basis for restrictions upon or derogations from constitutional rights, primarily freedom of movement. Unfortunately, the bill again suffered from unprofessional drafting and was an easy target for criticism. The shortcomings of the bill could have been remedied. The Constitutional Law Committee, headed by Antti Rinne from the same political party as Prime Minister Sanna Marin (Social Democrats), however, chose differently. Consensus between the cabinet and Parliament broke down, and re-emerged between the government coalition and opposition parties in Parliament. Unanimously, the Committee concluded that many of the central elements of the bill were not "deemed necessary" as required by s 23 of the Constitution. One can criticise this outcome as an error of logic, as the bill was not

25 'Government Decides to Supplement Action Plan for COVID-19 Hybrid Strategy' (Finnish Government press release, 25 January 2021) <https://valtioneuvosto.fi/-/10616/hallitus-linjasi-hybridistrategian-toimintasuunnitelman-taydentamisesta?languageId=en_US>.

about imposing radical restrictions upon freedom of movement but about *creating a legal basis* for such restrictions, should they become necessary and proportionate in respect of a health emergency. From the perspective of constitutionalism, it is remarkable that during an officially proclaimed state of emergency, Parliament plainly dismissed a centrepiece of the response proposed by the cabinet as not being necessary.

Finland being Finland, the return to business as usual was immediate. The cabinet withdrew the controversial bill and continued to address COVID-19 through communication and recommendations to the population; limited and inadequate powers under the Emergency Powers Act and the Communicable Diseases Act; piecemeal and usually unprofessionally crafted casuistic amendments to the latter Act; and continuing the de facto closure of Finland's borders without a proper legal basis. On 27 April 2021, the cabinet decided to discontinue the application of the (useless) Emergency Powers Act.

The episode just described entailed a shift of power and consensus-formation from the cabinet to Parliament. In Parliament, the two most important Committees have proven to be the Constitutional Law Committee and the Committee on Social Affairs and Health (chaired by Markus Lohi of the Centre Party, also in government). This power shift entails a move from mitigating the epidemic towards 'opening up' society and seeking consensus with the opposition, particularly the Coalition Party (conservatives). Throughout the epidemic, the Committee on Social Affairs and Health has proven to be sympathetic to the interests of the restaurant, hotel, travel and tourism industries. Through two consecutive amendments of the Communicable Diseases Act in March[26] and July[27] 2021, reflecting the power shift to Parliament, the de facto closure of Finland's borders without a proper legal basis was finally replaced by a regime based on COVID-19 certificates and uncontrolled entry from low-incidence countries. While the amendment to create a legal basis for measures at the border is welcome from a rule of law perspective, it was not supplemented by a framework of properly crafted powers that could be invoked if the epidemic got out of control.

Sadly, the highly contagious Delta variant landed in Finland exactly at the time when Parliament gave its finishing touch to the relaxed but law-based new regime at the borders. It came in with Finnish spectators who had travelled on coaches to the Euro 2020 football games played in St Petersburg, Russia. The seven-day average of new cases per million people shifted from 12 (17 June) to the nine-fold, but still modest, level of 108 (31 July). The Delta variant became dominant, kicking the idea of obtaining herd immunity through vaccinations into 2022, at the earliest. The latter outcome perhaps was unavoidable, but the episode demonstrates that

26 Government Bill 15/2021 (18 March 2021), Opinion 7/2021 by the Constitutional Law Committee, Report 6/2021 by the Committee on Social Affairs and Health, Act 224/2021 (26 March 2021).

27 Government Bill 105/2021 (18 June 2021), Opinion 26/2021 by the Constitutional Law Committee, Report 18/2021 by the Committee on Social Affairs and Health, Act 701/2021 (6 July 2021).

despite all its success, Finland remains unprepared, undecided and unprofessional in its response to COVID-19.

7.2 *Miracle or Mirage?*

This chapter has demonstrated that Finland's relative success in combatting COVID-19 has not resulted from mastery. So, is it a miracle or just a mirage?

The metaphor for a miracle is widely used in Finland as a non-religious but metaphysical expression of unexplained special characteristics of the Finnish nation or people that would make it almost invincible. 'The Miracle of the Winter War' is an expression of nationalist pride that refers to a 90-day war between the Soviet Union and Finland in 1939–1940, when Finland suffered heavy losses of people and territory but through perseverance (*sisu*) put up a military response against a country with ten-fold military strength, preserving its independence. Eighty years later, references to the Miracle of the Winter War are common in sports, as well as in politics, including during COVID-19. They crystallise, and psychologically explain, the unfounded tendency of many Finns to regard themselves as unaffected by grave threats.

There are several objective reasons for Finland's relative success, such as geographical location, low population density, and cultural features entailing avoidance of close physical proximity with most people, as well as longstanding factors, such as wealth, health care and a welfare state. A commitment to all categories of human rights and their interdependence is one important explanation as an achievement made by choice. The effect of decisions made by one particular government coalition in 2020–2021 was most likely less important. This does not mean that Finland has simply been 'lucky'. Good fortune is something shaped by one's own choices on the basis of the preconditions that you have. Finland's response did not represent mastery, except in avoiding grave errors that could have undone the fortune of advantageous factual circumstances. Together with that limited mastery, there has been a miraculous sequence of good luck, albeit accompanied by a risk that the success will prove out to be a mirage.

7.3 *Looking into the Crystal Ball*

The trajectory of the epidemic in 2021 is a race between vaccinations and new virus strains. Finland's communication-centred hybrid strategy may still be faced with an exponential rise of cases. If that were to happen, the Emergency Powers Act would not be fit for purpose as its usefulness has already proved very limited. A more adequate response could be based on the emergency powers provision in s 23 of the Constitution, for the quick enactment of tailor-made COVID-19 emergency measures.

There are, however, good reasons why this scenario is unlikely. The application of s 23 of the Constitution was already rejected in March 2021. Without a new strategic commitment to a suppression strategy that would justify the coherent and determined application of stricter measures for a very short period, new derogations from the Constitution are unlikely to pass the necessity test, if presented for the aim of mitigating the epidemic at a time when those at greatest risk already have been double vaccinated. It is more likely that the hybrid strategy of mitigation will shift towards a more typical western approach of 'opening up' society. This would not prove that Finland was wrong earlier, as 8,500 lives were already saved.[28]

The more likely scenario is that the more virulent strands do not become an unbearable problem in terms of deaths and hospitalisations and Finland manages to vaccinate its adult population, and ultimately also children. The human cost of 'opening up' will entail more deaths but not to a magnitude cancelling Finland's earlier relative success in a European comparison. Many more people will nevertheless face long-term illnesses and permanent disabilities. If this is indeed the trajectory, legislative attention should immediately shift to a careful and comprehensive review of both the Emergency Powers Act and the Communicable Diseases Act. These two legal instruments have been central in Finland's handling of the epidemic, but they have also both proven to be highly inadequate when the country is faced with an airborne pathogen that has a relatively high reproductive number and fatality rate. COVID-19 will not be the last pandemic with these parameters.

As Finland has been one of the EU countries that has de facto restricted intra-EU travel, it would be well placed to take the initiative towards creating a proper legal basis for the partitioning of the EU area during a public health emergency. It is absurd that while Member States may be imposing lockdowns internally, including by cordoning off parts of their territory, cross-border movement cannot be controlled through evidence-based decision-making but is outside everyone's competence because of what ultimately is an ideological commitment to the four economic freedoms of European integration. If the EU were a federal state hit by a deadly pandemic, then evidence and reason, rather than ideology and impotence, would govern its approach to freedom of movement.

Finally, governments, academics and international organisations should join forces in conducting a human rights assessment of strategies against COVID-19.[29] Doing so would better equip the world for future pandemics, as a human rights assessment could be built into all plans for preparedness and prevention.

28 By 24 July 2021, there were 980 COVID-19 deaths in Finland. Compared to the EU average of deaths per one million inhabitants, this means that 8,500 lives had been saved; see Ritchie and others (n 3) <https://ourworldindata.org/explorers/coronavirus-data-explorer?zoomToSelection=true&pickerSort=desc&pickerMetric=total_cases&hideControls=true&Metric=Confirmed+deaths&Interval=Cumulative&Relative+to+Population=true&Align+outbreaks=false&country=FIN~European+Union>.

29 Martin Scheinin and Helga Molbæk-Steensig, *Pandemics and Human Rights: Three Perspectives on Human Rights Assessment of Strategies against COVID-19* (EUI Working Paper LAW 2021/1). A revised version of Chapter 1 of the paper has been published as 'Human-Rights-Based Versus Populist Responses to the Pandemic' in Morten Kjærum, Martha F Davis and Amanda Lyons (eds), *COVID-19 and Human Rights* (Routledge 2021). See also chapter 9 in this volume.

12

A CRISIS OF RIGHTS AND DEMOCRACY IN INDIA

Thulasi K Raj

1. Introduction[1]

In the recent global history of constitutional democracies, it is difficult to name a single crisis that has plagued them simultaneously, until the COVID-19 pandemic. The calamity caused by the virus was universal. It presented an opportunity for crisis management without compromising principles of democratic governance and human rights guarantees. Some countries marginally succeeded in this test while in others, concerns about democratic decline and erosion of human rights were amplified. India unfortunately belongs to the latter camp.[2]

At the time of writing, there are reports from various parts of India of dead bodies queuing up at crematoriums for hours.[3] Hospitals have reached their full capacity,[4] patients continue to die for lack of oxygen supply,[5] and the attempt to vaccinate the population has been abysmal, with only 5.4% of the population fully vaccinated as of 12 July 2021.[6] India faces an unprecedented health emer-

1 All websites accessed on 12 July 2021.

2 This chapter is an extended version of Thulasi K Raj, 'COVID-19 and the Crisis in Indian Democracy' (*Verfassungsblog*, 26 February 2021) <https://verfassungsblog.de/covid-19-and-the-crisis-in-indian-democracy/>.

3 'At Delhi Crematoriums, Corpses Wait in 20-Hour Queues to Burn' (*Hindustan Times*, 27 April 2021) <https://www.hindustantimes.com/cities/delhi-news/at-delhi-crematoriums-corpses-wait-in-20-hour-queues-to-burn-101619522536735.html>.

4 Steve Inskeep, 'Doctor in India: Emergency Room is So Crowded, "It's Nearly Impossible to Walk"' (*NPR News*, 6 May 2021) <https://www.npr.org/sections/coronavirus-live-updates/2021/05/06/994145513/indias-covid-19-crisis-continue-to-get-worse?t=1624890596672>.

5 'Covid-19 in India: Cases, Deaths and Oxygen Supply' (*BBC News*, 29 April 2021) <https://www.bbc.com/news/world-asia-india-56891016>.

6 Johns Hopkins University Coronavirus Resource Center, 'Understanding Vaccination Progress' <https://coronavirus.jhu.edu/vaccines/international>.

DOI: 10.4324/9781003211952-14

gency and is placed by one authoritative ranking among the 20 worst affected countries in the world for COVID-19 mortality.[7] As one commentator ventured, because of mismanagement by the administration of Prime Minister Narendra Modi, "COVID-19 has brought India to its knees and tens of thousands of Indians to their deathbeds".[8]

Problems such as India's inadequate spending on health, the lack of social security measures and insufficient attention to medical research and development existed before the present regime. But much of the crisis is attributable to the flawed manner in which the government dealt with the pandemic. In this chapter, it is argued that the following features define the Indian response to COVID-19: lack of transparency, executive monopoly, curtailing rights and reckless management.

2. Lack of Transparency

The Indian response to COVID-19 was characterised by an absence of transparency in governance and crisis management. Transparency and access to information improve public trust. Open governments are considered to be more legitimate and accountable than those that resist public scrutiny. They perform more efficiently and reduce corruption.[9] However, the Indian government was reluctant to share data with the public, be it the details of national lockdowns or the number of COVID-19 cases. The government cultivated and perpetuated a rule of secrecy. Certain specific aspects are noteworthy.

2.1 A Lockdown Unannounced

On the evening of 24 March 2020, the prime minister announced a 21-day national lockdown which was set to begin within four hours. The lockdown was extremely harsh, leading to a complete ban on transport, including domestic and international travel; the closure of schools and non-essential shops; and prohibition of assemblies and events. The Oxford COVID-19 Government Response Tracker listed it as among the most stringent in the world.[10] This abrupt declaration without any prior notice left a country of almost 1.4 billion people in utter confusion and disarray.

7 Johns Hopkins University, Coronavirus Resource Center, Mortality Analyses (updated as of 12 July 2021) <https://coronavirus.jhu.edu/data/mortality>.

8 Prerna Singh, 'Op-Ed: How Democratic Politics Make India's COVID Calamity Worse' (*Los Angeles Times*, 8 May 2021) <https://www.latimes.com/opinion/story/2021-05-08/india-covid-pandemic-deaths-narendra-modi>.

9 Susan Rose-Ackerman, 'Redesigning the State to Fight Corruption: Transparency, Competition and Privatization' (World Bank, 1996) <https://openknowledge.worldbank.org/handle/10986/11627>.

10 University of Oxford, Blavatnik School of Government, 'Oxford Covid-19 Government Response Tracker' <https://www.bsg.ox.ac.uk/research/research-projects/covid-19-government-response-tracker>.

The unpreparedness of the state to meet the demands of such a lockdown was apparent. The shutdown led to a sudden halt in freedom of movement and access to resources. It caused disproportionate impact on groups in vulnerable circumstances such as students, women, the disabled, those on low incomes and the homeless. India's social safety net has proven to be vastly insufficient and during the pandemic, inadequate government spending and investment proved fatal.[11] The impact on poor migrant workers was especially striking; incomes stopped for most of the inter-state migrant workers constituting around 450 million people who had travelled from rural to urban neighborhoods seeking jobs. No arrangements for transport were made by the government, at least not until several weeks into the lockdown. Left with no other option, migrant workers resorted to walking hundreds of kilometres. For weeks, they walked to their homes, often carrying children and luggage and surviving on meagre food.[12] Numerous deaths were reported due to starvation and exhaustion.

The lockdown was extended several times – again without sufficient warning – and finally lifted, with some restrictions in place, on 31 May 2020. However, economists argue that the country both entered into and exited from lockdown too early.[13] A concern raised was that the lockdown trapped migrant workers in urban population centres, like Mumbai, in which the virus was spreading, before forcing them to return to the countryside, which had been virtually unaffected up to that point.[14] These tragedies could have been easily averted if the public had been given necessary warning and guidelines before the lockdown.

2.2 An Opaque Relief Fund

Purportedly to meet the demands of the pandemic, a Prime Minister's Citizen Assistance and Relief in Emergency Situations Fund (PM CARES) was set up by Narendra Modi in March 2020. Less than one week after being established, the Fund had collected a total amount of Rs. 30.76 billion (approximately US$415 million / €350 million) from corporate, institutional and individual donations, and this was later reported to have increased to Rs. 100 billion (approximately US$1.35 billion / €1.1 billion).[15]

11 Jayati Ghosh, 'A Critique of the Indian Government's Response to the COVID-19 Pandemic' (2020) 47 Journal of Industrial and Business Economics 519 <https://doi.org/10.1007/s40812-020-00170-x.

12 Vikas Pandey, 'Coronavirus Lockdown: The Indian Migrants Dying to Get Home' (*BBC News*, 20 May 2020) <https://www.bbc.com/news/world-asia-india-52672764>.

13 Gireesh Chandra Prasad, 'India Entered Into and Exited from Lockdown Way Too Early: Abhijit Banerjee' (*Livemint*, 15 August 2020) <https://www.livemint.com/news/india/india-entered-into-and-exited-from-lockdown-way-too-early-abhijit-banerjee-11597487108787.html>.

14 'Govt. Would Have Done Better Had it Listened to Experts: COVID-19 Task Force Report' (*The Wire Science*, 31 May 2020) <https://science.thewire.in/health/covid-19-task-force-joint-statement-migrant-exodus/>.

15 'Coronavirus: Secrecy Surrounds India PM Narendra Modi's "$1bn" Covid-19 Fund' (*BBC News*, 30 June 2020) <https://www.bbc.com/news/world-asia-india-53151308>.

The new scheme did not make use of the existing relief funds, such as the National Disaster Response Fund and the long-established Prime Minister's National Relief Fund, which would have given it a sound legal basis. Rather, the centralised system is opaque. The Right to Information Act 2005 (RTI) is legislation that enables citizens to gather information regarding public authorities. RTI applications, which sought details of the donors, spending and usage of the PM CARES Fund, were met with a refusal to give any information.[16] At the time of writing, the Fund is operating with an official .gov domain, with officers of the Prime Minister's Office administering and managing it. Yet, citizens remain in the dark about whether and how the money is being used for COVID-19 relief.

2.3 False Data, Misinformation and Underreporting

The governmental response during the pandemic was rife with misinformation and often false data. The number of reported cases was usually far from actual data, according to serological surveys.[17] The presence of community spread was not acknowledged by the central government even when record levels of 400,000 infections a day occurred in May 2021.[18] Similarly, COVID-19 fatalities were also deliberately undercounted by the government, with several major cities reporting far larger numbers of cremations and burials under coronavirus protocols than official death tolls showed.[19] Epidemiologist Bhramar Mukherjee described the official toll as "a complete massacre of data", venturing that the true number of deaths was two to five times higher.[20] In one instance, in the city of Kanpur, where 476 cremations took place in a single day, the number of deaths reported was three.[21] Medical personnel were asked to write "sickness" as the cause of death and not COVID-19.[22] A group of former civil servants known as the Constitutional Conduct Group lamented that authentic state-level data on testing, positive cases,

16 ibid.

17 The surveys are referred in Jean Drèze, 'India is in Denial About the COVID-19 Crisis' (*Scientific American*, 25 August 2020) <https://www.scientificamerican.com/article/india-is-in-denial-about-the-covid-19-crisis/>.

18 'Despite Record Number of Covid Cases, India Continues to Avoid Community Transmission Tag' (*Scroll*, 14 May 2021) <https://scroll.in/latest/994879/despite-record-number-of-covid-cases-india-continues-to-avoid-community-transmission-tag>.

19 Ezgi Toper, 'Massacre of Data': Experts say India is Undercounting its Covid Deaths' (*TRT News*, 27 April 2021) <https://www.trtworld.com/asia/massacre-of-data-experts-say-india-is-undercounting-its-covid-deaths-46256>.

20 Jeffrey Gettleman, Sameer Yasir, Hari Kumar and Suhasini Raj, 'As COVID-19 Devastates India, Deaths go Undercounted' (*The Economic Times*, 24 April 2021) <https://economictimes.indiatimes.com/news/india/as-covid-19-devastates-india-deaths-go-undercounted/articleshow/82234586.cms>.

21 Eric Feigl-Ding, 'Hugely Undercounting Deaths' (*Twitter*, 25 April 2021) <https://twitter.com/DrEricDing/status/1386124397300391940?ref_src=twsrc%5Etfw%7Ctwcamp%5Etweetembed%7Ctwterm%5E1386124397300391940%7Ctwgr%5E%7Ctwcon%5Es1_&ref_url=https%3A%2F%2F>.

22 Toper (n 19).

hospitalisations and deaths had not been publicly disseminated.[23] Therefore, the official figures on the COVID-19 pandemic were highly unreliable, jeopardising the planning of medical supplies and other essentials.

The health crisis also witnessed widespread misinformation and fake cures for the virus, which the executive did very little to curtail. At times, the government encouraged and actively promoted unscientific methods to prevent and cure the epidemic; for example, it encouraged the use of traditional Ayurvedic medicine, with no scientific evidence. This was described as "a fraud on the nation"[24] by the Indian Medical Association, the apex body of medical practitioners. The Science Ministry reportedly funded clinical trials to discover whether chanting of the Gayatri mantra, a Hindu religious hymn and yoga could cure COVID-19.[25] This was joined by fake optimism, including a plan for a vaccine by August 2020 by the government medical research body.[26] Various leaders from the ruling Bhartiya Janata Party advocated for baseless claims to fight COVID-19, such as drinking cow's urine, causing a real risk for desperate people.[27]

Unusually for constitutional democracies, the prime minister has not addressed a press conference for several years (except once in 2019, when he declined to answer questions).[28] This trend continued even during the days of the pandemic. At times, the Health Ministry also skipped media briefings without explanation.[29]

3. Executive Monopoly

The lack of transparency is exacerbated by a heavy concentration of powers and decision-making in the executive.

23 'Full Text: "India Needs Action Now" Say 116 Former Bureaucrats in Letter to Modi' (*Scroll.in*, 20 May 2021) <https://scroll.in/latest/995376/full-text-india-needs-action-now-say-116-former-bureaucrats-in-letter-to-modi?fbclid=IwAR2SrmwenOS6cziTuXQsBJ1UrACx_2F0nSjHn5gd0GDd0SQujQzHlwynGBQ>.

24 Priyanka Pulla, '"A Fraud on the Nation": Critics Blast Indian Government's Promotion of Traditional Medicine for COVID-19' (*Science*, 15 October 2020) <https://www.sciencemag.org/news/2020/10/fraud-nation-critics-blast-indian-government-s-promotion-traditional-medicine-covid-19>.

25 Jacob Koshy, 'Science Ministry Funds Trial on Effect of Gayatri Mantra in Treating COVID-19' (*The Hindu*, 20 March 2021) <https://www.thehindu.com/news/national/science-ministry-funds-trial-on-effect-of-gayatri-mantra-in-treating-covid-19/article34111676.ece>.

26 Murali Krishnan, 'Can India Really Have a Coronavirus Vaccine Ready by August?' (*Deutsche Welle*, 8 April 2020) <https://www.dw.com/en/coronavirus-vaccine-india/a-54089371>.

27 'Holy Smoke, Cow Urine, Yagna Chikitsa: BJP Leaders and Their Unscientific Claims on Covid Cure' (*The Indian Express*, 19 May 2021) <https://indianexpress.com/article/india/holy-smoke-cow-urine-yagna-chikitsa-bjp-leaders-and-their-unscientific-claims-on-covid-cure/>.

28 'At His First News Conference in India, PM Modi Declines Questions' (*Reuters*, 17 May 2019) <https://www.reuters.com/article/india-election-modi/at-his-first-news-conference-in-india-pm-modi-declines-questions-idUSKCN1SN224>.

29 Mukesh Rawat, 'Health Ministry Skips Media Briefings as Coronavirus Cases Soar. Why so Silent?' (*India Today*, 20 May 2020) https://www.indiatoday.in/news-analysis/story/health-ministry-skips-media-briefings-as-coronavirus-cases-soar-why-so-silent-1679920-2020-05-20.

3.1 Inadequate Laws and Misuse

The Indian Constitution does not provide for a health emergency. It permits, in Article 352, the declaration of emergency on grounds of war, external aggression or armed rebellion. It would have been difficult for the state to resort to this route in the context of COVID-19. However, a deadly pandemic required efficient and sustainable law-making for a large country like India. Under the Indian Constitution, civil and political rights are provided for in Chapter III. Chapter IV provides for non-justiciable socio-economic obligations for the state. The proportionality test of permissibility of infraction of rights consisting of legality, necessity, suitability and proportionality stricto sensu is recognised by Indian judicial practice.[30] Since the crisis required comprehensive management, the best modus operandi would have been to initiate specific and targeted legislation, similar to the United Kingdom[31] or Germany.[32]

A properly enacted law would have given sufficient clarity and accessibility to the population, and foreclosed, to some extent, possibilities for vague directions and misuse of powers. Instead, however, a series of restrictions was imposed via law-making by the executive, creating a patchwork of guidelines, ordinances and government orders. This vested an undue amount of discretion in the executive to decide on the nature and extent of the restrictions imposed on rights.

Existing legislation was also used to initiate and impose measures during the pandemic. This was, however, unsuitable. The Disaster Management Act, for instance, was originally enacted to govern natural disasters and did not contain provisions suitable for addressing a health crisis. Nevertheless, it was invoked and the authority under the Act was vested with wide powers. The Epidemic Diseases Act, a law from 1897, was also used with powers prescribed as widely as "measures" the state "deems necessary".[33] There were no rules specifically laid down for the COVID-19 pandemic management. As I wrote elsewhere, at the same time, the executive was vested with significant powers which were exercised in the form of executive orders.[34] Hence, the legislation was, simultaneously, excessive on one level and insufficient on another. Journalists were arrested under this law for accurately reporting issues related to the lockdown. Section 4 of the Act grants public authorities an absolute immunity from prosecution for actions taken under the Act.[35]

30 *Justice KS Puttaswamy (Retd) & Anr v Union of India & Ors* (2017) 10 Supreme Court Cases 1.

31 Coronavirus Act 2020.

32 'Germany: Amendments to Infectious Diseases Protection Act Enter into Force' (*Library of Congress*, 24 November 2020) <https://www.loc.gov/law/foreign-news/article/germany-amendments-to-infectious-diseases-protection-act-enter-into-force/>.

33 Parikshit Goyal, 'The Epidemic Diseases Act, 1897 Needs An Urgent Overhaul' (2020) 55(45) Economic and Political Weekly / EPW Engage <https://www.epw.in/node/157579/pdf>.

34 Thulasi K Raj, 'Rights During a Pandemic: The Indian Experience' (Global Roundtable of the International Association of Constitutional Law, 23 November 2020) <https://www.iacl-democracy-2020.org/blog/2016/3/23/blog-post-sample-9wntn-6ye75-hwawc-xx9lz-p6k2z-85m67-nkxzl-m76y3>.

35 This paragraph is based on Raj, ibid.

The criminal law framework was also used, leading to police violence in the guise of enforcing lockdown regulations and social distancing.[36] Section 144 of the Code of Criminal Procedure empowers judges to pass orders prohibiting unlawful assembly when nuisance or law and order problems are apprehended. Yet in the pandemic context, this law was enforced in several cities and gave police officers unfettered powers to control the movement of people. The police often abused street vendors, people who were simply outside to get essentials such as groceries and even doctors travelling for essential work. The police subjected those who violated lockdown restrictions to extra-judicial punishments such as forcing them to crawl on the street.[37]

3.2 A Dysfunctional Legislature

The executive monopoly was aided by a deliberate lack of legislative scrutiny. The number of sitting days of the Parliament had already seen a general decline before the pandemic.[38] But the pandemic made it convenient for the executive to suspend or shorten parliamentary sessions altogether. Usually, the Parliament sits in three sessions in a year. In March 2020, the session was cut short. The second session in September was prematurely interrupted. The last session of the year was suspended altogether, citing the pandemic, in spite of demands from members from the opposition.[39] No possibilities for virtual, reduced capacity or short-term sessions were explored, setting a dangerous precedent to suspend parliamentary sessions at the whim of the executive.

Even for the short duration for which the Parliament assembled, laws were passed practically without deliberation. The demands of the opposition to send Bills to committees and for individual voting were denied. In September 2020, two important laws – with far-reaching consequences for the agricultural sector and labour market – were passed without discussion.[40] The former was proposed to transform the agricultural sector and the latter was justified as a move to revive the labour sector from the economic problems posed by the pandemic. Both laws saw serious opposition from those affected; in fact, the labour codes were passed in the absence

36 Anisha Sircar, 'India's Coronavirus Lockdown Is Bringing Out the Worst in its Police Force' (*Quartz India,* 28 March 2020) <https://qz.com/india/1826387/indias-coronavirus-lockdown-brings-police-brutality-to-the-fore/>.

37 This paragraph is based on Raj (n 34).

38 Chakshu Roy, 'Explained: A Look at How and When Parliament is Convened' (*The Indian Express*, 23 December 2019) <https://indianexpress.com/article/explained/parliament-winter-session-lok-sabha-rajya-sabha-7107893/>.

39 'Covid Can't Be an Excuse to Avoid Assembly of Parliament' (*The Indian Express*, 12 January, 2021) <https://indianexpress.com/article/opinion/columns/winter-session-coronavirus-pandemic-budget-session-7142415/>.

40 Arathy R Jerath, 'Farm, Labour Bills Passed: Is This "End" of Parliamentary Debate?' (*The Quint*, 25 September, 2020) <https://www.thequint.com/voices/opinion/modi-govt-bjp-farm-bills-labour-bills-passed-rajya-sabha-parliamentary-affairs-dissent-democracy#read-more>.

of opposition members of parliament, who boycotted the session.[41] The farm laws were passed despite protests by the opposition that the required voting procedure, as specified by the Parliament's own rules, had not been followed in the upper chamber. The government's majority in the upper chamber was unclear given that smaller coalition partners had resigned from the coalition to oppose the farm bills.[42]

3.3 Limited Judicial Review

The Supreme Court's passive and deferential response to executive action is remarkable. The evasive approach of the Supreme Court has emerged in recent years: As I have argued elsewhere, "three distinct and recurrent tactics of evasion" can be identified.[43] First, when the court is called upon to decide on a matter, it refuses to give orders either way and chooses an indefinite adjournment. Second, the court defers to the executive when asked to answer legal questions, leaving it to decide on the validity of its own actions. Third, the court accepts the executive's version of events unquestioningly and closes cases without assigning substantial reasons.[44] During the pandemic, this trend became even more visible, leaving the executive's monopoly on power unchecked.

Prominent cases reached the Supreme Court concerning personal liberty, free speech and political assembly, but the court stayed aloof from rights adjudication in most cases. Activists, authors, student leaders and politicians were charged under anti-terrorism laws during and after the lockdown,[45] yet the court took a hands-off approach from interfering[46] or granting bail.[47] Constitutional challenge against labour laws passed during the pandemic was dismissed at the outset. Public trust in the court saw a significant decline,[48] arguably second only to its attitude during the national emergency in the 1970s.

41 'Parliament Passes Labour Bills Amid Boycott' (*The Hindu*, 23 September 2020) <https://www.thehindu.com/news/national/parliament-passes-three-key-labour-reform-bills/article32675729.ece>.

42 Shoaib Daniyal, 'Dubious Voice Vote to Pass Critical Farm Bills Severely Dents Indian democracy' (*Scroll.in*, 20 September 2020) <https://scroll.in/article/973588/use-of-a-dubious-voice-vote-to-pass-critical-farm-bills-severely-dents-indian-democracy>.

43 Thulasi K Raj, 'Helpless Spectators: How the Supreme Court Evades Administration of Justice' (*The Caravan*, 1 November 2020) <https://caravanmagazine.in/commentary/helpless-spectators>.

44 This paragraph is based on Raj, ibid.

45 Samir Yasir and Kai Schultz, 'India Rounds Up Critics Under Shadow of Virus Crisis, Activists Say' (*The New York Times*, 19 July 2020) <https://www.nytimes.com/2020/07/19/world/asia/india-activists-arrests-riots-coronavirus.html>.

46 'Bhima Koregaon Case: SC Denies Relief, asks Accused Gautam Navlakha and Anand Teltumbde to Surrender to Jail Authorities in a Week' (*Financial Express*, 8 April 2020)<https://www.financialexpress.com/india-news/bhima-koregaon-case-sc-denies-relief-asks-acused-gautam-navlakha-and-anand-teltumbde-to-surrender-to-jail-authorities-in-a-week/1922793/>.

47 'SC Refuses to Entertain Bail Plea by Activist Sudha Bharadwaj in Elgar Parishadi-Bhima Koregaon Case' (*The Indian Express*, 24 September, 2020) <https://indianexpress.com/article/india/sc-refuses-to-entertain-bail-plea-by-activist-sudha-bharadwaj-in-elgar-case-6608977/>.

48 Dushyant Dave, 'Credibility of Supreme Court Has Come Under Serious Threat' (*The Wire*, 13 November 2017) <https://thewire.in/law/supreme-court-judiciary>.

3.4 *Decline of Federalism*

The pandemic also saw concentration of powers at the central level, even when states were equipped to deal with the pandemic. For example, the powers exercised under the Disaster Management Act were made uniformly applicable and binding on all states. The states, with localised administration and better competence, were not given sufficient autonomy in decision-making. This led to conflict between the policies of the central and state governments. Moreover, the executive sought minimal or no involvement of the state representatives in taking significant decisions. For example, the prime minister decided to impose the initial lockdown in early 2020 without prior consultation with either key ministries, experts or the states.[49]

The shift in federal relations also deserves mention. At the beginning of the pandemic, the centre monopolised decision-making in matters of pandemic policy, leaving little for the state to regulate. After a year, however, by which time India was among the nations with the highest number of infections, the central government abdicated its responsibilities. For instance, it refrained from procuring vaccines and left it entirely for states and companies. As a result, state governments were left directly responsible for their vaccine procurement without any mechanism to do so and without the protection of price controls, which had been removed by the executive, allowing vaccine makers to sell them on the open market.[50] Until June 2021, India's vaccination policy was inequitable, with differential pricing which means that vaccines were sold at different prices to the Union and state governments, making it costlier for the latter. This vaccine policy was changed later where the Union agreed to centralised procurement, in response to widespread criticism.

4. Suppression of Civil Liberties

The pandemic period also saw serious curbs on civil liberties. Critics of the government or the ruling party were vilified and often criminally prosecuted. The repression was indiscriminate among politicians, academics, student leaders and writers. A policy of projecting a positive image of the government was prioritised above other concerns.

4.1 *Defusing Political Mobilisation*

In late 2019, the Indian Parliament passed the Citizenship Amendment Act granting citizenship to "illegal migrants" from certain neighbouring countries based on their religion. The law enumerated specific religious communities and excluded

49 'India Covid-19: PM Modi "Did Not Consult Before Lockdown"' (*BBC News*, 29 March 2021) <https://www.bbc.com/news/world-asia-india-56561095>.

50 Prabir Purkayastha, 'New Delhi Centralized Power but Blamed the States and Abdicated its Responsibility' (*National Herald*, 27 April 2021) <https://www.nationalheraldindia.com/opinion/new-delhi-centralised-power-but-blamed-the-states-and-abdicated-its-responsibility>.

Muslims, who were thus not eligible for citizenship, although there was no express singling out of Muslims in the law.[51] The Act was criticised as a measure to implement the Hindu nationalist ideology of the current government against the constitutional guarantees of secularism and non-discrimination.

Widespread protests broke out in various parts of the country against this law. The outbreak of the COVID-19 pandemic, however, put an abrupt end to the protests and presented a convenient opportunity for the government to distract the public from these concerns. This was one of the most disastrous consequences of the epidemic – it put dissent to rest and neutralised political movements. Making things worse, in February 2020, Delhi, the national capital, witnessed horrific riots mainly targeted at Muslim residents and often aided by the police.[52] Protests against the violence and support for the victims was cut short by the lockdown only one month later. This suppression aided the executive to also arrest journalists,[53] politicians and students. Many of those who criticised the Hindutva ideology were met with criminal charges. Participants in the protests against the citizenship law were targeted as well. The restrictions on assembly and freedom of movement made political mobilisation against the government repression almost impossible.

4.2 The Right to Dissent

Opposition leaders who condemned the government's handling of the pandemic were accused of not being united in the country's fight against the disease.[54] Constructive proposals and suggestions about health policy were dismissed. Health experts and economists widely criticised how India dealt with the crisis, from the unnecessarily harsh lockdown in 2020,[55] to the unequal vaccination policy in 2021. But the government continued to reject expert opinions on disease management. Writer Ramachandra Guha deplored the prime minister's "suspicion of experts and expertise" and his "explicit contempt for education".[56]

51 'Citizenship (Amendment) Act 2019: What Is It and Why Is It Seen as a Problem' (*The Economic Times*, 31 December 2019) <https://economictimes.indiatimes.com/news/et-explains/citizenship-amendment-bill-what-does-it-do-and-why-is-it-seen-as-a-problem/articleshow/72436995.cms?from=mdr>.

52 Amit Pandey and Shahid Tantrey, 'Hate Speech – A Hindu Rioter Speaks: Delhi Violence Was "Revenge" Against Muslims, Police Gave Free Reign' (*The Caravan*, 31 July 2020) <https://caravanmagazine.in/crime/delhi-rioter-testimony-hindu-revenge-muslims-police-free-reign>.

53 Mahtab Alam, 'Attacked, Arrested, Left Without Recourse: How 2020 Was for India's Journalists' (*The Wire*, 26 December 2020) <https://thewire.in/media/journalists-arrested-press-freedom-2020>.

54 Smriti Kak Ramachandran 'Covid-19: BJP Accuses Rahul Gandhi of Falsehood' (*Hindustan Times*, 27 May 2021) <https://www.hindustantimes.com/india-news/covid-19-bjp-accuses-rahul-gandhi-of-falsehood/story-1lcvrb2q8sSaBN75EgMilN.html>.

55 Prasad (n 13).

56 Karan Thapar, 'Modi's Leadership Main Reason for COVID Mishandling, He's a Megalomaniac: Ramachandra Guha' (*The Wire*, 20 April 2021) <https://thewire.in/government/watch-karan-thapar-ramachandra-guha-narendra-modi-covid-19-megalomaniac>.

The Indian government has now become infamous for its intolerance of accurate reporting and criticism. At the beginning of the pandemic, the prime minister told the owners of India's main media outlets that it was important to "tackle the spread of pessimism, negativity and rumour" implicitly discouraging them from objective reporting.[57] Journalists who made investigative reports were arrested or charged under the criminal law.[58] Citizens who put up posters opposing the government's vaccine export despite chronic domestic shortage were arrested.[59]

In April 2021, the government ordered social media platforms such as Twitter and Facebook to block content critical of government policy on the pandemic.[60] Twitter complied with the request to remove around 50 critical tweets.[61] The government sought to normalise press censorship and justified these infringements on speech on vague 'public order' grounds.[62] Both social media platforms and persons were victimised when reporting on lack of oxygen supplies or hospital beds.

In addition, the government was continuously engaged in putting forward a positive narrative through suppression. The Minister of External Affairs asked Indian ambassadors and high commissioners across the globe to "counter the one-sided narrative in international media" against the government's COVID-19 management policy.[63] When *The Australian* criticised the government's engagement with the crisis, the Indian High Commission wrote to the newspaper accusing it of publishing "completely baseless, malicious and slanderous" content.[64] When

57 Sagar, 'Speaking Positivity to Power' *(The Caravan*, 31 March 2020)<https://caravanmagazine.in/media/hours-before-lockdown-modi-asked-print-media-owners-editors-refrain-negative-covid-coverage>.

58 'How India's Government Tries to Suppress All Covid-19 Reporting' *(Reporters Without Borders*, 12 April 2020) <https://rsf.org/en/news/how-indias-government-tries-suppress-all-covid-19-reporting>.

59 Rohin Kumar, 'Anger in India over Arrests for Posters Asking Modi about Vaccine' (*Al Jazeera*, 18 May 2021) <https://www.aljazeera.com/news/2021/5/18/anger-in-india-over-arrests-for-posters-asking-modi-about-vaccine>.

60 Newley Purnell, 'India Accused of Censorship for Blocking Social Media Criticism Amid Covid Surge' (*The Wall Street Journal*, 26 April 2021) <https://www.wsj.com/articles/india-accused-of-censorship-for-blocking-social-media-criticism-amid-covid-surge-11619435006>.

61 'At Government Request, Twitter Takes Down Some Tweets Critical of Official COVID Handling' (*The Wire*, 24 April 2021) <https://thewire.in/tech/as-covid-19-crisis-deepens-twitter-takes-down-tweets-criticising-modi-government>.

62 Murali Krishnan, 'COVID: Why is India Censoring Media During Public Health Crisis?' (*Deutsche Welle*, 27 April 2021) <https://www.dw.com/en/covid-why-is-india-censoring-media-during-public-health-crisis/a-57353096>.

63 Nirupama Subramanian, 'Counter "One-Sided" World Media Narrative on Govt's Pandemic "Failure", Jaishankar tells Indian Diplomats' (*The Indian Express*, 30 April 2021) <https://indianexpress.com/article/india/counter-one-sided-world-media-narrative-on-govts-pandemic-failure-jaishankar-tells-indian-diplomats-7296036/>.

64 'Indian High Commission slams The Australian "Viral Apocalypse" report on COVID-19,' (*National Herald*, 27 April 2021) <https://www.nationalheraldindia.com/india/indian-high-commission-slams-the-australian-viral-apocalypse-report-on-covid-19>.

a ruling party member's tweet was flagged by Twitter as "manipulated media", its offices in the national capital were raided by the police.[65]

5. Reckless Management

In January 2021, the Prime Minister prematurely proclaimed that the country had "saved humanity from a big disaster by containing corona effectively".[66] However, instead of containing it, the government's reckless management multiplied the spread. It allowed mass gatherings without social distancing or precautions and was irresponsible in making adequate arrangements. The COVID-19 task force constituted by the central government in April 2020 failed to meet for several months after the first wave of the virus. The government showed criminal negligence in failing to take effective preparatory measures to contain another wave, in spite of having enough time. The government allowed the gathering of around nine million pilgrims for a Hindu religious festival called the 'Kumbh Mela' in April 2021. The event, unsurprisingly, turned to be a 'superspreader' of the pandemic, with thousands of attendees turning out to be COVID-19 positive. Critics said that Narendra Modi's reluctance to cancel the gathering was due to a possible backlash from Hindu religious leaders, who play an important role in mobilising Hindu votes during elections.[67] Similarly, the government exercised no restraint in organising large rallies for the elections to the state legislative assemblies. The prime minister himself led and encouraged such demonstrations.[68]

India's vaccine procurement and rollout also suffers from serious drawbacks. The lack of adequate vaccine orders with the manufacturers led to a vaccine shortage, while in February 2021, the government rejected the application by Pfizer for emergency use authorisation in India.[69] A significant order of 110 million doses for Covishield, the Indian version of the AstraZeneca vaccine, were only placed in April 2021.[70] The vaccine policy was aimed at fostering national pride rather

65 'Twitter Gets Police Visit After Agreeing With Congress that BJP Leader Used "Manipulated Media"' (*The Wire*, 24 May 2021) <https://thewire.in/tech/delhi-police-twitter-office-raid-sambit-patra-toolkit>.

66 Jeffery Gettleman et al., 'India's Coronavirus Crisis Tarnishes Modi's Image of Strength' (*The Seattle Times*, 1 May 2021) <https://www.seattletimes.com/nation-world/indias-coronavirus-crisis-tarnishes-modis-image-of-strength/>.

67 Geeta Pandey, 'India Covid: Kumbh Mela Pilgrims Turn into Super-spreaders' (*BBC News*, 10 May 2021).

68 'PM Modi Under Fire for Campaigning as India Reels from Covid Deaths' (*The Times of India*, 19 April 2021) <https://timesofindia.indiatimes.com/india/pm-modi-under-fire-for-campaigning-as-india-reels-from-covid-deaths/articleshow/82139423.cms>.

69 'Pfizer Covid Vaccine Not Recommended For Emergency Use "At This Stage": Expert Panel' (*NDTV*, 5 February 2021) <https://www.ndtv.com/india-news/expert-panel-had-rejected-emergency-use-to-pfizer-covid-vaccine-report-2364000>.

70 Manavi Kapur, 'The Indian Government Has Ordered its Vaccine Doses in Fits and Starts' (*Quartz India*, 6 May 2021) <https://qz.com/india/2005290/how-many-covishield-and-covaxin-doses-has-india-ordered/>.

than saving the most lives; while Pfizer's application was denied, the government allowed marketing of homegrown vaccines such as Covaxin before it had conducted phase three trials. As of May 2021, this vaccine had been approved neither by most other countries nor by the World Health Organisation but was being administered to thousands of Indians.

6. Conclusion

India paid a heavy price for the absence of transparency, unchecked executive action, reckless management and curtailing human rights. In their seminal work on famines and democracy, Amartya Sen and Jean Drèze point out that independent India has never seen a famine because democratic pressures push governments into action to prevent acute deprivation.[71] This success is based on transparency, democratic checks and balances, and free debate. The weakening of these pillars during the pandemic has led to crisis in India.

A major lesson of the COVID-19 pandemic for India, then, is to take deliberation and accountability seriously. The government must recognise the significance of transparency in governance. It is imperative to ensure that the regulatory systems such as parliamentary deliberation, judicial review of the executive and the federal structure are revived. Preservation of human rights is significant, and so are informal norms including public consultation and dialogue, respect for opposition and tolerance for dissent. India is already sliding away from its democratic set up and the need to reclaim it is vital.

71 Jean Dreze and Amartya Sen, *Hunger and Public Action* (Oxford University Press 1991).

13

DEALING WITH THE PANDEMIC AND SOCIAL UNREST

A Stress Test for Colombian Institutions

Julián Gaviria-Mira and Esteban Hoyos-Ceballos

1. Introduction[1]

The COVID-19 pandemic posed profound challenges to the Colombian constitutional system. This chapter reviews the main events that marked the institutional response to the pandemic and the implications that this response had for the Colombian constitutional system.[2] This analysis is complex because the pandemic was compounded by a pre-existing economic and social crisis that led, in turn, to social turmoil in Colombia.[3] The pandemic aggravated some of the country's historical social problems and deepened inequalities.[4] It also revealed the incapacity of the Colombian ruling class to address most of these issues. Therefore, the pandemic pushed people to retake the streets to demand social and economic rights,

1 All websites accessed on 8 August 2021.

2 This chapter is based on: Julián Gaviria-Mira and Esteban Hoyos-Ceballos, 'Pandemic and Executive Powers in Colombia: A Problem and a Modest Proposal' (*Verfassungsblog*, 17 April 2020)<https://verfassungsblog.de/pandemic-and-executive-powers-in-colombia-a-problem-and-a-modest-proposal/>; Esteban Hoyos-Ceballos and Julián Gaviria-Mira, 'Dealing with the Pandemic: A Stress Test for Colombian Political Institutions' (*Verfassugsblog*, 5 March 2021) <https://verfassungsblog.de/dealing-with-the-pandemic-a-stress-test-for-colombian-political-institutions/>.

3 Sandra Botero and Silvia Otero Bahamón, 'Colombia Is Having its Largest Wave of Protests in Recent Decades. Why?' (*The Washington Post*, 5 December 2019)<https://www.washingtonpost.com/politics/2019/12/05/colombia-is-having-its-largest-wave-protests-recent-decades-why/>.

4 National Administrative Department of Statistics (DANE), 'Pobreza y Desigualdad' (29 April 2021) <https://www.dane.gov.co/index.php/estadisticas-por-tema/pobreza-y-condiciones-de-vida/pobreza-y-desigualdad/>.

 DOI: 10.4324/9781003211952-15

especially for the youngest and the poorest, and the fulfilment of the social pact within the Colombian Constitution.[5]

The argument advanced in this chapter is that the institutional response to the pandemic, as well as to the social mobilisation that accompanied it, has been framed within an authoritarian drift in Colombia. Under this drift, the President of the Republic, Iván Duque, exceeded his executive powers. The executive unjustifiably restricted freedoms and fundamental rights by means of public order ordinary decrees. Most of these decrees eluded judicial and political controls given their ordinary character. Curfews and other restrictions on mobility were common and poorly justified. The Colombian national police also abused their powers to enforce restrictive measures to control both the pandemic and social mobilisation. All of the above was compounded by a weak system of checks and balances, which was not up to the challenge of stopping excessive executive actions. In sum, the public health and social crises were poorly confronted with public order and security measures rather than the required economic and social interventions.

Section 2 examines the social grievances prior to the arrival of the pandemic, while section 3 tracks the initial authoritarian response to it. Section 4 focuses on the weakness of the system of judicial and political checks and balances in dealing with the institutional response to the pandemic. Section 5 examines the problems of the supposedly independent supervisory organs which became captured by the executive before and during the pandemic. Section 6 examines the state's failure to address the impact of the pandemic on economic and social rights, while section 7 explores what lies ahead for Colombia after the institutional stress and social dislocation produced by COVID-19.

2. The Pre-Pandemic Context

Discussion about the pandemic in Colombia must take into account the particularities of the Colombian political and constitutional system, within the wider context of the economic situation of the country and the social crisis that had been brewing over the previous few years. The accumulation of problems became manifest in the events that occurred at the end of 2019, a few months before the arrival of the pandemic, when several demonstrations took place throughout the country.[6] People demanded, among other things, adequate funding of the public education system, as well as the protection of social leaders who had been targeted for assassination in several parts of the country after the signing of the peace agreement between the Colombian Government and the former guerrilla group FARC in 2016. In the midst of these protests, in November 2019, a high school

5 'The Riots in Colombia Hint at Deep Problems' (*The Economist*, 22 May 2021)<https://www.economist.com/the-americas/2021/05/22/the-riots-in-colombia-hint-at-deep-problems>.

6 Steven Grattan, 'Colombia Protests: What Prompted Them and Where Are They Headed? (*Al Jazeera*, 26 November 2019) <https://www.aljazeera.com/news/2019/11/26/colombia-protests-what-prompted-them-and-where-are-they-headed>.

student, Dilan Cruz, was killed by a member of the Colombian Riot Police Force. His death galvanised the protesters and added the rejection of police brutality to their grievances.[7]

In response to the mobilisations, the government called for a national dialogue to address social demands. This dialogue did not produce any visible results and proved frustrating for the protesters. A few months later, once COVID-19 arrived in Colombia, the protests went into hibernation and the institutional response to the pandemic began. This response was flawed from the beginning. Not only were the pandemic containment measures insufficient, but the chosen constitutional mechanisms were also dubious. In addition, only a very limited social protection plan was implemented.

The Colombian government adopted as its main control measure the confinement of the population. Although in general terms the population complied with these measures, the high rates of informal labour made it impossible for everyone to remain confined during the strict quarantine period. The quarantines decreed by the government placed the population under a great deal of pressure. The isolation that these measures entailed added to the existing economic crisis, pushing millions of people into poverty (as discussed in section 6). Before the pandemic, about 92% of Colombian households reported eating three meals a day; by May 2021, that number had fallen to 63%.[8]

In the midst of this panorama, the national government decided to promote a tax law reform that was taken by the general population as an attack on their already precarious situation.[9] The cycle of mobilisations, dormant for more than a year, revived. Thousands of people took to the streets on 28 April 2021. The government was forced to withdraw the tax reform that had generated the protests, but the social mobilisation – contained for so long – continued. The levels of police brutality used to control the protests were also exacerbated. In early June, Human Rights Watch reported at least 34 deaths in the context of the protests, of whom 20 "[appeared] to have been killed by the police".[10] A further 419 people had been reported missing, although the Attorney General's Office claimed to have found 304 of them in detention. As the next section explores, the arrival of the pandemic exposed longstanding economic and social problems and placed strain on Colombia's already fragile constitutional system.

7 'Dilan Cruz, Colombian Teenager Injured by Police Projectile, Dies' (*BBC News*, 26 November 2019) <https://www.bbc.com/news/world-latin-america-50557496>.

8 DANE, 'Encuesta Pulso Social' (May 2021) <https://www.dane.gov.co/index.php/estadisticas-por-tema/encuesta-pulso-social>.

9 Manuel Rueda, 'More Protests in Colombia as Government Unveils New Tax Plan' (*The Washington Post*, 20 July 2021) <https://www.washingtonpost.com/world/more-protests-in-colombia-as-government-unveils-new-tax-plan/2021/07/20/fd7b7b06-e9a1-11eb-a2ba-3be31d349258_story.html>.

10 Human Rights Watch, 'Colombia: Egregious Police Abuses Against Protesters' (9 June 2021) <https://www.hrw.org/news/2021/06/09/colombia-egregious-police-abuses-against-protesters>.

3. The Drift Towards Authoritarianism

Colombia's constitutional design has the dual purpose of establishing institutions that make the exercise of power possible, while creating an intricate network of relations between these established powers that allow for mutual control. The system works properly if power can be exercised and controlled effectively, so that citizens' rights and freedoms are protected. It is precisely this network of relationships that was weakened during the pandemic, a situation that led to an authoritarian drift in Colombia. Unfortunately, the pandemic and the response to the social outburst led to a concentration of power in the executive branch,[11] in a political system in which the balance of powers was already precarious, being characterised by a strong 'hyper-presidentialism', an abuse of the powers of exception and the dominance of the president in the legislative process.[12] This was aggravated by the executive's ability to evade constitutional controls along with poor justification of decisions that severely restricted fundamental rights.

The crisis generated by COVID-19 was undoubtedly an emergency. It demanded rapid action to deal with a pandemic for which little information was available and amid ever-changing conditions. The branch of government that was best placed to lead the pandemic response was the executive; the national government, with its decision-making apparatus concentrated in a few hands, had the possibility to assume extraordinary legislative powers, as well as budgetary control and technical and bureaucratic sufficiency. However, this process was not without problems.

As soon as the crisis began, under Article 215 of the Colombian National Constitution, the government declared a State of Economic, Social and Ecological Emergency,[13] which authorised it to issue legislative decrees that had the same legal status as laws enacted by Congress. In just a few months, President Iván

11 Roberto Gargarella, 'La Sala de Máquinas durante la Emergencia' (*Agenda Estado de Derecho*, 17 June 2021) <https://agendaestadodederecho.com/la-sala-de-maquinas-durante-la-emergencia/>.

12 Mauricio García Villegas and Rodrigo Uprimny-Yepes, '¿Controlando la excepcionalidad permanente en Colombia? Una defensa prudente del control judicial de los estados de excepción', Documentos de Discusión de 'DJS' Documento No 1 (Dejusticia, November 2005)<http://www.dejusticia.org/files/r2_actividades_recursos/fi_name_recurso.198.pdf. Revisado el 30 de marzo de 2019>; Mercedes García Montero, 'Presidentes y parlamentos: ¿quién controla la actividad legislativa en América Latina?' (Centro de Investigaciones Sociológicas 2009) and Ana Catalina Arango 'Mutaciones del presidencialismo. La transformación del poder presidencial en Colombia (1974–2018)' (2019) 17(2) Estudios Constitucionales 91.

13 Colombian Legislative National Decree 417 (17 March 2020) <https://dapre.presidencia.gov.co/normativa/normativa/DECRETO%20417%20DEL%2017%20DE%20MARZO%20DE%202020.pdf>. The Colombian Constitution provides for three states of exception: a state of internal commotion, a state of external war and a state of economic and social emergency. The particularity of the state of economic emergency is that the decrees adopted by the government are permanent (as opposed to the state of internal commotion, in which case the decrees remain in force only for the duration of the state of exception).

Duque issued 115 such legislative decrees[14] as part of the emergency legislation, a remarkable number considering that, in those few months, more legislative decrees were issued than in the entire previous decade. These legislative decrees were not the only constitutionally relevant decrees promulgated during this time. The executive branch adopted the controversial thesis that mass confinements – which involved strong restrictions on a multitude of rights – could be ordered through ordinary decrees, which were issued as the result of the regular exercise of police powers.[15]

4. Checks and Balances: Judicial and Political Inaction

The first image left by the pandemic in Colombia, at least from a constitutional point of view, was that of an executive exercising enormous normative powers which entailed strong restrictions of constitutional rights and liberties. Theoretically, this should have provoked an equally energetic action on the part of those other constitutionally authorised powers which have the important function of controlling the executive. One could say, following a well-known quote, that defence "must in this, as in all other cases, be made commensurate to the danger of attack".[16] Such control would include political scrutiny exercised by Congress, as well as control exercised by the judicial branch. However, this is not what happened in Colombia during the pandemic.

To start with, Congress played a secondary role in attending to the crisis and in controlling the national government. This is explained, at least in part, by the fact that at the beginning of the crisis there was intense discussion about the possibility that Congress could meet virtually, even though the rules of procedure of Congress did not expressly provide for such an eventuality. The debate was resolved and Congress began holding virtual sessions, but there were repeated complaints from some minority political parties[17] because they considered that virtual sessions precluded deliberation and the effective exercise of political control.[18] Consequently, there was a strong demand to resume in-person or mixed sessions. In the midst of this discussion, Congress neither exercised rigorous political control over the decrees issued by the President, nor approved relevant laws to control

14 Colombian Constitutional Court Report about Control of Executive Decrees during the Pandemic (7 December 2020) <https://www.corteconstitucional.gov.co/micrositios/estado-de-emergencia/estadisticas.php>.

15 Gaviria-Mira and Hoyos-Ceballos (n 2).

16 James Madison, 'Federalist Papers No. 51' (1788) <https://billofrightsinstitute.org/primary-sources/federalist-no-51>.

17 María José Pizarro, 'Nos Están Prohibiendo el Derecho Legítimo a Estar en el Congreso' (*El Espectador*, 7 May 2020) <https://www.elespectador.com/politica/nos-estan-prohibiendo-el-derecho-legitimo-a-estar-en-el-congreso-maria-jose-pizarro-article-918412/>.

18 At the local level, city councils and state assemblies moved to virtual sessions quickly, but their political control over local leaders was weak and mostly ineffective. This was significant, considering that many of the most restrictive measures that affected citizens directly were taken by local leaders.

the pandemic and its effects.[19] Meanwhile, the executive branch continued to issue decrees on various matters and to avoid discussion of its agenda in the legislature.

In the case of the judicial branch, the weakness in control may be explained by the volume and diversity of governmental decrees issued to control the pandemic. The Constitutional Court, for example, had to review the 115 legislative decrees mentioned above. While attending to this enormous task, the Court had to continue to fulfil its other constitutional functions in matters relating to the protection of fundamental rights and the judicial review of legislation.[20] The government's defeats before the Constitutional Court were partial. The most invasive measures against citizens' rights, which were the mandatory isolation decrees, were not even studied by the Constitutional Court.[21]

But the extraordinary legislative decrees were not the only ones issued by the national government. An immense number of decisions were adopted through ordinary decrees and resolutions. Among them were the decrees that ordered the mandatory preventive isolation of the entire population, a measure that most seriously affected the rights and freedoms of citizens. As these were ordinary decrees, the Council of State (*Consejo de Estado*), Colombia's highest administrative court, refrained from exercising automatic control over them and many of these decrees ended up not being subject to effective judicial control.

The lack of review of the executive branch's decisions had serious consequences. Both at the national and local levels, the main (and at times it seemed only) tool for controlling the pandemic was to regulate social interaction. To achieve this, the different levels of government severely restricted citizens' rights, often taking measures that seemed arbitrary or of dubious constitutionality. Constitutional democracy requires that power be exercised in accordance with the limits established by the Constitution itself. The reasonableness of the measures is not merely desirable, but something that the system itself demands. Rigorous judicial control over measures for which, at the very least, a justification should have been presented, was glaringly absent.

A notable exception to the weak judicial control of executive decisions can be found in the important (though solitary) ruling of the Bogotá Circuit Administrative Judge, Edith Alarcón-Bernal, who ruled in favour of a group of petitioners over 70 years of age.[22] In one of its decrees, the national government

19 'Un Congreso muy Regular: el Balance del Legislativo en el 2020' (*Semana*, 18 December 2020) <https://www.semana.com/nacion/articulo/un-congreso-muy-regular-el-balance-del-legislativo-en-el-2020/202049/>.

20 This is under article 241 of the Colombian National Constitution.

21 Juan Esteban Lewin, 'El examen de la Corte a los decretos de la emergencia crea un polémico precedente' (*La Silla Vacia,* 2 November 2020) <https://www.lasillavacia.com/historias/silla-nacional/el-examen-de-la-corte-a-los-decretos-de-emergencia-crea-un-polemico-precedente/>.

22 Esteban Hoyos-Ceballos and Rodrigo Uprimny-Yepes, 'Separated, Locked Down, and Unequal: The Grey Hair Revolution's Resistance to Draconian Quarantine in Colombia' (*Oxford Human Rights Hub*, 14 August 2020) <https://ohrh.law.ox.ac.uk/separated-locked-down-and-unequal-the-grey-hair-revolutions-resistance-to-draconian-quarantine-in-colombia/>.

had decided to severely restrict the mobility of older people, arguing that they were more susceptible to complications arising from the disease.[23] In her decision,[24] Judge Alarcón-Bernal concluded that although the objective set by the government was a legitimate one, the measures taken by the executive were disproportionate, discriminatory, inefficient and violated the petitioners' human dignity. This ruling, which was later upheld by the Administrative Tribunal of Cundinamarca,[25] was one of the few decisions that provided an effective counterweight to the decisions of the executive branch during the pandemic.

5. Checks and Balances: Metastatic Colonisation by the Executive

The increase in the executive's power did not occur exclusively as a consequence of the exercise of emergency powers. The government, in particular the president, has had the ability to dominate various spheres in which, in theory, independent powers should operate. Before the pandemic, President Duque appointed Francisco Barbosa, his former advisor, university classmate and personal friend, as Colombia's Attorney General. In the midst of the pandemic, he managed to have Margarita Cabello, his former Minister of Justice, elected Inspector General of Colombia, a role that involves overseeing the public conduct of officials and the correct functioning of government institutions. Finally, in September 2020, Carlos Ernesto Camargo Assis, also a friend and university classmate of the President, was sworn in as Colombia's National Ombudsperson, the country's national human rights institution.[26]

According to the Constitution, the president is directly involved in the election of all these high-level officials. In the case of the Attorney General, the president has to submit a shortlist of three candidates to the Supreme Court of Justice. For the Ombudsperson's office, the president has to send a shortlist of candidates to the House of Representatives. Finally, in the case of the Inspector General, the Senate chooses from a shortlist of candidates sent by the president, the Supreme Court of

23 These restrictions were established through a series of decrees and resolutions. Among them can be found Resolution 464 of 2020 of the Ministry of Health, Resolution 844 of 2020 Ministry of Health, and Presidential Decrees 749 of 2020 and 847 of 2020.

24 Juzgado 61 Administrativo – Bogotá. Tutela 061. Rudolf Manuel Hommes Rodríguez et. al vs Nación – Departamento Administrativo de la Presidencia de la República et al. Radicación: 110013343-061-2020-00111-00 (2 July 2020)<https://www.ramajudicial.gov.co/documents/7819920/40845311/ArchivoFirmado+%283%29.pdf/291e6ffe-14d0-4e67-b866-25637759e0a5>.

25 Tribunal Administrativo de Cundinamarca. Rudolf Manuel Hommes Rodríguez et al. vs Nación – Departamento Administrativo de la Presidencia de la República et al. Radicación: 110013343-061-2020-00111-00 (10 August 2020) <https://www.scribd.com/document/472157674/FalloSegundaInstanciaTutela061-2020-0111RudolfHommesRodriguezOtros#from_embed>.

26 According to the Constitution, the main function of the Colombian Ombudsperson's Office is to ensure the promotion and protection of human rights. This function is especially important in the case of human rights violations caused by state agents.

Justice and the Council of State. President Duque had the parliamentary majority to ensure the appointment of all these top officials.

The executive's capacity to interfere in these independent supervisory agencies is provided for in the Constitution (something that makes reform desirable, as will be seen below). However, the novelty in this case is due to a confluence of elements. The President, as we have seen, assumed immense power, a power that was not accompanied by the proper controls. This was aggravated by the way in which he exercised his power of appointment. Not only did he nominate people from his political realm, he also appointed people of his trust and, in most cases (as in the case of the Attorney General[27] and the Ombudsperson[28]), people who did not appear to have sufficient professional experience.

The proximity of the Ombudsperson to the government prevented the Ombudsperson's Office from fully fulfilling its role.[29] Neither was there a determined effort by the Attorney General's Office, which leads criminal action in Colombia, to conduct investigations against members of the security forces who had committed crimes in the control of social protest. The Attorney General's Office adopted the government's stigmatising discourse about social protest, which considers it as a criminal and even a terrorist threat.[30] These omissions legally legitimised the abuses by the police (or by private individuals who decided to take up arms against protesters, as in the southwestern city of Cali).[31] Finally, there is the case of the Inspector General, a former official of the Duque government, who did not exercise this function either.[32] All of these incidents of institutional

27 Juanita León and Juan Esteban Lewin, 'Barbosa: un fiscal sin experiencia ni posiciones fuertes, pero sin odios' (*La Silla Vacía*, 31 January 2020) <https://www.lasillavacia.com/historias/silla-nacional/barbosa-un-fiscal-sin-experiencia-ni-posiciones-fuertes-pero-sin-odios/>.

28 The Colombian Council of State (Consejo de Estado) admitted the lawsuit against the election of the Ombudsman Office (3 December 2020) <https://www.consejodeestado.gov.co/news/admitida-la-demanda-de-eleccion-del-defensor-del-pueblo>.

29 'Cuestionan papel del defensor del pueblo en medio de la crisis' (*El Tiempo*, 3 May 2021) <https://www.eltiempo.com/politica/gobierno/protestas-cuestionan-papel-del-defensor-del-pueblo-en-medio-de-la-crisis-585584>.

30 For example, as early as 4 May the Attorney General was already talking about terrorist infiltration of the protests without conducting any serious investigation; Colombia's Attorney General Office, 'Estructuras ligadas al narcotráfico, el ELN y las disidencias de las Farc serían las responsables de actos vandálicos en Cali: Fiscal General de la Nación' (4 May 2021) <https://www.fiscalia.gov.co/colombia/fiscal-general-de-la-nacion/estructuras-ligadas-al-narcotrafico-el-eln-y-las-disidencias-de-las-farc-serian-las-responsables-de-actos-vandalicos-en-cali-fiscal-general-de-la-nacion/>.

31 Joe Parkin Daniels, 'Cali is the Cockpit of Chaos as Colombia Protests Threaten to Spiral Out of Control' (*The Guardian*, 10 May 2021) <https://www.theguardian.com/global-development/2021/may/10/cali-colombia-protests-violence>.

32 Far from questioning the actions of the Colombian security forces in the protests, the first calls of the inspector general were in support of the police; 'Procuraduría envió un mensaje de respaldó a la fuerza pública en el marco de las protestas' (*Infobae*, 15 May 2021)<https://www.infobae.com/america/colombia/2021/05/17/procuraduria-envio-un-mensaje-de-respaldo-a-la-fuerza-publica-en-el-marco-de-las-protestas/e>.

paucity are risky on their own, but they become a serious threat to democracy when taken together.

6. The Economic Crisis Deepens

The pandemic that began in 2019 and that reached Colombia in the first months of 2020 led the nation into a severe economic crisis. The country went from a GDP growth in 2019 of 3.3% to a negative growth in 2020 of –6.8%.[33] According to the Colombian National Administrative Department of Statistics (DANE), from 2019 to 2020, 3.5 million people fell into poverty and 2.78 million into extreme poverty.[34] These figures mean that, as of 2020, 42.5% of the Colombian population was in poverty (an increase of 6.8 points compared to 2019) and about 15% was in extreme poverty (an increase of 5.5 points). In entire regions of the country, such as the departments of Chocó, La Guajira, Córdoba, Magdalena and Cesar, the population in poverty was around 60% and even exceeded this number.[35]

The pandemic deepened severe inequalities in Colombia. Unemployment skyrocketed and disproportionately affected women and young people. In April 2021, the unemployment rate was 15.1% and female unemployment reached 19.9%. Young women between 14 and 28 years of age corresponded to 43.1% of all the unemployed; while young men represented 42.9% of all the unemployed.[36] The pandemic also brought to light the inequality between publicly and privately educated children and young people in Colombia's education system.[37] According to figures from the Ministry of National Education, during the pandemic, 53,717 educational centres were closed; 82% (43,853) in the state sector and 18% (9,866) in the private sector.[38]

Amid these circumstances, social tension grew. To control the ensuing protests, the government tried to use the same strategy it had used in handling the protests of late 2019: a call to a national dialogue. Once again, the dialogue was ineffective due to its lack of methodology and the unrepresentativeness of the protest leaders involved.[39] The arrival of COVID-19 extinguished any remaining impetus for the

33 DANE, 'Producto Interno Bruto – Comunicado de Prensa' (15 February 2021)<https://www.dane.gov.co/files/investigaciones/boletines/pib/cp_PIB_IVtrim20.pdf>.

34 DANE, 'Pobreza y Condiciones de Vida' (29 April 2021) <https://www.dane.gov.co/index.php/estadisticas-por-tema/pobreza-y-condiciones-de-vida/pobreza-monetaria>.

35 ibid.

36 In order to contribute to the protection of the employment of Colombian workers during the COVID-19 health emergency, the national government, through Decree 677 of 2020, created a 'Payroll Subsidy' for employers. This subsidy was insufficient to address the unemployment crisis during the pandemic.

37 Mauricio García-Villegas, Jose Rafael Espinosa, Felipe Jimenez and Juan David Parra, 'Separados y desiguales: Educación y clases sociales en Colombia' (Dejusticia, 2013) 85.

38 Ángel Pérez, 'La pandemia: tragedia para la educación en Colombia' (*Razón Pública*, 12 April 2021) <https://razonpublica.com/la-pandemia-tragedia-la-educacion-colombia/>.

39 'Colombianos protestan y Duque inicia diálogo sin manifestantes' (*Deutsche Welle*, 5 May 2021) <https://www.dw.com/es/colombianos-protestan-y-duque-inicia-di%C3%A1logo-sin-manifestantes/a-57441940>.

government to continue discussions with protest organisers. The pandemic kept the social movement in suspension while the causes of social unrest worsened. Once the social outburst occurred, the government's reaction was to identify it with subversion and delinquency. The reaction of the state security forces was one of 'iron fist' and police excesses. Deaths during protests, disappearances and police abuse became regular news.[40]

The situation became particularly precarious due, on the one hand, to the government's inability and unwillingness to negotiate and, on the other hand, to the President's excessive influence over key institutions responsible for the oversight of an out-of-control police force. Despite the highly questionable actions of the Colombian police, the Ombudsperson's Office and the Inspector General's Office were conspicuous once again by their absence. When, concerned about the situation in Colombia, the Inter-American Commission on Human Rights announced a visit to Colombia, the initial government response was that it could only do so once these two institutions had carried out their investigations.[41] The Duque government showed great confidence in institutions that had shown few results in the investigation of the serious acts of violence that occurred during the protests, a confidence that, given his personal closeness to the officials who run these institutions, can be regarded with suspicion. The protests thus reinforced the authoritarian tendency already shown both by the exercise of the emergency powers and the severe rights restrictions that were the primary mechanism to control the pandemic.

7. What Is Next?

The enormous power exercised by the executive branch and the excesses that marked its response to social protests required a clear line of action from the other branches of government. We have seen, however, that Colombia's institutions were not up to the demands of a constitutional democracy. Yet there are possibilities to deal with the situation. First, Congress has the power to modify the decrees issued by the government through laws, which it has largely failed to do so far, and to exercise more strict political control over executive actions. Further, Congress should enact a law regulating the actions of the authorities when dealing with the pandemic.

In addition, a more active role for the judicial branch is necessary. Effective and reasonable control measures are not out of reach for Colombian judges. The Constitutional Court has shown enormous institutional courage on other

40 A particularly concerning issue is the use of so-called "military assistance", contained in Article 170 of the Colombian Police Code. This legal instrument allows the government to request "in a temporary and exceptional manner the assistance of the military force". The Colombian government requested this assistance for the control of the protests.

41 Sergio Gómez, 'Colombia se niega a aceptar, por ahora, visitas de la CIDH y OEA' (*El Tiempo*, 25 May 2021) <https://www.eltiempo.com/mundo/eeuu-y-canada/gira-de-marta-lucia-ramirez-colombia-no-aceptara-visitas-de-cidh-y-oea-590780>.

occasions,[42] and there is no reason to believe that this is impossible in the circumstances of a pandemic where it is so much required. The Court has at its disposal the important tool of reviewing *tutela* decisions; that is, constitutional complaints allowing citizens harmed by government (and in some cases private) actions in violation of their constitutional rights to sue the authorities.[43] This is no small matter given the restrictions on fundamental rights discussed above.

In the event that new emergencies are declared, as is now requested by some political sectors of the national government in order to deal with the crisis, the Constitutional Court also has the power to exercise automatic and strict control over the decrees issued by the government in accordance with its own jurisprudence. The system of judicial control in Colombia has been robust in the past, and the administrative jurisdiction also has ample powers to exercise control over the legality of administrative acts issued to contain the emergency, which it has so far not exercised sufficiently. Other constitutional judges in the country may also eventually protect the fundamental rights of citizens when their restriction is not clearly justified.

The social outburst unleashed by the pandemic has been, above all, a demand for compliance with the 1991 National Constitution – in particular, the fulfilment of constitutional promises regarding economic and social rights such as health, education and labour rights. However, and this is the call we have advanced together with other academic colleagues,[44] Colombia also needs to deepen local democracy and the mechanisms of citizen participation provided for in the Constitution.[45] The COVID-19 pandemic and the social unrest that preceded and accompanied it have shown that it is not enough for the authorities to make decisions; citizens must be directly involved in decision-making. It is not a matter of seeking constitutional change, but of deepening the participatory tools that the Constitution already provides for the fulfilment of the purposes of the state.

Yet, some legal and constitutional changes are necessary and even urgent. The reform of the police force (which has been, above all, a petition from the streets), is something that cannot wait.[46] Another very important reform would be, as seen in

42 This courage was shown, for example, by limiting the possibility of the re-election of the highly popular President Álvaro Uribe (Sentencia C-141 de 2010) or by demanding that the government adopt a public policy aimed at addressing the crisis caused by internal displacement (Sentencia T-025 de 2004).

43 David Landau, 'The Reality of Social Rights Enforcement' (2012) 53(1) Harvard International Law Journal 402.

44 'Universidades y academia proponemos democracia local frente a la crisis' (*Dejusticia*, 16 May 2021) <https://www.dejusticia.org/universidades-y-academia-proponemos-democracia-local-frente-a-la-crisis/>.

45 The Colombian Constitution is generous in citizen participation mechanisms. It establishes not only the possibility of calling referendums, but also allows for citizen consultations, open-town meetings and plebiscites (Article 103 of the Colombian Constitution).

46 Police reform in Colombia must address, among other issues, prevention, protection and respect for human rights by the security forces and the excessive use of force by the police. Another important issue is the change of location of the police force in the structure of the Colombian

this chapter, the way in which the heads of key supervisory agencies in Colombia are elected. It is unacceptable that the leaders of key institutions in charge of controlling the executive are former high-ranking government officials, without sufficient independence and autonomy to investigate the conduct of public servants who have violated human rights and disregarded the Constitution and national laws. Today, this contribution must insist that the health of the rule of law and protection of human rights in the country has been damaged by this public health and social crisis. At the same time, it is believed here that the Colombian Constitution has the tools and instruments to deal with it.

state government, as it is currently assigned to the Ministry of Defence. This was the position, for instance, of the Inter-American Commission on Human Rights in its working visit to the country: Organization of American States, 'IACHR Completes Working Visit to Colombia and Issues Observations and Recommendations' (7 July 2021) <https://www.oas.org/en/iachr/jsForm/?File=/en/iachr/media_center/preleases/2021/167.asp>.

14

THAILAND'S RESPONSE TO COVID-19

Human Rights in Decline and More Social Turbulence

Khemthong Tonsakulrungruang and Rawin Leelapatana

1. Introduction[1]

Thailand was the first country outside China[2] to detect COVID-19 cases, initially among Chinese tourists, as early as January 2020. The first wave peaked in March and April prompting the government to declare a nationwide emergency and impose a lockdown.[3] As of July 2021, Thailand remains under the emergency law, the 2005 Emergency Decree on Public Administration in Emergency Situation ('the 2005 Decree'), which was invoked on 26 March 2020. For a while, Thailand seemingly had the virus under control, with sporadic minor spikes. But from December 2020, the country faced a second wave and then a third in April 2021.[4] These waves proved highly contagious and have claimed 4,059 lives to date, with Thailand ranked by one authoritative measure as being among the 20 "most

1 All websites accessed on 22 July 2021 unless otherwise stated.

2 For general discussion, see deLisle and Kui, chapter 4.

3 This chapter draws on: Khemthong Tonsakulrungruang and Rawin Leelapatana, 'Health Before Rights and Liberties: Thailand's Response to COVID-19' (*Verfassungsblog*, 8 May 2020)<https://verfassungsblog.de/health-before-rights-and-liberties-thailands-response-to-covid-19/>; Khemthong Tonsakulrungruang and Rawin Leelapatana, 'Breeding More Social Turbulence? Thailand's Unprepared Response to the Second Wave of COVID-19' (*Verfassungsblog*, 23 February 2021)<https://verfassungsblog.de/breeding-more-social-turbulence-thailands-unprepared-response-to-the-second-wave-of-covid-19/>.

4 Sebastian Strangio, 'Thailand Buffeted by Third Wave of COVID-19 Infections' (*The Diplomat*, 12 April 2021) <https://thediplomat.com/2021/04/thailand-buffeted-by-third-wave-of-covid-19-infections/>.

 DOI: 10.4324/9781003211952-16

affected" countries in terms of mortality.[5] Numbers are increasing exponentially and official figures are probably understated.

COVID-19 was more than a public health crisis in Thailand; it had serious implications for the economy and social cohesion. It also exposed underlying socio-political problems and raised concerns over rampant human rights abuses. This chapter argues that the Thai government failed both to understand COVID-19 as a socio-political problem and to approach the crisis from a human rights perspective. A harsh, top-down and authoritarian approach, driven only by the imperative of disease control, in fact hindered the government from preventing subsequent and future waves and forestalled full recovery. The chapter asks two questions: first, why did the Thai government fail to take human rights into consideration when responding to COVID-19, and second, what was the consequence of that failure?

2. The Government's Response to COVID-19

Rather than proposing new legislation specific to COVID-19, the Thai government battled the pandemic using an existing emergency decree. Similar to martial law, the 2005 Decree consolidates all decision-making powers related to an exigency into the hands of the prime minister.[6] Originally, it was enacted to fight against Malay Muslim separatists in Southern Thailand.[7] Several of the powers it confers are vaguely worded and open-ended, thus posing the risk of abuse of power. Rising to his premiership through a military coup in 2014 and heading a military junta until elections in 2019, Prime Minister Prayuth adopted the slogan 'health before rights', indicating his willingness to tackle the pandemic through a "centralised, authoritarian-oriented approach".[8] Prayuth set up the Center for COVID-19 Situation Administration (CCSA) as the main taskforce under his command.[9] As of June 2021, 25 regulations had been issued under s 9 of the 2005 Decree. They imposed key COVID-19 response measures as follows: (i) semi-lockdown measures; (ii) preparedness measures; (iii) travel restrictions and border control; (iv) control of false and fake information; and (v) prophylactic measures. They were imposed, relaxed and re-imposed over time as the situation changed.

5 Johns Hopkins University Coronavirus Resource Center, 'Mortality Analyses' <https://coronavirus.jhu.edu/data/mortality>.

6 The Emergency Decree on Public Administration in Emergency Situation B.E. 2548 (2005), ss 4 and 5.

7 Andrew Harding and Peter Leyland, *The Constitutional System of Thailand: A Contextual Analysis* (Hart 2010) 114–115.

8 Rawin Leelapatana and Chompunoot Tangthavorn, 'Thailand: Emergency Responses or More Social Turbulence?' in Victor V Ramraj (ed), *Covid-19 in Asia: Law and Policy Contexts* (Oxford University Press 2021) 166.

9 PM Order 6/2563 (27 March 2020).

2.1 Semi-Lockdown Measures

The government initially adopted a centralised, 'one-size-fits-all' lockdown to tackle the first wave but showed greater caution after experiencing its devastating impact. The responses to the second and third waves were more measured and calibrated. Regulation no. 22 issued on 29 April 2021 re-categorised all COVID-19 zoning areas and measures across the country according to severity. Out of 77 provinces, Bangkok Metropolitan (six provinces, including Bangkok) was classified as a "maximum control area" with 45 provinces declared "high control areas" and the rest "control areas".[10] In all zones, educational institutions were closed, coupled with the strict prohibition of the use of their buildings;[11] social gatherings of more than 50 people were not allowed without the permission of the Bangkok or provincial governors;[12] and selling alcoholic beverages was strictly banned in all restaurants and serving places.[13] The prime minister permitted commercial stores and some essential services to remain open, subject to strict rules on social distancing and sanitation.

2.2 Preparedness Measures

Regulation no. 1, having been enforced since 25 March 2020, implemented several preparedness measures. These included the mandatory wearing of face-masks;[14] the prohibition of profiteering from the selling of face-masks and other protective equipment; the procurement of vaccines and other necessary medicines; and the preparation of quarantine places.[15] University facilities, hotels, private properties and convention centres could also be converted into field hospitals or quarantine places.[16] These measures were reaffirmed by Regulation no. 20 and no. 22 on 16 April and 29 April 2021, respectively.

2.3 Travel Restrictions and Border Control

Although Regulation no. 1 and no. 20 strongly discouraged domestic travelling, allowing police officers and soldiers to set up checkpoints on inter-provincial routes, the government did not ban travelling.[17] Meanwhile, initially, all inbound passengers were required to present a 72-hour medical certificate before boarding an aircraft. Upon arrival, they would be placed under a 14-day mandatory state

10 Regulation no. 22, s 2.
11 Regulation no. 20, s 1(1).
12 Regulation no. 20, s 1(2).
13 Regulation no. 20, ss 4(1)(gor) and 2(2)(gor).
14 Regulation no. 22, s 1.
15 Regulation no. 1, ss 4, 7(3),
16 Regulation no. 20, s 8.
17 Regulation no. 20, s 5.

quarantine.[18] However, since 1 July 2021, the government launched a 'sandbox tourism' model where tourists, with complete vaccination, may visit the island of Phuket and stay at a health-accredited hotel without quarantine.[19]

2.4 *Control of False and Fake Information*

Asserting the necessity to prevent the spread of 'false' or 'fake' COVID-related information which might provoke public fear and chaos, the government prohibited any dissemination of misleading information from 25 March 2020.[20] This measure allowed the CCSA to monopolise the spread of information regarding the virus and vaccinations.

2.5 *Prophylactic Measures*

Several prophylactic measures were introduced to mitigate the contagion. Regulation no. 1 required groups of "vulnerable people", namely people over 70 years of age, children under the age of five and people with chronic non-transmissible conditions, to stay inside their homes with the exception of those seeking medical care, travelling to discharge their duties as medical practitioners or purchasing necessary food.[21] Regulation no. 17, issued on 6 January 2021, urged all citizens to install COVID-19 mobile tracing applications – Mor Chana (Doctor wins) and Thai Chana (Thai wins).[22]

3. The Government's Weakness in Responding to the Health Crisis

Thailand's universal public health system, which provides basic coverage free of charge, is lauded internationally. Medical schools are world-class and a nationwide network of health volunteers helps monitor public health and disseminate information. All these mechanisms explain Thailand's early success in tackling COVID-19 that received praise from the World Health Organisation (WHO).[23] But as the crisis continued, the true extent of damage inflicted upon the populace, economy and society began to emerge and the WHO's praise appeared premature. Prayuth made a series of policy mistakes that resulted in hundreds of new clusters countrywide. Prolonged lockdown and unpredictable relief packages added emotional and economic strains upon the struggling public. Household debt rose significantly

18 'Traveling to Thailand During Covid-19: What You Need to Know Before You Go' (*CNN*, 15 July 2021) <https://edition.cnn.com/travel/article/thailand-travel-covid-19/index.html>.

19 No Quarantine Phuket Sandbox (Thai Embassy, 15 July 2021) <https://www.thaiembassy.com/travel-to-thailand/no-quarantine-phuket-sandbox-plan>.

20 Regulation no. 1, s 6.

21 Regulation no. 1, s 8.

22 Regulation no. 17, s 1.

23 'WHO Praises Thailand for Tackling Bug' (*The Bangkok Post*, 18 December 2020) <https://www.bangkokpost.com/thailand/general/2037147/who-praises-thailand-for-tackling-bug>.

and the suicide rate increased by at least 11%.[24] Meanwhile, Thailand failed to formulate an effective vaccination plan. Yet, the government refused to acknowledge its mishandling. This section examines three major components that contribute to the state's modus operandi.

3.1 Militarised Mentality

Since 2014, Thailand has been under the military (or, since 2019, military-dominated) government of Prayuth Chan-ocha, who ousted the democratically elected government of Yingluck Shinawatra. Despite the holding of elections in 2019, militarisation remains unchanged.[25] Prayuth's cronies, generals of the army, navy and air force, are appointed into every department and state enterprise, as well as political offices such as the Senate and independent agencies. The Secretary of the National Security Council was put in charge of the CCSA.

Militarisation goes beyond the governmental structure into how the government thinks and acts. Prayuth was himself the Army Commander from 2010–2014 and, as an authoritarian ruler, he has shown little respect for democracy and human rights while emphasising national security. Thailand has been described as a praetorian state, due to the long shadow of the military over the civilian government.[26] To justify its entrenchment in Thai society, the army has expanded its understanding of national security beyond conventional threats to include new challenges such as poverty, capitalism and lately the pandemic. The Prayuth administration initially set itself the overly simplistic goal of zero transmission to defeat the new 'public enemy' of COVID-19. The campaign from April to August 2020 was decisive and effective at controlling the spread of the virus, yet devastating as it did not account for the collateral damage caused by a rise in unemployment, business closures and bankruptcies.[27] Prayuth urged all Thais to make a sacrifice for national survival without offering adequate relief.[28] Those who failed to comply with the rules, for whatever reason, were labelled unpatriotic.[29] Migrant workers, especially Burmese and Cambodians, faced discrimination, being forced to quarantine in

24 'Covid-19 Takes Heavy Toll on Employment, Economy: Poll' (*The Bangkok Post*, 21 March 2021) <https://www.bangkokpost.com/thailand/general/2087251/unemployment-caused-by-covid-19-takes-heavy-toll-on-economy-suan-dusit-poll>; 'Suicides Rise in Thailand as Covid Decimates its Tourism Industry' (*The Telegraph*, 14 May 2021) <https://www.telegraph.co.uk/global-health/science-and-disease/suicides-rise-thailand-covid-decimates-tourism-industry/>.

25 Jacob Ricks, 'Thailand's 2019 Vote: The General's Election' (2019) 92 Pacific Affairs 443.

26 Puangthong Pawakapan, *Infiltrating Society: The Thai Military's Internal Security Affairs* (ISEAS-Yusok Ishak Institute 2021) 2–6.

27 Peter Janssen, 'Thailand's Covid Success Turns Economic Failure' (*AsiaTimes*, 14 August 2020) <https://asiatimes.com/2020/08/thailands-covid-success-turns-economic-failure/>.

28 For example, see 'COVID-19 Thailand: Thai PM "We Must Prepare Ourselves"' (*Travel Daily Media*, 23 December 2020) <https://www.traveldailymedia.com/covid-19-thai-pm-we-must-prepare-ourselves/>.

29 'Rash Edicts Spur Chaos at Airport' (*The Bangkok Post*, 5 April 2020) <https://www.bangkokpost.com/opinion/opinion/1893225/rash-edicts-spur-chaos-at-airport>.

factories and on building sites.[30] They were guarded by soldiers and left without enough food or access to proper medical care.

Another trait of the militarised mentality that exacerbated Prayuth's mistakes was the top-down style of decision-making that failed to appreciate the value of public participation. He paid no attention to the public's protest about his unreasonably harsh measures. As shown below, information about a vaccination plan was withheld from public and dissent suppressed, with the result that the government made decisions in an echo chamber of the like-minded. The frustrated public was kept in the dark about the government's next move.

3.2 *Ineffective Bureaucracy*

In addition to the military culture in the government, the bureaucracy, meaning all departments and agencies in the administrative branch, proved itself ineffective at dealing with a new and unforeseen crisis, which required a non-conventional and rapid response.

The cabinet is a fragile coalition, with seats allocated according to political quota rather than expertise, and infighting common. The Minister of Public Health, Anutin Charnvirakul, proved incapable of comprehending the seriousness of the pandemic, publicly lambasting medical personnel without providing any support; yet the politics of the coalition meant that he could not be fired.[31] For its part, the civil service suffers from favouritism. During the military dictatorship era, Prayuth, equipped with ultimate power, bypassed the merit system and appointed civil servants based on their allegiance to the regime. The result is a politicised, broken administration whose interest is in pleasing superiors, not serving the people.[32]

Prayuth's early response to COVID-19 exposed the weaknesses in his administration, which failed to work in unison. He neither issued guidance nor set a common goal for officials to follow. It was only after he invoked the 2005 Decree in late March 2020 that he was able to control the crisis.[33] But the 2005 Decree created its own problem by encouraging a culture of impunity, which is a deeply embedded characteristic of the Thai state.[34] Administrative agencies are risk-averse

30 Nanchanok Wongsamuth, 'Migrant Workers Face Tough Quarantine in Thailand as COVID-19 Cases Surge' (*Thomson Reuters Foundation*, 28 May 2021) <https://news.trust.org/item/20210528152739-huym4/?>.

31 'Anutin Criticises "Careless" Health Personnel, Apologises Again' (*The Bangkok Post*, 26 March 2021) <https://www.bangkokpost.com/thailand/general/1887115/anutin-criticises-careless-health-personnel-apologises-again>.

32 Prajak Kongkirati and Veerayooth Kanchoochat, 'The Prayuth Regime: Embedded Military and Hierarchical Capitalism in Thailand' (2018) 6 TRaNS 279, 289–292.

33 Khemthong Tonsakulrungruang, 'Two Prayuths Dilemma and COVID-19 in Thailand' (*CSEAS Corona Chronicles*, 5 May 2020) <https://covid-19chronicles.cseas.kyoto-u.ac.jp/post-010-html/>.

34 Tyrell Haberkorn, *In Plain Sight: Impunity and Human Rights in Thailand* (University of Wisconsin Press 2018) 5–7.

in taking critical decisions unless they are exempted from liability. Yet that also creates a moral hazard as an agency could make repeated mistakes without needing to correct them. Impunity had direct consequences in terms of virus transmission; all the major clusters detected in Thailand can be traced back to elite sectors of the society who held festivities defying the ban or to corrupt agencies allowing social gatherings such as gambling dens. Yet, the government officially condemned ordinary Thais for being careless and thus causing the new wave.[35]

3.3 State–Business Relations

The third factor that negatively affected the pandemic response was the state's amicable connection with some large business corporations. Evidence showed that these corporations benefited greatly from the junta's policies, even before the pandemic.[36] While fresh markets were ordered to close, department stores and convenience stores owned by large corporations were allow to open despite reports of cases.[37] Another area where favouritism was apparent was vaccines, which were acquired through a few channels controlled by either the Crown Property Bureau (CPB) or that of Prayuth's main business allies (see section 4.4). Several companies used their political connections to appropriate vaccines for their own personnel.[38]

4. The Impact of the Pandemic Response on Human Rights

The 2017 Constitution contains a standard set of civil and political rights: the right to life, the right to a fair trial, freedom of expression for individuals and the media, freedom of religion, the right to privacy, freedom of movement, the right to information and freedom of assembly.[39] The charter also acknowledges economic, social and cultural rights, including the right to receive public health services and state welfare and the right to engage in an occupation.[40] An indigent person must receive public health services free of charge.[41] A person is also entitled to be protected from, and treated for, dangerous communicable diseases without expense.[42] These rights are universally protected even when they are not expressly referred to in the charter. The 2017 Constitution also refers expressly to the duties of the state, which includes the duty to provide all citizens with efficient public health

35 Regulation no. 22, preamble.

36 Prajak Kongkirati and Veerayooth Kanchoochat, 'The Prayuth Regime: Embedded Military and Hierarchical Capitalism in Thailand' 2018 6(2) Trans – Regional and – National Studies of Southeast Asia 279, 293–297.

37 Regulation no. 23.

38 'Ministry Defends Decision to Grant ThaiBev Jab Support' (*The Bangkok Post*, 21 June 2021) <https://www.bangkokpost.com/thailand/general/2135423/ministry-defends-decision-to-grant-thaibev-jab-support>.

39 The 2017 Constitution, ss 28, 34, 35, 36, 39 and 41.

40 ibid, ss 47 and 40.

41 ibid, s 47.

42 ibid.

services, including prevention, control and recovery.[43] Whatever is not prohibited by the constitution is allowed.[44] The main grounds for restriction of rights and liberties are national security, public order and the rights and liberties of others. A restrictive measure must take into consideration the rule of law, the proportionality principle and the protection of human dignity.[45] All the aforesaid rights were impacted by the government's handling of the pandemic, some key aspects of which are highlighted below. Despite this guarantee, in 2021 Thailand, due to its government's militarised mentality, was demoted from 'partly free' to 'not free' by Freedom House.[46]

4.1 Right to Redress

Given the nature of the 2005 Decree, regulations issued under its auspices unsurprisingly prioritised national security concerns and favoured heavy-handed measures over human rights protection. Provisions expressly prevented possible redress and encouraged an unaccountable exercise of power, creating far-reaching immunities for operators of the emergency powers. Meanwhile, those with connections could flaunt the restrictions, to the devastating detriment of the majority.

Section 5 of the 2005 Decree empowers the prime minister, with the approval of the cabinet, to impose a 90-day state of emergency nationwide or in particular areas. This three-month imposition of a state of emergency, including its extension, was subject neither to parliamentary scrutiny nor judicial oversight. More problematically, the ouster clause enshrined in s 16 further exempts all emergency regulations issued by the prime minister from the Administrative Court's jurisdiction. Meanwhile, s 17 exculpates competent officials from liabilities, whether criminal, civil or disciplinary, for the performance of their duty if such acts were delivered in accordance with the duty of good faith, the rule against discrimination and the principle of proportionality. Not only do these far-reaching immunities undermine the right to remedies for human rights violations, but they also raise serious concerns over the increasing propensity for these violations.[47]

In the absence of parliamentary and judicial oversight, the state of emergency against COVID-19 imposed was extended by Prayuth continuously, reflecting "the normalisation of the exception".[48] Several measures were excessively sweeping and blatantly ran counter to the proportionality principle. For instance, it is questionable whether an absolute ban on selling alcoholic beverages can genuinely prevent the spread of the virus. However, if an individual seeks to challenge the legality of

43 ibid, s 55.

44 The Constitution of Thailand B.E. 2560 (2017), s 25 para. 1.

45 The 2017 Constitution, s 26.

46 Freedom House, 'Freedom in the World 2021' <https://freedomhouse.org/country/thailand/freedom-world/2021>.

47 Rawin and Chompunoot (n 8) 163–166.

48 Oren Gross and Fionnuala Ní Aoláin, *Law in Times of Crisis: Emergency Powers in Theory and Practice* (Cambridge University Press 2006) 237.

these regulations before the Administrative Court, the ouster clause would require their petition to be dismissed. Section 16 does not oust the jurisdiction of the court with general jurisdiction – the Civil Court. Yet, as a private law court, the Civil Court holds no authority to annul emergency regulations under the 2005 Decree. Plus, it had previously set a precedent in 2020 that all COVID-19 regulations could no longer be questioned on a ground of tort liability.[49]

4.2 Right to Political Participation

While social distancing is necessary to slow down transmission, the ban on public gathering provided an easy excuse to silence people and thereby ignore their grievances.[50] COVID-19 arrived in time to relieve the government of the burgeoning protests in February 2020 after the Constitutional Court dissolved the major opposition party, known as Future Forward.[51] It marked the beginning of nationwide protests after years of suppression under the military dictatorship. By March, however, protesters had to call off their activities due to rising case numbers and at the time of writing the ban on public assembly persists.

Protests and other forms of public assembly are regulated by the Public Assembly Act B.E. 2558 (2015), which requires the organisers to notify the authority at least 24 hours prior to the event. A protest must not cause disturbance to the government's facilities such as hospitals or schools. Failure to comply results in up to six months' imprisonment or a fine of up to 10,000 Thai baht (as of 26 July 2021, approximately US$300/€260). But the Public Assembly Act was suspended and replaced by the 2005 Decree, which completely banned all forms of assembly that would instigate disorder.

Despite this, the economic difficulty caused by COVID-19 mismanagement mobilised thousands of protestors to re-group and re-emerge as soon as the first wave subsided, demanding a complete overhaul of the government and the constitution.[52] Participants were seen wearing masks and applying hand sanitiser and organisers reminded them to keep socially distanced. Meanwhile, the police would read a warning statement according to the Emergency Decree and charge protesters with offences under both the Public Assembly Act and the 2005 Decree. The decision to charge double offences, regardless of the law, suggested that the police were using these laws intentionally to harass activists. Each time the new wave of COVID-19 struck, protesters lost momentum, buying Prayuth precious time to fortify his position.

49 The Civil Court's Dismissal Order of case no. p.1864/ 2563 (2020).

50 See International Crisis Group, *COVID-19 and a Possible Political Reckoning in Thailand* (Asia Report no. 309, 4 August 2020).

51 Khemthong Tonsakulrungruang, 'Anakot Mai: Lawfare and Future Forward Party's Legacy' (*New Mandala*, 28 February 2020) <https://www.newmandala.org/anakot-mai-lawfare-and-future-forward-partys-legacy/>.

52 Duncan McCargo, 'Disruptor's Dilemma? Thailand's 2020 Gen Z Protests' (2021) 53 Critical Asian Studies 175, 179.

4.3 *Right to Economic Relief*

The semi-lockdown and border control measures hit the Thai economy hard but the government had no tangible plan to compensate for any losses of business owners and employees. By the end of 2020, the government began to roll out an economic stimulus package. As the name suggested, the purpose was not to compensate for losses but to encourage spending. The government offered no long-term plan and stimulus packages were given in rounds with short notice. Only those whose yearly taxable income was below 300,000 Thai baht (approximately US$9,110/€7,715) were eligible and there were limited opportunities for registration and conditions on what the money could be spent on.[53] As of July 2021, because the government refrained from officially announcing another lockdown, there is virtually no subsidy or furlough money to prevent business shutdowns or layoffs. Nor did the government negotiate with major landlords to lower rents. Particularly vulnerable were those who were employed but with reduced wages, as they were not entitled to unemployment benefit.

4.4 *Rights to Good Public Health and Equality*

The state has fulfilled its constitutional duty in respect of public health by providing COVID-19 patients with free tests and treatment. COVID-19 patients were deemed emergency cases entitled to immediate admission, even to private hospitals, with the government reimbursing the cost.[54] Local health volunteers facilitated active monitoring and reporting of new cases.[55]

However, the early success could not be sustained without reinforcement, thus revealing that the 'health before rights' policy did nothing to ensure effective vaccine procurement and distribution. The public health system was maximised but the government proposed no follow-up plan. Funds were instead diverted to the military and the palace.[56] As of July 2021, doctors and nurses had yet to receive pending overtime payments.[57] Few additional hospitals were built and little equip-

53 **'โครงการเราชนะ'** ['We Win Together' project] <https://www.xn--b3c4a2a6ch6f.com/information>.

54 Ministry of Public Health Regulation on COVID-19 Patients B.E. 2563 (2020).

55 Montira Narkvichien, 'Thailand's 1 Million Village Health Volunteers – "Unsung Heroes" – Are Helping Guard Communities Nationwide from COVID-19' (*World Health Organisation*, 28 August 2020) <https://www.who.int/thailand/news/feature-stories/detail/thailands-1-million-village-health-volunteers-unsung-heroes-are-helping-guard-communities-nationwide-from-covid-19>.

56 **วจนา วรรลยางกูร** [Wajana Wanlayangkul], '**"งบประมาณทุกส่วนต้องตรวจสอบได้" เบญจา แสงจันทร์ กับคำถามต่อโครงการที่มีนามสกุล**' [Transparency of Government Budget: Bencha Saengchantra and Questions Over Cronyistic State Projects] (*The 101 World*, 15 June 2021) <https://www.the101.world/bencha-saengchantra-interview/>; 'Army Confirms Purchase of Airbus C295 Transport Plane' (*The Bangkok Post*, 22 June 2021) <https://www.bangkokpost.com/thailand/general/2136503/army-confirms-purchase-of-airbus-c295-transport-plane>.

57 'Does 2022 Budget Bill Answer the Country's Needs?' (*Thai PBS*, 28 May 2021) <https://www.thaipbsworld.com/does-2022-budget-bill-answer-the-countrys-needs/>.

ment was procured. The government, while making face-masks mandatory, did not secure sufficient supplies, some of which were found to have been hoarded by the Agricultural Deputy Minister's aide.[58] The government prohibited the public from accessing self-test kits.[59] As a result, when the pandemic entered the second year, the system showed signs of fatigue.

The third wave of COVID-19 starting in April 2021 revealed its full weakness. Exponentially rising numbers of cases from more active testing indicated that the previous, more positive statistics might have been an illusion created by under-testing. A shoddily and hastily set up call centre failed to handle numbers of calls and many people perished unable to contact medical hotlines as instructed.[60] Hospital beds soon filled up and even private hospitals closed down testing centres because of fears of bed shortages. By late July, corpses of COVID-19 patients began to appear on the streets. Doctors refused treatment to patients with low priority.

However, the most serious breach of a constitutional duty was the government's failure to procure good-quality vaccines. The 2017 Constitution guaranteed a free health service for contagious diseases but it did not require that service to be of good quality or to be delivered in a timely manner. In May 2021, it was revealed to the public that Prayuth had refused an early offer by Pfizer and an invitation to join the WHO-sponsored COVAX programme.[61] Instead, Thailand contracted only one manufacturer, AstraZeneca, to grant the Thai pharmaceutical company, Siam Bioscience, the rights to produce the vaccine domestically. Production was not due to begin until at least mid-2021, significantly behind the majority of the world. The deal was signed in secret and Siam Bioscience was later discovered to be owned by the CPB, a quasi-government agency that manages the property of the Thai monarchy. Criticism of the deal resulted in lèse-majesté charges.[62] To appease the public, Prayuth bought doses of the Chinese-made Sinovac as an emergency alternative. Sinovac, however, suffered credibility issues as the WHO had initially been reluctant to approve it. Moreover, it turned out that one of Prayuth's business allies, the Charoen Pokphand group, was a shareholder.[63] Certification of other vaccines was extremely slow.

58 'Deputy Agriculture Minister Thammanat in Trouble over Face Mask Controversy' (*Thai PBS*, 9 March 2020) <https://www.thaipbsworld.com/deputy-agriculture-minister-thammanat-in-trouble-over-face-mask-controversy/>.

59 'FDA Warns Lay Person Against Using COVID-19 Rapid Test Kit' (*The Nation*, 6 January 2021) <https://www.nationthailand.com/in-focus/30400755>.

60 Mongkol Bangprapa, 'Former E-Sport Player Dies of Covid-19 after Failing to Get Timely Help' (*The Bangkok Post*, 25 April 2021) <https://www.bangkokpost.com/thailand/general/2104999/former-e-sport-player-dies-of-covid-19-after-failing-to-get-timely-help>.

61 Thitinan Pongsudhirak, 'No Duopoly in Thai Jab Procurement' (*The Bangkok Post*, 27 May 2021) <https://www.bangkokpost.com/opinion/opinion/2122703/no-duopoly-in-thai-jab-procurement>.

62 Patpicha Tanakasempipat, 'Thai Govt Files Royal Insult Complaint after Criticism of its Vaccine Strategy' (*Reuters*, 20 January 2021) <https://www.reuters.com/article/us-thailand-politics-idUSKBN29P0RV>.

63 'The Inoculation Challenge' (*The Bangkok Post*, 18 January 2021) <https://www.bangkokpost.com/business/2052615/the-inoculation-challenge>.

The rollout of the vaccine was chaotic as shipments failed to arrive on time and those that did arrive were misallocated to politicians and well-connected corporate friends. To achieve the 70% vaccination benchmark, the government adamantly refused to acknowledge any side-effects of the vaccine, further scaring people away.[64] Migrant residents were not eligible for a vaccine. Prayuth repeatedly blocked the private sector's attempt to directly procure better vaccines.[65] To date, the vaccine rollout remains sluggish and with just over 5% of the population having been fully vaccinated to date, Thailand's performance is among the worst in Southeast Asia.[66]

4.5 Rights of Inmates

Thailand has one of the highest rates of incarceration in the world.[67] The sheer size of the prison population – almost 310,000 inmates as of July 2021 – posed a challenge to any attempt to contain COVID-19, despite a guideline ordering quarantine of newly arrived inmates and stricter hygiene protocols.[68] Stories about COVID-19 in places of detention only began to reach the public when political prisoners contracted the virus.[69] The high-profile nature of these cases drew public attention and the Ministry of Justice was forced to reveal the figures. Over a couple of days, the Ministry reported over 10,000 cases, indicating that the statistics must have been hidden months before the Justice Minister's admission.[70] These numbers were never included in the national tally. Accounts from former inmates revealed that prisons were under-resourced to deal with the pandemic, putting their and relatives' lives at risk,[71] and flouting international standards which view denial of inmates' access to health care as both degrading their human dignity and potentially violating their right to life.[72]

64 For example, see Apinya Wipatayotin, 'Health Official Dies after Being Vaccinated' (*The Bangkok Post*, 13 May 2021) <https://www.bangkokpost.com/thailand/general/2115147/health-official-dies-after-being-vaccinated>.

65 Thitinan Pongsudhirak, 'No Duopoly in Thai Jab Procurement' (*The Bangkok Post*, 28 May 2021) <https://www.bangkokpost.com/opinion/opinion/2122703/no-duopoly-in-thai-jab-procurement>.

66 Johns Hopkins University, Coronavirus Resource Center, Understanding Vaccination Progress (updated as of 26 July 2021) <https://coronavirus.jhu.edu/vaccines/international>.

67 World Prison Brief: <https://www.prisonstudies.org/highest-to-lowest/prison-population-total?field_region_taxonomy_tid=All>.

68 Department of Corrections' Guideline on COVID-19 Prevention (3 March 2020).

69 'Pro-democracy Lawyer Arnon Contracts Covid in Jail' (*The Nation*, 6 May 2021) <https://www.nationthailand.com/in-focus/40000594>.

70 'Thailand: Record Number of Covid Cases as Prison Clusters Grow' (*BBC News*, 17 May 2021) <https://www.bbc.com/news/world-asia-57139690>.

71 'Pandemic in Dark Land: Somyot Pruksakasemsuk' (*The 101 World*, 21 May 2021) <https://www.the101.world/somyot-pruksakasemsuk-interview/>.

72 World Health Organisation, 'UNODC, WHO, UNAIDS and OHCHR Joint Statement on COVID-19 in Prisons and Other Closed Settings' (13 May 2020) <https://www.who.int/news/

5. Conclusion

COVID-19 was undoubtedly a severe crisis for the Thai government. Not only did the pandemic seriously convulse the economy, but it also accelerated the erosion of human rights protections. Thailand thereby joined the club of authoritarian countries where the enforcement of disproportionately harsh emergency powers to resolve a national crisis came at the expense of human rights. Tragically, such sacrifices did not result in effective control of the virus, a successful vaccination programme or collaboration among government branches. The government's instinct was to prioritise the use of emergency powers over the art of persuasion and incentive. The distinctive nature of COVID-19, together with adverse impacts on human rights rendered by the 2005 Decree, ultimately require the Thai government to re-examine its constitutional design in order to achieve a decisive yet collaborative and effective response to any future global pandemic.

item/13-05-2020-unodc-who-unaids-and-ohchr-joint-statement-on-covid-19-in-prisons-and-other-closed-settings>.

15

POLITICAL OPPORTUNISM AND PANDEMIC MISMANAGEMENT IN KENYA

Tara Imalingat, Nerima Were and Allan Maleche

1. Introduction[1]

More than a year after its first COVID-19 case was confirmed, Kenya has not to date declared a state of emergency. The pandemic and the government's response to it has, however, exposed a blatant disregard for human rights and the rule of law in Kenya, witnessing a derogation from the constitutional ideal that all people are subject and answerable to the law.[2] With a three-armed government made up of the legislature, executive and judiciary, the separation of powers principle should regulate the exercise of powers by each arm and ensure that none acts outside of its powers and usurps the role of another. However, in the name of tackling a public health emergency, the executive, constituting the national government and 47 county governments whose authority is derived from the people, restricted human rights without due regard to the supremacy of the Constitution of Kenya, 2010.[3] This resulted in numerous violations, particularly against the most vulnerable and marginalised groups in the country. Additionally, weaknesses in Kenya's health and governance systems were further unearthed by this use of powers and its democracy threatened.

1 All websites accessed on 8 August 2021.

2 This chapter is based on: Allan Maleche, Nerima Were and Tara Imalingat, 'Excessive Law Enforcement in Kenya' (*Verfassungsblog*, 14 May 2020) <https://verfassungsblog.de/excessive-law-enforcement-in-kenya/>; Nerima Were, Allan Maleche and Tara Imalingat, 'COVID-19 in Kenya a Year Later: A Case of Déjà Vu' (*Verfassungsblog*, 29 April 2021) <https://verfassungsblog.de/covid-19-in-kenya-a-year-later-a-case-of-deja-vu/>.

3 Constitution of Kenya 2010, Article 2.

DOI: 10.4324/9781003211952-17

This chapter examines the pandemic response in Kenya, focusing on the role each arm of the state played. It critiques the state's failure to adopt a human rights-based approach, highlights the populations most affected, and concludes with recommendations to strengthen Kenya's constitutional democracy and future pandemic preparedness.

2. Overview of the COVID-19 Pandemic in Kenya

Kenya confirmed its first COVID-19 case on 12 March 2020. Days after the confirmation of two more cases, President Uhuru Kenyatta gave orders that hastened the government's plans to contain the virus. This included travel bans, self-quarantine requirements, the suspension of learning institutions and the establishment of the National Emergency Response Committee on Coronavirus formed by Executive Presidential Order on 28 February 2020.[4] The Committee was mandated to co-ordinate Kenya's preparedness, prevention and response to the virus and, at the time of writing, it continues to publish sporadic updates on the status of the virus and the recurrent response measures. At the onset of the pandemic, Kenya adopted the mantra "test, isolate, treat and trace" in the fight against COVID-19 as it worked to decrease the steady rise of positive cases.

In March 2020, the government introduced a series of rules and directives which disregarded statutory procedural processes, used mandatory quarantine as punishment for alleged breaches of the law, deployed police who used unreasonable force in the enforcement of curfews and introduced the use of preventive measures which disproportionately affected vulnerable communities.[5] In March 2021, despite a public outcry surrounding police brutality and the irregular implementation of COVID-19 measures, the country came full circle and saw a return to ultra vires actions by the state on account of the third wave of the virus, which led to a surge in the number of people testing positive and threw Kenya back into a state of disarray as poorly-resourced health facilities grappled with the rise in cases.[6]

Days after the anniversary of the first case in mid-March 2021, the country recorded its highest positivity rate of 22% of those tested, which had jumped from only 2% in January 2021.[7] The positivity rate climbed again to 26.6% in late March resulting in a partial lockdown of the COVID-19 hotspot counties.[8] In June 2021,

4 Executive Order No. 2 of 2020, National Emergency Response Committee on Coronavirus, 2020 <https://www.health.go.ke/wp-content/uploads/2020/06/Executive-Order-No-2-of-2020_National-Emergency-Response-Committee-on-Coronavirus-28.2.20.pdf>.

5 'Advisory Note on Ensuring a Rights-Based Response to Curb the Spread of COVID-19' (28 March 2021) <https://www.kelinkenya.org/wp-content/uploads/2020/03/letter2.pdf>.

6 Maleche, Were and Imalingat (n 2).

7 'The Fifteenth [15th] Presidential Address on The Coronavirus Pandemic' (26 March 2021) <https://www.president.go.ke/2021/03/26/the-fifteenth-15th-presidential-address-on-the-coronavirus-pandemic/>.

8 'The Sixteenth [16th] Presidential Address on The Coronavirus Pandemic' (29 June 2021) <https://www.president.go.ke/2021/06/29/the-sixteenth-16-th-presidential-address-on-the-coronavirus-pandemic/>.

the Western region of Kenya bore the brunt of the highly contagious Delta variant, and was forecast to be a precursor to a fourth wave in July and August 2021. At the time of writing, though there has been an increase in the positivity rate, the fourth wave has yet to peak, an effect attributed by experts to a lack of testing, under-reporting of data by the Ministry of Health and vaccination uptake,[9] although as of 8 August 2021, only 1.27% of the population is fully vaccinated.[10] To date, Kenya's per capita mortality rate is in the lowest 25% of states worldwide, although higher than most of its east African neighbours.[11]

3. The Executive and its Use of Powers in Response to Emergency

3.1 Unscrutinised Enactment and Implementation of Rules and Directives

The Constitution of Kenya 2010 grants the president powers to declare a state of emergency in line with Article 132(4)(d) read with Article 58(1), which provides that this power is exercised where the state is threatened by "war, invasion, general insurrection, disorder, natural disaster or other public emergency" and the declaration is "necessary to meet the circumstances for which the emergency is declared".[12] A state of emergency can only be declared prospectively, not for longer than 14 days without the approval of the National Assembly, and not for longer than two months at a time. The exercise of this power is subject to judicial scrutiny. As of August 2021, the president has not exercised this power but the conduct of the executive has led to questions around the legality of the manner in which such powers are being exercised, as discussed below.

At the start of the pandemic, the president opted instead to implement measures that ensured citizens could "continue with their lives", adding that a total lockdown of the country was the "last option on the table" and would not be needed "as long as we can strictly adhere to the measures already in place".[13]

As the president opted not to exercise his powers in terms of Article 132(4)(d), the Public Health Act[14] (the PHA) and Public Order Act[15] (the POA), enacted in 1921 and 1950, respectively, were the primary legal bases for the emergency power the executive utilised to introduce a series of new guidelines and directives. The

9 Hellen Shikanda, 'Kenya: Why COVID-19 Fourth Wave is Yet to Peak as Predicted' (*AllAfrica*, 20 July 2021) <https://allafrica.com/stories/202107210074.html>.

10 Johns Hopkins University Coronavirus Resource Center, Kenya Overview<https://coronavirus.jhu.edu/region/kenya>.

11 Johns Hopkins University Coronavirus Resource Center, Mortality Analyses<https://coronavirus.jhu.edu/data/mortality>.

12 The Constitution of Kenya, 2010, Article 58.

13 President of the Republic of Kenya, 'President Kenyatta Urges Kenyans to Observe Government Directives on Coronavirus' (7 April 2020) <https://www.president.go.ke/2020/04/07/president-kenyatta-urges-kenyans-to-observe-government-directives-on-coronavirus/>.

14 Chapter 242 of the Laws of Kenya.

15 Chapter 50 of the Laws of Kenya.

executive also implemented several prevention and management measures in the form of protocols in the fight against COVID-19. On 2 March 2020, the Cabinet Secretary for Health declared COVID-19 a notifiable disease under the PHA, meaning that the provisions of Part IV of the PHA dealing with the prevention, control and suppression of infectious diseases would be applicable. This declaration provided a legal justification for travel restrictions and isolation orders and further empowered the Cabinet Secretary to generate rules and guidelines for the management of the pandemic.

One immediate action taken by the government included a ban on all international flights which came into effect at midnight on 25 March 2020. International air travel resumed on 1 August 2020.[16] To facilitate the seamless return to air travel the Ministry of Transport, Infrastructure, Housing, Urban Development and Public Works developed a protocol which provided a framework for safe and secure aviation operations during the pandemic.[17] Notices on travelling requirements are issued by the Kenya Civil Aviation Authority and altered to reflect the COVID-19 infection rates of people travelling from selected countries.[18] Another measure was an order requiring individuals that entered Kenya after 22 March 2020 to undergo mandatory quarantine for 14 days at designated facilities at their own expense.[19]

In the exercise of the powers conferred by the POA, the Cabinet Secretary for Interior and Co-ordination for National Government ordered that, with effect from 27 March 2020 for a period of 30 days, the country would be subject to a 7:00pm – 5:00am curfew through Legal Notice 36 of 2020, Public Order (State Curfew) Order 2020. The order prohibited public gatherings and processions or movement, either alone or in a group, during the curfew period. Essential service workers were exempt from the provisions.

On 3 April 2020, the Cabinet Secretary for Health published the Public Health (Prevention, Control and Suppression of COVID-19) Rules 2020 and the Public Health (COVID-19 Restriction of Movement of Persons and Related Measures) Rules 2020, which instituted reporting obligations and guidance on burial procedures, and gave the Cabinet Secretary the power to declare any place an infected area, thereby regulating all conduct and activities therein. The rules applied for

16 Ministry of Transport, Infrastructure, Housing, Development and Public Works, 'Communique on the Resumption of International Air Travel on 1 August 2021' (31 July 2021)<https://www.kcaa.or.ke/sites/default/files/docs/covid_19/Min-of-Transport-33x3-1-8-20.pdf>.

17 Ministry of Transport, Infrastructure, Housing, Development and Public Works, 'Protocol for Air Travel Operations During the Covid-19 Public Health Crisis' (June 2020)<https://www.kcaa.or.ke/sites/default/files/docs/covid_19/Protocol-for-Air-Operations.pdf>.

18 Kenya Civil Aviation Authority, Notice (July 2021) <https://www.kcaa.or.ke/sites/default/files/covid-19/documents/exempted_states_3.pdf>.

19 The cost of quarantine was relative as the executive designated both private and public facilities as quarantine centres. This decision by the executive is, at the time of writing, the subject of a petition before the High Court challenging the use of mandatory quarantine, one of the issues highlighted being the cost. For more information please see details on *CM and others v the Attorney General and others* Petition 151 of 2020 <https://www.kelinkenya.org/wp-content/uploads/2020/05/communique-2.pdf>.

a specific period of time known as the 'restricted period' during which movement of persons into or out of an infected area or hotspot using any means was prohibited save for vehicles transporting food, certain cargo or ambulances. These rules were initially applied in five out of the 47 counties within the country; however, the cessation of movement rules were then diversely applied to several other counties in response to recorded positivity rates, while the nationwide dusk to dawn curfew remains applicable (as at August 2021) in all the counties with amendment (curfew is between 10:00pm – 4:00am).[20] These and other imposed public health and public order rules were extended and subject to variation almost unilaterally by the executive on account of parliamentary acquiescence and almost non-existent public participation as required by the constitution in the practice of state power.[21]

3.2 *Ultra Vires* Enforcement of Executive Directives

Any person that contravened the curfew order would be liable to a fine not exceeding 10,000 shillings (approximately US$90 or €78) or to imprisonment for a term not exceeding three months or both. Those that violated the cessation of movement rules would be liable to a fine not exceeding 20,000 shillings or to imprisonment for a period not exceeding six months, or both. However, despite this, the Ministry of Health, on 19 April 2020, announced that all those found to have breached the curfew would be assumed to have been in contact with suspected cases and would be placed under mandatory quarantine for a period of 14 days.[22] Thus, the state was using mandatory quarantine at one's own cost as a penalty for breaching the curfew.

The requirement of self-isolation and a valid negative COVID-19 test certificate swiftly replaced the mandatory quarantine practice for those entering the country save for some specific states as guided by the government.[23] However, mandatory quarantine, which placed people in sometimes unsanitary conditions (there were reports of water shortages and shared bathrooms with poor standards of hygiene), was weaponised against alleged breaches of law and was consecutively extended for an additional 14 days for all persons in certain facilities upon the discovery of positive cases or a breach of the guidelines around social distancing

20 'The Fifth Presidential Address on The Coronavirus Pandemic At State House, Nairobi Saturday, 25 April 2020' <https://www.president.go.ke/2020/04/25/the-fifth-presidential-address-on-the-coronavirus-pandemic-at-state-house-nairobi-saturday-25th-april-2020/>.

21 Article 10(2) of the Constitution of Kenya 2010 stipulates participation of the people as one of the national values and principles of governance. The obligation to facilitate public participation is discussed at length in *Republic v County Government of Kiambu; Ex Parte Robert Gakuru and Another* Judicial Review Case 434 of 2015 <http://kenyalaw.org/caselaw/cases/view/121953/>.

22 'Kenyans Who Break Curfew Rules to be Quarantined for 14 Days' (*NTV Kenya*, 19 April 2020) <https://www.youtube.com/watch?v=YgZ81loize0>.

23 Kenya Civil Aviation Authority, Notice (11 June 2021)<https://kcaa.or.ke/sites/default/files/docs/covid_19/exempted_states.pdf>.

within these facilities.[24] Some persons in quarantine were detained beyond the mandatory 14-day period because they were unable to pay for the cost of quarantine.[25] However, following complaints, the government announced that the cost of testing and staying in government quarantine facilities would be met specifically for those placed in quarantine by the Ministry of Health, but not those quarantined for violation of the curfew rules, with effect from 6 May 2020.[26]

This assurance was not fulfilled and civil society actors such as the Kenya Legal and Ethical Issues Network on HIV and AIDS (KELIN) filed a petition that challenged the forceful detention of patients for failure to pay for the costs of testing and medical treatment of COVID-19 while in isolation.[27] KELIN also raised concerns surrounding the rationality of decisions being devised by the government; for instance, the decision to quarantine persons who breached curfew was a penalty not provided for or guided by any legislative framework or existing power. Moreover, this decision was announced by the Ministry of Health and not the Ministry of Interior and Coordination of National Government, and was contrary to the principal legislation which specifies punitive measures.

3.3 Centralisation of the Pandemic Response

The executive's response to the pandemic was largely centralised, contrary to provisions in the constitution. Given Kenya's devolved system of governance and health, the initial marked silence from the county governments was concerning.[28] County health facilities contended with poorly stocked intensive care units and an oxygen shortage.[29] The sorry state of affairs in the county hospitals in the early months of 2021 was blamed on substandard planning, despite counties having had a year to address any anticipated obstacles.[30] In the latest county government press statement in April 2021, an intergovernmental health committee was formed between the

24 John-Allan Namu, 'Inside the Quarantine: Fears of Further Spreading the Virus Haunt the Confined' (*The Elephant*, 3 April 2020) <https://www.theelephant.info/features/2020/04/03/inside-the-quarantine-fears-of-further-spreading-the-virus-haunt-the-confined/>.

25 Katherine Houreld, 'Poor Kenyans Despair as Coronavirus Quarantine Extended over Unpaid Bills' (*Reuters*, 15 April 2020) <https://www.reuters.com/article/us-health-coronavirus-kenya-quarantine-idUSKCN21X2AT>.

26 National Emergency Response Committee on Coronavirus, 'Update of Coronavirus in the Country and Response Measures as at 6 May 2020, Day 55, Brief No 49' <https://www.health.go.ke/wp-content/uploads/2020/05/CS-Brief-No.-49.pdf>.

27 *JMK and 3 others v Kenyatta University Teaching, Referral and Research Hospital (Kutrrh) and 3 others* [2020] eKLR <http://kenyalaw.org/caselaw/cases/view/205616/>.

28 Morris Kiruga, 'Kenya's Fight against Coronavirus Difficult with its Two-Tiered Governance System' (*The Africa Report*, 17 April 2020) <https://www.theafricareport.com/26354/kenyas-fight-against-coronavirus-difficult-with-its-two-tiered-governance-system/>.

29 'Kenya: Counties Used Millions for Oxygen Plants, Delivered Air' (*AllAfrica*, 15 April 2021) <https://allafrica.com/stories/202104150687.html>.

30 Magdaline Saya, 'Oxygen Shortage Blamed on Poor Planning, Selfishness' (*The Star*, 8 April 2021) <https://www.the-star.co.ke/news/2021-04-08-oxygen-shortage-blamed-on-poor-planning-selfishness/>.

national and county government to coordinate a plethora of COVID-19 related issues; however, writing in August 2021, it remains to be seen whether this partnership will yield the desired results.[31]

4. Legislative Scrutiny and Oversight: Parliamentary Rubber-Stamping

To address the exceptional circumstances of the pandemic, the Pandemic Response and Management Bill 2020, which sought to provide a legal framework for a coordinated response for temporary measures and relief, was tabled before the Senate in April and passed in the Senate on 30 June 2020.[32] The Bill proposed the establishment of a National Committee and County Committees to co-ordinate the country's response through the implementation of strategies and measures to both combat and cushion the effects of the pandemic. The Bill also established a Pandemic Response Fund and laid down socio-economic protective measures for the public. On 28 July 2021, the Bill underwent its first reading before the National Assembly and at the time of writing is undergoing technical review. Because the Bill involves counties, it must go before both houses in Parliament and while the Senate was cognisant of the urgency to enact this Bill, the National Assembly has not been. No reasons have been given; however, it must be noted that in August 2020, many members of the National Assembly shifted their focus to a matter unconnected to the pandemic, the Building Bridges Initiative, which is concerned with reforming the constitution (see s 6).

Until the Bill is passed, the pandemic continues to be governed by rules derived from the PHA and POA. These rules are statutory instruments under the Statutory Instruments Act 2013 (SIA), as they are established in the execution of a power conferred by an Act of Parliament. As per the SIA (s 11), the regulations should be tabled before Parliament for approval or annulment within seven days of publication. Following this, statutory instruments are referred to the Committee on Delegated Legislation in the National Assembly, which may approve or annul them; if it opts to annul (partially or wholly), they shall be tabled to the National Assembly for consideration.

The National Assembly initially declined to approve the Public Health Act (Prevention, Control and Suppression of COVID-19) Rules 2020 and the Public Health (COVID-19 Restriction of Movement of Persons and Related Measures) Rules 2020 due to their punitive nature. However, they were later approved with little explanation and consultation as is required in the legislative process. The actions of the National Assembly have been mostly to rubber-stamp executive measures, and in the instance that parliamentarians interrogate the rules, this is done belatedly when the rules are already in force and being applied.

31 Press Statement on Coronavirus Pandemic, Council of Governors (1 April 2021) <https://www.cog.go.ke/media-multimedia/statements/category/109-covid-19>.

32 Twelfth Parliament (Fourth Session) The National Assembly (15 July 2020).

To date, Parliament has continued to rubber-stamp the actions of the executive and has in some instances wholly exempted some of the COVID-19 rules from scrutiny pursuant to s 14 of the SIA. Therefore, despite being mandated under the constitution to facilitate public participation, Parliament has allowed this function and its oversight role to be reduced to a cosmetic exercise. As of 29 June 2021, the fourth Public Order issued by the president prohibiting various gatherings and extending or modifying curfew has been published in response to the high positivity rates in the country.[33] The executive continues to validate an illegal process by publishing the rules without parliamentary approval, once again undermining the rule of law. Public participation requests have become 24-hour alerts relayed to only a few select persons or organisations to tick a compliance 'box' which does not constitute meaningful public participation.

5. Enforcing Constitutional Rights and Obligations: The Judiciary during the Pandemic

While the judiciary initially scaled down its operations, it quickly adapted to the 'new normal' and two weeks after the first COVID-19 case in Kenya, virtual court sessions started. The first online ruling was issued taking into account precautionary measures in accordance with the directive to suspend physical court proceedings issued by the then Chief Justice, David Maraga.[34] Practice rules to protect both court users, judicial officers and their staff were issued and resulted in the closure of courts and the use of technology for virtual sessions.[35] As of August 2021, these measures are still being used. However, requests are being made to develop a proper framework in the form of a Bill to better shield the digital courts from abuse.[36] Though the practice directions are comprehensive, they fail to provide any penalties for any possible privacy breaches or systems tampering, particularly with respect to the filing of sensitive court documents.

Despite a slow start, the judiciary began to play its role in checking executive power. There was, for example, uproar surrounding police brutality during the curfew period.[37] Police were recorded caning people who allegedly breached

33 'The Sixteenth [16th] Presidential Address on The Coronavirus Pandemic' (29 June 2021) <https://www.president.go.ke/2021/06/29/the-sixteenth-16-th-presidential-address-on-the-coronavirus-pandemic/>.

34 Martin Siele, 'Judge Holds Hearing Outdoors Over Coronavirus Fears' (*Kenyans.co.ke*, 17 March 2020) <https://www.kenyans.co.ke/news/50927-judge-holds-hearing-outdoors-over-coronavirus-fears-photos>.

35 Practice Notes for the Conduct of Court Business During the Global Coronavirus Pandemic (*Kenya Law Reports*, 21 April 2020) <http://kenyalaw.org/kl/index.php?id=10327>.

36 Jillo Kadida, 'CJ Maraga Launches e-filing Portal as Judiciary Goes Digital' (*The Star*, 1 July 2020) <https://www.the-star.co.ke/news/2020-07-01-cj-maraga-launches-e-filing-portal-as-judiciary-goes-digital/>.

37 'Kenya: Uproar Over Police Brutality During Virus Curfew' (*All Africa*, 28 March 2020) <https://allafrica.com/stories/202003300147.html>.

curfew and it was reported that at least 12 people died from police violence.[38] The High Court declared the unreasonable use of force by the police unconstitutional.[39] Additionally, the Ministry of Interior was ordered to include the Independent Policing Oversight Authority on the list of essential service providers in light of the need to closely monitor police engagement in efforts to curb the virus.[40]

Kenya's novel e-filing system was rolled out in July 2020. This digital migration was dictated by the trajectory of the COVID-19 pandemic. Thankfully, the wheels of justice could turn once again, albeit insufferably slowly. Since scaling down its operations in March 2020, the already overburdened judicial system continued to face a backlog of cases, including those initiated seeking to expose the ultra vires conduct of the executive and protect the rule of law. Many of these time-sensitive cases, filed under the stamp of urgency, remain unresolved. To date, KELIN has filed three petitions challenging the implementation of the COVID-19 response by government.[41] The first challenged the implementation of forced and mandatory quarantine; the second challenged the failure of various state and public entities to provide timely and accurate information during the pandemic; and the third (mentioned in section 3.2) concerned detention of patients held in isolation. Government in both cases failed to respond to the petitions despite court directions to do so. Despite the failure by the executive to respond, the court has to date continued to allow additional time, prejudicing the other parties and the interests of justice.[42] The continued disregard for judicial processes by the executive indicates a need to consider punitive measures within the rules of the judiciary to ensure that litigants are treated equally and the state cannot delay justice. Additionally, a specially constituted court should be established to hear pandemic-related cases if and when they arise to avoid delays in the delivery of court decisions, particularly those surrounding the fundamental rights and freedoms of citizens.

While the virtual court allowed the judiciary to remain available, the stark digital divide in Kenya called into question its accessibility. This divide was stretched further as marginalised and vulnerable groups of (potential) litigants were left further behind with no clear mitigation plans in sight. Access to both electricity and the internet, particularly within rural communities and informal settlements, highlighted the old adage of the 'haves' and the 'have nots'.

38 Andrew Wasike, 'Kenya Police Kill More during Curfew than COVID-19' (*Anadolu Agency*, 16 April 2020) <https://www.aa.com.tr/en/africa/kenya-police-kill-more-during-curfew-than-COVID-19/1807930>. 1

39 *Law Society of Kenya v Hillary Mutyambai Inspector General National Police Service and 4 others*; *Kenya National Commission on Human Rights and 3 others* (Interested Parties) [2020] eKLR.

40 Missing Voices <https://missingvoices.or.ke/facts-and-figures/>.

41 *CM and Others v AG and Others* (Petition No. 151 of 2020); *Erick Okioma and Others v The Attorney General and Others* (Petition No. 218 of 2020).

42 Declaration of interest: the authors represent KELIN.

6. Weak Leadership and Political Opportunism

Kenya's COVID-19 response can be summarised as follows. While the initial months of the pandemic were characterised by excessive law enforcement and use of mandatory quarantine as punishment, these issues improved as more about COVID-19 was understood, and due to push back within the civic space in Kenya, but quickly regressed with the third wave. To manage compliance with COVID-19 directives, a Special Enforcement Unit comprising the National Police Service and officials from the National and County Government was established.[43]

Despite these measures, laxity among the elite sections of society proved to be where the pandemic turned and irresponsible leadership was perhaps the most damning failure. 'Superspreader' rallies held across the country at the end of 2020 and the early months of 2021 fuelled the surge of COVID-19 infections as they attracted large audiences, creating an environment for the abrogation of COVID-19 protocols. The increase in politicking was due to the upcoming 2022 presidential elections and a political initiative geared towards efforts to make far-reaching amendments to the Constitution of Kenya 2010, dubbed the Building Bridges Initiative.[44] Parliament's independence also came into question with members of parliament and county assemblies organising and participating in political rallies, unaware or insouciant of the damaging role they were playing in the spread of COVID-19. Healthcare workers and the public at large suffered the consequences of this irrational decision-making.

Another illustration of this poor leadership was the Ministry of Health's failure to provide adequate information at the start of the pandemic.[45] This began to improve towards the second half of 2020 with more comprehensive information around the preparedness of the nation to manage the pandemic. However, during the third wave, which was announced in March 2021, government announcements reverted to providing only testing and vaccine numbers. This information vacuum was reversed in August 2021 after a three-month interruption and vaccination summary reports are, at the time of writing, published on a daily basis.

Significantly, the COVID-19 pandemic vaccination strategy further demonstrated the gaps in deploying a human rights-based approach, in its failure to consult with and accommodate vulnerable populations in its development and deployment. The strategy was scheduled to be deployed over an 18-month period

43 Mary Wambui, 'Sh20,000 Instant Fine for Flouting Covid Rules' (*Business Daily*, 5 November 2020) <https://www.businessdailyafrica.com/bd/news/sh20-000-fine-for-flouting-covid-rules-2732212>.

44 Peter Muiruri, 'Kenya's High Court Overturns President's Bid to Amend Constitution' (*The Guardian*, 27 May 2021) <https://www.theguardian.com/global-development/2021/may/27/kenyas-high-court-overturns-president-uhuru-kenyatta-bbi-bid-to-amend-constitution>.

45 Communique: *Erick Okioma and 12 others vs Mutahi Kagwe, Cabinet Secretary for Health and 8 Others for Health and 8 Others* <https://tikenya.org/wp-content/uploads/2020/07/Communique-Access-to-Information-petition.pdf>.

in three phases.[46] The first phase from late February 2021 was due to serve 1.25 million people, mainly frontline healthcare workers and staff; the second phase from July 2021 was targeted at some 9.7 million Kenyans above the age of 50 and those above 18 years with comorbidities; and the final phase, meant to run concurrently with phase two, was reserved for 4.9 million people from the most vulnerable groups in the country depending on vaccine availability.[47] This strategy was seemingly adapted, without any announcement or formal amendment of the strategy, with previously undisclosed populations falling into the definition of frontline workers, including teachers, uniformed personnel, religious leaders, diplomats, UN staff and political leaders. Further exacerbating the lack of clarity were persons using 'back door tactics' to receive the vaccine early, despite not fitting the prescribed criteria.[48]

The rollout of the government's haphazard vaccine deployment strategy on 5 March 2021 was further hampered by a derailed supply of vaccines, which raised concerns over whether the government could provide vaccinated persons with the required second dose.[49] Kenya received donations of vaccines from foreign countries, including funds from global organisations such as the World Bank to broaden inoculation coverage as rapidly as possible.[50] This vulnerability amplified the need for the development of local manufacturing capabilities in Kenya and within the East African region to reduce dependency on imported medical supplies and vaccines. As of August 2021, the government's latest strategy was to vaccinate the entire adult population of 26 million Kenyans by 2022.[51] However, as noted above, less than 2% of the population has been fully vaccinated to date.[52]

Finally, opportunism was illustrated through the misuse and misappropriation of government funds, a recurring theme within the Kenyan health sector during the COVID-19 pandemic. Despite large donations being made to fight the

46 Jemimah Mueni, '152 New Cases in Kenya as Govt Assures of Free Vaccines In Public Hospitals from Next Month' (*Capital News*, 20 February 2021) <https://www.capitalfm.co.ke/news/2021/02/152-new-covid-cases-in-kenya-as-govt-assures-of-free-vaccines-in-public-hospitals-from-next-month/>.

47 National Emergency Response Committee on Coronavirus, 'Update of Coronavirus in the Country and Response Measures as at January 29 2021, Day 319, Brief No 311' <https://www.health.go.ke/wp-content/uploads/2021/02/JANUARY-29-COVID-19-STATEMENT.pdf>.

48 Magdaline Saya, 'Vaccine Scandal: Rogue Staff Selling COVID-19 Jabs' (*The Star*, 23 March 2021) <https://www.the-star.co.ke/news/2021-03-23-vaccine-scandal-rogue-staff-selling-COVID-19-jabs/>.

49 'Uncertainty over Second Dose of Oxford/AstraZeneca Vaccine Rocks Kenya as COVID-19 Cases Increase' (*KTN News Kenya*, 20 April 2021) <https://www.youtube.com/watch?v=4OOkNAf2jAw>.

50 The World Bank, 'Kenya Secures $130 Million for COVID-19 Vaccines' (28 June 2021) <https://www.worldbank.org/en/news/press-release/2021/06/28/kenya-secures-130-million-for-COVID-19-vaccines>.

51 'The Sixteenth [16th] Presidential Address on The Coronavirus Pandemic' (29 June 2021) <https://www.president.go.ke/2021/06/29/the-sixteenth-16-th-presidential-address-on-the-coronavirus-pandemic/>.

52 Johns Hopkins University Coronavirus Resource Center (n 10).

virus, the government failed to keep track of funds and as a result over two billion US dollars was mismanaged and awarded to politically-connected individuals and businesses by the Kenya Medical Supplies Authority (KEMSA), the state corporation mandated to procure and distribute drugs and medical supplies for prescribed public health programmes.[53] Although a parliamentary committee on health investigated these allegations, it did not result in repercussions despite the committee's incriminating recommendations and increased oversight measures.[54] Furthermore, although the president gave investigative agencies 21 days to conclude investigations, this order fell on deaf ears and no prosecutions have taken place to date.[55]

7. Heightened Marginalisation of Vulnerable Communities

The result of the state's failures and inaction, particularly by the executive and legislature, has been the deepening of existing inequities within the country as a result of both the pandemic and the authorities' response to it.

7.1 Economic Fallout and Socio-Economic Crisis

In order to cushion Kenyans against economic shocks caused by COVID-19, Parliament endorsed and passed the 2020 Tax Laws (Amendment) Bill on 25 April 2020, which enabled Kenyans to enjoy COVID-19 tax relief in 2020.[56] In 2021, the country reverted to pre-COVID-19 tax rates, removing all tax concessions, as well as bringing to an end cash transfers of around 1,000 shillings (around US$9 or €8) per week to poor households.[57] Human Rights Watch estimated that, based on official data, the cash transfer programme provided support to less than 5% of socio-economically vulnerable families, which means that the government failed to guarantee the rights to social security and to an adequate standard of living, guaranteed by Articles 9 and 11 of the International Covenant on Economic, Social and Cultural Rights (ICESCR), to more than 95% of vulnerable households.[58] The president's addresses announcing the directives to combat the third

53 Emmanuel Igunza, 'Coronavirus Corruption in Kenya: Officials and Business People Targeted' (*BBC News*, 24 September 2020) <https://www.bbc.com/news/world-africa-54278417>.

54 Paul Wafula, 'At Long Last, Faces of COVID-19 Millionaires Start Emerging' (*Nation*, 24 November 2020) <https://nation.africa/kenya/news/at-long-last-faces-of-COVID-19-millionaires-start-emerging--3208076?view=htmlamp>.

55 Moses Odhiambo, 'Transparency International Renews Bid to have Kemsa Suspects Charged' (*The Star*, 21 April 2021) <https://www.the-star.co.ke/news/2021-04-21-transparency-international-renews-bid-to-have-kemsa-suspects-charged/>.

56 The Tax Laws (Amendment) Act 2020.

57 Edwin Mutai, 'State to End Free Sh1,000 Weekly M-Pesa Transfer in October' (*Business Daily*, 12 August 2020) <https://www.businessdailyafrica.com/bd/economy/state-to-end-free-sh1-000-weekly-m-pesa-transfer-in-october-2298444>.

58 Human Rights Watch, '"We Are All Vulnerable Here": Kenya's Pandemic Cash Transfer Program Riddled with Irregularities' (20 July 2021) <https://www.hrw.org/report/2021/07/20/we-are-all-vulnerable-here/kenyas-pandemic-cash-transfer-program-riddled>.

and fourth waves on 12 March 2021[59] and 29 June 2021[60] were silent on any contingency plan or a comprehensive framework to deal with the economic fallout occasioned by the pandemic.

Similarly, while the Kenyan government took some action to protect supply chains and distribute food to vulnerable populations, in the weeks after the government enacted the COVID-19 directives in 2020, unemployed Kenyans scrambled for food donations, and financial assistance was offered to only a few with no clear implementation plan or adequate transparency and accountability measures in place.[61] Therefore, many people, particularly in informal settlements, were left to fend for themselves. The foregoing coupled with a poor supply of water needed to combat the virus, meant that the government's lack of preparedness escalated into a socio-economic crisis.[62] Despite these lessons, the measures put in place in 2021 have been silent on securing food and water supplies to vulnerable families and communities.

This account indicates a failure by Kenya to meet its obligations not only under ICESCR but also under constitutional protections of the right to be free from hunger (Article 43(1)(c)), to be provided with adequate social security (Article 43(3)) and to have adequate housing and sanitation (Article 43(1)(b)), as well as analogous rights in the African Charter on Human and Peoples' Rights (the African Charter).

7.2 The 'Shadow Pandemic'

Kenya is fighting a second pandemic, dubbed 'the shadow pandemic', which refers to the violence being perpetrated against women and girls. Globally, data shows that there has been a surge in cases of gender-based violence since the onset of COVID-19.[63] In April 2020, civil society organisations sent an advisory opinion to government, which urged the taskforce on COVID-19 to ensure

59 'The Fourteenth Presidential Address on the Coronavirus Pandemic on Friday, 12 March 2021 at State House, Nairobi' <https://www.president.go.ke/2021/03/12/the-fourteenth-14th-presidential-address-on-the-coronavirus-pandemic-on-friday-12th-march-2021-at-state-house-nairobi/>.

60 'The Sixteenth Presidential Address on the Coronavirus Pandemic' (29 June 2021) <https://www.president.go.ke/2021/06/29/the-sixteenth-16-th-presidential-address-on-the-coronavirus-pandemic/>.

61 Thomas Bwire, 'They Used to Give Their Kids 3 Meals a Day: Then Came Coronavirus' (*NPR*, 11 May 2020) <https://www.npr.org/sections/goatsandsoda/2020/05/11/852423214/they-used-to-give-their-kids-3-meals-a-day-then-came-coronavirus>.

62 Duncan Miriri, 'Taps Run Dry in Kenya's Capital as Coronavirus Spreads' (*Reuters*, 14 May 2020) <https://www.reuters.com/article/us-health-coronavirus-kenya-water-idUSKBN22Q2JN>.

63 UN Women, *COVID-19 and Ending Violence Against Women and Girls* (2020) <https://www.unwomen.org/-/media/headquarters/attachments/sections/library/publications/2020/issue-brief-COVID-19-and-ending-violence-against-women-and-girls-en.pdf?la=en&vs=5006>. See also Donald and Leach, chapter 8.

that Kenya's response was gender sensitive.[64] Despite this, the country was slow to act and Kenya experienced a spike in gender-based violence cases, an increase in unintended pregnancies among teenagers and contraceptive shortages.[65] In late October, the government finally took heed of requests and enacted the Protection Against Domestic violence Rules 2020 to expedite complaints of suspected domestic violence cases; however, the implementation of these rules is yet to be seen.

7.3 Healthcare Workers Exposed

Healthcare workers, despite being vulnerable to infection, found themselves in an extended dispute with the government that resulted in a series of strikes by doctors, nurses and clinical officers between September 2020 and January 2021.[66] The strikes focused on the national and county governments' failure to provide a conducive and safe working environment through the provision of low-quality personal protective equipment and a failure to provide health insurance and isolation and treatment facilities for healthcare workers. Additionally, there were reports that infected healthcare workers had to attend to patients instead of isolating, putting patients at risk of contracting the virus.[67] It is therefore unsurprising that more than 60 healthcare professionals were among the 3,750 recorded positive cases that resulted in fatalities by March 2021.[68] By 31 July 2020, only 55.5% of the target population of almost 2,100,008 healthcare professionals had been fully vaccinated.[69] This data indicates that the Kenyan authorities failed to meet their positive obligation to protect the right to health of frontline healthcare workers under Article 12(2)(d) of ICESCR and their right to life under Article 6(1) of the International Covenant on Civil and Political Rights (ICCPR).

64 'The Shadow Pandemic: Kenyan Civil Society Demands Concrete Action to Protect Women and Girls During COVID-19' (*Equality Now*, 28 April 2020) <https://www.equalitynow.org/shadow_pandemic>.

65 Anna Mutavati and others, 'Fighting the Shadow Pandemic of Violence against Women and Children during COVID-19' (UNICEF, 25 April 2020) <https://www.unicef.org/kenya/stories/Fighting-the-shadow-pandemic>; Sophie Partridge-Hicks, 'Rise in Teenage Pregnancies in Kenya Linked to COVID-19 Lockdown' (*Global Citizen*, 19 August 2020) <https://www.globalcitizen.org/en/content/rise-in-teenage-pregnancies-during-kenya-lockdown/?template=next>.

66 'Health Workers in Kenya Set to Embark on Strike on December 7' (*Peoples Dispatch*, 25 November 2020) <https://peoplesdispatch.org/2020/11/25/health-workers-in-kenya-set-to-embark-on-strike-on-december-7/>.

67 Angela Oketch, 'Kenya: Revealed-Horror of COVID-19 Sick Doctors Forced to Treat Patients' (*All Africa*, 20 November 2020) <https://allafrica.com/stories/202011230128.html>.

68 Patrick Vidija, 'At Least 60 Healthcare Workers have Died of Covid, says Lobby' (*The Star*, 6 March 2021) <https://www.the-star.co.ke/news/2021-03-26-at-least-60-healthcare-workers-have-died-of-covid-says-lobby/>.

69 Ministry of Health, Updates on COVID-19 Vaccination Exercise (31 July 2021) <https://www.health.go.ke/wp-content/uploads/2021/08/MINISTRY-OF-HEALTH-KENYA-COVID-19-IMMUNIZATION-STATUS-REPORT-31ST-JULY-2021.pdf>.

7.4 The Right to Education Disrupted

Shortly after schools in the country were abruptly closed in March 2020, with less than one week's notice, the Ministry of Education developed the Kenya Basic Education COVID-19 Emergency Response Plan, which outlined interventions meant to prevent the spread of the pandemic and respond to educational needs during and after the COVID-19 crisis.[70] The plan acknowledged that the disruption of learning particularly impacts upon children with disabilities and financially disadvantaged children from informal settlements who cannot access remote learning tools, among other challenges. However, while the government provided free online, radio and television lessons, they were not differentiated to meet the varied learning needs of students, especially learners with disabilities, and infrastructure was lacking to sustain effective online teaching and learning.[71] Educational institutions reopened in January 2021, but promptly shutdown again in March due to the third wave. Where the country already had a great task ahead to bridge inequalities in access to and quality of education, this was further widened by the pandemic, and the full realisation of the right to education under Article 13 of ICESCR, especially for marginalised learners, has been set back. Not only that, but prolonged school closures and limited police presence also left girls at increased risk of sexual exploitation, domestic abuse and female genital mutilation.[72]

8. Conclusion and Recommendations

In analysing the experiences of various communities due to the pandemic and the authorities' response, it is evident that the state failed to meet both its constitutional and human rights obligations as codified in a number of treaty documents that Kenya is a party to, including the ICESCR, the ICCPR, the African Charter, and the Protocol to the African Charter on the Rights of Women. The executive's actions were largely unchecked with the legislature taking a back seat and the judiciary being slow in its response. While the president has not to date declared a state of emergency, he has often operated as though one was in place. The results of this have been excessive law enforcement; poorly executed mandatory quarantine; poor public participation practices; inadequate legislative scrutiny; misuse and misappropriation of government funds; deficient policing oversight; an absent contingency plan for economic fallout; and the blatant non-utilisation of a rights-based approach resulting in preventable human rights violations. The foregoing is evidence of the ultra vires use of powers and the mismanagement of

70 Ministry of Education, *Kenya Basic Education COVID-19 Emergency Response Plan* (May 2020) <https://www.education.go.ke/images/Kenya_basic_Education_COVID-19_Emergency_Response_Plan-compressed.pdf>.

71 Adrienne Monteath-van Dok, Anthony Davis and Nicholas Frost, *Education in Crisis: COVID-19 and Adolescents' Education in Fragile Contexts* (Plan International 2021) 40–41.

72 ibid 40.

the pandemic by the executive, despite being cautioned by civil society to employ a human rights-based approach.[73]

In preparation for future pandemics in Kenya, the following are some recommendations that should be considered. First, structural reforms within KEMSA are needed in order to improve transparency and accountability with respect to the use of funds in the procurement of medical supplies. Second, to facilitate access to justice, the judiciary should introduce penalties to mitigate the non-responsiveness of state agencies within the judiciary's rules during pandemic periods, as well as establishing specialised courts to sit during emergency periods. Third, the Pandemic Response and Management Bill 2020 centered on human rights should be enacted. Finally, there should be provision of economic cushion packages such as cash transfers to vulnerable communities, tax relief measures and business stimulus initiatives to protect Kenyans from the economic fallout of a pandemic and uphold economic and social rights.

Constitutionally, rights may only be limited by law and only to the extent that is reasonable and justifiable in an open and democratic society based on human dignity, equality and freedom. While the current situation calls for extraordinary emergency response strategies in line with the government's public health objectives, a human rights-based approach must still be employed.

73 Advisory Note on Ensuring a Rights-Based Response to Curb the Spread of COVID-19 (n 5).

PART III

The Rule of Law

Overview

Embodying the ideal that no one is above the law, not even in times of crisis and emergency, the rule of law is a foundational value of law and legal systems. It demands adherence to the principles of legality, legal certainty, equality before the law, access to justice and accountability for the prevention of the arbitrary use of power. However, the exigencies of global crisis have placed pressure on the expectation that systems should attain a high degree of compliance with the rule of law. One of the most immediate challenges of the pandemic was to balance the demands of rapid action with the procedural and substantive requirements of legal certainty and legality. Part III examines the impact of the pandemic on the rule of law, and the common and transversal concerns which have arisen, highlighting the experiences of Brazil, Sweden, Turkey, Hungary and Pakistan.

In the first thematic commentary, Joelle Grogan and Julinda Beqiraj outline the essential function of the rule of law in pandemic response. Adopting the principles which embody it as a framework for analysis, they expose concerning developments and weaknesses in national systems where the COVID-19 pandemic provided both a catalyst and a cover for further rule of law backsliding. At the same time, they highlight emerging best practices which not only helped engender public trust but also boosted the effectiveness of the pandemic response. They argue that the rule of law provides a "perimeter of legitimacy" to the restrictive measures taken in response to the pandemic, and that adherence to the rule of law can strengthen public trust in institutions, ultimately bolstering their effectiveness through increased compliance.

In the second thematic commentary, Hans Petter Graver considers the mode of assessment of governments' responses to COVID-19 from a rule of law perspective, arguing that the public health consequences cannot be the only, or even principal, measure of success (or failure). He argues for an approach assessing the

DOI: 10.4324/9781003211952-18

costs of the pandemic on democracy and the rule of law based on examining the consequent health of democratic institutions. Taking the diverse actions of Nordic states as case studies of well-established democracies adopting rationalist approaches, and with a particular emphasis on Norway, he evidences how legal and policy choices nevertheless exposed vulnerabilities in terms of excessive reliance on executive law-making, weak oversight mechanisms and opacity of decision-making. Where the COVID-19 pandemic is now a precedent for the action to be taken (or avoided) in future crises, he argues that critical assessment of the health of democratic institutions is essential.

In the first country chapter, Thomas Bustamante and Emílio Peluso Neder Meyer expose how the denialist approach adopted by the Bolsonaro government in **Brazil** is a case study in the consequences of populist and anti-science governance. Driven by two imperatives of being a 'model citizen' through commitment to Bolsonarism and a concept of liberty whereby freedom is decoupled from responsibility, the driving populist force of the federal government has negatively equated the rule of law with 'rule of the elite'. The authors examine and expose the irrationality of this attitude, dissecting the consequences for governance and pandemic response, and highlighting what capacity there is for legislative and judicial resistance to ensure the accountability of government to the law.

Sweden garnered worldwide attention for its approach to pandemic management, which notably diverged from its Nordic counterparts. Iain Cameron and Anna Jonsson Cornell analyse this strategy, characterised by a 'soft law' approach not to impose legal obligations or lockdowns in order to promote sustainable, voluntary adherence. They highlight how the decentralised approach of Swedish governance can promote a 'silo mentality' of responsibility among regional and administrative agencies, yet also how this mode of governance ensured relatively few concerns from a rule of law perspective.

Başak Çalı and Emre Turkut critically assess how the pandemic exacerbated and accelerated the process of executive aggrandisement and overreach in **Turkey**, with the new presidential system of governance catalysing its advancement. They lay bare and examine the (il)legality and legal (un)certainty of government action, the enforcement of rules with little or no legislative or judicial oversight, and the discriminatory application of the law, which evidenced critical failures in rule of law compliance.

In the case of **Hungary**, Kriszta Kovács exposes how the pandemic provided a further opportunity for Prime Minister Viktor Orbán to capitalise on a crisis to expand unchecked executive power. The near-permanent state of emergency engineered by Orbán's government and supermajority in Parliament, in addition to political control over the Constitutional Court, displaced the norms of governance based on rights, democracy and the rule of law. She underscores the limited, and decreasing, capacity for either domestic or supranational legal resistance to continuing autocratisation against the backdrop of the global health crisis.

Shaheera Syed and Nadia Tariq-Ali consider the response to the COVID-19 pandemic in **Pakistan**. Tracing the challenges faced within developing countries with inadequate healthcare structures and weak economic systems, which are still in the process of democratic and rule of law consolidation, they highlight the destructive 'battle of narratives' between the right to life and the right to livelihood across levels of government, which hindered any coordinated pandemic response. They question the effectiveness of both federal and provincial responses, characterised by centralised decision-making and non-democratic 'quick-fixes', which collectively undermined the capacity of the state to tackle the health emergency and exacted a heavy cost in terms of both the rights and well-being of citizens.

16

THE RULE OF LAW AS THE PERIMETER OF LEGITIMACY FOR COVID-19 RESPONSES

Joelle Grogan and Julinda Beqiraj

1. Introduction[1]

The COVID-19 pandemic exerted extreme strain on legal systems worldwide, as they struggled to adapt existing legislative frameworks, administrative functions and executive decision-making to the fast-changing and complex pandemic emergency.[2] The measures adopted worldwide, including mandates in the form of lockdowns and restrictions on gatherings as well as closures of educational and business institutions, were not only among the most widespread and restrictive limitations on rights seen in contemporary history, but also long-lasting and of uncertain duration. The social, political and regulatory environment created by pandemic conditions, including the speed at which action is needed, and the complex and changing demands of mitigating risk to the provision of healthcare, justice and supply chain services, can deprioritise the expectation of a high level of compliance with fundamental norms of governance based on the rule of law. Where a measure must be introduced quickly, little time is available for ex ante parliamentary scrutiny; where courts are closed due to the risk of infection, both ex post scrutiny and access to justice may be compromised.

However, in such an environment of incentivising rapid action without restraint, the danger of the (mis)use of powers during an emergency (far broader than only the use of *emergency* powers) was exposed, and where crisis propagated crisis, this proved a catalyst for further rule of law backsliding and democratic deconsolida-

1 All websites accessed on 8 September 2021.

2 This chapter draws from Joelle Grogan and Julinda Beqiraj, 'Rule of Law as a Perimeter of Legitimacy for COVID-19 Responses' (*Verfassungsblog*, 17 April 2021) <https://verfassungsblog.de/rule-of-law-as-a-perimeter-of-legitimacy-for-covid-19-responses/>.

DOI: 10.4324/9781003211952-19

tion.[3] It should be emphasised that this trend is not localised, but global in scope, as the extended emergency exposed the fragility of even well-entrenched democracies in times of crisis.[4]

However, even amid such stresses, the rule of law can and should inform responses to emergency, as much as it should guide the use of power in ordinary times.[5] The principles which form the foundation of the rule of law are no less relevant to situations of extreme uncertainty and risk and provide a perimeter of legitimacy for the restrictive measures taken in response to emergency. Taking the heads of rule of law principles as the framework of analysis – legality, legal certainty, accountability and the prevention of the misuse of power, access to justice and equality before the law – this chapter highlights deeply worrying trends, but also identifies where compliance with the rule of law can both inform and enhance effective strategies to manage risk, respond to emergency and prepare for future emergencies.

2. The Principle of Legality

That government should only act within the boundaries of the law is an axiomatic precept of the rule of law. As a principle, legality requires that state action is carried out in accordance with transparent and democratically enacted laws, not mere – and unconstrained – discretion. It also requires that the *process* for enacting laws is transparent, democratic and subject to scrutiny. However, the exigencies of an emergency can place pressure on governments to act, and act rapidly. The need for a decisive response during a pandemic can favour swift executive action over inevitably slower legislative or consultative processes. The speed of executive response and consequent control over the levels of infection, for example in Rwanda[6] and New Zealand,[7] evidenced the importance of early response to a developing pandemic.

Ensuring the security of the state and its democratic institutions, as well as the safety of its officials and population, are vital public and private interests, which deserve protection and may also require temporary derogations from cer-

3 See V-Dem Institute, 'Autocratization Turns Viral, Democracy Report 2021' <https://www.v-dem.net/media/filer_public/74/8c/748c68ad-f224-4cd7-87f9-8794add5c60f/dr_2021_updated.pdf>; and Daly, chapter 1 in this volume. See also Tom Daly, 'Democratic Decay: Conceptualising an Emerging Research Field' (2019) 11 Hague Journal on the Rule of Law 9.

4 OECD, 'Covid-19, Crises and Fragility' (29 April 2020) https://read.oecd-ilibrary.org/view/?ref=131_131938-b9ys3suiav&title=COVID-19-Crises-and-Fragility&_ga=2.200027374.1503018746.1629466595-1487165545.1629466595; see also Kim Lane Scheppele, 'Autocratic Legalism' (2018) 85 University of Chicago Law Review 545.

5 Nyasha Weinberg and Joelle Grogan 'Effective Pandemic Management Requires the Rule of Law and Good Governance' (*Verfassungsblog*, 4 November 2020) <https://verfassungsblog.de/effective-pandemic-management-requires-the-rule-of-law-and-good-governance/>.

6 Bikesha and Moore, chapter 26.

7 Knight, chapter 3.

tain human rights and an extraordinary, albeit time-limited, division of power.[8] However, and following the Council of Europe's Venice Commission, it should be underlined that: "State security and public safety can only be effectively secured in a democracy which fully respects the rule of law."[9]

At a global level, the majority of legal acts adopted in response to the pandemic were promulgated by the executive, rather than legislatures, again reflecting the balance in favour of rapid action over slower legislative processes. These executive-led legal responses to COVID-19 varied in form (e.g. orders, decrees, statutory instruments or regulations) and legal basis (e.g. based on powers under a constitutional state of emergency, prerogative powers or ordinary laws and legislation). That executive decision-making led the pandemic response is neither surprising nor innately concerning, just as emergency powers are not inherently problematic nor executive reliance solely upon ordinary law during a crisis always unproblematic.[10] However, where the use of these powers represents a shift (or an attempt to shift) the balance of powers decisively or permanently towards the executive (e.g. executive aggrandisement or "overreach"[11]), this *is* a problem from the perspective of legality and the rule of law.

To identify where risks to the rule of law arise, it is essential to focus on the *use* and not only the *form* of such measures. In a concerning number of countries, executive-made laws raised questions as to their legality where they rested on an uncertain legal basis or had no legal foundation whatsoever. Beyond violating a central tenet of the rule of law, this had concerning and tangible consequences for individuals where the measures carried sometimes severe penalties for non-compliance. For example, in Turkey, the plethora of presidential and ministerial circulars, public announcements and decisions of pandemic boards, which severely restricted constitutionally protected rights, were not provided for through parliamentary legislation as expressly required by the constitution.[12] Such a constitutional safeguard that requires restrictions on rights to be provided by law (and not secondary acts of government) can be an effective tool where used, but was all too often ignored or avoided during the COVID-19 pandemic.[13]

8 Emmons, chapter 30.

9 Venice Commission of the Council of Europe (2016) 'Rule of Law Checklist' (Council of Europe, 11–12 March 2016) <https://bit.ly/3cLPqpC>.

10 Joelle Grogan, 'States of Emergency: Analysing Global Use of Emergency Powers in Response to COVID-19' (2020) 22(4) European Journal of Law Reform 338.

11 David Pozen and Kim Lane Scheppele, 'Executive Overreach and Underreach in the Pandemic' in Miguel Poiares Maduro and Paul W Kahn (eds), *Democracy in Times of Pandemic: Different Futures Imagined* (Cambridge University Press 2020).

12 Article 13, Constitution of Turkey. Çalı and Turkut, chapter 20.

13 Jakub Jaraczewski 'The New Normal? – Emergency Measures in Response to the Second COVID-19 Wave in Poland' (*Verfassungsblog*, 24 March 2021) <https://verfassungsblog.de/the-new-normal-emergency-measures-in-response-to-the-second-covid-19-wave-in-poland/>; Roman Petrov and Bohdan Bernatskyi, 'Pandemic and Fragile Government: A Year of COVID-19 Fatigue and Disorder in Ukraine' (*Verfassungsblog*, 4 March 2021) <https://verfassungsblog.de/pandemic-and-fragile-government-a-year-of-covid-19-fatigue-and-disorder-in-ukraine/>.

Where pre-pandemic ordinary legislation was relied upon to provide for exceptional regulatory powers of government and also administrative agencies, it sometimes arguably provided for too great a degree of discretion for executive action. Take, for instance, the restrictive measures promulgated by the Indian government, which created a "patchwork of guidelines, ordinances and government orders" and allowed "an undue amount of discretion in the executive to decide on the nature and extent of the restrictions imposed on rights".[14] Such unrestrained discretion tests the limits of legality. An alternative and preferable response would have been to enact targeted legislation, providing for the delegation of powers but with the appropriate safeguards of limited action, necessity, proportionality, temporariness, and non-discrimination, as well as legislative and judicial oversight.

In many instances, however, safeguards were absent from legislation enacted in response to the pandemic and allowed virtually unconstrained discretion. Significant deference to government decision-making in the form of broad, discretionary, vague and open-ended provisions in COVID-19 legislation, often adopted in haste, allowed executives to take significant action with limited parliamentary scrutiny – both at the point of drafting[15] and of implementation and application.[16] In Germany, the initial legislative response by the *Bundestag* in March 2020 was to give the federal health ministry powers to announce COVID-19 measures by decree without set time limits (ostensibly contrary to the requirement of German constitutional law); these required explicit repeal by the Federal Parliament to end, rather than automatically expiring.[17] This was remedied a year later in March 2021, with the introduction of a sunset clause. The Swiss example in this context is revealing: the 'COVID-19 Act'[18] passed in September 2020 was "too vague for ordinary legislation" but when considered as emergency legislation created "a form of empowerment vis-à-vis the government that lacks a constitutional basis".[19] In this way, reliance on ordinary legislation is no obvious antidote to the overuse of emergency powers and legislation. While many such Acts have sunset clauses (providing a date at which the Act will expire without extension, typically by legislatures), where such Acts make permanent changes to other laws or are themselves made permanent, this can introduce a form of 'emergency creep', infecting governance beyond the immediate pandemic crisis.

In the context of states of emergency or exception[20] and the use of emergency powers, further challenges arise in the context of legality. Such emergency

14 Raj, chapter 12, 148.

15 Grogan, chapter 5.

16 Kovács, chapter 21.

17 Mangold, chapter 27.

18 Federal Act on the Statutory Principles for Federal Council Ordinances on Combating the COVID-19 Epidemic (COVID-19 Act) of 25 September 2020, 818.102.

19 Felix Uhlmann and Odile Ammann 'Switzerland and the COVID-19 Pandemic: A Look Back and a Look Into the Future' (*Verfassungsblog*, 11 March 2021) <https://verfassungsblog.de/switzerland-and-the-covid-19-pandemic-a-look-back-and-a-look-into-the-future/>.

20 The term 'states of emergency' is used broadly here to include constitutional and legal frameworks which designate the use of exceptional or emergency power by the executive, but please

frameworks are often framed in open-ended and broadly interpretable terms,[21] and sometimes with limited explicit provision for judicial oversight or parliamentary scrutiny.[22] Concerns about the potential misuse of emergency provisions become more pressing where the emergency is of extended duration – as we experience at the time of writing, 18 months into the COVID-19 pandemic. The near perpetual states of emergency or exception declared in Hungary (since 2016),[23] France (since 2015),[24] and Egypt (near continuously since 1967)[25] *prior* to the pandemic, and extended through it, violated the expectation of temporariness that should govern such emergency states. Each of these countries also showed a marked *intensification* of states of emergency: layering additional powers with fewer checks and balances.

Extended use of emergency power over time blunts any possible justification for its use and risks the normalisation of the exceptional – the "permanence of the temporary".[26] For ordinary citizens, this may mean that the exercise of ordinary rights without restriction is forgotten; and for governments, action with limited oversight may become the norm. Hungary, in particular, provides a troubling example, where successive 'crises' led to a "permanent state of emergency" to "consolidate power within the executive".[27] While pandemic legislation is frequently temporary in text, it risks becoming permanent in effect where governments (alone) determine when the need for emergency powers ends. The Hungarian government's extraordinary power during the pandemic was criticised for being broad in scope and without express temporal limit or strict rational connection to the areas where an urgent response to the pandemic was required.[28]

By contrast, Sweden diverged both from its Nordic neighbours and many states further afield in its approach to the containment of the virus and crisis management. The Swedish government did not impose a total lockdown, in the

---

note the challenge of categorisation: "Models of emergency power and the observed use of power during the COVID-19 emergency may be understood as existing on a spectrum ranging from constitutional declarations of emergency to extra-legal action, incorporating a wide range of (ostensibly) applicable safeguards and spanning an even wider range of application in practice." Joelle Grogan, 'The Impact of COVID-19 on Constitutionalism and Constitution-Building' in International IDEA Annual Report 2021 (forthcoming). See also Emmons, chapter 30; and Vedaschi and Graziani, chapter 31.

21 See e.g. Tonsakulrungruang and Leelapatana, chapter 14.

22 On emergency frameworks, see David Dyzenhaus, *The Constitution of Law: Legality in a Time of Emergency* (Cambridge University Press 2006); and Oren Gross and Fionnuala Ní Aoláin, *Law in Times of Crisis: Emergency Powers in Theory and Practice* (Cambridge University Press 2006).

23 Kovács, chapter 21.

24 Basilien-Gainche, chapter 35.

25 Ellaboudy, chapter 33.

26 David Dyzenhaus, 'The Permanence of the Temporary: Can Emergency Powers be Normalized?' in Ronald J Daniels and others (eds), *The Security of Freedom* (University of Toronto Press 2001).

27 Kovács, chapter 21, 260; and Gábor Halmai, Gábor Mészáros and Kim Lane Scheppele, 'From Emergency to Disaster: How Hungary's Second Pandemic Emergency will Further Destroy the Rule of Law' (*Verfassungsblog*, 30 May 2020) <https://verfassungsblog.de/from-emergency-to-disaster/>.

28 Kovács, chapter 21.

confidence that voluntary adherence to government recommendations over legal enforcement of restrictive measures, including mask-wearing and lockdowns, was necessary in order to be sustainable. In terms of the principle of legality, there was neither adoption of retrospective legislation nor interpretation of the law beyond what would have been acceptable. Legislation, even when adopted at speed, was temporary and did not involve wide discretionary powers delegated to government or administrative agencies. However, criticism was levelled at the Swedish government as to whether it should have adopted and exercised *more* powers – particularly in the light of the decentralised powers among administrative agencies which may have, at points, hindered effective action to contain the virus and protect vulnerable communities.[29]

On reflection, it can be argued that adherence to the principle of legality protects individuals from the arbitrary exercise of public power, and by ensuring that governance is exercised through rules and not discretion, guards the essence of the rule of law. Such compliance goes beyond formal authorisation by law and is an essential safeguard when circumstances of emergency put into question law's control over government action and challenge the balance between the empowerment of government and the protection of individual rights.

3. The Principle of Legal Certainty

The early stages of the pandemic were marked by an extreme degree of uncertainty as regards the nature and scale of the threat posed by COVID-19. Rapid lessons had to be learned about its virality and mode of transmission, and about the effectiveness of strategies to minimise community exposure and mitigate negative economic and social consequences. Common strategies were adopted worldwide including mask-wearing and social-distancing mandates, quarantine procedures and regional or national lockdowns. Nevertheless, the diversity of approaches as to when to introduce, reduce or remove measures, and how to enforce them, evidenced the uncertainty among decision-makers as to the most appropriate strategy to confront the global health crisis. However, even where there is *uncertainty* as to the most effective practice, this does not negate the need for *certainty* as to what the rules are, and what they require of people. Legal certainty in this context requires accessible, intelligible, clear, predictable and prospective laws in so far as is possible. It is also coupled with clear communication, as well as consistent and prospective application. Within the wider context of the 'infodemic' of fake news and misinformation, communication of the rationale underpinning measures is an important element to ensure they are understood and to boost compliance.

Certainty is needed for public administration, the private sector and citizens alike to ascertain what their rights and obligations are, as well as to prevent inconsistency or arbitrariness in the application of the law. Being strongly based upon the temporal dimension of laws and the prohibition of retroactivity, the princi-

29 Cameron and Jonsson Cornell, chapter 19.

ple of legal certainty is particularly relevant in the criminal law sector, as regards compliance with the 'no punishment without law' (*nulla poena sine lege*) principle. However, as seen in many of the states examined within this volume, governments have used the exigencies of the pandemic emergency crisis to introduce and apply punishment with little certainty,[30] and possibly even *without* law.[31]

Regulatory dysfunction results when people are unable to follow, or know, the laws which should guide their actions. A concerning trend observable worldwide was the rapid introduction of measures with little or no notice, or which were only published after they had come into force.[32] In some cases, this seems to have been a deliberate choice of executives rather than a necessity of circumstance: for example, Russian federal action via ordinance (which does not require publication) rather than decree (which requires publication) caused an absence of both communication and awareness of relevant COVID-19 rules on international travel.[33]

Further dysfunction caused by legal uncertainty was exposed where there was an unclear division of legal responsibility and powers between state institutions with conflicting mandates or where decisions were not published.[34] Uncertainties also resulted from political conflicts between levels of government.[35] Where there are sub-state regional differences, this can compromise both legal certainty and equality before the law, as happened for example with the divergent strategies of the Länder in Germany;[36] or the adoption of localised sanctions to a government mandate by the City of Kigali in Rwanda[37] which differed from neighbouring regions operating under the same mandate. A lack of coordinated strategy between central or federal powers and state, provincial or devolved legislatures in some cases had the effect of diminishing the effectiveness of pandemic response across at national level.

Even where localised authority to determine COVID-19 response can be merited to allow for adaptation to local social and epidemiological conditions, uncoordinated and uncommunicated divergence can cause uncertainty (and, by extension, lack of compliance) in both federal and devolved systems,[38] *particularly* where it stems from political disagreement as to the threat posed by the virus. The Brazilian example proves startling in this regard: the active dismissal of the threat of the disease, coupled with the promotion and funding of denialist campaigns by Bolsonaro's federal government, worked against state governments' measures

30 Grogan, chapter 5.
31 Tonsakulrungruang and Leelapatana, chapter 14.
32 See e.g. Grogan, chapter 5.
33 Kirill Koroteev, 'A Year of Zeros? Legal Responses to the COVID-19 Pandemic in Russia' (*Verfassungsblog*, 1 March 2021) <https://verfassungsblog.de/a-year-of-zeros-legal-responses-to-the-covid-19-pandemic-in-russia/>.
34 Darian, chapter 29.
35 Syed and Tariq-Ali, chapter 22.
36 Mangold, chapter 27.
37 Bikesha and Moore, chapter 26.
38 Grogan, chapter 5.

to limit community exposure and mitigate the impact of the health crisis.[39] This is an example of executive *under*reach,[40] and was matched by the downplayed response of the Trump administration.[41] Similarly, the conflict between the federal and provincial governments in Pakistan in gauging the threat of COVID-19 led to opposite policies and rhetoric – even as Prime Minister Imran Khan opposed lockdowns and pandemic measures which could impact the economy, lockdowns were introduced in the provinces of Sindh and Punjab, with partial lockdowns in Khyber Pakhtunkhwa and Balochistan.[42]

While the collective global experience of the pandemic reveals that there is no one constellation and timing of sanitary measures that has proven to be the most effective at containing transmission of the virus and reducing mortality, there are nevertheless clear lessons which emerged from comparative analysis on the more effective means of governance during the pandemic. Rationalised approaches based on clearly communicated measures support higher levels of support and trust and – arguably in so far as comparison can be made at this stage – are *more effective*. New Zealand's successful strategy of coherent and clear communication paired with early response and accountable, decisive and principled leadership provided a standard of approach revealing an effective mode of pandemic governance.[43]

4. Accountability and the Prevention of Misuse of Powers

4.1 Parliamentary Scrutiny

Limiting the possibility for (executive) misuse of powers during an emergency is a particular challenge for courts and legislatures, but this is precisely where the rule of law operates as a safeguard and should inform responses to an emergency. The function of both legislatures and the judiciary is to provide scrutiny and oversight of the practice of governments, particularly where they may severely, and over a long period, curtail the rights and liberties of citizens and residents, in order to hold executives to account and prevent the misuse of powers.

Social-distancing measures inevitably impacted the initial capacity of parliaments to meet,[44] and had the effect of limiting or removing their capacity to conduct oversight.[45] For many states, the involvement of legislatures in both the scrutiny of government action, and in legislating in response to the pandemic, remains at best "modest"[46] and at worst in effect all but suspended.[47] Cumulatively,

39 Bustamante and Meyer, chapter 18.
40 Pozen and Scheppele (n 11).
41 Graber, chapter 6.
42 Syed and Tariq-Ali, chapter 22.
43 Knight, chapter 3.
44 See e.g. Syed and Tariq-Ali, chapter 22; Balasubramaniam, chapter 34.
45 See e.g. Çalı and Turkut, chapter 20; and Kovács, chapter 21.
46 Labuschaigne and Staunton, chapter 28.
47 Malaysia.

the pandemic led to the marginalisation of parliaments;[48] nevertheless, legislative accountability in some instances proved to be an active source of resistance to illiberal governments that were dismantling of the rule of law (as in Brazil[49]).

During the pandemic, there was also evidence of democratic innovation,[50] and good practice principles which could and should be implemented in future pandemics or other emergencies: for example, Finland's standing practice of requiring real-time constitutional and parliamentary scrutiny of government regulations as both constitutional requirements and mandated under the Emergency Powers Act.[51] The Constitutional Law Committee of the Finnish Parliament exercises continuous scrutiny over both the constitutionality and human rights compliance of legislative bills and government regulations. Further good practice could be identified in Sweden, with the establishment of a Commission of Inquiry constituted of independent experts, reviewing actions taken across central, regional and local governmental levels; and with the further constitution of a cross-party parliamentary commission to review the actions of Parliament during the pandemic.[52] In Singapore, all control orders had to be presented to Parliament "as soon as possible", and they could be annulled by the passing of a resolution; similarly, any extension of powers had to be made by Parliament, not the minister for health.[53] The collective approach of New Zealand may prove exemplary in how to ensure accountability across the arenas of democratic, constitutional and "learning" (that is, "systematic improvement") accountability during a pandemic.[54]

4.2 *Judicial Review*

Judicial review can also play a pivotal role in ensuring the accountability of government action (or omission) and the prevention of misuse of power during a pandemic. In relation to challenges to emergency legislation, constitutional or other higher courts could be expected to play a key role in scrutinising such measures. In practice, there was wide variation globally in the intensity and scope of judicial review of compliance of new laws and their implementation with rule of law safeguards. The French *Conseil d'Etat* notably "downgraded the standard of its scrutiny"[55] to a corresponding minimal control, and did not evidence significant ex ante review of executive measures. The "passive and deferential"[56] attitude

48 See e.g. Tom Ginsburg and Mila Versteeg, 'Binding the Unbound Executive: Checks and Balances in Times of Pandemic' (2020) Virginia Public Law and Legal Theory Research Paper 2020–2052 and (2020) University of Chicago Public Law Working Paper 747.

49 Bustamante and Meyer, chapter 18.

50 Daly, chapter 1.

51 Scheinin, chapter 11.

52 Cameron and Jonsson Cornell, chapter 19.

53 Chua and Neo, chapter 7.

54 Knight, chapter 3, 40.

55 Basilien-Gainche, chapter 35, 443.

56 Raj, chapter 12, 150.

adopted by the Indian Supreme Court was in evidence prior to the pandemic,[57] and has only been heightened by it as the court declined to adjudicate in human rights cases.

There are examples, however, of where courts did critically scrutinise emergency legislation, for instance in relation to compliance with transparency, publicity and proportionality requirements, the correct use of legislative authority or the rationality of the laws. The Federal Supreme Court of Brazil, in particular, played a key role in assessing the constitutional legitimacy of COVID-19 measures and delivered important decisions, such as those restricting police raids in Rio de Janeiro's slums during the pandemic, supporting health policies concerning the pandemic as applied to indigenous people, and guaranteeing the constitutional right to access to information in relation to the publication of COVID-19 governmental data.[58]

A further challenge to effective judicial oversight is where there is no competence to review emergency measures or government actions: for example, decisions of the King regarding emergencies in Malaysia are unreviewable,[59] and wide immunities were granted to authorities in the ouster clause for all emergency regulations and actions taken under them in Thailand.[60] However, even where there is competence to review government actions, accountability through judicial review can be negated by excessive deference or the lack of judicial independence; for instance in Hungary, where judicial scrutiny of the emergency measures was de facto missing, as the Constitutional Court was captured by the political allies of Prime Minister Viktor Orbán and lacked independence and impartiality.[61]

Deference to decision-making in the context of the pandemic, however, can be a challenging aspect to consider within the context of accountability, since there can be good reasoning behind deference to political judgment or medical or scientific expertise. A point of difficulty exposed by the pandemic is where the line of judicial oversight begins, and scientific expertise ends. A lack of coherence in government strategy (particularly where there is inconsistency or contradiction between federal and sub-state responses) can bring the judicial branch in for adjudication, calling up officials' testimony as a means of scrutinising the government response. However, the risk is where the judicial branch ventures into evaluation (and criticism) of technical strategy, spending priorities and health expertise, raising questions about judicial *over*reach, as for example in Pakistan.[62]

57 Thulasi K Raj, 'Helpless Spectators: How the Supreme Court Evades Administration of Justice' (*The Caravan*, 1 November 2020) <https://caravanmagazine.in/commentary/helpless-spectators>.

58 Bustamante and Meyer, chapter 18.

59 Balasubramaniam, chapter 34.

60 Tonsakulrungruang and Leelapatana, chapter 14.

61 Kriszta Kovács, 'Hungary and the Pandemic: A Pretext for Expanding Power' (*Verfassungsblog*, 11 March 2021) <https://verfassungsblog.de/hungary-and-the-pandemic-a-pretext-for-expanding-power/>.

62 Syed and Tariq-Ali, chapter 22.

5. Access to Justice

Access to justice requires that everyone is able to challenge legal decisions adverse to their rights or interests and that the provision of justice is impartial, fair and timely. Courts have faced critical challenges during the pandemic, with some courthouses and buildings closing fully, even though for limited periods, and others only dealing with urgent or priority cases. COVID-19 also impacted upon the types and numbers of cases that could be challenged before courts, demanding a sort of 'triage' in the prioritisation of cases to be heard; for instance, courts faced an upsurge of cases related to sanctions imposed on individuals for breach of emergency measures, and offences such as domestic violence and corruption in the health sector, which increased during the pandemic. Case overload in Colombia caused by the sheer volume of governmental decrees paired with existing cases diminished the capacity of the Constitutional Court to review, while the *Consejo de Estado* (the supreme administrative court) declined to review the high number of ordinary decrees and resolutions which had mandated preventive isolation of the population.[63]

The extent to which judges were able to operate in person, virtually or not at all during the pandemic largely depended on the particular state's response to COVID-19 and whether the legislative framework provided for remote hearings while ensuring fair trial standards. For some, the balance was not found justified: in France, the *Conseil Constitutionnel* declared unconstitutional provisions allowing videoconferencing in criminal and juvenile courts without the defendant's agreement, and provisions allowing for the extension (and without provision to challenge) of pre-trial detention without judicial sanction.[64] Further practical challenges were exposed in the limited access of many populations to an adequate and secure internet connection, in addition to the technological literacy which would be necessary to enable remote hearings. This inevitably led to a negative impact on the resolution of disputes for poor and marginalised communities, as well as compounding the severity of the economic consequences for those involved. [65]

6. Equality before the Law

The rule of law can only be fully realised in an environment that respects and protects human rights. Laws should refrain from discriminating against individuals or groups and should guarantee equal and effective protection against discrimination on any ground, such as race, colour, sex, language, religion, political or other opinion, national or social origin, property, birth or other status. Related to this, equality before the law involves that all individuals are subject to the same laws, with no

63 Gaviria-Mira and Hoyos-Ceballos, chapter 13.

64 *Conseil Constitutionnel*, Decision n°2020/872 QPC, 15 January 2021; and *Conseil Constitutionnel*, Decision n°2020-878/879 QPC, 29 January 2021. Basilien-Gainche, chapter 35.

65 World Justice Project, *The Twin Crises of Public Health and the Rule of Law* (June 2020) <https://worldjusticeproject.org/sites/default/files/documents/Twin-Cities-Introduction.pdf>.

individual or group having special legal privileges. The principle of equality before the law adds a substantive dimension and provides context to the other rule of law components. Thus, for instance, it is not sufficient for restrictive measures to be formally authorised by laws, they should also comply with requirements regarding the protection of persons and the constraint of power.

In the context of responses to public health emergencies, measures should strike the right balance between specific conflicting rights, such as, on the one hand, the rights to liberty, freedom of movement, freedom of assembly, manifestation of religion or belief, privacy and the right to work and, on the other hand, the rights to life and health. In finding such a balance, governmental responses have been assessed against compliance with and respect for the general principles of necessity and proportionality. In Australia, for example, the Victorian Ombudsman found that the implementation of the targeted lockdown was wholly disproportionate and prejudicial to public housing residents, and oblivious of health and wellbeing issues, as well as cultural and linguistic diversity.[66] Such independent reviews investigating the proportionality of emergency executive measures play a crucial role, but they must be appropriately safeguarded and resourced, and receive due levels of consideration by governments.

Discriminatory application of legislation and restrictive measures was reported against certain individuals or groups due to their (perceived) nationality or ethnic origin and the severity of the pandemic in a particular country. In Colombia, the courts made a rare intervention in censuring discriminatory rules concerning the mobility of the elderly.[67] Selective enforcement of the law was also evidenced in Turkey, for example in the closure of public spaces and prohibition of public gatherings while still allowing pro-government assemblies to take place.[68] Unduly centralised and / or militarised COVID-19 responses create a risk of further alienating ethnic minorities and entrenching divisions in the population. The militarisation of response in Thailand,[69] the Philippines[70] and Egypt[71] correlated with the marginalisation of ordinary civilian administration, and was characterised by disproportionate and discriminatory application of laws, and the demand of mere obedience rather than offering justified reasoning and clear guidelines, as the strategy for public compliance.

7. The Rule of Law in a Global Health Emergency

Pre-existing threats to the rule of law were exacerbated and deepened by the pandemic, rather than caused by it. The tools used by autocratic or autocratising governments – limiting democratic oversight and review, and using laws to target

66 Rizzi and Tulich, chapter 37.
67 Gaviria-Mira and Hoyos-Ceballos, chapter 13.
68 Çalı and Turkut, chapter 20.
69 Tonsakulrungruang and Leelapatana, chapter 14.
70 Atienza, chapter 36.
71 Ellaboudy, chapter 33.

political enemies and opposition – were already in familiar hands: the pandemic only gave further capital and a guise of justification to accelerating these measures, and making them permanent beyond the pandemic. In times of increased vulnerability and disruption, it is as important as ever to demand adherence to the rule of law principles from those who exercise public power. However, instead, a false and damaging narrative became viral during the COVID-19 pandemic: the necessity of action in response to the pandemic emergency was asserted as legitimising *all* action undertaken by governments. 'Emergency creep', executive aggrandisement and overreach have now entered the vernacular of discussions on the impact of the COVID-19 pandemic, and this is an unwelcome legacy. Our expectations concerning the rule of law should not diminish in times of crisis; rather, adherence to it can strengthen public trust in institutions and consolidate the legitimacy of measures, ultimately bolstering their effectiveness through increased compliance.[72] Such adherence rests on a balance between accountable and rationalised executive decision-making, and active scrutiny and review of executive bodies by the legislature and judiciary. In this way, the rule of law provides a boundary of legitimacy to the restrictive measures taken in response to the pandemic. Beyond the measures of mortality and infection rates, we must also look to the surviving systems which will bear the consequences of the forms of governance adopted during the COVID-19 pandemic, and condition states' preparedness for future emergencies.

72 Jasanoff and Hilgartner, chapter 23.

17

BASELINING COVID-19

How Do We Assess the Success or Failure of the Responses of Governments to the Pandemic?

Hans Petter Graver

1. Introduction[1]

At the time of writing in August 2021, when the COVID-19 pandemic appears to be becoming manageable in many European countries, it is timely to discuss the relative successes and failures of the management of the pandemic. It is easy to concur with the European Commission when it stated that it is essential to "start with a critical look at what has been done, what has worked well and what has not".[2] Phrased differently, how successful have authorities been in their endeavours to contain and control the spread of COVID-19? And from a legal point of view, what are the constitutional and cultural legacies of a year of deploying war-like measures against the virus?

A widespread infectious disease that has serious if not fatal consequences for many of those infected affects society in many ways. Deaths and serious illnesses are human tragedies, require public health resources, affect employers and the economy and may cause serious disruptions in many fields. The same is the case with the measures society imposes in order to combat the disease and its consequences. These measures may be targeted directly at the spread of the disease, but may also have as their aim to alleviate the social or economic consequences of people getting ill. The choice of measures and their aims may in some cases seem inevitable, but are always the result of political considerations and decisions.

1 All websites accessed on 15 August 2021.

2 European Commission, 'Communication from the Commission to the European Parliament, the European Council, the Council, the European Economic And Social Committee and the Committee Of The Regions' (Brussels, 15 June 2021) COM(2021) 380 final 1 <communication150621.pdf (europa.eu)>.

DOI: 10.4324/9781003211952-20

Success and failure can be measured along many lines, and be seen from the perspectives of public health, economic impacts, political institutions and the rule of law, to mention but some. In this chapter, I examine how such evaluations depend and vary relative to the indicators chosen, with a particular emphasis on the rule of law and how the pandemic affects the 'health' of the institutions of democratic governance. I draw my examples mainly from the context of Europe with a specific focus on the Northern European countries, but I believe that the points I make have more general relevance. The Northern European countries have strong democratic institutions and high levels of trust, both between the citizens and the authorities, and between citizens. They should therefore be well equipped to endure a crisis such as the pandemic.[3] But even these countries may come weakened out of the pandemic.

I argue that it is misleading to see the physical effects of the disease as an indicator of failure or success. The number of infections and the fatality rates vary across countries and have no simple correlation with any given indicator. Some point to factors such as age and demography, the size of the population and the differences in gross domestic product (GDP),[4] whereas others emphasise the structure and strength of each nation's social contract and its role in framing how the response unfolded.[5] Public trust seems to be an important factor.[6] Among the high public-trust countries of Northern Europe, Sweden, nevertheless, appears to have failed compared to Denmark, Finland and Norway, if judged by the level of fatalities.[7] If the robustness of health systems – or avoiding health system collapse – is taken as a norm, the approach of Sweden of governing by persuasion, as opposed to a more coercive command-and-control approach taken by many other countries, was a success, since this norm has been upheld. If we exclude the most extreme cases where little or nothing has been done to combat the virus, the variations in performance along health indicators seem to be attributable to many different factors, where details in government policy and measures employed play but a minor role on important indicators such as hospitalisations and fatalities.[8] This means that

3 See Daly, chapter 1 in this volume.

4 Gabriele Sorci, Bruno Faivre and Serge Morand, 'Explaining Among-Country Variation in COVID-19 Case Fatality Rate' (2020) 10 Scientific Reports 18909.

5 Sheila Jasanoff, Stephen Hilgartner, Wilmot James and Lyal White, 'Learning from COVID-19: A 23-Nation Comparative Study of COVID-19 Response, with Lessons for the Future of Public Health' (January 2021) <https://iserp.columbia.edu/sites/default/files/National%20Comparative%20Study%20Synthesis%20Paper.pdf>.

6 See Jasanoff and Hilgartner, chapter 23.

7 Johns Hopkins University Coronavirus Resource Center, COVID-19 Dashboard <https://coronavirus.jhu.edu/map.html>. See also Scheinin, chapter 11; and Cameron and Cornell-Jonsson, chapter 19.

8 For the difficulties of measuring and drawing clear conclusions see, for example, Anjalika Nande and others, 'Dynamics of COVID-19 Under Social Distancing Measures are Driven by Transmission Network Structure' (2021) 17(2) PLoS Computational Biology e1008684; Hamid Khataee, Istvan Scheuring, Andras Czirok and Zoltan Neufeld, 'Effects of Social Distancing on the Spreading of COVID-19 Inferred from Mobile Phone Data' (2021) 11 Scientific Reports 1661.

it is difficult to claim that there are direct links between government policy and health-related indicators.

2. The Need for Clear Criteria

It is of the essence that there are clear criteria to guide decisions on whether to maintain, tighten or relax a lockdown. Governments, however, have not always been clear about the underlying aims of their interventions and restrictive policies to control COVID-19. This has made the rational basis for public policy less secure, diminished the possibility of proportionality tests of measures employed and made an assessment of the success or failure of government policy more difficult. In order both to implement proportionate measures and to evaluate their effectiveness, it is necessary to have a clear idea of what the relevant aims are.

All countries have adopted public health and social measures (PHSM) in response to the pandemic. Many of the measures adopted have been characterised as "the most extremely restrictive measures in modern history",[9] involving restrictions on human rights, such as the right to liberty and security and the right to a fair trial, the right to private life, freedom of conscience, freedom of expression, freedom of association, the right to education and children's welfare, the right to worship, and privacy and data protection.[10]

Measures have included personal protective measures and information; disease detection, investigation and tracing of contacts; restrictions on the holding of any public gatherings; restrictions on and closures of businesses and services, including educational services; restrictions on movement and social contacts; and, in the most extreme cases, stay at home orders and general curfews.[11] The measures have to a varying degree had severe impacts on social life and the economy.

In most countries there has been broad political consensus on the need to employ far-reaching restrictions and shut-downs, and the majority of the population have supported the measures employed by the authorities. Still, protests from professional workers, such as medical experts and lawyers, and political protests against lockdowns and other measures in many countries are evidence that many are sceptical of the use of more authoritarian measures.

Governments all over the world have stretched their legal powers to their limits and, indeed, sometimes beyond. The constitutional requirement that restrictions of fundamental rights must be according to law has thus been challenged by restric-

9 Joelle Grogan, 'States of Emergency: Analysing Global Use of Emergency Powers in Response to COVID-19' (2020) 22(4) European Journal of Law Reform 338.

10 See Council of Europe, 'Respecting Democracy, Rule of Law and Human Rights in the Framework of the COVID-19 Sanitary Crisis: A Toolkit for Member States', Council of Europe Information Documents, SG/Inf(2020)11 (7 April 2020). See also Donald and Leach, chapter 8.

11 World Health Organisation, 'WHO's Work in Health Emergencies: Strengthening Preparedness for Health Emergencies: Implementation of the International Health Regulations (2005)' A74/9 Add.1 (5 May 2021).

tions that have been enacted. In some cases, this has even been established by the highest court of the country.[12]

Whether the measures restrict a fundamental right or not, such measures should be applied only to the degree that they are effective and proportionate. In its guidance for the implementation of PHSMs, the World Health Organisation (WHO) states that: "Measures with the highest level of acceptability and feasibility and proven effectiveness – and which minimize the negative consequences on health and wellbeing of all members of society and the economy and – should be adopted."[13] Where a human right is restricted, a review of the proportionality is required in order to strike the right balance between the right to health and the right that is restricted by the measure.[14]

The proportionality of a measure is highly dependent on the definition of the aim that is pursued. The same is the case when evaluating whether a policy has been successful or not. Measuring success is always about choosing the baseline and the scale for what constitutes success and failure. When we are dealing with values, and incommensurable ones at that, the best measurement is by comparing the same values across different countries and to avoid drawing general conclusions about one country's performance across all values.

There are many dimensions to be compared: the spread and development in the number of confirmed cases of infection, the number of fatalities, the state of the economy, or the harm caused to people who are particularly vulnerable to the effects of lockdowns such as children, the elderly and socio-economically marginalised groups, etc. Governments can thus have many different aims with their responses to the pandemic, and the success of a society's response may be evaluated along many different lines. One may choose such different yardsticks as public health, economic development and alleviation of poverty, or compliance with human rights, to mention but a few.

While many policy documents, for instance the WHO guidance,[15] take the aim of protecting public health for granted, this choice is by no means obvious. The

12 See, for example, the Austrian Constitutional Court decisions: Verfassungsgerichtshof G 272/2020-11 ua.* (1 October 2020) and V 436/2020-15 (10 December 2020). See, further, Michele Di Bari, 'Let Judges Speak for Themselves: Can Comparative Constitutional Case Law Help Conceptualize Universal Standards in the Fight against COVID-19?' in Dirittifondamentali .it – Fascicolo 1/2021 (16 February 2021) <https://ssrn.com/abstract=3805599>; and Patricia Popelier and others, 'Health Crisis Measures and Standards for Fair Decision-Making: A Normative and Empirical-Based Account of the Interplay Between Science, Politics and Courts' (2021) European Journal of Risk Regulation 1.

13 World Health Organisation, 'Considerations for Implementing and Adjusting Public Health and Social Measures in the Context of COVID-19: Interim Guidance' (14 June 2021) 4 <https://apps.who.int/iris/bitstream/handle/10665/341811/WHO-2019-nCoV-Adjusting-PH-measures-2021.1-eng.pdf?sequence=1&isAllowed=y>.

14 Martin Scheinin proposes a model for this balancing in chapter 3 of Martin Scheinin and Helga Molbæk-Steensig, *Pandemics and Human Rights: Three Perspectives on Human Rights Assessment of Strategies against COVID-19*, EUI Working Papers LAW 2021/01.

15 World Health Organisation (n 13).

choice depends on how the policy area is defined. Defining the aim is therefore crucial both for the assessment of proportionality and for the benchmarking of performance. At the very general level, a central aim of measures that are implemented to combat the pandemic is the protection of public health. One could, of course, set other goals, such as the level of protection of human rights, or the uninterrupted functioning of sectors of the economy or public services, and regard the preservation of public health to avoid absences or excess costs as a set of means among others. Protection of public health can be a main value in itself, it can be but a means to obtain and protect other values, or it may be one aim among several, that may or may not be ordered in a hierarchy.

In defining the overarching aim, the sector involved in the policy-making matters. The aim of measures implemented by the health authorities will most often be related to public health. When the measures are decided and implemented by the highest political and regulatory levels of states, one needs to ask the question, however, if it is obvious that the sole aim should be public health. There are, after all, many activities that have profound effects on public health, but where regulatory policy is determined by a broader set of aims. It is enough to mention tobacco, sugar and road traffic, and the place in public policy that disadvantageous consequences to public health associated with such topics have, to substantiate this.

3. Public Health as the Overriding Aim

When the pandemic was declared in March 2020, most countries responded to it as a public health crisis, and most European countries went into a shut-down modus by closing their borders and applying strict PHSMs.[16] Measures directed towards other policy areas such as employment, securing essential supplies, protecting businesses and enterprises, etc., were not the main aim of public policy, but became necessary in order to mitigate the effects of the public health measures. From this perspective it is safe to assume that the main aim of public policy at the time was public health, and that economic and social aims were subsidiary aims, if they were aims at all.

The pandemic transformed society into a medical battlefield governed by the ethics and logic of the hospital, where policy and priorities are determined by the logic of triage. This understanding has been underpinned by daily reporting to the public on the number and rate of infections, the number of hospitalisations and fatalities, the capacity and resources of the health system and human-interest stories about people infected and suffering.

From a human rights perspective, one could argue that states were under an obligation in this way to put the protection of life and human health in the driver's seat. Scheinin and Molbæk-Steensig claim that "not acting to contain the virus or to alleviate suffering caused by it" is not "human-rights-wise acceptable".[17]

16 Grogan (n 9).

17 Scheinin and Molbæk-Steensig (n 14) 2.

Their main argument for this is that the right to life deserves primacy.[18] This begs the question, however, why a 'human rights-based' approach should determine this policy area, and entails a legalisation of policy that is by no means obvious. There are many threats to society and to the life and well-being of its members from various sources. Whereas the right to life is unarguably a human right, there is no right not to die. All threats can, of course, be analysed from the perspective of human rights. But one would be hard put to argue that international human rights determine what should be the priorities and the correct approach of polities to deal with fundamental threats and challenges. This does not mean that such issues cannot be framed in legal – and specifically in human rights – terms.[19] Nevertheless, there is far from agreement that determining the policy in such areas is a matter of law.

Grothe-Hammer and Roth argue that the response of many states to the pandemic has been governed by an underlying norm about protecting lives that implies that a death from COVID-19 is more important than deaths from other causes. The policy is therefore not about protecting lives per se, but about preventing people from dying specifically from or with COVID-19.[20] From this perspective, the apparent consensus that protecting public health should be the main and overriding aim of states' responses to the pandemic may seem surprising.

What is it in the threat of COVID-19 that calls for this response, not only from state authorities, but also from the media and the general public? It is true that in the short term, there is no other cause that results in the number of deaths and hospitalisations as COVID-19. In this way, the pandemic is exceptional. The threat of a plague has, furthermore, always led to widespread fears and to severe reactions from society and from governments. In this way, the reactions to the pandemic are both predictable and understandable. It should, nevertheless, be obvious that a human rights-based approach cannot demand that lives in the context of the pandemic should be valued or treated differently from lives in other contexts. Even in a public health emergency, a human rights-based approach must be based on the same standards as those that are applied under more normal circumstances.

The relationship between public health and human rights is more complex and nuanced than merely stating that the states have an obligation to promote public health as part of their obligation to respect and ensure the right to life. Mann points to three basic relations between human rights and public health.[21] First, public health measures often impose a burden on human rights by limiting activities and invading people's right to self-determination. Second, human rights viola-

18 ibid 3.

19 See Hans Petter Graver, 'Judging for Utopia: Climate Change and Judicial Action' (2020) 28(4) European Review of Private Law 885.

20 Michael Grothe-Hammer and Steffen Roth, 'Dying is Normal, Dying with the Coronavirus Is Not: A Sociological Analysis of the Implicit Norms Behind the Criticism of Swedish "Exceptionalism"' (2021) European Societies 23:sup1 S332.

21 Jonathan M Mann, 'Medicine and Public Health, Ethics and Human Rights' (1997) 27(3) Hastings Center Report 6, 9–10.

tions often have public health implications. And third, protecting and promoting human rights are inextricably linked with protecting and promoting health. Based on this one could claim that an equally relevant baseline for measuring the success of state measures against the pandemic, compared to the protection of public health, could be the extent to which they have respected and promoted human rights during the past year.

Even if we accept that public health should be the overriding concern of public policy during a pandemic, we are still left with many choices as to the definition of the aim and goals of different measures. Public health is a complex field that involves many subjects and targets at different levels. At its most general, public health is about people achieving "the highest possible level of physical, mental, and social well-being".[22] The goal of ensuring and protecting public health can be operationalised in many ways. Examples of such operationalisations are to save lives, to control the number of reported infections, to lower the rate of spread of the disease (the 'R-number'), to protect the most vulnerable and to protect the capacity of the acute health care system. Such operationalisations are necessary for the review of the proportionality of applied measures, to monitor their effectiveness and to assess and compare the success or failure of governments' responses to the pandemic.

4. The Problem of Shifting Aims

In many cases, a shift over time in public health goals can be observed. Initially, many governments were occupied with controlling the spread of the disease in order to protect the capacity of hospitals and health services to deal with people in need of treatment. Throughout the pandemic the aim shifted, and many governments monitored and developed their policies according to reported levels of transmission of the infection, or according to the level of immunity (mainly by vaccination) in the population. The number of deaths or hospitalisations was a central baseline to some countries, regardless of the actual effect on hospital capacity. In countries where the vaccination rate of the most vulnerable people increased, this yardstick lost importance as the foundation for public policy. The WHO, in its guidance from November 2020, recommends an assessment based on a matrix using transmission level and response capacity indicators to guide the adjustment of PHSM.[23] As long as the available health system response capacity is adequate, the WHO advocated for limited disruptions to social and economic activities. Governments do not always make clear in what way their policy goals differ from the WHO-matrix when they enact or keep in place more restrictive measures than those recommended by the WHO.

22 ibid 7.

23 World Health Organisation, 'Considerations for Implementing and Adjusting Public Health and Social Measures in the Context of COVID-19: Interim Guidance' (4 November 2020) 2 <https://apps.who.int/iris/bitstream/handle/10665/336374/WHO-2019-nCoV-Adjusting_PH_measures-2020.2-eng.pdf?sequence=1&isAllowed=y>.

Shifting aims are a challenge to the possibility of judicial review with the proportionality of measures employed by the government, as the fluidity allows the government to streamline its legal defence when challenged. Legal review is, in most cases, ex post facto where circumstances have changed by the time that the measures are reviewed. The case of the Norwegian owners of second homes in Sweden is illuminative. Their possibility to visit their homes in Sweden was curtailed by the first round of restrictions that were imposed on all parts of society in March 2020.

When the restrictions were originally imposed in March 2020, this happened without any substantial review of the benefits and disadvantages of the different measures. The restrictions of the second lockdown were supported by data and reports from the public health authorities, which included assessments of the proportionality of imposing restrictions on most activities in order to ensure social distancing. Now the baseline had shifted, however. Whereas the main argument for restrictions in March 2020 was to preserve the capacity of the health system, the government now argued for the necessity of preventing the import of the virus and eliminating the risk of increased spread of the disease. This led to a major difference in the review of the proportionality of the measures, affecting the possibility to challenge the restrictions by legal means. As the pandemic develops, the aims of the government change. This gives the government the possibility to adapt its legal defence and makes legal review more difficult.

5. The Challenge of Causality

If the problem of establishing the baseline for assessment of success or failure is overcome, there are still severe obstacles to determining a causal relationship between measures employed and developments in public health indicators. Studies seem to indicate, for instance, that variations in cross-country fatalities have more to do with variations in public trust in authorities than with the measures that these authorities have employed.[24] Countries with higher confidence in government values are associated with lower COVID-19 cases and deaths per million. Public trust increases the effectiveness of public information campaigns and increases voluntary compliance with PHSMs.

Sweden, with its vastly higher COVID-19-related deaths than neighbouring Denmark, Finland and Norway, seems to be an exception to this.[25] However, analysed more closely, the differences may relate more to differences in the aims that were set for government policy than differences in the effectiveness of the measures employed. Judged by its own aims to keep the health system from getting overburdened, Sweden's policy has at the time of writing been largely successful,

24 See Mohammad Reza Farzanegan and Hans Philipp Hofmann, 'A Matter of Trust? Political Trust and the COVID-19 Pandemic' (2021) CESifo Working Paper No. 9121 <https://ssrn.com/abstract=3863824>. See also Jasanoff and Hilgartner, chapter 23.

25 Johns Hopkins University Coronavirus Resource Center (n 7).

and Sweden has controlled the spread of the infection and the capacity of the health system much more successfully than most European countries.[26]

As pointed out by Burris and others, the usefulness of any measure depends not on its potential effectiveness under optimal conditions, but rather on its functioning and effects in the typical conditions of real life.[27] This means that assessing the effects of any measure must take into account social factors such as level of trust, control mechanisms, economic and cultural incentives and political and social resistance, among many other factors. Such factors vary across different societies, and may even differ over time, and probably explain more of the variations in the spread of COVID-19 across European countries than differences in the type and timing of government restrictions. In Norway, for instance, the population has been willing to accept some of the harshest border control and quarantine measures of Europe, whereas a proposal to impose a curfew, that has been accepted in many other countries, had to be dropped by the government.[28]

6. A Rule of Law Assessment

Thus, measuring the successes and failures of the management of the pandemic must first establish the criteria by which to perform the assessment. From a legal point of view, highly relevant criteria are those based on a core understanding of the rule of law, the principle of legality and the extent of independent control of the executive use of power. Such an assessment must be specific to a certain polity and legal order, but can, of course, be comparative in scope. Within the scope of a short chapter, it is possible only to scratch the surface. To illustrate the methodology, I will take the case of my own country, Norway, as an example.

In 1950, five years after the Second World War, and two years into the Cold War, Norway passed its Emergency Powers Act for Wartime and the Threat of War. Now, for the first time, after 70 years, the country is again ruled by emergency powers, albeit without a formal declaration of emergency. The government has challenged the constitutional requirement that restrictions of fundamental rights must be according to law by the restrictions that have been enacted. The government also altered the relationship between the legislative power (the *Stortinget*) and executive power by taking on wide law-making powers to deal with the pandemic.[29]

26 Grothe-Hammer and Roth (n 20) S335.

27 Scott Burris, Evan D Anderson and Alexander C Wagenaar, 'The "Legal Epidemiology" of Pandemic Control' (2021) 384 The New England Journal of Medicine 1973, 1974.

28 See Kristin Bergtora Sandvik, Hans Petter Graver and Peter Scharff Smith, 'The Pomp of Popular Constitutional Outrage: The Democratic Struggle over the Norwegian Covid-19 Curfew Proposal' (*Verfassungsblog*, 2 March 2021) <https://verfassungsblog.de/the-pomp-of-popular-constitutional-outrage/>.

29 See Hans Petter Graver, 'Fighting the Virus and the Rule of Law – A Country Report on Norway' (*Verfassungsblog*, 13 April 2020) <https://verfassungsblog.de/fighting-the-virus-and-the-rule-of-law-a-country-report-on-norway/>.

The government has introduced a practice of enacting binding regulations without complying with the normal procedures of public participation and deliberation. The consequences of this are to undermine the legitimacy of the law-making process and to risk flawed decisions due to the lack of input from outside the closed circle of decision-makers. The public engagement in relation to the curfew proposal circulated in January 2021 indicates that the public is able and willing to participate in the development of public policy in the field of COVID-19 restrictions.[30]

At the time of writing, the COVID-19 regulation has been amended more than 120 times.[31] None of these amendments was issued with advance notice. The same is the case for scores of local regulations issued by municipal authorities.[32] The de facto result of this is that by spring 2021 the country is in practice regulated by decrees and regulations through procedures and practices departing fundamentally from the open and inclusive decision-making that are the hallmarks of democratic governance. The embrace of a strategy of governance through piecemeal regulations and abrupt amendments engenders a need for a careful critical scrutiny of the strategy itself but also of the host of decisions on difficult ethical questions and the trade-offs embedded in these regulations.

The experiences of Norway are not particular to that country. On the contrary, they seem to fall into a general pattern of a use of emergency powers and short-circuiting of democratic procedures, even in stable democracies. A majority of countries have met the pandemic with formal emergency powers, and many of those who have not, have, like Norway, used their health legislation "to provide the legal basis for sweeping powers for detention, quarantine and even lockdown".[33] Even entrenched democracies with a "rationalist response" to the pandemic have experienced a side-lining of parliaments, excessive reliance on executive law-making with weak oversight and insufficient transparency.[34]

7. Beyond COVID-19

A year into the pandemic response, the Norwegian government's approach still enjoys broad public support. However, the success comes at a price: the government has established a precedent for extending legal powers in order to fight threats to society. The established legal requirement that restrictions of fundamental rights must be enacted according to law has been challenged. The government, with support from the *Stortinget*, has also weakened the parliamentary control over regulations issued under provisions on emergency powers. Finally, the authorities

30 Sandvik, Graver and Scharff Smith (n 28).

31 The regulations are available at <https://lovdata.no/dokument/SF/forskrift/2020-03-27-470>.

32 The local regulations are available at <https://lovdata.no/referanse/hjemmel?dokID=NL%2Flov%2F1994-08-05-55&kilde=LF>.

33 Grogan (n 9).

34 See Daly, chapter 1.

have based their regulatory activities on excessive exclusiveness and closed procedures.

It may be that in the short-term, the use of emergency or emergency-like powers and the departure from normal democratic and legal procedures have not set countries with strong institutions on the path to an erosion of democracy. How a society deals with crises is not necessarily a measure of how it functions under normal circumstances. Even democratic states based on the rule of law must sometimes employ oppressive measures in defence of democracy.

However, in dealing with the COVID-19 crisis, the state has also created pathways for future crisis responses. In one way, the pandemic has been an 'easy' crisis for democracies, in the sense that the need to deal effectively with the threat posed by the pandemic was so obvious. For this reason, departing from the safeguards of the rule of law may have seemed uncontroversial and unproblematic. The next crisis may be different – and perhaps subject to greater political controversy. When our political rulers set out to deal with such a crisis, they will do so with the legacy of the pandemic as precedent, unless we now review our experiences and enact measures to prevent this. When evaluating the rule of law aspects of the pandemic response, success can not only be measured through an assessment of how the law has dealt with economic turmoil, human suffering and the challenge of providing public services, but also by evaluating whether our institutions are better or worse equipped to meet future challenges.

18
BRAZIL
COVID-19, Illiberal Politics and the Rule of Law

Thomas Bustamante and Emílio Peluso Neder Meyer

1. Introduction[1]

The denialist approach that the Brazilian government adopted to the COVID-19 pandemic was based on a permanent strategy of exposing the population to the virus in the hope of achieving herd immunity, even after consensus had emerged on the inefficacy of such an approach.[2] We analyse, in this chapter, the central aspects of this response. We offer, in section 2, a reconstruction of the value of the rule of law, to show that Brazilian policies on COVID-19 failed to satisfy its demands. In section 3, we provide an account of the ethical commitments that motivate President Jair Bolsonaro's political project, while section 4 offers a panorama of the government's attitude toward the pandemic. Section 5 provides a concrete analysis of the Bolsonarist political machinery. In section 6, we describe the resistance of political institutions to Bolsonarism, and section 7 concludes.

2. Bolsonaro's Politics on COVID-19 and the Rule of Law

The federal government's approach to COVID-19 can be synthesised as a conscious decision to expose the population to the virus, in the hope of achieving herd immunity. President Bolsonaro's government had no fewer than four different ministers of health during the first 14 months of the pandemic, a sign that

1 All websites accessed on 18 July 2021 unless otherwise stated.

2 In a recent book about his experience as Minister of Health at the start of the pandemic, Luíz Henrique Mandetta summed up President Bolsonaro's position as expressed in the following statement: "Let's give [the people] this medicine, because with this little box of chloroquine in hand the workers will come back to activity, will produce again." See Luiz Henrique Mandetta, *Um paciente chamado Brasil: os bastidores da luta contra o coronavírus* (Objetiva 2020) 145, our translation.

DOI: 10.4324/9781003211952-21

only those who agree with his politics stay in office. In opposition to the response by the first of these ministers to the pandemic, Bolsonaro reacted with a denialist populist ideology.[3]

Norms and regulations proposed by the government, media strategies, official pronouncements and even judicial actions filed by Bolsonaro or his supporters on matters related to COVID-19 invariably pursued this goal, which was sustained by an ideology sceptical of science and public health measures.[4] This ideology, however, offered its supporters assurance through a communication apparatus that spread fake news about the risks of the disease, which was often portrayed as a "little flu", and a large-scale use of a combination of drugs without scientific evidence for their efficacy, which Bolsonaro's government officially endorsed as an "early treatment protocol".[5]

Bolsonarism's general approach to politics had an impact on the government's response to COVID-19, which was aimed at a "constitutional erosion".[6] A central aspect of Bolsonarism is an endeavour to undermine democracy from within, through an "incremental degradation" of the three constitutive elements of constitutional democracy: the rule of law, electoral competition and liberal rights.[7] Bolsonaro deepened the process of constitutional erosion in Brazil, attacking the constitutional identity defined by the 1988 Constitution.[8] It is an essential feature of illiberalism that it is at odds with the rule of law, once this value is understood in association with other values like democracy and liberal equality.

3. Ethical Commitments of Bolsonarism

Bolsonarism draws its political justification from two moral assumptions: first, the special dignity of persons committed to Bolsonarism, who are depicted as "model citizens"; second, a concept of liberty that decouples freedom from responsibility. These assumptions are aligned with a populist ideology that treats the rule of law as a euphemism for the rule of the elites.[9]

3 Deisy de Freitas Lima Ventura and Jameson Martins, 'Between Science and Populism: The Brazilian Response to COVID-19 from the Perspective of the Legal Determinants of Global Health' (2020) 17 Brazilian Journal of International Law 67.

4 Daniel Dourado and others, 'Les droits dans la pandémie: analyse juridique et sanitaire au Brésil' (2021) 28 Journal de Droit de la Santé et de l'Assurance Maladie 138.

5 Brazil, Ministério da Saúde, Nota Informativa nº 17/2020 – SE/GAB/SE/MS: Orientações do Ministério da Saúde para manuseio medicamentoso precoce de pacientes dom diagnóstico da Covid-19, 11 August 2020.

6 Emilio Peluso Neder Meyer, *Constitutional Erosion in Brazil* (Hart Publishing 2021) 7.

7 Tom Ginsburg and Aziz Huq, *How to Save a Constitutional Democracy* (University of Chicago Press 2018).

8 Meyer (n 6).

9 Paul Blokker, 'Populist Constitutionalism' in Clara De la Torre (ed) *Routledge Handbook of Global Constitutionalism* (Routledge 2018) 113.

The first prong of Bolsonarist ethics is the concept of the "model citizen" (*cidadão de bem*). Although the social base of Bolsonarism is pluralistic, the various groups that subscribe to it purport to belong to this idealised group, which claims a moral superiority over the rest of the political community.[10] A model citizen is held to possess a "social distinction", but it is important for Bolsonaro's political project that this distinction is easily earned. To be a model citizen is to be entitled to a special status based on what the model citizen is *not*: not corrupt, not leftist, not a scoundrel, not gay, not disorderly, not sensitive to petty victimisation (i.e. racial, gender or social injustice), not dependent on public welfare, etc.[11] By treating himself as a model citizen, the ordinary person claims to earn the entitlement to a special freedom, which is defined without the constraints imposed by the mainstream political thought.

The second prong is a pre-enlightenment conception of freedom. While liberalism's account of freedom is based on a Kantian ideal of autonomy that conceives agents as being constrained by reason,[12] Bolsonarism interprets liberty in a Hobbesian sense. Hobbes defines liberty as the "absence of opposition", i.e. "impediments to motion". Liberty is a concept that "may be applied no less to irrational, and inanimate creatures, than to rational", since a free man is any person who is not hindered from doing *all things* that, "by his strength and wit", he has a will to do.[13] The difference between Hobbes and Bolsonarism is that only the latter regards this freedom without responsibility as a value, that is, as something to be *retained* instead of traded by means of a social contract.

The concepts of model citizenship and freedom without responsibility work in tandem. For Bolsonarism, freedom is a license to act in an arbitrary way; a license that is not universal because it is granted only to a virtuous group.

4. The Government's Approach to COVID-19

Bolsonaro's response to the pandemic was described as "executive underreach", i.e. a "willful failure to address" relevant public concerns that the government is "legally and functionally equipped" to respond to.[14] From the early stages of the pandemic, Bolsonaro openly dismissed COVID-19 as a "little flu" and urged his supporters to ignore the sanitary recommendations of epidemiologists and scien-

10 Rafael Mafei, Thomas Bustamante and Emilio Meyer, 'From Antiestablishmentarianism to Bolsonarism in Brazil' in Andras Sajo, Stephen Holmes and Renata Uitz (eds) *The Routledge Handbook on Illiberalism* (Routledge 2022) 778–795.

11 Isabela Oliveira Kalil, *Quem São e no que Acreditam os Eleitores de Jair Bolsonaro* (Fundação Escola de Sociologia e Política de São Paulo 2018).

12 Immanuel Kant, 'Groundwork of the Metaphysics of Morals' in Mary Gregor and Jens Timmermans (eds) *Practical Philosophy* (Cambridge 1785/1996) 37.

13 Thomas Hobbes, *Leviathan* (John Gaskin (tr), Oxford 1651/1998) 139.

14 David E Pozen and Kim Lane Scheppele, 'Executive Underreach, in Pandemics and Otherwise' (2020) 114 The American Journal of International Law 608.

tific associations.[15] While local authorities attempted to enforce social distancing measures and impose limits on the circulation of people, the federal government spent public money on an advertisement campaign with the label "Brazil cannot stop", in which the president urged his supporters to "go back to work" and ignore the warnings of his own minister of health. He started a "hardball politics" against state governors and acted to undermine their efforts.[16] As the number of casualties rose, Bolsonaro forced upon the health system an "early treatment protocol" in which medicines with no efficacy against COVID-19 were widely distributed in the health system, with the potential to aggravate the condition of patients.[17]

In comparison with other science-sceptical governments, the hallmark of Bolsonaro's approach was the endurance of this discourse despite the failure of the attempt to achieve herd immunity, the mutations of the virus, the exponential rise in deaths and the development of vaccines. Instead of taking advantage of the fact that the pandemic arrived in Brazil several months after it had spread across Asia, Europe and the United States, Bolsonaro deliberately missed opportunities to secure vaccines at an early stage, declined to negotiate with vaccine producers at the appropriate time, and boycotted Chinese and Russian vaccines on ideological grounds.[18]

According to Bolsonaro's former Minister of Justice Luiz Henrique Mandetta, a trained physician who advocated a strictly technical epidemiologic protocol,

> for Bolsonaro the solution [to the COVID-19 pandemic] has always been simple: his project to fight the pandemic was to say that the government has a medicine and that whoever takes the medicine will be alright. Those who die are only the people that would die anyway.[19]

Even after vaccines were developed, the president held on to his denialism. He campaigned against the first vaccine that became available in Brazil, domestically produced through a collaborative agreement between a scientific entity publicly financed by the state of São Paulo and the Chinese company Sinovac. Despite the efficacy of the vaccine, measured by scientific research and attested by the Brazilian Health Regulatory Agency (ANVISA), Bolsonaro attempted to intimidate this agency during the process of authorising the vaccine's distribution and spread rumours against it, with a view to destroying the reputation of the governor of the state of São Paulo who opposed the president's denialist agenda.[20]

15 Amy Erica Smith, 'Covid vs. Brazil's Democracy: Brazil's Populist Playbook' (2020) 31 The Journal of Democracy 76.

16 Ventura and Martins (n 3) 74.

17 Hessley Machado Silva, 'The Brazilian Scientific Denialism Through "The American Journal of Medicine"' (2021) 134 The American Journal of Medicine 4.

18 Nathalie Passarinho, '3 Erros que Levaram à Falta de Vacinas Contra Covid-19 no Brazil' (*BBC News Brazil*, 23 February 2021) <https://www.bbc.com/portuguese/brasil-56160026>.

19 Mandetta (n 2) 145.

20 Emilio Peluso Neder Meyer and Thomas Bustamante, 'COVID-19 in Brazil: A Sick Constitutional Democracy' (*Verfassungsblog*, 22 February 2021) <https://verfassungsblog.de/covid-19-in-brazil-a-sick-constitutional-democracy/>.

While state governors and municipal authorities went to the Federal Supreme Court in order to force the government to adopt a nationwide vaccination plan, with a judicial declaration of a subsidiary power to make their own arrangements in case the federal government failed to do so, Bolsonarists filed a complaint at the court to defend a "freedom" not to be forcefully vaccinated by the government, which had in fact never been an issue in the mainstream debate about COVID-19.[21] Bolsonarists mocked the vaccines and spread rumours that they can produce mutations in their users, alter one's DNA, or secretly contain a device for taking control of one's mind. In some of his personal pronouncements, President Bolsonaro offered nothing more than anecdotes, which made fun of the national immunisation plan and advised his followers not to take the vaccine, to avoid the risk of turning oneself into a "crocodile".[22]

Bolsonarism's crusade against health measures also attributed a false cause to the economic consequences of the pandemic, blaming them on the social distancing measures instead of the virus itself.[23] Bolsonarist local authorities thus abused their power to classify certain activities as "essential" in order to skip anti-COVID regulations, opening fitness centres, hairdressers, churches, shopping centres, and the like. Moreover, in all 36 official events between 3 February and 10 March 2021, when the second wave of the pandemic was about to reach its peak, Bolsonaro appeared without a mask and making physical contact with his supporters.[24] At that time, confirmed cases and deaths were rising steeply and Brazil had one of the highest averages in the world.[25] A few months before, when asked about city curfews and restrictions on commerce and public transport, he responded thus: "I lament the deaths, but we all are going to die one day". In the same statement, he urged local authorities and courts to revoke restrictions and invoked homophobic language, complaining that "Brazil must cease to be a country of faggots".[26]

21 Thomas Bustamante, Emilio Peluso Neder Meyer and Felipe Tirado, 'Opposing an Idle Federal Government: The Brazilian Federal Supreme Court on Mandatory Vaccination' (*Verfassungsblog*, 23 December 2020) <https://verfassungsblog.de/opposing-an-idle-federal-government/>.

22 'Brazil's Bolsonaro Warns Virus Vaccine Can Turn People into "Crocodiles"' (*France24*, 18 December 2020) <https://www.france24.com/en/live-news/20201218-brazil-s-bolsonaro-warns-virus-vaccine-can-turn-people-into-crocodiles>.

23 Francisco Ortega and Michael Orsini, 'Governing COVID in Brazil: Dissecting the Ableist and Reluctant Authoritarian' (*Somatosphere*, 17 April 2020) <http://somatosphere.net/2020/governing-covid-in-brazil-dissecting-the-ableist-and-reluctant-authoritarian.html/>.

24 Guilherme Mazui and others, 'Usando Máscara, Bolsonaro Sanciona Lei que Facilita Compra de Vacinas contra a COVID-19' (*G1*, 10 March 2021) <https://g1.globo.com/politica/noticia/2021/03/10/usando-mascara-bolsonaro-sanciona-lei-que-facilita-compra-de-vacinas-contra-covid-19.ghtml>.

25 Our World in Data, 'Brazil: Coronavirus Pandemic Country Profile' <https://ourworldindata.org/coronavirus/country/brazil>.

26 PH Gomes, 'Brasil Tem de Deixar de Ser 'País de Maricas' e Enfrentar Pandemia de "Peito Aberto", Diz Bolsonaro' (*G1*, 10 November 2020) <https://g1.globo.com/politica/noticia/2020/11/10/bolsonaro-diz-que-brasil-tem-de-deixar-de-ser-pais-de-maricas-e-enfrentar-pandemia-de-peito-aberto.ghtml>.

In sum, the federal government exposed the population to COVID-19, with an attempt to achieve herd immunity. What is most striking, however, is the fact that even *after* it became evident that this attempt had failed, Bolsonaro *still* insisted on his denialist approach based on the intentional contamination of large populations, drug treatments without scientific evidence, failure to adopt a timely and effective vaccination programme and sabotaging of palliative measures introduced by state and local authorities. In a comprehensive study that analysed more than 3,000 normative acts, for instance, a leading research group in ethics and public health concluded that the federal government had enacted norms and regulations to "constantly obstruct" local responses to COVID-19.[27] The results were lethal: Brazil to date has the eighth-highest per capita COVID-19 mortality rate in the world, having confirmed more than 550,000 deaths.[28]

5. Microanalysis of COVID-Denialism

There are at least four aspects of Bolsonarism's illiberal approach to politics that explain its concrete response to the pandemic: media strategy; support from the medical class; appeal to a religious base; and attacks on scientific and political institutions.

In terms of its media strategy, Bolsonarism gained electoral competitiveness relatively recently, taking advantage of a global communications revolution that has enhanced the expansion of illiberalism.[29] Bolsonaro's media strategy eliminates intermediaries between himself and the population. It aims to deconstruct the institutional spaces where public reason can emerge to make ethical and empirical relativism more appealing than it would ordinarily be. It resorts to lies that attempt to unmake the certainties we need to share in order to live in a common reality.[30] As Hannah Arendt explains, history is full of examples of deliberate attempts to build a parallel reality in order to undermine a people's capacity to think and judge.[31] During Bolsonaro's presidential campaign, he established direct communication with his electors with the deliberate strategy of undermining this capacity, often relying on automated computer programmes known as 'bots' and messages specifically tailored to each of the groups that constitute his electoral base.[32]

27 Camila Lissa Asano, Deisy de Freitas Lima Ventura and others 'Editorial: Direito e Pandemia: Ordem Juridica e sistema Judiciario Nao Foram Suficientes Para Evitar Graves Violações' (2021) 10 Boletim Direitos na Pandemia – Conectas 1.

28 Johns Hopkins University, Coronavirus Resource Center, Mortality Analyses (updated as of 28 July 2021) <https://coronavirus.jhu.edu/data/mortality>.

29 Martin Moore, *Democracy Hacked: Political Turmoil and Information Warfare in the Digital Age* (Oneworld 2018).

30 Andrea Scoseria Katz, 'Lies in the Time of Corona: Attempts to Inoculate Truth from a Pandemic' *(I.CONnect,* 29 April 2020) <http://www.iconnectblog.com/2020/04/lies-in-the-time-of-corona-attempts-to-inoculate-truth-from-a-pandemic/>.

31 Hannah Arendt, 'Lying in Politics: Reflections on the Pentagon Papers' in *Crisis of the Republic* (Harvest 1972) 1.

32 Marco Aurelio Ruediger and others, 'Policy Paper 3: Bots and Brazil's Electoral System in the 2018 Elections' *(FGV DAPP,* 2018) <http://hdl.handle.net/10438/26229>.

After the election, this apparatus was used as an effective mechanism to maintain political support, attack opponents and advertise scepticism about COVID-19.[33] Bolsonaro's ideological appropriation of COVID-19 was fuelled by a campaign of disinformation by means of messages on WhatsApp and Twitter, which frame COVID-19 as "a political issue rather than a public health issue".[34]

The second aspect of Bolsonarism is the complicity of the medical class. Regardless of the scientific consensus that drugs like hydroxychloroquine and ivermectin were ineffective[35] and increased lethality,[36] the medical class offered little resistance to Bolsonaro's "early medical protocol". The Federal Council of Medicine did not expressly recommend their use, but formally authorised physicians to prescribe the drugs advertised by the president as part of their "medical freedom".[37] With the Council's endorsement of his conception of "liberty", Bolsonaro invested public funds to produce chloroquine pills to be used in the public health system[38] and employed the armed forces to further expand and distribute this production.[39]

On 5 April 2020, Bolsonaro convened a joint meeting of the head of ANVISA and several other authorities, such as the General Advocate of the State, the Ministry of Health and the Ministry of Science and Technology, to attempt to change the leaflet contained in packs of chloroquine in order to recommend its use against COVID-19.[40] Shortly afterwards, Bolsonaro fired the health minister and the new minister officially endorsed Bolsonaro's medical protocol against the virus.[41]

The third aspect of illiberal rule is the role of religion. Bolsonarism and the Brazilian Evangelical Movement coincide in their defence of three sets of values.[42] The first is an endorsement of values that have been defended by Brazilian

33 Meyer (n 6) 176.

34 Felipe Bonow Soares and others, 'Bolsonaro's Firehose: How Covid-19 Disinformation on WhatsApp Was Used to Fight a Government Political Crisis in Brazil' (2021) 2 Harvard Kennedy School Misinformation Review 1.

35 Markus Hoffmann and others, 'Chloroquine Does Not Inhibit Infection of Human Lung Cells with SARS-Cov-2' (2020) 585 Nature 588.

36 Catherine Axfors and others, 'Mortality Outcomes with Hydroxychloroquine and Chloroquine in COVID-19 from an International Collaborative Meta-Analysis of Randomized Trials' (2021) 12 Nature Communications 2349.

37 Conselho Federal de Medicina, Parecer CFM n. 04/2020, 16 Apr 2020.

38 Daniel Carvalho, 'Nobody Is Doing Anything Wrong' (*Folha de São Paulo*, 12 February 2021) <https://www1.folha.uol.com.br/internacional/en/scienceandhealth/2021/02/nobody-is-doing-anything-wrong-says-bolsonaro-about-brazils-chloroquine-production.shtml>.

39 Ministério da Defesa, 'Laboratórios das Forças Armadas ampliam produção de álcool em gel e cloroquina' *(SECOM,* 30 March 2020) <https://www.gov.br/defesa/pt-br/centrais-de-conteudo/noticias/ultimas-noticias/laboratorios-das-forcas-armadas-ampliam-producao-de-alcool-em-gel-e-cloroquina>.

40 Mandetta (n 2) 172–174.

41 Ministério da Saúde, Nota Informativa nº 17/2020 (n 5).

42 Brian Gordon Lutalo Kibuuka, 'Complicity and Synergy Between Bolsonaro and Brazilian Evangelicals in COVID-19 Times: Adherence to Scientific Negationism for Political-Religious Reasons' (2020) 4 International Journal of Latin American Religions 288.

Protestants since the 19th century, namely "the defense of the family, the fight against profanity of folklore and national festivals, demonization of African and indigenous culture, and fight against illicit drugs".[43] The second is the promotion of new values assimilated by neo-Pentecostal religions without resistance, such as the "policy of proliferation of weapons", moralisation and militarisation of politics and education, and attacks on democratic institutions. The third is an attachment to a "neoliberal economic agenda" that constitutes a central aspect of the "belief system of most evangelicals", in particular their conceptions of "freedom" and "meritocracy".[44] By endorsing these values, Bolsonarism used religion as a political platform, which gained force after the emergence of the pandemic. While advocates of social distancing measures were portrayed as religion-sceptics, a large network of Pentecostal media outlets, under the influence of Pastor Silas Malafaia (one of the most popular religious leaders in Brazil), treated the measures adopted by state governors, legislators, universities and courts as a violation of their religious liberty and saw in Bolsonaro a committed advocate of their spiritual identity.[45]

The fourth aspect of Bolsonarism is a coordinated effort to harass, expose, threaten and often prosecute scientists, physicians, journalists and university professors who issue opinions against the government. Scientists who denounced the inefficacy and harms of Bolsonaro's chloroquine-centred medical protocol were chased both by a mass of digital influencers and by prosecutors who questioned these scientific results and opened inquiries to defend the credibility of the president's campaign.[46] University professors were threatened with prosecution for criticising Bolsonaro, including the former president of the Federal University of Pelotas, Professor Pedro Hallal, who was summoned by the Office of Internal Control of the Executive branch to sign an agreement committing to abstain from making "offensive commentaries" against the president.[47]

Digital influencers and journalists who claimed that President Bolsonaro's choice to intentionally infect the population with the coronavirus makes him liable for human rights violations were also prosecuted for supposedly violating the National Security Act, a law inherited from the 1964–1985 dictatorship.[48]

43 ibid 290.

44 ibid.

45 ibid 302–310.

46 Lindzi Wessel, '"It's a Nightmare": How Brazilians Scientists Became Ensnared in Chloroquine Politics' (*Science*, 22 June 2020) <https://www.sciencemag.org/news/2020/06/it-s-nightmare-how-brazilian-scientists-became-ensnared-chloroquine-politics>.

47 Herton Escobar, '"A Hostile Environment": Brazilian Scientists Face Rising Attacks from Bolsonaro's Regime' (*Science*, 7 April 2021) <https://www.sciencemag.org/news/2021/04/hostile-environment-brazilian-scientists-face-rising-attacks-bolsonaro-s-regime>.

48 Fabricio Polido, and Emilio Peluso Neder Meyer, 'Disinformation, Digital Platforms and COVID-19: Making State Agents Accountable in Brazil' (*I.CONnect*, 26 March 2021) <http://www.iconnectblog.com/2021/03/disinformation-digital-platforms-and-covid-19-making-state-agents-accountable-in-brazil/>.

Bolsonaro's denialism contributed to amplifying attacks on journalists and the press, which have been on the rise since before the breakdown of the pandemic.[49]

In a similar vein, there were multiple attacks on the two Houses of Congress and the Federal Supreme Court. On 31 May 2020, for instance, far-right protesters rallied in front of the building of the Federal Supreme Court, carrying weapons and torches that mimicked those of the Ku Klux Klan. Later that day, Bolsonaro joined a small group of street demonstrators waving banners demanding a recess of the Federal Supreme Court. This episode led the Federal Supreme Court to open an inquiry to investigate supporters of the presidency that were posing threats to institutions and public officials.[50]

Finally, on 8 April 2021, the date of the peak of COVID-related deaths in Brazil, with more than 4,200 casualties in a single day, a vast virtual attack was noticed in multiple forms of social media, motivated by two decisions of the Federal Supreme Court: its decision to declare the right of the Senate's minority to open an inquiry against the executive omissions with regards to COVID-19; and a decision confirming the right of states and municipalities to restrict religious services to bring down the number of deaths.[51] As one of us commented, with this episode, the Bolsonarist media apparatus managed to turn two major judicial defeats into an opportunity for political gain, creating "a smokescreen to hide the more than 4,000 deaths in a single day".[52] Although Bolsonaro lost in court, he kept his supporters "permanently mobilized in defense of his mythological authority".[53]

6. Multi-Level Institutional Resistance

One of the distinctive features of the Brazilian political system is its fragmentation. The Brazilian system is normally described as a "coalitional presidentialism",[54] the central feature of which is a combination of a presidency "inspired by the US" with a parliament "modelled on Europe: that is: over-mighty executives on the one

49 Reporters Without Borders, 'RSF tallied 580 Attacks Against Media in Brazil in 2020' (*RSF Report*, 25 January 2021) <https://rsf.org/en/reports/rsf-tallied-580-attacks-against-media-brazil-2020>.

50 Emilio Pelusio Neder Meyer and Thomas Bustamante, 'Judicial Responses to Bolsonarism: The Leading Role of the Federal Supreme Court' (*Verfassungsblog*, 16 June 2020) <https://verfassungsblog.de/judicial-responses-to-bolsonarism-the-leading-role-of-the-federal-supreme-court/>.

51 Malu Gaspar, 'Decisões do STF Sobre Cultos e CPI da Covid Causam Revolta nas Redes Bolsonaristas' (*O Globo*, 9 April 2021) <https://blogs.oglobo.globo.com/malu-gaspar/post/decisoes-do-stf-sobre-cultos-em-igrejas-e-cpi-da-covid-causam-revolta-em-redes-bolsonaristas.html>.

52 Thomas Bustamante and Evanilda Nascimento de Godoi Bustamante, 'Negationism's "Day in Court": Bolsonaro between Legal Defeats and Threats to Judicial Independence' (*Verfassungsblog*, 11 April 2021 <https://verfassungsblog.de/negationisms-day-in-court/>.

53 ibid.

54 Sergio Abranches, *Presidencialismo de Coalizão: Raízes e Evolução do Modelo Político Brasileiro* (Companhia das Letras 2018).

hand, legislatures elected by proportional representation of votes – not the Anglo-Saxon first-past-the-post distortion of them – on the other".[55] Although this institutional design entails bargaining processes that are prone to produce instability,[56] analysts claim that it places Brazil in a favourable position to resist an illiberal government.[57] There are three institutional levels in which the executive has met resistance against Bolsonarism.

The first is legislative resistance, which has been capable of containing Bolsonaro in important ways. Congress approved, for instance, an emergency social benefit that played a crucial role in alleviating the economic consequences of the pandemic.[58] While Bolsonaro sent to the House of Representatives a modest social benefit to provide financial aid to persons affected by quarantine measures, the representatives responded to this proposal by tripling the amount to be paid to each citizen and allowing this revised value to be paid in double if the recipient is a single parent.[59]

By the same token, a minority of 31 (out of 81) senators in the Federal Senate was able to create a parliamentary inquiry commission in the aftermath of the deadliest week of the second wave of the pandemic (from 28 March to 3 April 2021), with a view to investigating the federal government's negligence to take action against the disease and reluctance to purchase vaccines.[60] This parliamentary investigation, which is based on a constitutional provision (Article 58, § 3°, of the 1988 Constitution) that establishes a right for a minority of a third of senators to initiate such an inquiry, was created only after a Federal Supreme Court injunction was issued in favour of the minority.[61] Nonetheless, after its creation it became a powerful mechanism to shed light on the human rights violations caused by the federal government's response to COVID-19.

Shortly after the inquiry began, the parliamentary inquiry commission was already playing an important role in holding the executive accountable for its denialism. The commission confirmed that the early protocol treatment (without scientific basis) was endorsed by the Ministry of Health (soon after Bolsonaro's first

55 Perry Anderson, *Brazil Apart: 1964–2019* (Verso 2019) 85.

56 Leonardo Avritzer, *Impasses da Democracia Brasileira* (*Civilização Brasileira* 2016).

57 Juliano Benvindo, 'The Party Fragmentation Paradox in Brazil: A Shield Against Authoritarianism?' (*I.CONnect*, 24 October 2019) <http://www.iconnectblog.com/2019/10/the-party-fragmentation-paradox-in-brazil-a-shield-against-authoritarianism/>.

58 Maria Lúcia Garcia and others, 'The COVID-19 Pandemic, Emergency Aid and Social Work in Brazil' (2021) 20 Qualitative Social Work 356.

59 Ligia Bahia and others, 'The Tragedy of Brazilian Coronavirus/COVID-19: An Analysis of the Federal Government's Misgovernment, 2020–2021', Report delivered to the Congressional Committee of Inquiry (CCI) for Covid-19 ofThe Federal Senate (28 April 2021) <https://www.clacso.org/wp-content/uploads/2021/05/The-Tragedy-of-brazilian-coronavirus_última.pdf>.

60 Deisy Ventura, 'A Parliamentary Commission of Inquiry (CPI) Will Investigate Brazil's Response to Covid-19 and the President's Liability for one of the Worst Death Rates in the World' (*Lex-Atlas COVID-19*, 27 April 2021) <https://lexatlas-c19.org/a-parliamentary-commission-of-inquiry-cpi-will-investigate-brazils-response-to-covid-19-and-the-presidents-liability-for-one-of-the-worst-death-rates-in-the-world/>.

61 Supremo Tribunal Federal, ADPF 881 MF dec. monocrática rel. min. Roberto Barroso j. 8/04/2021. See also Bustamante and Godoi Bustamante (n 52).

minister of health was removed from office), and found evidence that the president bypassed the technical directives of the Ministry of Health and listened only to a parallel cabinet formed by his most committed ideological advisers.[62] Furthermore, a representative in the Chamber of Deputies testified before the commission that he discovered suspicious operations for purchasing overpriced vaccines, and that the president was aware of this bargaining but did not take action to investigate it.[63] By the same token, in a hearing concerning accusations of corruption in the acquisition of vaccines, the spokesman of the parliamentary inquiry commission ordered the imprisonment of a witness that flagrantly lied in his testimony. Finally, several scientists that opposed Bolsonaro's policies were heard, allowing for public criticism towards the government.

The second level of resistance is offered through judicial review, which played a pivotal role in the enforcement of the measures adopted by the federal legislature and the states against COVID-19. In addition to the abovementioned decision on the Senate's inquiry commission, the Federal Supreme Court: (i) reversed Bolsonaro's attempt to extend indefinitely the validity of provisional measures of the executive, which would have given the government extensive emergency legislative powers;[64] (ii) reinforced the constitutional protection of indigenous people by demanding that the federal government offer adequate health policies concerning the pandemic – through a structural decision that ordered the executive to present a plan for protecting the indigenous populations and supervised its application;[65] (iii) protected the right to access to information, striking down an indefinite restriction on the publication of official COVID-19 data;[66] (iv) annulled a federal provision that limited the civil liability of officials that fail to adopt scientific and technical responses to the pandemic;[67] and (v) enforced the states' and municipal governments' autonomy to define measures of social distancing, quarantine and suspension of public activities.[68]

This last ruling contributed to the third level of institutional resistance, which was a strategy of "uncooperative federalism".[69] The resistance of states and munici-

62 Bryan Harris, 'Brazil's Covid Inquiry Puts Bolsonaro on the Back Foot' (*The Financial Times*, 17 June 2021) <https://www.ft.com/content/499bdf96-622a-4c14-8e91-faf4989f0113>.

63 'What Does Brazil's Vaccine Scandal Mean for Jair Bolsonaro?' (*The Economist*, 7 July 2021) <https://www.economist.com/the-economist-explains/2021/07/07/what-does-brazils-vaccine-scandal-mean-for-jair-bolsonaro>.

64 STF, ADPF 663 MC, rel. min. Alexandre de Moraes, 27/03/2020. Provisional measures are executive acts with statutory force, with capacity to modify or repeal legislative acts. Following the presidential enactment of a provisional measure, the National Congress must either convert these legislative measures into ordinary acts or repeal them, within sixty days (which can be the object of a single extension for an equal period).

65 STF, ADPF 709, MC, rel. min. Roberto Barroso, Pleno, 05/08/2020.

66 STF, ADPF 690, MC, rel. min. Alexandre de Moraes, Pleno, 30/03/2021.

67 STF, ADI 6421, MC, rel. min. Roberto Barroso, Pleno, 21/05/2020.

68 STF, ADI 6341 MC, rel. p/ acórdão min. Edson Fachin, 15/04/2020.

69 Jessica Bulman-Pozen and Heather K Gerken, 'Uncooperative Federalism' (2009) 118 The Yale Law Journal 1256.

palities against COVID-denialism was enhanced by the fact that the country has a 'unified health system' (*Sistema Único de Saúde* or SUS), which was built upon the principle that its funding and administration are *shared* among the federal, state and municipal governments. The judicial protection of state and local powers in the SUS system allowed states and municipalities to adopt local regulations on sanitary restrictions and the offer of health services, regardless of the federal government's stance.

7. Conclusion

COVID-19 reached Brazil during its most delicate political crisis since its re-democratisation in 1988. President Bolsonaro was elected with a promise to avenge the generation of supporters of the military dictatorship that lasted from 1964 to 1985. He openly defies democracy and nourishes his popularity from a populist defiance to the rule of law. His ideology is sceptical of science and entailed a denialist claim about COVID-19. The government denied the seriousness of the viral threat and adopted a policy marked by censorship, hate and manipulation. As of July 2021, scientific and political institutions (like courts and legislatures) are constantly under attack, as they are a natural firewall against Bolsonaro's authoritarian views. Nevertheless, these institutions have managed to contain Bolsonaro's commitment to provoke a more severe authoritarian rupture.[70] However, the epidemic remains uncontrolled due to Bolsonaro's denialist underreach, which has cost the country several opportunities to fight the disease and reduce the number of lives lost to COVID-19.

70 Emilio Peluso Neder Meyer and Thomas Bustamante, 'A Portrait of Bolsonaro's Crimes Against Humanity: The Legislative Investigative Committee Report on the COVID-19 Pandemic in Brazil' (*Verfassungsblog*, 5 November 2021) <https://verfassungsblog.de/a-portrait-of-bolsonaros-crimes-against-humanity/>.

19

DEALING WITH COVID-19 IN SWEDEN

Choosing a Different Path

Iain Cameron and Anna Jonsson Cornell

1. Introduction[1]

This chapter analyses the Swedish response to the COVID-19 pandemic and explains to what extent and why the Swedish response differed from that of other European states. Our chapter concentrates on the measures, binding or otherwise, which were taken and the institutional and legal framework for these measures.[2] The responsible administrative agency, the Public Health Agency (*Folkhälsomyndigheten* or FHM), in its reluctance to impose heavy restrictions such as lockdowns and mandatory face-masks, constantly referred to the lack of scientific support for such measures and the issue of sustainability as it was likely that measures would have to be in place for a long time. However, Sweden's responses changed over time, moving from being based largely on recommendations to also including legally binding measures. Therefore, we follow a broadly chronological approach. We also include issues of health law and the interface between policy-making and science.

1 All websites accessed on 14 July 2021.

2 This chapter draws on Iain Cameron and Anna Jonsson Cornell, 'Sweden and COVID 19: A Constitutional Perspective' (*Verfassungsblog*, 7 May 2020) <https://verfassungsblog.de/sweden-and-covid-19-a-constitutional-perspective/>; 'COVID-19 in Sweden: A Soft Power Approach' (*Verfassungsblog*, 24 February 2021) <https://verfassungsblog.de/covid-19-in-sweden-a-soft-power-approach/>. See also Ana Nordberg and Titti Mattsson, 'COVID-19 Pandemic in Sweden: Measures, Policy Approach and Legal and Ethical Debates' (2020) 1/2020 Biolaw Journal 731 and Henrik Wenander, 'Sweden: Non-Binding Rules against the Pandemic – Formalism, Pragmatism and Some Legal Realism' (2021) 12 European Journal of Risk Regulation 127.

DOI: 10.4324/9781003211952-22

2. The Constitutional Context

Sweden has collective rather than ministerial government,[3] and only a relatively small number of people are employed in government departments. Instead, central public administration is performed by semi-autonomous administrative agencies, which have a duty to obey government directives (RF 12:1). They are steered by government through ordinances which specify statutory requirements, budgetary means and guidelines. Agencies also have the constitutionally protected freedom to interpret and apply the law in individual cases (RF 12:2). This, together with the fact that the bulk of specialist knowledge is in the administrative agencies rather than government departments, is the core of the semi-autonomy of public administration. Except in cases where administrative agencies are specifically given oversight or appeal functions, they are not in any hierarchical position vis-a-vis one another. This constitutional setting has created a culture in which ministers tend to have a 'hands-off' approach towards the agencies which are under the supervision and control of their departments, reacting only when problems with political dimensions emerge. The pandemic was not initially considered to be of such a character. In normal times, the Swedish system of governance has several advantages. It can prevent political partisanship and foster rational and effective administration. However, it runs the risk of a type of 'silo' mentality, in agencies where no one takes a holistic responsibility.

The Swedish public system is decentralised in the sense that public services are to a large extent delivered by the 290 local authorities (*kommuner*), responsible inter alia for schools and care of the elderly, and 20 regional authorities (*regioner*) responsible for public transport and health care. Many of the tasks of regional and local authorities are regulated in national statutes and the autonomy of the local and regional authorities are stipulated in the constitution. The huge variations in size and population of local authorities cause problems when it comes to ensuring resources and a satisfactory minimal level of technical and administrative competence for local authority civil servants.

The system for crisis management in Sweden is horizontally collaborative and guided by three principles: (i) responsibility; (ii) parity; and (iii) proximity.[4] The principle of responsibility states that the actor responsible for a given activity under normal conditions is also responsible for that activity during a crisis. This is based on the idea that it is difficult to shift a modern network administration into a command-and-control mode in the event of a crisis.[5] Where, as is common,

3 RF 7:3. References to the Swedish constitution, the Instrument of Government (*Regeringsformen*, RF), are to the chapter and section number. For more background, see Thomas Bull and Iain Cameron, 'Sweden: Constitutional Foundations', in Armin von Bogdandy (ed), *Ius Publicum Europaeum – Constitutional Foundations, Evolution and Gestalt of European Constitutions* <https://papers.ssrn.com/sol3/papers.cfm?abstract_id=3782353>.

4 Per Bergling and others, *Krisen, myndigheterna och lagen: Krishantering i rättens gränsland* (Gleerups 2015).

5 Per Becker and Frederik Bynander, 'The System for Crisis Management in Sweden: Collaborative, Conformist, Contradictory', in Christian N Madu and Chu-Hua Kuei (eds), *Handbook of Disaster Risk Reduction and Management* (World Scientific Publishing 2017).

coping with a crisis involves several local authorities and/or administrative agencies, these are expected to cooperate with each other. Sectorial legislation seldom provides for a 'lead' agency, giving it control over other agencies. One disadvantage of this system is time-consuming collaborative processes. The parity principle follows on from the responsibility principle and provides that, as far as possible, the same structures, resources and organisation of activities should apply as apply under normal conditions. The proximity principle provides that a crisis should primarily be handled where it occurs, by those who are (geographically) closest to it.

There is no provision in the Swedish constitution for the declaration of a state of emergency in peacetime. Sweden's peaceful history largely accounts for this, together with the primacy given to Parliament in the constitution. Instead, the Swedish approach is to have emergency provisions in sector-specific statutes with delegations to the government and sub-delegations to administrative agencies (*författningsberedskap* or 'anticipatory statutorification').[6] Where these turn out to be inadequate, the solution (*konstitutionell beredskap* or 'constitutional readiness') is to rely upon the Parliament's willingness and capacity to legislate swiftly when needed.

Under RF chapter 8, statutes are required to regulate many areas. During the legislative process, draft laws are published and time is given for consultation with a variety of public bodies and civil society actors. Draft laws are also submitted to the Council on Legislation, which consists of temporarily seconded senior judges and checks the quality and constitutionality of proposals. The constitutionally-protected principle of access to official documents, together with a constitutional requirement (RF 7:2) to prepare governmental decisions (including bills) adequately, means that the Swedish legislative procedure, and policy making in general, have a high level of transparency.

Acts of Parliament are generally necessary to limit constitutional rights. The rights most directly relevant during the COVID-19 pandemic are the freedoms of assembly (RF 2:1, p. 3), demonstration (RF 2:1, p. 4), movement (RF 2:8), the protection of personal integrity and against arbitrary detention (RF 2:6), and the right to protection of private property (RF 2:15). These are all relative rights which can be limited by statute (RF 2:20–24), subject to necessity and proportionality tests. The freedoms of assembly and demonstration can only be restricted for specific purposes laid out in the constitution, including measures to combat an epidemic (RF 2:24).

3. The Public Health Agency and the Act on Protection Against Contagious Diseases

The FHM had a dominant role in determining the Swedish response to the COVID-19 pandemic. Until 2014, Sweden had a specialist epidemiological agency, the Institute of Prevention of Contagious Diseases. In 2014, this agency

6 Johan Hirschfeldt and Olof Petersson, *Rättsregler i kris* (Dialogos 2020).

was amalgamated with the FHM, which has a general mandate to promote better public health. Although the FHM is bound by its instruction to base any measures it might take on scientific research, it no longer has the same close links with academic research in epidemiology, virology and immunology.

The main legislation applicable is the Act on Protection Against Contagious Diseases (Smittskyddslagen (2004:168), SSL). According to the SSL, all measures taken should build on science, be evidence-based and proportional and respect the principle of equality and protect the personal integrity of individuals (SSL 1:4). Under SSL 2:1, all individuals have a responsibility to take measures to avoid infecting others. The SSL imposes a duty on each health region to appoint a 'prevention of contagion' doctor (*smittskyddsläkare*) with the powers to inter alia order the isolation of infected people (SSL 3:9) or smaller areas (SSL 3:10). Individuals subject to such decisions have a right of judicial review. The emphasis is firmly on the human rights of people who are, or are suspected of being, contagious.[7] The SSL further provides that the government, or the administrative agency specified by the government, may issue the additional regulations required for effective protection against contagion and for the protection of individuals (SSL 9:4). The government has sub-delegated this authority to the FHM.[8]

On 2 February 2020, the government classified COVID-19 as "dangerous to society", which meant that all the measures, including quarantine provisions, available in the SSL could be used. Quarantine, testing and contact tracing were, however, not used at the beginning of the pandemic. In this context, it should also be noted that prevention of contagion doctors have the legal authority to examine, and if needed quarantine, individuals that enter Sweden from a country with widespread contagious diseases (SSL 3:8, 9). These powers have not, to our knowledge, been used in Sweden in relation to COVID-19 as of June 2021.

The SSL does not provide for explicit powers to isolate healthy people, to protect them from contagion, or for a general and total lockdown. Instead, it is considered that non-binding and persuasive measures are more effective in changing behaviour and hence more sustainable. The HIV pandemic together with the swine flu (H1N1) epidemic in 2009[9] in this sense influenced the Swedish response to COVID-19.

4. The Measures Taken at the Beginning of the Pandemic: Soft Power

The FHM issued recommendations to the public to maintain 'social distancing' in all public places and on public transport. Employers were requested to ask work-

7 The *travaux préparatoires* (Prop. 2003/04:30 Ny Smittskyddslag) show that the measures adopted to deal with HIV-Aids were seen as an overreaction and, at times, not in accordance with human freedom and personal integrity, which explains the human rights approach in current legislation.

8 *Smittskyddsförordning* (2004:255), s 12. References to statutes and ordinances in force, *Svensk författningssamling*, SFS, are by year and statute/ordinance number.

9 To contain swine flu, Sweden embarked on a mass vaccination programme. A relatively large number of people (approximately 4,000, many of them young) suffered life-long side-effects, including narcolepsy, from the vaccine.

ers, where possible, to work from home. No shops, gyms or other businesses were ordered to be closed (this power at the time was not part of the SSL), but licensed premises such as restaurants and bars were only to allow table service and all businesses were requested to take steps to reduce over-crowding.[10]

The prime minister addressed the nation, emphasising that the government's main priority was the protection of the over 70s and other risk groups, and that it was vitally important that everyone took personal responsibility not to spread contagion, so as to ensure that hospital services (particularly intensive care beds) were not overwhelmed. A raft of economic measures was speedily adopted, providing for financial support to businesses, particularly to furlough employees. Some local authorities introduced a ban on visiting care homes. This was later supplemented by a national ban issued by the government, acting under the SSL.

Anonymised metadata surveys of mobile phones showed that there was a high level of compliance with the 'work at home' and 'social distancing' recommendations. Nonetheless, the virus spread quickly in March and April 2020, particularly in Stockholm. Many Swedes had been abroad during the winter break. The FHM did not recommend returning holidaymakers to get tested or self-isolate pre-emptively. Although the World Health Organisation recommended extensive testing and tracking, by March 2020 the FHM considered this of limited use because it believed that the virus in Sweden had already reached the pandemic stage. Moreover, the regions had insufficient resources and also considered testing, tracing and isolating to be a low priority. Elderly people in care homes, who are the frailest section of society, usually over the age of 85 and generally in poor health, began dying in large numbers. Particularly significant here is the fact that the workforce for elderly care is drawn partly from part-time workers from socially deprived areas, which have high levels of crowded accommodation and inter-generational living. Part-time workers did not have security of tenure, and so there were incentives to go to work even if infected. In the Stockholm area, they travelled mainly by public transport and at this time there was no recommendation to wear a face mask while using public transport. In areas inhabited mainly by immigrants, those working are in small businesses and service professions who could not easily work remotely. These areas consequently suffered disproportionally from the pandemic.

Another important factor in the initial high death rate in Sweden was the lack of protective personal equipment (PPE) and, initially, of reliable quick tests for staff working in care homes and providing care for elderly living in their own homes. The relevant laws provide for no central supervisory powers to check that the municipalities and regions are fulfilling their duties in this regard, and do not impose any sanctions for failure to meet these duties.[11] When international supply chains broke down the central government was slow to intervene. Eventually the

10 This was originally in the form of recommendations, backed up by the coercive power of the 'contagion doctors' to shut premises temporarily. However, in June 2020 an Act was passed (2020:526) providing powers to local authorities to shut premises not following distancing and other requirements.

11 See for local authorities, Act 2006:544, 3:1, for regions, Act 2017:30, 2:1.

regions themselves coordinated international purchases and subsequent distribution of PPE, with the central government financially underwriting the contracts. The situation illustrates the vulnerability of the so-called 'just in time' approach to the delivery and storage of medical supplies.

Early on, the existing powers under the Public Order Act (Ordningslagen (1993:1617), OL) allowing restrictions as to the number of participants in public meetings and events (including religious services) were put to use.[12] Initially the limit was set to 500 people; later (29 March 2020) the number was set to 50 (2020:114). Universities and high schools were ordered to go over to remote teaching (2020:115). Nurseries and primary/lower secondary schools (ages 6–15) were kept open, on the basis that the risks the virus posed to children were relatively small and counter-balanced by the major disruption that this would entail for society, particularly for essential workers with small children, and the mental health of children. As schools fall within the area of competence of local authorities, authorisation to the government to close high schools required the Parliament to enact a temporary Act (2020:148). The Act was framed more generally to include, if necessary, in the future, the closure of nurseries, basic schools and other learning facilities.

The other Nordic states' epidemiological agencies initially had a similar policy of containment,[13] as did the UK. However, in all these states in March 2020, politicians abandoned this policy and ordered lockdowns, in the UK after the publication of a study indicating that as many as 500,000 people could die of COVID-19.[14] Sweden did not. There are various explanations for this. The first is the Swedish governmental culture of indirect leadership and the existing legal framework. It would have been possible for the government to ask Parliament for additional powers, as happened in both Norway and Denmark (Finland already had powers under the constitution and statute to declare a state of emergency). But there was no guarantee that Parliament would give the minority government of the time new powers, especially if these were considered to be sweeping. Besides, the 'china shop' rule would apply to any change of policy, i.e. 'if you break it, it's yours'.

The FHM, with the state epidemiologist Anders Tegnell as a leading figure, was unequivocally against shutting down society.[15] If the government disagreed, it would have had to take responsibility for acting against its expert agency. In April

12 OL 2:15.

13 See the report to the Danish Parliament, Folketinget, *Håndteringen af covid-19 i foråret 2020 – Rapport afgivet af den af Folketingets Udvalg for Forretningsordenen nedsatte udredningsgruppe vedr. håndteringen af covid-19*, January 2021.

14 Neil M Ferguson, Daniel Laydon and others, 'Impact of Non-Pharmaceutical Interventions (NPIs) to Reduce COVID-19 Mortality and Healthcare Demand' (Imperial College, 16 March 2020) <https://www.imperial.ac.uk/media/imperial-college/medicine/sph/ide/gida-fellowships/Imperial-College-COVID19-NPI-modelling-16-03-2020.pdf>.

15 Unlike in other states, at least initially (e.g. the Scientific Advisory Group for Emergencies in the UK), the identity of the Swedish experts was published from the beginning, as was the content of their advice.

2020, a group of academics in epidemiology and related disciplines expressed harsh criticism of the FHM's predictions and policies. They advocated a shutdown to win time, particularly for PPE and testing resources to be built up, and in order to understand better how the virus was spreading and how it could be countered, epidemiologically and medically.[16] But there was no consensus in the academic community.[17] The Swedish government had no other public agency expertise besides the FHM to rely upon.[18] The FHM's broader mandate to promote public health probably also influenced its approach. According to the assessment of the FHM shutting down schools and society could result in long-term damage to pupils' learning, and mental illness, obesity, alcohol abuse problems and domestic violence would probably increase. Moreover, the FHM considered that the virus would spread anyway, at least in urban areas, as essential services and public transport would continue. The FHM took the view that dealing with COVID-19 would be a marathon rather than a sprint, calling for a long-term sustainable response.[19]

Bearing in mind the fact that protection of the most vulnerable group, the elderly, was central, it was strange that no one in Parliament at the time (February–April 2020) raised questions about what effects the government's COVID-19 strategy, or lack of it, was likely to have on this group. This is probably due to the consensus-oriented political culture in Sweden which is particularly strong during a crisis. Deaths and numbers of people needing intensive care in hospital peaked in April–May 2020. Hospital staff quickly redirected resources to intensive care facilities and scaled these up effectively. Nonetheless, the death rates meant that public pressure to do something mounted and on 4 April the government submitted to Parliament, in great haste, an amending bill to the SSL providing for certain temporary executive powers to issue ordinances to close or regulate malls, venues and transportation.[20] The proposal was simultaneously sent for consultation for a 24-hour period to a limited number of public bodies. The Council on Legislation and the parliament's Committee on the Constitution (*Konstitutionsutskottet*, KU) made proposals for amendments, insisting on necessity, proportionality and parliamentary oversight. The government accepted the amendments and reformulated the provisions accordingly. Thus, on this occasion, 'constitutional readiness' worked. However, the new powers were never used, probably due to the FHM's preference for voluntary measures, and they expired on 30 June 2020. This date also saw the government appoint a commission of inquiry, the 'Corona Commission'.[21]

16 Published in the newspaper *Dagens Nyheter*, 14 April 2020.

17 The independent Royal Academy of Sciences (KvA) recommended that the FHM appoint a reference group, to broaden its expertise and proposed a list of possible candidates, but when the FHM did so, it contained none of the candidates proposed by KvA.

18 The most relevant expertise would be the regional network of contagion doctors. We are not aware if they had a different view at the time (April 2020) from that of the FHM, but presumably not.

19 Johan Anderberg, *Flocken* (Bonniers 2021).

20 Prop. 2019/20:155. SFS 2020:241.

21 Coronakommissionen dir. [directive] 2020:74.

The government initially wished to leave all issues of accountability until after the pandemic. However, the opposition parties insisted on the appointment of an independent inquiry headed by a retired senior judge, rather than a parliamentary inquiry. Bearing in mind the fact that responsibility for the pandemic response is split between central, regional and local government, this was sensible. The Corona Commission was given a large number of factual and policy issues to consider, and was tasked to submit two partial reports and its final report by February 2022, seven months before the next parliamentary election.

5. The Second Wave – A Shift Towards More Legally Binding Measures

During the summer of 2020, infection rates decreased, albeit remaining at a relatively high level for Europe. The other Nordic states introduced entry requirements for Swedes, so the normal Nordic rules on freedom of movement were suspended, with exceptions being made for hospital personnel. The FHM had optimistic predictions that there were already relatively high levels of immunity in the population, at least in Stockholm. This was something of a paradox, because it also claimed that voluntary measures had been relatively effective in countering the spreading of the virus. The first surveys of antibodies in the population were therefore a disappointment, as they showed relatively low levels. The FHM, in line with most other states' predictions, also considered that the most likely scenario for the autumn was local outbreaks of the virus.

Testing and tracking were introduced after the summer of 2020. The regions had refused to bear the costs of testing people other than hospital personnel and only agreed to introduce large-scale testing and tracking when the government agreed to underwrite the costs, as this was not considered as health care according to the regions' interpretation of the law. Deaths peaked again in November 2020. Intensive care facilities were badly stretched, and health care workers were showing signs of fatigue. Public confidence in the FHM fell. However, it became clear that large-scale vaccination would soon be able to be introduced, meaning that restrictions would hopefully be short-lived. The government began introducing a number of legally binding measures. In December, serving of alcohol was forbidden after 20:00 hours. Permitted participants in public meetings were reduced to eight. Masks were made obligatory on peak hours of public transport, and a temporary entry prohibition into Sweden was issued.

A new bill was submitted to Parliament, again in a hurry, supplementing the SSL and containing more far-reaching powers compared to the changes made in April. The new COVID-19 Act (2021:4) was adopted on 8 January 2021 and at the time of writing is due to apply until 30 September 2021. It gave the government powers to regulate shopping malls, gyms and public transport; ban spontaneous private assemblies in specified areas; and shut off access to parks and similar public spaces. In all cases, such powers were to be proportional and required objective grounds for fearing that social distancing guidelines could not or would not be upheld. These powers, both to issue rules and to take decisions in individual cases, could be delegated to administrative agencies and local authorities, creating potential problems of legal certainty. The new powers stopped short of banning access to all public places. The law provided for administrative fines of up to €200 for individuals violating regulations issued under the law. As of June 2021, figures are unavailable on how often bans have been issued and fines imposed, but these have been relatively rare.

6. The 'Third Wave', Vaccination and Exit Strategies

Deaths declined in Sweden even before the vaccination programme began to be rolled out in January 2021. However, infection levels remained relatively high. Vaccination priorities were by age group. Groups at medical risk and hospital and care personnel received priority. The regions handled vaccination, again with financial support from central government. Vaccination was not made mandatory.[22] There are high levels of voluntary vaccination in Sweden, despite the negative experience of swine flu vaccination. Following scares during the spring of 2021 with serious side-effects from the AstraZeneca vaccine, the FHM decided that this vaccine should only be given to people over 65 years old.

With increased vaccination availability from March 2021 Sweden began opening up. From 1 June, licensing hours were extended. Permitted numbers of participants in public meetings and events were raised, and teaching at high schools and universities was expected to be normalised during the autumn semester 2021.

7. Evaluating the Swedish Measures from a Rule of Law Perspective

Whereas in most countries, public discussion was about unwarranted executive aggrandisement, in Sweden it was the opposite, namely whether the government should have taken, or exercised, *more* powers. Sweden showed a relatively high respect for the principle of legality. Existing powers were not subjected to dubious extensive interpretations. There was no retroactive legislation. New legislation was sometimes rushed, but it was temporary and did not, at least compared to most other European states, involve sweeping powers.[23]

As regards legislative oversight, Parliament continued to operate, as a result of voluntary agreement between the political parties, with a reduced physical presence of 55 MPs (down from 349). Meetings of committees and other parliamentary work were held online. As most measures initially were recommendations, there was no provision for parliamentary scrutiny or confirmation. As noted, the new binding executive powers provided for by statute were made subject to parliamentary confirmation, largely due to the intervention of the KU and the Council on Legislation. Both these bodies were fully operative during the pandemic and the KU held a series of public hearings in spring 2021 with government, administrative agencies and local authorities. The KU was unanimous, but relatively mild,

22 The constitutional right to personal integrity (RF 2:6) can be limited by statute. Labour law governs the issue to what extent, if at all, employers can require employees to be vaccinated.

23 See, however, below in this section on the right to life, regarding how the regions handled the availability of scarce intensive care.

in its criticism of six issues handled by the government response, including the visiting ban, assisting in the supply of PPE and testing and tracking.[24]

As regards judicial oversight, the courts continued to function, usually operating remotely. As regards the question of 'loyal cooperation' between central, regional and local government, this was not without difficulties, as indicated above. The division of responsibility between regions and local authorities for health care of the elderly in a pandemic was not entirely clear. The role of central government was mainly supportive. Problems were caused by the 'silo mentality' and time-consuming dialogue processes. As of June 2021, the Corona Commission has produced one report, on care of the elderly, which is important for the future debate on allocation of competence between central government, the regions and local authorities. The main finding in the report is that local authorities' care of the elderly must be improved by requiring a much greater presence of medically qualified staff, better pay and conditions for employees, and management reforms. While a significant number of local authorities failed to deliver safe standards of care, the Corona Commission stated clearly that the overall legal and political responsibility for this failure lies with the present, and former, central governments, which had failed for many years to deal with these known problems.

The constitutional rights of freedom of assembly and demonstration were limited, and no exception was made for religious services. During the second and third waves, people were fined for taking part in public demonstrations, and a few such demonstrations in Stockholm were broken up. An issue in a number of EU states was obligatory phone 'apps' to track contagion. No such apps were introduced in Sweden. The regions and the FHM considered that the concrete benefit of such an app was limited: it could only be voluntary, but it anyway entailed a restriction in private integrity. One private and family rights issue that arose concerns the government-issued ban on visiting elderly care facilities. The ban applied inflexibly over the whole country, even in areas where the spreading of the disease was low, and it was not subject to periodic evaluation. It was later delegated to the FHM to introduce local bans.

The right to life was also the subject of public debate, though it was not explicitly framed in legal terms or pursued in the courts. Accusations were levelled at some regions that during the first wave, a type of prioritisation of intensive care facilities took place. The Health and Social Care Inspectorate concluded[25] – disputed by the regions – that doctors on many occasions did not visit elderly care homes and were unfamiliar with residents and their medical records, but that they instead had, contrary to the law, made standardised assessments, relying on non-medically trained staff in care homes. The consequence was that some elderly patients received palliative care, instead of hospital care.

24 KU betänkande 2020/21:20, granskningsbetänkande 183–411.

25 IVO (Health and Social Care Inspectorate), 'Ingen region har tagit sitt fulla ansvar för individuell vård och behandling' (24 November 2020) <https://www.ivo.se/publicerat-material/nyheter/2020/ingen-region-har-tagit-fullt-ansvar-for-individuell-vard/>.

In many countries, property rights came before the courts. This is not (yet) so in Sweden. However, there have been many cases initiated by small businesses, which are not incorporated as companies, that there were major delays in paying out economic assistance and contributions towards furloughing employees, with the result that some went bankrupt.

8. Conclusion

Sweden has fared better than many other European states,[26] but it does not compare well to its Nordic neighbours. The pandemic has reminded us that societies are different, with different legal frameworks, levels of social capital and trust, structures of employment, levels of digitalisation and degrees of urbanisation. Above all, demographics, availability of health care and the general health of the population are important differences. Sweden, with a relatively high functioning welfare state with broad access to health care and a relatively high level of general health, should have had a good starting point for handling the pandemic. Still, Sweden, like many other countries, was not successful in protecting the most fragile, especially the elderly. In addition, the timing of responses is crucial: the policies chosen will depend upon what stage the contagion has reached and whether policies that are scientifically advisable are feasible to implement in practice. On at least three matters, Swedish measures have stood out in terms of timing: testing, self-isolation and quarantine, as well as face-mask recommendations were all imposed at a late stage compared to, for example, neighbouring Nordic states. Internationally, Sweden has served, and will continue to serve, as a 'counterfactual' example for states which subjected their populations to severe lockdowns.

26 Eurostat, 'Excess Mortality Starting to Fall Back in 2021, After a Large Death Toll' (*Eurostat*, 16 April 2021) <https://ec.europa.eu/eurostat/web/products-eurostat-news/-/ddn-20210416-2>.

20
TURKEY
Pandemic Governance and Executive Aggrandisement

Başak Çalı and Emre Turkut

1. Introduction[1]

Ever since the first officially reported COVID-19 case in the country in March 2020, Turkey, like most of the world, has taken drastic measures to control the pandemic.[2] The measures taken by Turkey included limitations on freedom of movement, closing schools and moving to online teaching at schools and universities, restrictions on business opening hours, cessation of prison and detention visits, prohibition of resignation for healthcare staff and, more stringently, the introduction of curfews.

These measures were taken against the backdrop of the coming into force of Turkey's new presidential system of government in 2018. Organised around vast presidential powers at the expense of the other branches of government,[3] the new regime was the culmination of the incremental and systemic efforts made by the President's Justice and Development Party (AKP) to undermine different forms of accountability in the past decade by executive aggrandisement.[4] Under this new

1 All websites accessed on 30 July 2021.

2 This chapter draws on Başak Çalı and Emre Turkut, 'Year One: Reflections on Turkey's Legal Responses to the COVID-19 Pandemic' (*Verfassungsblog*, 16 March 2021) <https://verfassungsblog.de/year-one-reflections-on-turkeys-legal-responses-to-the-covid-19-pandemic/>.

3 European Commission, 'Turkey 2019 EU Progress Report' (Communication) COM 260 final (2019) 29 May 2019, 5 (noting that the new regime "centralized power in the hands of the executive"); European Commission for Democracy through Law (Venice Commission), Opinion No 875/2017 on the Amendments to the Constitution Adopted by the Grand National Assembly on 21 January 2017 and to be submitted to a National Referendum on 16 April 2017, CDL-AD(2017)005, 13 March 2017, para 133 (highlighting "the dangers of degeneration of the proposed [presidential] system towards an authoritarian and personal regime").

4 Nancy Bermeo, 'On Democratic Backsliding' (2016) 27(1) Journal of Democracy 5; Tarunabh Khaitan, 'Executive Aggrandizement in Established Democracies: A Crisis of Liberal Democratic

 DOI: 10.4324/9781003211952-23

system, presidential decrees have been the main mechanism of rulemaking and the Parliament (controlled by the AKP and its small coalition partner, the Nationalist Movement Party (MHP)) is largely unable to exercise an effective oversight role. Over the first year of the COVID-19 pandemic, this apparent regression of oversight and accountability of the executive was put to the test. The institutional features of the presidential executive system, alongside the political and economic preferences of the government, therefore shaped the executive responses to the pandemic.

Turkey's legal response to the pandemic had four key features, which are examined in turn in this chapter. First, the wide-ranging response was primarily regulated by centralised executive measures in the form of presidential circulars, ministerial circulars and public announcements, alongside the decisions of provincial public health boards and provincial pandemic boards, raising credible doubts as to its legal basis. Second, these restrictions on fundamental rights followed a differentiated response in law and selective enforcement in practice. The measures categorically differentiated between individuals based on their ages and their ability to contribute to the economy, while the economic stimulus packages provided favoured employers rather than workers.[5] The application of measures was also selectively enforced in practice: for example, whilst public gatherings in closed and open spaces were banned, pro-government gatherings were allowed to take place. Third, there was almost no parliamentary involvement in and, as of July 2021, very limited judicial oversight of these executive measures. Finally, those who criticised the legality and the adequacy of the measures were subject to criminal legal proceedings under a broad range of charges.

2. The Legal Basis of Turkey's Pandemic Measures

As soon as the first COVID-19 case was reported in Turkey in early March 2020, the government rapidly resorted to wide-ranging extraordinary administrative measures, leveraging the country's previous knowhow in health emergency and disaster management.[6] In doing so, Turkey did not take the path of declaring a

Constitutionalism' (2019) 17(1) International Journal of Constitutional Law 342.

5 The efficiency of these 'employer-friendly' packages was questioned given the country's already collapsing economy even before the pandemic. For an analysis, see Ceyhun Elgin and Gökçe Basbug, 'Economic Stimulus Packages as a Response to the COVID-19 Pandemic: A Comparison & the Case of Turkey' (Heinrich Böll Stiftung Policy Paper, 18 April 2021) <https://www.istanpol.org/post/economic-stimulus-packages-as-a-response-to-the-covid-19-pandemic-a-comparison-the-case-of-turkey>.

6 For a detailed account of Turkey's institutional infrastructure for emergency preparedness, see World Health Organisation, 'Turkey's Response to COVID-19: First Impressions' (11 July 2020) <https://apps.who.int/iris/handle/10665/335803>. Following the emergence of the COVID-19 outbreak in China, the Turkish Ministry of Health also set up its Coronavirus Scientific Advisory Board – a consultative and decision-guiding body tasked with proposing prevention, mitigation and containment measures. The Board adopted several guidelines on COVID-19-related issues; see 'COVID-19 Guides', Turkish Ministry of Health, <https://hsgm.saglik.gov.tr/en/covid-19-ingilizce-dokumanlar/rehberler.html>.

state of emergency as provided for under Article 119 of the Turkish Constitution revised in the 2017 constitutional amendments.[7] Instead, it relied on the implied vast powers of the new presidential system and provisions of existing pieces of law, most notably the Law on Public Health No. 1593 (LPH)[8] and the Law on Provincial Administration No. 5442 (LPA)[9] to justify the wide range of executive measures restricting fundamental rights.

Under the Turkish Constitution, limitations of constitutional rights must either be enacted directly through an Act of Parliament in the shape of a statute or based on the express authorisation of such statute.[10] The government's direct and indirect reliance on existing laws, therefore, raised questions as to the legal basis of wide-ranging restrictions of fundamental rights under the Constitution since the start of the pandemic.

Of these laws, the LPH dates back to 1930. Although it is regarded as a comprehensive legal framework that formed the backbone of the nascent Turkish Republic's public health system at the time,[11] it is not a piece of law that has seen much practical application in the past 90 years and can best be qualified as 'rusty' to meet a pandemic erupting in 2020.[12] Specifically, the law focuses on measures that can be taken with respect to individuals "who are infected, suspected of being infected, or have been determined to be contagious", rather than measures affecting the population as a whole in the context of a public health emergency. This raised concerns as to whether this legislation could be the legal basis of extensive actions restricting constitutional rights by treating everyone as "suspected of being infected" in order to combat the pandemic.[13]

7 Under the amended Turkish Constitution, the power to declare a state of emergency belongs to the Turkish President. The President's emergency decision must be sent to the Parliament for approval on the same day. In addition to the authority to lift the state of emergency entirely, the Parliament can also shorten or extend emergency periods. The Turkish constitutional framework on states of emergency also gives the President a very broad authority to issue presidential emergency decrees having the force of law on "matters necessitated by the state of emergency" not confined by a specific area, contrary to ordinary presidential decrees. See Article 119 of the Turkish Constitution, as amended on 16 April 2017, Act No. 6771 <https://global.tbmm.gov.tr/docs/constitution_en.pdf>.

8 The Law on Public Health (*Umumi Hıfzıssıhha Kanunu*) No. 1593, adopted on 24 April 1930, published in the Official Gazette of Turkey on 6 May 1930.

9 The Law on Provincial Administrations (*İl Idaresi Kanunu*) No. 5442, adopted on 10 June 1949, published in the Official Gazette of Turkey on 18 June 1949.

10 The Turkish Constitution further stipulates that these limitations/restrictions shall not "be contrary to the letter and spirit of the Constitution and the requirements of the democratic order of the society and the secular republic and the principle of proportionality" – see Article 13 of the Turkish Constitution.

11 The LPH has in its entirety 15 sections and 309 articles and covers a wide number of public health related issues such as diseases, institutions and emergency contingency plans. For a history of public health in the early Turkish Republic, see Emine Evered and Kyle T Evered, 'Sin in the City: An Urban History of Medicine and Modern Morality in Turkey' in Igor Vojnovic and others (eds), *Handbook of Global Urban Health* (Routledge 2019) 68–84.

12 Çalı and Turkut (n 2).

13 Serdar Unver, 'Fighting COVID-19 – Legal Powers, Risks and the Rule of Law: Turkey' (*Verfassungsblog*, 15 April 2020) <https://verfassungsblog.de/fighting-covid-19-legal-powers

The LPA – most recently amended in 2018 – on the other hand confers wide-ranging powers on Turkish provincial administrative authorities to take all necessary measures to maintain public safety and order, including the power to prohibit anyone suspected of being a safety danger from entering and exiting provinces of Turkey for 15 days, and the power to temporarily close public places.[14] Here, too, it has been noted that treating everyone living in Turkey as a safety danger requires an extraordinarily broad interpretation of the LPA.[15] Even then, this law does not provide a clear legal basis for the authorisation of curfews or the imposition of inter-city travel bans for longer periods of time, or for the restriction of business hours. Yet, these obvious gaps in legal authorisation were not cured during the first year of the pandemic.

Despite these important concerns as to the legal basis of the restrictions as required by the Constitution, Turkey saw the adoption of countless ministerial circular orders to handle the pandemic. Whilst some of these measures can only be justified by adopting unduly broad interpretations, other measures cannot be justified in any way under the legal frameworks above. For example, the moratorium on the voluntary resignation of healthcare staff is a measure that can only be taken when a state of emergency is declared.[16] However, the governance of the pandemic has so far proceeded by way of adoption of 'state of emergency'-like measures by the executive and Parliament has not been called upon to ensure that measures taken meet the constitutional safeguard of legality of rights restrictions.

3. Differentiated Responses Across Age and Risk Groups, Economic Benefits, Gatherings and Assemblies

The Turkish response to the pandemic was based on the introduction of differentiated measures of rights restrictions. These differentiations were made not only based on health vulnerabilities, but also on economic benefits and political considerations. At the start of the pandemic, Turkey became the first country in the world to impose a 24-hour curfew (or 'targeted lockdown') on all individuals

-risks-and-the-rule-of-law-turkey/>; Kemal Gozler, 'Koronavirus Salginiyla Mucadele icin alinan tedbirler hukuka uygun mu?' [Are the measures taken to combat the coronavirus epidemic in compliance with the law?] (*Turk Anayasa Hukuku Sitesi*, 6 July 2020) <https://www.anayasa.gen.tr/korona-2.htm>.

14 See generally Article 11 of the LPA.

15 Venice Commission, Opinion No 842/2016 on the Legal Framework Governing Curfews, CDL-AD(2016)010, 13 June 2016, para 60 and 100ff <https://www.venice.coe.int/webforms/documents/default.aspx?pdffile=CDL-AD(2016)010-e>.

16 See Article 96 of the Turkish Law on Civil Servants (*Devlet Memurları Kanunu*) No. 657, adopted on 14 July 1965, published in the Official Gazette of Turkey on 23 July 1965. It should be noted that one of the most far-reaching emergency decrees adopted in the post-2016 coup period, Decree No. 684 of 25 August 2017, amended this Article. Previously, civil servants could not resign (or withdraw) from their duties until "their substitutes are appointed and take over from them". By way of the 2017 amendment, their resignation/withdrawal demands must also be "accepted" by relevant authorities.

with chronic conditions or over the age of 65.[17] This meant that those subject to a targeted lockdown were unable to leave their homes for weeks on end, even for a short stroll. Subsequently, this differentiated response was recalibrated, allowing those over 65 to leave their homes for a three-hour window during the day, requiring them to obtain special permits for inter-city travel and restricting their use of public transportation. Similar measures were put in place restricting the movement of individuals under the age of 20. These various restrictions were only fully lifted on 1 July 2021. As the pandemic worsened, Turkey also imposed weekend curfews requiring the whole population to remain indoors at the weekends. These differentiated responses based on age and health grounds, however, did not apply when restricted groups were active members of the workforce – a strategy dubbed as 'class-immunity' in ironic contrast to 'herd-immunity'.[18] When Turkey had to impose its first full lockdown in mid-April 2021 for three weeks in response to the soaring number of new infections, its definition of essential services that were allowed to remain open also remained broad compared to other countries, including, for example, hotels or other places of lodging.[19]

The Turkish authorities also pursued a differentiated response to business opening hours with the aim of keeping as many businesses open as possible, or closing some (such as restaurants and cafes) whilst keeping others open (such as hotels and shopping malls). Some of these decisions were criticised on grounds that they favoured the wealthy segments of Turkish society as well as any foreign tourists able to travel to Turkey.[20] For example, during the winter of 2020, hotels received special exemptions to remain open and admit customers over weekends. This meant that whilst the whole population was under a curfew and facing heavy fines (ranging from 392 to 3,150 TL – roughly US$45 to US$365 or €39 to €310 at the time of writing) if they left their homes, those individuals with reservations in ski resort hotels were exempted from the countrywide weekend curfew. In April 2021, foreign tourists were exempted from the full lockdown measures.[21]

17 During the first year of the pandemic, numerous circular orders for curfews were issued. For instance, see 'Circular on the curfew for those 65 and over and those with chronic illnesses', Turkish Ministry of Internal Affairs (21 March 2020) <https://www.icisleri.gov.tr/81-ilde-22052020-saat-2400-ile-26052020-saat-2400-arasinda-uygulanacak-sokaga-cikma-kisitlamasi>.

18 Evren Balta and Soli Özel, 'The Battle Over the Numbers: Turkey's Low Case Fatality Rate' (*Institut Montaigne*, 4 May 2020) <https://www.institutmontaigne.org/en/blog/battle-over-numbers-turkeys-low-case-fatality-rate>.

19 Gul Tuysuz, 'Turkey Enters First National Lockdown as Covid-19 Cases Rise' (*CNN*, 29 April 2021) <https://edition.cnn.com/2021/04/29/europe/turkey-enters-national-lockdown-intl/index.html>.

20 Julia Hahn, 'Tourists Exempt from Turkey's Coronavirus Lockdown' (*Deustche Welle*, 10 May 2021) <https://www.dw.com/en/tourists-exempt-from-turkeys-coronavirus-lockdown/av-57480517>.

21 Daren Butler, 'Turkey Welcomes Foreign Tourists While Locking Down Locals' (*Reuters*, 5 May 2021) <https://www.reuters.com/world/middle-east/turkey-welcomes-foreign-tourists-while-locking-down-locals-2021-05-05/>.

Executive restrictions also saw selective enforcement in practice, most visibly in the case of freedom of assembly. In many instances, the Turkish authorities issued bans on peaceful protests by rights activists including lawyers,[22] healthcare workers[23] and students[24] and arrested protesters. Despite all the legal restrictions in place, however, the Turkish government itself did not shy away from organising a number of mass gatherings over the past year. The inaugural Friday public prayer in Hagia Sophia, after its conversion to a mosque in July 2020, saw over 350,000 people attending.[25] In March 2021, the AKP organised numerous party rallies in multiple cities, where social distancing rules were not enforced and large-scale attendance was praised.[26]

Whilst the purported legitimate aim of all the enforced differentiated responses was the protection of public health and the right to life, they all raised questions concerning the proportionality of the measures and the discriminatory enforcement of rules, manifested, in particular, by bans on anti-government activities and lack of enforcement of rules for government condoned or supported activities with no accountability. As we discuss in the section below, however, the legal appraisal of these executive measures from the perspectives of legality, proportionality and non-discrimination by Parliament was absent and the role of the Turkish courts remained limited in the first year.

4. Lack of Legislative Oversight and Limited Judicial Oversight

The pandemic measures in Turkey were marked by a clear lack of an oversight role for the legislature and limited oversight by courts. Whilst the Parliament remained fully functional over the first year of the pandemic, it played no discernible role in pandemic governance either by exercising legislative oversight over the measures taken by the executive or by upgrading or improving pandemic-related legal frameworks. This is attributable both to the curbing of the oversight powers of the

22 'Turkish Police Block Dozens of Lawyers Marching to Ankara Against Bill' (*Al Arabiya*, 22 June 2020) <https://english.alarabiya.net/News/middle-east/2020/06/22/Turkish-police-block-dozens-of-lawyers-marching-to-Ankara-against-bill>.

23 Hamdi Firat Buyuk, 'Turkish Medical Workers Protest Over Handling of Pandemic' (*Balkan Insight*, 16 September 2020) <https://balkaninsight.com/2020/09/16/turkish-medical-workers-protest-over-handling-of-pandemic/>.

24 'Turkey: Dozens Arrested as Students Protest Erdogan University Pick' (*Deutsche Welle*, 6 January 2021) <https://www.dw.com/en/turkey-dozens-arrested-as-students-protest-erdogan-university-pick/a-56149287>.

25 Arwa Damon and Laura Smith-Spark, 'Turkey's Hagia Sophia Holds First Friday Prayers Since Conversion Back to Mosque' (*CNN*, 26 July 2020) <https://edition.cnn.com/2020/07/24/europe/hagia-sophia-mosque-friday-prayers-turkey-intl/index.html>. For a close reading of the Turkish Council of State's 2020 ruling to revert the Hagia Sophia into a mosque, see 'The Hagia Sophia Case' (2021) 134 Harvard Law Review 1278.

26 'AKP Draws Ire with Yet Another Congress in Complete Disregard of COVID-19 Measures' (*Duvar English*, 15 March 2021) <https://www.duvarenglish.com/turkeys-ruling-akp-draws-ire-with-yet-another-congress-in-complete-disregard-of-covid-19-measures-video-56642>.

Parliament by the new presidential system and the AKP–MHP bloc holding the majority in Parliament. Under the new system, the Parliament has reduced oversight functions due to the abolition of two effective accountability mechanisms under the old parliamentary system, namely, the vote of confidence and the possibility to put oral questions to the executive. The remaining three accountability mechanisms, namely, the right to put written questions, parliamentary inquiry and parliamentary investigations,[27] were frequently resorted to by the opposition MPs but remained unsuccessful. This is because the AKP–MHP majority was able to block the effective use of these mechanisms and the executive was unresponsive to pandemic-related questions.[28]

One notable exception to the parliamentary unresponsiveness to the pandemic was the introduction of early release legislation to reduce the chronic overcrowding in Turkey's prisons.[29] This law, however, differentiated between categories of prisoners and deliberately excluded thousands of prisoners charged under overly broad terrorism offences despite the European Court of Human Rights's repeated findings that such use is incompatible with the European Convention on Human Rights.[30] The early release law was passed in April 2020 by the AKP–MHP majority, and calls for significant amendments by opposition parties and civil society groups to broaden the scope of the law were ignored.[31]

There was no flurry of legal challenges before the Turkish courts regarding the wide-ranging measures taken to address the pandemic in the first year. In a handful of high profile and politically salient cases, the Turkish Constitutional Court (TCC) and the Turkish Council of State (Turkey's highest administrative court, TCS) chose to exercise judicial restraint concerning the actions of the executive. There were, however, also some court successes, concerning less politically costly pandemic measures.

27 See generally Article 98 of the Turkish Constitution.

28 The Turkish Parliament's statistics show that the overwhelming majority of the 581 written pandemic-related questions put by the opposition MPs over the past year remain unanswered. Moreover, the opposition parties lodged 80 motions for parliamentary inquiry, which, as of July 2021, still remain on the agenda of the Plenary Assembly. The final mechanism alive, parliamentary investigation, is tied to higher thresholds (three-fifths majority), which seems almost impossible to be attained in practice and this explains why no motion for opening parliamentary investigations was lodged by the opposition parties. The statistics are available on the website of the Turkish Grand National Assembly, under '*Denetim*' (Parliamentary Scrutiny): <https://www.tbmm.gov.tr/develop/owa/tbmm_internet.anasayfa>.

29 Turkey, Law No. 7242 on the Execution of Penalty and other Security measures amending certain legislations, adopted on 14 April 2020 published in the Official Gazette of Turkey on 15 April 2020.

30 See inter alia, *Parmak and Bakır v Turkey* App Nos. 22429/07 and 25195/07 (ECtHR, 3 December 2019) and *Selahattin Demirtaş v Turkey (No 2)* App no 14305/17 (ECtHR Grand Chamber, 22 December 2020).

31 Amnesty International, 'Turkey: Prison Release Law Leaves Innocent and Vulnerable Prisoners at Risk of COVID-19' (13 April 2020) <https://www.amnesty.org/en/latest/news/2020/04/prison-release-law-leaves-prisoners-at-risk-of-covid/>.

The TCC was seized to address both abstract norm review complaints (that can be initiated by the largest two political parties in Parliament or 120 members of Parliament) and individual applications concerning the pandemic restrictions. Turkey's largest opposition Republican People's Party (CHP) took the prisoner early release legislation to the TCC in April 2020 by lodging two separate applications. The first application concerned the legislation's form alleging that it served as a special amnesty (rather than an early release) law, which requires the three-fifth quorum for its approval as per Article 87 of the Turkish Constitution. The second application focused on the legislation's substance arguing that it violates the constitutional principle of equality as protected under Article 10 of the Turkish Constitution. Both applications were rejected by the TCC in July 2020 and July 2021, respectively.[32]

An individual application lodged before the TCC in April 2020 challenging the legal basis of the pandemic-related curfews imposed on citizens over 65 was similarly found inadmissible in June 2020.[33] In its decision, the TCC noted that a curfew in its nature is an administrative measure and that the applicant should first take this case before an administrative court.[34] As reported in Turkish media, in January 2021, an Istanbul-based association turned to the Istanbul Administrative Court for the annulment of the curfew on senior citizens, alleging its conflict with Article 23 of the Turkish Constitution (freedom of movement). The application was still pending when the curfews fully ended in July 2021.[35]

The TCS received further high-profile litigation when a Ministry of Interior circular limited the ability of the mayors of the three metropolitan cities of Turkey, Istanbul, Ankara and Izmir, all members of the opposition CHP, to maintain local services and distribute social assistance to those in need due to COVID-19. Initially, several initiatives taken by these CHP local authorities to fundraise for families affected by the lockdown received harsh criticism by President Erdogan, who accused the mayors of trying to create "a state within a state".[36] Following the president's cue, in an effort to prevent opposition municipalities from raising funds, the Turkish Interior Ministry issued a circular, banning the fundraising campaigns, blocking the collected funds in state-owned banks and

32 TCC, Constitutionality Review, App No 2020/44, Dec. No 2020/41 on 17 July 2020 (decision on the legislation's unconstitutionality with regard to its form) and Constitutionality Review, App No 220/53, Dec. No 2021/55 on 14 July 2021 (decision on the legislation's unconstitutionality with regard to its substance).

33 TCC, Individual Application (Senih Özay), App No 2020/13969, Dec. 9 June 2020<https://www.anayasa.gov.tr/media/6791/2020-13969.pdf>.

34 ibid, para 30.

35 'Turkish Association Files Lawsuit for Cancellation of Partial Curfew Imposed on Senior Citizens' (*Duvar English*, 25 January 2021) <https://www.duvarenglish.com/turkish-association-files-lawsuit-for-cancellation-of-partial-curfew-imposed-on-senior-citizens-news-56001>.

36 Tessa Fox, 'Brother Tayyip's Soup Kitchen' (*Foreign Policy*, 17 April 2020)<https://foreignpolicy.com/2020/04/17/erdogan-turkey-coronavirus-relief-politics-akp-chp-brother-tayyip-soup-kitchen/>.

informing the CHP mayors that they needed clear authorisation from local governors appointed by the President to carry out COVID-related social projects.[37] In response, the opposition mayors petitioned the TCS, requesting an order of stay of execution of this circular. The TCS, however, dismissed the request.[38] The court is expected to issue a full judgment later in 2021. This litigation points to the intolerance of any social support measures led by local authorities that are not coordinated centrally by the President's executive team through the new presidential system.

Individuals challenging the hefty fines or economic burdens imposed on them to combat the pandemic, on the other hand, had more success before domestic courts. In February 2021, the Turkish Court of Cassation (Turkey's supreme court of appeals) struck out an administrative fine imposed by the police on an individual for allegedly breaking COVID-19 rules by not wearing a mask on the ground that they do not possess such authority under the provisions of the LPH and the LPA in conjunction with the Turkish Misdemeanour Law.[39] Invoking this decision, a Turkish peace court (the lowest level of civil court) later invalidated another fine issued by the police to an individual for breaching the curfew rules.[40] These decisions, however, did not alter the fine regime, but merely instructed the executive to point to different legal provisions when issuing fines as their legal basis. In April 2021, teachers in state schools were successful before a first instance administrative court, when the court found the Turkish Ministry of Education's decision not to pay fees for supplementary courses to teachers due to the pandemic to be unjustified and unlawful and ordered the stay of execution of this decision.[41]

5. Criminalisation of Dissent and an Increase in Rights-Restricting Laws

From March 2020, concerns grew as to how COVID-19 was being handled in Turkey. The contradictory numbers released by government officials and the

37 'Turkish Gov't Bans Donation Campaigns of Opposition Municipalities' (*Sol International*, 2 April 2020) <https://news.sol.org.tr/turkish-govt-bans-donation-campaigns-opposition-municipalities-176639>.

38 'Danıştay'dan CHP'li belediyelerin bağış kampanyası hakkında karar' [Council of State's decision on funds raised by CHP] (*BirGün*, 24 June 2020) <https://www.birgun.net/haber/danistay-dan-chp-li-belediyelerin-bagis-kampanyasi-hakkinda-karar-305829>.

39 Turkish Court of Appeals, 19th Criminal Section, App No. 2020/4354, Dec. No. 2020/14250, 8 February 2021.

40 'Mahkeme, sokağa çıkma kısıtlamasına uymayan vatandaşa kesilen para cezasını iptal etti' [The court cancelled the fine imposed on a citizen who did not comply with the curfew] (*Cumhuriyet*, 6 October 2021) <https://www.cumhuriyet.com.tr/haber/mahkeme-sokaga-cikma-kisitlamasina-uymayan-vatandasa-kesilen-para-cezasini-iptal-etti-1804076>.

41 Mahkemeden öğretmenler için ek ders kararı: 'Pandemi nedeniyle kesilemez' [Court's decision on fees for additional courses: 'cannot be cut due to pandemic'] (*Cumhuriyet*, 27 April 2021) <https://www.cumhuriyet.com.tr/haber/mahkemeden-ogretmenler-icin-ek-ders-karari-pandemi-nedeniyle-kesilemez-1831494>.

under-reporting of coronavirus cases and deaths raised serious concerns alongside the government's organisation of, or attendance at, 'superspreader' events.[42] Another bone of contention was the introduction of some measures, such as an outright ban on the sale and transport of alcohol that arguably had little to no relevance to the pandemic.[43] The Turkish government also put considerable effort into containing the flow of information about the level of COVID-19 cases and targeted those who challenged the government's official line on the pandemic. Under the guise of combating 'fake news', 'incitement' or 'spreading fear and panic', hundreds of individuals, including social media users,[44] journalists,[45] doctors[46] and others who discussed the pandemic responses online, were investigated pursuant to criminal law provisions including Article 213 (threats to create fear and panic among the people), Article 216 (public incitement to enmity and hatred) and Article 217 (public incitement to break the law) of the Turkish Criminal Code.

In addition, whilst Parliament was largely sidelined in addressing the pandemic, it was active in introducing a wide range of laws restricting rights in contexts not related to the pandemic in the first year. For example, one piece of legislation adopted in summer 2020 tightened the governmental grip over social media platforms, allowing state authorities to remove content from these platforms (rather than blocking) and requiring social media giants to appoint a local representative to address authorities' concerns.[47] At the end of 2020, Parliament approved another law, which places onerous oversight rules on civil society organisations, and allows the Turkish Internal Ministry to replace the leaders of such organisations who face terrorism charges.[48]

42 Carlotta Gall, 'Istanbul Death Toll Hints Turkey Is Hiding a Wider Coronavirus Calamity' (*The New York Times*, 20 April 2020) <https://www.nytimes.com/2020/04/20/world/middleeast/coronavirus-turkey-deaths.html>; Sezer Kısa and Adnan Kısa, 'Under-reporting of COVID-19 Cases in Turkey' (2020) 35(5) The International Journal of Health Planning and Management 1009.

43 'Turkey Bans Alcohol Sales as Coronavirus Pandemic Measure' (*Deutsche Welle*, 30 April 2021) <https://www.dw.com/en/turkey-bans-alcohol-sales-as-coronavirus-pandemic-measure/a-57382148>. The Ankara Bar Association (ABA) took the alcohol ban to the TCS in April 2021, but as of July 2021, the decision was pending. The ABA's petition is available at <http://www.ankarabarosu.org.tr/HaberDuyuru.aspx?DUYURU&=11212>.

44 'Turkey Detains 19 People over "Provocative" Coronavirus Posts' (*Reuters*, 17 March 2020) <https://www.reuters.com/article/us-health-coronavirus-turkey-idUSKBN2140T9>.

45 Organization for Security and Co-operation in Europe, 'OSCE Media Freedom Representative about detention of several journalists following their reports on coronavirus crisis in Turkey' (23 March 2020) <https://reliefweb.int/report/turkey/osce-media-freedom-representative-concerned-about-detention-several-journalists>.

46 Owen Dyer, 'Covid-19: Turkey Cracks Down on Doctors who Doubt Official Figures' (2020) 370 British Medical Journal 2020;370:m3787 <https://www.bmj.com/content/370/bmj.m3787>.

47 Human Rights Watch, 'Turkey: Social Media Law Will Increase Censorship' (27 July 2020) <https://www.hrw.org/news/2020/07/27/turkey-social-media-law-will-increase-censorship>.

48 Freedom House, 'Turkey: Passage of NGO Law Strips Away Fundamental Rights and Freedoms' (4 January 2021) <https://freedomhouse.org/article/turkey-passage-ngo-law-strips-away-fundamental-rights-and-freedoms>.

6. Conclusion: Looking Ahead

Turkey's first year response to the pandemic was driven by its new executive presidential system, which places important barriers before legislative, judicial and effective civil society oversight of centralised executive action. Given this, the responses largely reflected the political and neo-liberal economic preferences of the government and were not tempered by checks and balances from other branches of government, often to the detriment of the protection of the rule of law, fundamental rights, equality and transparency. Moreover, centralised pandemic governance often appeared haphazard and disorganised.

The impact of the pandemic measures in their first year on the enjoyment of the full range of fundamental rights, in particular, the right to health, economic and social rights, women's rights, the right to education and democratic rights are yet to be studied in Turkey. An important challenge to this comprehensive impact assessment is the lack of release of adequate disaggregated data by the executive authorities.[49] There is some partial evidence that domestic violence rose in this period; data of the Istanbul Security Directorate in mid-2020, for example, revealed a 32.8% increase in domestic violence compared to 2019.[50] Paradoxically enough, in March 2021, President Erdogan issued a presidential decision officially withdrawing Turkey from the Council of Europe Convention on Preventing and Combatting Violence Against Women and Domestic Violence, known as the Istanbul Convention.[51] The impact of the extended school closures and the lack of internet access or proper technological devices on the right to education, in particular on the right to education of children coming from lower socio-economic backgrounds, also remains a major concern in the face of different remote learning policies adopted by the Turkish Ministry of Education in the past year.[52]

Overall, Turkey's pandemic response in the first year was shaped by the ongoing process of executive aggrandisement under its new presidential system. This was not only reflected in the centralised management of the pandemic measures by the executive team of the President with no or very limited oversight by Parliament, the courts or civil society, but also in the selective application of rules to the government and its critics, and legal harassment of those, including doctors and health workers, who criticised the measures taken or demanded more transparency and accountability.

49 Turkish Medical Association and others, 'Salgından Çıkışın Yolu Bellidir' [There is a way out of the pandemic] (30 July 2021) <https://www.ttb.org.tr/haber_goster.php?Guid=9851d19c-f132-11eb-9018-02370ea20223>.

50 'Domestic Violence Has Increased by 38.2 Percent in İstanbul' (*BIANET News*, 6 April 2020) <https://m.bianet.org/english/male-violence/222545-domestic-violence-has-increased-by-38-2-percent-in-istanbul>.

51 Presidential Decision No.3718, 20 March 2021 <https://www.mevzuat.gov.tr/MevzuatMetin/20.5.3718.pdf>.

52 OECD, 'School Education during COVID-19: Were Teachers and Students Ready?' Country Note: Turkey, 2020 <https://www.oecd.org/education/Turkey-coronavirus-education-country-note.pdf>.

21

THE COVID-19 PANDEMIC

A Pretext for Expanding Power in Hungary

Kriszta Kovács

1. Introduction[1]

The COVID-19 pandemic triggered unforeseen social and legal problems in the democratic world. Most governments were unprepared, and a lack of knowledge and infrastructure limited government responses. In some countries, the challenges were even more significant as pre-existing political and legal problems were aggravated by the pandemic. A prime example is Hungary, where the state of human rights, democracy and the rule of law – already grave in 2019[2] – was only exacerbated by the pandemic.[3] Nor has this approach proved effective at managing the virus: after initial success, Hungary has, at the time of writing, the second highest per capita death toll in the world.[4]

1 All websites accessed on 5 August 2021.

2 According to the World Justice Project Rule of Law Index 2020, Hungary was among the countries that experienced the largest average percentage drop in the rule of law between 2014 and 2019 <https://worldjusticeproject.org/our-work/research-and-data/wjp-rule-law-index-2020>. The Global State of Democracy 2019 produced by International IDEA listed Hungary among the countries that "has seen significant erosion of democratic checks and balances for the best part of a decade"; chapter 5, 222. <https://www.idea.int/sites/default/files/publications/chapters/the-global-state-of-democracy-2019-CH5.pdf>.

3 This chapter expands and revises my previous posts to the 2021 'Power and the COVID-19 Pandemic' and 2020 'States of Emergency' Symposia: Kriszta Kovács, 'Hungary's Orbánistan: A Complete Arsenal of Emergency Powers' (*Verfassungsblog*, 6 April 2020) <https://verfassungsblog.de/hungarys-orbanistan-a-complete-arsenal-of-emergency-powers/>; Kriszta Kovács, 'Hungary and the Pandemic: A Pretext for Expanding Power' (*Verfassungsblog*, 11 March 2021) <https://verfassungsblog.de/hungary-and-the-pandemic-a-pretext-for-expanding-power/>. The author has received funding from the European Union's Horizon 2020 research and innovation programme under the Marie Sklodowska-Curie grant agreement No 794368.

4 Johns Hopkins University, Coronavirus Resource Center, Mortality Analyses (updated as of 5 August 2021) <https://coronavirus.jhu.edu/data/mortality>.

DOI: 10.4324/9781003211952-24

Prime Minister Viktor Orbán strategically used the opportunity provided by COVID-19 to consolidate power within the executive and gain more unchecked power. This chapter demonstrates in section 2 how the Orbán government identified an ever-increasing number of alleged enemies against which the government equipped itself with practically unlimited powers by way of introducing various states of emergency. The government used these 'enemies' to justify restrictions on human rights and the stifling of political opposition. Section 3 examines the rights restrictions introduced by emergency decrees and the failure of Parliament and the courts to effectively check them. Instead, Hungary adopted an increasingly militarised response, as discussed in section 4. Finally, section 5 provides perspective on the possibilities for, and limitations of, legal and social resilience to protect human rights and the rule of law against further erosion.

2. A Permanent State of Emergency

Since the last free and fair elections[5] in 2010, Viktor Orbán has been working towards authoritarianism by using successive 'crises' to consolidate his hold on power. While doing this, Orbán has been perpetually on a war footing. He has made sharp distinctions between political friend and foe to maintain a sense of constant crisis and justify 'waging war' against the purported foes: "financiers", "illegal migrants", "terrorists", philanthropist George Soros who according to Orbán "obviously holds in his pocket the EU and the 'pro-refugee NGOs'"[6] and, most recently, COVID-19 itself. A whole array of processes was created after 2010 when Orbán was elected Prime Minister in response to these 'crises'.

The lightly entrenched democratic constitution of 1989 could be amended by a two-thirds vote of the Parliament, and Viktor Orbán's government had 68% of the seats, so in 2011, the parliamentary supermajority voted for a new constitution, officially called the Fundamental Law. Orbán justified its adoption with reference to the consequences of the 2008 global financial crisis and the country's high level of public debt.[7] The ruling majority gave its crisis management policy a constitutional rank: the Fundamental Law contains a debt ceiling and deprives the Constitutional Court of its power to review financial laws.[8] These measures remain in effect at the time of writing.

In 2016, faced with a sharp rise in the number of asylum-seekers arriving in Hungary, Viktor Orbán saw another opportunity to expand his power. Citing the threat posed by the 2015 'migrant crisis', the Orbán government, alone in the

5 Organisation for Security and Cooperation in Europe, 'Hungary, Parliamentary Elections, 11 April 2010: Election Assessment Mission Final Report' (9 August 2020) <https://www.osce.org/odihr/elections/hungary/117819>.

6 Viktor Orbán on Radio Kossuth on 22 May 2020 <https://2015-2019.kormany.hu/hu/a-miniszterelnok/beszedek-publikaciok-interjuk/orban-viktor-a-kossuth-radio-jo-reggelt-magyarorszag-cimu-musoraban-20200522>.

7 Kriszta Kovács, 'Hungary's Struggle: In a Permanent State of Exception' (*Verfassungsblog*, 17 March 2016) <https://verfassungsblog.de/hungarys-struggle-in-a-permanent-state-of-exception/>.

8 Article 37(4) of the Fundamental Law.

EU, declared a 'mass migration emergency' in a government decree.[9] Since then, Hungary has been in a continuous state of emergency. The 'mass migration emergency' is still in effect even though not a single migrant can legally enter Hungary's territory; the only legal way to trigger the asylum procedure is by submitting a 'declaration of intent' at the Hungarian embassy in Kyiv or Belgrade.[10] The government has renewed the emergency every six months; at the time of writing, the most recent extension was on 27 February 2021.[11]

The first reaction of the government to the COVID-19 pandemic was the introduction of a 'pandemic emergency' in a new government decree with a sunset clause of 15 days following its declaration if there were no parliamentary authorisation for its extension.[12] The decree cited both Article 15(1) of the Fundamental Law and the state of danger clause in Article 53, even though this article does not mention a pandemic as a source of danger. With the 15-day deadline looming, the government tabled the Act on Protecting against the Coronavirus,[13] labelled the 'Enabling Act' in public discourse in an echo of the Nazi era in Germany.[14] Although Parliament was in session, the Act enabled the government to issue decrees independently of Parliament and gave it the power to take extraordinary measures, including suspending or abrogating statutory provisions without parliamentary approval during the emergency.[15] The Enabling Act radically differed from its European counterparts in that the Hungarian government's extraordinary power was broad in scope and without express temporal limit or strict rational connection to the areas where an urgent response to the pandemic was required.[16] It has been subject to widespread criticism: international organisations including the Council of Europe Secretary-General,[17] the OSCE Office for Democratic Institutions and Human Rights,[18] the UN High Commissioner for Human

9 Government decree 41/2016. (III. 9). The government used Article 15(1) of the Fundamental Law – "The Government shall exercise powers which are not expressly conferred by laws on another state body" – to declare a state of emergency.

10 Sections 267–275 of the Act LVIII of 2020.

11 Government decree 93/2021. (II. 27).

12 Government decree 40/2020. (III. 11).

13 Act XII of 2020 on Protecting against the Coronavirus. An unofficial English translation is available here: <https://hungarianspectrum.org/2020/03/21/translation-of-draft-law-on-protecting-against-the-coronavirus/>.

14 The name refers to the 'Enabling Act' adopted in April 1933, which allowed the new German government led by Adolf Hitler to issue decrees independently of both Parliament and the then President, Paul von Hindenburg. In effect, the Act turned Hitler into a dictator.

15 Kriszta Kovács, 'Democracy in Lockdown' (2020) 87 Social Research: An International Quarterly 257.

16 Blackstone Chambers, 'Legal Opinion on Hungarian Covid-19 Legislation' (8 June 2020) <https://www.blackstonechambers.com/news/legal-opinion-hungarian-covid-19-legislation/>.

17 See letter sent by the Secretary General of the Council of Europe to Hungarian Prime Minister Viktor Orbán (24 March 2020) <https://rm.coe.int/orban-pm-hungary-24-03-2020/16809d5f04>.

18 See press release issued by the Director of the OSCE Office for Democratic Institutions and Human Rights (30 March 2020) <https://www.osce.org/odihr/449311>.

Rights[19] and the Civil Liberties Committee of the European Parliament[20] raised concerns about the Enabling Act's impact on the independence of democratic institutions and civil society. In response, in June 2000, the ruling parliamentary majority revoked the Enabling Act and the pandemic emergency; however, when it did so, it only transformed[21] it into a 'medical emergency' which functionally was identical to the provisions of the Enabling Act.[22]

When the second wave of COVID-19 arrived in September 2020, the country was already under a state of 'mass migration emergency' and a 'medical emergency'. Yet, the government introduced a third state of emergency, this time, a 'state of danger'.[23] The powers which can be exercised by the prime minister in the state of danger are in addition to those granted by the two previous emergencies.[24] Moreover, with a constitutional amendment[25] that substantially broadens the conditions in which emergencies can be declared[26] a further step was taken on the road to complete authoritarianism. Governing by decree became the default position as the constitutional amendment erased any meaningful role for Parliament in the oversight of government action. Decrees may suspend or deviate from statutory provisions and introduce other extraordinary measures, such as curfews. Thus, the Enabling Act and its stealthy continuation by a constitutional amendment and subsequent Acts gave Orbán unlimited emergency powers.[27] These powers are temporary in the text, but only the government, in effect the prime minister, can

19 Spokesperson for the UN High Commissioner for Human Rights, Rupert Colville, 'Press briefing note on Hungary' (27 March 2020) <https://www.ohchr.org/EN/NewsEvents/Pages/DisplayNews.aspx?LangID=E&NewsID=25750>.

20 European Parliament, 'EP Stands Up for Democracy in Hungary during Covid-19' (Press release, 24 March 2020) <https://www.europarl.europa.eu/news/en/press-room/20200324IPR75702/ep-stands-up-for-democracy-in-hungary-during-covid-19>.

21 Gábor Halmai, Gábor Mészáros and Kim Lane Scheppele, 'From Emergency to Disaster: How Hungary's Second Pandemic Emergency Will Further Destroy the Rule of Law' (*Verfassungsblog*, 30 May 2020) <https://verfassungsblog.de/from-emergency-to-disaster/>.

22 Government decree 283/2020. (VI. 17) and Act LVIII of 2020 on the Epidemiological Preparedness.

23 Government decree 478/2020. (XI. 3). This time, Article 53 of the Fundamental Law that regulates the state of danger was used as the basis for the emergency.

24 Viktor Z Kazai, 'Power Grab in Times of Emergency' (*Verfassungsblog*, 12 November 2020) <https://verfassungsblog.de/power-grab-in-times-of-emergency/>.

25 The Ninth Amendment to the Fundamental Law was adopted by the Hungarian Assembly on 15 December 2020.

26 Gábor Halmai, Gábor Mészáros and Kim Lane Scheppele, 'So It Goes – Part I' (*Verfassungsblog*, 19 November 2020) <https://verfassungsblog.de/so-it-goes-part-i/>.

27 The Ninth Amendment reduces the previous six categories of a "special legal order" to three categories: state of war, state of emergency and state of danger, but leaves the specification of most details to Cardinal Acts, that can only be amended by a two-thirds majority, which "could eventually raise some serious questions regarding the scope of powers of the State during states of exception"; Venice Commission, 'Opinion on the Constitutional Amendments Adopted by the Hungarian Parliament in December 2020' CDL-AD(2021)029, para 77. The Ninth Amendment entitles the government to issue decrees in all three situations. These provisions will enter into force on 1 July 2023.

determine when they are no longer necessary.[28] Hence, state actions are carried out not by transparent and democratically enacted laws but by mere discretion.

3. Unchallengeable Emergency Measures

During the first wave, governments across Central Europe introduced similar COVID-19 measures and coped well with the pandemic: they registered far lower levels of infection and mortality than in western and southern Europe.[29] Central European states all closed their borders and introduced lockdowns long before the virus reached them. But the Hungarian government went further: it cancelled by-elections already announced and closed the ordinary courts by declaring an 'extraordinary judicial holiday'.[30] The government also outlawed the obstruction of epidemiological control and criminalised the dissemination of falsehood and distorted facts "capable of interfering with the successful protection of the public".[31] Both provisions are vague enough to have a chilling effect[32] on any meaningful criticism of government action in response to the pandemic, and have been used in targeted attacks against critics.[33] Both of these provisions will remain part of the legal system even when the pandemic is over.[34]

During the second wave beginning in September 2020, Central European countries adopted various tactics to handle the pandemic. In contrast to the previously hard-line policies restricting access to the courts and suspension of by-elections, this time the Hungarian government tried to downplay the seriousness of the situation. Although it closed the borders to non-Hungarians (except for business and sportspeople) on 1 September 2020, it did not introduce further restrictive measures to protect the lives of populations at risk: schools, universities, shops and restaurants remained open, and there was no mask mandate or mass testing. The UEFA Super Cup took place in Budapest on 24 September 2020 with approximately 20,000 spectators. To facilitate the grandiose football event, the government made an exception to its own rules and allowed foreign fans to

28 For instance, government decree 26/2021. (I. 29) repealed the government decree 478/2020. (XI. 3) that declared the 'state of danger'.

29 Shaun Walker and Helena Smith, 'Why Has Eastern Europe Suffered Less from Coronavirus than the West?' (*The Guardian*, 5 May 2020) <https://www.theguardian.com/world/2020/may/05/why-has-eastern-europe-suffered-less-from-coronavirus-than-the-west>.

30 Government decree 45/2020. (III. 14).

31 Section 322/A(2) of the Act XII of 2020 on Protecting against the Coronavirus inserted s 337(2) into the Criminal Code.

32 Csaba Győry, 'Fighting Fake News or Fighting Inconvenient Truths?: On the Amended Hungarian Crime of Scaremongering' (*Verfassungsblog*, 11 April 2020) <https://verfassungsblog.de/fighting-fake-news-or-fighting-inconvenient-truths/>.

33 Alasdair Sandford, 'Hungary: "Critics Silenced" in Social Media Arrests as EU Abates Orban's Powers' (*Euronews*, 15 May 2020) <https://www.euronews.com/2020/05/14/hungary-critics-silenced-in-social-media-arrests-as-eu-debates-orban-s-powers>.

34 Constitutional Court decision 15/2020 (VII. 8) upheld the criminal provision on the dissemination of falsehood and distorted facts and thereby validated the suppression of criticism.

enter the country. A week of record-breaking hospitalisations and deaths changed the situation in early November 2020, and from 11 November 2020 to 23 May 2021, a general curfew and a ban on public events (except for church services and sporting events played to empty stands) was put in place.[35]

The third wave arrived in Hungary in mid-February 2021. At that time, the 14-day incidence value in Hungary (the rate of new cases in relation to the total population) was the highest in Europe.[36] Despite this, businesses (except for restaurants and bars), shopping malls and schools up to grade 8 (age 14) remained open. The government ordered non-essential businesses and primary schools to close only on 5 March.[37]

One of the most restrictive emergency measures adopted in response to these waves was the complete ban on public assemblies, which was stipulated by a government decree in November 2020.[38] In Hungarian law, assembly connotes "a public gathering held with at least two persons to express an opinion on a public affair".[39] Thus, it was a general ban, not a time, manner and place restriction, and it applied regardless of whether the two or more people followed COVID-19 regulations. Not only were public assemblies banned but the decree also prohibited any form of gathering even in open-air private places if more than ten people were present. Those who did not comply with the regulations faced hefty fines.[40]

The absolute ban on the right to gather, together with other rights restrictions, remained de facto unchallengeable because the once well-functioning democratic institutions had been either captured or abolished.[41] Following elections in April 2018, Orbán's party controlled two-thirds of the parliamentary seats, so the Parliament effectively rubberstamped the laws and constitutional amendments initiated by the government.

Judicial scrutiny of emergency measures was also severely lacking. Ordinary courts do not have the competence to review Acts and government decrees, although they can challenge the constitutionality of these laws by initiating proceedings before the Constitutional Court. This is what the Hungarian Helsinki Committee asked the Supreme Court to do in the so-called 'car demonstration' case, which arose after protestors who had driven around central Budapest in April and May 2020, honking their horns in opposition to the government's handling of

35 Government decree 484/2020. (XI. 10).

36 Zoltán Haszán, 'Egész Európában nálunk nő a legnagyobb ütemben a fertőzöttek száma' (*444.hu*, 21 February 2021) <https://444.hu/2021/02/21/egesz-europaban-nalunk-no-a-legnagyobb-utemben-a-fertozottek-szama>.

37 Government decree 104/2021. (III. 5).

38 Section 4(1) of Government decree 484/2020. (XI. 10).

39 Section 2(1) of the Act LV of 2018 on the right to assembly.

40 Gabriella Horn, 'Car Honking Protests Cancelled due to Astronomical Fines Handed out by Budapest Police' (*Átlátszó*, 25 May 2020) <https://english.atlatszo.hu/2020/05/25/car-honking-protests-cancelled-due-to-astronomical-fines-handed-out-by-budapest-police/>.

41 Kriszta Kovács and Kim Lane Scheppele, 'The Fragility of an Independent Judiciary: Lessons from Hungary and Poland—and the European Union' (2018) 51 Communist and Post-Communist Studies 189.

the pandemic, were heavily fined on grounds including breaking lockdown rules.[42] The protestors went before the Supreme Court to argue that the emergency decree banning public gatherings was unconstitutional and asking the Court to initiate proceedings before the Constitutional Court. The Supreme Court declined the petition,[43] but even if it had allowed it, the Constitutional Court, which has never opposed the Orbán government in politically sensitive cases, would probably have upheld the decree.[44]

While the Constitutional Court has the competence to review emergency decrees, as it is effectively packed with Viktor Orbán's political allies, it is no longer capable of fulfilling its role as a check on the executive. Its lack of independence and impartiality means that the government is free to introduce measures restricting fundamental rights with little fear of challenge before the Constitutional Court.[45] During the pandemic, several hundred decrees were introduced by the government. While some were meant to tackle the pandemic, others were designed to strengthen the executive power and weaken the already fragmented political opposition,[46] including bleeding opposition-led municipalities dry through a redirection of local funding.[47] Yet, the Constitutional Court has not, to date, declared any of these decrees unconstitutional; on the contrary, it upheld all those which reached its jurisdiction. For example, the mayor of an opposition-led small town, Göd, turned to the Constitutional Court after an emergency decree confiscated land owned by the municipality on which an industrial park (including a large Samsung plant) was based, thereby depriving the municipality of one-third of its annual revenue. The Constitutional Court upheld the decree, arguing that rapid and effective decisions were needed in a pandemic and that local governments should share the economic burden it caused.[48] Notably, such decrees were only targeted at opposition-led municipalities and not those where the leadership belonged to the ruling Fidesz party.[49]

42 Eötvös Károly Institution (EKINT), 'Concentration of Power Salvaged: Coronavirus Stocktaking. Assessing the Crisis Management of the Hungarian Government from the Perspective of Constitutional Law' <http://ekint.org/lib/documents/1595421967-EKINT_Concentration_of_Power_Salvaged_-_Coronavirus_Stocktaking_(analysis).pdf>.

43 Magyar Helsinki Bizottság, 'A Kúria meghajolt a kormány alapjogot sértő rendelete előtt' (*helsinki.hu*, 17 December 2020) <https://helsinki.hu/a-kuria-meghajolt-a-kormany-alapjogot-serto-rendelete-elott/>.

44 Gábor Attila Tóth, 'Legal Preconditions for Majoritarian Democracy: The Case of Hungary' (2021) 68 Zeitschrift für Politik 307.

45 Kovács and Scheppele, (n 41); Gábor Halmai, 'Dismantling Constitutional Review in Hungary' (2019) Rivista di Diritti Comparati 30.

46 Márta Pardavi and András Kádár, 'Hungary Should Not Become Patient Zero' (*Just Security*, 22 April 2020) <https://www.justsecurity.org/69780/hungary-should-not-become-patient-zero/>.

47 Government decree 136/2020. (IV. 17).

48 Constitutional Court Decision 8/2021. (III. 2).

49 Dániel Karsai, 'The Curious and Alarming Story of the City of Göd: How the Hungarian Government Misuses its Power in their Political Fights against Opposition-led Municipalities' (*Verfassungsblog*, 15 May 2020) <https://verfassungsblog.de/the-curious-and-alarming-story-of-the-city-of-goed/>.

4. Relying on the Military

Instead of relying solely on the actions of democratic institutions, the military played a prominent role in the 'fight' against the pandemic. It was involved in implementing COVID-19 measures, and heavily armed soldiers patrolled the streets in Hungarian cities to enforce curfew regulations.[50] The military sent control teams to the country's strategic companies to "ensure secure operations of key companies in telecommunications, transport and healthcare".[51]

From November 2020, there was an increased military presence in hospitals as 'hospital commanders' were placed in charge of medical resource questions.[52] The National Hospital Directorate-General was established by the interior minister to maintain state-run healthcare institutions and 'reform' healthcare.[53] Due to a shortage of qualified medical staff, the government required healthcare workers to sign new state contracts which increased salaries but imposed conditions such as limits on taking jobs outside the public health system. Some 5,500 healthcare workers resigned over the contracts, which they said offered unacceptable terms.[54]

While the government's Coronavirus Operational Corps led the response to COVID-19, medical expert bodies, including the Hungarian Medical Chamber, had no say in handling the virus. Public representation on the Coronavirus Operation Corps comprised two army commanders in uniform accompanied by one healthcare professional. Since photography and filming were not permitted within hospitals, and independent journalists were not permitted to interview medical personnel, the Corps was the only source of information on COVID-19 within Hungary. While the Corps regularly provided data on confirmed cases and deaths, it did not provide all relevant data, including the so-called R-value indicating how many people an infected person has infected further and data on the number of patients in intensive care. The numbers of trained medical personnel available for COVID-19 patients were also unknown. Nor did the figures for COVID-19-related deaths provided by the Corps reflect reality: investigative journalists revealed that the Central Statistical Office's (CSO) data contradicted the Corps' published data.[55] For example, the CSO's data demonstrated that the

50 Dániel Szűcs, 'Pécsen és Miskolcon a TEK páncélozott gépei védik az utcákat' (*szegeder.hu*, 11 November 2020) <http://szegeder.hu/pecsen-es-miskolcon-a-tek-pancelozott-gepei-vedik-az-utcakat/>.

51 MTI-Hungary Today, 'Coronavirus: Military Control Staff to Key Companies' (*Hungary Today*, 19 March 2020) <https://hungarytoday.hu/coronavirus-hungary-military-army-strategic-companies/>.

52 Government decree 499/2020. (XI. 13).

53 Government decree 287/2020. (VI. 17).

54 'Hungarian Hospital Staff Quit over New State Contract' (*France24*, 2 March 2021) <https://www.france24.com/en/live-news/20210302-hungarian-hospital-staff-quit-over-new-state-contract>.

55 Zoltán Haszán, 'Többen haltak meg január első hetében az elmúlt évek átlagánál' (*444.hu*, 3 February 2021) <https://444.hu/2021/02/03/tobben-haltak-meg-januar-elso-heteben-az-elmult-evek-atlaganal>.

number of deaths between October and December 2020 was 40% higher than the numbers of deaths in the same quarter of 2019, which was not reflected in the official report, indicating a degree of underreporting. However, even if we take the official reporting at face value,[56] with 30,032 fatalities to date in a country of less than 9.7 million people, Hungary's per capita death rate is by global comparison second only to Peru.[57]

5. A Way Out?

Protecting public health against epidemics is one of the state's chief duties, and the necessity of both medical and regulatory measures, lockdowns and severe consequences for breach of these measures are inevitable. Extraordinary situations require extraordinary responses. When taking action against a pandemic, the restriction of some fundamental rights (e.g. the rights to freedom of assembly and freedom of movement) in proportion to the danger may be justified. It might also be justifiable to adjust the functioning of democratic institutions, for instance, by limiting public access to court buildings. One can even imagine that the operation of democratic institutions might be temporarily suspended, and the distribution of powers modified in favour of the executive in order to manage the crisis. Still, COVID-19 cannot explain the scale or scope of actions undertaken by the Hungarian government, including depriving people of any right to protest peacefully or the right to go to an independent court to challenge government measures.

What can be done to stop these fundamental rights restrictions that are deeply problematic according to universal constitutional and international human rights standards? The near-complete erosion of the rule of law drastically limits the possibility of domestic legal resilience against restrictive emergency measures where courts have been politically captured or are otherwise incapable of responding due to a complete lack of judicial independence. What is left is a combination of legal resilience at the supranational level, including strategic litigation at the European Court of Justice and the European Court of Human Rights, and civil resistance at the domestic level.

One might wonder whether it makes a difference that rule of law backsliding[58] is happening in a European Union Member State. Among the conditions for membership in the Union is the protection of constitutional values: the existence of "stable institutions guaranteeing democracy, the rule of law, human rights and respect for and protection of minorities".[59] The primary sanctioning mechanism for values-based non-compliance with EU law is a political process identified

56 See the official website of the Hungarian government: <https://koronavirus.gov.hu>.

57 Johns Hopkins University (n 4).

58 The term describes the phenomenon when leaders who come to office within a democratic framework attack that framework when in office. Nancy Bermeo, 'On Democratic Backsliding' (2016) 27 Journal of Democracy 5.

59 The accession criteria were established by the Copenhagen European Council in 1993 <https://eur-lex.europa.eu/summary/glossary/accession_criteria_copenhague.html>.

in Article 7 of the Treaty on European Union. Article 7(1) allows the European Council to give a formal warning to a country if it finds a risk of a breach of the EU values. If that does not have the desired effect, the Council – subject to certain voting requirements – can impose sanctions and suspend voting rights under Article 7(2) and (3).

At the time of writing, the European Union has continued to stand by (as it has in the past), even as Viktor Orbán has assumed increasingly unlimited and unrestrained powers. Although in 2018, the European Parliament initiated the Article 7(1) process against Hungary, this procedure still hangs in the air because the Council has never seen fit to publicly condemn Hungary for failing to meet Europe's constitutional commitments. The other legal process for ensuring the uniform enforcement of EU law, including the infringement procedure,[60] allows the European Commission to bring a Member State to the European Court of Justice if it violates EU law. But infringement procedures have long been used for relatively technical violations – and nothing so wide in scope as a systemic threat to EU values. In 2018, the European Court of Justice elevated the infringement action so that it can be used to enforce EU constitutional values, giving the Commission a way to protect the constitutional commitments.[61] The legal basis of the emergency decrees (especially the constitutional amendment and the Enabling Acts) would have provided ample reasons to challenge Hungary through infringement actions. Of course, the Commission would have had to have been courageous to launch these actions. Yet, at the time of writing, there has been no sign of such courage. Since the Commission headed by Ursula von der Leyen took office in 2019, no infringement action has been launched against Hungary concerning the states of emergencies Hungary has declared.[62] Instead, a toothless new Rule of Law Review Cycle has been established,[63] with little indication of consideration of rule of law issues related to the COVID-19 pandemic.

Potential external support for the re-democratisation of Hungary is not limited to the European Union. Council of Europe bodies have condemned the use of the pandemic as a cover for unrelated illiberal measures.[64] The European Court of Human Rights is a venue for resisting further backsliding, yet the requirement to exhaust domestic remedies (and the absence of any time limit before the Constitutional Court for deciding complaints such as those by the sanctioned car

60 Article 258 Treaty on Functioning of the European Union.

61 Case C-64/16 *Associação Sindical dos Juízes Portugueses v Tribunal de Contas* [2018] EU:C:2018:117.

62 The only exception is the infringement procedure initiated against Hungary for the loose special public procurement rules of the 'mass migration emergency' <https://ec.europa.eu/commission/presscorner/detail/en/inf_20_2142>.

63 Laurent Pech, 'The Rule of Law' in Paul Craig and Gráinne de Búrca (eds), *Evolution of EU Law* (3rd edn, Oxford University Press 2021).

64 For example, Council of Europe Commissioner for Human Rights, 'Commissioner urges Hungary's Parliament to postpone the vote on draft bills that, if adopted, will have far-reaching adverse effects on human rights in the country' (20 November 2020) <https://www.coe.int/en/web/commissioner/-/commissioner-urges-hungary-s-parliament-to-postpone-the-vote-on-draft-bills-that-if-adopted-will-have-far-reaching-adverse-effects-on-human-rights-in->.

protesters) make this a slow and uncertain route to justice. Moreover, Hungary has failed to implement earlier rulings by the Strasbourg Court on rule of law backsliding.[65]

Most Europeans hope for the return to 'normalcy', that is, to a properly functioning constitutional democracy, when the pandemic finally ebbs. But what does return to 'normalcy' mean for Hungarians? A non-emergency authoritarian rule? Hard times can strengthen populist authoritarians. However, it may also happen that once the pandemic abates, the people's widespread discontent and anger will be directed against the politicians who abuse their powers. It is the people, not the plague, that can change the system. The dismantling of the rule of law leaves little room for legal resilience, but civil society can consider applying peaceful forms of democratic resistance. For instance, people may take advantage of the strategies of resistance developed during feudalism (e.g. the tradition of 'free cities') and socialism (e.g. 'samizdat' dissident activity).[66]

According to medieval traditions, free cities may function as islands of freedom and even exercise self-governance. Cities under opposition rule may reject and delegitimise the government's propaganda and directly tackle various problems related to the COVID-19 pandemic. Human dignity, freedom, democracy, equality, the rule of (local) law and respect for human rights may also be respected and exercised locally. It is significant, then, that just before the pandemic, on 16 December 2019, the so-called Free Cities Pact was signed by the mayors of Bratislava, Budapest, Prague and Warsaw to demonstrate their commitment to democratic values and increase their leverage against the national government.[67] Another form of resistance, widespread during socialism, is maintaining an 'alternative' sphere of public information. Social media naturally provides it, but collective or 'social' intelligence can also be used to generate verified information and reliable data.[68] In Hungary, 'samizdat' literature is again in circulation; Radio Free Europe is back on the scene,[69] and in March 2021, the German state broadcaster Deutsche Welle relaunched Hungarian-language news programmes for the first

65 For example, *Committee of Ministers, H46-11 Baka group v Hungary* (Applications No. 20261/12, 22254/14), CM/Del/Dec(2019)1355/H46-11, 25 September 2019.

66 See Kriszta Kovács and Boldizsár Nagy, 'In the Hands of a Populist Authoritarian: The Agony of the Hungarian Asylum System and the Possible Ways of Recovery' in Stijn Smet and Vladislava Stoyanova (eds), *Migrants' Rights, Populism and Legal Resilience in Europe* (Cambridge University Press, forthcoming).

67 Asenyina Dimitrova, 'Mayors of Bratislava, Budapest, Prague and Warsaw Sign Free Cities Pact' (*TheMayor.EU*, 17 December 2019) <https://www.themayor.eu/en/a/view/mayors-of-bratislava-budapest-prague-and-warsaw-sign-free-cities-pact-3945>.

68 Thamy Pogrebinschi, 'Might Social Intelligence Save Latin America from its Governments in Times of Covid-19?' (*Open Democracy*, 18 August 2020) <https://www.opendemocracy.net/en/democraciaabierta/puede-la-inteligencia-social-salvar-a-america-latina-de-sus-gobiernos-en-tiempos-de-covid-en/>.

69 'RFE/RL Relaunches Operations in Hungary Amid Drop in Media Freedom' (*RFE/RL*, 8 September 2020) <https://www.rferl.org/a/rfe-rl-relaunches-operations-in-hungary-amid-drop-in-media-freedom/30826537.html>.

time since 1999.[70] These developments may help ensure the free flow of information necessary to make the government more controllable and accountable.

6. Conclusion

In Hungary, the COVID-19 pandemic served as a pretext for the government to promote its goal of gaining more unrestricted power. Viktor Orbán sacrificed the rule of law and the functioning of democracy and conjured alleged 'enemies', including the COVID-19 pandemic itself, as existential threats to perpetuate a crisis that, according to his narrative, calls for a leader with extraordinary power to protect his people. A permanent state of emergency replaced rational discourse and a state operating within the bounds of fundamental rights, democracy and the rule of law. In order to stop further erosion of the rule of law, domestic democratic resistance and supranational legal actions would be necessary. Both have limited and ever-narrowing space. As doubts persist concerning the possibility of meaningful support from European institutions, no guarantee is within sight against deepening autocratisation.

70 'DW Magyar: Deutsche Welle Launches Program in "Old, New" Broadcast Language Hungarian' (*Deutsche Welle*, 28 April 2021) <https://www.dw.com/en/dw-magyar-deutsche-welle-launches-program-in-old-new-broadcast-language-hungarian/a-57358854>.

22

THE POLITICISATION OF HEALTH AND THREATS TO THE RULE OF LAW IN PAKISTAN

Shaheera Syed and Nadia Tariq-Ali

1. Introduction[1]

The COVID-19 pandemic was a global health emergency that wreaked medical, social and economic devastation across the world. The magnitude and intensity of the crisis left leaders in both developed and developing countries reeling. The challenge for developing countries like Pakistan, however, was greater.[2] In addition to struggling healthcare infrastructure and economic systems, Pakistan is still in the nascent stages of consolidating democracy and the rule of law and breaking from its history of post-colonial inspired centralised decision-making and over-reliance on non-democratic 'quick fixes'.

Pakistan experienced the outbreak of the pandemic as early as February 2020, which was unsurprising given that it shares borders with China, where the outbreak originated, and Iran, one of the first major outbreak epicentres outside Europe.[3] There was speculation that Pakistan could become a hotspot for COVID-19, being the world's fifth most populous country; however, to date it has avoided the very high levels of per capita mortality experienced by some of its neighbours

1 All websites accessed on 9 August 2021.

2 This chapter draws on Shaheera Syed and Nadia Tariq-Ali, 'Democratic Deficits of COVID-19 Crisis in Pakistan: Federal, Regional and Local Response and Coordination' (*Verfassungsblog*, 9 April 2021) <https://verfassungsblog.de/democratic-deficits-of-covid-19-crisis-in-pakistan/>.

3 Zulfiqar A Bhutta and others, 'Balancing Science and Public Policy in Pakistan's COVID-19 Response' (2021) East Mediterranean Health Journal (in press) <https://doi.org/10.26719/emhj.21.016>; for an analysis for the impact of COVID-19 on China from the viewpoint of democracy see deLisle and Shen, chapter 4.

DOI: 10.4324/9781003211952-25

(for example, as of 9 August 2021, the number of deaths per 100,000 people in Pakistan is 11.04, compared to 31.35 for India and 113.39 for Iran).[4] Nevertheless, dealing with COVID-19 has not been without challenges which could have been better dealt with or avoided altogether.

More than 70% of Pakistan's non-agricultural employment is in the informal sector, where the workforce is largely undocumented, depends on daily wages and has low levels of social security coverage. This meant that the authorities faced a trade-off between imposing lockdowns to flatten the curve and reduce the burden of the disease or risking over-straining the health sector by keeping the economy open to avoid death by poverty.[5] The 'lives versus livelihood' conundrum, which became apparent in Pakistan's COVID-19 response, is emblematic of the difficulties that accompany the balancing of conflicting rights in transitioning democracies. Moreover, as we examine in section 2, Pakistan's journey through the pandemic was mired in political contestation and power struggles between the provinces and the centre, which also allowed for the judiciary to play a larger role. As the crisis deepened in mid-2020, the social policies developed to respond to the pandemic became the site for centralising authority and there was an unprecedented flow of mis/disinformation. Section 3 proceeds to examine how structural challenges, like the absence of the local government systems to provide actionable data from the ground and inadequate parliamentary scrutiny, further exacerbated the crisis.

Another crucial facet of Pakistan's pandemic response was the rollout of vaccines; section 4 examines how the approach to vaccine distribution rendered large swathes of the population – such as stateless people – invisible, pushing them towards further deprivation. The result was a vaccine process conceived to 'leave no-one behind' but unwittingly accentuating the class divide, as well as raising human rights and rule of law concerns.

2. Rifts Between the Centre and the Provinces

2.1 Battle of the Narratives

Pakistan is a federation comprising four provinces: Punjab, Sindh, Khyber Pakhtunkhwa and Balochistan. The civil–military bureaucracy at the federal level has historically dominated, ensuring that the balance of power is tilted towards the centre, minimising the decision-making role of the provinces. The devolution process initiated through the 18th constitutional amendment in 2010 was a major step towards increasing the policy-making role of the provinces in areas such as health, taxes, policing and education, which were previously governed by the cen-

4 Johns Hopkins University, Coronavirus Resource Center, Mortality Analyses <https://coronavirus.jhu.edu/data/mortality>.

5 Sabah Shahid, 'Public Policy Lessons from Pakistan's Experience with COVID-19' (Observer Research Foundation, 25 September 2020) <https://www.orfonline.org/expert-speak/public-policy-lessons-pakistan-experience-covid19/>.

tre. The COVID-19 pandemic tested Pakistan's ability to make participatory decisions amidst the conflicting interests of the centre and the federating units, which brought the federalist principles of governance into direct conflict with centralisation and posed significant governance challenges for the country.

As COVID-19 cases started mounting towards the end of February 2020, the country's entire political system, comprising federal and provincial authorities and national and provincial parliaments, started crafting their responses. However, Prime Minister Imran Khan's initial steps were indecisive[6] and a lack of ownership of his approach by the provinces exposed the lack of coordination between the federal and provincial governments. For instance, initially, the Prime Minister asked the nation not to worry and publicly opposed the concept of lockdowns, severely underplaying the gravity of the situation.[7] The Sindh provincial government, meanwhile, asserted the need for a lockdown and in March 2020 announced one for the province, stating that saving lives was more important than the economy.[8] The public debate was, hence, reduced to a 'lives versus livelihoods' standoff.[9]

The inability of the federal government to see eye-to-eye with the opposition-ruled province of Sindh on the direction and pace of the province's aggressive but publicly-lauded steps to impose strict lockdown revealed the inability of the parties to move past their differences and resulted in the politicisation of public health. It was not just Sindh. When the Prime Minister announced that there would be no nationally ordered lockdown, the Punjab provincial government imposed one, while Khyber Pakhtunkhwa and Balochistan imposed partial ones.[10] These lockdowns were sporadically extended by provincial authorities through 2020 and into 2021.

2.2 Judicial Scrutiny of the State's Pandemic Response

The rifts between the centre and the provinces placed great emphasis on the role of the Supreme Court, the final arbiter of legal and constitutional disputes in Pakistan and an institution that is "equipped to provide clarity about the distribution of powers in the political system".[11] The lack of a coherent national pandemic

6 Madiha Afzal, 'The Pandemic Deals a Blow to Pakistan's Democracy' (*Brookings*, 6 August 2020) <https://www.brookings.edu/blog/order-from-chaos/2020/08/06/the-pandemic-deals-a-blow-to-pakistans-democracy/>.

7 Madiha Afzal, 'Pakistan Teeters on the Edge of Potential Disaster with the Coronavirus' (*Brookings*, 27 March 2020) <https://www.brookings.edu/blog/order-from-chaos/2020/03/27/pakistan-teeters-on-the-edge-of-potential-disaster-with-the-coronavirus/>.

8 International Crisis Group, 'Pakistan's Covid-19 Crisis' (6 August 2020) <https://www.crisisgroup.org/asia/south-asia/pakistan/b162-pakistans-covid-19-crisis>.

9 Syed and Tariq-Ali (n 2).

10 ibid.

11 Yasser Kureshi, '"Judicialising" the Pandemic in Pakistan' (Asian Legal Conversations – Covid-19, Melbourne Law School, 28 May 2020) 1 <https://law.unimelb.edu.au/__data/assets/pdf_file/0009/3392451/Kureshi_Judicialising.pdf>.

response created room for the Supreme Court to intervene and take a *suo moto* notice (where the court takes up a matter of public interest on its own initiative) – something which has been increasingly used as a tool for the expansion of the judicial power in Pakistan.[12] The court held widely publicised hearings and called in federal and provincial government officials as a means of scrutinising the state's response to the pandemic.[13]

While "oversight of the procedural aspects of the democratic process falls within the expertise of judges,"[14] and hence the court's highlighting of the need for better coordination between the various tiers of the government was merited, it became problematic when the court also started to raise "questions regarding the substance of technical policymaking [which] are not suited for judicial resolution".[15] The scathing criticism of the government in each hearing dominated the news headlines: for example, the Chief Justice publicly discussed removal of the federal government's top health official,[16] and questioned the transparency of the government's response stating: "Nothing is being told as to how departments are working. Everything seems to be just paperwork."[17] The court also commented explicitly on the government's spending priorities, stating that it "should not put all its resources for this one disease".[18]

The court's hearings also criticised the provincial governments for acting independently; this raised concerns about limiting the autonomy of the provinces in the "name of uniformity and coordination".[19] The provinces had gained autonomy after the 18th constitutional amendment, although, as the ultimate arbiter of the constitution, the Supreme Court can reinterpret the amendment in ways that reduce provincial autonomy. Hence, in relation to the exercise of both federal and provincial power, judicial oversight of the pandemic in Pakistan raised questions about judicial overreach and "centralisation of political authority" through "judicial interpretation".[20]

12 ibid 2.

13 Hasnaat Malik, "CJ Takes His First Suo Motu Notice on Corona Crisis" *(The Express Tribune*, 10 April 2020) <https://tribune.com.pk/story/2195087/1-top-judge-takes-suo-motu-notice-govts-measures-curb-coronavirus-crisis>.

14 Kureshi (n 11) 2.

15 ibid.

16 Hasnaat Malik, "SC Raises Questions Over Size of Federal Cabinet" (*The Express Tribune*, 13 April 2020) <https://tribune.com.pk/story/2196901/1-sc-asks-federal-govt-remove-dr-zafar-mriza-sapm-health>.

17 Hasnaat Malik, "Govt's Handling of Coronavirus Outbreak irks SC" (*The Express Tribune*, 4 May 2020) <https://tribune.com.pk/story/2213706/1-sc-expresses-dissatisfaction-govts-handling-coronavirus-outbreak>.

18 Suo moto regarding combating the pandemic of corona virus (COVID-19), SMC 01/2020 (Original jurisdiction, Supreme Court of Pakistan, 18 May 2020) [15] <https://www.supremecourt.gov.pk/downloads_judgements/s.m.c._01_2020_18052020.pdf>.

19 Kureshi (n 11) 3.

20 ibid.

2.3 The Pandemic Becomes an 'Infodemic'

Another aspect of the dislocation between different levels of government in Pakistan was confused public communication about the pandemic. The government did run a mass awareness-raising campaign about COVID-19; however, a sophisticated understanding of how the internet can shape the public discourse was missing from the wider government machinery.[21] Perhaps as a consequence, Pakistan saw an unprecedented volume of conspiracy theories, unverified claims and mis/disinformation about COVID-19 peddled through the internet and social networking sites, eroding public trust in the pandemic response.[22] The myths varied from "accusing the US of inventing the virus",[23] to the virus being a "conspiracy hatched by non-Muslims to keep believers from worshiping at mosques",[24] to COVID-19 vaccines being used as "an attempt by global powers to spy on the world population" or to install "nano-chips in people's bodies to gain power over 5G towers".[25] The sheer volume of mis/disinformation online crowded out accurate information, making it hard to distinguish between fact and fake content. Instead of taking control of the narrative, the constant rifts between politicians being played out live on prime-time television and the government's oft changing stance left its messaging muddled.[26] For instance, the government kept flipflopping regarding the severity of the crisis[27] and failed to clarify how strictly lockdown measures should be enforced which "led to various segments of society violating [them] or demanding outright relief".[28]

3. Structural Challenges in Dealing with the Pandemic

3.1 Creation of New Structures to Fill the Delivery Gaps

In line with many countries, COVID-19 forced the closure of Parliament in Pakistan in March 2020, a decision taken by the Parliamentary Committee on

21 'Covid Awareness' (*DAWN*, 18 May 2021) <https://www.dawn.com/news/1624222/covid-awareness>.

22 On the importance of public trust, see Jasanoff and Hilgartner, chapter 23.

23 Qamar Abbas, Fatima Mangrio and Sunil Kumar, 'Myths, Beliefs, and Conspiracies about COVID-19 Vaccines in Sindh, Pakistan: An Online Cross-Sectional Survey' (*Authorea*, 8 March 2021) <https://www.authorea.com/users/400163/articles/512518-myths-beliefs-and-conspiracies-about-covid-19-vaccines-in-sindh-pakistan-an-online-cross-sectional-survey>.

24 Daud Khattak, 'Pakistan's Confused Covid-19 Response' (*The Diplomat*, 9 July 2020) <https://thediplomat.com/2020/06/pakistans-confused-covid-19-response/>.

25 Hajira Maryam, 'Pakistan: Conspiracy Theories hamper Covid Vaccine Drive' (*Deutsche Welle*, 12 March 2021) <https://www.dw.com/en/pakistan-conspiracy-theories-hamper-covid-vaccine-drive/a-56853397>.

26 Syed and Tariq-Ali (n 2).

27 Khattak (n 24).

28 Ayesha Tanzeem, 'Lockdowns or No Lockdowns? Confusion Dominates Pakistan's Covid Response' (*Voice of America*, 1 May 2021) <https://www.voanews.com/covid-19-pandemic/lockdown-or-no-lockdown-confusion-dominates-pakistans-covid-response>.

Corona and the Speaker of the National Assembly of Pakistan. It reconvened in person in May to debate the pandemic response. Initially, no digital alternatives were offered but later a few hybrid meetings were held where some members attended the sessions remotely. Apart from a few minor closures, the Parliament continued to meet in person – a decision which was questioned by opposition members whenever COVID-19 infections peaked.[29] Nevertheless, certain changes were made to cater to the pandemic, such as testing members before they entered the building and introducing a set of standard operating procedures for the in-person sessions.[30] Although the Speaker of the National Assembly formed a special bipartisan Parliamentary Committee on Coronavirus Disease, the committee met only five times and parliamentary scrutiny did not make much headway due to the lack of consensus on the way forward.[31]

While there is a broad-based political consensus on federalism as the normative framework for governance in Pakistan, the government cited its limited capacity to respond to the pandemic as the basis for establishing a joint civilian–military body, the National Command and Operation Centre (NCOC). The NCOC fast tracked logistics, information gathering and real-time reporting of cases. This led to better oversight of the pandemic situation, streamlined procurement and rollout of personal protective equipment and eventually also facilitation of the vaccine rollout at the provincial and national levels. The low capacity and sluggish data gathering abilities of national and provincial public health institutions prevented timely gathering of population-based information from research. Consequently, many high-ranking military officers started playing an increasingly visible role[32] and enforced 'smart' lockdowns (a strategy adopted by the government to selectively close areas experiencing the worst infection rates) in hundreds of COVID-19 hotspots across the country.[33] The NCOC was visualised as a "nerve centre to synergize and articulate unified national effort against COVID-19".[34]

While the NCOC was successful in collating information, generating data flows and providing real time feedback to the federal and provincial governments, it did not help the situation that the NCOC was established in an ad hoc manner without any legal basis and without Parliament's approval and primarily operated outside the existing constitutional mechanisms responsible for inter-provincial

29 Amir Wasim, 'NA Session Begins Today Amid Spike in Covid-19 Cases' (*DAWN*, 29 March 2021) <https://www.dawn.com/news/1615230>.

30 Government of Pakistan, 'Guidelines for Holding National Assembly and Senate of Pakistan Sessions in Wake of COVID-19 Outbreak' (13 January 2021) <https://storage.covid.gov.pk/new_guidelines/13January2021_20210113_Guidelines_for_holding_National_Assembly_and_Senate_of_Pakistan_sessions_in_wake_of_COVID-19_outbreak_1502.pdf>.

31 'Opposition may Boycott Parliamentary Panel's Meeting on Covid-19' (*DAWN*, 23 November 2020) <https://www.dawn.com/news/1591905>.

32 Afzal (n 6).

33 'Smart Lockdown: A Better Option to Combat Covid-19' (*The News*, 4 May 2021) <https://www.thenews.com.pk/print/653861-smart-lockdown-a-better-option-to-combat-covid-19>.

34 Government of the Islamic Republic of Pakistan, National Command and Operation Center <https://ncoc.gov.pk>.

coordination such as the Council of Common Interests (CCI) and the Ministry of Inter-Provincial Coordination.[35] Unsurprisingly, some parliamentarians and federalism experts disagreed with this approach, arguing that since the 18th constitutional amendment, the CCI has become the heart of the Pakistani federation, whose proper functioning defines the health of the federation.[36] As per the Pakistani Constitution, the Council is mandated to formulate and regulate policies in relation to matters on Federal Legislative List-part-II (including energy, transport, industrial development and national economic planning, among others) and exercises supervision over related institutions. However, in the absence of formal representation from the military, the CCI lacked influence and convening power to meet regularly and roll out prompt responses to the pandemic. Veteran Senator Mian Raza Rabbani called for existing federal coordination mechanisms under the CCI to be strengthened and lamented that the concepts of federalism and parliamentary democracy were "eroding with each passing day".[37] While the cabinet's decision not to make an autonomous body such as the NCOC subservient to any specific ministry in the context of a fast-moving pandemic was positive, the cabinet was not the appropriate forum for such a decision. Inter-provincial coordination is part of the abovementioned Federal Legislative List Part-II and constitutionally such matters can only be decided by the CCI.

While there may be disagreements in the policy community about how essential the NCOC was to respond to the pandemic, creating additional structures without underlying institutional and legislative work creates administrative overlaps and conflicts that will have to be resolved in the post-COVID-19 world. The same concern surrounds the controversial move by the Prime Minister to establish the Corona Relief Tiger Force, a million-member force of volunteers providing relief and encouraging public adherence to preventive measures.[38] The outsourcing of such primary functions to unelected officials or volunteer forces further indicates the inability of the administration to deal with unexpected challenges. It is imperative that the government invests in strengthening existing structures and processes to develop greater preparedness for any future pandemic.

3.2 The Absence of Local Government

Another structural challenge that Pakistan faced while dealing with the pandemic was the lack of a functional local government system – in effect, an uneven patch-

35 Nazish Brohi, Danyal Adam Khan and Mosharraf Zaidi, 'Stress Testing Pakistani Federalism: Lessons from the Covid-19 Pandemic Response' (Tabadlab and Democracy Reporting International, 11 March 2021) <https://www.tabadlab.com/wp-content/uploads/2021/03/CGS-Tabadlab-Stress-Testing-Federalism-in-Pakistan-March-11.pdf>.

36 Aamir Yasin, 'Concept of Parliamentary Democracy Eroding in Pakistan: Rabbani' (*DAWN*, 13 March 2021) <https://www.dawn.com/news/1612172/concept-of-parliamentary-democracy-eroding-in-pakistan-rabbani>.

37 ibid.

38 'Tigers Unleashed' (*DAWN*, 14 October 2020) <https://www.dawn.com/news/1584954>.

work of arrangements that varies between provinces.[39] At the lowest rung of the federation, stopgap arrangements were unable to serve as a substitute for a local government elected through a consistent framework, which could offer robust service delivery. It is difficult to conceive and implement smart policies without a consistent flow of "clear insights, actionable data and implementable instructions" for district administration.[40] In effect, district commissioners and the bureaucracy of the Pakistan Administrative Service machinery under them had near total control of managing the pandemic at the ground level.[41]

Models where decision-making is in the hands of technocrats and administrators may provide a degree of efficiency, yet "many decades of experimentation with such structures reveals that [their] performance varies significantly across jurisdictions".[42] Put another way, power serves best when it is in the hands of people it is meant to serve. Brohi and others add that, "Local governments could have made a qualitative difference to the collection of data from neighbourhood, street and household levels, for which there can be no better source than elected representatives who are also residents of the area."[43] Such local representatives would also have been well-placed to counter misinformation and support the vaccine rollout.

3.3 *The Lack of Transparency*

Without well-functioning local government systems in place, it is nearly impossible to generate and process real-time data to feed into the policy-making cycle. Such was the case with COVID-19, and reliance on the NCOC became inevitable as it was the focal point for all data and information about the pandemic, including cases, deaths and vaccination rates. However, given Pakistan's historical civil–military divide, the fact that the NCOC's operations are under strict military control and the lack of objective sources corroborating official data left room for contestation as to whether the official narrative about the pandemic reflected reality on the ground.[44]

Similarly, due to the executive-led focus and lack of transparency surrounding other initiatives taken by the government, Pakistan's pandemic response was often under scrutiny. One of the most crucial steps to ease the economic blow of the pandemic, an ambitious Rs1.2 trillion (approximately US$7.5 billion/€6.3 billion) relief and fiscal stimulus package, was announced by the Prime Minister in March 2020. This step was taken to "revive the dwindling economy by provid-

39 Brohi, Kahn and Zaidi (n 35) 29–32.

40 ibid 32.

41 ibid.

42 ibid.

43 ibid.

44 Aliza Ayaz, 'The Actual Number of Covid 19 deaths in Pakistan' (*The Express Tribune*, 16 January 2021) <https://tribune.com.pk/story/2280133/the-actual-number-of-covid-19-deaths-in-pakistan>.

ing liquidity to firms, cash transfers to households and subsidies for firms' payroll expenditures".[45] From the start, the government was cognisant that labourers, daily wage earners, vendors and small shopkeepers would be hit particularly hard by the economic shutdown and hence the emergency cash-transfer programme would help mitigate their suffering.[46] The distribution of relief funds was placed under the Ehsaas programme, which was claimed by the government to be the biggest social security programme ever launched in Pakistan to uplift marginalised people.[47]

However, while the stimulus package was "seen as the fastest and easiest method to alleviate … hardship for beneficiaries in Pakistan",[48] the limited data available on the status of various components of the package and lack of transparency around the disbursement of funds tainted the overall reputation of the initiative. Many of the items which were included under the relief package were already part of the government's annual budget and yet were presented as a separate allocation.[49] Moreover, the government failed to leverage the vast outreach of civil society organisations engaged with the informal sector to identify potential beneficiaries and establish committees at local levels with diverse representation to make room for improved parliamentary, civil society and media oversight. This added layer of oversight would have improved transparency, and hence trust, in relation to such a massive public initiative. Thus, however well-intentioned, the ad hoc and temporary nature of the relief packages raised questions about their accountability and sustainability, especially if the pandemic proves to be protracted.

4. Rollout of the COVID-19 Vaccine

Pakistan's resource and policy gaps were visible from the outset of its immunisation drive, making a rapid and equitable rollout of COVID-19 vaccine highly improbable. The government received 500,000 Chinese Sinopharm doses in February 2021[50] and decided to start by inoculating frontline health workers. Surprisingly, though, a significant number of doctors and paramedics refused to

45 Nadia Farooq, 'Economic Impact of Government's Relief Package' (Democracy Reporting International, December 2020) <https://beta.democracy-reporting.org/uploads/publication/14741/document/dri-brief-eco-stimulus-package-smal-609e8fa287d32.pdf>.

46 'Jobless People Receive Rs12,000 Cash Aid Each Under Ehsaas Initiative' (*The Express Tribune*, 18 May 2020) <https://tribune.com.pk/story/2224423/jobless-people-receive-rs12000-cash-aid-ehsaas-initiative>.

47 Poverty Alleviation and Social Safety Division, Government of Pakistan, 'What is Ehsaas?' <https://www.pass.gov.pk/Detail92a7fc95-647d-43bd-a86c-477897e596e2>.

48 Iman Khan and Umair Javed, 'Evaluating EHSASS Emergency Cash Transfer Program: Successes, Oversights and Possibilities' (Democracy Reporting International, December 2020) 1 <https://democracy-reporting.org/wp-content/uploads/2021/01/DRI-Brief_Ehsaas_small.pdf>.

49 Neha Maqsood, 'On the Coronavirus, Pakistan's Government is Missing in Action' (*Foreign Policy*, 11 May 2020) <https://foreignpolicy.com/2020/05/11/on-coronavirus-pakistans-government-is-missing-in-action/>.

50 See Singh, chapter 2.

participate in the vaccination drive.[51] This hesitancy among medical professionals was due to the country's inability to independently evaluate the efficacy of newly developed antidotes to the previously unknown viral disease. The decision by the Drug Regulatory Authority of Pakistan to approve the Sinopharm vaccine for emergency was shrouded in contradictions.[52] In the absence of an official statement, it was not clear if its decision was based on data-driven analysis[53] or grounded in the fact that the vaccine was easier to access due to the country's strategic ties with China and did not require an elaborate distribution infrastructure.

4.1 Interplay with Legal Identity

When the Chinese vaccine arrived in early 2021, officials in Islamabad urged people to register themselves for vaccination through their national identity card numbers. This was despite the fact that nearly three million people in Pakistan, particularly women and people on the social periphery, such as Afghan refugees and other stateless people,[54] do not possess identity documents. The secretary-general of the Pakistan Medical Association urged the government to remove the condition and "simply let everyone get vaccinated"[55] – a critique that revealed the risk of treating the population as a homogenous group, overlooking significant group differences that created hierarchical citizenship and excluded marginalised segments in the rollout process.

4.2 Class Divides

Despite often living in abysmal poverty, some stateless people or others lacking identity documents tried to access privately imported Sputnik V vaccines from Russia, which were supplied to private medical facilities in the major urban centres of the country.[56] The Pakistani authorities had described their decision to involve the private sector to import and sell COVID-19 vaccines as a "deliberate policy tool" to help population segments which were not "part of the government's pri-

51 'Vaccine Hesitancy' (*DAWN*, 13 February 2021) <https://www.dawn.com/news/1607104>.

52 Rahul Basharat Rajput and Muhammed Nadeem Chaudhry, 'Pakistan Threatens Health Workers: Get the Chinese-Donated Vaccine or Get Fired!' (Health Policy Watch, 16 March 2021) <https://healthpolicy-watch.news/pakistan-threatens-health-workers-get-the-chinese-donated-vaccine-or-get-fired/!>.

53 ibid.

54 Aamir Saeed, 'For Pakistan's Over Three Million Stateless People, COVID-19 Jabs Out of Reach' (*Arab News Pakistan*, 25 May 2021) <https://www.arabnews.pk/node/1864586/pakistan>. See also Al Sabah and Gougsa, chapter 32.

55 '3 Million People in Pakistan Lacking IDs May Miss Out on Covid-19 Jabs' (*DAWN*, 22 May 2021) <https://www.dawn.com/news/1625073>.

56 ibid.

ority inoculation campaign".[57] Hence, while the state may have been negligent towards stateless people, it cannot be described as fully complicit in their exclusion from the vaccination programme. That said, the private procurement and distribution of Sputnik V had exposed "the rich-poor divide" in Pakistan; private hospitals were selling two doses for US$80, or more than two-thirds of the average worker's monthly salary.[58] This was despite the fact that the government had promised "to keep a check on prices instead of leaving it solely to free market dynamics".[59] If the idea of allowing private imports was to include people who were not yet considered a priority in the government inoculation campaign, it did not work in case of the stateless people who were willing to pay to be vaccinated but were excluded even from the programme managed by private hospitals because of their lack of identity documents needed to register for the vaccine.[60]

4.3 *Urban and Rural Dynamic*

As of July 2021, the country has allocated US$1.1 billion in the new fiscal year for vaccine procurement[61] with a target of vaccinating 70 million people by the end of 2021.[62] To date, Pakistan has fully vaccinated only 2.4% of the population.[63]

Given the huge disparity between medical facilities in the urban and rural areas, residents of Pakistan's remote towns were forced to travel to nearby cities to get vaccinated. The government created some mobile vaccination units, but this did not result in a significant increase in outreach since it mostly catered to elderly people in the cities who could not visit vaccine centres. The country could not devise an elaborate outreach strategy to immunise its rural population even after it had procured China's single-shot CanSino vaccine, which was easy to carry to remote settlements and would not have required follow-up visits by mobile teams.

This urban–rural divide was exacerbated by the absence of proper storage facilities for vaccines like Pfizer and Moderna, which Pakistan received under the World Health Organisation's COVAX programme. Such infrastructure con-

57 Naveed Siddiqui, 'Allowing Private Imports of Covid Vaccines is a "Deliberate Policy Tool": Govt' (*DAWN*, 24 March 2021) <https://www.dawn.com/news/1614332>.

58 Salman Masood, 'Pakistan's Private Vaccine Sales Highlight Rich-Poor Divide' (*The New York Times*, 22 May 2021) <https://www.nytimes.com/2021/05/22/world/asia/pakistan-private-vaccines.html>.

59 Siddiqui (n 57).

60 Saeed (n 54).

61 Aamir Saeed, 'Pakistan Hopes to Overcome COVID-19 Vaccine Shortages as More Doses Trickle In' (*Arab News*, 21 June 2021) <https://www.arabnews.com/node/1879841/pakistan>.

62 Mehtab Haider, 'Pakistan Targets Corona Vaccination for 70m People by Year End: Govt' (*The News*, 26 April 2021) <https://www.thenews.com.pk/print/826201-pakistan-targets-corona-vaccination-for-70m-people-by-year-end-govt>.

63 Data from John Hopkins University, Coronavirus Resource Center <https://coronavirus.jhu.edu/region/pakistan>.

straints became obvious amid reports of vaccine wastage[64] as the country started dealing with vaccines developed by countries other than China. Special refrigerators[65] became a necessity for Pakistan since the Chinese vaccines were not viable for international travel and people employed in other countries, particularly Middle East states, were desperate for Pfizer, Moderna and AstraZeneca vaccines to secure their livelihood. One such group stormed a mass vaccination centre in Islamabad in July 2021 after protesting about shortages of the AstraZeneca vaccine.[66] Similar protests were witnessed elsewhere. Addressing the issue was important since remittances by Pakistani workers form the backbone of the national economy. The government eventually announced it would administer Moderna shots to workers going abroad after the United States donated 2.5 million doses to the country.[67]

Despite the abovementioned weaknesses, provincial authorities announced punitive measures to increase the pace of Pakistan's immunisation campaign. The Sindh administration threatened to stop the salaries of public servants[68] and issued warning letters to frontline health workers with threats of cancellation of service contracts in case of non-compliance.[69] The Balochistan province decided not to entertain unvaccinated individuals at government offices or allow them to enter public parks or use public transportation.[70] Similarly, the Punjab provincial authorities decided to block the cell phones of unvaccinated individuals.[71]

Such public proclamations created a coercive atmosphere which was not conducive to running a convincing awareness campaign. Making vaccination a requirement for access to essential services, public spaces and economic opportunities is intrusive and limits people's choice and capabilities. It also contributes to multiple levels of marginalisation as those not given access to the vaccine are subsequently also denied access to other services. Given the inability of the federal and provincial governments to craft a unified lockdown policy already discussed in this chapter, the lack of coordination to ensure legal certainty and coherence of the punitive measures acquires added significance. The varied nature of these

64 Sumeera Riaz, 'Punjab to Procure Special Refrigerators for Pfizer and Moderna Vaccines – Health Officials' (*Arab News*, 3 July 2021) <https://www.arabnews.pk/node/1887711/pakistan>.

65 ibid.

66 Umar Farooq, 'Desperate Expatriate Workers Storm Islamabad Vaccination Centre' (*Reuters*, 29 June 2021) <https://www.reuters.com/world/asia-pacific/desperate-expatriate-workers-storm-islamabad-vaccination-centre-2021-06-28/>.

67 'Pakistan to Administer Moderna Vaccine to Citizens Going Abroad – Planning Minister' (*Arab News*, 3 July 2021) <https://www.arabnews.pk/node/1887756/pakistan>.

68 'Pakistan's Sindh Province Blocks Salary for Unvaccinated Employees' (*Arab News*, 3 June 2021) <https://www.arabnews.pk/node/1869901/pakistan>.

69 Rajput and Chaudhry (n 52).

70 'Pakistan Suspends 70 Paramilitary Troops for Refusing Vaccine' (*France24*, 1 July 2021) <https://www.france24.com/en/live-news/20210701-pakistan-suspends-70-paramilitary-troops-for-refusing-vaccine>.

71 Imran Gabol, 'Punjab Govt Decides to Block SIM Cards of People Refusing Vaccines' (*DAWN*, 10 June 2021) <https://www.dawn.com/news/1628625>.

punitive measures has a strong potential to breed frustrations, civil unrest and even democratic instability for provincial governments.

5. Conclusion

When compared with its neighbours, or even with developed countries like the United States, Pakistan has to date avoided catastrophe, at least as measured by its per capita mortality rate.[72] The government took some positive steps to mitigate the crisis, yet its response was not free of missteps. An effective pandemic response strategy would have been "nuanced, data-driven, transparent, robust and public health-led", with close parliamentary scrutiny to ensure equitable access to the system for all groups in vulnerable circumstances.[73] Instead, the pandemic response was driven more by the battle of narratives. In the early stages, when the response fell to provincial governments, there was a glimmer of hope that the crisis might actually help smoothen out political fault lines and enable democratic consolidation and strengthening of the rule of law in Pakistan. This did not happen. The pandemic opened a Pandora's box of "largely unconstructive and inconclusive debate"[74] on problems with provincial autonomy and the 18th constitutional amendment that granted it – with those critical of the law pushing back against the initial provincial control of the virus response. These skirmishes between the various tiers of government diluted the ability of the government at all levels to effectively deal with the crisis and resulted in the trade-offs between fundamental rights and the well-being of citizens. These trade-offs were not subject to systematic parliamentary scrutiny, since Parliament did not meet during March–May 2020 and even when it resumed afterwards, political differences overshadowed the debates. The lack of consensus between the various tiers of the government provided the opportunity for the Supreme Court to step in and call for a uniform response to the pandemic. However, the court's criticism expanded beyond proper oversight of the procedural shortcomings to questioning the technical soundness of policies, raising questions about judicial overreach and the separation of powers in accordance with the rule of law.

The creation of structures which were outside the constitutional ambit and the lack of transparency surrounding key government decisions from relief fund disbursement to vaccine procurement, raised further questions about the accountability and sustainability of the government's actions. A coordinated response requires building a political consensus; a unilateral approach to pandemic policy is impossible in a federation with a multi-party political system, as the likelihood that one political party will monopolise political authority at all tiers of government is narrow.[75] In today's world, where disinformation easily crowds out the truth,

72 Johns Hopkins University, Coronavirus Resource Centre (n 4).

73 Brohi, Kan and Zaidil (n 35) 2.

74 Afzal (n 6).

75 Syed and Tariq-Ali (n 2).

weak transparency and lack of ownership of narrative can be disastrous. Pakistan's experience shows that attempts to override and undermine federating units during national crises led to policy inertia, poor messaging and inconsistent enforcement. If it had handled matters better, Pakistan had the potential to be a relative success story for state responses to COVID-19. If history affords some leniency, it still could.

PART IV

Science, Public Trust and Decision-Making

Overview

The COVID-19 pandemic collapsed the boundaries between science on the one hand and politics and the law on the other: scientific experts were called upon to help design policies and legal measures, while politicians and judges had to weigh the merit of developing scientific findings and sometimes conflicting advice. Misinformation, fake news and the 'infodemic' plague public discourse and can have the effect of muting rational and evidence-based debate while undermining any trust in political discourse and efforts at collective pandemic response. While transversal lessons can be gleaned, it has to be underlined that *trust* in governance, institutions and expertise is vital, and this trust needs to be understood within the particular social and political context and legal culture in which it is realised. Part IV explores the complex and dynamic relationships between science, public trust and decision-making in pandemic governance, examining their interplay in Taiwan, Rwanda, Germany, South Africa and Iran.

In the first thematic commentary, Sheila Jasanoff and Stephen Hilgartner present interim findings of the Comparative Covid Response (CompCoRe) study, a global qualitative comparison of the highly varied policy responses to the pandemic adopted in 16 countries. They venture that COVID-19 simultaneously attacked biological, economic and political bodies and thereby constituted an acute stress test for governance, particularly in democracies. They identify three modes of governance which characterised governmental responses: *control*, *consensus* and *chaos* in the three examined arenas of health, economics and politics. The authors urge states to reform their existing institutional processes for integrating scientific and political consensus-building, since the legitimacy of public health expertise depends on the health of the entire body politic.

Ciara Staunton examines data transparency and governance in the second commentary. She identifies how the pandemic led to the expectation of an 'open sci-

DOI: 10.4324/9781003211952-26

ence' model of sharing data critical to the understanding of, and response to, the virus. This expectation of a rapid and open flow of information, Staunton argues, raises concerns relating to privacy, discrimination and inequitable access to new diagnostics, therapies and vaccines developed on the basis of shared data. She advocates for good data governance and stewardship, and a global agreement built on the principles of clarity, transparency and accountability.

In the first country chapter, Wen-Chen Chang and Chun-Yuan Lin analyse **Taiwan**'s successful control of COVID-19 to date, without the introduction of lockdowns or severely restrictive measures, evidencing a balance between the demands of pandemic control and the expectations of human rights, democracy and the rule of law. Essential to this success, they argue, was the Taiwanese model of 'dialogic constitutionalism', which ensured a transparent and responsive political process and active citizen engagement, prioritising the maintenance of public trust and democratic accountability.

Denis Bikesha and Allan T Moore analyse another standout case study of successful suppression of COVID-19, **Rwanda**, which generally surpassed its neighbours in Central and East Africa, as well as many high-income states. The authors identify Rwanda's pre-emptive efforts, informed by its experience of previous epidemics, coupled with the innovative use of technology to diagnose disease, collect data and communicate guidance that lay at the heart of the state's public health approach. They argue that some of these practices may be replicable elsewhere, yet others are less transferable, since they derive from Rwanda's unique historical and social context, including 20 years of transitional justice and reconciliation-based activities, as well as high levels of confidence in the healthcare system, and public trust in governance.

Analysis of the actions taken by federal and *Länder* governments in **Germany** is the focus of the third country chapter by Anna Katharina Mangold, who highlights how increasing knowledge and awareness of COVID-19 informed policy development and legislative reform. She analyses how both scientific and constitutional law expertise played a significant role in the approach adopted, assisted by the fact the parties making up the federal government were led by scientifically trained politicians. Yet, science did not dictate decision-making, which remained essentially political. Judicial review of the largely executive-led response, Mangold adds, centred on the proportionality of restrictive measures, with little consideration of substantive concerns about their unequal impact.

Melodie Labuschaigne and Ciara Staunton examine the challenging circumstances in **South Africa** which burdened the government's response to the pandemic, including a poorly resourced public healthcare system and a high percentage of the population living with comorbidities such as tuberculosis and HIV. They debate the rationality of the government's approach in relying on ministerial expert advisory committees and limiting parliamentary oversight, which meant that courts were the only effective check against arbitrary decisions. Highlighting the government's failure to recognise the importance of public debate for democracy during a public health crisis, Labuschaigne and Staunton decry the government's negative response to expert criticism of their pandemic approach. They underline the need for transparent, justifiable and reasoned decision-making as well as routes to accountability, both parliamentary and judicial.

The need for accountability is also a dominant theme in the final chapter of Part IV, in which Marzieh Tofighi Darian critically examines the response to COVID-19 in **Iran**. She explores how the establishment of the National Headquarters to Combat Corona, with a formidable array of powers and no meaningful parliamentary or judicial oversight, impacted negatively on the separation of powers between constitutional actors. She concludes that the institutional design formulated in response to the pandemic exposed structural weaknesses in the Iranian constitutional system, which necessitate the reimagination of institutional responses to emergencies, especially the creation of a greater role for the legislative and judicial branches.

23

A STRESS TEST FOR POLITICS

A Comparative Perspective on Policy Responses to COVID-19

Sheila Jasanoff and Stephen Hilgartner

1. Introduction[1]

The whole world perceived the COVID-19 epidemic of 2020 as an emergency. State after state enacted extraordinary measures to limit personal freedom and curtail economic and social activity to a degree never experienced in peacetime, and never on such a colossal scale. Travel across national borders came to a virtual halt in the pandemic's initial months, and even in early 2021 global air traffic was down more than 40% from its pre-pandemic level.[2] Lockdowns kept people homebound for months except on essential business. Schools closed and children lost access to teachers, playmates and recreational opportunities. Restrictions intruded into the most intimate areas of life, separating parents from grown children, keeping couples apart and leaving patients to die alone without the comfort of close relatives. Businesses suffered grievous losses, with impacts falling especially hard on small enterprises and on restaurants and hotels. With much of the world's population under enforced isolation, mental health declined, social grievances intensified and conspiracy theories took deeper root.[3]

1 All website links accessed on 13 June 2021.

2 E Mazareanu, 'Weekly Flights Change of Global Airlines due to COVID-19 as of January 2021' (*Statistica.com*, 13 January 2021) <https://www.statista.com/statistics/1104036/novel-coronavirus-weekly-flights-change-airlines-region/>.

3 This chapter is an expanded version of Sheila Jasanoff and Stephen Hilgartner, 'A Stress Test for Politics: Insights from the Comparative Covid Response Project (CompCoRe) 2020' (*Verfassungsblog*, 11 May 2021) <https://verfassungsblog.de/a-stress-test-for-politics-insights-from-the-comparative-covid-response-project-compcore-2020/>.

DOI: 10.4324/9781003211952-27

While the pandemic's effects were felt most immediately at local, even household, levels – through lockdowns, job losses, school closings, and illness and death – repercussions at transnational and global levels also emerged as significant concerns. The World Health Organisation (WHO) was seriously weakened by US President Donald J Trump's decision, in July 2020, to withdraw from membership in the very body whose task it was to investigate outbreaks and declare global pandemics. President Joseph R Biden's decision to restore US ties to the WHO on his first day in office, in January 2021, did not fully repair the damage to the world agency's standing and reputation. The WHO's investigation of the initial outbreak continued to be questioned, and its expert report on 30 March 2021 ruling the likelihood of a "lab leak" from the Wuhan Institute of Virology as "extremely unlikely"[4] proved insufficient to settle the controversy.

The Comparative Covid Response (CompCoRe) study, an ongoing qualitative comparison of policy responses to COVID-19 in 16 core countries, which began in April 2020, sought to identify and explain patterns of perceived success and failure in managing this multifaceted crisis.[5] The participating countries are Australia, Austria, Brazil, China, France, Germany, India, Italy, Japan, the Netherlands, Singapore, South Korea, Sweden, Taiwan, the United Kingdom and the United States. Additionally, teams from Indonesia and Peru, as well as an Africa Group, are included as CompCoRe affiliates. Our project concluded early on that this was a drama playing out simultaneously in three interlocking arenas: health, the economy and politics. The virus seemed to find and target weaknesses not only in vulnerable human bodies but also in the economic and political infrastructures that sustain societies. In doing so, it revealed tacit assumptions about science and public reason that guide governance in all three arenas. These assumptions typically are not codified in formal rules and regulations, but they are just as crucial to the constitutional orders that are taken for granted when a nation's collective life is functioning normally.

Early findings point to strong correlations between citizens' sense of solidarity and the state's ability to enact and enforce restrictive measures to fight the pandemic. Three broad – and dramatically different – patterns emerged over the first year of the pandemic, connecting policies and outcomes across national health, economic and political systems. Some countries achieved a coherent response and significant degree of *control* over the situation in all or most of the three arenas. Other countries achieved basic policy *consensus* about how to proceed, although trying to stall the epidemic entailed significant economic hardship. In still a third group of countries, policy *chaos* prevailed, with extensive conflict over policy goals and measures in all three systems. An interim report issued in January 2021 pointed to Taiwan as a paradigm case of a control country, Germany as a consensus

4 Javier C Hernández and James Gorman, 'Virus Origins Remain Unclear in W.H.O.-China Inquiry' (*The New York Times*, 29 May 2021) <https://www.nytimes.com/2021/03/29/world/asia/china-virus-WHO-report.html>.

5 Comparative Covid Response: Crisis, Knowledge, Politics <https://compcore.cornell.edu/>.

country and the United States (still in the Trump presidency) as a chaos country.[6] Subsequent phases of the epidemic, layered upon changes in politics (most dramatically in the United States in 2021), underscore the dynamic character of the object of inquiry. Our study's fundamental insights, however, remain constant: (1) an epidemic is a simultaneous attack on biological, economic and political bodies; and (2) as such, it poses an acute stress test for politics, perhaps most particularly in democracies.

2. Pandemic Performance: Keeping Score

Instability is the pandemic's most distinctive feature. As the virus spreads and mutates, economic conditions fluctuate and political winds blow unsteadily at best. Towards the end of 2020, for example, decades of scientific research bore fruit in the form of several hastily approved and efficacious vaccines, but that hugely promising development was soon engulfed by further crises: new variants that savagely attacked countries that had fought off earlier phases of the disease; production shortages and inequalities in distribution; and political resistance against mandatory vaccination. Just as policymakers had to monitor and continually adapt to the pandemic, so too did those studying pandemic policy constantly need to reappraise national and global efforts to manage this rapidly unfolding crisis.

Like the CompCoRe researchers, journalists around the world often adopted a comparative perspective, issuing instant scorecards casting nations as leaders or laggards in some imagined race to control the unruly virus. Indicators of success and failure remained bewilderingly diverse and mercurial, with anything measurable seemingly fair game for the near-daily tallies offered by the news media: the number of infections, pressure on intensive care beds, case-fatality rates, total deaths, deaths by demographic categories, length of lockdowns, unemployment levels, GDP estimates, and most recently the speed of vaccine rollout, the number of persons vaccinated and the percentages of the unvaccinated or unwilling. By some measures, powerful countries appeared to have traded places over the course of the pandemic's first year. China, where the virus got its deadly start, also achieved the quickest and most complete suppression of its spread.[7] In Europe's first phase, Germany was ahead in keeping infections and deaths relatively low and maintaining political consensus. In April 2021, gripped by a third wave, Germany's vaccination rate fell behind the United States, whose initially hesitant vaccination rollout soon became the envy of Europe (though deaths per million in Germany remained much lower).[8] At the same time, COVID-19 began surging with espe-

6 Sheila Jasanoff and others, *Comparative Covid Response: Crisis, Knowledge, Politics*, Interim Report (12 January 2021) <https://compcore.cornell.edu/publications/>; for analysis of these three states in this volume, see Chang and Lin, chapter 25; Mangold, chapter 27; Graber, chapter 6.

7 See also de Lisle and Shen, chapter 4.

8 Isabelle Mandraud and others, 'Covid-19: la Mortalité de la Pandémie est Encore Sous-Estimée dans le Monde' (*Le Monde*, 14 April 2021) <https://www.lemonde.fr/planete/article/2021/04/14/covid-19-dans-le-monde-une-mortalite-encore-sous-estimee_6076691_3244.html?xtor&

cially deadly effects in India after a period of relative calm, while Brazil faced ever greater political and public health chaos, along with the second highest number of COVID-19 fatalities.[9] Poorer countries vainly waited for vaccines while richer ones scrambled to satisfy their own increasingly restive populations.

Yet, this score-keeping by the numbers – almost as if pandemic response is a kind of involuntary spectator sport – leaves much to be desired in a world yearning not to repeat the trauma of 2020. For one thing, framing pandemic management as an international competition does not explain why the same country fared better or worse at different stages of the crisis. Such superficial comparisons also fail to grapple with CompCoRe's key insight, namely, that any serious assessment of policy efficacy must look not only at health impacts but also at impacts on politics and the economy, some of which may prove to be longer lasting and harder to cure than near-term control of the virus. Thus, in January 2021, the World Bank estimated that poverty would increase for the first time in 20 years as a result of the pandemic, with some 100 million new poor added to world rosters in 2020.[10] Time after time, one refrain has come to the fore: why did countries with top rankings in such preparedness metrics as the Global Health Security Index perform worse on multiple indicators than many lower-ranked countries?[11] Grappling with that question, too, might hold more promise for the future of global pandemic management than weekly or monthly country rankings according to arbitrarily selected indicators.

Our study demands, in effect, a reformulation of the central questions that need to be asked in the wake of the COVID-19 pandemic. The Spanish flu of 1918 left the world understandably preoccupied with what could be done to stop such a devastating disease from taking hold so widely and with such deadly effect. Given the past century's remarkable advances in biological knowledge and scientific medicine, as well as the intensification of global flows, we need to broaden the scope of our inquiry beyond disease prevention to encompass more deeply normative questions. When a pandemic hits, what resources do nations need to mitigate its worst effects, knowing that these will fall disproportionately on the most vulnerable members of society? In a world where the power to manage public health is still substantially located within national and local institutions, how can nations begin to cooperate better across geopolitical boundaries? And given that, in today's densely interconnected world, a virus knows no boundaries, what new norms are needed to ensure that knowledge and resources are shared equi-

&M_BT=40959345625355&x3D%3BEPR-32280629-%255Ba-la-une%255D-20210414-%255Bzone_edito_1_titre_1%255D>.

9 See also Raj, chapter 12 and Bustamante and Meyer, chapter 18.

10 Christoph Lakner and others, 'Updated Estimates of the Impact of COVID-19 on Global Poverty: Looking Back at 2020 and the Outlook for 2021' (World Bank, 11 January 2021) <https://blogs.worldbank.org/opendata/updated-estimates-impact-covid-19-global-poverty-looking-back-2020-and-outlook-2021>.

11 Global Health Security Index, *Building Collective Action and Accountability* (October 2019) <https://www.ghsindex.org/>.

tably, and that recovery and resilience for all are perceived as humankind's shared responsibility?

3. Politics of Trust

One axis of cross-national difference that our study addresses, and that is fundamental to building cooperative regimes, is the issue of trust. Trust is a factor that resists quantitative analysis but has influenced national performance in all three arenas of the COVID-19 crisis. Specifically, it affects people's willingness to heed health warnings, their confidence in economic resilience, and their allegiance to political leaders. As yet, however, trust has been narrowly construed in much public discourse, mainly as a matter of people's willingness to believe the scientific pronouncements of national health authorities.

We found a strong connection between trust in political institutions and trust in scientific expertise. Unsurprisingly, control and consensus countries fared better in this respect than chaos countries. In the divisive political environment of the United States, for instance, public health experts and the mainstream media blamed the runaway infection and death rates on the Trump administration's disregard for evidence and the public's loss of trust in science.

Trump himself seemed to offer living proof of such heedless denial. He often flouted the advice of his own expert advisers, eschewing masks and social distancing, for instance, even when he came down with the disease. Many political commentators therefore interpreted Biden's win in the 2020 presidential election as a victory for science pure and simple, but our research suggests a subtler reading: the election outcome expressed widespread disenchantment with a chaotic style of presidential politics that undermined faith in the government's commitment to a coherent and comprehensible pandemic policy.[12] A vote for Biden was less a vote for 'science' than for a steadier hand at the helm.

Cross-national comparison tells a nuanced story about the nature and role of trust during the pandemic. It suggests that the analytic starting point for understanding the phenomenon of trust has to be within national political systems and not in the technocratic domains of either health or economic expertise – let alone in some aggregated, survey-based, numerical index of public understanding of science. It is in the realm of politics that trusting relations are built among citizens, between citizens and the state, and among states and international organisations. And those relations in turn are mobilised when the public is asked to follow the recommendations of health experts who are advising the state or acting on the basis of their delegated sovereign authority.[13] Our study has documented on

12 Stephen Hilgartner, J Benjamin Hurlbut and Sheila Jasanoff, 'Was "Science" on the Ballot?' (2021) 371 Science 893.

13 Sheila Jasanoff, 'Pathologies of Liberty: Public Health Sovereignty and the Political Subject in the Covid-19 Crisis' (2020) 11 Cahiers Droit, Sciences, et Technologies 125 <https://journals.openedition.org/cdst/2982>.

the whole that countries with relatively high levels of trust in their government's ability to discern and serve the public interest have also generated fewer public controversies over scientific evidence. This group ranges from authoritarian to democratic, including for example China, the Netherlands, Taiwan, Singapore and Sweden.[14] By contrast, scientific controversies have proliferated in countries where a sizeable fraction of citizens has lost faith in the state's capacity to govern for the public good, such as Brazil and the United States.

4. Democracy under Fire

Our study further suggests that these variations in public trust across countries can be traced to the diverse ways in which modernity's social contract has been implemented in varied constitutional orders. We draw on decades of work in science and technology studies[15] showing that modern societies have adopted de facto constitutional settlements[16] in allowing experts to govern their lives.[17] Just as political constitutions set out the framework of delegated powers within which states and citizens exercise their rights and obligations, so these tacit "constitutions of modernity"[18] prescribe the principles by which societies delegate certain technical tasks to experts, while also holding them accountable for their judgments. Understandably, this parallel structure of governance has received far less theoretical attention than constitutional law as commonly understood, and yet the principles of delegation and accountability that constitute rule by experts in any society are as durable and as culturally embedded as more obviously political ideals of liberty, privacy or fairness enshrined in traditional constitutions.

Key to these settlements regarding expert rule are explicit and tacit delegations of power to knowledge-making institutions, most notably public health authorities.[19] No one today questions the need for experts to pass upon the safety of foods, the efficacy of drugs, the cleanliness of air and water or the need to adopt emergency measures against communicable diseases. Consequently, the exercise of state authority, and the production of what Timothy Mitchell, among others, has

14 For analysis of China, Taiwan, Singapore and Sweden, see also deLisle and Shen, chapter 4; Chang and Lin, chapter 25; Chua and Neo, chapter 7; and Cameroon and Jonsson Cornell, chapter 19.

15 Stephen Hilgartner, Clark Miller and Rob Hagendijk (eds), *Science and Democracy: Making Knowledge and Making Power in the Biosciences and Beyond* (Routledge 2015).

16 Sheila Jasanoff, 'In a Constitutional Moment: Science and Social Order at the Millennium' in Bernward Joerges and Helga Nowotny (eds) *Social Studies of Science and Technology: Looking Back, Ahead* (Kluwer 2003).

17 Sheila Jasanoff, *The Fifth Branch: Science Advisers as Policymakers* (Harvard University Press 1990).

18 Sheila Jasanoff, 'Constitutions of Modernity: Science, Risk, and Governable Subjects' in Maria Weimer and Anniek de Ruijter (eds) *Regulating Risks in the EU: The Co-Production of Expert and Executive Power* (Hart Publishing 2017).

19 Christopher Pollard, 'Explainer: the Ideas of Foucault' (*The Conversation*, 26 August 2019) <https://theconversation.com/explainer-the-ideas-of-foucault-99758>.

called state effects (the practices that make the state appear to exist),[20] frequently occur through consensus-building[21] or contention[22] among experts. The rules of the game by which experts negotiate differences among themselves and seek to persuade policymakers and wider publics of the merits of their arguments vary widely across countries. Indeed, these institutionalised modes of reasoning and reason-giving have proved sufficiently stable over time and across issue areas to serve as defining elements of a nation's political culture, or its prevailing civic epistemology.[23]

From the beginning of the crisis, national leaders in every country drew on a variety of prior understandings of how the state relates to citizens and vice versa, in other words, on deep-seated, and localised, constitutional understandings of citizenship. The metaphors leaders deploy tell part of this story. A quick survey of our 16 countries showed that heads of state in ten of them used war metaphors to rally their citizens, but with very different ideas of what their call to arms should inspire.[24] In China, the epitome of a control country in our analysis, appeal to a "People's War" against the virus legitimated the military precision and totalising sweep of the government's virus eradication policy. India's Prime Minister Narendra Modi likened the war against the virus to India's great war epic, the *Mahabharata*, thereby reinscribing his own standing as leader of the country's Hindu nationalists. Countries that rarely referred to war, and hence did not frame the viral challenge in terms of a battle to be won, included states already endowed with a high degree of social cohesion: Austria, Australia, Germany, the Netherlands and Sweden.[25] Germany's Angela Merkel did refer to World War II, but only to remind the nation of a historical period that had demanded solidarity and sacrifice in the face of an overwhelming challenge to established ways of life.

Policy contrasts across countries also underscore different underlying presumptions about the extent and nature of the authority delegated to the state and to its health authorities. In both the Netherlands and Sweden, for example, citizens expected to retain some freedom to judge for themselves the rationality of proposed regulations, even in the context of a public health emergency. Dutch Prime Minister Mark Rutte described his country's initial ban on large public gatherings in March 2020 as an "intelligent lockdown",[26] meaning one that depended on

20 Timothy Mitchell, 'The Limits of the State: Beyond Statist Approaches and their Critics' (1991) 85 American Political Science Review 77.

21 Stephen Hilgartner, *Science on Stage: Expert Advice as Public Drama* (Stanford University Press 2000).

22 David Kennedy, *A World of Struggle: How Power, Law, and Expertise Shape Global Political Economy* (Princeton University Press 2016).

23 Sheila Jasanoff, *Designs on Nature: Science and Democracy in Europe and the United States* (Princeton University Press 2005).

24 CompCoRe Chronicle, Issue 2 <https://compcore.cornell.edu/news-events/>.

25 For analysis of Australia, Germany and Sweden, see also Rizzi and Tulich, chapter 37; Mangold, chapter 27; and Cameron and Jonsson Cornell, chapter 19.

26 Reuters Staff, 'Dutch PM Rutte: Ban on Public Gatherings is "Intelligent Lockdown"' (*Reuters*, 23 March 2020) <https://www.reuters.com/article/us-health-coronavirus-netherlands-gather/

citizens to understand why such measures were needed and to comply in order to avoid more drastic curtailments. Such political buy-in has proved essential for the government. The following year, when Dutch citizens were dissatisfied with continued restrictions in the form of a curfew, their protests forced Parliament to enact a new law to put the measure on a firm legal footing that citizens could accept.[27] Sweden, which stood out early on for refusing to lock down its economy, routinely employs the doctrine of proportionality in its public health decisions. Extreme curtailments of liberty are permitted only when the country actually is at war – and, notably, our Swedish research team reported that their nation's political leaders never resorted to the discourse of war. Nonetheless, an early study suggested that levels of interpersonal and institutional trust rose in Sweden even when the country entered the acute phase of the pandemic in late summer of 2020.[28]

In the United States, by contrast, commentators zoomed in on loss of trust in expertise as a phenomenon of intense social concern, citing resistance to public health guidelines such as compulsory mask-wearing as evidence of denying science. Here again, our findings suggest that the interplay among the three arenas of health, economy and politics was highly significant. Political polarisation, already at historic highs, seeped into the assessment of the health risk from COVID-19. In March 2021, the Pew Research Center reported that only half as many Republicans (41%) as Democrats (82%) agreed that "the outbreak is a major threat to the health of the U.S. population as a whole".[29] Yet, roughly the same percentages of both parties (~82%) saw the pandemic as a major threat to the US economy. Unlike the virus, which seemed to devastate some regions while sparing others, shuttered businesses and lost jobs struck the entire country. People did not need to trust in mediating experts to feel these effects as serious. By the same token, even a revered scientist like Dr Anthony Fauci could not neutralise the distrust[30] of people whose friends and families were not sick, but who saw their economic futures teetering on the brink. Political polarisation left even Dr Fauci and, later, the health officials appointed by the Biden administration powerless to persuade loyal supporters of Donald Trump.

dutch-pm-rutte-ban-on-public-gatherings-is-intelligent-lockdown-idUSKBN21A39V>.

27 Mike Corder, 'Dutch Senate Approves Coronavirus Curfew Legislation' (*Seattle Times*, 19 February 2021) <https://www.seattletimes.com/business/dutch-government-in-2-pronged-bid-to-save-coronavirus-curfew/>.

28 Peter Esaiasson, Jacob Sohlberg, Marina Ghersetti and Bengt Johansson, 'How the Coronavirus Crisis Affects Citizen Trust in Institutions and in Unknown Others: Evidence from "the Swedish Experiment"' (2020) European Journal of Political Research (published online 9 September 2020) <https://doi.org/10.1111/1475-6765.12419>.

29 Katherine Schaeffer, 'Despite Wide Partisan Gaps in Views of Many Aspects of the Pandemic, Some Common Ground Exists' (Pew Research Center, 24 March 2021) <https://www.pewresearch.org/fact-tank/2021/03/24/despite-wide-partisan-gaps-in-views-of-many-aspects-of-the-pandemic-some-common-ground-exists/>.

30 John H Evans and Etszter Hargittai, 'Who Doesn't Trust Fauci? The Public's Belief in the Expertise and Shared Values of Scientists in the COVID-19 Pandemic' (2020) 6 Socius: Sociological Research for a Dynamic World 1.

Our study indicates that loss of trust in expertise is best understood not as an independent variable that undermines rational public policy but as an indicator of a country's capacity to hold together its constitutional settlement between knowledge and power in times of crisis. Countries with traditions of paternalistic or authoritarian government, such as Singapore and China,[31] maintained (or, in China's case, regained) public trust as long as they appeared to keep infections down and economies humming – even if some freedoms such as travel were sharply restricted. Countries with strong cultures of solidarity, like Germany and the Netherlands, also retained trust so long as leaders could persuade people that health measures were temporary and reasonable, as well as consistent with applicable law. By contrast, Brazil, a country in which politics rode roughshod over expert judgment, descended into prolonged chaos in health, economy and politics. And trust also frayed dramatically in the United States, where expert judgment drawing solely on the cultural authority of science proved insufficient to offset the sharp political divisions that increasingly gripped the country.

The pandemic also revealed serious weaknesses in global institutions' power to forge worldwide epistemic and normative agreements. Throughout the pandemic, there were few signs that national governments felt bound by global health or human rights regimes. The commitment to rapid sharing of outbreak information was undermined when Chinese officials initially suppressed news of the novel virus and punished whistleblowers for "spreading false rumors".[32] China's assertion of epistemic sovereignty renewed itself in its resistance to an independent investigation of the controversial 'lab leak' theory. Nationalism overrode concerns for the global common good in other respects as well. Early on, countries competed for limited supplies of personal protective equipment, and at the end of 2020 when vaccines became available, 'vaccine nationalism' privileging the citizens of producer nations became the word of the day.[33] The WHO's calls for international equity in vaccine distribution largely went unheeded (though the Biden administration announced a strategy for vaccine sharing in June 2021), and to a startling extent countries treated the pandemic as mainly a national political problem. A few threads of transnational solidarity were evident, including the publication of virus sequences and the exchange of information on novel variants of SARS-COV-2. But overall, the pandemic shows that national governments are still the central actors in this domain, not organisations like the WHO that are accountable to an imagined global 'we'.

As national and international authorities look to futures beyond COVID-19, a lesson emerging from our study is that they should revisit their established institutional processes for integrating scientific and political consensus-building. If free citizens are unable to see how expertise is serving the collective good, at all levels

31 See also Chua and Neo, chapter 7 and deLisle and Shen, chapter 4.

32 Verna Yu, '"Hero Who Told the Truth": Chinese Rage over Coronavirus Death of Whistleblower Doctor' (*The Guardian*, 7 February 2020) <https://www.theguardian.com/global-development/2020/feb/07/coronavirus-chinese-rage-death-whistleblower-doctor-li-wenliang>.

33 See also Singh, chapter 2.

of governance, they will sooner rebel against expert authority than give up their independence. Just as a sound mind is said to require a sound body, so COVID-19 has shown that the credibility and legitimacy of public health expertise depends on the health of the entire body politic. Global success in rising to the next pandemic demands that – following COVID-19 – we begin paying attention to humanity's social cohesiveness just as intently as we did to our biological vulnerability after the great Spanish flu pandemic of the previous century.

24

OPEN SCIENCE, DATA SHARING AND PANDEMIC PREPAREDNESS

Ciara Staunton

1. Introduction[1]

In a public health emergency, the need for rapid and timely access to data is clear.[2] Public health advisors need to know about the current epidemiological trends and capacity of the health system so as to provide the best advice. Policy makers need access to the data that has informed any public health advice and also data on the impact that any restrictions on civil liberties are likely to have on the population. The public should have access to this data so that it understands, trusts and supports the public health advice, regulations and restrictions on civil liberties. Researchers also require access to the most up-to-date research results, the genomic sequence of the virus, and any new mutations. This is dependent on access to biological samples and data on which to do research. Thus, a coherent public health response is in part contingent on access to and rapid sharing of data.

COVID-19 came at a time when there had already been an increase in the 'datafication' of health and the human body. Data has been used to identify hotspots and guide both national and localised responses, and access to data has been critical in developing new COVID-19 diagnostics, therapies and vaccines. COVID-19 is therefore very much the world's first 'digital pandemic'[3] and effective responses to it are reliant on access to and sharing of data.

From the outset of the pandemic, there were calls to make data and research results openly and quickly available. Many funders of science and prominent jour-

1 All websites accessed on 17 July 2021.

2 This chapter draws on a previous post by the author: 'Data Sharing and the Public Interest in a Digital Pandemic' (*Verfassungsblog*, 20 March 2021) <https://verfassungsblog.de/data-sharing-and-the-public-interest-in-a-digital-pandemic/>.

3 Steve Davis and Precious Matsoso, 'COVID-19 as a Digital Pandemic' (*Think Global Health*, 7 July 2020) <https://www.thinkglobalhealth.org/article/covid-19-digital-pandemic>.

DOI: 10.4324/9781003211952-28

nals signed a pledge urging researchers, journals and funders to share research findings and data that were relevant to informing public health responses.[4] In May 2020, the World Health Organisation (WHO) launched the COVID-19 Technology Access Pool (C-TAP) that aimed to "facilitate timely, equitable and affordable access ... [to] COVID-19 health products". It sought to achieve this in part through sharing knowledge and data.[5] There were also calls from researchers themselves to reduce barriers to data sharing "for research in the public interest".[6]

This call for data sharing is not new and the WHO Pandemic Influenza Preparedness Framework stresses the importance of data sharing in a pandemic.[7] However, during COVID-19 there was a shift in data practices; 'open science' and the rapid sharing of results of clinical trials, observational studies, operational research, routine surveillance and information on the virus and its genetic sequences, as well as the monitoring of disease control programmes, became the norm during the pandemic.[8] This resulted in an increase in international collaborative research,[9] accelerated the use of non-peer reviewed preprints that enabled rapid and free availability of data and results;[10] and importantly, was credited with the swift development of vaccines and diagnostics.[11]

It perhaps comes as no surprise, then, that at the World Health Assembly in May 2021, the World Health Organisation (WHO) Director-General, Dr Tedros Adhanom Ghebreyesus, called for a global pandemic treaty that would include, among other provisions, internationally agreed rules on data access during a pandemic.[12] This built upon a call in March 2021 by the science academies of the G7

4 'Coronavirus (COVID-19): Sharing Research Data' (Wellcome, 31 January 2020)<https://wellcome.org/press-release/sharing-research-data-and-findings-relevant-novel-coronavirus-ncov-outbreak>.

5 World Health Organisation, 'WHO COVID-19 Technology Access Pool' <https://www.who.int/initiatives/covid-19-technology-access-pool>.

6 'Open letter to the ICO, CMOs and UK Data Providers: Reducing Barriers to Data Access for Research in the Public Interest – Lessons from COVID-19' (6 July 2020) <https://www.ucl.ac.uk/health-informatics/sites/health-informatics/files/open_letter_improving_data_access_-_lessons_from_covid-19.pdf>.

7 World Health Organisation, 'Pandemic Influenza Preparedness Framework' (2011) <https://apps.who.int/gb/pip/pdf_files/pandemic-influenza-preparedness-en.pdf>.

8 European Commission, 'Coronavirus: Commission Launches Data Sharing Platform for Researchers' (20 April 2020) <https://ec.europa.eu/commission/presscorner/detail/en/IP_20_680>.

9 Ian Le Guillou 'Covid-19: How Unprecedented Data Sharing Has Led to Faster-than-Ever Outbreak Research' (*Horizon: the EU Research & Innovation magazine*, 23 March 2020) <https://horizon-magazine.eu/article/covid-19-how-unprecedented-data-sharing-has-led-faster-ever-outbreak-research.html>.

10 Liam Brierley, 'Lessons from the Influx of Preprints during the Early COVID-19 Pandemic' (2021) 5 The Lancet Planetary Health e115; Nicholas Fraser and others, 'The Evolving Role of Preprints in the Dissemination of COVID-19 Research and Their Impact on the Science Communication Landscape' (2021) 19 PLOS Biology e3000959.

11 'Editorial: Genomic Sequencing in Pandemics' (2021) 397(10273) The Lancet<https://www.thelancet.com/journals/lancet/article/PIIS0140-6736(21)00257-9/fulltext>.

12 'Wanted: Rules for Pandemic Data Access That Everyone Can Trust' (2021) 594 Nature 8.

group of the world's seven biggest economies (known as the S7) to develop data access rules for emergencies[13] either through a global pandemic treaty or internationally agreed data access rules. Such policies, provided they are internationally agreed, should facilitate data access and sharing in future pandemics. However, the rush towards global data sharing in a pandemic must not blind us to the fact that there are multi-faceted issues that must be addressed prior to data sharing during a pandemic.

This chapter seeks to address some of these issues. Section 2 considers three questions: privacy and data protection considerations; whether the call for global data sharing resulted in global benefits; and whether there is universal support for data sharing. Section 3 then turns to the proposed pandemic treaty itself and offers recommendations on a way forward.

2. Solidarity, Open Science and Data Sharing during COVID-19

Open science and data sharing have been an important part of COVID-19-related research, but this research is reliant on access to large quantities of data – often personal identifiable data. The legal, ethical and social concerns in accessing and sharing this data for research has long been discussed and often forms part of the opposition to unrestricted and open access data sharing.[14] However, throughout COVID-19, the importance of solidarity was continuously stressed. We are an interconnected world and in facing a common threat our individual response is for the collective benefit. It is for this reason that states' public health responses locked down our physical bodies but required our digital bodies to be moved and shared across borders: COVID-19 required a collective response and sharing data was necessary for the benefit of the collective.[15] Open science during the pandemic was therefore justified as being in the public interest.

However, the success of this collaborative sharing of data does not tell the full story. Sharing of personal data has considerable implications for fundamental rights and freedoms that include the rights to privacy and non-discrimination. COVID-19 demonstrated that the global sharing of data on the basis of solidarity does not necessarily result in a global benefit. Until structural factors and power asymmetries are addressed, global data sharing is largely for the benefit of researchers

13 Science Academies Group of Seven (G7) Nations, 'Data for International Health Emergencies: Governance, Operations and Skills' (31 March 2021) <https://royalsociety.org/-/media/about-us/international/g-science-statements/G7-data-for-international-health-emergencies-31-03-2021.pdf?la=en-GB&hash=E6AE132F624E4C01EB10BFC25CB83F1C>.

14 Anna Middleton and others, 'Global Public Perceptions of Genomic Data Sharing: What Shapes the Willingness to Donate DNA and Health Data?' (2020) 107 The American Journal of Human Genetics 743.

15 Angus Dawson and others, 'Key Ethical Concepts and Their Application to COVID-19 Research' (2020) 13 Public Health Ethics 127; Ciara Staunton and Deborah Mascalzoni, 'Solidarity, Trust and the Governance of Data Sharing during a Public Health Emergency' (*Journal of Medical Ethics blog*, 12 May 2021) <https://blogs.bmj.com/medical-ethics/2021/05/12/solidarity-trust-and-the-governance-of-data-sharing-during-a-public-health-emergency/>.

in high-income countries (HICs). This section will consider each of these issues in turn.

2.1 Data Sharing and the Right to Privacy

The pandemic saw the limitation of many rights including freedom of assembly and freedom of movement. The data-driven response that informed many states' pandemic policies was further reliant on access to large quantities of personal and other data, that has the potential to interfere with the right to privacy. The limitations on these rights were justified on the basis that they were necessary to enable states to respond to and suppress COVID-19: our collective interest required limitations on individual rights.

This 'public interest' was also used to frame and influence data practices and data use. However, in the context of these evolving practices and the surge in "techno-solutionism",[16] the narrative about the importance of data sharing must be balanced with the reality that the use of these data-driven technologies impacted upon the right to privacy and risked individual and group discrimination, racism and exploitation, and the systematic marginalisation of certain communities.[17] There was an ever-present danger that the emergency situation would be exploited to get access to this personal data for other purposes. Governments had an interest in accessing COVID-19-related data but this was not always for purposes that were directly linked to their COVID-19 response. For example, there were reports that in Hong Kong, samples for COVID-19 testing were used for forensic DNA profiling, and that data collected as part of contact tracing in Singapore may have been turned over to the police.[18] Private companies also see a commercial value in accessing and exploiting this data and Israel agreed to share disaggregated medical data with Pfizer in return for continued access to vaccines.[19] However, using data for a purpose other than what it was collected for is not only

16 Siddharth Venkataramakrishnan, 'Why Business Cannot Afford to Ignore Tech Ethics' (*The Financial Times*, 6 December 2020) <https://www.ft.com/content/f4d697d0-3a34-4ee8-a9d9-0dfdac1284ab>.

17 Gianclaudio Malgieri and Jędrzej Niklas, 'Vulnerable Data Subjects' (2020) 37 Computer Law & Security Review 105415; Francesca Forzano, Maurizio Genuardi and Yves Moreau, 'ESHG Warns against Misuses of Genetic Tests and Biobanks for Discrimination Purposes' (2021) European Journal of Human Genetics 1; Hannah E Knight and others, 'Challenging Racism in the Use of Health Data' (2021) 3 The Lancet Digital Health e144.

18 Forzano, Genuardi and Moreau (n 17); 'Singapore Says COVID-19 Contact-Tracing Data Can Be Requested By Police' (*NPR.org*, 5 January 2021) <https://www.npr.org/sections/coronavirus-live-updates/2021/01/05/953604553/singapore-says-covid-19-contact-tracing-data-can-be-requested-by-police>. On Singapore, see generally Chua and Neo, chapter 7.

19 Ulises Ali Mejias and Nick Couldry, 'Big Tech's Latest Moves Raise Health Privacy Fears' (*The Financial Times*, 7 December 2020) <https://www.ft.com/content/01d4452c-03e2-4b44-bf78-b017e66775f1>; Ilan Ben Zion, 'Israel Trades Pfizer Doses for Medical Data in Vaccine Blitz' (*AP News*, 20 April 2021) <https://apnews.com/article/international-news-israel-coronavirus-vaccine-coronavirus-pandemic-benjamin-netanyahu-b30f9af2139e64794ce66c6c9b367b7b>.

potentially an incursion on the right to privacy, but risks damaging public trust and support in the future use of data.

Therefore, there may be a public interest to access and share data that may limit the right to privacy, but there is an equal public interest in doing this in a way that respects and upholds human rights, notably the rights to privacy and to data protection. The use and sharing of personal data in the European Union to respond to COVID-19 without the consent of the data subject is potentially permitted on grounds of public interest under the General Data Protection Regulation (GDPR).[20] Article 6(1)(e) in combination with Article 9(2)(i) can provide a legal basis for the processing of health-related personal data in the public interest. The GDPR thus enables data sharing for research during public health emergencies. However, under Article 9(2)(i), this must be based on law and this law must provide for "suitable and specific measures to safeguard the rights and freedoms of the data subject". This caveat is crucial: the use of personal data in this context can limit many of the rights provided by the GDPR and can only be done in a manner that continues to safeguard fundamental rights and freedoms, which must continue to be applied to the use of personal data during a public health emergency. In this sense, the binary choice that was often presented as 'rights versus public health' presents a limited and purely biomedical view of the public interest that fails to reflect the inter-connectedness of health, economics and democracy. In the context of the use of personal data and data practices, the narrative should not be privacy *or* the public interest, but rather privacy *and* the public interest.

The importance of continuing to safeguard individual and collective privacy during the pandemic more accurately reflects the public interest in the preservation of privacy, even in an emergency situation. The WHO, the UN, the Organisation for Economic Co-operation and Development (OECD), the European Data Protection Supervisor, the Council of Europe and the Access to COVID-19 Tools (ACT) Accelerator (a global collaboration to accelerate the development and production of, and equitable access to, COVID-19 tests, treatments and vaccines) have all emphasised the importance of using personal data in accordance with the right to privacy and the principles of data protection.[21] They recognise that

20 European Data Protection Board, 'Guidelines 03/2020 on the Processing of Data Concerning Health for the Purpose of Scientific Research in the Context of the COVID-19 Outbreak' (21 April 2020) <https://edpb.europa.eu/sites/default/files/files/file1/edpb_guidelines_202003_healthdatascientificresearchcovid19_en.pdf>.

21 United Nations Global Pulse, 'Joint Statement on Data Protection and Privacy in the COVID-19 Response' (18 November 2020) <https://www.un.org/en/coronavirus/joint-statement-data-protection-and-privacy-covid-19-response>; Organisation for Economic Cooperation and Development, 'Ensuring Data Privacy as We Battle COVID-19' (14 April 2020) <https://www.oecd.org/coronavirus/policy-responses/ensuring-data-privacy-as-we-battle-covid-19-36c2f31e/>; European Data Protection Supervisor, 'EDPS Response to the COVID-19 Outbreak' (undated) <https://edps.europa.eu/data-protection/our-work/subjects/covid-19_en>; Council of Europe, 'COVID-19 and Data Protection' (undated) <https://www.coe.int/en/web/data-protection/covid-19-data-protection>; Access to COVID-19 Tools Accelerator 'Framework for the Governance of Personal Data for the Access to COVID-19 Tools Accelerator'

although the right to privacy can be limited, privacy interests must continue to be safeguarded during a pandemic. Thus, any restriction of the right to privacy and the right to data protection must be necessary for the purpose of the use of the personal data and must be a proportionate limitation to achieve the specified aim. Moreover, the restriction must be time-bound and limited to the duration of the pandemic or when the purpose of the data use has been achieved, whichever is first. Importantly, if a particular aim or purpose can be achieved without limiting the right to privacy, then that option must be pursued. Thus, data sharing during a pandemic must be rooted in human rights and this must be embedded in any pandemic treaty. The exceptional nature of the restriction in these conditions must be emphasised, otherwise there is a risk of the normalisation on the limitations of rights and freedoms in data practices.

2.2 Data Sharing on the Basis of Solidarity: Who Benefits?

The public interest can provide a legal basis on which to share data, but the call for global data sharing has also been justified on the basis of "solidarity".[22] In biomedical research, the principle of solidarity is gaining prominence and is characterised as a "commitment to carry costs … to assist others".[23] In the context of COVID-19, solidarity emphasises individual adherence to public health measures and participation in COVID-19 research because it is in the collective interest.[24] Thus, we commit to carrying a cost by sharing our data in the hope that it will assist others through the development of new tests, treatments and vaccines.[25]

This global pandemic required a global response. It required not just the sharing of data, but the *global* sharing of data. As the virus evolved and new variants emerged, the sharing of data related to these new variants was essential for surveillance, but the efficacy of tests, treatments and vaccines on these new variants also had to be tested and shared.[26] Research must also be done on, and data collected from, populations across the globe to ensure that dosage and frequency can be tailored to suit local populations.[27]

(January 2021) <https://www.finddx.org/wp-content/uploads/2021/01/ACT-A-Dx-data-governance-framework_15.01.2021.pdf>.

22 World Health Organisation, 'Solidarity Call to Action' (29 May 2020)<https://www.who.int/initiatives/covid-19-technology-access-pool/solidarity-call-to-action>.

23 Barbara Prainsack and Alena Buyx, *Solidarity in Biomedicine and Beyond* (Cambridge University Press 2017).

24 Dawson and others (n 15).

25 Staunton and Mascalzoni (n 15).

26 Houriiyah Tegally and others, 'Emergence and Rapid Spread of a New Severe Acute Respiratory Syndrome-Related Coronavirus 2 (SARS-CoV-2) Lineage with Multiple Spike Mutations in South Africa' (2020) medRxiv <https://doi.org/10.1101/2020.12.21.20248640>.

27 Kelly Chibale, 'OPINIONISTA: Africa Should Be at the Forefront of Covid-19 Vaccine Trials — and Should Be Providing Scientific Leadership' (*Daily Maverick*, 29 July 2020)<https://www.dailymaverick.co.za/opinionista/2020-07-30-africa-should-be-at-the-forefront-of-covid-19-vaccine-trials-and-should-be-providing-scientific-leadership/>.

This global sharing of data must be matched with global benefits. In a public health emergency, these benefits must, at a minimum, be equitable access to tests, treatments and vaccines. The evidence suggests that the solidarity-based approach in the sharing of data has not been met with equitable distribution of the fruits of this data sharing. Vaccines have predominately been administered in HICs and the cost of some vaccines in low- and middle-income countries (LMICs) were double that of HICs.[28] The "self-centred approach" of hoarding vaccines and preferring to vaccine younger age groups rather than share vaccines for vulnerable populations in LMICs is a real failure in securing global equity and not reflective of solidarity.[29] The solidarity-based call to action resulted in an imbalance between the erosion of individual rights in the name of the public interest vis-a-vis results that were, in fact, distributed in the pursuit of national and private interests and economic gain. Data use and data practices during the pandemic reinforced the social gradient of health and rather than serving the global public interest[30] instead served the interests of the Global North, reinforcing existing healthy inequity and power asymmetries. A pandemic treaty must therefore start from the premise that global data sharing must yield global results. If we are to share data on the basis of solidarity and limit our rights in the public interest, solidarity must be embedded in the proposed governance framework throughout the data life-cycle. This starts from data collection, through to data use, and ultimately the benefits that accrue from this data.

2.3 Data Sharing and Equity of Access

The pre-pandemic push for open science was largely advocated by funders, scientists and other organisations that are based in HICs. Not all researchers have been supportive of this approach, particularly due to concerns that the primary data collector will not receive any credit.[31] Research in many resource-limited settings has a history of exploitative or so-called 'parachute' research, whereby biological samples and data are sent to laboratories in HICs for research.[32] As a result, valuable biological samples and data are not available for local researchers to develop

28 'Covid-19 Tracker' (*Bloomberg*, updated daily) <https://www.bloomberg.com/graphics/covid-vaccine-tracker-global-distribution/>; 'Experts Warn of Third Covid-19 Wave in South Africa amid Vaccination Delay: Report' (*Businesstech*, 24 January 2021) <https://businesstech.co.za/news/trending/462986/experts-warn-of-third-covid-19-wave-in-south-africa-amid-vaccination-delay-report/>.

29 Marguerite Massinga Loembé and John N Nkengasong, 'COVID-19 Vaccine Access in Africa: Global Distribution, Vaccine Platforms, and Challenges Ahead' (2021) 54(7) Immunity 1353.

30 Allison Crawford and Eva Serhal, 'Digital Health Equity and COVID-19: The Innovation Curve Cannot Reinforce the Social Gradient of Health' (2020) 22 Journal of Medical Internet Research e19361.

31 Virginia Gewin, 'Six Tips for Data Sharing in the Age of the Coronavirus' (*Nature*, 28 May 2020) <https://www.nature.com/articles/d41586-020-01516-0>.

32 Billie-Jo Hardy and others, 'South Africa: From Species Cradle to Genomic Applications' (2008) 9 Nature Reviews Genetics S19.

their capacity and expertise, and biological materials are used for research on diseases that are not for the benefit of the local population but rather populations in HICs.[33] Shaped by these historical exploitative research practices, and more recent examples of unethical data use,[34] researchers in some resource-limited settings have legitimate concerns that international collaborations forged during the COVID-19 pandemic will lead to exploitation.[35]

During a pandemic, particularly one that is global in nature, research must be conducted on populations throughout the world. Dosages and frequency of vaccines and therapies must be tailored to local populations, but also conditions on the transport and storage of any interventions must be feasible and suit local conditions. Scientific validity, particularly in genetic studies, depends in part on access to large quantities of data[36] and this must be combined with efficient and rapid data analysis.[37]

However, there have been reports of a push back from some researchers in Africa towards open data sharing during COVID-19. This is due to the aforementioned concerns around exploitation, lack of acknowledgment of the local data collector and fears of inequitable use.[38] Open dating sharing that requires the data collector to relinquish all rights to the data has been described as exhibiting a "neo-colonial mentality".[39] This reluctance, even in a public health emergency, cannot come as a surprise. Due to past experiences in influenza outbreaks, during the H_5N_1 (avian influenza) outbreak, Indonesia refused to share its samples with the WHO without a legally binding agreement on intellectual property rights and benefit sharing.[40] During the West Africa Ebola outbreak, samples were shipped to HICs and as a result the scientific papers and patents based on these samples went to researchers based at institutions in HICs.[41] It can therefore come as no surprise

33 Ciara Staunton and Jantina de Vries, 'The Governance of Genomic Biobank Research in Africa: Reframing the Regulatory Tilt' (2020) Journal of Law and Biosciences 1.

34 Erik Stokstad, 'Major U.K. Genetics Lab Accused of Misusing African DNA' (*ScienceMag*, 30 October 2019) <https://www.sciencemag.org/news/2019/10/major-uk-genetics-lab-accused-misusing-african-dna>.

35 Nchangwi Syntia Munung, Bongani M Mayosi and Jantina de Vries, 'Equity in International Health Research Collaborations in Africa: Perceptions and Expectations of African Researchers' (2017) 12 PLOS ONE e0186237.

36 Christine L Borgman, 'The Conundrum of Sharing Research Data' (2012) 63 Journal of the American Society for Information Science and Technology 1059.

37 Safia Mahomed and Ciara Staunton, 'Ethico-Legal Analysis of International Sample and Data Sharing for Genomic Research during COVID-19: A South African Perspective' (2021) 21 BioLaw Journal – Rivista di BioDiritto 261.

38 Amy Maxmen, 'One Million Coronavirus Sequences: Popular Genome Site Hits Mega Milestone' (2021) 593 Nature 21.

39 'Opinion: Data Imperialism in a Pandemic: How to Make Things Fall Apart' (*IOL*, 1 May 2021) <https://www.iol.co.za/news/opinion/data-imperialism-in-a-pandemic-how-to-make-things-fall-apart-f707fe96-fc6f-4866-aa9f-7c0aaa1f97db>.

40 Xinqing Zhang and others, 'Attitudes towards Transfers of Human Tissue Samples across Borders: An International Survey of Researchers and Policy Makers in Five Countries' (2010) 11 BMC Medical Ethics 16.

41 Amy Maxmen, 'Science under Fire: Ebola Researchers Fight to Test Drugs and Vaccines in a War Zone' (2019) 572 Nature 16.

that the OECD has identified a lack of trust between data communities and a lack of policy coherence as the main barriers to data sharing. However, there are examples of good practice.[42] For example, by April 2020, more than 1.2 million coronavirus genome sequences from 172 countries had been deposited with the Global Initiative on Sharing Avian Influenza Data (GISAID). Its success is due in part to terms of access that seek to guard against exploitation by requiring the scientists who uploaded the data to be acknowledged.[43] These best practices in the ethical and equitable sharing of data must be assessed and built upon as we take data sharing into the next pandemic.

3. Data Access and an International Pandemic Treaty

As we entered the second year of the pandemic in 2021, conversations began to shift towards developing a pandemic treaty, with data sharing to be included in such a treaty. The question is thus not *whether* we should include data sharing as part of a pandemic treaty, but *how*.

The first step in these discussions is the acknowledgment that ethical and equitable data sharing cannot happen if the infrastructure, tools and appropriately trained personnel are not in place across the world to rapidly process and share data. Collaborations such as that between the Africa Centres for Disease Control and Prevention, the European and Developing Countries Clinical Trials Partnership and the Foundation for Innovative New Diagnostics, which seeks to train epidemiologists and biostatisticians to conduct surveillance, public health research and support timely responses to disease outbreaks in Africa, should continue to be supported and funded.[44] The S7 recognises that data sharing rules are contingent on improving data literacy, statistics, privacy awareness and cybersecurity skills. The S7, however, needs to go beyond the recommendation to "support low-resource countries in developing and using examples of best practice, including through grant aid and technological cooperation".[45] Home-grown initiatives are essential and must be supported because, as noted by Loembé and Nkengasong, "models based on solidarity and philanthropy from wealthier nations have proven unsuccessful".[46]

The further development of equitable collaborations and more local initiatives must also include investment in capacity in law and ethics to ensure the appropri-

42 Organisation for Economic Cooperation and Development, 'The Digitalisation of Science, Technology and Innovation: Key Developments and Policies (11 February 2020) <https://www.oecd-ilibrary.org/science-and-technology/the-digitalisation-of-science-technology-and-innovation_b9e4a2c0-en>.

43 Maxmen (n 38).

44 African Union and Africa CDC, 'EDCTP and Africa CDC Collaborate to Develop Capacity for Outbreak and Epidemic Response in Sub- Saharan Africa' <https://africacdc.org/news-item/edctp-and-africa-cdc-collaborate-to-develop-capacity-for-outbreak-and-epidemic-response-in-sub-saharan-africa/>.

45 Science Academies Group of Seven (G7) Nations (n 13).

46 Loembé and Nkengasong (n 29)

ate governance of such initiatives. This will help inform what can be considered to be "best practice" in data use. Current so-called best practices are embedding global power asymmetries in data practices and the "data use for a common social benefit"[47] is, in fact, for the benefit of certain geographical areas. Thus, conversations on data use in a pandemic should not be led by HICs. The development of good governance of data in a pandemic requires a recognition of the structural, cultural, legal and ethical barriers to data sharing. A necessary first step in the development of data rules as part of a pandemic treaty should be wide and *global* engagement. This must include the data provider, researchers, public health experts, policy makers, lawyers, ethicists, funders and, importantly, the public, in order to identify the issues and challenges. It is this process that must be the foundation for any discussion on data practices in a pandemic treaty.

Turning to the pandemic treaty itself, data sharing should be overseen by robust governance frameworks. Conditions of data access must be grounded in human rights in order to ensure that any limitations on rights are proportionate, legitimate and necessary. Global engagement on best practices can identify the substantive values that should guide data practices, but it is essential that they are backed up by procedural values that include accountability, transparency and engagement. Key in the implementation of these principles will be the drafting of procedures on the appropriate use and development of accountability mechanisms in the event of a breach by any researcher, institution or country of these data practices. Trust is essential for the sharing of data.[48] Trust, however, is too elusive a concept to guide the use and sharing of data. Trust and solidarity without appropriate governance procedures are a potential breeding ground for exploitative data practices. It is good governance that can help strike this balance between individual rights and collective interests in the area of public health.[49] Without accountable governance, data practices during a pandemic will perpetuate global health inequity. Therefore, a key question that will need to be answered in these discussions is where responsibility for holding those to account should sit.

Finally, a pandemic treaty must address how data collected and shared during a pandemic should be managed and shared in a post-pandemic world. Data collected during any public health emergency will be of benefit to researchers, governments and commercial entities and can be used to inform states' pandemic preparedness and future pandemic responses. After the pandemic, the circumstances will have changed but the data will remain. The public interest can no longer serve as a legal basis on which to justify the limitation of rights, and data practices must reflect these changed circumstances. Previous experiences from the West Africa Ebola epidemic demonstrated that a lack of coordination and accountability mechanisms

47 Science Academies Group of Seven (G7) Nations (n 13).

48 Middleton and others (n 14).

49 Effy Vayena, 'Value from Health Data: European Opportunity to Catalyse Progress in Digital Health' (2021) 397(10275) The Lancet 652 <https://www.thelancet.com/journals/lancet/article/PIIS0140-6736(21)00203-8/abstract>.

made tracking the availability and use of the data after the pandemic challenging.[50] It is currently unclear whether the private sector, which includes pharmaceutical companies, will continue to support access to and sharing of the data for research if there is no clear economic return in a post-pandemic world.

To ensure the long-term sustainability of and continued access to the data, there is a need for appropriate stewardship of it. Data stewardship is an approach to management of data that ensures the "long term care" of the data.[51] It seeks both to protect and promote the use of the data and conveys a level of responsibility in its use.[52] An important part of data stewardship is unpacking what is meant by the 'appropriate' use of this data. Data that was given on the basis of solidarity that it would be used in the public interest must continue to be used in this way if we are to honour the social contract between the public and those using their data in research.

Discussions on the appropriate stewardship of this data in a post-pandemic world must be part of any discussion on data practices during a pandemic. The public's expectations about the use of their data in research must be determined, and it is particularly important to involve groups in vulnerable and marginalised circumstances in this discussion. If industry is expected to continue to make data available, this must be made known, particularly as data will have been shared with them on the basis that it will be used for global benefit. The interests and justifications in accessing and using the data will have changed and the data practices must equally change to reflect this. The sustainable use of data collected during a pandemic will in part depend on identifying and balancing these new competing interests between industry that may want to profit from the data, policy makers that may want to share the data for further research and the public who may no longer wish their data to be shared in a post-pandemic world.

4. Conclusion

COVID-19 has demonstrated the clear need for rapid data access and rapid data sharing. Equally, it has also shown that mistakes in data practices from previous public health emergencies continue to be repeated. Research requires access to data across the world, but largely continues to be conducted for the benefit of those who can pay. In reality the limitation of rights across the world has primarily benefited HICs. A global pandemic treaty could be a solution, but only if it meaningfully addresses inequity in global health and global health research. The drafting of best practices in data sharing as part of a pandemic treaty must first

50 Nchangwi Syntia Munung and others, 'Perspectives of Different Stakeholders on Data Use and Management in Public Health Emergencies in Sub-Saharan Africa: A Meeting Report' (2021) 6 Wellcome Open Research 11.

51 Mark D Wilkinson and others, 'The FAIR Guiding Principles for Scientific Data Management and Stewardship' (2016) 3 Scientific Data < https://doi.org/10.1038/sdata.2016.18>.

52 Sara Rosenbaum, 'Data Governance and Stewardship: Designing Data Stewardship Entities and Advancing Data Access' (2010) 45 Health Services Research 1442.

identify the various barriers to data sharing and that must be done through wide engagement of the data provider, researchers, public health experts, policy makers, lawyers, ethicists, funders and, importantly, the public. As part of this engagement, discussions must be had on the good governance of data during a pandemic. Clear, transparent and, most importantly, *accountable* data practices must form the basis of any framework. Finally, agreement must be reached on how best to steward the use of this data in a post-pandemic world so that it can inform and improve our pandemic preparedness.

25

TAIWAN'S EFFECTIVE PANDEMIC CONTROL WITH DIALOGIC CONSTITUTIONALISM

Wen-Chen Chang and Chun-Yuan Lin

1. Introduction[1]

Taiwan successfully controlled the COVID-19 pandemic outside its border for more than 18 months until May 2021, when the Alpha variant led to a sudden outbreak, resulting in more than 500 locally transmitted cases per day and an increase of 9,000 cases in one month alone.[2] In a mere three months, however, Taiwan again saw fewer than ten locally transmitted cases per day, and achieved this without seriously restrictive measures or lockdowns. Meanwhile, due to the difficulty in accessing vaccines, only 30% of the population has received at least one dose of a COVID-19 vaccine at the time of writing,[3] which means that just under 3% of the population is fully vaccinated, well below the global average.[4]

Taiwan's first COVID-19 case was confirmed on 21 January 2020. Before the outbreak in May 2021, Taiwan kept its globally acclaimed record of zero locally transmitted cases for nearly eight months. Daily life proceeded without substantial interruption,[5] scheduled elections were held, court hearings continued in-person, and government services were delivered without compromise. All these factors

1 All websites accessed on 18 August 2021.

2 Taiwan Centers for Disease Control (CDC) <https://www.cdc.gov.tw/En>.

3 Keoni Everington, 'Taiwan's 1st-Dose Vaccination Rate Surpasses 30%' (*Taiwan News*, 30 July 2021) <https://www.taiwannews.com.tw/en/news/4261089>.

4 Johns Hopkins University Coronavirus Resource Centre, Understanding Vaccination Progress <https://coronavirus.jhu.edu/vaccines/international>. On the issue of Taiwan's access to vaccines, see Singh, chapter 2.

5 Our World in Data, 'COVID-19: Stringency Index'<https://ourworldindata.org/grapher/covid-stringency-index>.

DOI: 10.4324/9781003211952-29

led to a 3% growth in gross domestic product (GDP) in 2020,[6] the best among advanced economies.[7] Even after the spike of infections in May 2021, Taiwan's GDP was projected to grow by 5.16% in 2021,[8] despite the fact that schools changed to online teaching, some employees began working from home, and certain business sectors were suspended. Mandatory face-mask wearing was imposed, social distancing kept and outdoor gatherings limited with exceptions for religious activities.

This chapter analyses how Taiwan achieved this level of success in pandemic control despite its barred access to the World Health Organisation (WHO) and its geographic proximity and close economic ties to China.[9] We argue that legal preparedness after the 2003 SARS epidemic helped to some extent, but other than law, a comprehensive national healthcare system with affordable care, a high level of digital technology with cautious application and a vibrant civil society actively engaged in regulatory process and pandemic control were pivotal. In addition, the key mechanism keeping government power under control was not any particular pre-existing law. Rather, the role that the law, including the constitution, served was to channel and even to initiate open and vibrant political dialogue with horizontal and vertical separations of powers between various government branches, and more importantly, between the government and wider society. This mechanism is what we call the model of 'dialogic constitutionalism' in pandemic control.[10]

2. Controlling the Pandemic: Law, Healthcare, Technology and Society

As early as 31 December 2019, when the world was barely aware of COVID-19 as a deadly infectious disease, Taiwan's Centers for Disease Control (CDC) quickly detected it and imposed onboard inspections of all direct flights arriving from China's metropolitan city of Wuhan, the then epicentre. On 15 January 2020, the CDC declared COVID-19 as a Category 5 disease under the Communicable Disease Control Act (CDC Act) last amended in 2019.[11] On 20 January 2020, the

6 'Taiwan 2020nian GDP Changzhanglu 2.98%, Yikaifaguojia zui jia, 30 nian lai shoudu chaoyue China' [The 2.98 % GDP growth of Taiwan in 2020 is the best among the developed countries, exceeding China for the first time in 30 years] (*The News Lens*, 30 January 2021) <https://www.thenewslens.com/article/146741>.

7 Keoni Everington, 'Taiwan Sees Lowest Economic Impact from Coronavirus in World' (*Taiwan News*, 14 September 2020) <https://www.taiwannews.com.tw/en/news/4008495>.

8 Matthew Strong, 'Taiwan Think Tank Sees Economy Grow by 5.16% in 2021' (*Taiwan News*, 20 July 2021) <https://www.taiwannews.com.tw/en/news/4252914>.

9 The chapter draws on Wen-Chen Chang and Chun-Yuan Lin, 'Legislative/Judicial Deference Versus NGOs/Citizens Activism: Taiwan's Successful Fight against Covid-19' (*Verfassungsblog*, 21 April 2021) <https://verfassungsblog.de/legislative-judicial-deference-versus-ngos-citizens-activism-taiwans-successful-fight-against-covid-19/>.

10 For analysis of Taiwan's dialogic constitutionalism beyond judicial dialogue, see Jiunn-rong Yeh, *The Constitution of Taiwan: A Contextual Analysis* (Hart Publishing 2016).

11 Chunaranbing Fanzhi Fa [Communicable Disease Control Act].

Central Epidemic Command Center (Central Command or CECC)[12] was created to coordinate inter-agency efforts and provide for regulatory measures.

2.1 Legal Preparedness since SARS

Like all other laws involving technology governance, the CDC Act is filled with broad delegations to the Health Ministry and experts. One such provision, however, was challenged before the Constitutional Court after the 2003 SARS outbreak.[13] While upholding the constitutionality of the government's broad power, the Constitutional Court nevertheless instructed the legislature to provide further details, a time limit, and compensation for the restrictions. Accordingly, the revised CDC Act of 2003 incorporated some mechanisms for emergent public health events from the already appealed Temporary Act for Prevention and Relief for Severe Acute Respiratory Syndrome (SARS).

The current CDC Act authorises the government to create a Central Command and delegate it with broad power to quickly respond to an emergent public health event, including the power to expropriate or requisition private products, buildings, devices, facilities, pharmaceuticals and medical devices for disease control practices with adequate compensation.[14] Article 20 requires the government to prepare and stock a sufficient quantity of various pharmaceuticals, devices and protective equipment for communicable disease control. In addition, the CDC Act includes provisions against possible discrimination and human rights infringements in the name of disease control.[15] The legal framework balances the need for human rights protection with the government's need for legal and regulatory capacity in combating severe transmittable diseases, including bird flu, Zika virus, swine flu and, this time, COVID-19.

Aside from the CDC Act, the Special Act for Prevention, Relief, and Revitalization Measures for Severe Pneumonia with Novel Pathogens (Special COVID-19 Act) was enacted on 25 February 2020. The Special COVID-19 Act set a time limit of 15 January 2020 to 30 June 2021. Because the CDC Act already equipped the government with significant power for combating the pandemic, most provisions of the Special COVID-19 Act were enacted for relief, compensation and economic stimulus. Accordingly, a budget of TWD 60 billion (approximately US$2.15 billion or €1.84 billion) was authorised.

Two provisions of the Special COVID-19 Act, however, caused serious concern. The first was Article 7, which granted the Central Command the power to

12 Central Epidemic Command Center <https://covid19.mohw.gov.tw/en/cp-4771-53696-206.html>.

13 *JY Interpretation No. 690*, 30 September 2011, Constitutional Court, Judicial Yuan, ROC.

14 Article 17, 52-57 of the CDC Act.

15 Article 10 protects the privacy and information autonomy of patients and suspected patients. Article 11 emphasises the right to be respected and to non-discrimination of all patients, individuals under quarantine, and their families. Article 12 requires the government, civic groups, enterprises or individuals not to deny patients' rights to education, employment, nursing care or housing, or impose any other unfair treatment.

implement necessary measures for pandemic control. Unlike other provisions in the CDC Act, this provision granted a broad power subject only to necessity. Wary of criticism, the Central Command seldom referred to this provision, except for a travel ban issued to medical personnel.[16] The other controversial provision was Article 8, which gave the Central Command the power to release personal data if an individual violated a quarantine or isolation order. This was an exception to Articles 10 and 11 of the CDC Act, under which those having access to personal data are banned from disclosure. Facing mounting pressure from human rights groups, a clause was eventually added, requiring deletion of personal data at the end of pandemic according to the Personal Data Protection Act.[17]

2.2 The National Health Insurance System and Affordable Care

Taiwan's National Health Insurance (NHI) system provided the necessary infrastructure and capacity against the pandemic. Established in 1995, the NHI covers 99.6% of the population, including indigenous peoples, low-income families, persons with disabilities and even eligible foreigners, and provides high-quality medical services at affordable cost, making it one of the best in the world.[18] Affordable healthcare reduced the concerns of possible carriers seeking medical help and treatment and prevented widescale community transmission. The digital NHI database provided the infrastructure for coordination between medical institutions and inter-agency efforts. From the beginning of 2020, the NHI instructed all hospitals to impose compulsory temperature checks and a mask-wearing policy for anyone entering hospitals. Referring to Articles 31 and 32 of the CDC Act, which requires medical personnel to ask patients for their travel histories and personal contacts, and obliges patients to make full disclosure, the CECC further integrated the NHI database and the immigration database in February 2020 to allow medical personnel to be instantly informed of the travel histories of their patients. If a patient had a travel history in the previous 14 days, the integrated database would notify the doctors. This measure proved effective in protecting medical personnel and substantially reducing the risk of infection in medical facilities. It also facilitated the work of contact tracing, orders for quarantine and the later process of vaccination.

The NHI continued to facilitate testing and vaccination after the outbreak in May 2021. However, the sudden increased need for testing and treatment overwhelmed the capacity of the health system. The limited nursing staff delayed test-

16 Ministry of Health and Welfare, 'Fangyi Qijian Yiyuan Yishirenyuan ji Shegong Chuguo yu Xiangguan Buchang Guiding' [Rules of compensation for medical personnel and social workers during the pandemic] (27 May 2020) <https://www.mohw.gov.tw/cp-16-51720-1.html>.

17 Yenzhong Teshu Chunaranxing Feiyen Fanzhi Ji Shukun Zhenxing Tebie Tiaoli [Special Act for Prevention, Relief and Revitalization Measures for Severe Pneumonia with Novel Pathogens], art 8 cl 3 ('Special Act').

18 Sophie Ireland, 'Revealed: Countries with The Best Health Care Systems 2021' (*CEOWORLD Magazine*, 27 April 2021) <https://ceoworld.biz/2019/08/05/revealed-countries-with-the-best-health-care-systems-2019/>.

ing and vaccination and the shortage of hospital beds resulted in delayed treatment of COVID-19 patients. The mounting pressure under the sudden outbreak also exposed the long existing problems of nurses' working conditions and inadequate pay.[19] These factors triggered an exodus of nurses from the profession in Taiwan, exacerbating the shortage of medical personnel.

2.3 Digital Technology and its Cautious Application

Digital technology was used to facilitate government enforcement of regulatory measures and reduce compliance costs.[20] Yet because such technology raises privacy concerns, the government was cautious in its use.

The application of digital technology facilitated border control and resource distribution. On 3 February 2020, the government took precautionary measures to ensure a sustainable supply of medical resources for the general public. The minister of the economy and the vice premier coordinated key manufacturers to collaborate on mask production according to Article 54 of the CDC Act. In order to ensure a sustainable and fair supply for all citizens, the authority used the NHI MediCloud database to enable a personalised 'real-name' distribution system of face-masks on 6 February.[21] An app developed by a citizen engineer revealing the available number of face-masks around Taiwan inspired the digital minister, who later scaled up the system to increase its fairness and efficiency in distributing face-masks and other medical supplies.[22] Owing to this system, while other countries faced a severe shortage of masks and other medical equipment, Taiwan's supplies steadily increased. This system also facilitated the tracing of confirmed patients or patients with suspected symptoms based on their travel histories and contact information.

Digital technology was also used to ensure compliance with COVID-19 regulatory measures.[23] In mid-March 2020, an 'electronic fence' system started to track

19 Han Cheung, 'Taiwan's Nursing Conditions in Poor State of Health' (*Taipei Times*, 21 July 2020) <https://www.taipeitimes.com/News/feat/archives/2020/07/21/2003740278>.

20 See, for example, Jobie Budd and others, 'Digital Technologies in the Public-Health Response to COVID-19' (2020) 26 Nature Medicine 1183; Sara Gerke and others, 'Regulatory, Safety, and Privacy Concerns of Home Monitoring Technologies during COVID-19' (2020) 26 Nature Medicine 1176.

21 In 2013, the National Health Insurance Administration had installed the MediCloud system to electronically store medical records to improve data transfer efficiency for decentralised health-care providers. All persons, including foreigners with an identification card or visa, could get masks at a reasonably low price at authorised pharmacies, health centres and convenience stores; Taiwan Centers for Disease Control (6 February 2020) <https://www.mohw.gov.tw/cp-16-51370-1.html>.

22 Yeh Su-ping and Chiang Yi-ching, 'Japanese Media Praises Taiwan Minister for COVID-19 Prevention Efforts' (*Central News Agency*, 1 March 2020) <https://focustaiwan.tw/politics/202003010004>.

23 Andreas Kluth, 'If We Must Build a Surveillance State, Let's Do It Properly' (*Bloomberg Opinion*, 22 April 2020) <https://www.bloomberg.com/opinion/articles/2020-04-22/taiwan-offers-the-best-model-for-coronavirus-data-tracking>; Ravi Aron, 'Combating COVID-19: Lessons from

quarantined people through mobile phone signals to ensure they remained in designated places. In order to accommodate privacy concerns, this system did not disclose personal information unless and until an individual violated the quarantine or isolation order. When isolated or quarantined individuals left their designated shelter locations or turned off their mobile devices, the system would notify the police, civil and health authorities. To reduce privacy concerns, the system disclosed the name, phone number and address of the violators only to the first responder. On 1 April 2020, the Central Command deployed cell broadcasting technology to alert people in a crowded area of the risk of potential exposure. Relying on the cell tower data, the cell broadcasting system disclosed no personal data in order to fulfill the requirement of Article 10 of the CDC Act.[24]

The government used digital technology again to increase people's compliance to control the outbreak in May 2021. When the level 3 alert was imposed, the Central Command required everyone to register when entering stores and public agencies. In order to reduce the cost of compliance and the risk of infection, the digital minister developed a real-name mobile messaging system on 19 May 2021 to simplify the process of providing contact information.[25] People scanned QR codes and sent the code of the location to the system through a message without disclosing their name or mobile phone number to the store. Telecom providers collected and stored the information and deleted it after 28 days.[26] When information derived from the mobile message system was allegedly to be misused for criminal investigation by the police, the Central Command soon determined that all information should be used for contact tracing only.[27]

2.4 Social Solidarity and Civil Society

Previous public health crises, including the SARS outbreak in 2003, motivated Taiwanese society to foster a sense of interdependence against transmittable diseases.[28] This social foundation successfully mobilised the public to comply with the law and participate in collective efforts to prevent COVID-19 transmission. Taiwanese society displayed great moral conviction regarding mutual protection

Singapore, South Korea and Taiwan' (*Knowledge*, 21 April 2020)<https://knowledge.wharton.upenn.edu/article/singapore-south_korea-taiwan-used-technology-combat-covid-19/>.

24 Chi-Mai Chen and others, 'Containing COVID-19 Among 627,386 Persons in Contact With the Diamond Princess Cruise Ship Passengers Who Disembarked in Taiwan: Big Data Analytics' (2020) 22(5) Journal of Medical Internet Research e19540.

25 Keoni Everington, 'Taiwan Launches New QR Code for Real-Name Registration System' (*Taiwan News*, 19 May 2021) <https://www.taiwannews.com.tw/en/news/4206312>.

26 'Taiwan Launches Mobile Message Service for Contact Tracing' (*Focus Taiwan*, 19 May 2021) <https://focustaiwan.tw/sci-tech/202105190014>.

27 Shelley Shan, 'COVID-19: SMS System Not Used by Police' (*Taipei Times*, 22 June 2021) <https://www.taipeitimes.com/News/taiwan/archives/2021/06/22/2003759599>.

28 Ming-Cheng M Lo and Hsin-Yi Hsieh, 'The "Societalization" of Pandemic Unpreparedness: Lessons from Taiwan's COVID Response' (19 September 2020) American Journal of Cultural Sociology 1 <https://doi.org/10.1057/s41290-020-00113-y>.

and generated a sense of an 'epidemic-proof' community in which no one was an outsider. While the mandate of mask-wearing encountered resistance in the US and some European countries, Taiwanese people generally see hand-washing, mask-wearing and exercising precautions in public and private gatherings as part of a civic duty during the pandemic. Local organisations actively participated in the network of implementing quarantine orders, disseminating information to residents and supporting people under isolation or quarantine orders.[29] Citizens also collected supplies for medical personnel when surgical masks were in short supply.[30]

Civic cooperation would not have continued without public trust in decision-making processes and authority; the transparency of the Central Command contributed to the shaping of social solidarity.[31] In addition, it also actively sought to mitigate social cleavage by emphasising the importance of equal protection and inclusion. For example, Health Minister Chen urged the public to stop witch-hunting carriers, saying, "our enemy is not the person, but the virus".[32]

Yet, as the experience of other countries showed, existing social inequalities worsened during the pandemic.[33] Taiwan did not escape this phenomenon. Because the May 2021 outbreak started in local sex teahouses in the Wanhua district of Taipei, the communities of sex workers, migrants, the homeless and older people were blamed and stigmatised.[34] Several scandals of privileged access to vaccination also invited severe criticism from the public.[35] These cleavages became the vulnerable spot for the virus spreading and undermined the otherwise strong social solidarity against the pandemic.

3. Controlling Power: Checks and Balances with Dialogue

The expansion and concentration of administrative power inevitably raised concerns about the rule of law. While legislative delegation and judicial deference

29 Chang-Ching Fu, 'Lessons from Taiwan's Experience of Covid-19' (*Atlantic Council*, 7 April 2020) <https://www.atlanticcouncil.org/blogs/new-atlanticist/lessons-from-taiwans-experience-with-covid-19/>.

30 Hsu Jen-hui, 'People Come Together to Overcome Mask Crisis' (*Taipei Times*, 20 February 2020) <http://www.taipeitimes.com/News/editorials/archives/2020/02/20/2003731291>.

31 On the importance of public trust, see Jasanoff and Hilgartner, chapter 23.

32 'Taiwan Health Minister Urges the Public to Stop "Witch-Hunting" Virus Patients' (*Taiwan News*, 20 April 2020) <https://www.taiwannews.com.tw/en/news/3919283>.

33 Faheem Ahmed, Na'eem Ahmed and others, 'Why Inequality Could Spread COVID-19' (2020) 5(5) The Lancet e240 <https://doi.org/10.1016/S2468-2667(20)30085-2>; Beckie Malay and Pradeep Baisakh, *Impact of COVID-19 Pandemic on Inequalities in Asia* (Global Call to Action against Poverty 2020) <https://gcap.global/wp-content/uploads/2020/11/Impact-of-COVID-19-on-Inequalities-in-Asia-GCAP-11-Nov.pdf>.

34 Cheng Ming-hsiang and Jake Chung, 'Sex Worker Advocacy Blasts "Discrimination"' (*Taipei Times*, 21 May 2021) <https://www.taipeitimes.com/News/taiwan/archives/2021/05/21/2003757790>.

35 Jason Pan, 'Good Liver Clinic's "Jab Hookup" Probed' (*Taipei Times*, 11 June 2021) <https://www.taipeitimes.com/News/taiwan/archives/2021/06/11/2003758987>.

risked weakening the constitutional function of checks and balances, the dynamics between the different levels of government, and between the government and society, contributed to a dialogical process that ensured the accountability of decision-makers and led to better regulatory solutions.

3.1 Legislative Delegation and Oversight

The legal framework established in the CDC Act and later the Special COVID-19 Act enabled the government's swift and effective response through broad legislative delegation. While adopting less stringent ex ante scrutiny for legal vagueness and explicit authorisation, Taiwan attempted to balance this approach with ex post legislative oversight. To increase the level of congressional oversight, Article 18 of the Special COVID-19 Act[36] requires the government to issue a written report three months after promulgation and the premier to report to the legislature in person about the pandemic situation and extraordinary budget expenditure after six months. It also requires a dedicated government website[37] for updated information on relevant laws, regulations or government orders.

Accordingly, in April and September 2020, Premier Tseng-Chang Su reported to the legislature on the COVID-19 special budget and updates, and on 8 June 2021 he delivered his most recent report to date before the legislature, including on the progress of vaccination. On 24 March 2021, initiated by the main opposition KMT party, the legislature passed a resolution to authorise the forming of an inspection committee to acquire all relevant documents concerning vaccination procurement.[38] Despite these efforts, legislative oversight remained weak because the majority of the legislature belongs to the same Democratic Progressive Party as the executive branch.

3.2 Judicial Deference

Regulatory measures for pandemic control, including inspection, contact-tracing, quarantine and inbound and outbound travel restrictions, inevitably raised human rights concerns. Of particular note was the strict imposition of 14-day quarantine on those thought to be infected or those – nationals and non-nationals alike – entering into Taiwan from the countries listed on the Travel Notice announced by the CDC. Those under quarantine orders were required to report their health status to the local health authority regularly. Non-compliance with quarantine orders was subject to civil penalties. Although compensation was provided for quarantined individuals who did not receive a salary or other subsidies, 14-day quarantine

36 Special Act (n 17) art 18.

37 Ministry of Health and Welfare, 'Crucial Policies for Combating COVID-19' <https://covid19.mohw.gov.tw/en/mp-206.html>.

38 'LiYuan Chengli Yimiao Caigou Diaoyue Xiaozu, Chen Shih-Chung: ZunZhong' [The legislature established an inspection committee on vaccination procurement, Chen Shih-chung: respect] (*NOWnews*, 24 March 2021) <https://www.nownews.com/news/5220401>.

orders were undoubtedly a substantial restriction of personal freedom guaranteed by Article 8 of the Constitution, a core fundamental right whose protection was extended to non-nationals by the Constitutional Court in *JY Interpretation No 708*.[39] The use of digital technology in monitoring compliance also raised concerns about privacy and personal data protection.

There have to date been several judicial challenges to these quarantine orders or the imposition of civil penalties. None of these challenges, however, succeeded in the courts. For example, the first habeas corpus challenge was brought in August 2020 by an individual returning from Hong Kong, arguing that the quarantine order was illegal as it was not imposed in compliance with the due process guaranteed by Article 8 of the Constitution[40] and the 2014 Habeas Corpus Act.[41] The District Court dismissed the challenge, and the Taiwan High Court sustained the dismissal.[42] Another habeas corpus challenge was brought in December 2020 by an individual who was confirmed with COVID-19 infection and quarantined in a hospital, arguing that the requirement of consecutive negative RT-PCR tests for release from hospital was too stringent and hence the resulting extension of quarantine for more than 30 days was unnecessary and illegal. Again, the challenge was not accepted by the court.[43] Most other challenges were made to civil penalties imposed for violating quarantine orders, and none succeeded.

Detained foreign nationals brought other judicial challenges pending deportation. By the Constitutional Court decision in *JY Interpretation No 708*, a foreign national facing deportation and being temporarily detained was given the right to seek judicial redress. In May 2020, a migrant worker pending deportation to Vietnam challenged his temporary detention order that had been extended due to the pandemic. He argued for release from the detention centre pending his deportation as the crowded situation in the centre increased his risk of infection. Having balanced all relevant factors, including the detention centre's hygiene measures, the court denied the request. Other similar requests were also rejected.[44]

Also noteworthy are criminal sanctions for spreading pandemic misinformation. Both Article 14 of the Special COVID-19 Act and Article 63 of the CDC Act impose criminal penalties, including fines of up to TWD 3 million (approximately US$108,000 or €91,760) on those who disseminate rumours or incorrect information concerning epidemic conditions or communicable diseases that result in damages to the public or others. There have been quite a number of cases regarding pandemic misinformation, and expectedly, judicial deference to such criminal prosecutions is also generously provided.

39 *JY Interpretation No. 708*, 6 February 2013, Constitutional Court, Judicial Yuan, ROC.
40 Constitution of the Republic of China (Taiwan), art 8.
41 Tisheng Fa [Habeas Corpus Act].
42 Gaodeng Fayuan [Taiwan High Court] 31 August 2020, Minguo 109 (Kang) No. 1425 Criminal Ruling.
43 Taibei Difang Fayuan [Taiwan Taipei District Court] 12 January 2021, Minguo 110 (Ti) No. 1 Ruling.
44 Hsinchu Difang Fayuan [Taiwan Hsinchu District Court] 13 May 2020, Minguo 109 (Yi) No. 3 Ruling.

Several opposition politicians brought a case after the May 2021 wave of infection, arguing that the Central Command was legally obliged to provide sufficient vaccines to them and the public. The court rejected the case and held that the plaintiffs had no public right and legal basis for requiring such an obligation.[45]

In sum, the courts in Taiwan were restrained in not finding COVID-19 measures illegal and deferring discretion to the competent authorities. This judicial deference is understandable in the COVID-19 context; however, courts should carefully examine each case and explain their underlying reasoning to the relevant agencies and the public.

3.3 Power Dynamics Between Central and Local Governments

As global experience showed, the pandemic frequently triggered tension between central and local governments. On the one hand, centralised power may deliver more consistent policies and mobilise resources. On the other hand, local governments were on the frontline of the crisis and required more discretion to deal with reality on the ground. At the start of the pandemic, the Central Command enjoyed the highest power in coordinating the efforts against a pandemic based on s 3, article 37 of the CDC Act. Local governments could adopt measures different from the Central Command, yet they eventually adjusted such measures when the Central Command dissented. For example, the health bureau of Chang-Hua County had conducted undisclosed general testing during the first wave of the pandemic and contradicted the Central Command's decision not to carry out general testing. While some epidemiologists supported the measure, the testing, as a part of a government-funded research project, failed to undergo the proper review process and raised ethical concerns.[46] The testing was subsequently suspended on the ground that it violated the 2016 Human Subjects Research Act.

When the May 2021 outbreak challenged the capacity of the Central Command, it authorised the city and county authorities to disclose the tracing of confirmed cases under pressure from local governments. This delegation empowered local competence to challenge the authority of the Central Command and also created political competition for the best practice, enhancing checks and balances between central and local governments.

Local governments had voiced their dissent against the Central Command. Some required more discretion and resources, and some demanded more precise rules and procedures. These voices pushed the Central Command to coordinate with local authorities and to adjust its measures. When the level 3 alert was declared, the Central Command held a National Epidemic Prevention Meeting with city and county governments on 21 May 2021 to coordinate regulatory

45 Taipei High Administrative Court, Szuzi 110, No. 623 Ruling.

46 'Taiwan's Changhua Conducted Undisclosed Coronavirus Tests for Six Months: CECC' (*Taiwan News*, 20 August 2020) <https://www.taiwannews.com.tw/en/news/3991295>.

measures and the distribution of testing resources.[47] Another example was Kinmen County's policy of imposing mandatory COVID-19 testing on all passengers entering the island. The central command revoked the order based on article 37 of the CDC Act. Yet considering the limited medical resources of this outlying island, the Central Command then compromised by agreeing to test all passengers in the main island's airports before they flew to outlying islands.[48]

The dialectical process also prevented local governments from abusing their power. When the Miaoli County government prohibited all migrant workers from leaving their dormitories, the Central Command urged it to follow the rules of the level 3 alert and facilitated testing to lift the controversial ban.[49]

In addition, competition among local governments also became a mechanism to check each other's power. The genuine effort of local governments, such as hotspot general-testing in New Taipei City, created a feedback loop to the central and other local governments to expand their own testing. Competition between local governments for more efficient vaccination also initiated a process of mutual learning.

In dealing with the rapid spread of the pandemic, different levels of government embody different merits and limits. Centralised power may better coordinate policies and mobilise resources on a large scale, yet be incapable of dealing with a sudden outbreak. Local delegation may better cope with local variations and mobilise local resources, yet fragmented implementation may result in unequal treatment and inconsistency. In the face of the pandemic, neither central nor local government alone guaranteed the best policy. The dialectical process between different levels of government in Taiwan suggested an alternative approach to create accountability and compete for better coordination. Fortunately, with no major election to be held in 2021, the dialectical process was not overly politicised so as to undermine rational deliberation.

3.4 Open and Transparent Public Dialogue

As previously mentioned, human rights NGOs were active in voicing concerns about legislative and regulatory measures. It was due to their persistence that the deletion of relevant personal data and the security of data transmission were promised and eventually written into law.[50] In another instance, when the

47 Centers for Disease Control, 'National Epidemic Prevention Meeting Report at Morning Press Conference on 21 May' (21 May 2021)<https://www.cdc.gov.tw/En/Bulletin/Detail/V5_1p7SPS5FJ9vt9WzmXRA?typeid=158>.

48 Matthew Strong, 'Compulsory COVID Tests at Airports on Taiwan's Outlying Islands Are Illegal: CECC' (*Taiwan News*, 1 June 2021) <https://www.taiwannews.com.tw/en/news/4214233>.

49 Centers for Disease Control, 'In response to cluster infections in electronics factories in Miaoli County, CECC provides details about COVID-19 control measures adopted by incident command post' (6 June 2021) <https://www.cdc.gov.tw/En/Bulletin/Detail/SQeL9I-JHXpfZRWt1haipg?typeid=158>.

50 Special Act (n 17).

Central Command required all inbound passengers, including nationals, to provide an RT-PCR test report before arriving at airports in Taiwan, NGOs and human rights lawyers – citing one's fundamental right to return home – successfully pushed the Central Command to make changes overnight.[51]

The existence of a vibrant civil society also contributed to a more transparent and responsive decision-making process. Primarily consisting of medical professionals, the Central Command was keenly aware of the importance of maintaining public trust and democratic accountability in a pandemic. It held daily live-broadcast press conferences to provide updates on the pandemic to dispel fake news and misinformation from the day it was established.[52] In addition, the Central Command made its decision-making process transparent, evidenced-based and open to public scrutiny, taking as many questions as possible from journalists and reporters. All relevant information on COVID-19 can be quickly verified with supporting materials on the official website. Transparent and accurate information worked as an effective method of minimising public panic in the face of uncertainty.[53]

Civil society activism further pushed the Central Command to reduce possible infringements from the public and private sphere. For example, as the first confirmed case of an illegal migrant worker was reported, the Ministry of Labour was ready to expel illegal migrant workers to prevent a possible loophole under public criticism. At the press conference, the Central Command reminded the public of the contributions of migrant workers to Taiwan's healthcare system, and the negative impact that harsh enforcement policies had on illegal migrant workers and on pandemic control.[54]

Taiwan's vibrant civil society has thus been a crucial counterbalance to government power, weakening the tendency of power concentration that has been seen in other countries where democratic backsliding or authoritarian governance was

51 The right of returning home has been recognised by the Constitutional Court as a constitutional right. See JY Interpretation No. 558 (official English translation)<https://cons.judicial.gov.tw/jcc/en-us/jep03/show?expno=558>. Huang Guo su, Guoren Fantai Wu Yinxingzhengming [Returning Taiwanese nationals may sign affidavit to replace a negative RT-PCR testing record] (*Mandarin Daily News*, 1 December 2020)<https://www.mdnkids.com/search_content.asp?Serial_NO=%20118852>.

52 Victor Pu, 'The Coronavirus Outbreak: How Democratic Taiwan Outperformed Authoritarian China' (*The Diplomat*, 27 February 2020)<https://thediplomat.com/2020/02/the-coronavirus-outbreak-how-democratic-taiwan-outperformed-authoritarian-china>; Jaron Lanier and EG Weyl, 'How Civic Technology Can Help Stop a Pandemic' (*Foreign Affairs*, 20 March 2020)<https://www.foreignaffairs.com/articles/asia/2020-03-20/how-civic-technology-can-help-stop-pandemic>.

53 Sean Lin, 'Virus Outbreak: Supplies of Food, Daily Necessities Sufficient' (*Taipei Times*, 21 March 2020) <https://www.taipeitimes.com/News/taiwan/archives/2020/03/21/2003733109>.

54 Ming-cheng Lo, 'Taiwan's State and its Lessons for Effective Epidemic Intervention' (*Contexts*, 25 March 2020) <https://contexts.org/blog/the-global-coronavirus-epidemic-commentary-on-east-asias-response/?fbclid=IwAR0StexTlroZ7c3lOBGFo68U8i7EhDuqtEmiVsHn8MXyFYIbEUJO9foczLY#lo>.

revived in the name of pandemic control.[55] Although extraterritorially produced disinformation attempted at undermining public trust in the wake of the sudden outbreak in May 2021, the Central Command continued to rely on open and transparent dialogues with reasoned responses, in addition to investigating disinformation.[56]

4. Conclusion

The COVID-19 pandemic turned the world upside down – and effective legal and regulatory responses required innovation. In Taiwan, the key to preventing tyranny in pandemic control was a transparent and responsive political process in which citizen activism was crucial.

Notwithstanding its broad legislative delegation and judicial deference to regulatory restrictions, the CECC was keenly aware of the importance of maintaining public trust and shouldering democratic accountability during the pandemic. Taiwan's experience suggested a new model of democratic legitimacy for pandemic governance, a model we call pandemic control with dialogic constitutionalism. While broad legislative delegation and judicial deference may not serve as sufficient constitutional checks and balances, and risk human rights violations, NGO and citizen activism form a critical counterbalancing power and may provide a means of counterbalancing the worst aspects of 'pandemocracy'.

55 See Jonathan Schwartz, 'Compensating for the "Authoritarian Advantage" in Crisis Response: A Comparative Case Study of SARS Pandemic Responses in China and Taiwan' (2012) 17(3) Journal of Chinese Political Science 313.

56 'Fake News Alert: Taiwan Fights Disinformation as COVID Surges' (*Al Jazeera*, 28 May 2021) <https://www.aljazeera.com/news/2021/5/28/disinformation-goes-viral-as-taiwan-battles-new-covid-surge>; Matthew Strong, 'Taiwan Investigates 144 People for Fake News About COVID Outbreak' (*Taiwan News*, 4 June 2021) <https://www.taiwannews.com.tw/en/news/4216214>.

26

PUBLIC HEALTH, TECHNOLOGY AND SOCIAL CONTEXT IN RWANDA'S COVID-19 RESPONSE

Denis Bikesha and Allan T Moore

1. Introduction[1]

Rwanda is a small, landlocked country in central-east Africa with a hybrid legal system including elements of civil law, common law and customary law.[2] This makes Rwanda an interesting case study when considering emergencies such as the COVID-19 pandemic, as it has the potential to draw on a wide range of potential legal responses that nations with more fixed legal traditions may not consider appropriate, including a combination of codified provision, case precedent and modernised indigenous mechanisms.

As of 27 July 2021, Rwanda is recorded as being in the top quarter of countries in terms of lowest confirmed COVID-19 deaths per capita (45th out of 181 countries), with a record comparable to or better than nations in the region including Uganda, Somalia, Sudan and Malawi, and far better than many high-income countries.[3]

Section 2 of this chapter outlines Rwanda's initial response to COVID-19, where themes of prior experience of epidemic preparedness, public health and use of technology become evident. Section 3 examines the legitimacy of the use of executive powers in creating and implementing measures that are enforceable against the Rwandan population. In Rwanda there has been devolution of powers to deal with COVID-19 to the regional and local level, in keeping with constitutional provisions, and section 4 discusses these provisions and their legal basis.

1 All websites accessed on 27 July 2021.

2 Jean-Marie Kamatali, *Introduction to Rwandan Law* (Routledge 2020) 13–14.

3 Johns Hopkins University, Coronavirus Resource Center, Mortality Analyses <https://coronavirus.jhu.edu/data/mortality>.

 DOI: 10.4324/9781003211952-30

Section 5 analyses the human rights implications of the COVID-19 response with a focus on the balance between fulfilling state obligations to protect the lives and health of the population at the expense of restricting other rights. In section 6, a snapshot is provided of the use of technology in Rwanda's pandemic response, while section 7 explores the historical, social and political context, without which Rwanda's COVID-19 response is unlikely to have been as successful as it was. Section 8 concludes with insights from Rwanda's relative success for other states.

2. Overview of the Legal and Political Response and Adaptation to COVID-19

As awareness increased globally regarding a pandemic spreading at pace in early 2020, the Rwandan authorities were able to draw upon previous experience in response to epidemics such as the Ebola virus disease. In late January 2020, nearly two months before the first COVID-19 case was confirmed in Rwanda, the government introduced thermal scanning of all travellers entering the country through airports or land borders, with healthcare workers documenting information and travel history related to any suspected cases.[4] Already at this preliminary stage, then, there were indications of three intersecting themes: the pre-existing context (the Ebola epidemic); the use of executive powers (the specific approach being ordered by the government); and technology (the use of thermal scanners for early detection). All three of these themes continued to be crucial in Rwanda's COVID-19 response.

The authorities' clear awareness of the potential severity of the virus was shown when, in February 2020, one of Rwanda's most modern health centres, in Kanyinya on the outskirts of Kigali, was pre-emptively converted to become a COVID-19 treatment centre.[5] Subsequently, one of Kigali's largest hotels was similarly repurposed and all 80 of Rwanda's public hospitals were required to prepare isolation rooms for any suspected cases of COVID-19.[6]

As the situation escalated globally during March 2020, clarification was made that Rwanda's strategic response would primarily be driven by the executive with three ministerial departments explicitly named – the Office of the Prime Minister, the Ministry of Health, and the Ministry of Local Government. However, it was not confirmed whether it was envisaged that the response would be purely one of general policy or of binding law. A joint taskforce was established[7] and Rwanda's 'National Preparedness and Response Plan, March–August 2020' was published by the Rwanda

4 Elizabeth Farah Louis and others, 'Rwanda's Response During COVID-19' (2020) 12(5) Psychological Trauma: Theory, Research, Practice, and Policy 565; James Ngamije and Callixte Yadufashije, 'COVID-19 Pandemic in Rwanda: An Overview of Prevention Strategies' (2020) 13(8) Asian Pacific Journal of Tropical Medicine 333.

5 Naz Karim, 'Lessons Learned from Rwanda: Innovative Strategies for Prevention and Containment of COVID-19' (2021) 87(1) 23 Annals of Global Health 3.

6 ibid.

7 ibid 2.

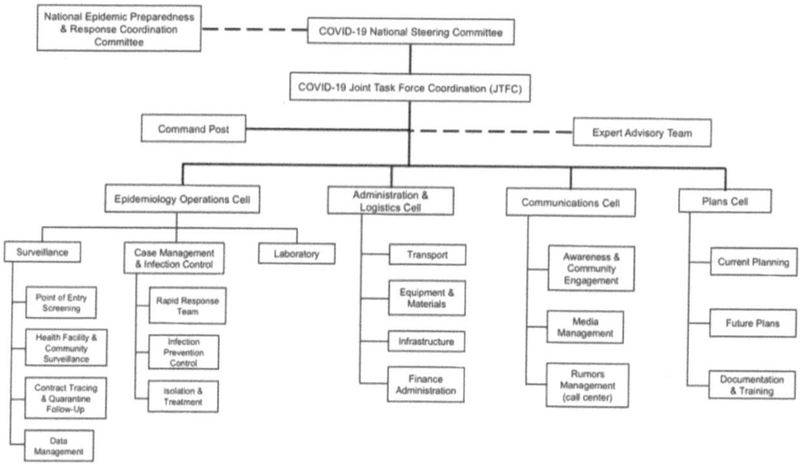

Figure 26.1 Rwanda COVID-19 Incident Management System Coordination Structure. ibid 5.

Biomedical Centre, listed as being a joint publication of the Centre and the Ministry of Health.[8] It was here that Rwanda's COVID-19 response was comprehensively outlined. A vertical hierarchy was established, with a National Steering Committee at the highest point and a Joint Taskforce reporting to the Committee. The activities of the taskforce were divided into four key strands; 'Epidemiology Operations', 'Administration and Logistics', 'Communications' and 'Plans', and within each strand there was a set of activities and responsibilities listed (see Figure 26.1).[9]

On 14 March 2020, the first case of COVID-19 was confirmed in Rwanda.[10] President Paul Kagame tweeted that: "… panic in this situation does not help. Focus and simple but effective measures are key to keeping each other and everyone safe".[11] A cabinet communiqué on 1 April announced that, with the exception of those providing essential services, "All employees (public and private) shall continue to use technology to work from home";[12] that "Electronic payments and online banking services should be used whenever possible";[13] and, crucially in the context of this chapter, that "The minister for ICT and Innovation briefed cabinet about technology tools being used in the fight against COVID-19 and available

8 Daniel M Ngamije and Sabin Nsanzimana, 'Coronavirus Disease 2019, National Preparedness and Response Plan March – August 2020' (2020) Rwanda Biomedical Centre and Rwanda Ministry of Health.

9 ibid 5.

10 World Health Organisation (Rwanda), 'First Case of COVID-19 Confirmed in Rwanda' (15 March 2020) <https://www.afro.who.int/news/first-case-covid-19-confirmed-rwanda>.

11 President Paul Kagame (*Twitter*, 14 March 2020) <https://twitter.com/PaulKagame/status/1238803616544239618>.

12 Prime Minister Edouard Ngirente, Cabinet communiqué, 1 April 2020 3 (e).

13 ibid 3 (l).

e-learning tools for education".[14] Evidently, then, the Rwandan executive had planned from the early stages of the pandemic for technology to form a core element of their public policy response.

The evidence was strengthened as communiqués established at the end of April that mass screening and testing was to be expanded nationwide.[15] As identified by Musanabaganwa and others, individuals were screened for symptoms and provided samples on the spot and then received their results via text message within eight to 24 hours,[16] arguably exceeding the technological response that many more developed countries implemented at the same stage. Here, the intersection between public policy, science and technology is clear. Indeed, as Musanabaganwa and others argue, any suggestion that Rwanda's comparatively low number of COVID-19 cases might have been due to cases being missed or overlooked is unsustainable, given not only the systematic testing of suspected cases, but also extensive random community sampling.[17]

3. The Executive and the Use of Powers in Response to Emergency

Rwanda's key responses to the COVID-19 pandemic were developed and communicated by the executive rather than the legislature. As characterised by Binagwaho, on the day that the first confirmed COVID-19 case emerged in March 2020 "the government rapidly responded without waiting for a second case to emerge. Immediately, systematic contact tracing and testing were conducted, and the country implemented a national lock-down the following day."[18] These measures were compulsory, binding and enforceable.[19] Whilst the requirement for such enforceable provisions to be scrutinised by a legislature would ordinarily be expected, this ordinary process does not lend itself to emergency situations, where a delay of even a few days has been shown to result in exponentially increasing levels of risk. As such, the rapid nature of the executive response was arguably justified.

Importantly, however, the question remains of whether or not there was a pre-existing legal basis for such use of executive powers in Rwanda. On examination of the 2003 Constitution of the Republic of Rwanda as amended in 2015, Article 61 provides for a formal separation of powers between the legislature, executive and judiciary, and outlines that the "three branches are separate and independent from each other but are all complementary".[20] Like many constitutions, there are existing provisions that allow for unusual circumstances to provide a basis for laws

14 ibid 5.

15 Prime Minister Edouard Ngirente, Cabinet communiqué, 30 April 2020 4 (a).

16 Clarisse Musanabaganwa and others, 'One Hundred Thirty-Three Observed COVID-19 Deaths in 10 Months: Unpacking Lower than Predicted Mortality in Rwanda' (2021) 6 BMJ Global Health e004547 2.

17 ibid.

18 Agnes Binagwaho, 'We Need Compassionate Leadership Management Based on Evidence to Defeat COVID-19' (2020) 9(10) International Journal of Health Policy Management 413.

19 ibid 414.

20 Rwanda's Constitution of 2003 with Amendments through 2015, Art 61.

to be created at the executive level. For example, Article 108 gives authority for the President to declare war, siege or a state of emergency, and Article 112 allows for the creation and implementation of presidential orders if approved by the cabinet. Further, Article 92 provides for presidential decrees to be adopted and given the same legal standing as an ordinary law if the Parliament is unable to sit. Thus, several constitutional routes can give a legal basis for binding executive action to be implemented complementary to, or in replacement of, the ordinary legislative process.

Beyond the technical details, there are also cultural provisions within Rwanda's Constitution that could be argued to apply to the COVID-19 context, particularly as contained in Article 11, which states that "Rwandans, based on their values, initiate home-grown mechanisms to deal with matters that concern them"[21] and that "Laws may establish different mechanisms for home-grown solutions".[22]

Of further importance, Article 3 of the Constitution provides that, "The Constitution is the supreme law of the country"[23] and Article 95 clarifies explicitly that international treaties or agreements are placed third in a hierarchy behind organic law and – of highest importance – the Constitution itself. There is no room for ambiguity if laws in different positions of the hierarchy come into conflict, as Article 95 states that "a law cannot contradict another law that is higher in hierarchy".[24] As such, any external principles or international obligations would be held to be of secondary consideration under Rwandan law unless enshrined under the terms of Article 168, which gives force of law to such agreements. The practical effect here is that if an international law comes into conflict with an organic law or a provision from within Rwanda's constitution, then the latter two would be upheld by a Rwandan court over the former.

4. Regional and Local Responses

Rwanda has a system of devolving aspects of law to the regional or local level. This is necessary as only 17% of the population live in an urban setting, with 83% still living and working in rural locations.[25] The legal basis for such devolution of powers is found in Article 6 of the Constitution, which notes that "Public powers are decentralised at local administrative entities in accordance with provisions of law".[26] One such law is found in Article 9 of the law governing the City of Kigali, which provides that the Council of the City of Kigali is "responsible for taking decisions, putting in place strategies and issuing instructions on administrative sanctions to be imposed on those who fail to comply with regulations of the

21 ibid Art 11.
22 ibid.
23 ibid Art 3.
24 ibid Art 95.
25 Karim (n 4).
26 Rwanda's Constitution of 2003 with Amendments through 2015, Art 6.

Council in accordance with the law".[27] Since population density may exacerbate a public health problem, affecting certain areas more than others, it is unsurprising that provisions may vary across the country, in keeping with principles of decentralisation.

The City of Kigali Council implemented its own administrative measures to allow for sanctions to be taken against individuals observed to have contravened national guidelines on lockdown, curfew, social distancing, or any other instruction. On 31 August 2020, the Council issued the first enforceable instructions orienting the public on what specific administrative sanctions could be taken against any person that breached the guidelines.[28] The measures were questionable in three respects. First, referring to the instructions themselves, there is arguably no legal basis for the Council to issue instructions of the specific nature of the ones created. The Council, in Article 1 of its developed instructions, provides that the aim is to sanction persons who do not comply with measures developed *by the Government of Rwanda*. However, according to Article 9 of the law governing the City of Kigali as discussed previously, the Council only has existing competence to sanction those who do not comply with *their own* regulations. To the best of the authors' knowledge, the Council has not issued city-specific COVID-19 regulations; thus, issuing sanctions on measures created by *the government* is not within its legal mandate.

Second, among the sanctions included in the Kigali City measures there are *ibindi bihano bishobora kwiyongera ku ihazabu* (additional sanctions to a fine). The instructions provide that a person who has not complied with the government's pandemic measures may be taken to an identified place for up to 24 hours and be given 'civic knowledge' on COVID-19 prevention. This is comparable to the detention of a person who is suspected of committing a criminal offence, yet again the Council does not have a legal mandate to issue such sanctions. As discussed below in the context of human rights considerations, Article 24 of the Constitution stipulates that no one shall be detained unless provided for *by the law in force* at the time the offence was committed, while Article 29 provides that no one shall be detained on account of any act that *does not constitute an offence* (emphasis added). In the case of the existing COVID-19 guidance, it can be argued that the government measures are not tantamount to an offence since they do not appear in any promulgated law. If they had appeared in the law, and there was a general expectation of enforceable sanction for breaches of the instructions, then this should have been provided for in the *national* guidance or as an amendment to the law governing crimes and punishments in general. Although there is provision for ordinary restrictions such as fines to be administered for breaches of local

27 Law No 22/2019 of 29/07/2019 Governing the City of Kigali, O.G., no. Special of 31 July 2019.

28 Amabwiriza No 90 yo ku wa 31 Kanama 2020 y'Inama Njyanama y'Umujyi wa Kigaliyerekeye Uburyo bwo Guhana Abatubahirije Ingamba zo Kwirinda Ikwirakwiza ry'icyorozo cya COVID-19 mu Mujyi wa Kigali <https://kigalicity.gov.rw/fileadmin/templates/Documents/cok_Council_Resolutions/2020/Amabwiriza_y_Inama_Njyanama_y_Umujyi_wa_Kigali_agena_ibihano_kubatubahiriza_ingamba_zo_kwirinda_koronavirusi.pdf>.

measures, there is no existing legal text that allows local or regional administrative institutions to order detention among those sanctions.

Third, the Rwandan Constitution and other ratified international legal instruments provide for equality of persons before the law. In consideration of this principle, and the need for legal certainty, it appears inconsistent in law to sanction people differently for the same 'offence' depending solely on their geographic location, particularly with a sanction as serious as detention.

However, the Government of Rwanda has not made any official comment on these apparent legal anomalies, either in support or in criticism of the local measures. This may have been taken to be a tacit approval, as since the City of Kigali's localised approach has been implemented some other regions have likewise developed their own specific sanctions.[29]

5. Human Rights and Civil Liberties

Before we close our discussion of the lawfulness of sanctions, we must consider the legal basis on which human rights and civil liberties are granted in Rwanda, and the extent to which they may be restricted. Chapter IV of the Rwandan Constitution confirms that there are various human rights and freedoms that anybody in the country is entitled to rely upon, including the right to liberty and security whereby an individual may only be detained, arrested or punished under an existing law at the time an action is carried out;[30] and the right to due process, including the right to legal representation, together with a presumption of innocence until proven guilty.[31]

However, chapter IV also specifies obligations of the state that, whilst normally complementary, could come into conflict with certain rights held by individuals. For example, where chapter IV sets out that everybody has the right to good health[32] and to live in a clean and healthy environment,[33] or where it refers to the state as having an obligation to respect, protect and defend human beings,[34] there is an acceptance that in order for these obligations to be met, this may require that some individual rights and freedoms are restricted in the process.[35] Crucially, no

29 Sylidio Sebuharara, 'Rubavu: hashyizweho ibihano ku batubahiriza amabwiriza yo kwirinda COVID-19', (*Kigali Today*, 4 June 2020) <https://www.kigalitoday.com/amakuru/amakuru-mu-rwanda/article/rubavu-hashyizweho-ibihano-ku-batubahiriza-amabwiriza-yo-kwirinda-covid-19>.

30 Rwanda's Constitution of 2003 with Amendments through 2015, Art 24.

31 ibid Art 29.

32 ibid Art 21.

33 ibid Art 22.

34 ibid Art 13.

35 Article 41. See also Art 45 on the state having the duty to mobilise the population for activities aimed at good health, and Art 51 which provides that the state has a duty to protect vulnerable groups including the elderly and those with disabilities. As the COVID-19 virus has been shown to be especially dangerous for precisely those groups, this provision could be argued to be applicable during the pandemic.

specificity is provided on whether the intention is for these to be read as obligations only on the national authorities, or whether such responsibility also extends to local bodies such as the Council of the City of Kigali. With this being open to interpretation, then, and in the context of a pandemic with severe implications for life and health, it could be argued that such restrictions are in fact *lawfully* implemented where those restrictions can be argued to be necessary in order for the state, at both national and local levels, to meet its obligation to protect the population as a whole.

Importantly, there have been no legal challenges to existing COVID-19 restrictions or measures heard in the Rwandan courts. Neither have there been any significant challenges made by political opposition, probably due to the consensus democracy and power-sharing structures that are ingrained within Rwanda's political system, and so the analysis remains hypothetical in nature.

6. Rwanda's Approach to Public Health and Technology

Cahan identifies several hallmarks of Rwanda's healthcare system: use of technology; the principle that no citizen should be denied access; and the principle of equity, which ensures that coverage is universal and free to those who cannot afford to pay for it.[36] Coverage is high in terms of the overall population, with McNeil reporting that 84% of Rwandans have public health insurance, and 6% have coverage through other types of insurance.[37]

In December 2019, upon first learning about the possibility of a pandemic, the government established a team of medical professionals responsible for the fight against COVID-19, who would receive specialist training on the spread of the pandemic and how best to manage it in a clinical setting.[38] Additionally, to prevent health services becoming overwhelmed, approximately 5,000 specially trained youth volunteers were deployed around Rwanda to encourage public respect for preventative guidelines. Predominantly posted to hotspots with a greater concentration of people, particularly the City of Kigali where 800 are based in markets, bus depots and other busy locations, the volunteers are tasked to work through polite reinforcement, with no authorisation to use force or enforce sanctions.[39]

With respect to technology, Musanabaganwa and others venture that Rwanda has been "one of the advanced countries in promoting IT in the region … apply-

36 Eli M Cahan, 'Rwanda's Secret Weapon Against COVID-19: Trust' (2020) 371 British Medical Journal 1.

37 Donald G McNeil, 'Rwanda's Health Care Success Story' (*The New York Times*, 4 February 2013) <https://www.nytimes.com/2013/02/05/science/rwandas-health-care-success-story.html>.

38 James Tasamba, 'Rwanda Uses Ebola Experience to Combat COVID-19' (*Anadolu Agency*, 22 April 2020) <https://www.aa.com.tr/en/africa/rwanda-uses-ebola-experience-to-combat-covid-19/1813902>.

39 James Tasamba, 'Rwanda Youth Volunteers Helping Fight against COVID-19' (*Anadolu Agency*, 6 June 2020) <https://www.aa.com.tr/en/africa/rwandan-youth-volunteers-helping-fight-against-covid-19/1867456>.

ing technologies in surveillance and control of epidemics especially in COVID-19 containment".[40] Specifically the authors highlight the use of robots from the early stages of the pandemic, supplied by the Ministry of Health and funded in part by the United Nations Development Programme. Again, knowledge and the experience gained from past epidemics in Africa have been invaluable to Rwanda. For example, the disproportionate number of deaths of frontline medical personnel during the Ebola epidemic[41] prompted the use of robots programmed to keep health records, carry out basic diagnostic work such as temperature checking and transport essentials such as food and medicines between healthcare professionals and patients. All of these functions minimised the need for physical contact and reduced the likelihood of transmission of COVID-19.[42] Musanabaganwa and others add that Rwanda's strategy has included the use of drones for broadcast of important public health information including preventative measures, symptoms, how to access testing for COVID-19 and dispelling of myths and misinformation;[43] and the use of contact tracing and hotspot detection through the development of a mobile phone application downloadable by anybody in the country.[44]

Nachega and others explain that elements of the public health strategy, such as contact tracing, were also devolved locally,[45] and conclude that Rwanda's comprehensive response to COVID-19 encompassed a combination of factors including the understanding at an early stage that responses have to be adapted in line with local challenges; drawing upon experiences of previous epidemics; and adapting existing platforms that already follow a public or community health approach (such as for HIV-AIDS). Further, Rwanda's use of technology was used to improve decision-making through accuracy and precision of data.[46]

7. The Historical, Social and Political Context

Rwanda's pandemic response strategy extended beyond scientific public health measures, underlining that a "multidisciplinary approach is needed to integrate technical, social, political and regulatory issues in addressing COVID-19",[47] factors that are crucial in the Rwandan context.

40 Clarisse Musanabaganwa and others, 'Use of Technologies in COVID-19 Containment in Rwanda' (2020) 2(2) Rwanda Public Health Bulletin 8.

41 Joanna Raven, Haja Wurie and Sophie Witter, 'Health Workers' Experiences of Coping with the Ebola Epidemic in Sierra Leone's Health System: a Qualitative Study' (2018) 18 BMC Health Service Research 2.

42 Musanabaganwa and others (n 41).

43 ibid 9.

44 ibid.

45 Jean B Nachega and others, 'Contact Tracing and the COVID-19 Response in Africa: Best Practices, Key Challenges, and Lessons Learned from Nigeria, Rwanda, South Africa, and Uganda' (2021) 104(4) American Journal of Tropical Medicine and Hygiene 1180.

46 ibid 1180–1182.

47 Ngamije and Nsanzimana (n 8).

Rwandans born before 1994 lived through the genocide against the Tutsi[48] that took place between April and July of that year, resulting in the death of approximately one million people, the majority belonging to the formerly officially designated Tutsi ethnic group.[49] Prior to 1994, in every decade since the 1950s, there had also been eruptions of conflict stemming from colonial, ethnically driven policies.[50] Since 1994, Rwanda has been transformed as a country through the ongoing efforts of governance and justice institutions at all levels that have allowed ordinary citizens to interact with both local and national politicians, members of the judiciary and other stakeholders regarding a range of issues, allowing their voices to be heard and policies shaped according to the communicated needs of the citizenry.[51] In the context of emergency public health laws, Cahan explains that citizens understand that public health guidance has no political motivation; rather the measures are intended to protect the wellbeing of the population.[52] More specifically on the intersections between governance, trust and use of science and technology, Cahan goes on to argue that:

> when the government closes the borders and sends everyone home—when it deploys health workers to people's homes, robots to their treatment centres, and drones to their skies (as it has done)—the people must know these actions are not against them, but for them. That's the only way they'll comply with the guidance—enforcement gets you only so far.[53]

The assertion that public trust is as important, if not more important, than knowledge about science and technology is reinforced by data on public attitudes to science and health published by the Wellcome Trust in 2019, less than a year before the COVID-19 pandemic.[54] Significantly, the data indicates that while Rwandans have on average the lowest self-assessed knowledge about science in the world (although less so in younger age groups),[55] they have the highest confidence in

48 The specific term of 'genocide against the Tutsi' is the correct title for events that took place in Rwanda between 6 April 1994 and 17 July 1994 as per 'ICTR Appeals Chamber takes Judicial Notice of Genocide in Rwanda' United Nations International Criminal Tribunal for Rwanda, 20 June 2006 <https://unictr.irmct.org/en/news/ictr-appeals-chamber-takes-judicial-notice-genocide-rwanda>.

49 Allan T Moore, 'Words and Power in Conflict: Rwanda Under MRND Rule' (2020) 27(2) Peace and Conflict Studies 6.

50 Aalyia Feroz Ali Sadruddin and Marcia C Inhorn, 'Aging, Vulnerability and Questions of Care in the Time of COVID-19' (2020) 12(1) Anthropology Now 19.

51 See institutions and organisations including the National Unity and Reconciliation Commission <https://www.nurc.gov.rw/index.php?id=83> and Never Again Rwanda <https://neveragain-rwanda.org/>.

52 Cahan (n 37).

53 ibid.

54 Simon Chaplin and others, 'Wellcome Global Monitor 2018: How Does the World Feel about Science and Health?' (*Wellcome*, 18 June 2019) <https://wellcome.org/sites/default/files/wellcome-global-monitor-2018.pdf>.

55 ibid 32.

their healthcare system (97%), and near universal agreement about the effectiveness of vaccines, findings that are attributed to the "extraordinary improvements in the country's healthcare system"[56] and "tremendous success"[57] in its vaccination programme over the past two decades. This data echoes broader observations about the trust in state institutions built up amongst the majority of Rwandans in the aftermath of the 1994 genocide,[58] and the positive trajectory the country has been on since then, resulting in trust in other authority figures who assist with the development of national policy, such as scientists in the context of the COVID-19 pandemic. This trust has been established through a pre-existing context which was always likely to result in higher levels of compliance with unusual restrictions on normally held rights and liberties.

8. Looking Forward: Insights on Governance, Democracy, Human Rights and the Rule of Law

The factors examined in this chapter – experience of previous pandemics; high levels of confidence in authority and the healthcare system; and the intersection between law, policy and trust stemming from the nation's recovery after the 1994 genocide – created the particular context which resulted in Rwanda's relative success in suppressing transmission of COVID-19. On the other hand, there may be lessons that the rest of the world could learn from Rwanda. The first is recognition that a purely national as opposed to a partly devolved approach, although easier to implement, may not be the most effective in the event of any future pandemic. Second, consideration should be given to what may be learned from how other pre-existing non-pandemic-related clinical conditions that rely on public or community health approaches are already being dealt with in a strategic or organisational sense, in order to avoid unnecessarily reinventing the wheel. Third, Rwanda's success at using of technology from the outset, both in the clinical setting and for information and prevention purposes, may be replicable elsewhere. These are some of the simpler recommendations to implement. More challenging is the complete mindset change advocated by Cahan who argues that:

> Covid-19 has shown that the Western world and the global north are not the best at doing everything. It's time to revisit why they're doing what they're doing. The culture of individualism, the lack of solidarity—it's losing trust with the people. And it's making people sick.[59]

56 ibid 68.

57 ibid 113.

58 Pamela Abbott and Claire Wallace, 'Happiness in a Post-Conflict Society: Rwanda' in Helaine Selin and Gareth Davey (eds), *Happiness Across Cultures: View of Happiness and Quality of Life in Non-Western Cultures* (Springer 2012); see also Firoz Khan and Pregala Pillay, 'Corruption and its Repercussions on Employment, Poverty and Inequality: Rwanda and South Africa Compared' (2019) 8 Journal of Reviews on Global Economics 1203.

59 Cahan (n 37).

It is this context of solidarity that is difficult to create artificially; a nation such as Rwanda, which had been through more than two decades of transitional justice and reconciliation programmes before the pandemic, may be better placed to genuinely appreciate the benefits that such solidarity can bring. Attempts to foster a similar sentiment in a society which has individuality engrained would have to be a long-term vision with no certainty as to how it might be achieved.

In respect of the use of law, a degree of ambivalence remains. It is difficult to know if the lack of precision in the Rwandan Constitution regarding the definition of 'the state' for specific purposes of devolution of powers is intentional to allow for interpretation in the event of abnormal situations, or a weakness of vague drafting that has only coincidentally allowed for this. Likewise, on the one hand it could be argued that Rwanda as a state has prima facie breached individual human rights that are constitutionally protected as discussed in section 5. On the other hand, non-absolute rights may legitimately be restricted on the basis of legality, necessity and proportionality for the greater community benefit. When considering not only that general principle, but also the specific obligations that the Rwandan state has a constitutional duty to uphold, on balance it is argued that the approaches taken by the Rwandan state at national and local levels have been lawful. The questions for other states looking to mirror Rwanda's approach would be whether their own constitutional arrangements allow for similar flexibility in interpretation of provisions, and whether they are willing to open themselves up to potential scrutiny or challenges to legality should there be any disagreement on that basis.

27

GERMANY AND COVID-19

Expertise and Public Political Deliberation

Anna Katharina Mangold

1. Introduction[1]

In January 2020, information about a highly contagious virus in Wuhan started to get public attention in Germany.[2] Initially, as can be expected in times of crisis, it was mostly executive bodies that took action. Due to federal competence allocation in Germany, local authorities acted first in their capacity as health authorities, soon joined by the governments of the federal states (*Länder*) and the federal government. To date, legislative amendments have formed a massive body of COVID-19 legislation,[3] covering various aspects of economic and social life in Germany. The debate in Germany has mainly focused on questions of vertical and horizontal separation of powers, the role of expertise in the COVID-19 response and restrictions of fundamental rights as adjudicated by courts.

2. The Legal Responses to COVID-19

As a first response, on 30 January 2020, the federal health ministry issued a decree mandating reports of any infections with the "novel coronavirus that first appeared in Wuhan/People's Republic of China in December 2019",[4] based on the until

1 All websites accessed on 5 August 2021.

2 This paper is based on a blog post for the 'Power and the COVID-19 Pandemic' symposium: Anna Katharina Mangold, 'Germany and COVID-19: A Most Eventful Year' (*Verfassungsblog*, 7 April 2021) <https://verfassungsblog.de/germany-and-covid-19-a-most-eventful-year/>.

3 A helpful and astonishing overview has been collected at Wikipedia (in German): <https://de.wikipedia.org/wiki/Liste_der_infolge_der_COVID-19-Pandemie_erlassenen_deutschen_Gesetze_und_Verordnungen>.

4 Verordnung über die Ausdehnung der Meldepflicht nach § 6 Absatz 1 Satz 1 Nummer 1 und § 7 Absatz 1 Satz 1 des Infektionsschutzgesetzes auf Infektionen mit dem erstmals im Dezember 2019 in Wuhan/Volksrepublik China aufgetretenen neuartigen Coronavirus (2019-nCoV) of 30

DOI: 10.4324/9781003211952-31

then little known Infection Protection Act (IPA) of 2000[5] and its § 15.[6] During February and March 2020, federal and *Länder*, including communal, executives continued to respond to the pandemic by issuing decrees, mostly without the involvement of parliaments, mandating contact restrictions and closure of schools, universities and shops.

In March 2020, a supplementary federal budget[7] made available €122.5 billion and allowed further borrowing of up to €156 billion. This money was designated to help companies and employees, and to cushion the social repercussions of the pandemic. For example, urgent financial help to pay employees was an important tool to prevent mass layoffs; the so-called *Kurzarbeitergeld*, co-funded by employer and state, covers 60% (for employees with children, 67%) of the usual wage.[8]

Thus, from the very beginning of the pandemic, the social effects of the measures taken to fight the virus were considered, and arguably the gravest consequences were addressed. The promised COVID-19 aid funds, however, took a long time to reach businesses and companies.[9] On closer inspection, further disparities appear, especially when considering what has not been addressed in the legal responses to the pandemic. The closure of schools and social support systems for children will most likely lead to significant inequalities in educational progress. Neglect of schools and pupils resulted in even bigger disparities, as success at school to a large extent depends on parents' ability to substitute for teachers or to provide digital infrastructure.

In keeping with the principles of German federalism (Articles 83 and 84 of the Basic Law (BL)[10]), the IPA is primarily implemented by the *Länder*, which initially relied on it to impose measures by executive decree. These measures were designed to prevent the transmission of the virus, detect infections at an early stage and prevent their further spread, in order to prevent deaths and an overburdening of the health system. Measures included a minimum 1.5-metre physical distance between individuals; contact restrictions; bans on leaving one's home (apart from for outdoor exercise); curfews; prohibition of meetings, assemblies, religious and political gatherings; closure of kindergartens, schools and universities, businesses, shops and

January 2020, Federal Gazette (FG) Official Part (OP) 31 January 2020 V1, which has meanwhile expired.

5 The German version in its current form can be found online <https://www.gesetze-im-internet.de/ifsg/index.html>.

6 § 15 IPA allows the federal health ministry to stipulate obligations to report infections in an epidemic situation and adapt such obligations as need arises.

7 Gesetz über die Feststellung eines Nachtrags zum Bundeshaushaltsplan für das Haushaltsjahr 2020 (Nachtragshaushaltsgesetz 2020) of 27 March 2020, Federal Law Gazette (FLG) I 556.

8 The Federal Employment Agency provided an overview how the complex legal situation works in practice at <https://www.arbeitsagentur.de/m/corona-kurzarbeit/>.

9 FAZ/dpa, 'Corona-Hilfen für Unternehmen sollen wieder normal laufen' (*Frankfurter Allgemeine Zeitung*, 12 March 2021) <https://www.faz.net/aktuell/wirtschaft/corona-hilfen-fuer-unternehmen-sollen-wieder-normal-laufen-17240908.html>.

10 Official English translation of the 'Grundgesetz' available at: <https://www.gesetze-im-internet.de/englisch_gg/englisch_gg.html>.

restaurants, museums and theatres and sports and cultural facilities; restrictions on visits to hospitals, retirement homes and other social institutions; prohibition of travel for private reasons and to second homes; and finally, as late as the end of April 2020, an obligation to wear a face-mask indoors, and later also outdoors in public.[11] Considerable variations in the *Länder* decrees allowed for exceptions or further restrictions. Eventually, this multitude of regulations converged into a catalogue of standard measures. But they continued to be based on a very general provision in § 28 IPA, which originally was designed to permit individual measures in relation to infectious or possibly infectious people – not far-reaching measures targeting the population at large.

3. The Four 'Acts on the Protection of the Population in the Event of an Epidemic Situation of National Significance'

At the end of March 2020, the first Act on the Protection of the Population in the Event of an Epidemic Situation of National Significance[12] introduced a new § 5 into the IPA, providing the federal health ministry with far reaching powers to announce COVID-19 measures by decree. These powers were triggered by the Federal Parliament (*Bundestag*) declaring an "epidemic situation of national significance" in plenary session; they were to cease as soon as Parliament declared the end of such a situation. No definition was given, though, of what constituted such an "epidemic situation of national significance". The bill was rushed through Parliament, and Parliament declared an "epidemic situation of national significance" that would have to be explicitly repealed in order to end.

The new § 5 IPA was heavily criticised for transferring decree powers to the federal health ministry without setting limits, as constitutionally demanded by Article 80(1) BL. If the ministry is empowered to issue decrees that can deviate from and even change the requirements set by other Acts of Parliament, then this puts into question the democratic rule of law itself. Nonetheless, in May 2020, the Second Act on the Protection of the Population in the Event of an Epidemic Situation of National Significance[13] brought few changes to the problematic transfer of powers to the federal health ministry.

It was not until November 2020 that the Third Act on the Protection of the Population in the Event of an Epidemic Situation of National Significance[14] introduced a definition of the "epidemic situation of national significance" and added

11 This obligation was introduced in the 16 *Länder* but the federal government announced its introduction nationwide on 29 April 2020: <https://www.bundesregierung.de/breg-de/themen/coronavirus/maskenpflicht-in-deutschland-1747318>.

12 Gesetz zum Schutz der Bevölkerung bei einer epidemischen Lage von nationaler Tragweite of 27 March 2020 FLG I 587.

13 Zweites Gesetz zum Schutz der Bevölkerung bei einer epidemischen Lage von nationaler Tragweite of 19 May 2020 FLG I 1018.

14 Drittes Gesetz zum Schutz der Bevölkerung bei einer epidemischen Lage von nationaler Tragweite of 18 November 2020 FLG I2397.

the new and complex § 28a IPA. This law finally introduced a proper legislative basis for the standard COVID-19 measures and provided an extensive catalogue of permissible measures to be implemented by the *Länder*, essentially transforming into an Act the previous measures issued by decree.

At the end of March 2021, the Federal Parliament decided to again formally declare the "epidemic situation of national significance" – now, however, introducing a change to the mechanism in the IPA with a sunset clause so that the epidemic situation would end automatically three months after its declaration if Parliament did not explicitly decide to continue it.[15] On 11 June 2021, Parliament declared the "epidemic situation of national significance" as continuing.[16]

In Spring 2021, both the *Länder* governments and the population became tired of more and stricter measures, even though infection rates still were high and predicted to rise again due to the Easter holidays. In this situation, no new nationwide agreements could be reached. The federal government decided to introduce a 'federal emergency brake' (*Bundesnotbremse*) into the IPA. Just after Easter 2021, the Fourth Act on the Protection of the Population in the Event of an Epidemic Situation of National Significance introduced an automated mechanism with the new § 28b IPA:[17] if infection rates rose above 100 per 100,000 inhabitants in a seven-day average for a period of three consecutive days in a county, severe restrictions would automatically enter into force in that county until the infection rates fell again. Both the legal regulation mechanism and the measures introduced were heavily criticised, especially the night-time curfew. By the end of May 2021, the breath-taking number of 424 constitutional complaints were lodged against the federal emergency brake at the Federal Constitutional Court (FCC).[18] § 28b(10) IPA enshrined an automatic end to the emergency brake mechanism on 30 June 2021; hence, the measures no longer apply.

4. Horizontal and Vertical Separation of Powers

While it was the *Länder* executives that first reacted to the pandemic, soon, federal and *Länder* governments started to coordinate their activities. The regular meetings of the heads of government under the leadership of Chancellor Merkel (*Bund-Länder-Konferenzen*) became much awaited media events. The steps agreed in these meetings were issued in decrees by the *Länder* governments; to the

15 Gesetz zur Fortgeltung der die epidemische Lage von nationaler Tragweite betreffenden Regelungen of 29 March 2021 FLG I 370.

16 See 'Bundestag stellt Fortbestehen epidemischer Lage von nationaler Tragweite fest' <https://www.bundestag.de/dokumente/textarchiv/2021/kw23-de-epidemische-lage-845692>.

17 Viertes Gesetz zum Schutz der Bevölkerung bei einer epidemischen Lage von nationaler Tragweite of 22 April 2021 FLG I 802.

18 Bundesverfassungsgericht, 'Mehrere Eilanträge und Verfassungsbeschwerden gegen Vorschriften des Vierten Bevölkerungsschutzgesetzes ("Bundesnotbremse") erfolglos', Press release 47/2021 (2 June 2021) <https://www.bundesverfassungsgericht.de/SharedDocs/Pressemitteilungen/DE/2021/bvg21-047.html>.

extent the *Länder* parliaments were involved at all, they merely executed what had been decided in the government meetings. The Federal Parliament only slowly took it upon itself to even discuss the COVID-19 measures and the situation with the aforementioned Acts on the Protection of the Population and other laws.

At times, the *Bundestag* merely followed what the government representatives had decided behind closed doors. § 28a IPA, for example, appeared to be a step in the right direction because finally Parliament legislated a catalogue of measures. However, as legal experts pointed out in a public hearing in the *Bundestag*,[19] § 28a IPA merely rubber-stamped the measures previously imposed by executive bodies and did not properly define the conditions under which they could be ordered.

As the meetings between federal and *Länder* governments continued, there was also growing criticism over their closed-door nature, which set them apart from public deliberation in Parliament.[20] Decisions were then implemented by way of executive decrees, leaving little or no room for public debate ex post facto. German political culture thus appeared to shift towards executive decision-making. Early in 2021, however, *Länder* parliaments requested more involvement and *Länder* governments started to report to parliaments on the situation and their actions.[21]

In March and April 2021, Germany faced a severe third wave of infections, now mainly of the B.1.1.7 mutation. In early March 2021, counterintuitively, the federal and *Länder* governments decided to loosen the restrictions and set higher thresholds in infection rates, raising them from 35 or 50 respectively to 100 – a new threshold that was not mirrored in the legal basis of the restrictions (§ 28a(3) IfSG). This could be interpreted as an inclination of the executive to get rid of legislative restraints.[22] Before Easter 2021, the meeting of the federal and *Länder* governments had decided to add two holidays as a 'circuit breaker' lockdown to stop that third wave (*Osterruhetage*).[23] This measure, introduced late at night during an 11-hour long meeting on 23 March 2021, was apparently not legally checked,

19 Expert hearing of the Health Committee of the German Federal Parliament, 12 November 2021. Reports of the experts: <https://www.bundestag.de/ausschuesse/a14/anhoerungen>.

20 Johannes Gallon, 'Informeller Föderalismus statt öffentlicher Deliberation: Oder: Warum die Öffentlichkeit bei der Bund-Länder Koordination in der Pandemiebekämpfung beteiligt werden sollte' (*Verfassungsblog*, 9 February 2021) <https://verfassungsblog.de/informeller-foderalismus-statt-offentlicher-deliberation/>.

21 Christian Rath, 'Landtage wollen mitentscheiden' (*Taz*, 20 January 2021) <https://taz.de/Coronamassnahmen-und-Demokratie/!5745583/>.

22 Johannes Gallon, 'Schutzverpflichtungen aus dem Infektionsschutzgesetz: Warum Landesregierungen und Gesundheitsämter bei Überschreitung der gesetzlichen Schwellenwerte die Corona-Bekämpfungsmaßnahmen verschärfen müssen' (*Verfassungsblog*, 3 March 2021) <https://verfassungsblog.de/schutzverpflichtungen-aus-dem-infektionsschutzgesetz/>.

23 Official press release of the meeting of the federal and *Länder* governments of 23 March 2021: <https://www.bundesregierung.de/breg-de/themen/coronavirus/bund-laender-beschluss-22-03-1879986>.

resulting in an astonishing apology by Chancellor Merkel,[24] who took back the extra holidays just a day later.

After Easter 2021, the federal and *Länder* government meetings essentially came to an end. With infection rates again rising due to the Delta variant of the virus at the time of writing, it is predicted that they will be taken up again in late summer and autumn 2021.

5. The Effectiveness of Judicial Scrutiny

A search in the legal database *Juris* (where many, but not all, German court decisions are reported) using the terms 'Corona', 'COVID-19' and 'SARS-CoV-2' leads to the remarkable number of 6,241 decisions (as of 26 July 2021), of which 4,388 were delivered by administrative courts or the Federal Constitutional Court (FCC) over the past year. Due to the rapid factual and legal developments, most of these decisions concerned requests for interim relief against specific measures or packages of measures, usually based on claims of fundamental rights violations. In the fully constitutionalised legal order in Germany, any administrative court is bound by the human rights and civil liberties enshrined in the bill of rights in the Basic Law (Article 1-19 BL). Article 19(4) BL guarantees a right to judicial review for any violations of human rights and civil liberties.

When deciding about interim relief, the courts do not fully review the case in substance, but base their decision on an assessment of probability: which decision will be more detrimental if later proven wrong? In this situation, courts seemingly tend to focus on procedural and formal 'mistakes' made by the administration when imposing COVID-19 measures: is there a proper legal basis for the measures that is sufficiently clear? Even though most measures were based on the insufficient § 28 IPA (as the new § 28a IPA was only introduced in November 2020), the courts in summer and autumn 2020 were still very hesitant to repeal imposed measures on grounds of an inadequate legal basis. The only exemption to that rule was the night-time curfew that many courts considered unconstitutional as too far reaching in its restrictions of fundamental rights.[25] In interim decisions, the FCC – sitting for the first time during the pandemic as the full First Senate of the FCC with eight Justices instead of a chamber of only three Justices – did not temporarily strike down the curfew.[26] The final decision is expected late in 2021 or early in 2022.[27]

24 Martin Schmidt, 'Kanzlerin Merkel entschuldigt sich für "Osterruhe"' (*Tagesschau*, 24 March 2021) <https://www.tagesschau.de/multimedia/video/video-840769.html>.

25 For constitutional analysis of this measure with references to court decisions, see: Anna Katharina Mangold, 'Grundrechtliche Bewertung einer Ausgangssperre zur Pandemiebekämpfung: Kurzgutachten' (*Gesellschaft für Freiheitsrechte*, 20 April 2021) <https://freiheitsrechte.org/home/wp-content/uploads/2021/04/GFF-Gutachten-Ausgangssperren.pdf>.

26 FCC, Decision of the First Senate of 5 May 2021, docket Nos. 1 BvR 781/21, 1 BvR 805/21, 1 BvR 820/21, 1 BvR 854/21, 1 BvR 889/21 <https://www.bundesverfassungsgericht.de/SharedDocs/Entscheidungen/DE/2021/05/rs20210505_1bvr078121.html>.

27 Disclosure: acting as legal representative, I have lodged constitutional complaint docket No. 1 BvR 805/21 for a number of complainants on behalf of the *Gesellschaft für Freiheitsrechte* (GFF;

6. Protecting Human Rights and Civil Liberties

Apart from this, when it came to civil liberties and human rights, the proportionality test took centre stage. This test requires measures (i) to have a legitimate aim and (ii) to be suitable to achieve this aim; further, it asks (iii) whether other less intrusive measures could have been chosen; and finally (iv) whether there was a proportionate relationship between the restriction of the fundamental right and the legitimate aim pursued – the famous balancing act. Considering the highest rank ascribed to the right to life, courts were understandably hesitant to find against measures on grounds of them not being proportionate, i.e. stage (iv). Rather, they focused on stages (ii) and (iii) which require scientific assessment more than legal evaluation.

For example, during the first lockdown governments had generally prohibited all religious services and assemblies, including political demonstrations, without exemptions, even though they are especially protected in Articles 4 and 8 BL. Throughout April 2020, the FCC struck down such overly broad prohibitions,[28] arguing that a less intrusive measure was to require appropriate hygiene regimes. During the summer, this led some administrative courts to allow huge demonstrations against COVID-19 measures involving widespread travel activities to go ahead, even though it was clear that participants would probably not follow hygiene measures because they did not believe that the virus was dangerous at all. In a side note, early on the FCC had clarified that such demonstrations could very well be prohibited for reasons of pandemic safety.[29]

Concerns over unequal treatment also played a major role in public debates. As everybody is equally affected by the virus, unequal sharing of the burdens of preventing it from spreading has increasingly turned into a veritable problem for the legitimacy of the measures. This fundamental question has also resulted in legal cases relying on the equal protection of the law under Article 3(1) BL. However, other than requiring reasonable justification of unequal treatment (in this sense, similar to the *Wednesbury* doctrine[30]), this legal review has unsurprisingly not resulted in many tangible corrections of measures to date, and has led to vastly differing evaluations even of those measures setting highly questionable

Society for Civil Liberties), an NGO for strategic litigation to defend civil liberties and human rights in Germany.

28 FCC, Decision of the First Chamber of the First Senate of 15 April 2020, docket No. 1 BvR 828/20, <http://www.bverfg.de/e/rk20200415_1bvr082820.html>; FCC, Decision of the First Chamber of the First Senate of April 17, 2020, docket No. 11 BvQ 37/20 <http://www.bverfg.de/e/qk20200417_1bvq003720.html>; FCC, Decision of the Second Chamber of the First Senate of 29 April 2020, docket No. 1 BvQ 44/20, <http://www.bverfg.de/e/qk20200429_1bvq004420.html>.

29 FCC, Decision of the First Chamber of the First Senate of 16 May 2020, docket No. 1 BvQ 55/20, <http://www.bverfg.de/e/qk20200516_1bvq005520.html>.

30 Court of Appeal of England and Wales, *Associated Provincial Picture Houses v Wednesbury Corporation*, [1947] EWCA Civ 1, [1948] 1 KB 223, [1947] 2 All ER 680, [1948] KB 223, per Lord Greene MR.

and seemingly arbitrary thresholds (e.g. a maximum of 800 square metres for shops[31] to be allowed to reopen). It seems that the traditional preponderance of freedom rights over substantive equality concerns in judicial review also played out here.[32]

7. The Role of Expertise and Public Deliberation

2021 is an election year. With several *Länder* elections and the federal general elections in September 2021, the political situation in Germany is, at the time of writing, volatile. The federal election will bring the end of Angela Merkel's chancellorship after 16 years. During the pandemic, Merkel's science background – she holds a PhD in physics – played a decisive role because she simply understood what exponential growth means. Merkel's second in command, head of the chancellor's office Helge Braun, is a trained physician and understands the medical aspects very well. The Social Democratic party, currently in a coalition with Merkel's conservative Christian Democratic Union, has Karl Lauterbach among its members of parliament, a Harvard trained epidemiologist and Professor of Health Economics at the University of Cologne. The Grand Coalition thus mostly worked together in a science-based approach to contain COVID-19 infections.

From early on, public health experts, epidemiologists and virologists were invited for hearings before political bodies,[33] but it was not always scientific evidence that guided decisions. This was particularly noticeable after the summer of 2020 had brought a measure of relief, allowing public life to return to some semblance of normalcy. In September and October 2020, the second wave of infections was well under way; eminent experts such as Prof Dr Christian Drosten, a virologist at Charité Berlin, had warned of its coming already in early August.[34] But the second lockdown was delayed until November 2020, because the politicians were hesitant to impose restrictions yet again, only six months after the first, rather strict lockdown. Arguably, this delay contributed to numerous deaths in the second wave, whereas the first wave had been managed much better with the stricter and earlier lockdown.[35] Political choices very obviously depend on sci-

31 FCC, Decision of the Second Chamber of the First Senate of 29 April 2020, docket No. 1 BvQ 47/20 <http://www.bverfg.de/e/qk20200429_1bvq004720.html>.

32 For a doctrinal proposal to take into account unequal factual consequences of the COVID-19 measures, see Anna Katharina Mangold, 'Relationale Freiheit: Grundrechte in der Pandemie', Veröffentlichungen der Vereinigung Deutscher Staatsrechtslehrer 80 (2021), forthcoming.

33 In Germany, the Robert-Koch-Institute (RKI) advises the federal government in matters of infectious diseases. The RKI is the central scientific institution in the field of biomedicine, has the task of safeguarding public health in Germany and hosts topic-specific World Health Organisation Collaborating Centres, see <https://www.rki.de>.

34 Christian Drosten, 'Ein Plan für den Herbst' (*Zeit Online*, 5 August 2020) <https://www.zeit.de/2020/33/corona-zweite-welle-eindaemmung-massnahmen-christian-drosten/komplettansicht>.

35 Michael Hörz, Robert Meyer and Moritz Zajonz, 'Alle Zahlen und Grafiken zum Coronavirus' (*ZDF*, 25 July 2021) <https://www.zdf.de/nachrichten/heute/coronavirus-ausbreitung-info-

ence[36] and growing knowledge about the exponential development of the virus and its mutations. The hard facts of the pandemic could not be denied, and political wishful thinking to return to 'normal' life could not change the parameters of exponential growth. Yet this reality did not always impinge on decision making, as was evident in Summer 2021 when, with the Delta variant looming on the horizon, politicians proved unwilling to engage in pandemic management decisions, a situation exacerbated by the ongoing election campaigns leading up to the federal general elections in September 2021.

The deeply political and ethical nature of choices between measures such as partial or full lockdown, closure of economic sectors and educational facilities, and mass testing and vaccinations, thus once again became evident in the pandemic. From a deontological standpoint, on which human dignity as a fundamental right is based, deaths have to be prevented by all means, economic repercussions notwithstanding ("every death is one too many", as Bavarian Minister President Markus Söder[37] famously phrased it in March 2020). Article 1(1) BL protects human dignity, which is the essential human right and the basis for all legal regulation in Germany; hence, the deontological approach is much more common in Germany. A more utilitarian approach holds that liberal societies accept certain deaths all the time,[38] for example when allowing dangerous activities such as driving a car. Such utilitarian assessments seem to be more common in the English-speaking world, especially when propagating herd immunity by way of infections; however, such assessments gained ground in Germany, too, during the pandemic.[39]

In Germany, the issue of triage – that is, whether a law should be introduced to decide which patients should get access to intensive care if not all could be accommodated – brought the ethical challenges of the pandemic to the fore: should human dignity be the starting point or are utilitarian considerations better suited to allocate sparse resources? Criminal lawyers and philosophers alike discussed the philosophical and practical questions,[40] and the media debated triage scenarios,

---

grafiken-102.html>; see graph 'Neuinfektionen in Deutschland' (new infections in Germany) with exponential growth starting in summer 2020.

36 Indeed, expert knowledge plays an ambiguous role in democracies but in practice forms an essential part of parliamentary and governmental workings; see Laura Münkler, *Expertokratie: Zwischen Herrschaft kraft Wissens und politischem Dezisionismus* (Mohr Siebeck 2020).

37 Widely reported in the press; see e.g. 'Massive Ausgangsbeschränkungen für ganz Bayern ab Samstag' (*Süddeutsche Zeitung*, 20 March 2020) <https://www.sueddeutsche.de/gesundheit/gesundheit-muenchen-massive-ausgangsbeschraenkungen-fuer-ganz-bayern-ab-samstag-dpa.urn-newsml-dpa-com-20090101-200320-99-404727>.

38 David Lanius and Christoph Schmidt-Petri, 'Und was ist mit den Folgen der Krise? Die gängige Ethik bedenkt sie zu wenig' (*Neue Zürcher Zeitung*, 30 April 2020) <https://www.nzz.ch/feuilleton/und-was-ist-mit-den-folgen-die-gaengige-ethik-bedenkt-sie-zu-wenig-ld.1554154>.

39 Targeting herd immunity by vaccination is compatible with concepts of human dignity of each individual person. Encouraging people to get infected as a means to achieve the greater good, namely herd immunity, arguably is not compatible with such an individualistic understanding of human dignity.

40 Tatjana Hörnle, Stefan Huster and Ralf Poscher (eds), *Triage in der Pandemie* (Mohr Siebeck 2021).

even though virtually no actual triage happened since hospitals were able to cope.[41] Here, a strange interest in extreme scenarios put philosophical expertise in the spotlight.

However, it is not only triage situations that warrant a thorough ethical and political analysis. The same is true for decisions about which businesses and activities are to halt temporarily so as to stop the virus from spreading. Such decisions are taken with possible consequences and repercussions in mind. It became increasingly apparent in Germany that closure of schools caused highly gender-specific effects: it was mostly women who stayed at home to take care of children and stood in as ad hoc teachers.[42] If such an effect becomes discernible (surprisingly for some), it is a political choice to retain a specific measure and refrain from changing the situation for the women affected. In this example, it was interesting to note that gender experts warned early on of the gendered effects of the pandemic[43] but they did not get the appropriate time in the spotlight. Indeed, the Leopoldina, the distinguished German Academy of Sciences,[44] offered a multidisciplinary expert opinion on appropriate reactions to the pandemic in April 2020,[45] without giving due respect to gendered aspects of the situation.[46] Partly, this can be explained by the focus on individual freedom rather than substantive equality in German discourse.

Yet in the end, the pandemic continued to be a feast mostly for constitutional law experts. Public debate focused very much on the principle of proportionality, which was widely used to assess the constitutionality of specific COVID-19 measures and the situation more generally. Some constitutional law professors voiced strongly worded opinions early on ("fascist-hysterical hygienic state";[47] "state of exception"[48]). However, more measured constitutional law professors appeared

41 Astrid *Prange*, 'Corona: In Deutschland geht es ohne Triage' (*Deutsche Welle*, 16 April 2021) <https://www.dw.com/de/corona-in-deutschland-geht-es-ohne-triage/a-57217358>.

42 Bettina Kohlrausch and Aline Zucco, 'Die Corona-Krise trifft Frauen doppelt: Weniger Erwerbseinkommen und mehr Sorgearbeit' (2020) 40 WSI <https://www.boeckler.de/de/faust-detail.htm?sync_id=8906>.

43 Eg Gunda Windmüller, 'Alle Frauen weg? Wie die Corona-Krise zum Backlash für Gleichberechtigung wird' (*Ze.tt*, 16 May 2020) <https://ze.tt/alle-frauen-weg-wie-die-corona-krise-zum-backlash-fuer-gleichberechtigung-wird-feminismus-genderstudies/>.

44 The Leopoldina was founded in 1652 as a classical scholarly society and became the National Academy of Sciences in 2008. Its task is to provide "policymakers and the public with science-based advice". For further information, see <https://www.leopoldina.org>.

45 National Academy of Sciences Leopoldina, Ad-hoc-statement 3 April 2020: 'Coronavirus Pandemic – Measures Relevant to Health' <https://www.leopoldina.org/uploads/tx_leopublication/2020_04_08_2ad_hoc_statement_coronavirus_en_final_01.pdf>.

46 Amory Burchard, Interview with Jutta Allmendinger on the Leopoldina recommendations: 'Das Wohlergehen der Frauen wird nicht adressiert' (*Der Tagesspiegel*, 14 April 2020) <https://www.tagesspiegel.de/wissen/kritik-an-leopoldina-empfehlung-das-wohlergehen-der-frauen-wird-nicht-adressiert/25739444.html>.

47 Hans Michael Heinig, 'Gottesdienstverbot auf Grundlage des Infektionsschutzgesetzes: Verfassungsrechtliche Rechtfertigung und Grenzen' (*Verfassungsblog*, 17 March 2020) <https://verfassungsblog.de/gottesdienstverbot-auf-grundlage-des-infektionsschutzgesetzes/>.

48 Uwe Volkmann, 'Der Ausnahmezustand' (*Verfassungsblog*, 20 March 2020) <https://verfassungsblog.de/der-ausnahmezustand/>.

regularly in the media, shaping and framing the public debate about the pandemic. Considering their prominence in public debate, unsurprisingly the role of constitutional law expertise was hotly debated. The advice of constitutional law experts was less welcomed by politicians when it emphasised the importance of having proper legal bases for the measures and clear definitions of measures as a rule of law requirement. The chairman of the legal committee of the federal parliament even singled out two leading experts on public health law on Twitter,[49] insinuating that they were cooperating with the far-right party *Alternative für Deutschland* (AfD) and with COVID-19 deniers; he later tried to justify this outrageous and unprecedented personal attack in a blog post.[50] The strains showed in the pandemic: the discussion about 'expertocracy' and democratic law is far older than the pandemic, but was relit by it.

8. Future Outlook

As I write in late July 2021, a strategy on how mutations of the virus may be kept under control in the EU and its Member States, including Germany, is still awaited. A team of scientists under the label #NoCovid[51] proposed a model of green and red zones, following the successful examples of Australia and New Zealand. It has yet to gather real political momentum in Germany.

Inevitably, the fight against the virus has become a topic in the election campaigns. For some politicians, loosening restrictions appears as a political strategy to attract voters, while others push for stricter measures. Some parties, especially the AfD, outrightly deny the dangers of the virus, likening it to a mere influenza. When the elections take place in September, in all likelihood the Delta variant will hit Germany in a fourth wave of infections. Once again, the deeply political nature of COVID-19 measures will become evident.

49 Heribert Hirte (*Twitter*, 19 January 2021) <https://twitter.com/hhirte/status/1351485097854316544>. Astonishingly, Heribert Hirte is himself a Professor of Commercial Law at the University of Hamburg.

50 Heribert Hirte, 'Auch Sachverständige tragen Verantwortung für die Gesellschaft und sind Teil der politischen Willensbildung' (*Verfassungsblog*, 23 January 2021) <https://verfassungsblog.de/auch-sachverstandige-tragen-verantwortung-fur-die-gesellschaft-und-sind-teil-der-politischen-willensbildung/>.

51 'No-COVID: Controlling the Pandemic through Green Zones' <https://nocovid-europe.eu/>.

28

THE RATIONALITY OF SOUTH AFRICA'S STATE OF DISASTER DURING COVID-19

Melodie Labuschaigne and Ciara Staunton

1. Introduction[1]

Across the globe, governments' responses to COVID-19 have included measures aimed at containing the spread of the virus (such as the closing of borders and restrictions on movement), public health measures (such as contact tracing and testing policies) and measures targeted at providing short-term economic relief (such as income support). The rationality of a government's response, as this chapter addresses, may be determined by a consideration of the rationality of legislative and decision-making processes during the pandemic. South Africa's response to the pandemic, traced by the authors of this chapter since the reporting of South Africa's first confirmed case of COVID-19 in March 2020,[2] reveals interesting, yet conflicting developments. This chapter considers the rationality of the South African government's choice of opting for a state of national disaster instead of a state of emergency, followed by a critical examination of the suspension of Parliament's role and the rationality of decision-making by the pandemic oversight structures, including that of the criminalisation of breaches of lockdown regulations. The chapter concludes with recommendations that emphasise the importance of the role of courts and public debate during COVID-19 and future pandemics.

1 All websites accessed on 19 July 2021.

2 This chapter draws on two posts by the authors: 'COVID-19: State of Disaster in South-Africa' (*Verfassungsblog*, 11 April 2020) <https://verfassungsblog.de/covid-19-state-of-disaster-in-south-africa/>; 'COVID-19 in South Africa: A Year in Review' (*Verfassungsblog*, 11 March 2021) <https://verfassungsblog.de/covid-19-in-south-africa-a-year-in-review/>.

DOI: 10.4324/9781003211952-32

South Africa is an unequal society with only 16% of its population having access to private medical aid,[3] with the rest reliant on a poorly resourced public health care system[4] that is buckling under a heavy tuberculosis (TB), HIV and HIV/TB co-infection burden.[5] While strategies such as social distancing, self-isolation, quarantine, testing and lockdown proved successful in limiting, and at times containing, the spread of the virus elsewhere, South Africa's socio-economic realities, including the prevalence of poverty and malnutrition,[6] posed a serious threat to the effectiveness of these measures. With 13% of all households located in dense, informal settlements that often lack access to running water,[7] self-isolation and quarantine for millions forced to share a bedroom or even a bed seemed near impossible.[8] There was, thus, justified concern that South Africa's already overstretched public healthcare system would be unable to cope with increasing COVID-19 infections, making preventing and containing the spread of the virus in South Africa a critical national priority.

Following the World Health Organisation's declaration of COVID-19 as a pandemic on 11 March 2020 and the first reported case of community transmission in South Africa, President Cyril Ramaphosa declared a national State of Disaster[9] on 15 March 2020. At the time of writing, South Africa has entered the third wave of the virus, which led to the introduction of a higher alert level with stricter limitations on social gatherings and personal movement.[10] The rationale for this is clear from South Africa's COVID-19 statistics on 28 June 2021, which show 32,125 infections per million and 998 deaths per million (or 3.2%) of the population.[11] The severity of the situation is clear from the same-day comparison with Nigeria, the African continent's most populous country, which reveals 793 infections per million and ten deaths per million (or 1.3%) of its population.[12] To date, South

3 Council for Medical Schemes, 'Annual Report' (2015/2016).

4 Office of Health Standards Compliance, 'Annual Inspection Report 2016–2017' (Pretoria, 2018).

5 'The Number: HIV and TB in South Africa (*Spotlight*, 4 July 2018) https://www.spotlightnsp.co.za/2018/07/04/the-numbers-hiv-and-tb-in-south-africa/.

6 President Cyril Ramaphosa, 'Escalation of Measures to Combat Coronavirus COVID-19 Pandemic' (Speech, 23 March 2020).

7 Socio-Economic Rights Institute of South Africa, 'Informal Settlements and Human Rights in South Africa: Submission to the United Nations Special Rapporteur on Adequate Housing as a Component of the Right to an Adequate Standard of Living' (May 2018).

8 Statistics South Africa, 'Inequality Trends in South Africa: A Multidimensional Diagnostic of Inequality' (14 November 2019) <http://www.statssa.gov.za/?p=12744>.

9 Disaster Management Act 2002, Declaration of a National State of Disaster, Government Gazette No 43096 15 March 2020.

10 A 14-day adjusted lockdown alert level 4 was instituted on 28 June 2021. This is the second highest alert level of the five-tiered risk adjusted strategy which regulates permitted retail and service operations and personal movement. See COVID-19 Online Resource and News Portal (Department of Health), 'COVID-19 Risk-Adjusted Strategy' <https://sacoronavirus.co.za/covid-19-risk-adjusted-strategy/>.

11 Coronavirus Statistics: South Africa (*epidemic-stats.com*, updated daily) <https://epidemic-stats.com/coronavirus/south-africa>.

12 Coronavirus Statistics: Nigeria (*epidemic-stats.com*, updated daily) <https://epidemic-stats.com/coronavirus/nigeria>.

Africa's COVID-19 deaths constitute 42% of all COVID-19 deaths on the African continent.[13]

2. The Rationality of Declaring a National State of Disaster

Having decided that "urgent and drastic" measures were necessary to limit the spread of COVID-19,[14] President Ramaphosa had two options: to declare a state of emergency or a state of disaster. The first-mentioned, which derives from s 37 of the Constitution, must be declared within the terms of the State of Emergency Act 64 of 1997[15] and may only be declared when, among other things, "the life of the nation is threatened by war, invasion, general insurrection, disorder, natural disaster or other public emergency". Certain rights under the Bill of Rights may be derogated from, excluding the non-derogable rights to dignity, life and fair trial.[16] Although only declared for 21 days initially, Parliament may, by a majority, extend it by three months. Further extensions require a 60% majority in Parliament. Since the validity of a state of emergency, its extension or any regulations promulgated under it may be reviewed by any court within South Africa, Parliament and the courts, thus, retain a supervisory role.

A state of emergency has not been declared since the commencement of the constitutional democracy in South Africa in 1994. The last state of emergency, which was declared under the then apartheid regime in 1985 and lasted until 1990, enabled the government to rule by decree, detain citizens without trial, restrict freedom of movement and gave the police and military significant powers. As a declaration of a state of emergency is conventionally declared to restore peace and order, it is not necessarily the first choice for a public health emergency. One may speculate that its association with the apartheid era may have persuaded President Ramaphosa to opt instead for a state of disaster.

The executive power to declare a national state of disaster does not derive from the Constitution but from the Disaster Management Act 57 of 2002.[17] A "disaster" is defined as a "progressive or sudden, widespread or localised, natural or human-caused occurrence which causes or threatens to cause death, injury or disease; damage to property, infrastructure or the environment; or disruption of the life of a community". COVID-19 clearly falls within this definition. The Act provides the relevant minister (in the case of COVID-19, the Minister of Cooperative Governance and Traditional Affairs) the power to impose limitations

13 Reuters COVID-19 Tracker: Africa <https://graphics.reuters.com/world-coronavirus-tracker-and-maps/regions/africa/>.

14 South African Government, 'President Cyril Ramaphosa: Measures to Combat Coronavirus COVID-19 Epidemic' (15 March 2020) <https://www.gov.za/speeches/statement-president-cyril-ramaphosa-measures-combat-covid-19-epidemic-15-mar-2020-0000#>.

15 State of Emergency Act 64 1997.

16 Section 37(5) of the Constitution of the Republic of South Africa 1996.

17 Disaster Management Act No. 57 of 2002, Government Gazette (No 24252) of 15 January 2003.

on individuals' rights and freedoms through the promulgating of regulations.[18] A National Disaster Management Centre must be established (in this case within the Department of Cooperative Governance and Traditional Affairs) which, among other duties, makes recommendations on draft legislation. Although the exercise of its powers and duties falls to the relevant minister, it is the national executive (i.e. the cabinet) that is primarily responsible for coordination and management of the disaster. A state of disaster lasts three months and may be extended by the minister for one month at a time. Unlike under a state of emergency, regulations promulgated under a state of disaster must conform to the Bill of Rights. Although rights may be limited, they may not be derogated from under a state of disaster. Parliament has no oversight role during a state of disaster, but the courts have the power to review and strike down the declaration of the state of disaster or related regulations.

Consequently, a series of regulations restricting, among other things, the movement of persons, goods and the dissemination of information was promulgated in March 2020.[19] On 1 May 2020, a five-tier risk adjusted strategy,[20] consisting of varying restrictions depending on the situation at a given point in time, was introduced. The criteria for the alert levels,[21] officially published in the Government Gazette on 7 August 2020, are informed by COVID-19 epidemiological trends, the capacity of the health system to respond, and any other factor influencing the level of infection, hospitalisation and mortality. Substantial changes in the alert levels are communicated via broadcast statements by the President,[22] fondly known as "family meetings".[23] They are welcomed in general and seen to promote transparency regarding lockdown restrictions, as well as social solidarity, the latter described as a feature of South African nationhood.[24]

3. The Rationality of Pandemic Oversight and Decision-Making

As stated above, Parliament's direct oversight role during the management of COVID-19 was suspended and delegated to the Minister for Cooperative Governance and Traditional Affairs, Nkosazana Dhlamini-Zuma, under the 2002

18 South African Government, 'Regulations and Guidelines—Coronavirus COVID-19' <https://www.gov.za/covid-19/resources/regulations-and-guidelines-coronavirus-covid-19>.

19 ibid.

20 COVID-19 Online Resource and News Portal (Department of Health) (n 10).

21 Directions issued in Terms of Regulation 3(3) of the Regulations Made under s 27(2) of the Disaster Management Act 2002 (Act No. 57 of 2002): Criteria to Guide the Determination of Alert Levels. Government Gazette No. 43599 (Regulation Gazette 11158 of 7 August 2020).

22 All speeches are available on the South African Government website <https://www.gov.za/speeches>.

23 Thabi Madiba, 'Ramaphosa to Host Family Meeting at 19:30' (*Polity*, 30 March 2021) <https://www.polity.org.za/article/ramaphosa-to-host-family-meeting-at-7pm-2021-03-30>.

24 'This Is Social Solidarity in Action, a Feature of Nationhood' (*City Press*, 23 March 2020) <https://www.news24.com/citypress/news/this-is-social-solidarity-in-action-a-feature-of-our-nationhood-ramaphosa-20200323>.

Act. On 16 April 2020, Parliament resumed work relating to the oversight of the government's COVID-19 response using virtual platforms. The National Coronavirus Command Council (NCCC) was established on 17 March 2020, comprising cabinet ministers and experts and chaired by the President. NCCC decisions are presented to cabinet for approval before being announced by President Ramaphosa.

Scientific advice informs much of the decision-making through the creation of Ministerial Advisory Committees (MACs). The National Health Act 61 of 2003 provides that, in consultation with the National Health Council, the minister of health may establish an advisory committee deemed necessary to achieve the objectives of the Act.[25] In total, three advisory committees were established: the MAC on COVID-19 (established on 30 March 2020); the MAC on Social and Behavioural Change (established on 16 June 2020); and the MAC on COVID Vaccines (established on 14 September 2020). When a MAC is established, the minister must gazette, among others, its terms of reference, function and working procedures.[26] However, concern was expressed that the establishment of the MACs was not gazetted[27] and that the terms of reference for the appointment of members on the MAC on COVID-19 were not made available by the National Department of Health.[28]

Although the NCCC is under no obligation to follow the advice of the MACs, the government stated on 28 August 2020 that it had followed more than 95% of the advice rendered to the NCCC.[29] In an apparent effort to improve transparency and following pressure from the media and civil society, all of the MACs' "advisories" or guideline documents were published by the National Department of Health on 27 August 2020. As of 28 June 2021, the MAC on COVID-19 had published 90 advisories.[30]

In addition to the initial questions raised with regard to the functioning of the MAC on COVID-19, public criticism by MAC members regarding the government's handling of the pandemic led to a backlash by the Department of Health. In May 2020, Professor Glenda Gray (President of the South African Medical Research Council (SAMRC) and then a member of the MAC on COVID-19) criticised the government's phased exit from the lockdown as "unscientific and nonsensical".[31] In response, the Minister of Health issued a public statement argu-

25 National Health Act 61 of 2003, s 91(1).

26 ibid s 91(2).

27 Jerome Amir Singh, 'How South Africa's Ministerial Advisory Committee on COVID-19 can be Optimised' (2020) 110(6) South African Medical Journal 439.

28 ibid.

29 Kabous Le Roux, 'Newly Released MAC documents: Govt Mostly Followed Advice, with Vital Exceptions' (*Cape Talk*, 28 August 2020) <http://www.capetalk.co.za/articles/394565/newly-released-mac-documents-govt-mostly-followed-advice-with-a-few-vital-exceptions>.

30 COVID-19 Online Resource and News Portal (Department of Health), 'MAC Advisories' <https://sacoronavirus.co.za/category/mac-advisories/page/3/?fbclid=iwar3trqhhklmpf_bnr2l3n3neuebzbvy5hjozfvbla_ggjk_p1rvpgznz8j0>.

31 Azarrah Karrim and Sarah Evans, 'Unscientific and Nonsensical: Top Scientist Slams Government's Lockdown Strategy' (*News24*, 16 May 2020) <https://www.news24.com/news24/SouthAfrica

ing that Professor Gray had made "factually incorrect and unfounded statements".[32] The Department then requested the SAMRC to conduct an investigation into Professor Gray on the basis that she had "made a number of false allegations against the media" that were "damaging to the government's COVID-19 response".[33] This was met with an outcry from the scientific community and concerns were expressed about the right of academic freedom.[34] In September 2020, 14 of the 50 MAC members on COVID-19 were removed, whom Minister Mkhize stated had to be replaced by experts from additional sectors, including social behavioural scientists, to influence the behavioural change that was required to mitigate against the spread of COVID-19.[35] Although the addition of behavioural scientists on the committee was welcomed, the axing of the three experts most openly critical of the government's handling of the pandemic raised some eyebrows.[36]

Any regulations promulgated under the state of disaster must pass the test of rationality. This is a rule of law requirement and it is irrelevant whether the decisions or regulations were made mistakenly or in good faith.[37] On this point, in June 2020, certain lockdown regulations on levels 3 and 4 were struck down as unconstitutional by the Gauteng Division of the High Court, but the declaration of the state of disaster was upheld.[38] In reviewing the regulations, the court observed that some of the regulations caused many who work in the informal sector, and who would have limited interactions with others, to lose their right to "eke out a livelihood", whereas minibus taxis, on the other hand, could continue to operate with people sitting in close proximity.[39] It also found that restricting physical exercise to "arbitrarily determined time periods is completely irrational".[40] The court held

/News/unscientific-and-nonsensical-top-scientific-adviser-slams-governments-lockdown-strategy-20200516>.

32 COVID-19 Online Resource and News Portal (Department of Health), 'Health Minister's Statement on Prof Glenda Gray's Public Attack of Government Based on Inaccurate Information' (20 May 2020) <https://sacoronavirus.co.za/2020/05/20/health-ministers-statement-on-the-prof-glenda-grays-public-attack-of-government-based-on-inaccurate-information/>.

33 Liezel Human and Nathan Geffen, 'Health Boss Wants Investigation into Scientist Critical of SA's Lockdown' (*Times Live*, 22 May 2020) <https://www.timeslive.co.za/news/south-africa/2020-05-22-health-boss-wants-investigation-into-scientist-critical-of-sas-lockdown/>.

34 '250 Senior Academics Issue Statement to Support Prof Glenda Gray and "the Principle of Academic Freedom"' (*Maverick Citizen*, 15 May 2020) <https://www.dailymaverick.co.za/article/2020-05-25-250-senior-academics-issue-statement-to-support-prof-glenda-gray-and-the-principle-of-academic-freedom/>.

35 'Mkhize Disbands Ministerial Advisory Committee on COVID-19' (*Citizen*, 25 September 2020) <https://citizen.co.za/news/covid-19/2362959/mkhize-disbands-ministerial-advisory-committee-on-covid-19/>.

36 'Mhkize Culls his Critics in order to "Strengthen" the MACs' (*Medical Brief*, 30 September 2020 <https://www.medicalbrief.co.za/archives/mkhize-culls-his-critics-in-order-to-strengthen-the-macs/>.

37 *Khosa v Minister of Defence* [2020] BCLR 816 (GP) [5] High Court of South Africa.

38 *De Beer and Others v Minister of Cooperative Governance and Traditional Affairs* [2020] BCLR 1349 (GP).

39 ibid [5.2].

40 ibid [7.2].

that, although the government's approach was focused on reducing the incidence of COVID-19, little or no consideration of whether the limitation on rights was justifiable was evident. It found the government's approach to be paternalistic and not constitutionally justified.[41]

In January 2021, regulations that restricted exercise to certain hours and the ban on the sale of hot food in shops were found to be invalid for failing to meet this test of rationality. In the case of *Esau and Others v Minister of Co-Operative Governance and Traditional Affairs and Others*, the Supreme Court of Appeal held that the regulation prohibiting supermarkets from selling hot food was "invalid to the extent that they prohibited the sale of hot, cooked food otherwise than for delivery to a person's home".[42] The effect of this regulation was that "while a supermarket could sell, to in-store customers, a salad or a cold pie, it could not sell a hot piece of chicken or a hot pie. The latter items could only be sold if they are delivered to the customer's home."[43] The court added that "[i]t is arbitrary in the extreme to draw a distinction, to put it at its crudest, between a hot piece of chicken and a cold piece of chicken".[44] Moreover, the regulation restricting the movement of persons was found to be invalid to the extent that it limited exercise to walking, running and cycling between 6am and 9am and within a five kilometre radius of a person's home.[45] The court referred to the "systemic encroachments" on the common law right to freedom of movement in the past; for example, "the pass laws, influx control, race-based restrictions on interprovincial movement, banishments and house arrests under the security laws during apartheid".[46] The court indicated that the link between the infringement of the right to freedom of movement and the right to human dignity was "clear and direct".[47] Not only did the judgment question why only three types of exercise were permitted but the rationale for the five kilometre radius limitation was also interrogated.[48] The court held that, in the absence of justifications for these limitations, "there is no rational explanation to justify them".[49]

At various times during the state of disaster, the sale of cigarettes was prohibited. This ban was successfully challenged in the Western Cape High Court on 11 December 2020. The court held that the ban was unconstitutional and that regulation 45 of the Disaster Management Act — under which the cigarette prohibition was put in place — "cannot and does not withstand constitutional scrutiny".[50] In

41 ibid.
42 *Esau and Others v Minister of Co-Operative Governance and Traditional Affairs and Others* [2021] ZASCA 9 [161].
43 ibid [151].
44 ibid [152].
45 ibid [161].
46 ibid [121].
47 ibid [120].
48 ibid [161].
49 ibid [146].
50 Matthew Savides, 'Lockdown Cigarette Ban was "Not Necessary" and Unconstitutional, Says WC High Court' (*Times Live*, 11 December 2020) <https://www.timeslive.co.za/news/south

addition, it was found that the ban did not achieve its stated purpose (to reduce the incidence of smoking) and that the Minister had not demonstrated that the constitutional rights of smokers, tobacco farmers and tobacconists had not been violated.[51] As of 28 June 2021, the government was appealing this ruling.[52] A similar ban on the sale of alcohol was also being challenged on the basis that it goes beyond what is reasonable and necessary to stop the spread of COVID-19 and that it removes the right of adults to responsibly consume beer safely in the privacy of their own homes.[53]

These legal challenges demonstrate the important role of the courts in ensuring the soundness of the pandemic response, protecting against potentially arbitrary decisions and providing for some accountability mechanisms. Misuse of the additional powers by governments, whether for financial or political benefit, further exacerbates the risk of human rights abuses. The implementation of lockdown measures in South Africa has been marked by corruption and a lack of clear coordination.[54] There have been reports of police officers confiscating tobacco and liquor; councillors of the ruling African National Congress (ANC) looting food relief destined for those at risk of starvation; and senior ANC figures enriching themselves through COVID-19 tenders.[55] The relevant criminal justice structures exist to address fraud and corruption arising during a pandemic, but bringing those guilty to account is a slow and often frustrating process.[56] Managing a pandemic requires trust between governments and citizens, which should be strengthened by transparency and accountability.

From March 2020 to 28 June 2021, more than a hundred legal challenges relating to the lockdown regulations were brought by various individuals, political parties and lobby groups, and this trend looked set to continue. As South Africa enters a second year of COVID-19 and a third wave of COVID-19 at the time of writing, questions must be asked about whether it is appropriate for the courts to

-africa/2020-12-11-lockdown-cigarette-ban-does-not-withstand-constitutional-scrutiny-says-wc-high-court/>.

51 Samantha Filby, Kirsten Van der Zee and Corné Van Walbeek, 'The Temporary Ban on Tobacco Sales in South Africa: Lessons for Endgame Strategies', BMJ Tobacco Control (published online, 20 January 2021) <http://doi:10.1136/tobaccocontrol-2020-056209>. The authors conclude that the ban is inappropriate, as the government should first have the illicit tobacco market under control before doing so.

52 Bloomberg, 'Government's Tobacco Case Appeal Raises Fears of Another Cigarette Ban in South Africa' (*Businesstech*, 5 January 2021) <https://businesstech.co.za/news/lifestyle/459136/governments-tobacco-case-appeal-raises-fears-of-another-cigarette-ban-in-south-africa/>.

53 'Government Given Ultimatum on Further Alcohol Bans for South Africa' (*Businesstech*, 9 May 2021). <https://businesstech.co.za/news/business/488943/government-given-ultimatum-on-further-alcohol-bans-for-south-africa/>.

54 Melodie Labuschaigne, 'Ethicolegal Issues Relating to the South African Government's Response to COVID-19' (2020) 13(1) South African Journal of Bioethics and Law 6.

55 Bonga Dlulane, 'ANC Set to Ask Members Implicated in COVID-19 Tender Allegations to Step Aside' (*Eyewitness News*, undated) <https://ewn.co.za/2020/08/04/anc-nec-resolves-to-ask-members-implicated-in-covid-19-tender-corruption-to-step-aside>.

56 Labuschaigne (n 54) 23–28.

remain the only branch with direct oversight powers. Access to the courts remains a crucial balancing check on the power that remains centralised to the minister in charge and the NCCC. The longer the period that Parliament is not directly involved with the management of the COVID-19 pandemic, the greater the risk that the vital principle of checks and balances with the executive may be jeopardised, opening the door for possible excesses of power and abuse or mismanagement of public health resources made available as part of the pandemic response.

4. The Rationality of the Criminalisation of COVID-19 Regulation Breaches

South Africa's COVID-19 response shows an overreliance on the criminal law with insufficient consideration of how to foster trust and enable compliance with the public health measures. The announcement of the first lockdown in March 2020 saw President Ramaphosa appearing in military fatigues, which set a militarised tone for future enforcement. Failure to comply with some of the lockdown restrictions may result in imprisonment of up to six months, a fine or both. For example, regulations published as recently as 27 June 2021 criminalise the convening of any gathering or selling of liquor, among other things.[57]

Not only was the South African National Defence Force (SANDF) bestowed with additional powers and deployed to support the South African Police Force, but a military presence became a familiar scene across South Africa in enforcing the regulations. Within the first few days of the lockdown, reports of the SANDF and the South African Police Service using rubber bullets[58] and allegations of abuse surfaced.[59] Eight people were reported to have been killed by the police during the first week of the lockdown in enforcing the COVID-19 regulations, which at that time was more than the number of deaths related to the virus.[60] An entire group of almost 50 wedding guests, including the bride and groom, were arrested in the first week of April for breaking the ban on public gatherings[61] and two doctors who tested positive for COVID-19 were forced into quarantine at a medical facility.[62] However, in June 2020, the North Gauteng High Court issued an order

57 Disaster Management Act, 2002. Regulation Gazette 11299 of 27 June 2021 (No. 44772), reg 30.

58 Jason Burke, 'South African Police Fire Rubber Bullets at Shoppers amid Lockdown' (*The Guardian*, 28 March 2020) <http://www.theguardian.com/world/2020/mar/28/south-africa-police-rubber-bullets-shoppers-covid-19-lockdown>.

59 Andisiwe Makinana, 'DA Calls for Investigation into "Gross Violations" by Soldiers Policing Lockdown' (*SowetanLIVE*, 30 March 2020) <https://www.sowetanlive.co.za/news/south-africa/2020-03-30-da-calls-for-investigation-into-gross-violations-by-soldiers-policing-lockdown/>.

60 Daneel Knoetze and Citizen reporter, 'Eight People Allegedly Already Killed by Police during Lockdown—More than the Virus' (*The Citizen*, 3 April 2020) <https://citizen.co.za/news/south-africa/crime/2265100/eight-people-allegedly-already-killed-by-police-during-lockdown-more-than-the-virus/>.

61 'Lockdown Wedding Ends in Arrest of Bride and Groom' (*BBC News*, 6 April 2020) <https://www.bbc.com/news/world-africa-52183152>.

62 Azarrah Karim, '2 Doctors Allegedly Forced into Quarantine after "Bringing Coronavirus to Limpopo"' (*News24*, 3 April 2020) <https://m.news24.com/SouthAfrica/News/watch-2

prohibiting government from forcing those who tested positive for COVID-19 into state quarantine facilities if they were able to self-isolate. The High Court held that a person is "only required to be quarantined or isolated at a state facility, or other designated quarantine site, when that person is unable to self-isolate, or refuses to do so, or violates the self-quarantine or self-isolation rules".[63]

The degree to which South Africa learned from other pandemics, notably of HIV and TB, and used this experience to inform its initial COVID-19 response, must be questioned. Criminalising the transmission of other infectious diseases such as HIV is generally considered to be a counterproductive policy, lacking in any evidence base. It only serves to stigmatise the disease, discriminates against those who have it[64] and results in potential human rights abuses.[65] There is concern that criminalisation could exacerbate public health challenges,[66] and have a devastating impact on already marginalised, stigmatised or criminalised communities.[67] South Africa fortunately resisted any attempts to criminalise HIV, but it is unclear why there has been a different response to COVID-19.

South Africa has also learned that prevention, testing and treatment campaigns must involve the community and that community-based services are essential in achieving results. Public engagement is thus essential at both a macro level in the formation of policy and at a micro level whereby community engagement can help support the implementation of policy. At a macro level, any guidance must be contextualised to take account of local healthcare systems, beliefs and traditions. For the COVID-19 measures to succeed, it is necessary to know what different communities need to do to comply with these measures, and an important component is community engagement. South Africa should have drawn on its considerable experience of conducting community engagement to ensure that the regulations address COVID-19 effectively, and do not result in stigma and discrimination or disproportionately affect those on low incomes and perpetuate

-doctors-allegedly-forced-into-quarantine-after-claim-of-bringing-coronavirus-to-limpopo-20200403>.

63 'Another Court Loss for NDZ as COVID-19 Patients May Not Be Forced into State Quarantine' (*The Citizen*, 3 June 2020) <https://citizen.co.za/news/south-africa/courts/2296197/another-court-loss-for-ndz-as-covid-19-patients-may-not-beforced-into-state-quarantine/>.

64 The Lancet HIV, 'Editorial: HIV Criminalisation Is Bad Policy Based on Bad Science' (2018) 5(9) Lancet HIV <https://www.thelancet.com/journals/lanhiv/article/PIIS2352-3018(18)30219-4/fulltext>.

65 UNAIDS, 'Rights in the Time of COVID-19—Lessons from HIV for an Effective, Community-Led Response' (2020) 20; Gill Black, 'COVID-19 Community Engagement in South Africa: The Time Is Now' (Sustainable Livelihoods Foundation, 10 April 2020) <http://livelihoods.org.za/2020/04/10/covid-19-community-engagement-in-south-africa-the-time-is-now/>.

66 Kristin B Sandvik, 'Governing Global Health Emergencies: The Role of Criminalization' (*PRIO Blogs*, 2 March 2020) <https://blogs.prio.org/2020/03/governing-global-health-emergencies-the-role-of-criminalization/>.

67 HIV Justice Network, 'HIV Justice Worldwide Steering Committee Statement on COVID-19 Criminalisation' (25 March 2020) <http://www.hivjustice.net/news/hiv-justice-worldwide-steering-committee-statement-on-covid-19-criminalisation/>.

health inequity.[68] A community-centred response for COVID-19 at the outset should have been adopted.[69] Although President Ramaphosa stated in his March 2020 address to the nation that he consulted with business and industry, there appeared to be a lack of consultation with those living in cramped, informal settlements who struggled to comply with these restrictive measures, putting them at risk of breaching lockdown regulations that carry a criminal sanction.[70]

On both a macro and micro level, stigma reduction campaigns are essential during a pandemic response.[71] Key to this is stopping the spread of disinformation, particularly as a vaccine roll-out programme begins. South Africa has considerable experience from its exposure to the HIV epidemic, marked by a history of false cures for HIV that included garlic, beetroot and holy water, to name but a few.[72] Stopping the spread of disinformation and informing the public about the virus is essential. Shocking disinformation by influential figures, such as the comments made by South Africa's Chief Justice, Justice Mgoeng Mgoeng in December 2021, must be strongly condemned. Mgoeng CJ observed during a gathering that, "[i]f there be any (COVID-19) vaccine that is the work of the devil, meant to infuse 666 in the lives of the people, meant to corrupt their DNA … it [ought] to be destroyed by fire".[73] His regrettable refusal to correct his irrational stance on COVID-19 vaccines led to a health advocacy group, African Alliance, filing a formal complaint against him with the Judicial Services Commission.[74] As a highly visible and senior member of society, with a significant following, the group argued that his comments risked serious social harm and undermined the public's confidence in life-saving and scientifically tested vaccines.

5. Conclusion

Balancing competing legal interests during a pandemic is a delicate exercise that has to consider both societal and individual interests. It is sometimes necessary to take extreme measures that result in the limitation of certain human rights

68 Peter A Newman and others (2015) 'Towards a Science of Community Stakeholder Engagement in Biomedical HIV Prevention Trials: An Embedded Four-Country Case Study' 10(8) PLoS ONE e0135937.

69 UNAIDS (n 64); Black (n 65).

70 Ciara Staunton, Carmen Swanepoel and Melodie Labuschaigne, 'Between a Rock and a Hard Place: COVID-19 and South Africa's Response' (2020) 7(1) Journal of Law and the Biosciences 1.

71 Carmen Logie and Janet Turan, 'How Do We Balance Tensions Between COVID-19 Public Health Responses and Stigma Mitigation? Learning from HIV Research' (2020) 24(1) AIDS and Behavior <https://doi.org/10.1007/s10461-020-02856-8>.

72 Keymanthri Moodley and others, 'The Psychology of "Cure"—Unique Challenges to Consent Processes in HIV Cure Research in South Africa' (2019) 20(9) BMC Medical Ethics <https://doi.org/10.1186/s12910-019-0348-z>.

73 Chris Roper, 'Mogoeng's Vaccine Apocalypse' (*Financial Mail*, 17 December 2020) <https://www.businesslive.co.za/fm/features/2020-12-17-chris-roper-mogoengs-vaccine-apocalypse/>.

74 Andrea Chotia, 'Formal Complaint Filed against Chief Justice Mogoeng for "Vaccine Prayer"' (*MSN News*, 14 January 2021) <https://www.msn.com/en-za/news/national/formal-complaint-filed-against-chief-justice-mogoeng-for-vaccine-prayer/ar-BB1cKjwj>.

and freedoms, such as bodily integrity, privacy, freedom of association and freedom of movement. In constitutional democracies such as South Africa, however, such restrictions have to be consistent with the limitation provisions in the Constitution.[75] A consideration of rationality is important, not only as a requirement of the principle of legality, but to ensure that a decision, whether legislative or executive, is rationally related to a legitimate governmental purpose, otherwise it will be arbitrary and inconsistent with the Constitution.[76]

South Africa's response in the first 18 months of the COVID-19 pandemic saw an overreliance on the criminal law in ensuring compliance, and insufficient consideration of the socio-economic reality that a large segment of the South African population lives in overcrowded, informal settlements and, as a consequence of COVID-related restrictions, found itself with either no or limited access to employment or social support.

As South Africa continues to manage the pandemic, lessons must be learned. The first is that South Africa must draw from its considerable experience of addressing HIV and TB and identify measures that can inform its pandemic preparedness. Second, as was identified early on in the HIV and TB pandemic, behavioural and social scientists must inform policy making. Third, South Africa must realise that informed criticism and public debate are crucial in a functioning democracy and particularly during a public health crisis. The focus should be on stopping the spread of misinformation and not the suppression of debate. Finally, judicial oversight of executive action alone is not enough; consideration should be given to strengthening the scrutiny and decision-making roles of Parliament during a state of disaster, particularly when it lasts for an extended period of time.

75 Section 36 of the Constitution.

76 *Pharmaceutical Manufactures: In re Ex parte Application of the President of the Republic of South Africa* [2000] SA 674 (CC) [85].

29

IRAN'S COVID-19 RESPONSE

Who Calls the Shots?

Marzieh Tofighi Darian

1. Introduction[1]

At the time of writing, Iran is among the 20 worst affected countries in the world for COVID-19, having the ninth worst case-fatality rate of those states and the 11th worst per capita mortality rate.[2] This also made Iran the worst affected state in the Middle East. Iranian officials finally confirmed the first COVID-19-related death on 19 February 2020, after days of denial.[3] The government's sluggish response in the early days of the pandemic was a preview of what was yet to come: refusing to quarantine the city of Qom, the first domestic COVID-19 epicentre; rejecting calls to postpone parliamentary elections; and continuing to receive flights from China,[4] all of which contributed to the rapid spread of the virus across the country.

The repeated failure to impose a full lockdown brought about a fourth wave of COVID-19 in April–June 2021, with a fifth wave threatened. The Iranian government's response was mostly reactive, delayed and ineffective. In fact, unlike many other countries which faced anti-lockdown protests, in Iran, the general public and health professionals repeatedly called for a more robust and interventionist

1 All websites accessed on 19 July 2021.

2 Johns Hopkins University Coronavirus Resource Center, Mortality Analyses <https://coronavirus.jhu.edu/data/mortality>.

3 A short version of this chapter was originally published as 'Iran's COVID-19 Response: Who Calls the Shots?' (*Verfassungsblog*, 12 March 2021) <https://verfassungsblog.de/irans-covid-19-response-who-calls-the-shots>.

4 Maysam Bahravesh, 'The Untold Story of How Iran Became An Epicenter' (*Foreign Policy*, 24 March 2020) <https://foreignpolicy.com/2020/03/24/how-iran-botched-coronavirus-pandemic-response/>.

DOI: 10.4324/9781003211952-33

official response.[5] The government's tactical error in refusing to impose a lockdown or at least a ban on domestic travel during the most important national holiday (Persian New Year in March 2021) once again led to infections spiralling out of control. This brought almost the entire country to its highest level of alert within only a few days, forcing the government to backtrack from its decision to allow travel. However, although other restrictive measures were sporadically put in place, their enforcement was relatively loose or, at best, inconsistent.[6]

The government's reluctance to enforce full lockdown was partly attributed to the country's economic crisis in the wake of US-imposed sanctions, and its inability to sustain people financially via unemployment benefits or other substitutes.[7] The sanctions also disrupted and delayed the timely purchase of vaccines, making it harder to manage the spread of the virus and its variants.[8] Notwithstanding this, however, the domestic mismanagement of the crisis is undeniable.

This chapter focuses on Iran's institutional response to the COVID-19 crisis and examines how the new institutional setup relates to the existing constitutional system. It also seeks to explore what impacts might be felt in terms of constitutional rights and future relations between different branches of government. Section 2 examines the creation of the National Headquarters to Combat Corona (NHCC) and its related constitutional status. Section 3 reviews the legal grounds and the scope of the NHCC's decisions, and the potential dangers of overreach, while section 4 highlights the ramifications of this institutional arrangement in terms of Parliament's law-making and supervisory powers. In conclusion, it is argued that the institutional design created in response to the pandemic has again exposed the structural defects and limits of Iran's constitutional system, especially with respect to the division of power between the executive branch and the Supreme Leader on the one hand, and Parliament and other specialised constitutional councils on the other.

2. The Creation of the National Headquarters to Combat Corona

Shortly after the public confirmation of the first cases of COVID-19 in Iran, the Supreme National Security Council (SNSC) took matters into its own hands.

5 Patrick Wintour, 'Iran's President Has Left Nation Open to Second Covid-19 Wave – Critics' (*The Guardian*, 13 April 2020) <https://www.theguardian.com/world/2020/apr/13/irans-president-has-left-nation-open-to-second-covid-19-wave-critics>; Maziar Motamedi, 'Iran Imposes Nationwide COVID-19 Restrictions But No Lockdown' (*Al Jazeera*, 21 November 2020) <https://www.aljazeera.com/news/2020/11/21/iran-imposes-nationwide-covid-19-restrictions-but-no-lockdown>.

6 ibid.

7 'Iran's Covid-19 Death Toll Is Rising. Show Mercy Mr. Trump' (*The New York Times*, 13 October 2020) <https://www.nytimes.com/2020/10/13/opinion/iran-trump-sanctions-covid.html>.

8 Miriam Berger, 'U.S. Sanctions Could Impede Iran's Access to Coronavirus Vaccines, Experts Say' (*The Washington Post*, 7 December 2020) <https://www.washingtonpost.com/world/middle_east/iran-covax-coronavirus-vaccine-sanctions/2020/12/07/61a721f8-3632-11eb-9699-00d311f13d2d_story.html>.

Behind closed doors, it issued an order to set up the National Headquarters to Combat Corona (NHCC). It also announced that the NHCC's orders enjoyed the same degree of authority as those of the SNSC. The SNSC's role as immediate decision-maker was constitutionally consequential in this case, signalling that the pandemic was rapidly designated as a national security threat, instead of a crisis that could have been handled through existing legal frameworks. This is particularly significant as some officials, including the Supreme Leader himself, had tiptoed around the idea of suggesting bioterrorism as a cause of the pandemic in its early days.[9]

The SNSC consists of the heads of the three branches of government; the Chief of the Supreme Command Council of the Armed Forces; the officer in charge of planning and budgetary affairs; two representatives nominated by the Supreme Leader; the Ministers of Foreign Affairs, the Interior and Intelligence; and, when necessary, other relevant ministers and the highest-ranking officials from the Armed Forces and the Islamic Revolutionary Guards Corps.[10] Although the SNSC is presided over by the sitting president, it is not officially considered part of the executive. The Constitution explicitly states that the SNSC's decisions shall only become effective upon the Supreme Leader's approval, making it clear that the ultimate legitimacy of the Council's decisions is derived from the broader powers of the Supreme Leader under the Constitution.[11]

The Constitution, in Article 79, gives the government the power to temporarily impose certain necessary restrictions in cases of war or other emergencies.[12] However, such an invocation is conditional upon the approval of Parliament, and needs to be reauthorised every 30 days. The Guardian Council, the organ of constitutional review and interpretation, has not delivered any opinion on Article 79. Thus, it is not clear whether a public health crisis can be characterised as the kind of emergency warranting the invocation of this Article. However, there is nothing in the constitutional text itself to bar such an understanding. In fact, constitutional law scholars have contemplated the exact relationship between the emergency powers, as stated in Article 79, and the broad scope of the SNSC's mandate under Article 176 of the Constitution. For example, Hashemi has sought to reconcile the two by arguing that, after the setting of the general national security policies by the SNSC, if the aforesaid policies infringe upon or restrict any individual rights, the government must present the matter to Parliament. It is only upon receiving Parliament's permission that the final enactment can be submitted to the Supreme Leader for his approval through the SNSC mechanism.[13] Despite this argument,

9 The Office of Supreme Leader, Commander-in-Chief's Order to the Supreme Command Council of the Armed Forces to Combat Corona, 12 March 2020 <https://www.leader.ir/fa/content/24345/فرمان-فرمانده-کل-قوا-به-رئیس-ستادکل-نیروهای-مسلح-در-زمینه-مقابله-با-کرونا>.

10 Constitution of Islamic Republic of Iran, 1989, art 176.

11 ibid, art 110.

12 ibid, art 79.

13 Mohammad Hashemi, *Constitutional Law of Islamic Republic of Iran Sovereign and Political Institutions*, vol 2 (7th edn, Mizan 2003) 536.

which implies the preservation of some role for Parliament in cases of the curtailment of individual rights, in practice, the SNSC has not seen itself as bound by this provision, nor by any other legislative oversight. Therefore, the establishment of the NHCC through the SNSC effectively transferred powers from the two elected branches to a more restricted group, with the ultimate power of approval given to the Supreme Leader. This last feature was to become a double-edged sword in the fight against COVID-19.

Under Iran's Constitution, the Supreme Leader enjoys a significant share of executive power. He is the Commander-in-Chief, sets the state's general policies, and holds significant military and civilian appointment powers. On 12 March 2020, the Supreme Leader ordered the Supreme Command Council of the Armed Forces to set up temporary hospitals and take necessary measures to treat patients in order to prevent the further spread of the virus.[14] He instructed the military to cooperate with the government, in particular the Ministry of Health and Medical Education. He also lent his full support to the establishment of the NHCC, and stated that following the NHCC's orders was both a legal and religious obligation.[15] This support was critical in the NHCC's decision to close the Holy Shrines in Qom and Mashhad, and to suspend Friday religious congregations in almost all cities for quite some time, a decision that was initially met with strong resistance. It is evident that, had it not been for his support, the NHCC would probably have failed to enforce these religiously sensitive decisions in the face of fierce resistance within more conservative segments of the population and political entities.[16]

The bifurcated system of governance between the president (as the head of the executive) and the Supreme Leader has been laid bare in the management of the COVID-19 crisis. While the Supreme Leader has the final say on SNSC decisions, unlike the president, he is insulated from direct electoral accountability. Although the Supreme Leader's support reinforced the NHCC's authority, at the same time, it exposed the limits and fragility of this relationship. This imbalance of power meant that the Supreme Leader's clear opposition, or even his silence, could trouble the enforcement of NHCC decisions. The controversy over vaccination made this tenuous situation manifest. In a speech in January 2021, the Supreme Leader unequivocally announced a ban on importing US and UK vaccines.[17] Many healthcare professionals, including those within the Scientific Committee of the NHCC, and even more tacitly the president himself, expressed their discontent

14 The Office of Supreme Leader (n 9).

15 Interview with Saeed Namaki, 'Complying with the NHCC's Orders Were the Results of the Supreme Leader's Support' (Supreme Council of Cultural Revolution, 30 April 2020) <https://sccr.ir/News/11090/1/تبعیت-از-تصمیمات-ستاد-ملی-مبارزه-با-کرونا-نتیجه-حمایت%E2%80%8Cهای-رهبر-معظم-انقلاب-بود>.

16 Parliament's News, interview with Babak Negahdari, advisor to the Parliament's Spokesperson (*Parliran*, 29 June 2020) <https://www.parliran.ir/majles/fa/Content/_/تنها-اولویت-مجلس-یازدهم-مشکلات-مردم-و-منافع-ملی-است-تحول-یعنی-بازگشت-مجلس-به-ریل-اصلی-خود>.

17 Erin Cunningham, 'Iran's Khamenei Bans the Import of US and UK Coronavirus Vaccines' (*The Washington Post*, 8 January 2021) <https://www.washingtonpost.com/world/2021/01/08/iran-khamenei-bans-us-uk-coronavirus-vaccines/>.

with this decision.[18] Nonetheless, in the wake of his speech, some pre-orders were reportedly cancelled,[19] and the NHCC's attention shifted to Russian, Chinese and Cuban vaccines. The possibility of cooperating with these countries to reach self-sufficiency in producing domestic vaccines was also raised. At the time, this resulted in public outrage, with one of the nation's top infectious disease specialists publicly announcing that she would not get a Russian vaccine.[20] Similar contentions were also raised over the regulation of major religious events such as Muharram, for which hundreds of thousands of mourners ordinarily gather each year. Although the Supreme Leader clearly stated that he deferred to the decision of the NHCC, he made it clear that those officials who appreciated the value of prayer[21] should make the final call. In the end, the NHCC issued a set of guidelines[22] and urged religious centres to scale back their events and comply with the Ministry of Health's protocols. However, the poor execution of these protocols, combined with a lack of sufficient enforcement, led to several mass gatherings occurring.

3. The Legal Grounds for the NHCC's Power and its Potential Overreach

The NHCC's mandate makes this institution the sole decision-maker when it comes to the COVID-19 outbreak. These decisions range from public health protocols (such as social distancing and mask mandates) to economic relief measures (like giving out loans and cash payments and lease moratoria), and restrictive measures that are sanctioned under the law, such as limiting freedom of movement (by imposing curfews or temporarily banning inter-provincial travel). Other decisions adopted by the NHCC included collecting patient data and sharing it with public and private institutions to prevent citizens from boarding planes or entering governmental offices.[23] With such a broad mandate, and in order to understand the scope of its power, the institution that created the NHCC – the SNSC – must be examined: what powers does the SNSC have under the Constitution, and what share of these could be handed over to an ad hoc independent institution? Moreover, what supervisory mechanisms are in place to ensure that both institutions stay within the bounds of the law?

18 'Minoo Mohraz Rejected Ayatollah Khamenei's Comments on the Coronavirus Vaccine' (*BBC Persian*, 27 January 2021) <https://www.bbc.com/persian/iran-55694318>.

19 'Iran Bans Import of UK and US Covid-19 Vaccines, Saying They're "Completely Untrustworthy"' (*France 24*, 9 January 2021) <https://www.france24.com/en/middle-east/20210109-iran-bans-import-of-uk-and-us-covid-19-vaccines-saying-they-re-completely-untrustworthy>.

20 Maziar Motamedi, 'Purchase of Russia's Covid Vaccine Sparks Debate in Iran' (*Al Jazeera*, 3 February 2021) <https://www.aljazeera.com/news/2021/2/3/vaccine-debate-rages-as-russias-sputnik-v-heads-for-iran>.

21 The Office of Supreme Leader, Supreme Leader's Speech to the NHCC' (10 May 2020) <https://www.leader.ir/fa/speech/24452/بیانات-در-ارتباط-تصویری-با-ستاد-ملی-مبارزه-با-کرونا>.

22 The Office of Presidency, 'Compilation of NHCC's Enactments' 30th session, s 1 (2020) 46 <http://media.cabinetoffice.ir/uploads/org/2021/01/23/161139553089692800.pdf>.

23 ibid, session 5-50.

The SNSC is not merely an advisory council; rather, it is interpreted to have some form of law-making power. The constitutional provision states that the SNSC has the power to set state national security policies, coordinate activities in this area and use all resources to combat any security threat. However, the last section of Article 176 introduces the 'enactments' of the Council and makes them conditional upon the Supreme Leader's approval.[24] The exact characterisation of the SNSC's enactments is unclear. Are they considered executive regulations, given the composition of the Council, or legislation? Furthermore, what is the relationship between the SNSC's enactments and those of the executive or legislative branches, particularly given the secrecy of the Council's decisions? The ambiguity over the law-making power of the SNSC begets two sets of problems. First, do the SNSC's enactments pre-empt the field for parliamentary legislation? If so, is this partial or total? Secondly, are the SNSC's enactments subject to regular judicial review mechanisms? If not, what can guarantee that the Council will not act ultra vires or infringe on fundamental rights?

From the relatively sparse available data, it can be concluded that, in the eyes of the Guardian Council, the organ of constitutional review, the SNSC is authorised to legislate, and its legislation pre-empts that of the Parliament. In a few instances, the Guardian Council, reviewing legislation, raised objections that some of the provisions in the law under review were not compatible with the enactments of the SNSC, and directed Parliament to resolve the inconsistencies.[25] Certain scholars have also concluded that subsequent legislation by the SNSC, if in conflict with existing law, will repeal parliamentary legislation.[26] To put it differently, SNSC enactments can trump existing executive regulations and legislation, and cannot be overturned by any of them subsequently.[27] The Court of Administrative Justice has confirmed this conclusion in its 2012 opinion, in which the Court rejected the plaintiff's argument that that SNSC's enactment was impliedly repealed by the adoption of the Civil Service Management Law in Parliament, stating that "the SNSC's enactments that the Supreme Leader approves may not be overturned by legislation".[28]

Not only are the two political branches thus subject to the SNSC's higher authority, but there is also no judicial oversight over the Council's enactments. National security cases are generally viewed as requiring more deference to the political branches.[29] However, exempting a Council with the power to legislate in

24 See Kevjn Lim, 'National Security Decision-making in Iran' (2015) 34 Comparative Strategy 149, 154–157.

25 Guardian Council's Objections to the Fifth Development Plan No. 89/30/40968 (2010) 3 <http://nazarat.shora-rc.ir/Forms/FileLoad.aspx?id=VXVS6q6T1xQ=&TN=l7tLyhyOobj0SooAFUE3m5rC3iufWLR1csaqpt/F9Oo=&NF=bHiIRfspeW0=>.

26 Mohammad Hashemi, *Constitutional Law of Islamic Republic of Iran Sovereign and Political Institutions*, vol 2 (7th edn, Mizan 2003) 537.

27 Mehdi Moghaddasi and Ehsan Akbari, 'The Legal Status of SNSC's Enactments in Iran's Constitutional System' (2017) 47 Public Law Studies 873, 890.

28 ibid 882.

29 Aziz Huq, 'Against National Security Exceptionalism' (2009) Vol. 2009-1 The Supreme Court Review 225.

secret, free from the purview of any judicial oversight, can lead to severe encroachments on constitutional rights. The SNSC's enactments certainly do not qualify as ordinary legislation, and therefore, are not subject to the Guardian Council's constitutional review powers. On the other hand, nor can the SNSC's decisions merely be classified as executive or administrative decisions. In fact, Article 12 of the Law on Organisation and Procedure of the Court of Administrative Justice (as amended in 2013) clearly states that the SNSC's decisions are outside the purview of the Court's jurisdiction.[30] With nobody specifically in charge of ensuring that the Council is not acting ultra vires, then, there seems to be no legal safeguard other than the Supreme Leader's interpretation of the SNSC's mandate.

Against this backdrop, the legal authority of the National Headquarters to Combat Corona's decisions and available remedies for potential violations of individual rights and freedoms becomes significant. In its order to establish the NHCC, the SNSC indicated that NHCC's decisions carried the same weight as those of the SNSC. In fact, the Interior Minister said that NHCC's decisions were more authoritative than law.[31] President Hasan Rouhani, in a televised speech, also emphasised that all measures approved by the NHCC were to be treated as law and must be implemented.[32] However, the exact nature of the NHCC as an ad hoc institution is not entirely spelled out. Article 176 authorises the SNSC to create sub-councils, such as the Defence Council or the Domestic National Security Council, as it sees fit. Such designation is of significance because, under the Constitution – and unlike the SNSC itself – Parliament can determine the scope of these sub-councils' jurisdictions. Yet, in the more than three decades since its inception, the SNSC has not established any sub-council other than the Domestic National Security Council. Instead, it has increasingly empowered and expanded its own secretariat, a practice that itself has been the subject of criticism.[33]

Is the NHCC, then, a sub-council subject to Parliament's power, or is it a separate, ad hoc institution fully under the SNSC's control? If considered a sub-council, Parliament can provide an additional layer of oversight and regulate the scope of NHCC authority and, if necessary, prevent it from law-making in certain areas. Absent a constitutional interpretation, a definitive answer cannot be provided. However, the sub-councils mentioned in the text of the Constitution seem to share two features: they cover general and permanent themes such as defence and security. The NHCC does not share these characteristics. Moreover, it is not the first time that the SNSC has created an ad hoc body to tackle what it has designated as an urgent national security problem. For example, after the SNSC

30 Law on Organisation and Procedure of the Court of Administrative Justice 2013.

31 'Minister of Interior: NHCC's Enactments Are Regarded as the SNSC's Enactments' (*Etemad Online*, 16 November 2020) <https://etemadonline.com/content/445668/مصوبات-ستاد-کرونا-در-حکم-مصوبات-شورای-عالی-امنیت-ملی-است-آمارسازی-و-مخفی-کاری-در-کار-نباشد>.

32 Motamedi (n 5).

33 Mohammad Mohsen Roozitalab and Kheyrollah Parvin, 'Legal Reflection on the Structure and Jurisdiction of the Secretariat of the Supreme National Security Council in terms of Passing Resolutions' (2021) 3 Quarterly Journal of Public Law Knowledge 105.

created a Task Force on Special Measures Against Sanctions, the Guardian Council objected to legislation that aimed to regulate the Task Force's decisions. In its decision, the Guardian Council stated that it was the SNSC that had established this Task Force and determined the scope of its powers. Thus, the Task Force's decisions were seen as being under the SNSC's oversight.[34] This decision came after an earlier advisory report to the Guardian Council which had raised doubts about the exact nature of this Task Force, but had concluded that if the Task Force did not fit within the sub-council concept, Parliament could not regulate its activities.[35]

To view the NHCC as an ad hoc institution that enjoys the same level of authority as the SNSC poses another question: on what basis can the SNSC have transferred its power to another institution? There is nothing in the Constitution that provides such authority for the SNSC, outside of the sub-council scheme. Moreover, the SNSC, by its nature, is composed of a limited number of high-ranking individuals who can be trusted with handling national security issues. Some scholars have rejected the application of the delegation doctrine in the expansion of the SNSC's secretariat.[36] The argument is even more applicable to an external, ad hoc institution.

With no real restriction over the scope of the NHCC's authority and no judicial review power over its enactments, it is only the SNSC and the Supreme Leader that can, at their discretion, monitor the NHCC's operations within the bounds of the law. The lack of an oversight mechanism may thus facilitate NHCC overreach. For example, when it comes to data collection and privacy concerns, the Information and Communications Technology (ICT) Ministry may decide to pass executive regulations under the rubric of the NHCC, instead of utilising the regular bureaucratic process, thus shielding these regulations from judicial review or conflicting legislation. In fact, such encroachments have already occurred. As explained in the following section, the NHCC unilaterally amended the amount of economic relief passed in Parliament. On another occasion, it was reported that President Rouhani, in order to implement the Law Requiring the Government to Pay Subsidies for Essential Goods, ordered the sale of government shares in the stock market to three banks. Some accused the president of passing this "unrelated bill" via the NHCC to circumvent potential objections by the Head of the Central Bank, who presides over the Economic Council.[37] It is additionally possible to be concerned about the extension of the NHCC's decisions far beyond the pandemic. President Rouhani, in one of his speeches, acknowledged that the NHCC's decisions are temporary and specific to the handling of the pandemic. However, he

34 Bill on Removing Obstacles to Competitive Production and Promoting the Country's Financial System, Guardian Council's Opinion No. 93/102/3811, 7 March 2015, s 9.

35 Opinions of the Legal Advisory Council with regard to Bill on Removing Obstacles to Competitive Production and Promoting the Country's Financial System No. 9312035, 23 February 2015, 25–27.

36 Mohammad Mohsen Roozitalab and Kheyrollah Parvin (n 33) 116–119.

37 'Governance Failure for an Administration that Claimed to Prioritize Rational Decision-making' (*Fars News*, 22 May 2021) <https://www.farsnews.ir/news/14000301000102/ابتذال-حکمرانی-در-دولتی-که-مدعی-تدبیر-و-عقلانیت-بود-از-قرارگاه-مرغ-تا>.

added that some of these measures might become permanent after being adopted by other bodies.[38] In any event, there is nothing to bar the SNSC from adopting any of the COVID-19-era restrictions as a permanent measure, except for the Council's own discretion and the Supreme Leader's consent.

The centralisation of power in the NHCC did not, however, result in swift and aggressive measures to combat the pandemic. In November 2020, in the face of the third wave of the COVID-19 outbreak, the NHCC adopted the Comprehensive Plan for COVID-19 Restrictions,[39] which created a targeted and smart response system to the spread of the virus. The NHCC's main body, which makes the final decisions, consists mainly of political figures including cabinet members (the President, Ministers of Interior, Health, Transportation, Education, etc), a member of the Budget and Planning Organisation, and a member of the Guardian Council and the armed forces.[40] The NHCC does have sub-committees with epidemiologists and experts serving on them, but the political appointees have the upper hand in the decision-making process. This set-up has sometimes led to contradictory voices coming out of the NHCC, with public health experts challenging the adequacy of the NHCC's decisions, most significantly over its vaccination and lockdown decisions.[41]

The delayed nature and insufficiency of the NHCC's decisions is just one part of the story, however. As time passed, the NHCC began to adopt more aggressive measures in some areas, such as collecting data[42] from those who tested positive and using smart national ID cards to screen people.[43] In October 2020, the NHCC required all medical centres to transfer information about those diagnosed with COVID-19 to the Ministry of Health's central database. It also required infected individuals to self-report to the Ministry of Health, download the authorised tracking application and not break quarantine. In November, the NHCC passed a resolution requiring government offices to use smart ID cards before rendering any service. In the same session, the NHCC authorised the ICT Minister to track the data of those diagnosed, and to notify the Ministry of Health if they broke quarantine. In December, the Ministry of Health announced that hotels, travel agencies, organisations and even shopping malls could designate a contact person to connect to the centralised database of COVID-19 patients. They also proposed to share data with ride-sharing applications. As of June 2021, it was not clear to what extent these measures had been operationalised. Nevertheless, it was

38 President Rouhani, 'Speech during the NHCC's session' (20 February 2021)< https://www.president.ir/fa/119753>.

39 President Rouhani, 'Statement on Restrictive Measures Against the Third Wave of Corona' (15 November 2020) <https://www.president.ir/fa/118177/printable>.

40 List of the members appointed to the NHCC <https://www.tabnak.ir/fa/tags/181101/1/ستاد-مقابله-با-کرونا>.

41 Motamedi (n 5).

42 Shadi Karimi, 'Regulating Electronic Means to Fight the Spread of Covid-19' The Law Library of Congress No. 2020-019000 (June 2020) 167, Section on Iran < https://www.loc.gov/item/2020714995/>.

43 The Office of Presidency, 'Compilation of NHCC's Enactments' 30th session, s 1 (2020) 46.1

reported[44] that 700 individuals had been barred from boarding flights using this mechanism. A report released[45] by the ICT Ministry catalogues the data collection measures employed in countries like China, South Korea, Taiwan and Singapore,[46] indicating that the NHCC may move more aggressively to follow their direction. In its report, mirroring the South Korean model, the ICT Ministry suggested using the Central Bank's financial transaction data to contact-trace those infected with the virus.

4. The Marginalisation of Parliament

Absent from these discussions so far is the role of Parliament. The political and constitutional developments during the COVID-19 crisis once again confirmed the understanding that Parliament has mostly been sidelined and increasingly co-opted within the Iranian legal system. Although crisis management requires swift actions that are characteristics of the executive, invoking emergency powers could have given some supervisory power to Parliament, at least in having a say over how long the emergency measures would continue. On 7 April 2020, as cases were rapidly increasing, a few MPs unhappy with the government's failure to declare a lockdown introduced a bill to shut down the country for a month.[47] The deputy spokesperson soon rejected the proposal, saying that the bill violated Article 79 of the Constitution on emergency powers, since it was the executive that needed to initiate emergency power declaration, not Parliament.

The decision not to characterise the NHCC as a sub-council, as provided under the Constitution, also excluded Parliament from setting the scope of the Council's authority. It also has no power to pass legislation conflicting with that of the NHCC. Moreover, no legislator is reported to be in the composition of the NHCC's main body, even though a representative of the Guardian Council and armed forces are present. Notwithstanding this, Parliament is not kept in the dark; its various commissions regularly meet with relevant cabinet members, although at the time of writing no major legislation has passed in this regard.

Aside from modifications to the Budget Law, the only other legislative attempt was a bill proposed in November 2020 requiring the government to provide essential goods in case of lockdown, and to compensate struggling businesses.[48] It also included a provision extending lease contracts up to three months after the

44 'Mask Application To Identify Corona Patients' (*Irinn*, 2 December 2020)<https://www.irinn.ir/fa/news/805415/اپلیکیشن-ماسک-برای-شناسایی-مسافران-مبتلا-به-کرونا>.

45 Office of Presidency Centre for Strategic Studies 'Assessing Iran's Experience in Using New IT and Communication Capacities in the Management of Corona' (*Coronomy*, 1 January 2021)<https://coronomy.ir/detail/1283/ایران-چگونه-از-ict-در-مدیریت-کرونا-بهره-گرفت؟>.

46 For discussion of China, Taiwan and Singapore, see deLisle and Shen, chapter 4; Chang and Lin, chapter 25; Chua and Neo, chapter 7.

47 Radio Farda, 'Iran's Parliament Rejects Bill To Introduce One-Month National Lockdown' (*Radio Farda*, 7 April 2020) <https://en.radiofarda.com/a/iran-parliament-rejects-bill-to-introduce-one-month-national-lockdown/30540091.html>.

48 Bill on Regulations on the Corona Outbreak 19 November 2020.

end of the pandemic, with a maximum 20% increase in rents. As of June 2021, this bill had not yet passed in Parliament. However, the NHCC periodically ordered the extension of lease contracts on its own. The same month, Parliament passed a law on Requiring the Government to Pay Subsidies for Essential Goods.[49] As a result of the US's crippling sanctions, cash payments are not new in Iran. The law did not explicitly name COVID-19, but it was clearly passed with the pandemic's economic impact in mind, and provided a very modest payment (less than $6 per individual, and half of that for those with fixed incomes) to a total of 60 million Iranians for six months. Instead of enforcing the law, and in the face of MPs' objections, the NHCC modified the terms and eventually passed a resolution to pay roughly $4 per individual to 40 million people for four months.[50]

The passage of the Budget Law precipitated a legislative crisis in March 2020, as the NHCC almost forced Parliament to cancel its sessions due to the outbreak. With time running out to pass the budget, the parliamentary spokesperson wrote a letter to the Supreme Leader asking for his authorisation to pass the law in the Joint Commission instead of the Parliament's plenary session, as they were unable to reconvene.[51] At the time, the Supreme Leader authorised this move, and Parliament subsequently revised its Rules of Procedure to allow for the use of video conferencing. However, the idea of an ad hoc institution created by the SNSC forcing the closure of Parliament set off alarm bells.

5. Conclusion

The COVID-19 outbreak created a playbook for handling future crises, whether public health-related or otherwise. The Expediency Council, which is in charge of setting the state's general policies, has already issued an order to draw from the COVID-19 experience to reform the state's general policies in the areas of public health and national security, with a specific focus on bioterrorism.[52] The institutional setup created to combat the pandemic, including the enormous powers given to the National Headquarters to Combat Corona with no meaningful legislative or judicial oversight, exposed the shortcomings of the constitutional system and highlighted the potential for further power grabs and infringement of constitutional rights. It also shed new light on the Supreme National Security Council's jurisdiction and its broad law-making powers that can, at times, be misused. More than anything else, Iran's pandemic experience necessitates the reimagination of institutional responses to emergencies, while preserving some role for the legislative and judicial branches.

49 Law on Requiring the Government to Pay Subsidies for Essential Goods 27 November 2020.

50 NHCC's 49th Session's Amendment (23 December 2020) <https://coronomy.ir/detail/1224/اصلاحیه-جلسه-49-ستاد-ملی-مقابله-با-بیماری-کرونا>.

51 Supreme Leader's Letter Permitting the Adoption of the Budget Law in the Joint Commission (3 March 2020) <https://www.parliran.ir/majles/fa/Content/_/اذن-رهبر-معظم-انقلاب-برای-عبور-از-تنگنای-بودجه-سال-۹۹-متن-نامه>.

52 The Expediency Discernment Council, 'Five Expediency Council Measures to Examine Ways to Accelerate Corona Fighting' (24 March 2020) <http://maslahat.ir/index.jsp?siteid=3&fkeyid=&siteid=3&fkeyid=&siteid=3&pageid=382&newsview=1176>.

PART V

States of Emergency and Exception

Overview

States of emergency or exception allow for the exceptional use of power by (typically) the executive outside of the normal constraints of law-making and governance. Models of emergency power and the observed use of power during the COVID-19 emergency may be understood as existing on a spectrum ranging from constitutional declarations of emergency to extra-legal action, incorporating a wide range of applicable safeguards and spanning an even wider range of application in practice. A common element has been the question of the limitation of power: recognising both the extraordinary scope of powers which can be delegated to the few, and negative historical experiences of the misuse and abuse of powers under the pretext of emergency. Most frameworks for emergency power envision them to be temporary and incorporate procedural and substantive safeguards which act as a 'quarantine' on the use and prolonged extension of the exceptional use of powers. Examination of state action, however, reveals a concerning tapestry of abuse and lip-service to safeguards, to the ultimate end of executive aggrandisement and the normalisation of emergency powers. Part V examines how states of emergency and exception have shaped political and legal discourse during the pandemic, through three thematic commentaries and five chapters examining their use (and abuse) in Egypt, Malaysia, France, the Philippines and Australia.

In the first thematic commentary, Cassandra Emmons frames the international obligations on regimes for states of emergency, acknowledging the unique and difficult task for governments of balancing protections for individual human rights against the necessity of upholding the common and collective good. Where international law provides guidelines for derogation from certain rights, she highlights the limited and selective use of these provisions during the COVID-19 crisis. In evaluating these gaps in effective implementation and ultimately protection of

DOI: 10.4324/9781003211952-34

rights, she identifies the preparation needed for future pandemics, and the essential role of international bodies in this process.

Arianna Vedaschi and Chiara Graziani offer a closer examination in their commentary of how emergency powers and frameworks emerged during the COVID-19 pandemic in Western European democracies. They offer a categorisation of the forms and uses of emergency power frameworks across the selected states, which challenge prior assumptions about how states would respond based on their pre-existing laws. Indeed, Vedaschi and Graziani highlight a preference for 'alternative' strategies than those within the existing constitutional frameworks, and examine the reasoning behind these choices. They propose recommendations for how emergency frameworks must be reformed post-pandemic.

In the final commentary, Rasha Al Saba and Samrawit Gougsa expose endemic inequalities in the experience of minorities and indigenous peoples during the COVID-19 pandemic. Emergency measures introduced by governments in response to the pandemic disproportionately affected these communities, leading to increased risk of infection, unemployment and forced labour. They evidence how discriminatory practices and the lack of social protection, as well as inequitable provision of health services and access to vaccines, only served to exacerbate this inequity. Al Saba and Gougsa advocate the path forward: realising the guarantee of universal health coverage and designing and implementing mitigation measures with the participation of minorities and indigenous peoples in this process.

Ahmed Ellaboudy analyses the legal and political response to the pandemic in **Egypt** which has been in a near-continuous state of emergency declared by successive regimes since 1967. The virtually exclusive reliance on emergency regimes in response to ongoing security concerns as the default mode of governance exposed the inadequacy of alternative tools to address the health crisis. Ellaboudy examines legal reforms targeting the economic and public health challenges in Egypt, and highlights the essential role of civil society and litigants in forwarding the right to health.

R Rueban Balasubramaniam exposes the fragility of constitutional democracy in **Malaysia**. Already in the midst of political crisis with the collapse of the pro-democracy government in 2020, the uncertainty caused the constitutional monarch (both legally and politically unaccountable) to determine the formation of government: an interim administration that resisted the establishment of democratic legitimacy. With courts unable or unwilling to review emergency measures, and the construction of a system masking undemocratic political decision-making, Balasubramaniam underlines how the pandemic amplified an 'ethno-authoritarian' trajectory within Malaysia which is designed to entrench Malay dominance.

The normalising of exception is also a dominant theme of Marie-Laure Basilien-Gainche's account of executive decisions taken over the course of the pandemic in **France**. In the enactment of a new 'state of health emergency', the delegation of wide discretionary powers to the executive and administrative authorities enables the severe restriction of rights with minimal checks. This 'security-focused' management of pandemic continues the expansion of exceptional regimes in France, leading to the dominance of the executive with insufficient institutional oversight.

Maria Ela L Atienza exposes a similar executive dominance in the **Philippines**, combined with an inept pandemic response. Having introduced one of the longest lockdowns in the world, the Philippines nevertheless has to date had one of the highest infection rates in Southeast Asia. The delegation of emergency powers – although limited in form – in practice served to further executive aggrandisement, in tandem with a Congress which failed to exercise its oversight functions. Ineffective, punitive and discriminatory practices – often targeting the opposition and marginalised communities – further undermined both citizens' rights and effective containment of the virus. However, Atienza argues that innovation through community-based initiatives of citizens and local government was a positive step towards the management of the pandemic and the mitigation of its impact on communities.

In contrast to the Philippines, **Australia**'s response to COVID-19 has to date been relatively successful in limiting the infection rate. Yet, as Marco Rizzi and Tamara Tulich venture, it nevertheless caused concerns from a rule of law perspective. They highlight the exercise of executive powers following the declaration of a state of emergency and the near absence of appropriate checks and balances on the use of these powers. Prolonged international isolation following the closure of borders strained institutional and legal frameworks, which were only further pressured by sustained states of emergency throughout the country.

30

RESPONDING TO COVID-19 WITH STATES OF EMERGENCY

Reflections and Recommendations for Future Health Crises

Cassandra V Emmons

1. Introduction[1]

At the time of writing, the fight against the COVID-19 pandemic is far from over.[2,3] After 18 months, over 181 million cases of the novel SARS-CoV-2 virus have been reported to the World Health Organisation (WHO) including more than 3.9 million fatalities.[4] In the throes of unfathomable death tolls and overwhelmed emergency rooms and morgues, governments attempted to 'stop the spread' by closing borders, schools, businesses and places of worship all in the name of public health and safety. Others went so far as to limit access to and penalise dissemination of (mis)information about the virus. Lockdowns became the 'new normal' and, where broadband internet was accessible, 'Zoom rooms' the venue for everything from birthdays to court hearings to memorial services.

In some – but crucially not all – countries, these changes were implemented through states of emergency. States of emergency or 'states of exception' provide governments the necessary flexibility to protect the nation from unanticipated,

1 All websites accessed on 29 July 2021 unless otherwise stated.

2 This chapter builds upon a blog post for the symposium on COVID-19 and States of Emergency, 'International Human Rights Law and COVID-19 States of Emergency' (*Verfassungsblog*, 25 April 2020) <https://verfassungsblog.de/international-human-rights-law-and-covid-19-states-of-emergency/>.

3 The numbers and progress in the fight against COVID-19 referred to in this chapter are current as of 30 June 2021.

4 WHO Coronavirus Dashboard <https://covid19.who.int>.

DOI: 10.4324/9781003211952-35

"apocalyptic" threats.[5] A crisis event is one that "cross[es] a threat severity threshold, necessitating *urgent*, *exceptional*, and, consequently, *temporary* actions by the state not permissible when *normal conditions* exist" (emphasis added).[6] As summarised by the International Commission of Jurists (ICJ), "the state of emergency is the counterpart in international law of self-defence in penal law".[7] Objectively, the circumstances around the novel COVID-19 virus – its unknown transmission methods, uncertain risk factors and susceptibilities and absence of proven treatment protocols – do certainly appear to qualify, though state approaches varied dramatically.[8]

By declaring states of emergency for COVID-19 response, governments were able to offer stimulus packages with unemployment benefits and small business loans, repurpose funds for quick procurement of personal protective equipment and medical equipment,[9] activate national guards for manning vaccination sites and expedite vaccine testing, among other things. Many of these actions were proportionate, rational responses to the crisis. Unfortunately, states of emergency – for public health or otherwise – can also be abused by governments and enable corruption, particularly in places where governance practices are already weak. COVID-19 emergency decrees have been used by leaders to further political ambitions in places like Hungary and the Philippines and to curtail rights for prolonged – and by most criteria unnecessary – time periods.[10]

While states bear the responsibility of protecting their nations, international human rights law (IHRL) was designed precisely to protect people from governments that would otherwise abuse their power and/or take advantage of situations to renege on their human rights commitments. International human rights treaties categorise rights that can and cannot be suspended even in the case of emergencies. They also have clear reporting procedures and can monitor government actions and usually rule on the necessity of such measures in international courts. Altogether, these checks are meant to restrain governments and guarantee rights even in dark moments of crisis.

At this juncture given the (albeit small and privileged) distance from COVID-19's initial onset, we can meaningfully reflect upon government responses to the pandemic, the international guidelines and procedures that worked well and the ones that did not perform as expected. This chapter identifies gaps between the restraints

5 Bruce Ackerman, 'The Emergency Constitution' (2004) 113 Yale Law Journal 1029, 1038.

6 Alan Green, *Permanent States of Emergency and the Rule of Law: Constitutions in an Age of Crisis* (Hart Publishing 2018) 33.

7 International Commission of Jurists, *States of Emergency: Their Impact on Human Rights* (1983) 413.

8 Alan Green, 'Derogating from the European Convention on Human Rights in Response to the Coronavirus Pandemic: If Not Now, When?' (2020) 3 European Human Rights Law Review 262. For comparisons, see Vedaschi and Graziani, chapter 31.

9 Michael Meyer-Resende, 'The Rule of Law Stress Test: EU Member States' Responses to COVID-19' (*Verfassungsblog*, 24 May 2020) <https://verfassungsblog.de/the-rule-of-law-stress-test-eu-member-states-responses-to-covid-19/>.

10 Kriszta Kovács, 'Hungary and the Pandemic: A Pretext for Expanding Power' (*Verfassungsblog*, 11 March 2021) <https://verfassungsblog.de/hungary-and-the-pandemic-a-pretext-for-expanding-power/>; see also in this volume Kovács, chapter 21 and Atienza, chapter 36.

human rights treaties were meant to place on government prerogative during crises and the degree to which states have engaged and complied with them during the COVID-19 pandemic. It touches upon some of the unique complications to derogating or otherwise limiting rights during public health pandemics. The chapter concludes with a discussion of enforcement and suggests changes to the way we identify, classify, respond to and behave during future health emergencies.

2. Derogations, Limitations and Positive Rights to Health in International Human Rights Law

States are subject to an intricate web of international human rights treaties. Since its adoption in 1948, the Universal Declaration of Human Rights has served as the foundation for over 70 global and regional treaties guaranteeing human rights.[11] At the universal level are the International Covenant on Civil and Political Rights (ICCPR) with (to date) 173 parties and six additional signatories and the International Covenant on Economic, Social and Cultural Rights (ICESCR) with 171 parties.[12] Regionally, the American Convention on Human Rights (AmCHR) compounds these commitments for 24 states in the western hemisphere.[13] The European Convention on Human Rights (ECHR) does the same for 47 and the European Social Charter (ESC) for 34 European countries.[14] The African Charter on Human and Peoples' Rights (ACHPR) covers 54 African states.[15] Lastly, and most recently, the Arab Charter on Human Rights (ArCHR) has 17 parties with three additional signatories.[16]

These overlapping instruments compound the legal obligations of their ratifiers, creating unique conditions for each state when emergencies strike. Despite these particularities, we can summarise the general experiences of state regimes and citizens under this non-exhaustive list of international commitments during the COVID-19 pandemic. There are three types of clauses that are specifically relevant for states facing the COVID-19 crisis: derogation and limitations clauses[17] and those guaranteeing the positive right to health.

11 Universal Declaration of Human Rights (adopted 10 December 1948) UNGA Res 217 A(III).

12 ICCPR (adopted 16 December 1966, in force 23 March 1976) 999 UNTS 171; ICESCR (adopted 16 December 1966, in force 3 January 1976) 993 UNTS 3.

13 AmCHR (adopted 22 November 1969, in force 18 July 1978).

14 ECHR (adopted 4 November 1950, in force 3 September 1953) EU; ESC (revised, adopted 3 May 1996, in force 1 July 1999) CoE 163.

15 ACHPR (adopted 27 June 1981, in force 21 October 1986).

16 ArCHR (adopted 22 May 2004, in force 15 March 2008). The ArCHR has come under considerable criticism for failing to meet minimum qualifications of a human rights instrument, specifically concerning the rights of children and prohibition of the death penalty for children. It is included in this analysis given its formal standing as a fully ratified treaty enforceable at the international level.

17 On the distinction, see Oren Gross, '"Once More unto the Breach": The Systemic Failure of Applying the European Convention on Human Rights to Entrenched Emergencies' (1998) 23 Yale Journal of International Law 437, 445–448.

Table 30.1 Non-Derogable Rights in International Human Rights Treaties

	ICCPR (Art. 4(2))	*ECHR (Art. 15(2))*	*AmCHR (Art. 27(2))*	*ArCHR (Art. 4(2))*
Right to life	✓	✓	✓	✓
Prohibition of torture	✓	✓	✓	✓
Prohibition against slavery	✓	✓	✓	✓
Require prior provision of the law	✓	✓	✓	✓
Right to legal personality	✓		✓	✓
Freedom of thought	✓			✓
Freedom of religion	✓		✓	✓
Freedom of conscience	✓		✓	✓
Right to domestic remedies via judicial processes	✓*			✓
Prohibition of the death penalty	restrictions†	✓‡		
Prohibition of imprisonment for failure to pay debt or fulfil contractual obligation	✓			✓
Freedom from double jeopardy		✓§		✓
Right to humane treatment while in custody			✓	✓
Right to nationality			✓	✓
Prohibition against forced labor			✓	✓
Freedom from human trafficking			✓	✓
Rights of the child			✓	
Rights of the family			✓	
Right to a name			✓	
Right to participate in government			✓	
Right to seek political asylum				✓

Notes for Table 30.1: *Human Rights Committee General Comment Number 29. †Article 6(2,5). See also the second optional Protocol. ‡Protocol 13, Article 2. § Protocol 7, Article 4(3)

Derogation clauses outline the conditions under and process by which states can temporarily suspend individual rights during national emergencies. Five of these treaties have such clauses in effect: the ICCPR (Article 4), the ECHR (Article 15), the ESC (Article F), the AmCHR (Article 27) and the ArCHR (Article 4). All but the ESC identify a subset of rights that are non-derogable and must be guaranteed at all times – including and especially during crises. The specific non-derogable rights vary across the four charters (see Table 30.1). All four expressly guarantee the right to life, freedom from slavery, prohibition of torture and non-retroactive application of the law.[18] Besides those listed in Table 30.1, all other rights enshrined

18 Agreement across the charters on these core rights is sometimes, problematically, interpreted as evidence of customary international law. See Joan Hartman, 'Derogation from Human Rights Treaties in Public Emergencies' (1981) 22 Harvard International Law Journal 1, 15.

in these four charters and the entire ESC – including the right to work, to property or to certain provisions while in detention and/or awaiting trial – can be derogated from if the exigent situation warrants it.

Being 'exceptions', derogations are bound by a few criteria as set out in these clauses and further interpreted by the International Law Association (ILA) and the American Association for the ICJ (AAICJ).[19] They should respond to a formally recognised crisis; be proportionate to that crisis and necessary for protecting the nation and responding to the threat; not discriminate on the basis of race, colour, sex, language, religion or social origin; remain compatible with the state's other international legal obligations; and last only as long as necessary.[20] The final requirement is notifying the relevant international body. Generally, states are required to do so at least twice, when the derogation begins and again when the crisis has been resolved or the situation changed such that emergency measures – including the derogation – are no longer necessary.[21] The initial notice should specify the reason for suspending rights under the respective article and might note which rights have been derogated.[22] Uniquely, the AmCHR also requires the government to provide the "set date for the termination of each suspension" in the initial notice, again since states of emergencies are supposed to be *temporary* diversions.[23] The other four agreements do not request an estimated expiration, but they do require subsequent notice alerting the organisation that the situation no longer poses an existential threat and the state's legal commitments to individual rights have been restored. Governments that prolong or amend their states of emergency may also be expected to update the relevant secretariat after the initial notice is given.

Not all emergency situations require derogations from rights; instead, some treaties allow governments to *limit* the exercise of rights in the name of public safety, health or morals, public order or national security. 'Limitations clauses' essentially allow governments to weigh the rights of individual persons against the rights of the larger community. Typically, limitations are rights-specific, identified throughout the charter. Table 30.2 lists the rights subject to limitation for public health under the ICCPR, the ECHR, the AmCHR, the ACHPR and the ArCHR; the ESC permits restrictions on *any* rights for public health.[24] These clauses provided an alternative path for governments to combat COVID-19 without declaring an emergency.[25]

19 Richard Lillich, 'The Paris Minimum Standards of Human Rights Norms in a State of Emergency' (1985) 79 American Journal of International Law 1072; see also AAICJ, Siracusa Principles on the Limitation and Derogation Provisions in the ICCPR (1985).

20 ICCPR Art 4(1), AmCHR Art 27(1), ECHR Art 15(1), ESC Art F(1), ArCHR Art 4(1); AAICJ (1985) (n 19).

21 ICCPR Art 4(3), AmCHR Art 27(3), ECHR Art 15(3), ESC Art F(2), ArCHR Art 4(3).

22 AAICJ (1985) (n 19).

23 Art 27(3).

24 Art G(1).

25 See Dominic McGoldrick, 'The Interface between Public Emergency Powers and International Law' (2004) 2 International Journal of Constitutional Law 380.

Table 30.2 Rights Subject to Limitation for Public Health or Safety

	ICCPR	*ECHR*	*AmCHR*	*ArCHR*	*ACHPR*
Freedom of assembly	21	11(2)	15	24(6,7)	11
Freedom of association	22(2)	11(2)	16	24(5–7)	
Freedom of movement	12(3)	2 (Protocol 4)	22		12(2)
Freedom of residence	12(3)		22		12(2)
Freedom of information	19(3)b		13(2)b	32(2)*	
Freedom of expression			13(2)b		
Freedom of thought			13(2)b		
Right to manifest one's religion or belief	18(3)	9(2)	12(3)	30(2)	
Property rights					14
Public pronouncement of judgments		6(1)			
Respect for privacy and family rights		8(2)			
Right to participate in government, public affairs and elections				24(1–3,7)	
Right to form and join trade unions				35	

*In direct contradiction to Article 4(2), which protects freedom of thought and conscience.

Originally, limitations clauses had few formal restrictions to their use, unlike derogation clauses. The charters do not provide any parameters around what 'protecting public health' means nor are reporting procedures specified. In the 1980s, the AAICJ issued guidelines for interpreting the limitations clauses in the ICCPR, that the UN Economic and Social Council endorsed, though these are non-binding.[26]

While derogations and limitations clauses prohibit governments from certain actions, several international covenants and charters also implore them to guarantee a *positive right* to health. The ICESCR[27] mandates signatory governments to protect the public from epidemic diseases, as does the ESC.[28] The ACHPR also requires signatories to "protect the health of their people",[29] while the ArCHR requires parties to take "efforts to control disease".[30] COVID-19 thus presented a unique challenge: balancing commitments to individual human rights and freedoms with the duty to guarantee the positive right to health.

26 See AAICJ (n 18); Katherine Todrys, Erin Howe and Joseph Amon, 'Failing Siracusa: Governments' Obligations to Find the Least Restrictive Options for Tuberculosis Control' (2013) 3 Public Health Action 7.

27 Art 12(2)c.

28 Art 11(3).

29 Art 16(21).

30 Art 39(2)b.

3. Derogation Clause Procedures During COVID-19: Adherence and Divergence

Among the states that declared formal states of emergency to fight COVID-19, we can critically assess whether the measures taken meet the minimum requirements for derogation outlined above. The first point of departure is determining whether COVID-19 warranted emergency government as a crisis. A crisis, again, must be "sudden, unforeseen, and of unknown duration"[31] and threaten the "life of the nation" (ICCPR, ECHR, ArCHR) or the "independence or security of a State" (AmCHR). Given the unexpected and unanticipated nature of crises, no national constitution – or international human rights treaty – proscribes an exhaustive list of circumstances that warrant emergency government. Most constitutions afford the executive prerogative over determining whether a situation qualifies and what emergency provisions are necessary and proportionate – an interpretive power that is quite risky.

The classification and necessity criteria are better evaluated on a case-by-case basis, as can be found in other chapters of this volume. Briefly, Alan Green made a compelling case for derogating from human rights commitments because of COVID-19, at least in early 2020.[32] However, while COVID-19 did prove to spread quickly, it did not impact or overwhelm all states simultaneously. The lagged effect theoretically provided some governments adequate time to prepare or at least made breakouts more predictable, bringing into question the true necessity of *new* states of emergency for the crisis once the pandemic was in its second year.

The second and more comparatively observable gap is between the states that did and did not follow the reporting procedures when derogating for the emergency. To date, only ten of the 47 ECHR parties have reported their derogations to the Council of Europe's (CoE) Secretary General.[33] Fifteen of the current 24 AmCHR parties have notified the Organization of American States (OAS) Secretary General of their derogations.[34] Twenty-four state parties to the ICCPR have formally derogated by informing the United Nations (UN) Secretary-General.[35] No state has formally notified the CoE Secretary General about

31 Harold Relyea, *National Emergency Powers* (Report No. 98-505 GOV, US Congressional Research Service 2001).

32 Alan Green, *Emergency Powers in a Time of Pandemic* (Bristol University Press 2020); Green (n 8).

33 Council of Europe, Reservations and Declarations of Treaty No.005 <https://www.coe.int/en/web/conventions/full-list/-/conventions/treaty/005/declarations>; Council of Europe, Notifications under Article 15 of the Convention in the context of the COVID-19 pandemic as of 30 April 2021 <https://www.coe.int/en/web/conventions/full-list/-/conventions/webContent/99943603>.

34 Organization of American States, Department of International Law, 'Recent Suspensions of Guarantees Regarding Multilateral Treaties' <http://www.oas.org/en/sla/dil/inter_american_treaties_suspension_guarantees.asp>.

35 UN Treaty Collection, Status of Treaties, <https://treaties.un.org/Pages/ViewDetails.aspx?src=TREATY&mtdsg_no=IV-4&chapter=4&clang=_en>.

derogating from the provisions laid out in the ESC,[36] nor has the Arab League been notified of its parties' derogations.

There is some optimism in these reporting patterns. First, many of the reporters were 'first-timers' indicating a new level of engagement with these international bodies in light of the crisis. Second, many remained in regular communication with the relevant international bodies about the status of IHRL commitments. Some reported to their regional organisations about extensions either in time or to different parts of their territories (Armenia, Georgia, Latvia, North Macedonia, Romania and San Marino for the ECHR; Argentina, Bolivia, Chile, Colombia, Dominican Republic, Ecuador, Guatemala, Honduras, Panama, Paraguay and Peru for the AmCHR).[37] Third, there was a high degree of reporting to both the regional and UN bodies: 60% of the American states that notified the OAS also notified the UN, while 80% of the European states that notified the ECHR also notified the UN.[38] Argentina is the only state that extended its emergency and reported it to the OAS but *not* to the UN, suggesting a possible norm among the states that follow the regional procedures of informing both.

Clearly, though, there are large gaps between the number of states that reported derogations and those that derogated or otherwise limited citizens' rights. Many states derogated from these treaties without ever notifying the relevant bodies. Bulgaria, Cyprus, the Czech Republic, Greece, Hungary, Luxembourg, Portugal, Slovakia and Spain have not submitted any formal notice to the CoE or the UN about their emergency derogations from the treaties – and all did declare formal emergencies under their constitutional provisions.[39] Other states notified the relevant bodies after prolonged delays. For instance, Togo declared its public health state of emergency on 16 March 2020 but did not notify the UN until 9 October 2020 via a *note verbale* and not in writing until 17 May 2021. Unfortunately, none of the treaties specifies *how soon after* a state of emergency is declared the organisation needs to be informed. In its case law, the European Court of Human Rights has determined three and four months were unnecessarily long delays, but this precedent is far from a universally accepted norm.[40]

Recall that the goal of emergency regimes is not to eliminate a crisis; it is to allow government the *temporary* flexibility to respond. At the time of writing, we

36 Kushtrim Istrefi, 'To Notify or Not to Notify: Derogations from Human Rights Treaties (*OpinioJuris*, 18 April 2020) <http://opiniojuris.org/2020/04/18/to-notify-or-not-to-notify-derogations-from-human-rights-treaties/>.

37 Because the AmCHR requires states to indicate the expiration of the state of emergency, follow up notices might be more common than in other regions.

38 Exceptions: Argentina, Bolivia, Honduras, North Macedonia and Panama.

39 Democracy Reporting International, 'The Rule of Law Stress Test: EU Member States' Responses to COVID-19' (May 2020). This measure is conservative: an additional eight states that do not have constitutional provisions for states of emergency used statutory provisions to limit rights but did not report these measures either.

40 *Greece v United Kingdom* App no 176/56 (Report of the European Commission of Human Rights, 26 September 1958) [158]; *Denmark, Norway, Sweden and the Netherlands v Greece* App nos 3321-4/67 (Report of the European Commission of Human Rights, 5 November 1969) [81(3)].

have reached the point where we can start asking whether any of these emergency regimes have outlasted their necessity. All but one ECHR notice have been formally withdrawn. However, none of the AmCHR derogations have been withdrawn and only 13 of the 29 ICCPR derogation notices have been withdrawn. New notices are still being submitted to the latter two. Again, unfortunately, the treaties do not stipulate time frames for restoring derogated rights at a crisis's conclusion, though the Siracusa Principles emphasise it should be immediate.

Despite standard-setting efforts in the 1980s, derogation clauses are not foolproof guarantees for individual rights and the rule of law during emergencies. In fact, there are many examples of emergency government and rights limitations becoming 'normalised' or 'permanent' rather than transient exceptions to the rule.[41] Crises are not always resolved quickly, which has historically invited "extended", "entrenched" or even "permanent" emergencies.[42] Not only does this pose a threat to the rule of law and good governance, but when emergencies become entrenched and new emergent situations arise, governments are even less well able to adjust to the new threat.[43]

4. International Checks on Rights: Pitfalls and Promises

While the hope is that governments will abide by their commitments, international bodies associated with these treaties typically have some oversight and enforcement powers. The legitimacy of derogations can be challenged in two ways at the international level: international courts and active monitoring. COVID-19 demonstrated that these provisions are inadequate as designed, at least in public health emergencies, but also displayed promising innovation.

Violations under the ECHR and AmCHR can be brought to the respective international courts. Since 1998, the European Court of Human Rights (ECtHR) can be directly addressed by individuals who have exhausted domestic remedies.[44] The American Court of Human Rights (IACtHR) only hears cases from citizens through the Inter-American Commission on Human Rights (IACHR), though state parties can bring one another before the Court directly.

Courts have several shortcomings when it comes to emergencies. Across the board, human rights courts have been reticent to pass judgments on the legality of emergency powers; when they do, they have tended to defer to the government.[45] A main issue with juridical approaches boils down to expediency. Given the ECHR

41 Clinton Rossiter, *Constitutional Dictatorship: Crisis Government in the Modern Democracies* (first published 1948, 6th edn, Transaction Publishers 2009); Green (n 6).

42 Gross (n 17); Myriam Feinberg 'States of Emergency in France and Israel: Terrorism, "Permanent Emergencies", and Democracy' (2018) 28 *Zeitschrift für Politikwissenschaft* 495; Green (n 6).

43 See Ellaboudy, chapter 33.

44 Protocol no. 11 to the ECHR (1994), Art. 34–35.

45 Gross (n 17); Natasha Holcroft-Emmess 'Derogating to Deal with Covid: State Practice and Thoughts on the Need for Notification' (*EJIL: Talk*, 10 April 2020) <https://www.ejiltalk.org/derogating-to-deal-with-covid-19-state-practice-and-thoughts-on-the-need-for-notification/>.

and AmCHR require domestic remedies be exhausted and the lengths of time accused governments have to respond to either court or committee, this option hardly rises to the challenge of addressing abuses of rights under states of emergency. Even relaxing the domestic remedies requirement would not meaningfully shorten the process of a case when facing such a fast-paced threat. COVID-19 posed a unique challenge as courts struggled to adjust time-honoured procedures in pursuit of justice while simultaneously taking health precautions.

To date, the ECtHR has received several hundred applications for interim measures – urgent measures which apply where there is an imminent risk of irreparable harm – related to pandemic restrictions. Three cases were deemed inadmissible; one violation that was supported was a case of inhuman treatment.[46] Sixteen cases are pending, dealing with inhuman treatment, right to a fair trial and freedom of religion, expression, assembly and movement.[47] The IACtHR has not heard any cases pertaining to COVID-19. Slow court response times, worsened by the transition to online hearings and learning new technologies, make this option a stretch for those whose rights were being unjustifiably violated.

Monitoring is another method for international bodies to enforce human rights.[48] Speed is its comparative advantage. Compliance with the ICCPR is monitored by the Human Rights Committee. An optional protocol to the ICCPR, currently ratified by 116 states and signed by an additional three, grants individuals in any signatory state the right to address the Human Rights Committee directly about violations of their rights under the Covenant after exhausting domestic remedies.[49] The AmCHR is monitored by the IACHR, which can also be addressed by individuals.[50] The CoE's member states are monitored by the Commissioner for Human Rights, the Secretary General and a variety of other entities.[51] In support of these efforts, the ILA's committee on enforcement of human rights produced a framework for critically evaluating actions taken under the guise of states of emergency called the 'Queensland Guidelines';[52] another active committee began analysing this very topic prior to COVID-19.[53]

While monitors can outpace judicial actors, their main shortcoming is that they have very few punitive tools. The *modus operandi* for monitors is to call attention to a problem and 'name and shame' the actors, sometimes also providing information

46 *Feilazoo v Malta* App no 6865/19 (ECtHR, 11 March 2021).

47 European Court of Human Rights, 'COVID-19 Health Crisis Factsheet' (June 2021) <https://www.echr.coe.int/Documents/FS_Covid_ENG.pdf>.

48 Joan Fitzpatrick, *Human Rights in Crisis: The International System for Protecting Rights During States of Emergency* (University of Pennsylvania Press 1994).

49 First Optional Protocol to the ICCPR (adopted 16 December 1966, in force 23 March 1976).

50 AmCHR, Art 44.

51 See Council of Europe, 'Administrative Entities: Human Rights' <https://www.coe.int/en/web/portal/human-rights>.

52 International Law Association, *Queensland Guidelines for Bodies Monitoring Respect for Human Rights During States of Emergency* (1990).

53 International Law Association, 'Committees' <https://www.ila-hq.org/index.php/committees>.

that allows cases to reach the courts. During COVID-19, these international actors struggled to perform their same duties, having such tight restrictions on travel and difficulties reaching areas hardest hit without putting staff at risk.

Monitoring bodies adapted quickly to the COVID-19 conditions, though and several promising innovations deserve recognition. The IACHR developed multiple 'Rapid Integrated Response Coordination Units' to compile guidelines, offer recommendations for the region and devise new methods of observing and collecting information in areas with acute, compounding political and social crises including the United States, Colombia and Peru.[54] Other actors kept pressure on governments through regular virtual appearances on webinars and at hearings. UN High Commissioner for Human Rights Michelle Bachelet actively promoted her office's guidelines for protecting vulnerable populations[55] and CoE Commissioner for Human Rights Dunja Mijatovic continued pressuring governments to guarantee media freedom and rights for minorities.[56] These innovations are exemplary of the unique role supra- and international bodies can play during emergencies.

5. Confronting Future Public Health Pandemics: Recommended Changes for Enforcement

Reflecting upon the way IHRL met or failed expectations during this pandemic is one of the primary goals of this volume. Given these lessons, I conclude here with some suggested changes to better prepare for future emergencies: expanding international institutions' competences, revisiting norms and procedures for limitations and derogations and increasing information provision.

First, international institutions should play a more central role in identifying the onset and conclusions of public health crises. The WHO is the most logical existing institution to take on such responsibility, given its explicit focus on combatting international health emergencies through coordination and collaboration. The WHO declared COVID-19 a 'Public Health Emergency of International Concern' on 30 January 2020 and a pandemic on 11 March, but some governments continued to publicly doubt COVID-19's severity. Given their expertise in epidemiology, WHO scientists are among the best-suited to identify the type of behavioral restrictions necessary to quell the spread of this and any future disease. The WHO's risk classifications should therefore be treated more consistently as non-partisan metrics for executives to determine national risk levels.[57] Reassigning

54 Organization of American States, 'The IACHR Presents Progress Report for 2020' (27 February 2021) <https://www.oas.org/fr/CIDH/jsForm/?File=/en/iachr/media_center/PReleases/2021/045.asp>.

55 UN Office of the High Commissioner for Human Rights, 'Guidance Memorandum' (15 April 2020) <https://www.ohchr.org/Documents/Issues/Women/COVID-19_and_Womens_Human_Rights.pdf>.

56 Council of Europe Commissioner for Human Rights, *Annual Activity Report 2020* (21 April 2021).

57 This was a recommendation in the Siracusa Principles (1985) (n 19) para 26.

this role from national governments with widely different capabilities reduces the possibility that national officials with less or no expertise will (mis)interpret events. It also avoids negative spillovers of poor or politically motivated policies or, worse, intentional abuse of the situation. Deference to the expertise of an international institution should also apply when determining that conditions are improving and restrictions can be lifted in a non-political, or at least less political, manner. Such changes might reduce the occurrence of entrenched emergencies resulting from public health emergencies.

For the abovementioned competence expansion of the WHO to be palatable to state parties, the funding scheme could be revamped guaranteeing no undue influence over the institution from any one participant. At present, the WHO is funded by a combination of assessed and voluntary contributions that come from both governments and non-governmental actors like GAVI (the Vaccine Alliance) and the Bill and Melinda Gates Foundation. Voluntary contributions are typically earmarked for specific projects; these preconditions could feasibly be loosened during pandemics. Greater oversight and investment during non-pandemic times can also promise better preparedness for the next crisis.

International institutions have proven they monitor well, but when travel and in-person interactions are limited, they can rely on their networking and coordination skills. By fostering relationships with actors in local communities as well as national and international public and private institutions, international institutions offer a unique brokerage. They can elevate the concerns of certain communities that may otherwise have no recourse. International institutions can also set priorities for governments that incorporate human rights protections. For instance, the Office of the High Commissioner for Human Rights issued a set of guidelines for guaranteeing gender equitable COVID-19 responses.[58] The High Commissioner's work could be supplemented – though should not be duplicated – by regional bodies through greater inter-agency relationships.

Second, international human rights institutions might revisit their derogation and limitations procedures in light of what we have learned from government responses to COVID-19. Given the pros and cons of each clause, there is good reason for institutions to encourage formal derogation during global public health pandemics rather than relying on hard-to-monitor limitations clauses. Public health derogations would then explicitly become subject to the proportionality criterion and be temporary. Alternatively, parties to international human rights treaties might introduce parameters for the various limitations clauses similar to derogation clauses. Derogation clauses are imperfect, as has been shown, but they are attractive models because state parties are already familiar with and might reflexively abide by them. These institutions should pay particular attention to the ILA committee on this topic.[59]

Lastly, in the absence of appetite for expanding powers of the institutions or changing international procedures, the institutional agents themselves can con-

58 UN Office of the High Commissioner for Human Rights (n 55).

59 International Law Association (n 53).

tinue to find creative ways of disseminating up-to-date information to the public. Recall that the right to information can be limited during a public health emergency (Table 30.2). Early in the pandemic when the science was less certain, restricting information was a cautiously plausible tactic. However, as the scientific community gained confidence in its understanding of the disease, it had to combat misinformation and, in some places, fight to have its information disseminated at all. The political implications of free information are clear: "Providing the public with access to fact-based information about current events is one of the best ways to combat authoritarian power."[60] Bolstering these organisations' platforms would thus ensure accurate, consistent messaging and strengthen the collective response to a public health pandemic as well as ward against democratic decay and declining rule of law.

60 Freedom House, *Nations in Transit 2021: The Antidemocratic Turn* (2021) 19.

31

COVID-19 AND EMERGENCY POWERS IN WESTERN EUROPEAN DEMOCRACIES

Trends and Issues

Arianna Vedaschi and Chiara Graziani

1. Introduction[1]

This chapter addresses legal reactions in the fight against COVID-19, focusing on selected Western European democracies. The aim of the chapter is to highlight some common trends in the use (or non-use) of emergency powers against COVID-19.

Section 2 offers a survey of whether and how the constitutions of these European democratic countries regulate resort to emergency powers and identifies some 'emergency models', attempting to categorise constitutional emergency powers. Section 3 considers whether or not these 'emergency constitutions' were applied as legal bases for anti-pandemic measures, focusing on Spain, France, Germany and Italy. It finds that triggering constitutional emergency powers has been the exception, rather than the rule, since many jurisdictions have preferred alternative strategies. Concluding remarks in section 4 take stock of the findings of the previous sections – showing an 'escape' from existing emergency powers in the fight against COVID-19 – and discuss what changes might be introduced, once the crisis is over, to improve emergency frameworks and make them suitable to face future global emergencies.

2. Constitutional Emergency Models

Constitutions of Western European democracies can be categorised at least into two main macro-models based on their approach to emergency.[2] The first macro-

1 All websites accessed on 18 July 2021.

2 For a detailed analysis of emergency models, see Arianna Vedaschi, *À la Guerre Comme à la Guerre? La disciplina della guerra nel diritto costituzionale comparato* (Giappichelli 2007).

 DOI: 10.4324/9781003211952-36

model – or rather, a 'non-model' – is a legacy of some constitutional charters of the 19th century and includes constitutions that do not provide a systematic and well-structured regulation of emergency. The second macro-model features constitutions that govern recourse to emergency powers.

The 1948 Italian Constitution belongs to the 'non-model'. It was drafted in the aftermath of the Second World War, with terrible memories of the Fascist regime still fresh in the minds of the members of the Constituent Assembly. Consequently, the centralisation of power in the hands of a single body, especially of the executive, was opposed as it might have paved the way for new forms of authoritarianism. As a consequence, Italy lacks a well-defined constitutional emergency paradigm, albeit the Italian Constitution does contain some emergency clauses. The foremost is Article 77[3] concerning decree laws. Originally conceived to manage cases of natural disasters, throughout history it has been used for a number of different emergencies or sometimes even to address situations that hardly fall within the definition of an emergency. Article 78 is specifically focused on war, even though the latter is minimally regulated.[4] Similarly, the 1949 German *Grundgesetz* (Fundamental Law), until a 1968 constitutional amendment introducing detailed emergency provisions, fitted the 'non-model'. The choice not to regulate emergency explicitly, due to the horrors of Nazism, was imposed by political forces occupying the Western part of the country after Germany's defeat in the Second World War.[5]

The second macro-model, which expressly addresses emergency powers, features two sub-models: constitutions that regulate emergency in general terms (the 'general clause' model) and those that do so in more detail (the 'rationalised' model). An example of the general clause model is Article 16 of the 1958 French Constitution,[6] vesting the President of the Republic with vague (and, thus, highly discretionary) powers in times of political crisis. Constitutions of the rationalised model instead regulate emergency through detailed provisions. For example, the

3 Art 77 of the Italian Constitution reads: "The Government may not, without an enabling act from the Houses, issue a decree having force of law. When the Government, in case of necessity and urgency, adopts under its own responsibility a temporary measure, it shall introduce such measure to Parliament for transposition into law. During dissolution, Parliament shall be convened within five days of such introduction. Such a measure shall lose effect from the beginning if it is not transposed into law by Parliament within sixty days of its publication. Parliament may regulate the legal relations arisen from the rejected measure." (All translations of the Italian Constitution are by the Italian Senate).

4 Art 78 reads: "Parliament has the authority to declare a state of war and vest the necessary powers into the Government."

5 Mario G Losano, *Le Tre Costituzioni Pacifiste: il Rifiuto della Guerra nelle Costituzioni di Giappone, Italia e Germania* (Max Planck Institute for European Legal Studies 2020).

6 Art 16, para 1, of the French Constitution reads: "Where the institutions of the Republic, the independence of the Nation, the integrity of its territory or the fulfilment of its international commitments are under serious and immediate threat, and where the proper functioning of the constitutional public authorities is interrupted, the President of the Republic shall take measures required by these circumstances" (Translation by the French Constitutional Council.)

1949 German *Grundgesetz*, after the 1968 constitutional amendment, enshrines several emergency regimes and the choice among them is determined by the intensity of the threat arising from a particular source.[7]

Other constitutional texts – still belonging to the rationalised model – embody emergency patterns that do not depend on the increasing intensity of a threat stemming from one single cause, but on what circumstances provoked the emergency. For instance, Article 116 of the 1978 Spanish Constitution envisages the state of alarm (*estado de alarma*), the state of exception (*estado de excepción*) and the state of siege (*estado de sitio*), which can be applied in case of neutral emergencies (such as epidemics), political emergencies and war, respectively. The substantive aspects of these regimes are regulated by Ley Orgánica 4/1981.

3. The COVID-19 Pandemic and Emergency Powers

Constitutional emergency clauses – whose prototypes are described in section 2 – were hardly ever resorted to during the 'waves' of the COVID-19 pandemic that loomed over Europe from early 2020 (if not earlier, according to some studies).[8] Among Western European democracies, only Spain and Portugal invoked the *estado de alarma* and the *estado de emergência* (which is a constitutional regime embedded in the Portuguese Constitution) respectively.[9] Other countries, even those with detailed emergency provisions in their constitutions, preferred different strategies.[10] This section identifies four main trends:[11]

(i) The use of constitutional emergency powers – as noted, only Spain and Portugal, among the countries considered in this chapter, took this option.
(ii) Countries – such as France – that, although having pre-existing constitutional and/or statutory frameworks to deal with emergency, decided to

7 The German Constitution regulates political emergencies through the state of tension (Art 80a, para 1), the alliance clause (Art 80a, para 3) and the state of defence (Art 115a, para 1). The latter can be equated to a state of war. Moreover, the German Constitution governs 'neutral' or 'technical' emergencies (i.e. non-political emergencies) through Arts 35, paras 2–3; 87a, paras 2–4; and 91.

8 Gemma Chavarria-Miró and others, 'Sentinel Surveillance of SARS-CoV-2 in Wastewater Anticipates the Occurrence of COVID-19 Cases' (2020) MedRxiv <https://doi.org/10.1101/2020.06.13.20129627>.

9 Art 19 of the Portuguese Constitution. See Teresa Violante and Rui T Lanceiro, 'The Response to the COVID-19 Pandemic in Portugal: A Success Story Gone Wrong' (*Verfassungsblog*, 4 March 2021) <https://verfassungsblog.de/the-response-to-the-covid-19-pandemic-in-portugal-a-success-story-gone-wrong/>.

10 Arianna Vedaschi, 'Il Covid-19, l'Ultimo *Stress Test* per gli Ordinamenti Democratici: Uno Sguardo Comparato' (2020) DPCE Online 1453.

11 For different 'categorisations' of COVID-19 reactions, see Tom Ginsburg and Mila Versteeg, 'The Bound Executive: Emergency Powers during the Pandemic' (2020) Virginia Public Law and Legal Theory Research Paper No 2020-52; University of Chicago, Public Law Working Paper No 747 <https://papers.ssrn.com/sol3/papers.cfm?abstract_id=3608974>; Joelle Grogan, 'Analysing Global Use of Emergency Powers in Response to COVID-19' (2020) 4 European Journal of Law Reform 338.

adopt new emergency laws, creating ex novo emergency regimes specifically aimed at tackling COVID-19.

(iii) Jurisdictions, such as Germany and Austria, that relied on statutory emergency tools already in force, but amended them during the pandemic itself.

(iv) States, such as Italy, where a variety of tools were used – not always consistently – giving rise to a fragmented situation, due to the lack of a clear constitutional model specifically designed to tackle emergency and public health crises.

3.1 The (Uncommon) Use of Constitutional Emergency Clauses: Spain

Among the (few) countries using constitutional emergency powers, Spain serves as a case study. A state of alarm can be triggered in Spain, inter alia, in case of 'health crises, such as epidemics'.[12] On 14 March 2020, a state of alarm was declared by the Council of Ministers.[13] The Spanish government's decision to resort to the state of alarm might appear as a choice taken 'by the book', ie exactly following legal provisions, which explicitly list health emergencies among the grounds to activate this regime. Nevertheless, much criticism arose around the Spanish state of alarm. Some scholars[14] claimed that, while Article 11 of Ley Orgánica 4/1981 authorises mere 'limitation' of rights and freedoms during a state of alarm, the measures imposed by the Spanish government de facto amounted to fully-fledged 'suspension' of some rights and freedoms. And, they argued, suspension is only possible when an *estado de excepción* – and not of alarm – is in place.[15] The *estado de excepción* allows more guarantees since, to be invoked, it has to be preventively authorised by the Congreso de los Diputados (the lower house of the Spanish Parliament), while the *estado de alarma* is declared directly by the government and only its (potential) extensions require ex ante parliamentary authorisation.[16] Despite this criticism, the state of alarm was extended several times (at the time of writing, the latest extension took place on 3 November 2020 and lasted until 9 May 2021). Therefore, for more than one year,[17] it was the main tool on which Spain relied to fight COVID-19.

12 Art 4, Ley Orgánica 4/1981. Translation by the authors.

13 Real Decreto 463/2020, 14 March 2020. On early Spanish responses to COVID-19, Lorenzo Cotino Hueso, 'Los Derechos Fundamentales en Tiempos del Coronavirus. Régimen General y Garantías y Especial Atención a las Restricciones de Excepcionalidad Ordinaria' (2020) El Cronista 88.

14 Remedio Sánchez Ferriz, 'Reflexiones Constitucionales Desde el Confinamiento' (2020) Actualidad Jurídica Iberoamericana 16.

15 Art 13, Ley Orgánica 4/1981.

16 However, it should be noted that the state of exception can only be triggered in case of political distress. Nevertheless, in July 2021, the Spanish Constitutional Court upheld the claims brought by some political forces and ruled the first declaration of the state of alarm unconstitutional. At the time of writing, the full decision has not been published yet, so it is not possible to further analyse the reasoning of constitutional judges. See Tribunal Constitucional de España, Nota Informativa no 72/2021.

17 With a stop from 21 June to 25 October 2020.

In the Spanish regional system – which in 'ordinary times' is based on wide autonomy of its political-administrative divisions, namely the autonomous communities (*communidades autonomas*), to the point that Spain is sometimes defined as 'quasi-federal'[18] – the state of alarm, especially during the 'first wave' of COVID-19, implied a significant centralisation of powers.[19] For example, public purchase of medical equipment – a competence of the *communidades*[20] – was transferred to the central executive; and quarantine measures were fully decided by central authorities, causing clashes with the executive bodies of some autonomous communities that, instead, called for either more or less severe lockdowns over time.[21] In the light of such conflicts between central and regional (or even local) authorities, a path towards less strict centralisation was taken in October 2020, during the 'second wave' of COVID-19, when Real Decreto 926/2020 authorised territorial authorities to decide the extent of restrictions they deemed necessary, still within the framework of a centrally declared state of alarm.

At the end of the state of alarm, on 9 May 2021, the shift towards decentralisation was completed, as the transition 'back to normalcy' was left totally to the autonomous communities. This step may seem a natural one once the emergency was (partially) over, but after months of centralised measures, an abrupt turn to decentralisation presented some challenges. After 9 May 2021, the Spanish autonomous communities took fragmented and diverging approaches (even more than between October 2020 and April 2021). In some of them, partial lockdowns were still in place,[22] while in others almost no restrictions were imposed.[23] This fragmentation was due to the fact that, with the state of alarm no longer into force, the autonomous communities had no legal framework on which restrictions could be grounded, except for Ley 33/2011 (General Law on Public Health) and Ley 14/1986 (General Law on Healthcare). According to them, the executives of the *communidades autonomas* can restrict freedoms in cases of 'imminent and extraordinary risk to health',[24] on the authorisation of local courts. As a consequence, different courts may take different stances – and they in fact did so.[25] To try to put an end to this fragmented situation, the Spanish government partially restored

18 Alicia Cebada Romero and Elvira Dominguez Redondo, 'Spain: One Pandemic and Two Versions of the State of Alarm' (*Verfassungsblog*, 26 February 2021) <https://verfassungsblog.de/spain-one-pandemic-and-two-versions-of-the-state-of-alarm/>.

19 Alba Nogueira López and Gabriel Doménech 'Fighting COVID 19 – Legal Powers and Risks: Spain' (*Verfassungsblog*, 30 March 2020) <https://verfassungsblog.de/fighting-covid-19-legal-powers-and-risks-spain/>.

20 Art 148 of the Spanish Constitution.

21 E.g. Catalonia and Murcia.

22 E.g. Asturias.

23 E.g. Castilla y León.

24 Ley 14/1986, art 26. Similarly, art 54 of Ley 33/2011 provides that measures can be taken "if there are reasonable indications of risk to health". Translation by *Lex-Atlas: Covid-19*.

25 Among 'restrictive' courts, Tribunal de Justicia de las Islas Canarias, judgment 138/2021 of 6 May 2021; among 'relaxed' tribunals, Tribunal Superior de Justicia del País Vasco, judgment of 6 May 2021.

centralisation, by adopting a royal decree law allowing the Spanish Supreme Court (Tribunal Supremo) to hear appeals of decisions of local courts concerning the authorisation of restrictions.[26]

The Spanish experience showed that transition from advanced centralisation to (almost full) decentralisation may not be beneficial in terms of the uniformity of responses and legal certainty. Had the legal framework provided for a clearer allocation of competences from the beginning of the state of alarm, a patchy situation at a particularly sensitive stage, that is the return to 'normal life', would probably have been avoided.

3.2 New Emergency Powers Embodied in New Legislation: France

The second trend consists of countries that adopted 'brand new' emergency regimes, explicitly designed to tackle the pandemic. Paradigmatically, France[27] did not rely on Article 16 of the Constitution to address COVID-19, because this provision is considered to be designed to deal with *political* distress, and not with *technical* emergencies, such as a pandemic. Neither did the French authorities invoke Law 55-385, which sets a statutory framework for an *état d'urgence* and was applied between 2015 and 2017 against the international terrorist threat,[28] albeit, according to some scholars, they could legitimately have done so.[29] Actually, the *état d'urgence* can be used, inter alia, in case of events that "because of their nature or gravity, can be qualified as *public crises*" (emphasis added),[30] a definition that, in some views, encompasses public health emergencies.

However, after handling the pandemic through existing provisions of the Code de la Santé Publique for a few weeks, France enacted Law 2020-290, amending the Code itself and other sources and creating a new kind of emergency, the *état d'urgence sanitaire*.[31] Law 2020-290 resembles, in some aspects, Law 55-385. In both cases, the declaration of emergency is made through a decree of the Council of Ministers and can be extended by a law. Nonetheless, the *état d'urgence* governed by Law 55-385 only lasts 12 days, after which it expires, if a law does not reauthorise it, while the *état d'urgence sanitaire* set up by Law 2020-290 remains in place for one

26 Real Decreto Ley 8/2021 of 4 May 2021. The Spanish Supreme Court, pursuant to this decree, confirmed some restrictive measures imposed by the authorities of the Canarias and ratified by the local court. Tribunal Supremo, judgment 3375/2021 of 24 May 2021.

27 See Basilien-Gainche, chapter 35.

28 Arianna Vedaschi, 'The Multilevel Governance of Emergency in Counterterrorism: The "Globalization" of the Law of Exception?' in Arianna Vedaschi and Kim Lane Scheppele (eds), *9/11 and the Rise of Global Anti-Terrorism Law. How the UN Security Council Rules the World* (Cambridge University Press 2021).

29 Krisztina Binder and others, 'States of Emergency in Response to the Coronavirus Crisis: Situation in Certain Member States' (2020) European Parliamentary Research Service PE 649.408.

30 Art 1, Law no 55-385.

31 See Basilien-Gainche, chapter 35.

month[32] before needing extension. Therefore, parliamentary scrutiny over emergency tools is less strict than that provided by the regulation of the 'traditional' *état d'urgence*. Moreover, while the 1955 law requires that the *état d'urgence* automatically ends if the Assemblée Nationale (the lower house of the French Parliament) is dissolved or the government resigns, the same guarantee is not provided by the law on the *état d'urgence sanitaire*. Once again, the 2020 regime offers a lower level of safeguards than the 1955 framework.

The *état d'urgence sanitaire* was declared for the first time on 23 March 2020 and then extended several times up to 10 July 2020, when it was replaced by a transitory regime.[33] The *état d'urgence sanitaire* was declared again to face the 'second wave' of COVID-19 in October 2020 up to 1 June 2021. Starting from 2 June 2021, a second transitory regime, governed by Law 2021-689 of 31 March 2020, was in place.

The French example demonstrated that enacting brand new emergency powers during an emergency might not be a rational choice, since there is the risk of accentuating the drawbacks that are common in situations of emergency, such as the lack of meaningful parliamentary scrutiny.

The French approach did not remain isolated: the United Kingdom, too, 'created' a new emergency regime (Coronavirus Act 2020), instead of applying the existing Civil Contingencies Act 2004.[34] The Irish Oireachtas did something similar by adopting a new emergency scheme through the Health (Preservation and Protection and other Emergency Measures in the Public Interest) Act 2020.[35] And in the Netherlands, no constitutional state of emergency was invoked, yet a Temporary Corona Act set new rules.[36]

3.3 Amending Existing Emergency Legislation During the Pandemic: Germany

A third trend consisted of countries that invoked existing primary legislation on emergency, but amended part of it during the COVID-19 emergency.

32 Indeed, the first declaration was exceptionally set to last for two months.

33 Law 2020-856 of 9 July 2020. On legal issues of the transitional regime, see Sylvia Brunet, 'The Hyper-Executive State of Emergency in France' in Konrad Lachmayer, Matthias C Ketteman (eds), *Pandemocracy in Europe* (Hart Publishing 2022).

34 See Grogan, chapter 5. See also – criticising several aspects of the Coronavirus Act and the choice not to trigger the Civil Contingencies Act – Clive Walker and Andrew Blick, 'Coronavirus Legislative Responses in the UK: Regression to Panic and Disdain of Constitutionalism' (*Just Security*, 12 May 2020)<https://www.justsecurity.org/70106/coronavirus-legislative-responses-in-the-uk-regression-to-panic-and-disdain-of-constitutionalism/>.

35 Oran Doyle and others, 'Ireland's Emergency Powers during the COVID-19 Pandemic', Report prepared for The Irish Human Rights and Equality Commission by The COVID-19 Law and Human Rights Observatory (2020).

36 Manon Julicher and Max Vetzo, 'COVID-19 in the Netherlands: of Changing Tides and Constitutional Constants' (*Verfassungsblog*, 22 April 2021) <https://verfassungsblog.de/covid-19-in-the-netherlands-of-changing-tides-and-constitutional-constants/>.

Germany[37] did not rely on its 'emergency constitution', but grounded its responses to COVID-19 on a federal law, the Protection against Infection Act 2000. Pursuant to it, in the event of a health crisis, appropriate measures shall be taken by the *Länder*, with the supervision and coordination of the federal government. In fact, lockdown orders were adopted by the *Länder*'s executives, which had previously stipulated agreements with the federal government to ensure uniform responses across the country.

At first, this model seemed successful, showing a working example of 'cooperative federalism'. However, at the beginning of the pandemic, a 'centralising will' became evident. In March 2020, the federal government proposed an amendment – which then became law – to the 2000 federal statute, providing for a stronger role for the federal minister of health.[38] The latter has new powers, among which, to impose border control rules and to limit patents of certain drugs, if useful to fight COVID-19.

An even stronger centralising effort could be detected in April 2021. At this stage, the federal government and the *Länder* had agreed that the latter could decide how and to what extent to ease their restrictions, based on the number of COVID-19 cases. Yet some *Länder* – under public pressure to get back to 'normal life' – pushed ahead with re-opening. On the one hand, this caused a lack of uniformity, since some federated states had more relaxed measures while others were stricter. On the other hand, in the more 'permissive' *Länder*, the infection rate increased. As a consequence, the federal government made a proposal to amend further the Protection against Infection Act, introducing a 'federal emergency brake'.[39] The changes imply that the *Länder*, as well as cities and districts, with high incidences of COVID-19 cases – according to parameters established by the law itself – can be legally required to apply rules decided by the federal government. The bill swiftly became law[40] at the end of April 2021. It represented a turning point in Germany's anti-COVID-19 efforts, which, during the first year of pandemic, were mainly based on a cooperative attitude. From April to June 2021, the 'federal emergency brake' was triggered in several territories to impose curfews, limitations on sports and trade and school closures. Due to the improvement of the situation, the federal government let the emergency brake expire on 30 June 2021.

Overall, Germany adopted an evident change of strategy during the pandemic: from being praised as a well-functioning example of decentralisation (albeit with the federal authorities as a considerable driving force), it turned to strong centralisation to combat the spread of the disease. Germany thus took a quite different path to Spain, which went from centralisation to increasing decentralisation.

37 See Mangold, chapter 27.

38 Infektionsschutzgesetz 2000, s 5.3, amended in 2020.

39 'German Cabinet Approves Uniform COVID Measures Nationwide' (*Deutsche Welle*, 13 April 2021) <https://www.dw.com/en/german-cabinet-approves-uniform-covid-measures-nationwide/a-57178073>.

40 Viertes Gesetz zum Schutz der Bevölkerung bei einer epidemischen Lage von nationaler Tragweite, 22 April 2021.

Germany also differed from France, in that it did not create a new state of emergency from scratch, but rather relied on existing legislation, adapting it to what the political branches considered to be the current needs.

It should be noted that also Austria followed a similar path, with more than twenty amendments to existing statutes regulating emergency.[41] The risk of taking overly hasty decisions still remains, although, in the case of Germany, the amendment of emergency legislation, resulting in the centralisation of powers, has at the time of writing contributed to a decrease in COVID-19 cases.[42]

3.4 'Patchwork' Responses to the COVID-19 Emergency: Italy

A fourth path consisted of using a variety of tools to tackle COVID-19, so creating a fragmented pattern. Italy can be placed within this trend. As noted in section 2, Italy does not have a clearly articulated constitutional framework governing emergencies. After declaring a state of emergency (still in place as of July 2021) pursuant to an existing act, Legislative Decree 1/2018, a number of decree laws – which in Italy have the same legal force as statute law – were adopted to react to COVID-19.

However, these decrees deferred the enactment of measures strongly limiting personal freedoms to decrees of the President of the Council of Ministers (i.e. the head of the executive). In the hierarchy of Italian legal sources, such decrees have a lower rank than statutes, are adopted by the head of the executive alone and do not receive any check from Parliament or from other bodies, namely the President of the Republic or the Constitutional Court. Therefore, their use raised a number of issues. First, they restricted freedoms (e.g. freedom of movement) that should be limited only by law or sources with the same legal force.[43] Second, the choice of such decrees as a one-size-fits-all solution to combat COVID-19 resulted in the marginalisation of Parliament in favour of the head of the executive. Indeed, at the beginning of the pandemic, the legislative Assembly was almost cut off from decisions. Afterwards, some oversight mechanisms were introduced, but they were weak, because, among other reasons, the Houses could only adopt a resolution – which is a non-binding tool – on measures to be enacted.[44] Third, decrees of the President of the Council of Ministers are unlikely to be scrutinised by any court. They fall outside of the jurisdiction of the Constitutional Court, which can only review primary sources,[45] while administrative courts, despite being, in

41 Francesco Palermo, 'La gestione della crisi pandemica in Austria: regolarità costituzionale e qualche distonia politica' (2020) DPCE Online 1743.

42 Berlinen Morgenpost, 'Coronavirus Monitor' <https://interaktiv.morgenpost.de/corona-virus-karte-infektionen-deutschland-weltweit/>.

43 Art 14 of the Italian Constitution.

44 Arianna Vedaschi, 'The Marginalisation of Parliament in Facing the Coronavirus Emergency: What about Democracy in Italy?', in *Pandemocracy in Europe* (n 33).

45 Art 134 of the Italian Constitution reads: "The Constitutional Court shall pass judgement on controversies on the constitutional legitimacy of laws and enactments having force of law issued by the State and Regions".

theory, entitled to review them, in practice either exercised their role with (often excessive) deference or were prevented from scrutinising them by procedural or timing reasons.[46] After a new government took office in February 2021, limitations of rights and freedoms were rarely adopted through said decrees, but rather through decree laws, partially overcoming the abovementioned problems. Decree laws, having the same legal force as law, involve the houses of Parliament – which are called to determine whether or not to convert them into law – and are subject to the scrutiny of the Constitutional Court.[47]

This change in terms of legal source did not solve further problems that characterised the Italian response to the pandemic from the very beginning. One of them is territorial fragmentation. This was a major issue during the first weeks of the pandemic in 2020. At this stage – due also to the complex allocation of public health competences in the Italian Constitution[48] – there were significant inconsistencies between the approach of the central government and that of several regional and even local administrations.[49] To reduce these concerns, a first response had been provided by the government led by Giuseppe Conte with Decree Law 9/2020, requiring that local measures that contradict central ones shall be considered without effect.[50] Yet, this norm failed to clearly settle regional fragmentation, which was managed through dialogue with regional authorities before adopting measures. This approach tried to implement the principle of loyal cooperation in a mutual relationship between different levels of government, inferred from Articles 5 and 120 of the Constitution. However, both before and after the new government was sworn in in February 2021, the situation was challenging, with attempts by regions and by lower levels to depart from centrally imposed rules.

The Italian experience was thus paradigmatic of how, in the absence of a well-defined emergency framework, the uncertainty as to the legal tools to be deployed and the authority – or at least the level of government – that should take certain decisions may entail legal and practical challenges. A stance very much akin to the Italian one was adopted in Belgium, where, lacking a constitutional state of emergency, the COVID-19 crisis was mainly managed by ministerial decrees and significant fragmentation was entailed.[51]

46 Among others, Regional Administrative Tribunal for Lazio, order 3453 of 4 May 2020.

47 See further Arianna Vedaschi, 'Italy and COVID-19: A Call for an "Italian Emergency Constitution"?' (*Just Security*, 12 May 2020) <https://www.justsecurity.org/70081/italy-and-covid-19-a-call-for-an-italian-emergency-constitution/>.

48 Per art 117, para 3 of the Italian Constitution, both the state and the regions can legislate on health protection, with the state determining general principles and the regions adopting detailed rules. Sometimes the boundary between 'general principles' and 'detailed rules' is blurry, increasing the possibility of conflict.

49 Arianna Vedaschi and Chiara Graziani, 'Coronavirus, Health Emergencies and Public Law Issues' (*Verfassungsblog*, 6 March 2020) <https://verfassungsblog.de/coronavirus-health-emergencies-and-public-law-issues/>.

50 The same provision was reiterated by Decree Law 19/2020, replacing the previous Decree Law.

51 Maaike de Ridder, 'Belgium's Accordion Response to COVID-19' (*Verfassungsblog*, 10 March 2021) <https://verfassungsblog.de/belgiums-accordion-response-to-covid-19/>.

4. Conclusion

In examining the four trends in emergency reactions by Western European democracies, several points should be highlighted.

First, the analysis shows an 'escape' from existing emergency frameworks, both constitutional and statutory, which were put aside to leave room for 'brand new' emergency rules, if not regimes. Paradoxically, in Spain, where constitutional emergency powers were resorted to, much criticism arose as to the chosen emergency regime.

Second, either by creating new emergency regimes or amending existing ones, countries such as France and Germany did something that is commonly considered unwise. Emergency rules should be drafted in ordinary times, to ensure thoughtful and in-depth consideration and unemotional debate, with the best balance of interests at stake. Adopting or amending emergency tools during an emergency is usually regarded as risking the introduction of hasty and ill thought-out provisions. The experience of France, and to a lesser extent Germany, confirmed this risk: many flaws can be detected in their new anti-COVID-19 emergency provisions, including excessive marginalisation of parliamentary bodies, overreach of executives,[52] and lack of clarity as to whether central or local approaches need to be taken.

Third, in countries such as Italy, where no systematic and well-structured emergency framework exists, similar and even more serious problems can be identified: doubts about which legal sources to apply in an emergency and about which level of government is better placed to decide; failure to comply with the principle of loyal cooperation; and difficulties in challenging emergency measures before courts.

Against this background, some general considerations stand out. The 'escape' from existing emergency powers might stem from the fact that these rules, drafted years ago in very different historical and political contexts, might have been perceived as unsuitable to deal with the pandemic. Thus, it appears necessary to rethink – not during an emergency, but in 'ordinary' times – new emergency paradigms, for instance including well-functioning cooperative mechanisms to address 'global' emergencies. A fortiori, countries like Italy, without a structured emergency regime, should seriously consider creating one. In doing so, they should take into account the global reach of current emergencies (not only pandemics, but also international terrorism or financial turmoil that crosses national boundaries).

In general, to allow new, 'global' emergency schemes to work at the state level, it would be desirable that – by learning from what has not worked properly during this pandemic – inter-state cooperative protocols to be applied in times of emergency are strengthened[53]. In other words, to ensure successful emergency provisions, isolated approaches by single states are no longer enough and intensive cooperation should be built with other levels of governance.[54]

52 Yet in other contexts executive 'underreach' has been highlighted. Kim Lane Scheppele and David Pozen, 'Executive Underreach, in Pandemics and Otherwise' (2020) 114 American Journal of International Law 608.

53 See many United Nations resolutions against the terrorist threat.

54 Vedaschi (n 28).

32

EXPOSING INEQUALITIES

The Experience of Minorities and Indigenous Peoples During COVID-19 Emergencies

Rasha Al Saba and Samrawit Gougsa

1. Introduction[1]

Although everyone is at risk of the COVID-19 virus, some populations have been worse affected than others. The disproportionate impact of COVID-19 on minority and indigenous peoples across the globe has been well documented.[2] Where disaggregated data is available, it shows that members of these communities have experienced systemically higher levels of severe COVID-19 illness and higher mortality rates. This trend has been documented in several countries, including the United States (US), the United Kingdom (UK), Sweden, Brazil, Spain and South Africa.[3] The causes of these disparities can be complex and multi-layered, yet social determinants of health play a crucial role in health disparities, especially in the ways that they intersect with ethnicity, religion, gender, disability and immigration status.[4] A report by Public Health England investigating the unequal impact

1 All websites accessed on 11 August 2021.

2 Rasha Al Saba, 'Inequality and the Impact of Covid-19: How Discrimination is Shaping the Experiences of Minorities and Indigenous Peoples During the Pandemic' (Minority Rights Group International 2020); Rasha Al Saba and Samrawit Gougsa, 'COVID-19, Minorities, and Indigenous peoples: The Litmus Test of Equality' (*Verfassungsblog*, 24 April 2021) <https://verfassungsblog.de/covid-19-minorities-and-indigenous-peoples-the-litmus-test-of-equality/>.

3 Maria Melchior and others, 'Migrant Status, Ethnicity and COVID-19: More Accurate European Data are Greatly Needed' (2021) 27(2) Clinical Microbiology and Infection 160. See also, in this volume, Graber, chapter 6 (United States); Grogan, chapter 5 (United Kingdom); Cameron and Jonsson Cornell, chapter 19 (Sweden); Bustamante and Meyer, chapter 18 (Brazil); and Labuschaigne and Staunton, chapter 28 (South Africa).

4 Lauren Paremoer and others, 'Covid-19 Pandemic and the Social Determinants of Health' (2021) British Medical Journal 372:n129.

DOI: 10.4324/9781003211952-37

of COVID-19 on minorities in the UK suggested that racism and discrimination could be a factor in the increased risk for ethnic minorities in contracting and dying from the virus.[5] Our research has shown that the impact of public health measures primarily designed to mitigate the health crisis, including related restrictions on freedom of movement and access to remedial measures and relief packages, were experienced differently by many minorities and indigenous people worldwide. More than anything this signals the urgent need for a reorientation of public health priorities and systems.

Emergency measures by states ostensibly designed as a pandemic response, when framed in discriminatory social and economic policies, have not only fuelled pre-existing inequalities but may have exacerbated the barriers to minorities' and indigenous peoples' enjoyment of rights. While COVID-19 vaccinations provide an opportunity to overcome the pandemic, the way in which they are distributed have not, at the time of writing, adequately considered the vulnerabilities of minorities and indigenous peoples to the virus.

This chapter seeks to review how lockdowns and restrictions on freedom of movement – two measures commonly implemented by countries to curb the spread of COVID-19 – have disproportionately impacted the health, security and economic situations of people from minority and indigenous communities globally. In addition, this chapter reviews recovery policies supposedly designed to mitigate the impact of the pandemic, examining the extent to which these have been inclusive and responsive to the specific challenges faced by minorities and indigenous peoples. As vaccines become a vital global tool in controlling the spread of COVID-19, data emerging in 2021 demonstrates that vaccination rates among ethnic and religious minorities are still markedly lower than those among the majority groups.[6] The final section of this chapter therefore also assesses key issues regarding equitable access to vaccines and factors determining vaccine uptake by minorities and indigenous peoples. It concludes by providing recommendations to policy makers on systemic issues concerning economic and social protection and vaccination efforts.

2. Impact of Emergency Measures

Since the efficacy of 'stay at home' orders depended heavily on individuals' living conditions, practicing physical distancing and self-isolation has often been nearly impossible in contexts where minorities and other marginalised groups reside, as typified by the experience of migrants and refugees living in camps.[7] While it is

5 Public Health England, *Beyond the Data: Understanding the Impact of Covid-19 on BAME Groups* (2020) 38–39 <https://assets.publishing.service.gov.uk/government/uploads/system/uploads/attachment_data/file/892376/COVID_stakeholder_engagement_synthesis_beyond_the_data.pdf>.

6 Al Saba and Gougsa (n 2).

7 Nidhi Subbaraman, '"Distancing is Impossible": Refugee Camps Race to Avert Coronavirus Catastrophe' (*Nature*, 24 April 2020) <https://www.nature.com/articles/d41586-020-01219-6>.

clear that the situation of individuals belonging to different minority communities varies tremendously, they are, as a class of individuals, often more likely to live in densely populated or overcrowded areas. These are conditions that support the spread of COVID-19, so while government orders to 'stay at home' may have been well intentioned, mandating individuals to remain confined in such living conditions, without specific additional advice on how to mitigate these conditions, particularly in the context of clusters of people living in close proximity to an essential worker, may have instead increased the risk of COVID-19 infection within the home and community.

Enforcement of lockdown measures, including restrictions on freedom of movement, was in many cases achieved through an increase in the use of extreme force – a facet of the discriminatory policing that is often a feature of minorities' lived experience. For instance, the enforcement of lockdown measures introduced by France's *Décret* (decree) n° 2020-264[8] disproportionately impacted poorer areas, which have a higher proportion of residents from ethnic minority groups.[9] For some minority communities, extreme enforcement of quarantines led to stigmatisation and further societal alienation. Thus, in Bulgaria and Slovakia authorities placed entire Roma settlements under compulsory quarantines using armed military personnel in April 2020, deeming it necessary for the protection of the public's health and safety.[10] Targeting entire communities without evidence of infection rates or other scientific rationale behind the claim signals a blanket extension of a discriminatory practices under cover of the pandemic.[11]

The COVID-19 pandemic elucidated the extent to which societies rely on certain so-called 'frontline workforces' often characterised by low wages. From bus drivers to meat packers, several jobs designated 'essential' were ones in which minorities and indigenous peoples across the globe are overrepresented, mainly as a consequence of entrenched structural discrimination that bars entry to other professions. While we did not detect a unified definition of an 'essential worker', with varied practice across jurisdictions, global lockdown experiences confirm that such workers were exempted from lockdown regulations because their roles were deemed crucial for society. As well documented,[12] this requirement on individuals to continue exposing themselves to a higher risk of infection increased

8 Décree 2020-264 du 17 mars 2020 (FR) (*Légifrance*, 18 March 2020). See also Basilien-Gainche, chapter 35.

9 Nathalie Revenu, 'Coronavirus en Seine-Saint-Denis: un nombre record d'amendes, police et justice durcissent le ton' (*Le Parisien*, 19 March, 2020) <https://www.leparisien.fr/seine-saint-denis-93/coronavirus-en-seine-saint-denis-un-nombre-record-d-amendes-police-et-justice-durcissent-le-ton-19-03-2020-8284008.php>.

10 'Stigmatizing Quarantines of Roma Settlements in Slovakia and Bulgaria' (Amnesty International, 17 April 2020).

11 Bernard Rorke and Jonathan Lee, *Roma Rights in the Time of COVID* (European Roma Rights Centre 2020).

12 Miriam Mutambudzi and others, 'Occupation and Risk of Severe COVID-19: Prospective Cohort Study of 120 075 UK Biobank Participants' (2020) 78 Occupational and Environmental Medicine 307.

their likelihood of coming into proximity with other persons or places carrying the virus. In many instances, these individuals were even forced to fulfil their jobs without adequate prioritisation for personal protective equipment (PPE).

The ease with which the virus transmits, the fact that higher proportions of minorities worked in essential jobs and the lower socio-economic affluence of such individuals in their personal living conditions, meant that it was not only the individual worker at risk of contracting the virus, but also the family and by association the entire community in which the person was embedded. This was evidenced in the commune of Seine-Saint-Denis in the northern suburbs of Paris, France, one of the poorest areas in the country, where a majority of its residents are of Black or North African origin. Seine-Saint-Denis had one of the highest COVID-19 death rates in France due to dismally overcrowded housing conditions and a higher number of commune residents working in jobs deemed 'essential' during the lockdown.[13]

Unemployment, reduced income and a growth in human insecurity were also major consequences of lockdown measures. According to the International Labour Organisation, an estimated 8.8% of global working hours were lost in 2020 alone, equivalent to 255 million full-time jobs.[14] While many jobs in the formal sector were protected through government schemes, jobs in the informal sector, which make up 61.2% of the world's workforce,[15] and where minorities and indigenous peoples are overwhelmingly represented, were impacted harder. Unlike the formal economy, the nature of the informal economy means that workers do not have secure employment contracts, access to labour protections or social protection through employment,[16] leaving them in precarious positions and exposed to significant financial instability. The gendered nature of the informal economy also needs to be emphasised: 92% of women in low-income countries are employed in the informal sector.[17] In Colombia, most displaced Venezuelan women work in the informal economy and 78% of them work in industries highly impacted by the COVID-19 pandemic compared to 57% of employed Venezuelan men and 59% of employed Colombian women.[18] There is also growing evidence that the pandemic resulted in significant movements of minority workers from the formal economy to the informal economy.[19] In Brazil, for example, indigenous peoples and Black Brazilians became vulner-

13 Catherine Mangeney and others, 'La Surmortalité Durant l'Épidémie de COVID-19 dans les Départements Franciliens' (Observatoire Régional de Santé 2020).

14 International Labour Organisation, *ILO Monitor: COVID-19 and the World of Work* (7th edn, 2021).

15 International Labour Organisation, *Women and Men in the Informal Economy: A Statistical Picture* (3rd edn 2018).

16 Rajneesh Narula, 'Policy Opportunities and Challenges from the Covid-19 Pandemic for Economies in Large Sector' (2020) 3 Journal of International Business Policy 302, 303.

17 Florence Bonnet, Joann Vanek and Martha Chen, 'Women and Men in the Informal Economy: A Statistical Brief' (Women in Informal Employment: Globalizing and Organizing (WIEGO) 2019).

18 Jimmy Graham and Martha Guerrero Ble, 'The Impact of COVID-19 on the Economic Inclusion ofVenezuelans in Colombia' (Center for Global Development 2021).

19 Tomoya Obokata and others, 'Good Practice in Protecting People from Modern Slavery During the Covid-19 Pandemic' (Modern Slavery and Human Rights Policy and Evidence Centre 2021).

able to unemployment and thus sought employment in the informal sector.[20] This shift from formal to informal sectors underscores an increased vulnerability imposed on minorities and indigenous peoples by the pandemic.

Of course, some sectors experienced an increased demand for products and services, a notable example being manufacturers of PPE, which reportedly fuelled abusive working conditions and labour rights violations of minorities. Several companies in China, for example, were implicated in the exploitation of Uyghurs who were forced to produce medical masks in conditions that fit within the parameters of forced labour.[21] Similarly in Gulf countries, the pandemic drove steep increases in labour abuses, including 'wage theft' against migrant workers by employers.[22] Challenging employers and governments in the Gulf region for wage theft of migrant workers has been hindered by extensive COVID-19 repatriation programmes, highlighting the vulnerability these workers face and the close to weak or inexistent protection they receive in employment contracts that often steer power towards employers.[23] The situation demonstrates that while forced labour and exploitative practices existed prior to the pandemic, the economic crisis that has emerged as a result created conditions for its exacerbation.

3. Social and Economic Responses to the Crisis

Many minorities and indigenous people were hit especially hard by the socio-economic impact of the pandemic. This was largely due to historical and contemporary contexts of marginalisation which have ossified structural discrimination, leaving these communities with few means to face an economic crisis of the dimension experienced. Data from the US,[24] the UK[25] and Canada[26] show that many ethnic minorities live in vulnerable socio-economic situations that predate the pandemic, leaving them with inadequate resilience to face this crisis. Research conducted by

20 The Freedom Fund, 'Global Pandemic, Local Devastation: Frontline Efforts to Support the Most Vulnerable' (2020) <https://freedomfund.org/our-reports/global-pandemic-local-devastation/>.

21 Muyi Xiao and others, 'China Is Using Uighur Labor to Produce Face Masks' (*The New York Times*, 19 July 2020).

22 Isobel Archer and Danielle McMullan, 'COVID-19: Spike in Allegations of Labour Abuse Against Migrant Workers in the Gulf' (Business and Human Rights Resource Centre, 23 September 2020) <https://www.business-humanrights.org/en/blog/spike-in-allegations-of-labour-abuse-against-migrant-workers-in-the-gulf/>; Equidem, *The Cost of Contagion: The Human Rights Impacts of COVID-19 on Migrant Workers in the Gulf* (2021).

23 Laura Foley and Nicola Piper, 'Returning Home Empty Handed: Examining How COVID-19 Exacerbates the Non-Payment of Temporary Migrant Workers' Wages' (2021) Global Social Policy <https://doi.org/10.1177%2F14680181211012958>.

24 Don Bambino Geno Tai and others, 'The Disproportionate Impact of COVID-19 on Racial and Ethnic Minorities in the United States' (2021) 72(4) Clinical Infectious Diseases 703.

25 Rohini Mathur, 'Urgent Action and Policies Needed to Address COVID-19 among UK Ethnic Minorities' (2020) 396(10266) The Lancet 1866.

26 Statistics Canada, 'Economic Impact of COVID-19 Among Visible Minority Groups (2020) <https://www150.statcan.gc.ca/n1/pub/45-28-0001/202001/article/00042-eng.htm>.

University College London, just before the first wave of COVID-19 infections hit the UK, showed that youth from ethnic minorities were 47% more likely to work on so-called 'zero-hours contracts'.[27] To mitigate the economic impact of the pandemic and to provide the means for these individuals to absorb such impact, governments sought to develop new schemes or expand on existing ones.[28] The narrative focused on different countries' approaches and their comparative success in governing but paid less attention to the efficiency of these responses in protecting vulnerable groups and those at most acute risk within wider society. One way to examine the effectiveness of responses during the pandemic through a minority and indigenous lens is by assessing the extent to which these schemes were available, adequate and accessible to members of these communities. To be effective in such a crisis, responses clearly need to acknowledge the vulnerable socio-economic situation that many minorities and indigenous people depart from.

One particular area of concern lies with the measures designed to combat the mass unemployment that became associated with lockdowns and limited economic activity. Popular governmental measures aimed at restricting the impact of this phenomenon were through job retention schemes, in which governments helped retain employees by subsidising a percentage of their income. Although these measures played a major role in reducing the number of jobs at risk, especially during the confinement phase of the pandemic, their benefit beyond firm-related human capital is significantly in question. The evidence suggests that such schemes mainly targeted workers in the formal economy and, apart from few countries, were not designed to cater to those working in informal jobs.[29] The consequence was that many minorities and indigenous people who are overrepresented in the informal or non-standard economy had no access to the job security these measures could offer.[30]

The structuring of job security around standardised jobs is merely one facet of indirect discrimination against minorities and indigenous people. Their inadequacy and lack of sustainability is another determinant of how governmental responses were insensitive to the social position of minorities and indigenous peoples. The question ahead is whether these measures are likely to provide adequate compensation to sustain a decent income, especially for low-wage workers. Although most governments' responses associated with COVID-19 were perceived as attempts to manage the crisis and therefore temporary in nature, the ones that targeted vulnerable groups and populations appeared to be even shorter in duration. This included cash transfer and food assistance schemes to vulnerable people including informal

27 Georgina Bowyer and others, *Race Inequality in the Workforce: Exploring Connections Between Work, Ethnicity and Mental Health* (Carnegie Trust 2020).

28 Tomoya Obokata and others, 'Good Practice in Protecting People from Modern Slavery During the Covid-19 Pandemic' (Modern Slavery and Human Rights Policy and Evidence Centre 2021).

29 Organisation for Economic Cooperation and Development, 'Job Retention Schemes during the COVID-19 Lockdown and Beyond' (October 2020) <https://www.oecd.org/coronavirus/policy-responses/job-retention-schemes-during-the-covid-19-lockdown-and-beyond-0853ba1d/>.

30 Narula (n 16).

workers, self-employed persons, refugees, people living in rural areas and returned migrant workers.[31] Although cash transfers were implemented to unprecedented levels during the pandemic, they were still perceived as inadequate and ad hoc.[32] South Africa, Chile and Pakistan, for example, provided temporary cash grants and cash assistance to vulnerable populations, yet such forms of assistance were often considered insufficient with the amounts provided under the national poverty line in these countries.[33] A similar trend was witnessed in Egypt where grants made available to vulnerable groups were equal to the individual extreme poverty line of the years 2017 and 2018, which had most likely increased dramatically since then due to inflation.[34]

Too often, discrimination and exclusion were couched in terms of regularised status and citizenship, terms that shaped eligibility for services well before the pandemic. Documents that certified individual status, such as identification documentation, are one long-standing discriminatory requirement that excludes access to services for many minorities and indigenous peoples. Although some governments relaxed eligibility for social protection schemes, these barriers persisted throughout the pandemic when accessing much needed health services and social protection. For some Roma community members in Ukraine, for instance, the barrier in registering with family doctors is a direct result of their lack of birth certificates, which is a prerequisite for the service.[35] Similarly, in many cases access to social protection measures requires individuals to provide ID or some form of financial identification prior to access. In Argentina, for example, while workers in the informal economy were eligible for a singular cash payment, they needed to provide a bank account to be able to benefit from the scheme.[36] This meant that many migrants, minorities and indigenous peoples who lack these benefits because of long histories of marginalisation, were left without vital support. Although some of these conditions were said to be needed to improve outreach and reduce the possibility of financial fraud,[37] the narrowness of the scope of eligibility in design, cou-

31 Ugo Gentilini and others, 'Social Protection and Job Responses to COVID-19: A Real-Time Review of Country Responses' (World Bank, July 2020), 73, 98, 282, 328, 351, 380, 393, 460.

32 Ugo Gentilini, 'A Game Changer for Social Protection? Six Reflections on COVID-19 and the Future of Cash Transfers' (World Bank, 11 January 2021).

33 Special Rapporteur on Extreme Poverty and Human Rights, 'Looking Back to Look Ahead: A Rights Based Approach to Social Protection in the Post COVID-19 Economic Recovery' (September 2020) para 27 <https://www.ohchr.org/Documents/Issues/Poverty/covid19.pdf>. See also, on Pakistan, Syed and Tariq-Ali, chapter 22.

34 Hussein Suleiman, 'COVID-19 and Households in Egypt: Implications, Policy Response, and Recommendations' (Center for Mediterranean Integration, October 2020).

35 International Charitable Organization Roma Women's Fund, *COVID-19 Response Action for Roma in Ukraine* (Minority Rights Group Europe, December 2020).

36 Francisco Aldaya, 'Argentina Scraps Cash Distribution for Emergency Welfare' (*S&P Global*, 12 June 2020) <https://www.spglobal.com/marketintelligence/en/news-insights/latest-news-headlines/argentina-scraps-cash-distribution-for-emergency-welfare-59066760>.

37 Jens Arnold, Paula Garda and Alberto Gonzalez-Pandiella, 'Reaching Out to Informal Workers in Latin America: Lessons from COVID-19' (OECD, 9 June 2020) <https://oecdecoscope.blog/2020/06/29/reaching-out-to-informal-workers-in-latin-america-lessons-from-covid-19/>.

pled with administration and implementation impacted by prejudice, is expected to have a great impact on deepening inequalities.

Poorly designed administrative mechanisms and infrastructure in implementing COVID-19 related responses played a crucial role in denying access to services for minorities and indigenous peoples. Poor administration and reductive implementation created or deepened inequalities within communities. In the Philippines, for example, local officials delegated the distribution of aid to tribal leaders in some cases.[38] This practice increased the risk of ethnic tensions since evidence shows it favoured those with strong tribal ties.[39] The design and effectiveness of the communication in addition to its mode of dissemination was another factor that determined the success of a response in reaching those entitled to services. While many governments were sensitive to delivering messages and making information available in indigenous languages, others struggled to adopt such an approach in their communication. This is illustrated in Kenya, where a survey showed that while the government was successful in making COVID-19 related prevention information available to indigenous peoples, less than a third were aware of the economic assistance packages theoretically available to them.[40] There is a continued fear that barriers preventing minorities and indigenous peoples from accessing health services and social protection will hinder universal coverage of protection through vaccination.

4. Vaccine Distribution Plans and Equitable Access

Vaccination became the most critical measure to confront and control the COVID-19 pandemic.[41] For vaccination to achieve its full potential benefit, along with prioritising the most vulnerable and those at risk, at least 70% of a country's population would need to have been vaccinated to hinder further transmission.[42] At the time of writing, although vaccination efforts have been escalated,[43] inequi-

38 US Department of State, '2020 Country Reports on Human Rights Practices: Philippines' (Bureau of Democracy, Human Rights and Labor, 2020) <https://www.state.gov/reports/2020-country-reports-on-human-rights-practices/philippines/>. See also Atienza, chapter 36.

39 Nina Rayana Bahjin-Imlan, 'The Pandemic's Forgotten Faces: The Plight of Muslims, Women, and Other Minorities' (*Philippine Daily Inquirer*, 24 April 2020) <https://opinion.inquirer.net/129176/forgotten-muslims-and-other-minorities>.

40 UN Office of the High Commissioner for Human Rights, 'Kenya: Leaving No One Behind in the COVID-19 Crisis Human Rights Impacts in Indigenous Communities' (December 2020) <https://www.ohchr.org/Documents/Countries/KE/OHCHR-DC_December2020.pdf>. See Imalingat, Were and Maleche, chapter 15.

41 Committee on Economic, Social and Cultural Rights, 'Statement on universal and equitable access to vaccines for the coronavirus disease (COVID-19)' (27 November 2020) para 1. <https://www.ohchr.org/Documents/HRBodies/CESCR/E_C_12_2020_2_AUV.docx>. See also Singh, chapter 2.

42 Organization of American States, 'Inter-American Commission on Human Rights and its SRESCER Call on American States to Make Public Health and Human Rights the Focus of All their Decisions and Policies Concerning the COVID-19 Vaccine' (5 February 2021).

43 World Health Organisation, 'WHO Director-General's Opening Remarks at the Media Briefing on COVID-19' (5 February 2021).

table access to COVID-19 vaccines within and across countries raises significant concern about its efficacy in containing the pandemic. While wealthier countries in the Global North continue the practice of purchasing and hoarding large quantities of the vaccines, countries in the Global South face acute shortages in production and rising prices of the vaccines.[44] For a country such as Kenya, lack of equitable global access to vaccines means it will not be until 2023 that 30% of its population will be vaccinated against COVID-19.[45] To think of unequal access to vaccines is thus to ask the question, a vaccine for whom? More specifically, it is vital to ascertain whether vaccines would reach those who are marginalised, especially the most vulnerable to the virus among minorities and indigenous people.

The monopoly of wealthier countries on vaccine production in conjunction with global shortages in supply chains pushed some countries in the Global South to look for alternative measures and to authorise vaccination programmes emanating in the private sector. In Pakistan,[46] for example, commercial imports of COVID-19 vaccine were approved, allowing the private sector to offer vaccines to everyone for a price.[47] As vaccines became increasingly commodified, access to vaccination became dependent on an ability to pay, producing significant inequalities and leaving many minorities and indigenous peoples beyond reach. In the context of manufactured scarcity, where needs are put in competition against each other, accountability becomes even harder to achieve. Some countries introduced additional measures to control the parallel private sector roll out programme, as in the Philippines, where the government allowed the private sector to procure COVID-19 vaccine agreements with the government.[48] It remains too soon to assess the efficacy of such steps.

Data on interaction with COVID-19 related health services disaggregated by ethnicity and other factors of identity, such as religion, is limited.[49] Yet in countries privileged enough to secure COVID-19 vaccines for their populations, and where disaggregated data is available, disparities in the vaccination uptake has occurred across many communities. According to a survey conducted in the UK in November and December 2020, a high percentage of ethnic minorities

44 David Meyer, 'AstraZeneca is Finding it Hard to Keep its COVID-19 Vaccine Promises' (*Fortune*, 25 January 2021) <https://fortune.com/2021/01/25/astrazeneca-covid-vaccines-europe-deliveries-south-africa-price/>.

45 Nita Bhalla, '"Pricing out the Poor": Fears over COVID-19 Vaccine Access as Kenya Lets in Private Sector', (*Reuters*, 25 March 2021) <https://www.reuters.com/article/us-health-coronavirus-kenya-vaccine-idUSKBN2BH2Q9>.

46 See Syed and Tariq-Ali, chapter 22.

47 Syed Hassan, 'Young Pakistanis Rush to Purchase Russian Vaccine as Private Sales Open' (*Reuters*, 4 April 2021).

48 Department of Health, Philippines, 'DOH, NTF: Private Sector Allowed to Procure COVID-19 Vaccines via Tripartite Agreements' (22 March 2021) <https://doh.gov.ph/doh-press-release/DOH-NTF-PRIVATE-SECTOR-ALLOWED-TO-PROCURE-COVID-19-VACCINES-VIA-TRIPARTITE-AGREEMENTS>.

49 Al Saba and Gougsa (n 2).

were unlikely to take the vaccine.[50] Similar trends were detectable among ethnic minorities in the US, where the white population was twice more likely to take COVID-19 vaccination compared with Hispanic and African Americans.[51] However, a different picture emerges among indigenous people in the US, who were also hard hit by the virus. Data from the Center of Disease Control (CDC) in the US shows that as of 5 April 2021, about 30% of Americans who self-identify as American Indian and Alaskan Native (AIAN) had received at least one dose of COVID-19 vaccine, compared to only about 19% of white Americans, 16% of Asian Americans, 12% of African Americans and 9% of the Hispanic population.[52] According to a survey conducted by the Urban Indian Health Institute, about 75% of participants from tribal and indigenous background deemed themselves willing to receive the vaccine.[53] This brings to the forefront the crucial role of community mobilisation and outreach in disastrous scenarios including health emergencies.

Factors determining vaccine uptake are various and complex. Managing information has proven to be one of the biggest challenges and ought to be regarded as equally important as the availability of medical infrastructure, including vaccines, during the pandemic. What has been perceived as 'vaccine hesitancy' and distrust in health systems among minorities and indigenous people is often entrenched in a long history of structural racism and discrimination that persists and shapes their daily lived experience. There is significant evidence of historical research abuses and medical harm perpetrated against minorities and indigenous people which have contributed to ongoing scepticism towards COVID-19 vaccines.[54] While correcting vaccine-related misinformation, communicating information can be co-implemented with community members through organising, trust building and tailored messages. Over-reliance on web-based vaccine registration systems in countries such as the US[55] and India[56] also disadvantaged minorities such as

50 Elaine Robertson and others, 'Predictors of COVID-19 Vaccine Hesitancy in the UK Household Longitudinal Study' (2021) 94 Brain, Behavior, and Immunity 41.

51 Nambi Ndugga and others, 'Latest Data on COVID-19 Vaccinations Race/Ethnicity' (*KFF*, 26 May 2021) <https://www.kff.org/coronavirus-covid-19/issue-brief/latest-data-on-covid-19-vaccinations-race-ethnicity/>.

52 Latoya Hill and Samantha Artiga, 'COVID-19 Vaccination among American Indian and Alaska Native People' (*KFF*, 9 April 2021) <https://www.kff.org/racial-equity-and-health-policy/issue-brief/covid-19-vaccination-american-indian-alaska-native-people/>.

53 Urban Indian Health Institute, 'Results from a National COVID-19 Vaccination Survey: Strengthening Vaccine Efforts in Indian Country' (28 January 2021) <https://www.uihi.org/projects/strengthening-vaccine-efforts-in-indian-country/>.

54 Erin Blakemore, 'The Little-Known History of the Forced Sterilization of Native American Women' (*JSTOR Daily*, 25 August 2016) <https://daily.jstor.org/the-little-known-history-of-the-forced-sterilization-of-native-american-women/>; 'What Is Behind the Low Covid-19 Vaccine Take-up in Some Ethnic Minorities?' (*The BMJ Opinion*, 8 April 2021) <https://blogs.bmj.com/bmj/2021/04/08/what-is-behind-the-low-covid-19-vaccine-take-up-in-some-ethnic-minorities/>.

55 Jacinda C Abdul-Mutakabbir, 'A Three-Tiered Approach to Address Barriers to COVID-19 Vaccine Delivery in the Black Community' (June 2021) 9(6) The Lancet: Global Health e749.

56 Bhavya Dore, 'In India's COVID-19 Crisis, the Internet Is Both a Lifeline and a Barrier' (*The New Humanitarian*, 25 May 2021) <https://www.thenewhumanitarian.org/news/2021/5/25/india-COVID-19-digital-divide-hampers-vaccine-and-healthcare-access>.

African Americans and non-native English speakers, many of whom may not have adequate access to technology or the necessary language skills to independently utilise such systems.

Where segments of society have been the target of state violence, COVID-19 vaccines were instrumentalised to further oppress these groups. Thus, despite a legal obligation under the Fourth Geneva Convention to the people under its jurisdiction, the Israeli authorities[57] continued to follow discriminatory policies against Palestinians living in Israel and in the occupied Palestinian territory. While celebrating its record-setting vaccination drive, the Israeli government discriminated against Palestinian prisoners and detainees in its custody and denied their right to be protected from the virus.[58] Furthermore, Israel denied vaccines to the 4.5 million Palestinians living in the occupied territories while reaching out to settlers in the West Bank.[59]

Often overlooked by governments, minority and indigenous communities hold distinctive values that can support diverse thinking around public health measures. For example, the indigenous Khoikhoi of Southern Africa have a principle of distributive justice, which describes what society owes individuals. This philosophy obliges the government to remedy unacceptable distribution of essential resources amongst the population, providing valuable insight for the conversation around global vaccine hoarding and distribution, since it requires global cooperation to overcome the pandemic. Governments should pay greater attention to these views, which offer valuable insight and ideas to design and implement vaccination strategies.[60] Ultimately, as argued by Ewuoso and Cordero-Rodrigues, "[T]here is a need for a holistic approach that takes into account the economic and health situation of all".[61]

5. Conclusion

In the face of multiple complexities such as those imposed by COVID-19, a profound shift towards actions targeting minorities and indigenous is needed. Ending the public health crisis starts from guaranteeing access to universal health coverage, while dismantling structural barriers that prevent anyone, including minorities and

57 'Israel: Provide Vaccines to Occupied Palestinians' (Human Rights Watch, 17 January 2021) <https://www.hrw.org/news/2021/01/17/israel-provide-vaccines-occupied-palestinians>.

58 'Civil Society Calls for Urgent Release of Palestinian Prisoners and Detainees in Israeli Prisons' (*Civicus*, 22 April 2020) <https://www.civicus.org/index.php/media-resources/news/4382-on-palestinian-prisoners-day-civil-society-calls-for-urgent-release-of-palestinian-prisoners-and-detainees-in-israeli-prisons>.

59 Matthias Kennes, 'In Israel, You're 60 Times More Likely to Have a COVID Vaccine than in Palestine' (Médecins Sans Frontières, 22 February 2021) <https://www.msf.org/stark-inequality-covid-19-vaccination-between-israel-and-palestine>.

60 Cornelius Ewuoso and Luis Cordeiro-Rodrigues, 'Khoikhoi Perspectives on Public Health: Indigenous Values For a COVID-19 Response in South Africa' (2021) 11 Journal of Global Health 03032.

61 ibid.

indigenous people, from accessing health care. In light of the unprecedented and extended crisis, it is imperative to ensure that emergency measures are justified by reasonable public health objectives and are legally grounded, proportionate, necessary and non-discriminatory. The extension of lockdowns and other emergency measures should be accompanied by avenues to access health and financial support services, as well as access to justice. This requires providing support and protection to workers vulnerable to conditions of forced labour and exploitation, particularly ethnic and religious minorities, indigenous peoples, women and migrant workers. To protect these groups against the extended economic crisis associated with the pandemic, it is vital that social protection measures are adequate and universally accessible – regardless of legal status. However, there cannot be equitable responses until the voices, knowledge and experiences of minority groups and indigenous people are heard and used to 're-imagine' public policies. Mechanisms of accountability during administration of economic and social aid should be also developed.

Equitable access to COVID-19 vaccines remains key to tackling the crisis. Countries must collaborate to expand manufacturing capacity and advocate for the global community to fairly share COVID-19 vaccine and treatment technologies. Additionally, national health equity in prioritising vaccines should be ensured by focusing attention on the hardest hit by the virus, including minorities and indigenous people and those systemically disadvantaged and marginalised. This is especially important in contexts where vaccines and supplies are limited. To combat the ever-increasing misinformation, efforts must focus on providing accurate and consistent information on public health and protection measures that are accessible in minority and indigenous languages.

The crisis provoked by the pandemic provides governments in general and public health authorities in particular with the opportunity to address issues of mistrust. This can be done by acknowledging historical and current harms caused by unethical medical treatment and research. For vaccination programmes to reach the most vulnerable, the dependency on web-based registries should be balanced by offering alternatives such as walk-in vaccination centres that do not require online registrations in areas populated by minorities and indigenous people, especially in deprived urban and rural areas. Finally, evidence shows that it is crucial to the success of vaccination programmes to be grounded by ensuring the engagement of community members at multiple levels, including community outreach and the development of culturally accepted messages.

33

WHEN EMERGENCY IS PERMANENT

Egypt's Legal Response to COVID-19

Ahmed Ellaboudy

1. Introduction[1]

As COVID-19 caused states around the world to introduce emergency laws and regulations, the question of how to achieve a balance between restricted emergency measures, ordinary governance arrangements and protection of human rights and civil liberties was at the heart of global legal discourse. The legal implications of living under emergency regulations are considered conventional within the legal practice of contemporary Egypt. In fact, Egypt is a landmark case study with regards to 'normalising the exception', having relied on emergency regulations continuously for decades.[2] As a predictable consequence of such a situation, a state of emergency declared in 2017 in response to the bombing of churches was repeatedly extended up to 2020. Hence, on 14 February 2020, when Egypt recorded its first confirmed COVID-19 case, the inevitable question arose: with a de facto permanent state of emergency, what else could be done?

Some legislative amendments to the existing emergency law, among other procedures, were introduced to respond to the economic damage and public health concerns arising from COVID-19. Significantly, however, no specific legal response was adopted which might have altered the regular decision-making process or power arrangements between different branches of the state. Rather, Egypt's approach to managing the pandemic was the adoption of the minimum possible actions, which neither harmed the state's economic plan, nor changed the way the legal and political system functions.[3] This chapter focuses on the harmful con-

1 All websites accessed on 4 July 2021.

2 Sadiq Reza, 'Endless Emergency: The Case of Egypt' (2007) 10(4) New Criminal Law Review 532.

3 This chapter draws on the following: Ahmed Ellaboudy, 'Emergency Law Amendments to Fight Covid-19 in Egypt: Putting the Poison in the Honey' (*Verfassungsblog*, 19 May 2020)<https://ver-

DOI: 10.4324/9781003211952-38

sequences of the long-standing application of emergency regulations on Egypt's ability to respond to the real threat of the pandemic. To do so, section 2 provides a historical contextualisation of the circumstances that shaped the quasi-permanent state of emergency in Egypt. It also outlines the basic features of the existing emergency law and the 2014 constitutional framework that regulates emergency measures. Section 3 examines the executive and legislative response to the COVID-19 crisis, focusing on the emergency law amendments and relevant legislative efforts to contain the pandemic's impact. Section 4 assesses the human rights concerns that were raised during the pandemic, especially those related to the right to health. Finally, section 5 analyses Egypt's efforts related to conducting the House and Senate elections and fulfilling its constitutional obligations during the time of the COVID-19 crisis, while there was a chance to postpone the Senate elections to minimise health risks.

2. Contextualising the State of Emergency in Egypt

How has the extended use of emergency powers become the main feature of contemporary legal practice in Egypt? An overview of the nature and composition of the newly-established republic following the abolition of the monarchy in 1953 provides the answer. In July 1952, a military coup, led by the Free Officers Movement, surprisingly succeeded in overthrowing King Farouk, ending the era of the Muhammad Ali dynasty in Egypt. Immediately after the establishment of the republic, there were only two paths for Egypt's political future: the return of the military to barracks after achieving the reforms required to establish democracy or the creation of a military state controlled by security-minded officers. The latter path was the choice that determined Egypt's political and legal practice for the next seven decades.

In order to protect the newly established regime, Hazem Kandil observes that "the political leadership – headed by President Nasser – needed military and/or security support to preserve its power should the masses refuse to obey".[4] Meanwhile, he adds, "the security establishment understood that its influence was contingent on the persistence of autocracy, that transition to democracy would spell its downfall from power".[5] Consequently, reliance on the extended use of exceptional powers was the fundamental tool that was used as a carte blanche for the executive to ensure internal stability, in the context of an exceptionally conflict-heated region.[6] In other words, the military background of each of the

fassungsblog.de/emergency-law-amendments-to-fight-covid-19-in-egypt-putting-the-poison-in-the-honey/>; Ahmed Ellaboudy, 'When Emergency Is Permanent, What Else Could be Done? A Year of Sanitary Crisis in Egypt' (*Verfassungsblog*, 15 April 2021) <https://verfassungsblog.de/when-emergency-is-permanent-what-else-could-be-done/>.

4 Hazem Kandil, *Soldiers, Spies, and Statesmen: Egypt's Road to Revolt* (Verso Books 2012) 11.

5 ibid.

6 The Martial Law No 533 of 1954, which was one of the early pieces of legislation that featured exceptional executive powers.

state organs at that time drove the creation of a legal system that allowed for permanent extraordinary measures, such as arbitrary detentions and the establishment of special courts, as the best way of governing. As a result, a state of emergency was activated in Egypt for almost 12 of the 15 years from 1952 to 1967.

What is more, Emergency Law No 162/1958 was drafted to expand the executive powers during exceptional circumstances such as wars and internal unrest. In practice, however, it has been used for the purpose of giving the President of the Republic unlimited powers to repress any kind of popular opposition.[7] Accordingly, a state of emergency was declared in 1967 during the Arab–Israeli war and endured for 13 years. It was lifted, briefly, in 1980, but following the assassination of President Sadat in 1981, his successor President Mubarak continually extended the state of emergency for the next 30 years that he stayed in power until 2011.[8]

It is worth mentioning that the decisive shift from a military to a police state that evolved during the mandate of President Mubarak was a central factor which created a perfect environment for the continuous application of emergency regulations. Indeed, it would be accurate to state that the long-standing abuse of emergency powers was the backbone of Mubarak's authoritarian regime.

2.1 The Colonial Features of the 1958 Emergency Law

Emergency Law No 162/1958 is still the principal normative framework that regulates emergency power in Egypt. The origins of the current emergency regulations can easily be traced back to the period of British martial law, which was adopted after the declaration of Egypt as a British protectorate in 1914. Unsurprisingly, the basic features of martial law were characterised by arbitrary and totalitarian rule, in keeping with its colonial origin. Measures such as the unrestricted scope of time to apply emergency measures, searching people and places, censoring the press, prohibiting meetings and assemblies, restricting freedom of movement and seizing assets were allowed according to the law, without even the need for written orders.[9]

Despite the apparent difference in the purpose behind enacting an emergency law by a colonial authority and a liberation movement, the 1958 Emergency Law was similar to the British martial law and included many of its arbitrary measures which impose unjustified restrictions on fundamental rights. In the words of Kandil,

> the law allows for extended detention without trial, denies detainees habeas corpus, bans labour strikes, prohibits demonstrations without police permission, justifies press censorship and sanctions trial of political

7 Ellaboudy, 'Emergency Law Amendments to Fight Covid-19 in Egypt' (n 3).

8 ibid.

9 Reza (n 2) 535–536.

prisoners by special courts that deliver 'swift justice' and restrict defendants' right to appeal.[10]

Moreover, the 1958 Emergency Law authorises the president to declare a state of emergency "whenever public security or order are threatened"; however, such a vague phrase provides no clear criteria for what a state of emergency means or when it shall be declared.[11] The law contains a non-exclusive list of events that might trigger a state of emergency such as "war, internal disturbances, natural disasters, or the spread of an epidemic";[12] in practice, however, the only kind of emergencies that constructed Egyptian practice related to security concerns, which, as discussed below, had important implications when a non-security emergency – the COVID-19 pandemic – occurred.

2.2 The 2014 Constitutional Framework: A Good Text Alone Is not Enough

The quasi-permanent state of emergency, which has been in place for almost five decades, was one of the main catalysts for the escalation of grievances in 2011, which led to a popular revolution. The 2014 Constitution was drafted in its shadow. The emergency provisions it contains were concerned with avoiding a repetition of the endless state of emergency. Hence, whilst Article 154 of the Constitution gives the president the power to declare a state of emergency, it requires prior consultation with the cabinet; in addition, such a declaration must be submitted to the House of Representatives within the following seven days for approval by a majority.[13] Further, a state of emergency must be declared for a specified period not exceeding three months, which can only be extended by another similar period upon the approval of two-thirds of members of the House. In all cases, the House of Representatives cannot be dissolved while a state of emergency is in force.[14]

Although the drafters of the 2014 Constitution had intended the limited duration of a state of emergency and the requirement for a two-thirds majority for any extension to be important safeguards against a permanent state of emergency, the current Egyptian regime has in practice succeeded in rebuilding an unlimited state of emergency. In April 2017, a state of emergency was declared for three months following a terrorist attack that targeted two churches and left 44 people dead.[15] Since then, until the time of writing, the state of emergency has been systemati-

10 Kandil (n 4) 233.

11 Emergency Law No 162 of 1958, Art 1.

12 ibid.

13 Article 154 of the 2014 Constitution of Egypt, ratified on 18 January 2014.

14 Ellaboudy, 'Emergency Law Amendments to Fight Covid-19 in Egypt' (n 3).

15 Taha Saker, 'Egypt's State of Emergency in 2017: Constitutional Enforcement and Consequences' (*Egypt Independent*, 10 April 2017) <https://egyptindependent.com/egypt-s-state-emergency-2017-constitutional-enforcement-and-consequences/>.

cally renewed every three months.[16] To avoid the constitutional requirement for an extension to be approved by the House of Representatives, the president would typically wait until a couple of days after the end of the three-month period and then declare a new state of emergency. From a formalistic and procedural point of view, such a declaration is not a violation of the Constitution. As the Parliament is effectively controlled by the executive, approving a state of emergency every three months has become a routine rubber-stamping exercise.

Indeed, one could learn an important lesson from the Egyptian experience as it relates to states of emergency: a good constitutional text alone is not enough. As Sajó ventures, "rule of law seems to be more of a cultural practice (a set of practices) than anything else".[17] Hence, there is no doubt that the continuous reliance on emergency powers, as a default way of governing for decades, has infected the whole Egyptian legal culture with what might be termed the 'activated emergency disease' and manoeuvres around constitutional texts are only the symptoms of this disease.

3. Egypt's Response to the COVID-19 Pandemic

Like many countries, Egypt adopted several exceptional measures aiming to tackle the rapid outbreak of COVID-19. From 19 March 2020, borders were closed and a nationwide night-time curfew was imposed. Measures such as limiting business activities, closing schools and minimising the work of state institutions were also implemented.[18] At the same time, there was a pressing need for legislative initiatives to respond to the unexpected health crisis. However, unlike other countries in the region that adopted new legislation focused solely on regulating the health emergency,[19] the ongoing emergency mode in Egypt and its embedded security concerns appeared to leave no options for such a move; rather, major amendments to the existing emergency law were the inevitable choice.

3.1 Emergency Law Amendments: New Presidential Powers to Contain the Pandemic – and what else?

Emergency Law No 162/1958 always considered "the spread of an epidemic" as one of the events that allows a state of emergency to be declared.[20] Therefore, it was predictable that the amendments, approved by Parliament on 22 April 2020,

16 'Egypt Extends State of Emergency for Ninth Time' (*Al-Monitor*, 18 July 2019) <https://www.al-monitor.com/originals/2019/07/emergency-egypt-law-state-security-extension-terrorism.html>.

17 András Sajó, 'The Rule of Law as Legal Despotism: Concerned Remarks on the Use of "Rule of Law" in Illiberal Democracies' (2019) 11(2-3) Hague Journal on the Rule of Law 371, 372.

18 Prime Ministerial decisions No 606,719, and 724 of 2020 (March 2020).

19 For instance, in Morocco new legislation has been adopted only for the purpose of regulating health emergencies measures. See Decree No 2.20.292, published on 23 March 2020.

20 Emergency Law No 162/1958, Art 1.

provided more powers to the president, as head of the executive, to contain the impact of the spreading virus – not just from the public health perspective, but also taking into consideration the economic and social impact that this special case of emergency would have on people's lives. Consequently, the amendments empowered the president to suspend or shut down schools, universities and government agencies; and to oblige returning Egyptian expats to commit to quarantine measures.[21] Moreover, the president now had the power to allocate cash and in-kind assistance to individuals and families; offer financial support to medical research; provide financial and in-kind support to damaged economic sectors; and postpone the payment of certain taxes.[22] Although most of these measures had been already taken before the formal approval of the amendments due to the urgency of events, it was essential that they be prescribed by law, in recognition of the principle of legality.[23]

However, as the political aphorism goes, one should 'never let a good crisis go to waste', and the new amendments appeared to take this maxim to heart. One of the new emergency powers given to the president was "*prohibiting* all public and private meetings, assemblies, protests, parades and any other forms of assemblies" (emphasis added).[24] Taking into consideration the more-or-less permanent state of emergency in Egypt, this provision could be easily invoked to eliminate the right to freedom of assembly. Given that the Emergency Law already authorised the president to "*restrict* people's freedoms of movement and assemblies" (emphasis added), inserting such a provision could be seen as a new weapon in the authoritarian legislative arsenal that has been under construction for decades.[25]

Further, the Emergency Law allows the creation of emergency state-security courts, which are composed of judges in addition to military officers who can be added to the bench by the President.[26] According to the amendments passed in the context of COVID-19, the military prosecution now has jurisdiction to investigate all events and crimes that are caught by military officers, and the president has the power to transfer any investigation regarding violations of emergency law to military prosecution.[27] The very nature of emergency measures includes extraordinary limitations on fundamental rights, but these measures ought to be capable of achieving their purpose with minimal alteration of normal rules and procedures. Hence, the unnecessary expansion of the competencies of military courts, among amendments that are supposedly aiming to combat the spread of a virus, could be easily characterised as disproportionate and illegitimate and raise concerns regarding their real purpose.

21 ibid Art 3.
22 ibid.
23 Ellaboudy, 'Emergency Law Amendments to Fight Covid-19 in Egypt' (n 3).
24 Emergency Law No 162/1958, Art 3.
25 ibid.
26 Emergency Law No 162/1958, Art 7.
27 Emergency Law No 162/1958, Art 4.

3.2 Mandatory 'Donations' and Clinical Medical Regulation

The key actions of Egypt in response to the COVID-19 crisis were economic and financial in nature. As previously explained, several provisions within the amendments to the Emergency Law were concerned with supporting individuals and economic sectors with financial and in-kind assistance. The question of providing the required funds for such support was at the heart of the state reaction to the crisis. Hence, in August 2020, a new law proposing to cut a fixed percentage of employees' salaries in order to finance the state plan and the precautionary measures to stop the spread of the virus was approved by Parliament.[28] Specifically, the law allows a deduction of 1% from the net monthly income of all employees in the public and private sectors and a deduction of 0.5% from pensioners' net monthly income for one year.[29]

Many concerns have been raised regarding the legitimacy of this law; however, the question of the constitutionality of these 'donations' has not been examined by any court. While some commentators argue that the law can be an expression of solidarity and a means of sharing the burden of the pandemic, these 'donations' are arguably a form of taxation, since the state is deducting net income by law. Awad El-Morr, the former chief justice of the Egyptian Supreme Constitutional Court, rightly argues that "the mere need of the state to increase its resources by taxes, is not a conclusive factor in determining [the law's] … constitutionality".[30] Further, one can see that the adoption of such legislation comes as a predictable consequence of the state's failure with respect to its constitutional commitment regarding the health sector. According to the Egyptian Constitution, "the state commits to allocating a percentage of government expenditure that is no less than 3% of (GDP) to health".[31] However, since the adoption of the constitution in 2014, this required percentage of government expenditure has never been allocated for the health sector, within any annual state budget.[32] Hence, it should be noted that the government must fulfil such a constitutional obligation and consider it as an inevitable means of improving the health sector and preparing for any future health crisis.

A more welcome initiative by the Egyptian legislature during the COVID-19 crisis was the adoption of Law No 214/2020, which regulates clinical medical research in Egypt. After two years of controversial debates over the law which began pre-pandemic, and which led President El-Sisi, for the first time, to use his presidential veto to object to some of its provisions, the law was approved in December 2020. Significantly, the extensive punitive provisions which did not consider the nature of scientific research, in addition to the required bureaucratic

28 Law No 170 of 2020, published on 13 August 2020.

29 ibid.

30 Awad El-Morr, *Judicial Review on Constitutionality of Laws* (Renee Centre 2003) 290.

31 Art 18 of the Egyptian Constitution of 2014.

32 'The Absence of Corona in the Government's Plan for 2020–2021' The Egyptian Initiative for Personal Rights, Position Paper (1 July 2020) 13–14 <https://bit.ly/3ytso2i>.

process that needs to be fulfilled to conduct medical or clinical experiments, were the main reasons behind the President's disapproval of the law in 2018.[33] Accordingly, the 2020 version of the Law was amended to avoid such objections, easing clinical medical research procedures.

The significance of this law comes from the fact that Egypt has extensively contributed to the clinical trials related to the Chinese COVID-19 vaccine. Therefore, there was a pressing need to establish a legal framework that allows such medical research, and in addition, respects people's right to life and the sanctity of the human body. In fact, prioritising regulation of clinical medical research at such a time marks a paradigm shift in the Parliament's legislative performance and indicates that the Egyptian legislature is genuinely concerned with the contemporary health care needs of the society at a time of a global pandemic.

4. Fundamental Rights Under the Spotlight

In October 2020, the inter-governmental Permanent High Committee for Human Rights, created in 2018 and headed by the foreign minister, announced its decision to draft the first comprehensive national strategy for human rights in Egypt. According to the Committee, the strategy is focused on challenges that face the current Egyptian human rights situation, including civil and political rights and economic, social and cultural rights, in the light of all the recommendations that Egypt has received from regional and international entities.[34] Yet, the initiative did not translate to any actual steps on the ground. While the COVID-19 crisis was at its peak, arresting and detaining political opponents never stopped and even included doctors who criticised the state's performance regarding the health crisis.[35] Interestingly, in response to national and international criticism regarding the human rights situation in Egypt, the state consistently called for a focus not only on civil and political rights, but also socio-economic rights.[36] Therefore, there is no more relevant moment than a global pandemic to evaluate the state's willingness to promote socio-economic rights and, at the heart of these rights, the right to health.

Coincidentally, in the year of a global pandemic, Egypt was planning to launch its comprehensive health care system in 2020, which was expected to provide health care insurance for all Egyptians within 15 years.[37] Indeed, in recent years,

33 'Sisi Objects to Some Articles of Medical and Clinical Research Draft Law' (*Egypt Today*, 3 October 2018) <https://www.egypttoday.com/Article/1/58440/Sisi-objects-to-some-articles-of-medical-and-clinical-research>.

34 Yasmine Hassan, 'Egypt Draws Up First "National Human Rights Strategy"' (*Egypt Today*, 18 October 2020) <https://www.egypttoday.com/Article/1/93199/Egypt-draws-up-first-National-Human-Rights-Strategy>.

35 Maged Mandour, *Repression and Coronavirus Response in Egypt* (Carnegie Endowment for International Peace, 15 July 2020).

36 'Human Rights Not Limited to Political Aspects: Sisi' (*Egypt Today*, 6 November 2019) <https://www.egypttoday.com/Article/1/77531/Human-rights-not-limited-to-political-aspects-Sisi>.

37 In light of the Law No 2 of 2018 concerning the establishment of the comprehensive health care system.

state actions on public health, including initiatives for the early detection and free treatment of several diseases, have been impressive compared to all previous attempts to upgrade the health system in Egypt. It was surprising, then, that the state's response to the most significant challenge at the time of writing – the COVID-19 vaccination campaign – seemed to be hesitant and lacking in momentum, as exemplified by two remarkable episodes.

First, in a televised statement, health officials stated that the COVID-19 vaccine would be available for free only to medical staff and economically vulnerable groups who are registered within the database of the Ministry of Social Security, estimated to be around 15 million people out of a total population of 100 million. This meant that the vast majority of Egyptians would have needed to pay for vaccination. In response, a group of petitioners brought a lawsuit before the Cairo Administrative Court challenging the state policy regarding the vaccination plan and demanded free vaccination for all Egyptians.[38] One of the arguments introduced to the court was that the right to health contains entitlements such as the right to prevention, treatment and control of diseases; thus, the right to free COVID-19 vaccinations must be enshrined at such a time of health emergency.[39] The petitioners further argued that the state's development plans would be pointless without protecting the "development" of people's lives in the first place. As of June 2021, the case is still pending and no further statements have been made regarding paying for the vaccine. However, signifying a possible retreat from its original policy, in March 2021, the government slightly expanded its vaccination programme, which was delivered free for anyone and everyone who had been registered in the online system.[40]

Second, another lawsuit calling for prisoners to be able to register for the COVID-19 vaccination was filed in May 2021. Remarkably, a few days later and before any judicial decision had been issued, the health minister announced that the government would soon begin vaccinating all prisoners against COVID-19 across the country and that 5,000 elderly detainees had already been vaccinated.[41] While this was a welcome development, the episode illustrated the absence of any meaningful dialogue between the government and civil society organisations in Egypt. In spite of its quick and positive official response to the substance of the lawsuit, the Egyptian state still looked suspiciously at civil society initiatives and recommendations, labelling them as a national threat.[42] Therefore, if there is a les-

38 Case No 28585 of judicial year 75, The Cairo Administrative Court.

39 This argument is supported by the Committee on Economic, Social and Cultural Rights, 'Statement on Universal and Equitable Access to Vaccines for COVID-19' E/C.12/2020/2, 27 November 2020, para 4, which states that vaccines should be provided free of charge, "at least for lower income persons and the poor".

40 Ahmed Ellaboudy, 'When Emergency Is Permanent, What Else Could be Done?' (n 3).

41 'Government to Start Vaccinating All Prisoners Against Coronavirus Soon: Health Minister' (*Ahram Online*, 17 May 2021) <https://english.ahram.org.eg/NewsContent/1/64/411273/Egypt/Politics-/Government-to-start-vaccinating-all-prisoners-agai.aspx>.

42 Human Right Watch, 'Egypt Crackdown on Civil Society' (undated) <https://www.hrw.org/tag/egypt-crackdown-civil-society>.

son the government could learn from the ongoing health crisis, it is that direct and honest dialogue with civil society is an essential condition for the establishment of a stable state based on rule of law principles.

5. 'Democracy' First: Two Elections During the Pandemic

Given the weak role of upper chambers in the history of Egypt's parliamentary life, in addition to the high financial costs, the 2014 constitutional drafters refused to adopt the bicameral model of parliament. However, constitutional amendments in 2019 reintroduced the Senate, the second chamber of Parliament, to the Egyptian political system. The state then exhibited a surprising desire to fulfil its constitutional commitment and conduct Senate elections without delay, despite the absence of any legislative authority of the new Senate and its merely consultative competence. Hence, amidst warnings of the second wave of COVID-19, the elections were held in August 2020, with a participation rate of just over 14%.[43]

Moreover, between October and December 2020, during the peak of the second wave of COVID-19 in Egypt, further elections took place to the House of Representatives. Once again, the goal of the elections was neither high participation rates (it was estimated at 29.5%) nor having a fair and competitive process, but rather, fulfilling the formal constitutional requirements at the appointed time, whatever the cost. Distinct from the Senate elections, the Egyptian Constitution sets a clear procedural deadline for the House elections, stating that "elections for a new House are held during the 60 days preceding the end of its term".[44] Since the end of the previous House term was approaching in January 2021, there was a constitutional obligation to hold the House elections at the end of 2020; thus, the state decided in favour of holding the elections at the appointed time. Accordingly, wearing face masks and adhering to social distancing were among the mandatory restrictions adopted during the election. Also, it should be noted that in-person voting was the only available option since the government's infrastructure was never prepared for the adoption of any alternative voting method (e.g. postal voting). Nevertheless, there was no indication that holding the elections led to any rise in the COVID-19 infections numbers or affected the health emergency situation.

Indeed, holding parliamentary elections during these exceptional circumstances was not challenged before any court. However, other cases considered the question of holding elections to non-state bodies during the health crisis. In August 2020, the same month as the Senate elections, the Cairo Administrative Court found that holding elections to the Egyptian Writers' Union threatened the life of its members; thus, the election was postponed based on the prime ministerial decision on the suspension of all events that involve the assembly of citizens. In its reasoning, the court was concerned with the poor precautionary measures which might

43 Amr Rabea, *2020 Egyptian Senate Elections: Outcomes and Challenges to its Role in Politics* (Emirates Policy Centre, 27 September 2020).

44 Article 106 of the Egyptian Constitution of 2014.

surround the election procedures, considering the absence of any alternative voting methods such as electronic or mail-in voting. Responding to the defendants' arguments in respect of the more wide-scale election which was being run by the state at the same time, the court justified this action on the basis that the Senate election was "necessary" for the state to fulfil its constitutional commitment and for democratic life in Egypt and asserted that it was applying its proportionality analysis test to balance the benefits and harms of each decision through a case-by-case approach.[45] Four months later, during the second wave of COVID-19, the same court allowed in-person elections to the subsidiary Bar Association Board and refused all arguments to delay the poll due to the pandemic. Despite the similarities between the two cases, the court did not provide adequate reasoning for its findings, apart from briefly addressing the significance of trade unions' independence in managing their internal business.

Such contradictory findings concerning similar cases could be seen as a predictable result given the lack of a proportionality analysis test within Egyptian judicial practice. Egyptian courts do not provide a consistent framework concerning their proportionality analysis test which could be systematically followed by all courts or even apex courts.[46]

6. Conclusion

Living in a permanent state of emergency is not just a threat to the enjoyment of fundamental rights and a back door for the abuse of exceptional powers: it also leaves the entire legal system in a state of confusion when a genuine emergency takes place. In 2020, Egypt found itself in the middle of a global health emergency, but both the mentality and skills of crisis management of the authorities were, through long engrained practice, geared towards security concerns. Attempts to contain the social and economic impact of the pandemic were made; however, the consequences of the quasi-permanent emergency, which was used as a repressive tool, were inescapable. If one could provide some recommendations at such a critical time, the first would be ending the continuous state of emergency that has been activated since 2017. Keeping emergency regulations in force eliminates any chance for the establishment of the rule of law and democracy in Egypt. The ongoing state of exception constructs a constitutional and legal foundation for unlimited presidential powers and legitimises the continuous functioning of exceptional courts.[47]

Indeed, Egypt needs a transformative vision regarding the use of emergency powers, which requires in turn a comprehensive revision of the current emergency

45 Ellaboudy, 'When Emergency Is Permanent, What Else Could be Done?' (n 3).

46 The principle of proportionality was introduced within Egyptian constitutional jurisprudence in 1995. However, the Egyptian Supreme Constitutional Court showed a notable attitude towards the proportionality analysis test, ignoring its full application and relying on other techniques of analysis.

47 Ellaboudy, 'When Emergency Is Permanent, What Else Could be Done?' (n 3).

laws. Further, Egypt should put an end to the 'unhealthy harmony' between the executive power and Parliament, which results in unconditional approval for the continuous emergency declarations. To do so, Egypt needs sincere political will that prioritises the importance of political pluralism and human rights and that sees citizens and civil society organisations as partners in the decision-making process, not as a potential danger threatening the stability of the state.

34

THE COVID-19 EMERGENCY

Malaysia's Fragile Constitutional Democracy

R Rueban Balasubramaniam

1. Introduction[1]

When Malaysia gained independence from British rule in 1957, law and politics were to be regulated by a legally supreme written constitution with features generally associated with constitutional democracy. The constitution stipulates a Westminster model of democracy in which the prime minister and cabinet are appointed from the majority party in Parliament. In addition, in recognition of the pre-colonial standing of Malay Royalty comprising Sultanates of 11 Malaysian states, the constitution created the office of the Yang di-Pertuan Agong, the king, a constitutional monarch and formal head of state who would exercise powers on the advice of the prime minister representing a democratically-elected government. Finally, the constitution imposes constraints on state power in the form of an expansive bill of rights and provisions dividing authority between the organs of government according to the principles of federalism and the separation of powers, including an independent judiciary. The overall constitutional framework anticipates the basis for political rule subject to the discipline of the principles of democracy and the rule of law.

However, a potential problem with the design of the constitution is the granting of vast emergency powers, potentially allowing government to operate outside the discipline of constitutional legality.[2] Article 150 sets out the emergency powers framework and authorises the king to proclaim a state of emergency if satisfied that there is a serious threat to "security", "economic life" or "public order". If

1 All websites accessed on 16 July 2021.

2 Early academic reviews of the constitution identified risks posed by the emergency-powers framework, see especially S Jayakumar, 'Constitutional Limitations on Legislative Power in Malaysia' (1967) Malaya Law Review 96.

DOI: 10.4324/9781003211952-39

Parliament is not sitting during the emergency, the king can rule by decree in derogation of the constitutional bill of rights. Importantly, the king's subjective judgment that there is an emergency and how to respond to that emergency are deemed immune from judicial review. In addition, Article 150 expressly declares that any law enacted during the emergency shall not be invalid "on the ground of inconsistency with the Constitution". Hence, the constitution appears to grant a carte blanche to the king to exercise legally uncontrolled power. In practice, since the king exercises emergency powers on the advice of the prime minister, the risk is that the constitution might allow an authoritarian government to use emergency powers to protect its political position and to undermine constitutional democracy.

Unfortunately, throughout Malaysia's political history, this risk has materialised. From 1957 to 2018, the United Malay National Organisation (UMNO), a Malay nationalist party committed to the doctrine of ethnic 'Malay Dominance', had controlled government and practised ethnocratic rule whereby the primary role of government was to define and defend the identity and interests of the ethnic Malay majority, while those ineligible for membership within the dominant ethnos were deemed politically unequal or 'second-class'. Opponents of ethnocracy have been subject to legal, political and social controls such that the record of ethnocracy has been generally authoritarian. While there remains some space for authentic democratic politics, Parliament and the courts have been rendered ineffective and subordinate to executive authority. Within this context, various declarations of emergency proved pivotal to the rise of authoritarian and ethnocratic politics and detrimental to constitutional democracy. Emergency powers have become a crucial modality for authoritarian rule in Malaysia.[3]

The COVID-19 pandemic triggered a formal declaration of emergency in Malaysia that is arguably likely to continue this trend towards authoritarian rule in Malaysia.[4] Strikingly, the emergency coincided with reversals of the political wheel beginning with UMNO's surprising loss in the 2018 general elections to a political coalition committed to democratic change, followed by the equally unexpected collapse of the reformist government in March 2020 when the pandemic began. This chapter proceeds with an account of these events in section 2 before spotlighting, in section 3, how the confluence of political upheaval and the public health emergency enhanced the status of the king as a crucial source of constitutional and political legitimation in a manner that threatened the democratic authority of parliament. In section 4, the chapter explains how ideologues

3 As Lee notes, emergency powers pose problems of "profound significance" for constitutionalism in Malaysia. See H P Lee, *Constitutional Conflicts in Contemporary Malaysia* (2nd edn, Oxford University Press 2017) 155.

4 This chapter expands upon R Rueban Balasubramaniam, 'Covid-19: Malaysia and the Return of Rule by Law' (*Verfassungsblog*, 16 May 2020) <https://verfassungsblog.de/covid-19-malaysia-and-the-return-of-rule-by-law/>; R Rueban Balasubramaniam, 'Covid-19: Malaysia's Fragile Constitutional Democracy' (*Verfassungsblog*, 2 March 2021) <https://verfassungsblog.de/covid-19-malaysias-fragile-constitutional-democracy/>.

used the COVID-19 emergency to construct an authoritarian re-description of the notion of constitutional legality in a bid to legitimise ethno-authoritarian rule. The chapter concludes that the prospects for constitutional democracy are bleak and that the post-pandemic political dispensation is likely to mark a return to ethno-authoritarian rule.

2. The Fall of the 'New' Malaysia and COVID-19

In 2018, the Pakatan Harapan (PH), a coalition of parties committed to democratic change, unexpectedly defeated UMNO at the polls despite the fact that general elections had historically been 'free but unfair' to favour the latter's victory. UMNO lost because the party had become egregiously corrupt, kleptocratic and inept. The then Prime Minister Najib Razak was implicated in a global scandal called '1MDB', involving the theft of billions of dollars from a national investment fund. The scandal attracted international attention and involved a transnational investigation, recounted in a best-selling book.[5] It caused massive embarrassment while damaging the economy. Voters thus deserted UMNO in droves to put the PH into power, giving rise to what many dubbed the 'New' Malaysia.

Unfortunately, the PH government lacked a coherent plan for governance and was reluctant to undo ethnocratic political structures. For instance, despite initially promising to ratify the International Convention on the Elimination of Racial Discrimination, the PH backtracked on this promise and repeated an argument used by ethnocrats to defend Malay Dominance, the argument that the constitution embodies a 'social contract' – a social-political agreement between the country's founding fathers – that affirms a 'sacrosanct' principle of Malay Dominance.[6] The PH worried about alienating ethnic Malays and thus appeared ambivalent about constitutional democracy. To make matters worse, PH rulers were preoccupied with a battle for leadership and the position of prime minister rather than the business of governance. Ultimately, this political infighting led to a series of political machinations and defections that caused the PH to fall apart just as the World Health Organisation formally declared a global pandemic. The dream of a 'New' Malaysia came to an abrupt end.

A major lesson to draw from the PH's collapse is that the public political culture – the general package of ideas that frame questions of legal and political legitimacy – privileges ethnic and religious values as sources of political legitimacy associated with Malay and Muslim identity over the values linked to constitutional democracy. The PH was too weak to resist ensuing pressures to conform to ethnocracy, leading to a loss of legitimacy that encouraged internal battling over leadership

5 Tom Wright and Bradley Hope, *Billion Dollar Whale: The Man Who Fooled Wall Street, Hollywood, and the World* (Little, Brown Book Group Ltd 2018).

6 See my analysis of this argument as presupposing an authoritarian philosophy of law in R Rueban Balasubramaniam, 'Malaysia's Blocked Social Contract Debate' in Andrew Harding and Dian Shah (eds) *Law and Society in Malaysia: Pluralism, Religion, and Ethnicity* (Routledge 2018).

and its ultimate downfall. The implicit political dynamics that led to this conclusion would only be amplified by the political and public health emergency caused by COVID-19, especially by increasing the authority of the king as a symbol of Malay political power.

3. The Pandemic Response and Emergency Rule

Under the Malaysian Constitution, the king has the authority to appoint the prime minister and cabinet, who are appointed from the majority party in Parliament, a decision that typically certifies the result of a general election.[7] But when the PH fell, the king undertook the unusual process of interviewing all the members of parliament to figure out which party had a political majority sufficient to form government. The process was secret and filled with intrigue, with leading political figures meeting the king claiming to have a sufficient majority in an opportunistic battle for the position of prime minister. The outcome was the appointment in March 2020 of a new coalition government comprising the remnants of the PH and including UMNO but this time as junior partner in the coalition called the Perikatan Nasional (PN). Because of the unorthodox process, the PN was widely viewed as illegitimate and pejoratively labelled a 'backdoor' government.

While the king may well have acted in good faith to stabilise a politically volatile situation made more urgent by the pandemic, the situation posed serious problems at the level of constitutional principle keeping in mind the vast emergency powers that accrue to the king's office. Supposing that the king's decision to appoint government coincides with an official declaration of emergency that is not subject to judicial review, and is thus free of meaningful constitutional control, the king would wield an arbitrary power not even curbed by democratic political considerations. Given such unusual conditions, the king would not be acting on the advice of the prime minister since in effect he would be appointing the government of the day. Even if the king were acting in good faith, the danger remains that groups bearing an authoritarian political agenda might co-opt the king's office to exercise that agenda by successfully petitioning the king.

As the pandemic began to play out, it grew clearer that the PN would indeed use the office of the king to resist democratic pressures to establish authentic legitimacy for its claim to the office of government. However, this playing out would only follow a series of mismanaged responses to the pandemic that ultimately required the official declaration of an emergency – mismanagement that in part issued from the PN's focus on defending its political position rather than taking serious steps to address the public health crisis.

Thus, initially, the PN government used ordinary legislation and did not seek a formal declaration of a state of emergency. The government relied on the

7 Article 43(2)(a) empowers the king to appoint as prime minister "a Member of the House of Representatives who in his judgment is likely to command the confidence of the majority".

Prevention and Control of Diseases Act 1988 (PCDA 1988), which allows for the use of Movement Control Orders (MCOs) to limit freedom of movement to contain the spread of the virus. MCOs can be flexibly calibrated to allow for more or less restrictions on movement depending on the seriousness of infection rates in a given area. Until September 2020, the government adopted a medically informed approach that appeared effective. The numbers of cases at this early stage was relatively low compared to many other countries.[8]

However, ever mindful of its dubious political legitimacy, the PN chose to hold an ill-advised state by-election in the East Malaysian state of Sabah, the country's poorest state. As Sabah is notoriously a vote-bank for the federal government, usually led by UMNO, the goal was to secure an electoral victory to shore up its legitimacy. However, this move proved reckless from a public health perspective. The election led to a massive surge in infections that overwhelmed the already weak public health care system. Weaknesses in testing, treatment, personnel and infrastructure in the impoverished, mainly rural state created a humanitarian crisis.[9] The PN won the Sabah by-election but was reluctant to reconvene Parliament fearing a vote of confidence by the opposition.

In addition, to make matters worse for the PN, UMNO was unhappy with its status as junior partner in the coalition and disgruntled by the fact that Prime Minister Muhyddin Yassin had not called off investigations into UMNO leaders, including former Prime Minister Najib Razak, begun under the PH. Indeed, UMNO elites began to agitate for a general election, calculating that if snap elections were held, their party could win and take back control of government. This was very worrying for the PN because UMNO still had significant influence amongst ethnic Malay voters and posed a serious threat to its position.

Meanwhile, a second wave of COVID-19 hit the country, revealing that the existing response to the pandemic was inadequate. Federal-state coordination regarding pandemic relief was weak and there were large deficits with testing, tracing and treatment. By the end of September 2020, the public health situation had deteriorated such that MCOs were reinstated in almost every Malaysian state. The decision was not popular because of the significant economic toll. Notably, the government-backed national oil company, a major source of revenue for government, suffered huge losses.[10] Hence, the PN was caught between a political rock given its weak legitimacy and a public health hard place wrought by the worsening effects of the pandemic.

8 Vinod Sekhar, 'Where America's Covid-19 Response Failed, Malaysia's Succeeded' (*Toronto Star*, 6 July 2020) <https://www.thestar.com/opinion/contributors/2020/07/06/where-americas-covid-19-response-failed-malaysias-succeeded.html>.

9 Bridget Welsh, 'Emerging Humanitarian Crisis in Sabah' (*Bridget Welsh*, 25 October 2020) <https://bridgetwelsh.com/uncategorized/emerging-humanitarian-covid-19-crisis-in-sabah/>.

10 Prem Kumar, 'Malaysia's Petronas Suffers $5bn Net Loss' (*Nikkei Asia*, 4 September 2020) <https://asia.nikkei.com/Business/Energy/Malaysia-s-Petronas-reports-5bn-net-loss-for-April-to-June-period#:~:text=KUALA%20LUMPUR%20%2D%2D%20Malaysia's%20state,oil%20prices%20and%20weak%20demand>.

To manage the former, the prime minister petitioned the king, asking for him to declare a formal state of emergency under Article 150. But to his chagrin, the king refused the prime minister's request. However, the number of deaths and illnesses continued to rise significantly and by January 2021, there were serious worries that the public health care system would be overwhelmed. Upon a further request to the king, a formal state of emergency rule was declared on 12 January 2021.

Keen to assuage the perception that emergency rule was a mere façade designed to evade a test of political legitimacy, the prime minister assured citizens that civilian rule would continue. However, empowered to introduce legislation while bypassing parliamentary processes under emergency rule, the PN government enacted new regulations to control speech criticising the government, including speech that called into question the political legitimacy of the emergency declaration. The Emergency (Essential Powers) (No. 2) Ordinance 2021 (known as the 'fake news' ordinance) under the 12 January Proclamation of Emergency, made it a criminal offence to "create, publish, or disseminate 'fake news'" relating to COVID-19 or the proclamation of emergency, or to fail to remove such materials at the request of the government. The law also purported to govern individuals "anywhere in the world" and was widely criticised domestically and internationally, including by Human Rights Watch.[11] The passing of the 'fake news' ordinance showed that the PN government was willing to use authoritarian means to stay in power.

While there was a legitimate public health emergency, it was nevertheless far from clear that the emergency also required the ongoing suspension of Parliament. The PN regime refused to allow Parliament to sit, citing the risk of spreading COVID-19. This was a specious argument given the availability of technological solutions as well as the fact that legislatures elsewhere in the world had figured out safety protocols to continue legislative activity. To make matters worse, the opposition and critics of government even agreed not to challenge the PN through a vote of confidence and to place the focus on how to improve the pandemic response. Yet, the PN remained stubborn and unwilling to recall Parliament, indicating its deep political insecurity.

By May 2021, and despite the rolling out of vaccines in Malaysia, more infectious and threatening variants of the COVID-19 virus posed a significant danger. Increasing cases, deaths and clusters of infection threatened to overwhelm the public health system. Consequently, the PN government announced that the country would be placed under total 'lockdown' for two weeks from 1 June and announced a massive stimulus package to support citizens. Nevertheless, the public was angered not only because of the economic price they would pay but also because it was evident that the use of MCOs and further lockdown were blunt tools against the pandemic.

Given the clear impression that the PN's priority was to cling to power, rather than the effective management of the pandemic, the leader of the political oppo-

11 Human Rights Watch, 'Malaysia: Revoke 'Fake News' Ordinance: New Law Criminalizes Expression, Violates Privacy Rights' (Human Rights Watch, 21 March 2021) <https://www.hrw.org/news/2021/03/13/malaysia-revoke-fake-news-ordinance>.

sition, Datuk Seri Anwar Ibrahim, met the king to plead that emergency rule should not be unnecessarily prolonged.[12] While the details of that meeting were confidential, Anwar indicated that the subject of a change of government was not raised. The meeting was evidence of the enhanced position of the king as having immense power to determine who could form government. The king not only met with Anwar but also other leaders vying for leadership, in addition to meeting Prime Minister Muhyddin. The meetings signalled that in a genuine moment of political and public health emergency, powers had concentrated in the office of the monarch who could not only determine whether the government would stand or fall but also exercise influence over governance in the face of the pandemic while the deliberative powers of Parliament had been suspended.

The political and public health situation was now dire. These dynamics were very troubling since it became clear that the prime minister, the leader of the opposition and other leaders of political parties were all weak and operating more like pressure groups lobbying the king to gain access to power, rather than political parties committed to advancing the common good of all citizens. Indeed, it was troubling that Anwar chose to frame his meeting with the king by emphasising the threat to the economy rather than the ongoing threat posed by the emergency to constitutional democracy.

That the fate of Malaysian politics now lay in the hands of the king is a significant fact given that the king is a symbol of Malay political power. Relevant to bear in mind is that over the last two decades, the Malay Royalty has grown far more assertive in Malaysian politics. In some instances, the Royalty has even determined the outcome of state by-elections in favour of UMNO, leading to the worry that UMNO elites would look to the Royalty to reverse their loss in the 2018 elections. While this did not take place, if the king has absolute authority to decide who forms a government in an emergency, then there is a serious structural problem for constitutional democracy, since ethnocratic forces seeking to subvert genuine democratic processes could manipulate the king's decision-making. This danger is amplified by ongoing ideological efforts to re-describe the general notion of constitutional legality to establish that Royal decisions are also sufficient to establish democratic legitimacy absent authentic democratic processes of legitimation.

4. The Authoritarian Re-description of Constitutional Democracy

It is not possible to delve into all the twists and turns behind ideological efforts by ethnocrats who, at the time of writing in 2021, are trying to re-describe the Malaysian Constitution and reframe questions of constitutional legitimacy by reference to sources of legitimation that favour ethnocratic rule. Suffice to note

12 Terrence Tan and Austin Camoens, 'Anwar: I Pleaded with King Not to Extend Emergency Beyond Aug 1 as it Will Bring Adverse Economic Effects' (*The Star*, 9 June 2021) <https://www.thestar.com.my/news/nation/2021/06/09/anwar-i-pleaded-with-king-not-to-extend-emergency-beyond-aug-1-as-it-will-bring-adverse-economic-effects>.

that such efforts have been long-standing as ideologues have attempted to shift the conceptual register that frames questions of legal and political legitimacy to sources of legitimacy favourable to ethnic Malay-Muslim identity, not the values of constitutional and democratic legality. The pivotal role of the king provided an occasion for an ideological defence of that role.

In this connection, consider the argument made by Abdul Harun Idris, who was appointed parliamentary Speaker by Prime Minister Muhyddin when the PN was appointed by the king to take charge of government in March 2020. Prior to this appointment, Harun, better known as 'Art Harun', was a public intellectual who was also held in esteem as a respected human rights lawyer and articulate critic of the UMNO-led government. But when the PN took charge, the prime minister – without deliberation or a vote by parliament, as is customary for the appointment of the Speaker's role – appointed Harun. The appointment was shocking given Harun's reputation as a critic of government. Indeed, Harun had been appointed by the fallen PH government to spearhead reform of general elections as chairman of the Election Commission. The feeling was that Harun had traded in his principles to cloak the 'backdoor' government with a veneer of legitimacy.[13]

Sadly, Harun turned his knowledge of the law towards advancing a narrow constitutional perspective that proffers a reading of the Malaysian Constitution that detaches the constitutional framework from the values of constitutional democracy. Ironically, he offered a view that de-emphasised the legitimacy of parliament in favour of bestowing the king – in reality, the prime minister – with legally and politically uncontrolled power during an emergency in a way that proved congenial to a pseudo-democratic and populist perspective.

This perspective was evident in an unusual intervention by Harun in the press addressing political rulers seeking to petition the king and to undo the declaration of emergency in a bid to have parliament reconvene.[14] The intervention begins with an epigraph from the 18th century political philosopher Thomas Paine, observing that the legitimacy of a written constitution derives from the ultimate exercise of "sovereignty" by "the people". The reference invokes the ideal of democracy as the legitimating ideal of a written constitution. However, Harun articulates a rather perverse understanding of the principle of the separation of powers as part of the Malaysian Constitution. As a general matter, the separation of powers is widely viewed as integral to constitutional democracy and is arguably a corollary of the rule of law if one supposes that the point of the rule of law is to constrain arbitrary power. Yet, Harun trivialises the principle and states that it is "not a legal principle" but is "merely a political theory". Therefore, the doctrine

13 Syed Jaymal Zahiid, 'Why did Perikatan Pick Art Harun as New Speaker? Pundits Suggest Part of Bid to Woo Urbanites' (*Malay Mail,* 29 July 2020) <https://www.malaymail.com/news/malaysia/2020/07/29/why-did-perikatan-pick-art-harun-as-new-speaker-pundits-suggest-part-of-bid/1889010>.

14 Azhar Harun, 'Danger of Quoting the Constitution Selectively for Political Purposes' (*Malaysianow,* 30 May 2021) <https://www.malaysianow.com/opinion/2021/05/30/danger-of-quoting-the-constitution-selectively-for-political-purposes/>.

of the separation of powers is not legally enforceable and may be qualified by the constitution, which he describes as the "mother of all laws". Accepting that the separation of powers may be limited, Harun argues that the constitution empowers the king, under the advice of the prime minister, to formally proclaim an emergency, including deciding whether Parliament should or should not sit and where such decisions cannot be questioned in court. Correspondingly, public officials are under a solemn duty to uphold the ideals of constitutional supremacy and the rule of law and to absolutely obey the king's decisions and respect the "law as it is".

Harun's argument echoes the disreputable judgments of the Malaysian courts that have previously held that Parliament may abrogate the separation of powers and thereby free the executive of constitutional controls on state power that should otherwise be enforceable by Malaysian judges via judicial review.[15] These judgments were a surprising self-emasculation of judicial power. Harun's argument is tantamount to a self-emasculation of legislative power, a power that, as Speaker, he was constitutionally supposed to safeguard. But what makes his argument dangerous is that it yokes constitutional authority to the democratic will of "the people" and then reaches the conclusion that the constitution would allow for the subversion of the legislature's democratic authority.

Of course, the invocation of 'the people' or the notion of popular sovereignty as the foundational legitimating basis of the constitution resonates with the type of justification given by ethnocrats for constitutional legitimacy. The claim that the constitution is predicated upon an ethnocratic 'Malay Dominance' social contract implies that 'the people' refers to a unified ethnic 'Malay-Muslim' community, where those who are not part of that community are deemed 'other'. This argument is dangerous because it resonates with ethno-populist justifications for pseudo-executive dictatorship where political power concentrates in the executive, not Parliament.

The fact of weak coalition governments and a weak opposition, coupled with the enhanced role of the king as possessed of what appears to be a legally and politically unlimited power to decide who can form government, poses a serious threat to democracy keeping in mind the populist trajectory behind the ethnocratic position. Here, it is worth noting that UMNO, a political party with a dismal record when it comes to constitutional democracy, is at the time of writing pushing for a general election. The political dynamics are such that actors who think they have sufficient power to form government would like to use the trappings of democracy to legitimate some form of ethno-authoritarian rule.

All this resonates with the kind of authoritarian political logic set out by the conservative German thinker and political theorist Carl Schmitt. Any serious study of how ethnocratic rule and the use of emergency powers have eroded the potential for constitutional democracy in Malaysia would benefit from a close study of Schmittian ideas. For now, let me mention the most well-known sentence of

15 R. Rueban Balasubramaniam, 'Has Rule by Law Killed the Rule of Law in Malaysia?' (2008) 8(2) Oxford University Commonwealth Law Journal 211.

Schmitt's work: "Sovereign is he who decides on the exception."[16] This sentence is especially relevant as of 2021, given the ongoing state of emergency in Malaysia in the midst of political upheaval and public health emergency. According to Schmitt, politics is defined by an existential battle between groups about the identity of the state that can only be resolved by a sovereign whose decision asserts a distinction between 'friend' versus 'enemy', thereby constituting the identity of the former while vanquishing the latter. The sovereign is thus a dictator whose decision is made in a moment of 'exception' where there is an existential threat to society and where the legitimacy of that decision flows from the ex post facto ratification of that decision by an ethnically homogeneous and socially salient group willing to act politically as the 'people'. Schmitt's work offers the intellectual resources needed to engage in precisely the kind of authoritarian re-description of constitutional democracy now taking place in Malaysia.[17] For now, however, the point to be underlined is that given the emergency that is ongoing as of June 2021, there a serious danger that power politics will play out in a way that favours a return to ethno-authoritarian rule, facilitated by a sufficiently powerful group petitioning the king to install that group into the office of government while proclaiming that any such installation would be democratically legitimate as an expression of the will of an ethnocratic people.

Whether this happens will depend in part on at least one key issue; that is, how far the king and public officials accept the constitutionally orthodox view that emergency powers are not subject to constitutional constraints on power. While the moral character of the king may be unimpeachable, the question is about how far the office of the king will be attuned to the idea of constitutional role morality; that is, the idea that the king's official role is that of constitutional monarch so that the king remains bound by implicit values associated with constitutional democracy that inform the legitimacy of the constitution and thus condition the king's emergency powers. This would also require rejecting Harun's arguments about the separation of powers and accepting that the legitimacy of the Malaysian Constitution is founded in the rule of law, not the idea of popular sovereignty. Any resistance to the authoritarian political dynamics that could potentially unfold given the present situation has to begin with an assertion of constitutional legality as a concept wholly defined as internal to the rule of law or legality.

5. Conclusion

At the time of writing, it has become clear that the PN government has mishandled the COVID-19 pandemic response. While vaccines are slowly rolling out, the country is presently under lockdown as the rate of illness continues to climb,

16 Carl Schmitt, *Political Theology: Four Chapters on the Concept of Sovereignty* (George Schwab trs, University of Chicago Press 2005) 5.

17 Lars Vinx, 'Carl Schmitt and the Authoritarian Subversion of Democracy' (2021) 47(2) Philosophy and Social Criticism 173.

a problem made worse by the rampaging Delta variant of the virus. It is difficult to resist the impression that politicians have been too busy protecting their self-interest in accessing and retaining positions of power to focus on the unfolding public health emergency. In this regard, it is difficult to separate this botched response from the pathological political context and to ignore how the underlying pathologies that have subverted constitutional democracy are likely to be amplified at the cost of human life. Unfortunately, citizens may only have the opportunity to register their displeasure with ruling elites at the next general election, which will probably not be held until 2023 as the constitutionally mandated end of the five-year period since the holding of the previous general election.

The facts suggest that citizens may not have appealing options as to who should form the next government. The potentiality is that the PN will continue to rule for another two years despite doubts about its legitimacy. And given the continuous political musical chairs taking place within coalition configurations in both the PN and the opposition, it is very difficult to predict what lies in store in the short to medium term for Malaysian politics. What is clear is that constitutional democracy is on the back foot because there appears to be an absence of democrats. Consider that the PH has indicated that it is willing to work with UMNO to compete in the next general election; in other words, the party that was once committed to democratic change is now willing to hold hands with ethnocrats to gain power. Additionally, in keeping with long-term trends, the Malaysian courts are refusing to review the constitutional legality of the proclamation of emergency and laws enacted thereunder are not subject to judicial review. Hence, the absence of democrats coincides with the general reluctance of even judges tasked to defend the rule of law to take up that task. In sum, the prospects for constitutional democracy look very poor. Instead, the evidence points to a post-pandemic political dispensation likely to take some form of reconfigured ethno-authoritarian government.

35

THE FRENCH MANAGEMENT OF COVID-19

Normalisation of Regimes of Exception and Degradation of the Rule of Law

Marie-Laure Basilien-Gainche

1. Introduction – From Exception to Exceptions[1]

To cope with the COVID-19 crisis, the French Parliament adopted on 23 March 2020 Statute Law n°2020-290 creating a new emergency powers regime: the state of health emergency. This, first, confers important powers and wide discretion on the executive branch and the administrative authorities, to a degree far more worrying than those provided by the traditional state of security emergency, contained in the 1955 Statute Law. Second, the state of health emergency enables the executive to severely restrict rights and freedoms with minimal checks and balances. What makes the new state of exception all the more concerning is that France has been governed since the coordinated terrorist attacks of November 2015 in Paris by successive states of exception.

This trend to deploy, multiply and intensify states of exception at the expense of legal normality is worrying, especially as the adequacy, necessity and proportionality of the measures adopted in order to tackle the COVID-19 crisis are disputed. According to Mireille Delmas-Marty,[2] we observe a "normative insanity" ("*une folie normative*") that resulted in an escalation of restrictions of rights and liberties, all in the name of defending them. For instance, while (at the time of writing) 11 bills of legislative reform related to the state of health emergency have been transmitted to the Parliament since March 2020, executive acts have been adopted

1 All websites accessed on 27 July 2021.

2 Mireille Delmas-Marty, 'Nous Basculons Vers un Droit Pénal de la Sécurité, qui Traite le Suspect en Criminal' (*Le Monde*, 23 October 2020) <https://www.lemonde.fr/idees/article/2020/10/23/mireille-delmas-marty-nous-basculons-vers-un-droit-penal-de-la-securite_6057057_3232.html>.

 DOI: 10.4324/9781003211952-40

in a frenetic manner and modified on a weekly basis, generating a complex and constantly shifting corpus of exceptional rules.[3] Nor are the measures transparent: the French Senate website lists the ordinances, regulations and decrees the government adopted in application of Statute Law n°2020-290, but the inventory unfortunately does not go beyond 17 May 2020. Moreover, these laws promoted an illusion of security, while substantially limiting liberties.

To expose how security-focused the management of the health crisis was in France, this chapter exposes the expansion of exceptional regimes in France under the guise of the pandemic challenge (section 2); the escalation of the executive powers that limit and suspend rights and freedoms (section 3); and the lack of any genuinely effective institutional oversight (section 4).

2. The Expansion of Exceptional Regimes: Confronting or Using the Health Crisis?

Facing the COVID-19 crisis, the French Parliament examined in four days the bill proposed by the government establishing a new emergency powers regime and adopted Statute Law n°2020-290. The state of health emergency is contained in Articles 1 to 8 of the Statute Law and is codified in the Public Health Code (PHC).[4] This exceptional regime was activated by the Law itself that creates it (though the text disposes that the state of health emergency is declared by the President) and was extended by Statute Law n°2020-946 of 11 May 2020 until 9 July 2020. Yet the first measures responding to COVID-19 were adopted under legal bases that were already available in the French legal order. Thus, the creation of this exceptional regime, which allowed significant restrictions of rights and freedoms, was concerning and of dubious necessity.[5]

2.1 The Creation of Another State of Exception: Was the Emergency Regime Needed?

The health minister adopted on 14 March 2020, on the basis of Article L.3131-1 PHC, Decree n°2020-247 which closed establishments open to the public (shopping centres, restaurants, cinemas, theatres, museums, etc); banned any gathering, meeting or activity bringing together more than 100 people in a closed or open environment; and closed childcare establishments and educational and higher education institutions. Subsequently, the prime minister, health minister and home

3 Paul Cassia, 'Coronafolie' (*Mediapart – Le Blog*, 20 January 2021) <https://blogs.mediapart.fr/paul-cassia/blog/180121/coronafolie>.

4 Article L 3131-14 to Article L 3131-12 PHC.

5 Jacques Petit, 'L'État d'Urgence Sanitaire' (2020) 15 Actualité juridique. Droit Administratif 833; Vincent Sizaire, 'Un Colosse aux Pieds d'Argile: Les Fondements Juridiques Fragiles de l'Urgence Sanitaire' (2010) Revue des Droits de l'Homme <https://doi.org/10.4000/revdh.8976>.

affairs minister established a nationwide lockdown and criminalised breaches of it:[6] a fourth class minor offence was created, punishable by a maximum fine of €750, which could be upgraded to a fifth class offence in case of recidivism within 15 days, punishable by a maximum fine of €1,500.[7] It also became a criminal offence, punishable by six months in prison and a fine of €3,750, to commit at least three violations within 30 days.[8]

The necessity of creating a new exceptional regime was doubtful and contested.[9] Nevertheless, the government chose to create the new state of health emergency regime arguing that the health emergency powers enounced in Article L.3131-1 PHC provided the health minister, but not the prime minister, with the authority to adopt "any measure proportionate to the risks and appropriate to the circumstances of time and place in order to prevent and limit the consequences of possible threats to the health of the population".[10] Thus, the French Parliament adopted under the fast track legislative procedure the Emergency Response to the COVID-19 Epidemic Statute Law n°2020-290. This text includes various measures: some designed to manage the epidemic; others to give the government the power to adopt, within three months and in defined legal areas, the urgent measures necessary to mitigate the economic fallout of the epidemic; and others to postpone the second round of the municipal elections, which had been due to take place on 22 March 2021. While under Article 38 of the French Constitution, the government may ask Parliament for authorisation, for a limited period, to take measures by ordinance that are normally the preserve of statute law; under powers conferred by Statute Law n°2020-290, the government adopted no fewer than 110 ordinances (as of 22 May 2021), some introducing worrying reforms[11] to judicial procedures (such as automatic extension of the duration of pre-trial detention without any judicial intervention)[12] and administrative procedures (extension of the cases in which the administrative courts can pronounce by order, i.e. with a formation composed of a single judge).[13]

6 Decree n°2020-260 of 16 March 2020, amended by Decree n°2020-264 of 17 March 2020 and Decree n°2020-279 of 19 March 2020; see Article L 3136-1 PHC.

7 Article 131-13(4) Criminal Code.

8 Article 131-8 Criminal Code.

9 Sébastien Platon, 'Reinventing the Wheel … and Rolling over Fundamental Freedoms? The Covid-19 Epidemic in France and the State of Health Emergency' (2020) 8(3) The Theory and Practice of Legislation 293; Olivier Beaud and Cécile Guérin-Bargues, 'L'État d'Urgence Sanitaire: Était-il Judicieux de Créer un Nouveau Regime d'Exception?' (2020) Recueil Dalloz 891.

10 The conformity of this provision with constitutional law and with the international obligations of France is doubtful, as its vague wording and uncertain scope do not offer the required guarantees that constitutional and international obligations impose when restrictions on rights and liberties are extended. Stéphanie Renard, *L'Ordre Public Sanitaire* (Thèse de Droit Public, Université Rennes 1 2008).

11 Paul Cassia, 'En République Française, le Gouvernement Légifère' (*Médiapart – Le Blog*, 8 June 2020) <https://blogs.mediapart.fr/paul-cassia/blog/070620/en-republique-francaise-le-gouvernement-legifere>.

12 Ordinance n°2020-303, Decree n°2020-427, Ordinance n°2020-557.

13 Ordinance n°2020-305, Ordinance n°2020-405, Ordinance n°2020-558.

2.2 Implementation of the State of Health Emergency: How Exceptional Is the Exception?

The state of health emergency was applied twice,[14] some transitory emergency mechanisms being used in between. The way in which the exceptional regimes have become the 'new normal' without challenge is striking. Different elements should be highlighted: the introduction of new exceptional regimes;[15] the successive extensions of the state of health emergency under the accelerated legislative procedure; the normalisation of the new state of health emergency regime as Statute Law n°2021-160, which at the time of writing has been extended to 31 December 2021; and the presentation by the government in December 2020 of a legislative proposal to establish a permanent health crisis management regime (whose provisions were particularly concerning as they essentially consist of normalising the power the executive disposes of under the state of health emergency).

Scholars criticised the normalisation of the state of health emergency regime:[16] the circumstances of the epidemic were, after the first wave, not unexpected; there was no catastrophe, in the legal meaning of the term;[17] and nor was a threat putting in danger France's institutions, population or territory.[18] Yet, considering that the state of health emergency aimed at eradicating the epidemic, this inevitably resulted in making the exception permanent. While the recourse to exceptional regimes is portrayed as a means of coping with the crisis that reassures the public, the way they are used in practice can be as perilous as the danger they are sup-

14 The implementation of the state of health emergency proceeded as follows: first from 23 March 2020 to 9 July 2020 when declared by Statute Law n°2020-290 and extended by Statute Law n°2020-946 of 11 May 2020 until 10 July 2020; and second, from 17 October 2020 when declared by the President of the Republic by Decree n°2020-1257 of 14 October 2020 with a first extension until 16 February 2021 by Statute Law n°2020-1379 adopted on 14 November 2020, and a second until 1 June 2021 by Statute Law n°2021-160, adopted on 15 February 2021. The state of health emergency was declared a third time on 14 July 2021 in La Réunion and Martinique.

15 E.g. the state of health emergency with Statute Law n°2020-290; the regime organising the way out of the state of health emergency with Statute Law n°2020-856; the regime aiming at managing the way out of the sanitary crisis with Statute Law n°2021-689; and the regime organising the management of the health crisis resolution with Statute Law n°2021-1040.

16 Stéphanie Renard, 'L'État d'Urgence Sanitaire: Droit d'Exception et Exceptions au Droit' (2020) 13 Revue des Droits et Libertés Fondamentaux <http://www.revuedlf.com/droit-administratif/letat-durgence-sanitaire-droit-dexception-et-exceptions-au-droit/>; Rosalie Lafarge, 'L'état d'Urgence Sanitaire: d'un Régime d'Exception à un Régime Permanent ?' (*France Culture*, 19 January 2021)< https://www.franceculture.fr/politique/letat-durgence-sanitaire-dun-regime-dexception-a-un-regime-permanent>; Paul Cassia, 'L'État d'Urgence Sanitaire: Remède, Placebo ou Venin Juridique' (*Médiapart – Le Blog*, 24 March 2020) <https://blogs.mediapart.fr/paul-cassia/blog/230320/l-etat-d-urgence-sanitaire-remede-placebo-ou-venin-juridique>.

17 The *Conseil d'Etat* admitted this when it authorised the second extension of the second state of health emergency in Opinion n°401919 of 11 January 2021 on Statute Law n°2021-160.

18 François Saint-Bonnet, 'De la Banalisation de Nos États d'Urgence' (*Jus Politicum*, 9 January 2021) <https://blog.juspoliticum.com/2021/01/09/de-la-banalisation-des-etats-durgence-par-francois-saint-bonnet/>.

posed to tame. For example, in order to protect people from COVID-19, the French authorities developed a concerning tendency towards legal uncertainty, with a proliferation of measures adopted at different administrative levels that were constantly modified; one decree (Decree n°2020-1262 of 16 October 2020) was amended no fewer than 35 times up to 25 May 2021. Moreover, the powers offered by the state of health emergency to the executive were so numerous and intense that they could diminish, even extinguish, rights and liberties.

3. The Escalation of Executive Powers: How Far Should Rights Be Limited?

According to Article L.3131-15 PHC, whenever and wherever the state of health emergency is declared, the prime minister has ten powers that can be activated by regulatory decree for the sole purpose of guaranteeing public health. These are the powers to (i) restrict or prohibit the movement of people and vehicles; (ii) prohibit people from leaving their homes; (iii) order quarantine of persons likely to be affected; (iv) order isolation of persons actually affected; (v) order the temporary closure of establishments open to the public; (vi) limit or prohibit gatherings in public places; (vii) order the requisition of all goods and services necessary to tackle the health emergency; (viii) take temporary control of prices to prevent or correct tensions in the market; (ix) take all measures to make available appropriate medicines to patients; and (x) take by decree any other regulatory measure limiting rights and freedoms.

3.1 Invasive Restrictions of Rights and Freedoms: How Far Can They Be Tamed?

These powers vested in the government under the state of health emergency differ qualitatively from the ones the state of security emergency allows: the administration can adopt not only specific measures aimed at particular individuals or places, but also general measures covering the whole of French territory and the entire population.[19] Moreover, the tenth power listed above is particularly troubling as it provides the executive with a *carte blanche*. The health minister can prescribe regulatory measures relating to the organisation and operation of the health system aimed at ending the health disaster, as well as individual measures necessary for the application of any measures prescribed by the prime minister. Local representatives of the executive are also empowered to adopt measures that extend curfew hours, restrictions on movement and transport and so forth. During the first and the second uses of the state of health emergency, drastic restrictions on rights and

19 Estelle Chambas and Thomas Perroud, 'France: Legal Response to COVID-19' in Jeff King and Octavio Ferraz (eds), *The Oxford Compendium of National Legal Responses to COVID-19* (Oxford University Press 2021).

freedoms were adopted and implemented.[20] Decrees established lockdowns, which forbade all movement and transport of persons; prohibited all gatherings; closed all non-essential activities; closed all educational institutions – elementary, secondary and superior; controlled the price of some goods, such as hand sanitiser; and requisitioned masks for health professionals as well as products necessary to health facilities, such as medicines, painkillers and antibiotics. Afterwards, Decree n°2021-699 of 1 June 2021 created the sanitary pass/digital COVID certificate, whose scope was extended by Decree n°21-955 of 19 July 2021.

The national lockdowns were the main vehicle by which rights and freedoms were restricted: the first occurred from 17 March to 11 May 2020; the second lasted from 30 October 2020 to 15 December 2020.[21] Curfews were also introduced by the French authorities.[22] The rights and freedoms affected were numerous: individual liberty, with the imposition of lockdowns, curfews, quarantine or isolation; freedom of association and freedom of expression, with the prohibition of gatherings and assemblies; freedom of religion, by closing all places of worship or imposing limitations on the number of attendees at religious services; freedom of education, with the closure of universities, theatres and museums and the promotion of remote learning without securing access for all students to the necessary infrastructure; freedom of movement, with the requirement to leave one's home only for a permitted reason during the two lockdowns; and freedom of commerce, with the closure of non-essential establishments like bars, restaurants, sport facilities and the imposition of quotas of employees allowed to be physically present in workplaces.

3.2 Overwhelming Executive Power: Why Security-Focused Measures Are Concerning

The use of the state of health emergency was of dubious efficacy. On the one hand, executive and administrative authorities obtained wide-ranging powers, at the expense of the separation of powers and the guarantee of rights – all in the name of controlling the epidemic. On the other hand, the authorities invested with such powers seemed unable to develop effective policies to tackle the health crisis. The efficacy of using security-focused measures to tackle a health crisis was

20 The restrictions of rights and freedoms during the first state of emergency were regulated by Decree n°2020-293 of 23 March 2020, Decree n°2020-337 of 26 March 2020, and Decree n°2020-370 of 30 March 2020; and during the second one by Decree n°2020-1257 of 14 October 2020 and Decree n°2020-1310 of 29 October 2020.

21 Paul Cassia, 'Le Confinement: 67 millions de Privations Arbitraires de la Liberté de Circuler' (*Médiapart – Le Blog*, 13 May 2020) <https://blogs.mediapart.fr/paul-cassia/blog/120520/le-confinement-67-millions-de-privations-arbitraires-de-la-liberte-de-circuler>.

22 The curfews registered in France evolved as follows: from 8 pm to 6 am from 15 December 2020 to 15 January 2021, with the exception of Christmas Day; from 6 pm to 6 am from 16 January 2021 to 19 March 2021; from 7 pm to 6 am from 20 March 2021 to 18 May 2021; from 9 pm to 6 am from 19 May 2021 to 30 June 2021.

questioned: there have been problems with the supply of masks, respirators, tests and vaccines.[23] France ranks among the worst 20% of countries in the world for the per capita mortality rate from COVID-19 as of July 2021,[24] and the French answer to the health emergency created not only a socio-economic crisis but also another type of crisis affecting mental health due to the measures taken to tackle the COVID-19 crisis (for instance, the lockdown imposed a situation of isolation on vulnerable persons who developed depressive disorders for which adequate treatment is not available).[25]

As many measures adopted under the state of health emergency restricted rights and liberties, the question of their legality, necessity and proportionality is crucial and unfortunately was not appropriately addressed by the political and judicial authorities. Foremost concerns related to the compatibility of the measures with constitutional, European and international instruments protecting human rights. This was highlighted by national human rights institutions, such as the *Commission Nationale Consultative pour les Droits de l'Homme* (CNCDH), which established an observatory of the state of health emergency;[26] and published several opinions expressing its deep concern that the state of health emergency was incompatible with international and regional instruments of human rights protections and that restrictions on rights and freedoms, as well as the concentration of powers in the executive, were not in line with the standard of what is acceptable in a democratic society. Another institution, the *Défenseur des Droits*, expressed alarm related to some infringements of rights and freedoms, in particular of vulnerable people and the weakness of the institutional control of the measures and the policies deployed.[27] Yet the observations that these two institutions, among others, made no manifest impact on the security-focused manner in which the executive decided to manage the health crisis.

4. The Weakness of Institutional Control: Who Guards the Guardians?

The political and judicial scrutiny of the measures adopted by the executive to manage COVID-19 was so weak that significant concerns about the rule of law and democratic principles exist in France. The restrictions on rights and freedoms

23 'Masques, Tests, Vaccins: Un An de Polémiques en France en Trois Actes' (*Le Télégramme*, 19 January 2021) <https://www.letelegramme.fr/coronavirus/masques-tests-vaccins-un-an-de-polemiques-en-france-en-trois-actes-19-01-2021-12690993.php>.

24 Johns Hopkins University Coronavirus Resource Center, 'Mortality Analyses'<https://coronavirus.jhu.edu/data/mortality>.

25 Éric Péchillon, 'Confinement et Santé Mentale: Quand l'Impensable se Heurte à l'Irrationnel' (2020) 76 Revue Générale de Droit Médical 145; Stéphanie Renard, 'L'état d'Urgence Sanitaire: d'un Régime d'Exception à un Régime Permanent?' (n 16).

26 Commission Nationale Consultative pour les Droits de l'Homme (CNCDH), 'Observatoire de l'État d'Urgence Sanitaire et du Confinement' (4 June 2020) <https://www.cncdh.fr/fr/travaux-en-cours/observatoire-de-letat-durgence-sanitaire-et-du-confinement>.

27 Défenseur des Droits, Opinion 20-10, 3 December 2020.

occurred in an already deteriorated situation of the rule of law, since the country had already been under the state of security emergency for two years prior to the pandemic and had seen many provisions adopted under such state of exception encapsulated in ordinary law.[28] The state of health emergency is flawed, due to the patent imbalance between the expansive powers conferred on executive authorities and the paucity of safeguards provided to control the adopted measures.[29]

4.1 Insignificant Parliamentary Oversight: What Happened to the Balance of Powers?

Under Article L.3131-13 § 1 PHC, Parliament has limited powers under the state of health emergency – more limited than the ones it has under the state of security emergency: (a) the extension of the state of health emergency must be authorised by Parliament beyond one month (and not beyond 12 days);[30] (b) there is no sunset clause provided for in the case of the state of health emergency, similar to Article 4 of the 1955 Statute Law (the Act of Parliament extending the state of security emergency lapses after 15 days following the resignation of the government or the dissolution of the National Assembly); (c) executive and administrative authorities are not required to send to Parliament copies of all the Acts they adopt under the state of health emergency, unlike a state of security emergency; and (d) Parliament seemed less willing to exercise its control powers during the state of health emergency. During the state of security emergency that lasted from November 2015 to October 2017, the Law Commission of the National Assembly obtained means of information and investigation similar to those of an inquiry committee, allowing real-time monitoring of the use by the executive of its exceptional powers. Yet, only a simple 'information mission' regarding the state of health emergency application was established in National Assembly on 27 March 2020, whose oversight was not significant and whose dissolution was decided on 27 January 2021.[31]

Though the Parliament was operational during the states of health emergency, the scrutiny the assemblies exercised on the executive handling of the health crisis was paltry. This resulted from the political concordance between the executive branch and the parliamentary majority (*fait majoritaire*) and from its intensification by the 2008 constitutional reform, so much so that the executive has many tools to control parliamentary work (such as control of the assemblies' agenda).[32]

28 This occurred with Statute Law n°2017-1510 of 30 October 2017 reinforcing the internal security and the fight against terrorism, whose provisions were extended by Statute Law n°2020-1671 of 24 December 2020 for some until 30 June 2021 and for others until 31 December 2021.

29 Adélaïde Jacquin and Emmanuel Daoud, 'L'Etat d'Urgence Sanitaire ou l'Etat de Droit Mutilé' (April 2020) 4 Actualité Juridique Droit Pénal 191.

30 The *Conseil d'Etat* – in its function of adviser to the government – suggested departing from the 12-day deadline and preferred a one-month deadline for involving Parliament.

31 Its first report was published on 3 June 2020, and a second on 3 December 2020.

32 Céline Vintzel, *Les Armes du Gouvernement dans la Procédure Législative* (Dalloz 2011); 'Renforcer le Parlement Français: Les Leçons du Droit Comparé' (*Jus Politicum*, 17 January 2017) <http://

The tendency to devalue Parliament is highlighted by the manner in which the executive framed the examination by the Houses of the different bills relating to the state of health emergency, requiring their examination to be conducted under the accelerated legislative procedure.[33] Yet in the Senate some resistance appeared against the adoption of the second authorisation of extension of the second state of health emergency. However, the absence of compromise between the two chambers in the joint committee formed to scrutinise the text ensured that the text as adopted by the National Assembly prevailed (Article 45 Al. 4 of the 1958 French constitution).

4.2 Deficient Judicial Review: Is the Council of State at the Service of the Government?

If parliamentary oversight appeared insignificant, judicial review of the adopted measures was also deficient. The weakness of judicial review was first evident from the way the Constitutional Council exercises its role. The *Conseil Constitutionnel* (CC) examines legislative acts when seized ex ante (in abstracto) or ex post (in concreto) via the *Question prioritaire de constitutionnalité* (QPC) procedure, assessing the compatibility of the provisions with constitutional norms (not with EU law, the European Convention on Human Rights or international law). The ex ante constitutional scrutiny was exercised on the extension of the first state of health emergency;[34] the organisation of the way out of the state of health emergency;[35] and the first extension of the second state of health emergency.[36] The constitutional judges performed their control in a cautious and restrained way: they refused to fully consider whether the normative measures relating to the state of health emergency respected the principles of necessity and proportionality, asserting that the measures fulfilled these requirements as their goal was the preservation of public health and thus a matter of public interest. In their ex post decisions, the constitutional judges appeared to be a feeble guardian of the separation of powers and the protection of rights. A ruling of May 2020 declared that ordinances the government adopts under Article 38 of the Constitution acquired the status of Statute Law, even where

juspoliticum.com/article/Renforcer-le-Parlement-francais-Les-lecons-du-droit-compare-1146.html>.

33 Elina Lemaire, 'Le Parlement Face à la Crise du Covid-19', Part 1 (2 April 2020) and Part 2 (*Jus Politicum*, 13 April 2020) <https://blog.juspoliticum.com/2020/04/13/le-parlement-face-a-la-crise-du-covid-19-2-2-par-elina-lemaire/>; 'La Procédure Accélérée ou la Regrettable Normalisation d'une Procédure Dérogatoire' (*Jus Politicum*, 5 July 2017) <https://blog.juspoliticum.com/2017/07/05/la-procedure-acceleree-ou-la-regrettable-normalisation-dune-procedure-derogatoire-par-elina-lemaire/>.

34 CC, Decision n°2020-800 DC, 11 May 2020.

35 CC, Decision n°2020-803 DC, 9 July 2020.

36 CC, Decision n°2020-808 DC, 13 November 2020.

they were not ratified by Parliament within the timeframe fixed in the legislation that conferred the considered powers, heightening the imbalance between the executive and legislature.[37] The Council did declare unconstitutional some provisions of Ordinance n°2020-303: those which allowed trials to be conducted by videoconference in criminal or juvenile courts without the agreement of the defendant;[38] and those which provided for the extension of all pre-trial detentions that expired during the first state of public health emergency without any judicial intervention,[39] and without the possibility of challenge.[40] Yet, these decisions may be regarded as too little, too late.

Similarly, the *Conseil d'Etat*, intervening ex ante by giving opinions on the government's bills, appeared reluctant to defend rights and freedoms.[41] As the supreme administrative jurisdiction, the institution downgraded the standard of its scrutiny (*contrôle de l'erreur manifeste d'appréciation*, that corresponds to minimum control) and exercised only the slightest control of the executive and administrative measures adopted to tackle the health crisis, refusing to order their suspension or annulment. Decisions issued in September 2020 are illustrative:[42] an administrative police measure (which imposed the compulsory wearing of a mask in any public space) was considered legal because of its simplicity and clarity, without taking into account its necessity and proportionality, which were both doubtful as this measure applies to anyone, anytime, anywhere, irrespective of the context.[43] As several academics noted,[44] the administrative jurisdiction's decisions were characterised by the poverty of their reasoning and by the overreliance on documents and arguments provided by the government. Moreover, some inconsistencies appeared: examining Decree n°2020-1310 re-establishing the lockdown which forbade all public

37 CC, Decision n°2020-843 QPC, 28 May 2020.

38 CC, Decision n°2020/872 QPC, 15 January 2021.

39 The delay was of two to three months in correctional matters and of six months on criminal matters.

40 CC, Decision n°2020-878/879 QPC, 29 January 2021.

41 CE, 18 March 2020, avis sur le projet de loi organique d'urgence pour faire face à l'épidémie de COVID-19; 18 March 2020, avis sur le projet de loi d'urgence pour faire face à l'épidémie de COVID-19; 9 June 2020, avis sur le projet de loi organisant la sortie de l'état d'urgence sanitaire; 21 December 2020, avis sur le projet de loi pérennisant le dispositif de l'état d'urgence sanitaire et reportant la caducité des regimes institués; 14 January 2021, avis sur le projet de loi autorisant la prorogation de l'état d'urgence sanitaire et reportant la caducité des régimes institués; 28 April 2021, avis sur le projet de loi relatif à la gestion de la sortie de la crise sanitaire.

42 CE, 6 September 2020, Ord. n°443750, Ord. n°44351.

43 Paul Cassia, 'Port Obligatoire du Masque: la Volte Face du Conseil d'Etat' (*Médiapart – Le Blog*, 14 September 2020) <https://blogs.mediapart.fr/paul-cassia/blog/130920/port-obligatoire-du-masque-la-volte-face-du-conseil-d-etat>.

44 E.g. Florence Chaltiel, 'A propos de l'État d'Urgence Sanitaire, Textes et Contextes', 155a3 (2020) 155a3 Les Petites Affiches 16; Loïc Vatna, 'Le Juge Administratif et la Crise de la Covid-19' (October 2020) Revue des Droits de l'Homme <http://journals.openedition.org/revdh/10542; DOI: https://doi.org/10.4000/revdh.10542>.

gatherings, the *Conseil d'Etat* demanded that the government nuance its measures regarding assemblies in churches;[45] but not for universities[46] and theatres.[47]

5. Conclusion

The restrictions of rights and liberties in France via the state of security emergency made it easier for the executive authorities to decide to limit them further in the name of the protection of public health when facing the COVID-19 pandemic. Moreover, by deploying inadequate oversight, the Parliament and judiciary validated the restraints on rights and freedoms without exercising genuine control of the legality, conventionality, necessity and proportionality of the measures. The security-focused management of COVID-19, whose efficacy has not been proven, needs therefore to be questioned in Michel Foucault's terms, as the state of health emergency offers the executive the opportunity to establish a worrying system of control, a concerning *panopticon*. For instance, the *Préfet de Police* in Paris decided without any legal basis to use drones to enforce lockdown measures and physical distancing, the *Conseil d'Etat* validating this illegal police measure by refusing to sanction it.[48] Yet, the *Conseil Constitutionnel* considered that Article 46 of the bill concerning global security was not totally in conformity with constitutional obligations: the *Conseil* admits that the legislature could authorise the capture, recording and transmission of images by drones for the purposes of investigating, recording or prosecuting criminal offences or maintaining public order and security; but it sanctioned the absence of special safeguards to protect the right to privacy with regard to the implementation of such surveillance systems.[49] The *raison d'etat* when becoming the *raison de la santé* can be used to legitimate every suspension, restriction or suppression of rights in the name of the preservation of life, the authorities seizing every incentive to avoid scrutiny by exploiting the legal tools of exception at their disposal.

45 CE, 29 November 2020, Ord. n°446930 and others.

46 CE, 10 December 2020 Ord. n°447015.

47 CE, 23 December 2020, Ord. n°447698; Paul Cassia, 'Fermeture des Théâtres et Cinémas: Comédie au Conseil d'Etat' (*Médiapart – Le Blog*, 28 December 2020) <https://blogs.mediapart.fr/paul-cassia/blog/281220/fermeture-des-theatres-et-cinemas-comedie-au-conseil-d-etat>.

48 CE, 18 May 2020, Ord. n°440442 and n°440445.

49 Jean-Baptiste Perrier, 'Le Droit Pénal du Danger' (7 May 2020) 17 Recueil Dalloz 937.

36

THE PHILIPPINES UNDER LOCKDOWN

Continuing Executive Dominance and an Unclear Pandemic Response

Maria Ela L Atienza

1. Introduction[1]

The Philippines has to date had one of the longest lockdowns[2] and one of the longest states of emergency[3] in response to COVID-19. This chapter reviews what happened following the declaration of emergency and imposition of lockdown in March 2020,[4] focusing on the main legal and political issues as well as prospects in the country with, at the time of writing, the second highest total number of

1 All websites accessed on 30 July 2021.

2 Aie Balagtas See, 'Rodrigo Duterte Is Using One of the World's Longest COVID-19 Lockdowns to Strengthen His Grip on the Philippines' (*Time*, 15 March 2021) <https://time.com/5945616/covid-philippines-pandemic-lockdown/>.

3 International IDEA, *The Global State of Democracy in Focus Special Brief: Taking Stock of Global Democratic Trends Before and During the COVID 19 Pandemic* (December 2020) 9 <https://idea.int/publications/catalogue/global-democratic-trends-before-and-during-covid19>.

4 This is an expanded version of the author's blog post: Maria Ela L Atienza, 'The Philippines a Year under Lockdown: Continuing Executive Dominance, Threats to Democracy, and Unclear Pandemic Response' (*Verfassungsblog*, 26 April 2021) <https://verfassungsblog.de/the-philippines-a-year-under-lockdown/>. Some sections are updated from two previous works: Atienza, Aries A Arugay, Jean Encinas-Franco, Jan Robert R Go and Rogelio Alicor L Panao 'Constitutional Performance Assessment in the Time of a Pandemic: The 1987 Constitution and the Philippines' COVID-19 Response' (2020) International IDEA Discussion Paper 3/2020 <https://doi.org/10.31752/idea.2020.36>; Atienza, 'Emergency Powers and COVID-19: The Philippines as a Case Study' (2020) (Melbourne Forum on Constitution-Building 2020 organised by International Institute for Democracy and Electoral Assistance (IDEA) and Constitution Transformation Network, Melbourne, September 2020) <https://law.unimelb.edu.au/__data/assets/pdf_file/0011/3474344/MF20-Web1-Philippines-Ela-FINAL.pdf>.

DOI: 10.4324/9781003211952-41

COVID-19 cases in Southeast Asia.[5] Section 2 provides an overview of legal and political responses and adaptation to the pandemic. This is followed by analysis of the executive branch and use of powers (section 3), the effectiveness of judicial and legislative scrutiny and oversight (section 4), responses of regional and local governments (section 5) and the impact on human rights and civil liberties (section 6). Section 7 ends with discussion of the prospects for governance, democracy, human rights and the rule of law.

2. Overview of Legal and Political Responses and Adaptation to COVID-19

2.1 Response of the Executive Branch

The first imported case of COVID-19 was detected in the Philippines in late January 2020. Initially, the national administration downplayed the virus and claimed that the country was on top of the situation. However, by early February, the government relented to pressure from some legislators, media and interest groups and imposed a travel ban on flights from Wuhan, Macau and Hong Kong. By 10 February, voluntary repatriation of Filipinos from Wuhan started.

Following the first cases of local transmission, President Rodrigo Duterte declared a state of public health emergency in the country on 8 March 2020 (Proclamation No 922). This declaration adheres to the 1987 Constitution, particularly the state's policy to protect and promote the right to health,[6] and the Law on Reporting of Communicable Diseases (Republic Act [RA] No 11332), which provides that the Philippine President shall declare the state of public health emergency in case of an epidemic of national and/or international concern that threatens national security. It also enables the President to mobilise agencies and resources to address the threat.

Schools were suspended on 8 March 2020. A partial lockdown of Metro Manila from 15 March to 14 April was announced, together with suspension of travel to and from the capital. On 16 March, the entire Luzon group of islands was placed under enhanced community quarantine (ECQ), effectively a total lockdown and the strictest category of lockdown imposed in the country. In the following months, the government imposed various types of quarantine and the list of allowed and disallowed activities outside homes evolved based on the changing evaluations of the Inter-Agency Task Force for the Management of Emerging Infectious Diseases (IATF), which was organised earlier in 2014 through Executive Order 168 of then President Benigno Aquino III to assess, monitor, contain, control and prevent the spread of any potential epidemic in the Philippines.

5 Center for Strategic and International Studies, 'Southeast Asia Covid-19 Tracker' (2021) (as of 30 July 2021) <https://www.csis.org/programs/southeast-asia-program/southeast-asia-covid-19-tracker-0>.

6 Philippines, 1987 Constitution, Article II, sec 15.

On 16 March 2020, the President signed Proclamation No 929 placing the country under a state of calamity due to COVID-19 for six months, again adhering to the Constitution[7] and the Philippines Disaster Risk Reduction and Management Act (RA No 10121). The proclamation allows the national and local governments ample leeway to utilise appropriate funds in their disaster preparedness and response efforts to contain the spread of COVID-19 and continue provision of basic services to their respective populations.

After 15 May, there was a gradual easing of lockdown in certain areas depending on the number of COVID-19 cases, with the main aim of enabling economic recovery. Metro Manila's ECQ was lifted on 1 June and was replaced by general community quarantine (GCQ), which allowed some economic activities to resume and limited public transportation to operate. However, for certain periods in 2020, some areas were put under a 'modified ECQ' (MECQ) or stricter lockdown,[8] which further limited economic activities due to a spike in cases and demands by health workers' associations to allow the health system to recover. By the end of 2020, most of the country was under modified general community quarantine (MGCQ), the loosest quarantine phase that permits many businesses and other activities to open with some limitations.

The initial period of the country's state of calamity was further extended by Proclamation No 1021 (dated September 2020) to 12 September 2021, making it at that point the world's longest state of emergency in response to COVID-19.[9] Due to a further spike of cases from January 2021, continued limitations in the capacity of effective contract tracing, testing and resources of health facilities, as well as delays in the purchase and arrival of both purchased and donated vaccines from the World Health Organisation-sponsored COVAX programme, restrictions began to increase again. Metro Manila and neighbouring provinces were once again placed under ECQ, the strictest level, from 29 March to 11 April and under MECQ from 12 April until 14 May.

2.2 Response of the Legislative Branch

In March 2020, the two Houses of Congress, upon the request of the Office of the President, approved the Bayanihan to Heal as One Act (RA No 11469), also known as Bayanihan 1 Act. (*Bayanihan* is a Filipino cultural value used to refer to a spirit of communal unity and cooperation.) The law gave the President certain emergency powers for the duration of three months to optimise the pandemic response as support to the two presidential proclamations on national health emergency and national calamity. The law has eight policy objectives, namely mitigating the transmission of the virus; mobilising the provision of basic necessities to those affected

7 ibid.

8 'MECQ now in Effect in Metro Manila and Four Provinces until August 18' (*CNN Philippines*, 4 August 2020) <https://www.cnn.ph/news/2020/8/4/metro-manila-four-provinces-back-in-MECQ-today.html>.

9 International IDEA (n 3).

by the imposition of quarantine; undertaking measures to prevent overburdening of the healthcare system; providing immediate and ample healthcare to those affected by the virus; providing recovery and rehabilitation through social amelioration and provision of safety nets to affected sectors; ensuring adequate and readily available funding; partnering with the private sector and others to deliver measures quickly and efficiently; and promoting and protecting the collective interests of Filipinos.

The law expired on 25 June 2020 and the Office of the President requested the two Houses of Congress once again to pass a second Bayanihan law, this time focused on recovery. By September 2020, the Bayanihan to Recover as One Act (RA No 11494 or Bayanihan 2 Act), which lays out the country's COVID-19 response and allocates funds (a PhP165 billion – equivalent to around US$3.272 billion or €2.776 billion – stimulus package) to help struggling sectors cope with the pandemic's impacts, had been approved by Congress and signed by the President. Bayanihan 2 expired in December 2020 but appropriations made under the law were extended up to June 2021.

As of June 2021, the House of Representatives has passed on third reading the Bayanihan to Arise as One bill, the third stimulus package aimed at addressing the social and economic impact of the pandemic. However, the Senate did not pass a counterpart bill by end of June, considering that there were still unspent funds under Bayanihan 2 that could no longer be used after June.

3. The Executive and the Use of Powers in Response to Emergency

Temporary emergency powers of the President are constitutional when obtained through legislative enactment specifically to allow the executive branch to better address a particular threat facing the Philippines and its people by means of a declaration.[10] During war or other national emergencies, the two Houses of Congress may, by law, "authorize the President, for a limited period and subject to such restrictions as it may prescribe, to exercise powers necessary and proper to carry out a declared national policy".[11]

Emergency powers were granted to the President by the Bayanihan 1 and 2 Acts. Other declarations regarding the health emergency and the state of calamity mentioned earlier are based on earlier legislation. This was not the first time that Congress had granted special temporary emergency powers to the President and to the executive branch of government under the Constitution to address a crisis. In the past, Congress granted emergency powers to the President for a limited time to address economic reconstruction due to a mutiny and rebellion of some factions in the military (1989); construction of irrigation projects to halt an impending agricultural crisis (1991); entering into negotiated contracts to address

10 Jorge V Tigno 'A Primer on Bayanihan to Heal as One Act of 2020: 26 Questions' University of the Philippines Diliman Department of Political Science (15 April 2020) <https://polisci.upd.edu.ph/resources/bayanihan-primer/>.

11 Philippines, 1987 Constitution, Article VI, sec 23.

a power shortage (1993); and a water crisis (1995).[12] However, the Bayanihan 1 and 2 Acts were the first national health emergency powers legislated by Congress for the President to exercise since the ratification of the 1987 Constitution.

The declaration of the national health emergency in the respective laws did not invalidate the Constitution or any of its provisions, particularly the Bill of Rights.[13] However, as examined in this chapter and based on a constitutional performance assessment during the period of the pandemic,[14] despite the constitutional and other legal safeguards in the exercise of emergency powers, there was greater consolidation of powers in the executive branch and a further weakening of the separation of powers. Executive dominance had already been noted in a pre-pandemic performance assessment of the Constitution,[15] and the trend was exacerbated by COVID-19. The executive branch dominated the pandemic response, for better or for worse, and its implementation resulted not only in a poorly planned and coordinated response to the pandemic but also in the further weakening of other democratic institutions, processes and principles.

The cabinet was disproportionately led by former or retired military and police generals and they largely dictated national responses to the pandemic.[16] Thus, a hierarchical, top-down, peace-and-order approach became a feature of the government's COVID-19 response. Citizens were mostly instructed to 'obey' the rules even if some of these were lacking in clarity, instead of harnessing cooperation, civic duty and the true *bayanihan* spirit of community and helping fellow citizens. Civilian health and other experts had difficulties getting their analyses and suggestions to the executive branch. Instead of providing concrete plans and comprehensive reports related to the pandemic response, the President's weekly public briefings and the daily press briefings of cabinet members and departmental representatives were used to attack and discredit critics, the opposition, activists and some media groups and businesses accused of being enemies of the government.

4. The Effectiveness of Judicial and Legislative Scrutiny and Oversight

4.1 Scrutiny and Oversight of Congress

While Congress passed the two Bayanihan Acts swiftly since the President certified them as urgent, the Constitution and the law obliged the President's office to

12 Tigno (n 10).

13 Philippines, 1987 Constitution, Article III.

14 Atienza and others (n 4).

15 Maria Ela L Atienza and others, 'Constitutional Performance Assessment of the 1987 Constitution: Summary of Findings' (International IDEA and University of the Philippines Center for Integrative and Development Studies 2020) <https://www.idea.int/publications/catalogue/constitutional-performance-assessment-1987-philippine-constitution>.

16 Vince Ferreras, 'Duterte Defends Military Men in War vs. COVID-19: You Need Not Be a Doctor Here' (*CNN Philippines*, 25 March 2021) <https://www.cnnphilippines.com/news/2021/3/25/Duterte-defends-military-men-in-war-vs.-COVID-19--You-need-not-be-a-doctor-here.html>.

account to Congress for all actions taken throughout the period of national emergency and to submit regular reports of all acts performed, including the amount and utilisation of funds pursuant to addressing the pandemic. The two Houses of Congress, after all, exercise oversight functions over the other two branches of government.

Yet, even prior to the pandemic, both Houses were dominated by blocs allied with the President. In a country with weak political parties and personality-oriented politics, most traditional legislators and politicians ally themselves with a popular chief executive, who appeared to enjoy high trust ratings even in surveys conducted during the pandemic. Even in the midst of a pandemic, Congress in July 2020 passed the Anti-Terrorism Act of 2020 (RA No 11479) which had questionable provisions that define terrorism too vaguely and broadly, limit the roles of the judiciary and the Commission on Human Rights in cases covered by the law and threaten the rights of people "suspected" of committing "terrorist" acts. In July 2020, Congress controversially denied a new franchise to ABS-CBN, the largest broadcast network with the widest reach in the country, and accused it of having "displeased" the President for its supposed bias in reporting and campaign coverage, on the basis of certain technicalities like operating a cable channel and the supposed role of foreign investors.[17]

During the pandemic, there was little information as to the extent to which Congress scrutinised the weekly reports submitted by the Office of the President as regards the use of the emergency powers or how much deliberation surrounded their submission.[18] Both Houses' leadership and the Congressional Oversight Committee declared satisfaction with the executive branch's performance as regards the Bayanihan 1 Act, despite the opposition's insistence on the need for more scrutiny, especially with regards to the spending of substantial amounts of funds on the pandemic response.

What was more obvious from 2020 was the targeting of investigations into specific departments. For instance, the two Houses conducted committee hearings related to the Department of Health's (DOH) readiness and continuing responses to the pandemic,[19] and corruption allegations in the Philippine Health Insurance Corporation.[20] But save for a few resignations of some officials in the insurance corporation, there was so significant impact on the direction of the DOH's pandemic response. However, in early May 2021, a group of senators sent a formal 'bipartisan request' to the Senate President to reconvene the Committee of the

17 Jason Gutierrez, 'Philippine Congress Officially Shuts Down Leading Broadcaster' (*The New York Times*, 10 July 2020) <https://www.nytimes.com/2020/07/10/world/asia/philippines-congress-media-duterte-abs-cbn.html>.

18 Atienza and others (n 4).

19 Rambo Talabong, '"We are Failing": House Highlights Duterte Admin's Mishandling of the Pandemic' (*Rappler*, 31 March 2021) <https://www.rappler.com/nation/highlights-house-hearing-duterte-government-mishandling-pandemic>.

20 Jenny Lei Ravelo, 'Corruption Allegations Rock Philippine Health Insurance Corporation amid COVID-19' (*Devex*, 14 September 2020) <https://www.devex.com/news/corruption-allegations-rock-philippine-health-insurance-corporation-amid-covid-19-98048>.

Whole to review the executive branch's pandemic response and vaccination roll-out. At the time of writing, the Senate President has not decided whether to grant this request.[21] Some senators also noted in June 2021 the large amount of unspent funds under Bayanihan 2.[22]

4.2 The Role of the Courts

Since President Duterte assumed power in 2016, the Supreme Court and the judiciary have weakened in terms of independence vis-à-vis the executive and legislative branches, highlighted by the Court's removal of the Chief Justice appointed by the previous President through an unprecedented *quo warranto* petition filed by the Solicitor General in 2018.[23] Actors in the justice system have also been individually threatened to an unprecedented degree: 61 lawyers, judges and prosecutors were killed in the first five years of the Duterte administration, more than the combined number (49) of those killed during the administrations from Ferdinand Marcos and ending with Benigno Aquino III, which is equivalent to 44 years.[24]

In 2020, the Supreme Court, dominated by Duterte appointees,[25] denied a petition seeking to declare the Bayanihan 1 Act unconstitutional, rejecting the argument that it showed grave abuse of discretion. However, proof that various groups still see the Supreme Court as the last bastion of democracy and human rights was the number of petitions (37) filed by various groups against the controversial Anti-Terror Law.[26] Oral arguments began, amidst observation of strict safety measures and delayed by various forms of lockdown, in February 2021. As of July 2021, the public awaits the verdict of the Court. In an unprecedented move and giving in to demands for decisive action from lawyers, the Supreme Court *en banc* issued a statement in March 2021[27] condemning the killings of

21 Maila Ager, 'Senators Seek "Review" of Gov't Pandemic Response' (*Philippine Daily Inquirer*, 19 May 2021) <https://newsinfo.inquirer.net/1433857/senators-seek-review-of-govts-pandemic-response>.

22 Nestor Corrales, 'Senators Want Gov't to Spend Bayanihan 2 Budget' (*Philippine Daily Inquirer*, 21 June 2021) <https://newsinfo.inquirer.net/1448596/senators-want-govt-to-spend-bayanihan-2-budget>

23 Imelda Deinla, Veronica Taylor and Steven Rood, 'Philippines: Justice Removed, Justice Denied' (*The Interpreter* (published by the Lowy Institute), 17 May 2018) <https://www.lowyinstitute.org/the-interpreter/philippines-justice-removed-justice-denied>.

24 Lian Buan, 'Lawyers Killed: 61 under Duterte, 49 from Marcos to Aquino' (*Rappler*, 15 March 2021) <https://www.rappler.com/nation/lawyers-killed-duterte-marcos-aquino-administrations-data-studies>.

25 Artemio V Panganiban, 'Duterte's Appointees to Dominate SC' (*Philippine Daily Inquirer*, 21 July 2019) <https://opinion.inquirer.net/122750/duterte-appointees-to-dominate-sc>.

26 Michael Beltran, 'Battle Over Anti-Terror Law Opens at the Philippines' Top Court' (*The Diplomat*, 4 February 2021) <https://thediplomat.com/2021/02/battle-over-anti-terror-law-opens-at-the-philippines-top-court/>.

27 Supreme Court of the Philippines, 'A Statement of the Members of the Court En Banc Responding to Calls for Action on the Killings of Lawyers and Threats to our Judges' (23 March 2021).

lawyers, judges and prosecutors, and vowed to look into institutional changes to better protect them.[28]

Lower courts have ruled on issues related to alleged violations committed by executive agencies in the enforcement of the national health emergency powers. Despite their operations being affected by the pandemic,[29] courts in several instances pointed out that the police and local law enforcers had committed errors in their application of policies related not only to the Bayanihan Acts but also to quarantine laws and related local ordinances, particularly in arresting supposed violators, who were mostly community organisers and people living precariously on low incomes who were trying to continue making a living despite the pandemic.[30]

The judiciary, despite its many challenges even before the pandemic, stepped up its innovations as a result of COVID-19.[31] In order to decongest jails and limit the spread of COVID-19, the Supreme Court revised procedures and instituted videoconferencing hearings to release qualified inmates at the earliest possible time, particularly low-level offenders and sick and elderly prisoners or those detained but qualified to be released based on Supreme Court guidelines. However, human rights groups stated that more inmates, especially political detainees, needed to be released.[32] Courts restarted full operations on 1 June 2020 but only with essential (skeletal) staff for many courts around the country depending on the lockdown status of the locality; videoconferencing hearings continued for cases involving accused who were detained and certain other cases. The Supreme Court also allowed the e-filing of complaints, petition for bail and submission of requirements for bail to minimise physical contact in judicial proceedings during the strict lockdown period. These were significant developments that allowed the courts to continue operating in a pandemic in order to not result in further delays in delivering justice, though access to justice for all sectors remains an issue in the country.

28 Lian Buan, 'Amid Pressure, Supreme Court Condemns Lawyer Killings and Vows Changes' (*Rappler*, 23 March 2021) <https://www.rappler.com/nation/supreme-court-looks-institutional-change-protect-lawyers-after-pressure>.

29 Angelica Carballo Pago, 'Eyes on the Court: Access to PH Justice System Suffers Amid the Lockdown' (Philippine Center for Investigative Journalism, 22 May 2020) <https://pcij.org/article/4090/covid-19-worsens-already-limited-access-to-justice>.

30 See, for example, Lian Buan, 'Court Clears Activists in Quarantine Case: Use of "Broad" Law Improper' (*Rappler*, 10 June 2020) <https://www.rappler.com/nation/court-clears-activists-quarantine-case-notifiable-disease-law-improper>.

31 Atienza and others (n 4).

32 Ellie Aben, 'Philippines' Top Court Moves to Decongest Jails Across the Country over COVID-19 Fears' (*Arab News*, 2 May 2020) <https://www.arabnews.com/node/1668696/world>; Alvin Murcia, 'Phl Judiciary Reports Release of 22.5K PDL' (*Daily Tribune*, 29 May 2020) <https://tribune.net.ph/index.php/2020/05/29/phl-judiciary-reports-release-of-22-5k-pdl/?__cf_chl_jschl_tk__=pmd_7e8ec15c2a864c486f81a2a0fe4919c585a47d22-1627386583-0-gqNtZGzNAmKjcnBszQb6>.

4.3 *The Role of the Commission on Audit*

Another possible source of oversight is the Commission on Audit, one of the independent accountability institutions established in the Constitution that stayed relatively independent even when Duterte became President.[33] However, its auditing report on government spending, particularly for the Bayanihan laws, will only be available after some time. For instance, the Commission only began flagging specific government agencies for underspending Bayanihan funds and some questionable procurements after the prescribed period of the effectiveness of the laws. Thus, while it determined what had not been spent for certain purposes, the opportunity had already been lost to provide immediate assistance to vulnerable sectors as the prescribed period of spending had passed.

5. Regional and Local Government Responses

From the beginning of COVID-19, there were a number of local government units (LGUs) led by fast-thinking and innovative mayors, which were proactive not only in trying to mitigate the spread of the virus in their localities, but also in dealing with the dislocation of constituents and other effects of the lockdown.[34] Some of these LGUs had good coordination with national agencies, but some had to work with the private sector and other civil society groups in the absence of clear instructions from the national government, particularly at the beginning of the pandemic. These LGUs and mayors had at their disposal relatively large budgets and resources compared to other LGUs, as well as skilled local bureaucracy, good data management and evidence-based decision-making, good partnerships with the private sector and civil society groups and participatory mechanisms. However, other LGUs failed to meet the challenges of COVID-19 during the crisis because of limited resources, lack of good management skills, the dominance of patronage politics and corruption.

The inequity in capacity and access to resources among LGUs and how it impacts consistency in effective service delivery, despite significant powers devolved to LGUs since the 1991 Local Government Code (RA No 7160), was further highlighted by the pandemic.[35] Perhaps one beneficial development arising from the pandemic is that there might in the future be a greater role for regional bodies or groupings of LGUs, going beyond administrative coordination and development planning and extending to making and implementing plans appropriate to local conditions, developing coordinated and appropriate services for their constituents

33 Atienza and others (n 4).

34 See, for example, Angelica Villanueva, 'LGUs in Action against COVID-19' (*Manila Standard*, 29 May 2020) <https://www.manilastandard.net/mobile/article/324805>; Samantha Bagayas, 'How to Fight the Pandemic: Women Mayors Don't Sugarcoat How Deadly the Virus is' (*Rappler*, 11 July 2020) <https://www.rappler.com/newsbreak/in-depth/fight-pandemic-women-mayors-do-not-sugarcoat-deadly-virus>.

35 Atienza and others (n 4).

and sharing resources with other LGUs. Regional Inter-Agency Task Forces were also eventually created to be the IATF's local counterparts, although they were supervised by a cabinet member assigned to the region by the President.[36] The newly reconstituted Bangsamoro Autonomous Region in Muslim Mindanao, the only autonomous region with a regional government created as a result of a peace agreement between the Philippine government and Muslim rebels, also worked on the additional challenges posed by COVID-19 in trying to combat the spread of the virus in a poor area where peace is fragile; for example, Friday prayers were suspended and mass gatherings prohibited even during Ramadan.[37]

6. Human Rights and Civil Liberties

The Philippine Constitution's Bill of Rights (Article III) enshrines an extensive list of civil, political and other rights. The Constitution also created an independent Commission on Human Rights. The country is a party to the International Covenant on Civil and Political Rights and the International Covenant on Economic, Social and Cultural Rights. However, despite all these legal instruments and commitments, many of these rights have not been evenly and uniformly implemented since the promulgation of the 1987 Constitution. Extrajudicial killings and other human rights violations have also increased since 2016 when Duterte assumed the presidency.[38]

The pandemic response of the national government certainly curtailed a number of civil, political, social and economic rights. Generally, most people obeyed the lockdown rules for fear of becoming infected with COVID-19. However, many people, especially those on low incomes and without secure employment, required better support for the loss of livelihood as well as equal access to health and other services. The poorly planned and uncoordinated response of the government left a large number of people uninformed, stranded, jobless and without access to proper health services and social welfare. Some had to beg on the streets and try to earn income despite the lockdown. The plight of poorly paid and overworked health workers, especially in public health facilities, came under additional focus due to the pandemic.[39] Even returning overseas Filipino workers, who contributed to the economy from their remittances but lost their jobs abroad due to the pandemic,

36 Ruth Abbey Gita-Carlos, 'IATF Names new Heads of Covid-19 Regional Task Groups' (*Philippine News Agency*, 14 April 2020) <https://www.pna.gov.ph/articles/1099824>.

37 Bai Shaima Baraguir, 'Covid-19 in the Philippines: The Bangsamoro Government's Trial by Fire' (Italian Institute for International Political Studies, 29 May 2020) <https://www.ispionline.it/en/pubblicazione/covid-19-philippines-bangsamoro-governments-trial-fire-26364>.

38 Atienza and others (n 15).

39 Christian Deiparine, 'Health Workers on Gov't Pandemic Response a Year Later: "Inefficient, Negligent, Failure"' (*Philippine Star*, 31 January 2021) <https://www.philstar.com/headlines/2021/01/31/2074334/health-workers-govt-pandemic-response-year-later-inefficient-negligent-failure>; Sofia Tomacruz and Aika Rey, '"Underpaid, Overworked, Unappreciated": PH Deployment Ban Scars Nurses during Pandemic' (*Rappler*, 16 April 2020) <https://www.rappler.com/newsbreak/in-depth/philippines-deployment-ban-scars-nurses-coronavirus-pandemic>.

faced significant challenges. In the middle of 2020, the country experienced its first recession in 29 years,[40] with the unemployment rate in January 2021 at 8.7%.[41] About 4.5 million Filipinos lost their jobs in 2020.[42]

What was also worrying was the punitive, top-down and unequal response to citizens accused of violating curfew and lockdown policies by enforcement authorities (mostly police and local enforcers). The national pandemic response was characterised by executive dominance and a militaristic response instead of a public health and crisis response. Illegal arrests and detention were cases in point, with reports of curfew violators being placed in dog cages, or forced to sit under the midday sun and some even being killed.[43] Even students and volunteers providing feeding programmes and Labour Day protestors were subjected to so-called 'red-tagging' and arrested even though most protests by civil society followed physical distancing protocols. However, inequality in treatment was most clearly evidenced where a majority of those arrested or punished for violations were people from deprived neighbourhoods, while political influencers, government officials and wealthy people who also violated COVID-19 measures were treated humanely and accorded with courtesies by the enforcing authorities.[44] Moreover, extrajudicial killing of suspected drug users and pushers and the 'red-tagging' of critics and those labelled as part of the opposition continued, even extending to university students and professors, entertainers, members of legitimate civil society groups, farmers, indigenous peoples and professionals.

The above observations are substantiated by global indices. The V-Dem Pandemic Democratic Violations Index identified the Philippines as one of seven countries with a high risk of pandemic backsliding.[45] The International IDEA's COVID-19 Monitor, meanwhile, pointed out three worrying areas for the Philippines in the area of rights, namely freedom of expression, media integrity and predictable enforcement of the law.[46]

40 Enrico dela Cruz and Neil Jerome Morales, 'Philippines Suffers First Recession in 29 Years: Braces for Grim Year on Virus Woes' (*Reuters*, 6 August 2020) <https://www.reuters.com/article/us-philippines-economy-gdp-idUSKCN25208X>.

41 Philippine Statistics Authority (PSA), 'Employment Situation in January 2021' (9 March 2021) <https://psa.gov.ph/content/employment-situation-january-2021>.

42 'Philippines Suffers Worst Job Losses in 15 years due to Covid-19 and Lockdown' (*The Straits Times*, 4 December 2020) <https://www.straitstimes.com/asia/se-asia/philippines-suffers-worst-job-losses-in-15-years-due-to-covid-19-and-lockdown>.

43 'Philippines: Curfew Violators Abused' (Human Rights Watch, 26 March 2020) <https://www.hrw.org/news/2020/03/26/philippines-curfew-violators-abused>.

44 Aie Balagtas See, '"They Treated Me like I Murdered Someone": Lockdown Arrests Mark 1st Year of PH Pandemic Response' (Philippine Center for Investigative Journalism, 15 March 2021) <https://pcij.org/article/4836/they-treated-me-like-i-murdered-someone-lockdown-arrests-mark-1st-year-of-ph-pandemic-response>.

45 V-Dem, 'Pandemic Backsliding: Democracy During COVID-19 (March to December 2020)' (2020) <https://www.v-dem.net/en/analysis/PanDem/>.

46 International IDEA, 'Global Monitor of COVID-19's Impact on Democracy and Human Rights: Philippines' (26 May 2021) <https://www.idea.int/gsod-indices/#/indices/countries-regions-profile?rsc=[840]&covid19=1>.

7. Looking Forward

Urgent issues for the Philippines now and beyond the pandemic include the need to exert more active pressure on the executive branch to be accountable for its actions as regards health emergencies and other matters. Such pressure should come from legislators using and strengthening the exercise by Congress of its legislative and oversight functions and a more independent judiciary exercising greater scrutiny and becoming more accessible to citizens. In addition, there needs to be more extensive civilian oversight over the military and the police and stronger political parties and reforms to the electoral system to increase representation. Further, independent accountability institutions like the Commission on Human Rights and the Commission on Audit need to be protected; the rights of citizens upheld; accurate public information and education promoted; and equitable economic development pursued. Another imperative is to strengthen the spirit of community[47] and active citizenship[48] that has been on display so prominently since the pandemic.

The pandemic is a 'game changer' in the immediate future of the Philippines. The 2022 national and local elections, which were already in the minds of both voters and politicians as early as 2020, will add to the complexities of decision-making, including the continuing response to the pandemic. COVID-19 will be an election issue, whether candidates and parties like it or not. There are already indications that since 2020, some citizens and groups are mobilising to push for more effective and equitable responses to the pandemic as well as more progressive multi-sectoral groupings in preparation for the elections. It remains to be seen how successful these will be, given the threats to democracy and the rule of law that predated the pandemic but intensified during it. The pandemic also highlighted the challenge facing progressive and grassroots organisations that were severely weakened by the increasing dominance of elite politicians as the post-1986 euphoria of 'people power' waned, especially under Duterte; their efforts continue to offer a participatory, inclusive and democratic alternative to the current populist and punitive national leadership.

47 Samantha Bagayas, 'Pandemic Can't Stop Bayanihan: How Filipinos Took Action on Urgent Issues in 2020' (*Rappler*, 31 December 2020) <https://www.rappler.com/moveph/times-filipinos-acted-issues-yearend-2020>.

48 Raul Dancel, 'Community Pantries Sprout Across the Philippines Amid Flailing Govt Response to Covid-19 Pandemic' (*The Straits Times*, 20 April 2021) <https://www.straitstimes.com/asia/se-asia/fuelled-by-flailing-govt-response-to-pandemic-community-pantries-sprout-across-the>.

37

ALL BETS ON THE EXECUTIVE(S)! THE AUSTRALIAN RESPONSE TO COVID-19

Marco Rizzi and Tamara Tulich

1. Introduction[1]

Appraising the Australian legal and political response to the COVID-19 pandemic is a difficult task: it has, at the time of writing, been very successful in containing the spread of the disease, yet patchy at best from a rule of law perspective and liable to indefinitely isolate the country from the rest of the world.[2] The first pivotal move was the formation of a new intergovernmental forum, the National Cabinet, tasked with leading a coordinated response to the pandemic. In parallel, multiple states of emergency were declared at both federal and state levels, triggering extraordinary executive powers, including limitations on movement and border closures. While Australia, at the time of writing, has been largely successful in curtailing community transmission of COVID-19, it has done so at the cost of side-lining mechanisms of executive accountability and parliamentary scrutiny, imposing significant restrictions on basic freedoms with little independent oversight. These democratic deficits presented serious challenges, particularly as the National Cabinet became permanent, the vaccination rollout lingered and states of emergency looked set to endure for the foreseeable future.

1 All websites accessed on 9 August 2021.

2 This chapter is based on: Tamara Tulich, Marco Rizzi and Fiona McGaughey, 'Cooperative Federalism, Soft Governance and Hard Laws in Australia's State of Emergency' (*Verfassungsblog*, 10 April 2020) <https://verfassungsblog.de/fighting-covid-19-legal-powers-and-risks-australia/>; Marco Rizzi and Tamara Tulich, 'The Australian Response to COVID-19: A Year in Review' (*Verfassungsblog*, 22 February 2021) <https://verfassungsblog.de/the-australian-response-to-covid-19-a-year-in-review/>. The authors wish to thank Amy Thomasson (UWA Law School) for her outstanding research assistance. All mistakes remain our own.

DOI: 10.4324/9781003211952-42

2. The Executive and the Use of Powers in Response to the Emergency

2.1 The Federal Level: The National Cabinet and the 'Closed Borders' Doctrine

The National Cabinet was formed on 13 March 2020 as a new intergovernmental decision-making body to lead a unified and coordinated response to COVID-19 across Australia. It comprises the Prime Minister of Australia, the Premiers of the six Australian states and the Chief Ministers of the two territories. It is advised by the National Coordination Mechanism[3] on non-health aspects of the pandemic and by the Australian Health Protection Principal Committee[4] on medical issues.

The National Cabinet had some moderate initial success in providing coordinated crisis leadership, resulting in a comparatively manageable first wave of the pandemic.[5] For this reason, in May 2020, the Prime Minister announced that it would become a permanent feature of the Australian political landscape,[6] forming the core of the newly established National Federation Reform Council.[7] The National Cabinet is a prime example of an emergency body becoming crystallised into the institutional framework of the country. It also raises serious questions of transparency and accountability and its operation remains fundamentally opaque.[8]

After its initial success, the National Cabinet suffered major failures, such as the inability to secure a coordinated approach to interstate travel within Australia. Internal border closures restricting movement between states and territories remained entirely at the whim of state and territory governments, and so did decisions on restrictions and lockdowns, generating confusion and alarm amongst Australians.

To implement National Cabinet decisions and contain the spread of COVID-19, all Australian governments relied on emergency executive powers. At the Federal level, successive states of emergency were declared by the Governor

3 Australian Government, 'Emergency Management' (Department of Home Affairs, 29 June 2021) <https://www.homeaffairs.gov.au/about-us/our-portfolios/emergency-management/about-emergency-management/national-coordination-mechanism>.

4 Australian Government, 'Australian Health Protection Principal Committee (AHPPC)' (Department of Health, 28 May 2021) <https://www.health.gov.au/committees-and-groups/australian-health-protection-principal-committee-ahppc>.

5 Stephen Duckett and Anika Stobart, 'Australia's COVID-19 Journey Takes a Turn for the Worse' (Grattan Institute, 12 August 2020) <https://grattan.edu.au/news/australias-covid-19-journey-takes-a-turn-for-the-worse/>.

6 Prime Minister of Australia, 'Update following National Cabinet meeting' (29 May 2020) <https://www.pm.gov.au/media/update-following-national-cabinet-meeting>.

7 This body replaced the Council of Australian Governments (COAG).

8 See below 3.1. Tamara Tulich, Ben Reilly and Sarah Murray, 'The National Cabinet: Presidentialised Politics, Power-Sharing and a Deficit in Transparency' (*AusPubLaw*, 23 October 2020) <https://auspublaw.org/2020/10/the-national-cabinet-presidentialised-politics-power-sharing-and-a-deficit-in-transparency/>; Janina Boughey, 'Executive Power in Emergencies: Where is the Accountability?' (2020) 45(3) Alternative Law Journal 168.

General.[9] The first declaration of a 'human biosecurity emergency' was made on 18 March 2020 and the ensuing state of emergency was extended for successive periods of three months up to the time of writing.[10] Upon the making of such a declaration, the Minister for Health was granted expansive powers under the Biosecurity Act 2015 (Cth) ('Biosecurity Act') to "take any necessary measures to prevent and control COVID-19, and protect the health of all Australians".[11] The Minister issued a number of Determinations, pursuant to s 477 of the Biosecurity Act, including to restrict cruise ship movement[12] and stringently restrict both outgoing ('overseas travel ban')[13] and inbound international travel.[14]

The Minister was expressly permitted to impose requirements that "restrict or prevent the movement of persons, goods or conveyances in or between specific places",[15] subject to a broad proportionality test under s 477(1) and (4). An extraordinary exercise of this power occurred with the Determination known as the 'India travel pause', when the Federal Government banned its own citizens and permanent residents from travelling back to Australia from India between 3 and 15 May 2021[16] during India's devastating second wave. This entailed not only stopping all flights from India to Australia, but the provision of criminal sanctions for citizens and permanent residents returning to Australia who had been in India in the previous 14 days.[17] Faced with significant backlash both internally and internationally,[18] the Prime Minister informed the press that "the likelihood

9 On the advice of the Federal Executive Council, and upon recommendation of the Minister for Health under the Biosecurity Act 2015 (Cth) s 474 (Health minister to be satisfied that declaration is necessary).

10 Biosecurity (Human Biosecurity Emergency) (Human Coronavirus with Pandemic Potential) Declaration 2020 (Cth). The latest extension commenced on 11 June: Biosecurity (Human Biosecurity Emergency) (Human Coronavirus with Pandemic Potential) Variation (Extension No 2) Instrument 2021 (Cth).

11 The Hon Greg Hunt MP, 'Extending the Human Biosecurity Emergency Period by Three Months' (Department of Health, 8 December 2020) <https://www.health.gov.au/ministers/the-hon-greg-hunt-mp/media/extending-the-human-biosecurity-emergency-period-by-three-months>.

12 Biosecurity (Human Biosecurity Emergency) (Human Coronavirus with Pandemic Potential) (Emergency Requirements for Cruise Ships) Determination 2020 (Cth).

13 Biosecurity (Human Biosecurity Emergency) (Human Coronavirus with Pandemic Potential) (Overseas Travel Ban Emergency Requirements) Determination 2020 (Cth).

14 Australian Government, 'Coronavirus (COVID-19) Advice for International Travellers' (Department of Health, 17 June 2021) <https://www.health.gov.au/news/health-alerts/novel-coronavirus-2019-ncov-health-alert/coronavirus-covid-19-restrictions/coronavirus-covid-19-advice-for-international-travellers>.

15 Biosecurity Act (n 9) s 477(3)(b).

16 Biosecurity (Human Biosecurity Emergency) (Human Coronavirus with Pandemic Potential) (Emergency Requirements – High Risk Country Travel Pause) Determination 2021 (Cth), s 2(1). See also Raj, chapter 16.

17 Per s 479 of the Biosecurity Act (n 9), a person who does not comply with "emergency requirements and directions" such as the travel pause can be liable to a penalty of up to five years in jail, a AUD$66,000 (approximately US$48,575 or €41,290) fine, or both.

18 Daniel Hurst, 'UN Raises Serious Human Rights Concerns over Australia's India Travel Ban' (*The Guardian*, 5 May 2021) <https://www.theguardian.com/australia-news/2021/may/05/un-raises-serious-human-rights-concerns-over-australia-india-travel-ban>.

of people being prosecuted for breaching the ban was 'pretty much zero' and 'very remote'".[19] This created a rather peculiar situation in which the very executive that created a specific criminal sanction publicly stated that the sanction would not be enforced two days after its entry into force.

As of 2 July, Australia allowed international travel free of restrictions only with New Zealand ('Trans-Tasman travel bubble'),[20] provided that travellers to New Zealand intended to either solely return to Australia or not return to Australia at all (to avoid the risk of New Zealand being used as a 'hub' for further international travel). Practically, New Zealand was considered an extension of Australian territory for travel purposes, leaving all the inconsistencies and uncertainties of internal border closures between states and territories still in place. The bubble was subject to constant suspension and reopening as outbreaks began and ended in the different states and territories, as well as in New Zealand itself.[21]

The Federal Budget for 2021–2022 assumed a "gradual return of temporary and permanent migrants" from mid-2022; the continued limitation of international arrivals due to quarantine caps "over 2021 and the first half of 2022"; and international travel "expected to remain low through to mid-2022" even applying the hypothesis of a successful vaccine rollout.[22] The budget hinted at the introduction of more 'bubble arrangements', referring to passengers from Safe Travel Zones as an exception to the quarantine caps.[23] However, an outbreak of the Delta variant in the State of New South Wales (NSW) has since plunged the entire east coast of the country into prolonged lockdown, prompting further tightening of border control measures. This included draconian restrictions on Australian citizens resident overseas returning for temporary visits, requiring them to apply for governmental permit to both re-enter and leave Australia.[24]

2.2 The State Level: States of Emergency and Fragmented Approaches

As responsibility for public health resides primarily with the states and territories, all sub-national governments, except NSW,[25] declared states of emergency under

19 Andrew Probyn, 'Indian Travel Ban Headed to Court as Australian Stuck in Bangalore Launches Legal Challenge' (*ABC News*, 5 May 2021) <https://www.abc.net.au/news/2021-05-05/legal-challenge-federal-government-court-india-covid-travel-ban/100115540>.

20 Biosecurity (Human Biosecurity Emergency) (Human Coronavirus with Pandemic Potential) (Overseas Travel Ban Emergency Requirements) Amendment (No 1) Determination 2021 (Cth), and as of 18 April 2021 Biosecurity Legislation (Human Coronavirus with Pandemic Potential) Amendment (No 1) Determination 2021 (Cth). See also Knight, chapter 3.

21 Note that New Zealand suspended the bubble indefinitely on 31 July 2021 in the aftermath of an outbreak of the Delta variant in NSW.

22 Commonwealth of Australia, *Budget 2021–22: Budget Strategy and Outlook* (Budget Paper No 1, 11 May 2021) 36 (Budget).

23 ibid 36.

24 Biosecurity Determination (n 20), Schedule 1 – Amendments.

25 Section 7(1) of the Public Health Act 2010 (NSW) provides that emergency powers are exercisable when there is a "risk to public health", without the need for emergency declarations.

their respective public health laws and/or emergency legislation. For example, in Western Australia (WA), a 'State of Emergency' was declared by the Minister for Emergency Services from 16 March 2020 under s 56 of the Emergency Management Act 2005 (WA), and was extended for 14 days up to the time of writing. Emergency powers thus activated included electronic monitoring of persons in quarantine and powers to direct the closure of premises.[26]

A 'Public Health State of Emergency' was also declared in WA on 23 March 2020, by the Minister for Health under the Public Health Act 2016 (WA), and had similarly been extended every 14 days up to the time of writing. These declarations provided the WA executive with a wealth of powers, including the ability to issue medical directions to individuals and other measures relating to movement and quarantine.[27]

The most significant emergency policy adopted in WA, implemented under ss 67, 70 and 72A of the Emergency Management Act 2005 (WA), was the 'controlled border'.[28] It included measures ranging from an entry pass, health screening and quarantine requirements, to a 'hard interstate border' whereby entry was refused to travellers from other Australian jurisdictions and New Zealand when there are outbreaks, with limited and rigidly regulated exemptions. These measures could apply retrospectively to whomever was in WA territory at the time of adoption and could be made legally binding without any form of parliamentary oversight. Directions adopted under the Act were subject to a bland requirement of being "published in the manner that the Minister considers suitable in the circumstances of the emergency",[29] and failure to do so did not invalidate the direction.[30] However, failure by an individual to comply with any direction constituted an offence punishable by imprisonment for up to 12 months (this penalty was specifically introduced in response to COVID-19)[31] or a very significant fine of up to AUD$50,000 (US$37,400 or €31,500).[32] Breaches of quarantine directions were successfully prosecuted in WA, but custodial sentences were overturned on appeal.[33]

Other states that experienced higher levels of community transmission deployed other restrictive emergency measures, the most significant being the hard lockdown imposed in Melbourne under the Public Health and Wellbeing Act 2008

26 Emergency Management Act 2005 (WA), pt 6.

27 Public Health Act 2016 (WA), pt 12, div 5.

28 Christopher John Dawson, Commissioner of Police and State Emergency Coordinator, 'Controlled Border for Western Australia Directions' (Government of Western Australia, 13 November 2020) <https://www.wa.gov.au/sites/default/files/2020-11/20201113ControlledBorderforWADirections.pdf>. As at 28 June 2021, the 'Controlled Border for Western Australia Directions' are in their 28th iteration – cfr 'Controlled Border for Western Australia Amendment Directions (No 28)'.

29 Emergency Management Act 2005 (WA), s 77(2A)(c).

30 ibid s 77(3).

31 Emergency Management Amendment (COVID-19 Response) Act 2020 (WA), s 13(1)(b).

32 Emergency Management Act 2005 (WA), s 86.

33 *Vander Sanden v Johnson* [2020] WASC 331; *Johnson v Vander Sanden* [2021] WASCA 27; *Tonkin v Busby* [2021] WASC 61

(Vic) in August 2020.[34] Both the WA hard border and the Victorian lockdown were subject to court challenges as discussed below.

From the start of 2021, several states adopted the strategy of imposing short 'snap' or 'circuit breaker' lockdowns of a few days to crush emerging outbreaks in response to as little as one case of community transmission.[35] While this strategy was implemented with a certain degree of consistency in WA, Queensland and the Northern Territory, the more populous states of Victoria and NSW tended to delay lockdowns until community transmission was more established. In particular, the NSW response to an outbreak of the so-called Delta variant in June 2021 attracted severe criticisms and arguably caused a domino effect of subsequent restrictions adopted in most other states and territories.[36]

2.3 The Vaccine Rollout Strategy

The vaccine rollout strategy has been, to date, a resounding failure, plagued by insufficient supply,[37] chaotic communication with erratic shifts in policy targets[38] and growing levels of hesitancy.[39] At the end of June 2021, Australia had the lowest percentage of fully vaccinated population among OECD countries – a grim 4.7%.[40]

It is difficult to disentangle politics from laws and norms in this space, but technically the rollout was administered pursuant to the Australian Vaccination and Treatment Strategy and the Rollout Strategy[41] adopted by the National

34 Holly Mclean and Ben Huf, 'Emergency Powers, Public Health and COVID-19' (2020) Department of Parliamentary Services Research Paper No 2 <https://www.parliament.vic.gov.au/publications/research-papers/send/36-research-papers/13962-emergency-powers-public-health-and-covid-19>.

35 For example: Queensland Government, 'Restrictions for Impacted Areas – South East Queensland, Townsville (including Magnetic Island and palm Island)' (2 July 2021) <https://www.qld.gov.au/health/conditions/health-alerts/coronavirus-covid-19/current-status/public-health-directions/restrictions-impacted-areas>. Similar measures were adopted by Western Australia and the Northern Territory around the same dates.

36 Aisha Dow and Melissa Cunningham, 'NSW Too Slow to Lock Down so Borders Should be Closed: Epidemiologists' (*The Age*, 28 June 2021) <https://www.theage.com.au/national/victoria/nsw-too-slow-to-lock-down-so-borders-should-be-closed-epidemiologists-20210628-p584y4.html>.

37 'What's Gone Wrong with Australia's Vaccine Rollout?' (*BBC News*, 17 June 2021) <https://www.bbc.com/news/world-australia-56825920>. See also Singh, chapter 2.

38 Inga Ting, Nathanael Scott and Alex Palmer, 'Untangling Australia's Vaccine Rollout Timetable' (*ABC News*, 30 May 2021) <https://www.abc.net.au/news/2021-05-28/untangling-australia-s-covid-vaccine-rollout-timetable/100156720>.

39 Nicholas Biddle and others, 'Vaccine Willingness and Concerns in Australia: August 2020 to April 2021' (2021) ANU Centre for Social Research & Methods Research Paper <https://csrm.cass.anu.edu.au/sites/default/files/docs/2021/5/Vaccine_willingness_and_concerns_in_Australia_-_August_2020_to_April_2021.pdf>.

40 Our World in Data, 'Coronavirus (COVID-19) Vaccinations' (Statistics and Research, 30 June 2021) <https://ourworldindata.org/covid-vaccinations>.

41 Australian Government, 'COVID-19 Vaccine and Treatment Strategy' (Department of Health, 27 January 2021) <https://www.health.gov.au/initiatives-and-programs/covid-19-vaccines/about-covid-19-vaccines/covid-19-vaccine-and-treatment-strategy>.

Cabinet. The fifth element of the strategy is the Australian COVID-19 Vaccination Policy,[42] which was implemented through the Australian Government COVID-19 Implementation Plan, with each state and territory responsible for "developing jurisdictional implementation plans".[43] The strategy created 'priority populations' and a phased rollout approach based on vulnerability levels identified by the Department of Health after consultation with the Australian Technical Advisory Group on Immunisation (ATAGI).[44] Decisions on prioritisation were described by the policy as "difficult and contentious".[45] Crucially, none of the documents mentioned here were expressed as being made pursuant to any written law. In response to a specific inquiry as to the legal basis of the Strategy, the Department of Health COVID-19 Vaccine Taskforce confirmed that "policy decisions of National Cabinet regarding priority cohorts do not require legislation or any other legislative instruments to support their implementation".[46]

As of 2 July 2021, there has been little national consistency in the rollout, with states and territories opening and closing vaccination to different age groups regardless of the original prioritisation scheme.[47] Concerns have also been raised about several aspects of the rollout strategy, including supply flows from the national to the state level and potential age discrimination as young people were turned away from empty vaccination centres.[48] Further problems may arise should the government move in the direction of easing restrictions (such as quarantine requirements for returning travellers) for fully vaccinated individuals, as envisaged in the vaccination policy. Indeed, it is unclear what (if any) mechanisms of accountability, such as judicial review, may be available in this regard.

3. Legislative Scrutiny and Judicial Oversight

3.1 The National Cabinet: Amorphous and Unchallengeable?

As noted in section 2.1, the National Cabinet raises questions of transparency and accountability. First, it is established as a Committee of the Federal Cabinet.[49]

42 Australian Government, 'Australian COVID-19 Vaccination Policy' (13 November 2020) 2 <https://www.health.gov.au/sites/default/files/documents/2020/12/covid-19-vaccination-australian-covid-19-vaccination-policy.pdf>.

43 ibid 7.

44 Australian Government, 'Australia's COVID-19 Vaccine National Roll-out Strategy' (7 January 2021) <https://www.health.gov.au/sites/default/files/documents/2021/01/covid-19-vaccination-australia-s-covid-19-vaccine-national-roll-out-strategy.pdf>.

45 Australian Government (n 42) 11.

46 Email from COVID-19 Vaccine Taskforce to the lead author (17 June 2021).

47 Sarah Swain, 'Can You Get a COVID-19 Vaccination Yet? State-by-State Guide' (*9News*, 17 June 2021) <https://www.9news.com.au/national/coronavirus-vaccine-update-australia-state-by-state-guide-who-can-get-covid19-vaccine-explainer/103ad605-d711-4b06-8334-8f26731561b1>.

48 Luke Beck, 'Vaccine Rollout Looks Discriminatory Against Young People' (*The Sydney Morning Herald*, 13 June 2021) <https://www.smh.com.au/national/vaccine-rollout-looks-discriminatory-against-young-people-20210613-p580m2.html>.

49 Commonwealth of Australia, 'Cabinet Handbook' (Department of Prime Minister and Cabinet, 16 October 2020).

A cabinet is the primary decision-making organ of executive governments in Australia and is held accountable to Parliament through the convention of responsible government. Yet, important aspects of this convention – cabinet *confidentiality*, *solidarity* and *collective cabinet responsibility* – are disrupted by the National Cabinet.

Cabinet confidentiality protects internal discussions and documents from disclosure. Cabinet documents and deliberations, including those of the National Cabinet, are classified as exempt documents under State and Federal freedom of information (FOI) legislation[50] – shielded from a key mechanism for ensuring democratic accountability of executives in Australia.[51] Senator Rex Patrick of South Australia, after being denied access to National Cabinet documents several times, applied to the FOI Division of the Administrative Appeals Tribunal (AAT) for review. On social media, Senator Patrick explained that he is fighting for transparency, for "the preservation of responsible government" and for the right to access information pertaining to intergovernmental meetings.[52] On 5 August, the AAT handed down a decision in favour of Senator Patrick,[53] in what is arguably the first instance of substantive pushback against the otherwise unfettered dominance of the executive since the start of the pandemic. The Tribunal found that the National Cabinet cannot benefit from FOI exemptions "merely because the Prime Minister of the day has purported to establish it as [a federal Cabinet committee]".[54] At the time of writing, the Federal Government is considering whether to appeal the decision.

As for the principle of *cabinet solidarity*, this requires cabinet members to show public support for its decisions, regardless of their individual views. Additionally, cabinets are normally accountable through *collective cabinet responsibility* to the Parliament from which they are drawn. However, because the National Cabinet is an intergovernmental body, its members are not collectively responsible to one Parliament, but individually responsible to nine separate parliaments and the interests of their constituencies. The principles of collective responsibility and solidarity are therefore ineffective in this context.

3.2 Delegated Legislation and Parliamentary Scrutiny in States of Emergency

Parliamentary scrutiny and oversight of delegated legislation, or legislative instruments, enables accountability of executive action taken under states of emergency across Australia. As of 17 June 2021, the Commonwealth Senate Standing Committee for the Scrutiny of Delegated Legislation (SCSDL) found that 494

50 Freedom of Information Act 1982 (Cth); every state and territory has analogous legislation.

51 Boughey (n 8) 168.

52 Senator Rex Patrick, '*Rex v Scott*: An Important Fight' (*Facebook*, 22 May 2021) <https://www.facebook.com/permalink.php?story_fbid=927206971173053&id=193047494589008>.

53 *Patrick and Secretary, Department of Prime Minister and Cabinet (Freedom of Information)* [2021] AATA 2719 (5 August 2021).

54 ibid [67].

legislative instruments had been made in response to COVID-19,[55] a significant number of which are exempt from disallowance. This meant that they were protected from parliamentary scrutiny. The SCSDL, in its interim report into the exemption of delegated legislation from parliamentary oversight, observed that between 1 January and 31 July 2020, 20% of all instruments made in response to COVID-19 were exempt from disallowance.[56] By the end of 2020, the percentage of exempt instruments remained at 17%.[57] In its interim report, the SCSDL formed the view that emergency-related delegated legislation engaging individual rights and liberties should not be quarantined from parliamentary scrutiny and oversight, including through disallowance procedures.[58]

Parliamentary oversight and scrutiny were further curtailed by suspensions in parliamentary sittings.[59] In 2020, the National Parliament was suspended from 23 March to 11 August,[60] far exceeding the number of sitting days cancelled in Canada, France, Germany, New Zealand, Spain, the UK and the US despite the incomparably lower impact of the pandemic in Australia.[61] Six out of Australia's eight sub-national parliaments also cancelled sitting days due to the pandemic.[62] This stands in contrast to parliamentary sittings during World War I, World War II and the Spanish Flu when suspensions did not occur.[63]

At the Federal level, the exemption of legislative instruments from disallowance has flow on effects for parliamentary scrutiny of human rights pursuant to the Human Rights (Parliamentary Scrutiny) Act 2011 (Cth). In 2011, Australia introduced a parliamentary scrutiny model of human rights protection at the Federal level,[64] whereby bills and delegated legislation are scrutinised for their compli-

55 Parliament of Australia, Senate Standing Committee for the Scrutiny of Delegated Legislation, 'Scrutiny of COVID-19 Instruments' (26 June 2021) <https://www.aph.gov.au/Parliamentary_Business/Committees/Senate/Scrutiny_of_Delegated_Legislation/Scrutiny_of_COVID-19_instruments>.

56 Parliament of Australia, Senate Standing Committee for the Scrutiny of Delegated Legislation, *Inquiry into the Exemption of Delegated Legislation From Parliamentary Oversight – Interim Report* (Parliament of Australia 2020) 48.

57 Yee-Fui Ng and Stephen Gray, 'Wars, Pandemics and Emergencies: What Can History Tell Us About Executive Power And Surveillance In Times Of Crisis?' (2020) 44(1) UNSW Law Journal 227, 259.

58 ibid.

59 ibid 257.

60 Both Houses of Parliament returned to consider COVID-19 related legislation on 8 April and 12 to 14 May 2020.

61 Parliament of Australia (n 56) 40. See also Basilien-Gainche, chapter 35 (France); Mangold, chapter 27 (Germany); Knight, chapter 3 (New Zealand); Grogan, chapter 5 (United Kingdom); Graber, chapter 6 (United States).

62 Parliament of Australia (n 56); Nicholas Horne, 'COVID-19 and Parliamentary Sittings' (*FlagPost*, 2 April 2020) <https://www.aph.gov.au/About_Parliament/Parliamentary_Departments/Parliamentary_Library/FlagPost/2020/April/COVID-19_and_parliamentary_sittings>; Ng and Gray (n 57) 257.

63 Ng and Gray (n 57) 259.

64 See generally: George Williams and Daniel Reynolds, 'Parliamentary Human Rights Vetting and Deliberation' in Ron Levy, Hoi Kong, Graeme Orr and Jeff King (eds), *The Cambridge Handbook*

ance with human rights contained in seven international instruments identified in s 3(1). However, the Act excludes from this scrutiny any legislative instrument exempt from disallowance.[65] Notwithstanding, under s 7 the Parliamentary Joint Committee on Human Rights examines legislative instruments for compatibility with human rights and reports to Parliament on the issue. The joint committee has taken this function seriously, examining and reporting on the instruments exempt from disallowance under the Biosecurity Act. However, the legislative exemption from provision of a statement of compatibility for exempt instruments has hamstrung its role – leaving unanswerable "whether all of the measures are reasonable, necessary and proportionate".[66]

3.3 *Judicial and Other Independent Forms of Oversight*

At the time of writing, measures adopted by federal and state governments have attracted relatively little litigation and, more importantly, governments have almost always prevailed, except for the AAT decision on FOI.

3.3.1 Court Challenges to Federal Measures

Two court challenges were brought before the Federal Court of Australia against national measures: the 'India travel pause' and the 'overseas travel ban'. Both failed.

In the first case,[67] a Melbourne man challenged the India travel pause claiming that it either infringed on a common law right of citizens to re-enter the country,[68] or that it was beyond power as laid out in the Biosecurity Act. This was broken down into two arguments. First, that the Minister for Health had not complied with the proportionality requirements outlined in the Act,[69] and secondly, that the travel pause had an impermissible extraterritorial effect.

The Federal Court rejected the first argument, finding that a sufficient intent to abrogate the common law right to re-enter Australia could be found in the wording of s 477.[70] The Court referred to it being a "necessary incident of the scheme contemplated by Ch 8 [of the Biosecurity Act] that a person may be prevented from both entering and leaving Australia".[71]

---

of Deliberative Constitutionalism (Cambridge University Press 2018) 72; Stephen Gardbaum, 'The New Commonwealth Model of Constitutionalism' (2001) 49(4) American Journal of Comparative Law 707.

65 Human Rights (Parliamentary Scrutiny) Act 2011 (Cth), s 9(1).

66 Parliamentary Joint Committee on Human Rights, *Human Rights Scrutiny Report* (Commonwealth of Australia, Report 12 of 2020).

67 *Newman v Minister for Health and Aged Care* [2021] FCA 517 (*Newman*).

68 Australia does not have a constitutional or statutory bill of rights at the Federal level. Queensland, Victoria and the ACT are the only jurisdictions to have introduced human rights legislation. No constitutional right of entry for citizens exists.

69 Biosecurity Act (n 9) s 477(4).

70 *Newman* (n 67) [82].

71 ibid.

The Court also rejected the second argument, that the minister's actions were disproportionate,[72] finding the travel pause "no more restrictive or intrusive than is required in the circumstances".[73] This conclusion was justified on the basis that the minister had received and considered advice from the Commonwealth's Chief Medical Officer, who said that banning travel from India was necessary to protect public health.[74] The Court also found that the measure did not operate extraterritorially, as it simply made it an offence to enter Australian territory and "[l] egislation does not operate extraterritorially merely because it might have some relationship to events which occur overseas, such as boarding a flight".[75]

In the second case before the Federal Court, the thinktank LibertyWorks initiated a judicial review challenge to the international travel ban,[76] arguing that the Minister for Health only had the power to stop an individual from leaving the country,[77] rather than a group of individuals such as all permanent residents and Australian citizens via a Determination under s 477(1). The Court concluded that to interpret the Minister's power as subject to such limitations would "eviscerate" or "at least emasculate" it and "frustrate the Parliament's clear intention in enacting emergency powers".[78] The Court explained that such an interpretation would be completely impractical and effectively require biosecurity control orders to be made for every individual who planned to leave the country.[79]

LibertyWorks submitted that its argument was supported by the principle of legality and Article 12 of the ICCPR (freedom of movement).[80] The Court rejected this submission because it proceeded on the basis that the right is absolute, while it is not given that restrictions on various grounds, including public health, are expressly permitted.[81] The Court concluded that the proportionality requirements of s 477(4) of the Biosecurity Act are sufficient to protect freedom of movement.[82]

3.3.2 Court Challenges to State Measures

At the state level there were three main court challenges to pandemic executive measures. All saw the relevant state government emerge victorious. The most important challenge was brought in the High Court of Australia by mining magnate Clive Palmer against WA's 'hard interstate border'.[83] Palmer claimed that the directions

72 ibid [52], [59], [61].
73 ibid [61].
74 ibid.
75 ibid [63].
76 *LibertyWorks Inc v Commonwealth of Australia* [2021] FCAFC 90 (*LibertyWorks*).
77 A power granted under s 96 of the Biosecurity Act (n 9).
78 *LibertyWorks* (n 76) [63].
79 ibid [64].
80 ibid [70].
81 ibid [71].
82 ibid.
83 *Palmer v Western Australia* [2021] HCA 5. See also *Palmer v State of Western Australia (No 4)* [2020] FCA 1221 for factual findings in the case.

and/or the empowering provisions in the Emergency Management Act 2005 (WA) authorising the border closure violated s 92 of the Australia Constitution that provides "trade, commerce, and intercourse among the states … shall be absolutely free". The High Court dismissed the claim, finding that s 56 of the Emergency Management Act (the power to declare a state of emergency) and s 67 (the power to prohibit the movement of persons into a declared emergency area) of the Act did not impermissibly infringe upon s 92 of the Constitution. The Court accepted that s 67 burdened interstate movement, but that this burden was justified in the circumstances:

> the restrictions are severe, but it cannot be denied that the importance of the protection of health and life amply justifies the severity of the measures.[84]

The second challenge was brought to the High Court by a hotel owner in Melbourne, against a direction of the Victorian government limiting the movement of individuals to 25km from their home. The argument was that the Australian Constitution establishes an implied freedom of movement of residents within a state, allegedly contravened by the direction. The Court however was not satisfied that such an implication could be drawn from the text and structure of the Constitution and dismissed the case.[85]

Finally, a challenge was brought in the Victorian Supreme Court by a cafe owner in Melbourne. She argued that curfews imposed in Victoria breached the rights to freedom of movement and liberty enshrined in the Charter of Human Rights and Responsibilities Act 2006 (Vic). While acknowledging that measures such as curfews represent major restrictions on individual rights, the Court dismissed the claim finding curfews a proportionate curtailment of such rights for the protection of public health in an emergency.[86]

George Williams observed that Australia has "a long record of deferring to government at a time of national crisis".[87] Deference in this context has translated into a significant margin of manoeuvre left to executive governments at all levels, particularly in the absence of an agreed national containment strategy.

It is finally worth noting a parallel line of cases that have tackled the impact of COVID-19 restrictions on freedom of association and political communication. Litigation in NSW challenging restrictions on the Black Lives Matter protests that took place in June–July 2020 brought this issue to the fore with variable results.[88]

84 ibid [81].

85 *Gerner v Victoria* [2020] HCA 48.

86 *Loielo v Giles* [2020] VSC 722.

87 George Williams, 'No Good Reason to Hide Powers from Parliament's Eye' (*The Australian*, 6 December 2020) <https://www.theaustralian.com.au/commentary/no-good-reason-to-hide-powers-from-parliaments-eye/news-story/3cba3f7c9539f8dafc999d4cac41b5af>.

88 *Raul Bassi v Commissioner of Police (NSW)* [2020] NSWCA 109; *Commissioner of Police v Gray* [2020] NSWSC 867; *Commissioner of Police (NSW) v Supple* [2020] NSWSC 727; *Commissioner of Police (NSW) v Gibson* [2020] NSWSC 953.

These cases involved a complex balance between free speech and the protection of public health.[89] Protests are typically characterised as non-essential activities and are not the subject of exemptions during lockdowns, despite other activities such as community sports being permitted, which has contributed to courts taking a permissive approach in some cases.[90] Rather than seeking to ban protests, other states opted for a softer approach of urging people not to attend, emphasising existing COVID-19 restrictions limiting outdoor gatherings.[91]

3.3.3 Other Forms of Independent Oversight

The Victorian Ombudsman conducted a thorough investigation into the detention and treatment of public housing residents during a COVID-19 'hard lockdown' in July 2020 in Melbourne.[92] This measure preceded the hard lockdown imposed on the entire metropolitan area later in August and was specifically aimed at the residents of nine public housing towers across two inner suburbs of Melbourne. The investigation made several distressing findings, showing that the implementation of the targeted lockdown was wholly disproportionate and prejudicial to the affected residents. It was oblivious to health and wellbeing issues, as well as to cultural and linguistic diversity, both of which should have been a prime concern given the nature of the premises. The Victorian government acknowledged the findings and recommendations of the reports in December 2020.[93] At the time of writing, it remains unclear what, if any, material consequence will ensue.

4. The 'New Normal'?

At the time of writing, Australia is in a peculiar position. From a public health perspective, it has so far successfully prevented the spread of COVID-19 through blunt instruments such as lockdowns and border closures. However, the cost has been a staggering level of uncertainty, with states driving the response internally through different strategies and the Federal Government receding to external border control and unsuccessful attempts at rolling out vaccination.

89 Maria O'Sullivan, 'Protest in a Pandemic – The Special Status of Public Spaces' (*AusPubLaw*, 27 July 2020) <https://auspublaw.org/2020/07/protest-in-a-pandemic-the-special-status-of-public-spaces/>.

90 ibid.

91 Eliza Laschon, 'Coronavirus Rules Mean Protesters Should Not Attend Black Lives Matter Rallies, WA Premier Says' (*ABC News*, 9 June 2020) <https://www.abc.net.au/news/2020-06-09/coronavirus-rules-black-lives-matter-protest-warning-wa-premier/12334446>.

92 Victorian Ombudsman, *Investigation into the Detention and Treatment of Public Housing Residents Arising from a COVID-19 'Hard Lockdown' in July 2020* (17 December 2020) <https://www.ombudsman.vic.gov.au/our-impact/investigation-reports/investigation-into-the-detention-and-treatment-of-public-housing-residents-arising-from-a-covid-19-hard-lockdown-in-july-2020/>.

93 Premier of Victoria, 'Statement on Victorian Ombudsman Housing Report' (17 December 2020) <https://www.premier.vic.gov.au/statement-victorian-ombudsman-housing-report>.

A striking feature of this period was the absolute prevalence of the executive (federal and state) over other branches of government and of political expediency over legal processes and guarantees. The 'India travel pause' judgment highlighted the meagre substance of fundamental rights attached to Australian citizenship and permanent residency. As colourfully put by counsel for the Australian Government in the case, the Biosecurity Act is a "legislative bulldozer".[94] This is a fitting metaphor. Over the past eighteen months the Federal bulldozer (and its state equivalents) pushed aside rights and guarantees while leaving little room for challenge and accountability. The absence of substantive fundamental rights protection in Australia was certainly an important factor in the customary deference shown by courts to executive action. In this context, the recent AAT decision allowing FOI requests on National Cabinet documents could represent a first step towards re-establishing checks and balances, at least for the purpose of transparency.

We finished drafting this chapter at the beginning of July 2021, surrounded by states and territories continuing to plunge into hard lockdowns, a lagging vaccine rollout and no clear idea of how long this 'new normal' will endure. For how long the current unfettered prevalence of the executive(s), coupled with the mix of internal fragmentation and international isolation, will be sustainable is a pressing question, exacerbated by the increasingly uneven distribution of the social and financial cost of restrictions.

As the prospect of a prolonged state of emergency is no longer an abstraction but a concrete reality, Australia must interrogate its institutional, legal and political architecture to not merely deliver prompt muscular responses, but transparent processes, clear guarantees and substantive protections.

94 Elizabeth Byrne, 'Federal Court Throws Out Part of Challenge to Federal Government's India Travel Ban' (*ABC News,* 10 May 2021) <https://www.abc.net.au/news/2021-05-10/federal-court-judge-throws-out-part-of-india-travel-ban/100129520>.

BEYOND THE PANDEMIC

38

LESSONS FOR A 'POST-PANDEMIC' FUTURE

Joelle Grogan and Alice Donald

1. Introduction

It is difficult to imagine readers in the future, sitting without face-masks, in close proximity to each other and with distant memories of the restrictions and isolation which existed at the height of the COVID-19 pandemic. As we write for them now – with trepidation – about such a 'post-pandemic' future, our one certainty is that it is essential for us to learn the lessons of our pandemic present. Some of these lessons are hard: the pandemic aggravated endemic socio-economic inequalities and exposed geopolitical fault lines. Nationalism and self-interest generally trumped global action, welfare and solidarity. Desperate populations lost their livelihoods and found no social safety net. Authoritarian governance and 'anti-truth' politics burgeoned. Other lessons are more hopeful: democratic institutions seized opportunities (and technologies) for innovation and renewal, and communities and institutions at different levels of governance mobilised in mutual support.

While this volume aimed to analyse the *law* and the COVID-19 pandemic, as evidenced within every chapter, it is impossible to separate the law from the wider social, economic and political contexts in which it operates. The capacity of healthcare, administrative, regulatory and justice systems to function and adapt, and the political courage of leaders to respond quickly and with sustainable effect, were as relevant to effective pandemic response as whether or not there was a provision on the statute books or in a constitution to regulate action in during a health emergency. Similarly, in democracies, commitment to upholding fundamental constitutional values depended on the willingness of executives to adhere to them and, crucially, a healthy separation of powers to ensure scrutiny of the drastic restrictions that, almost overnight, separated families and closed borders and places of work and education. Beyond these systems is the wider social and human dimension: the communities, the civil society and the *citizen* living in the pandemic world and their trust, or distrust, in the institutions that govern them.

DOI: 10.4324/9781003211952-44

Trust depends in part on the existence of a shared language and commitment to truth and reason in public discourse. Many competing narratives framed the responses to COVID-19, and these will doubtless be reinvented in the years ahead. These narratives were frequently adversarial and reductive, simplifying complex systems and values to straw men and anaemic shades of thought: 'autocracy is more effective than democracy during a pandemic', 'health trumps rights' and 'lives versus livelihoods' were some of the regrettable tropes that sought to influence policy choices during the first two years of the pandemic.

It is imperative, then, to draw lessons from the pandemic that eschew fallacious and simplistic narratives in favour of those based on evidence, in all its complexity. In the same vein, examining what was done, and what should have been done, in a single national context is insular. By examining collective experience, critical insights can be provided about the health of national and global governance institutions and their capacity and preparedness to respond effectively to health emergencies and pan-global crisis. Below, we reflect on the lessons that emerge from the rich accounts of pandemic responses in this volume and the imperatives we draw from this experience to guide future action and ensure that the world is better prepared for the next emergency.

2. Lessons about how States Performed During the Pandemic

A connecting theme of this volume is the extent to which assumptions about how states would perform in the face of COVID-19 – based on regime type, pre-existing legal frameworks or assessments of preparedness – proved to be unreliable. This is not to say that the pandemic transformed legal systems, institutions or governments or set in motion a pattern of democratic deconsolidation that was not already visible. Rather, it generally had the effect of accelerating pre-existing trends and exposing the true character of regimes (witness, for instance, how China's response reflected deeply entrenched features of its law and governance). As chapters in this volume attest, pre-commitment to accountability, transparency and good governance tended to be reflected in a pandemic response that maintained these values (Finland, New Zealand, Taiwan), while autocratising or militarised states frequently seized upon the virus as a pretext to entrench power at the centre and treated it as a security problem as much as a health crisis (India, Hungary, the Philippines, Thailand, Turkey). Likewise, states habituated to forms of emergency rule continued that unfortunate trajectory (Egypt, France, Hungary, Malaysia).

Nevertheless, regime type was not a sure predictor of either the *form* of state response or its *outcome* in terms of suppressing infections or deaths: states on the spectrum from democracy to autocracy proved equally, and unpredictably, vulnerable in terms of both health and institutional outcomes. The breadth of pandemic responses across political systems (and the kaleidoscope of experience within each regime type) exposes this variation. Some autocrats used COVID-19 as a pretext for disproportionate restrictions and power grabs which did not, however, prevent catastrophic mortality rates (Orbán in Hungary); others cost lives through their inaction, denial and fantastical thinking (Bolsonaro in Brazil). Some established democracies modelled a response that protected both public health and the 'health' of legal and political institutions (Finland, New Zealand, Taiwan); others fell disastrously short on both these counts (the United Kingdom, the United States under Trump). In states on the spectrum between authoritarianism and democracy, the pandemic appeared to pull systems in different and sometimes unexpected directions: towards democratic consolidation (Singapore) or along the opposite path (Malaysia).

Nor were pre-existing legal frameworks necessarily a reliable guide for what actions countries would take once the pandemic hit. Some states utilised existing statutory or constitutional emergency frameworks (Colombia, Thailand) but others did not invoke such frameworks (India, Turkey), or rapidly amended them (Germany). Other states swiftly enacted laws specifically designed to respond to COVID-19 (France, the United Kingdom) or created centralised bodies to do so, sometimes without properly delegated authority (Iran, Pakistan). By contrast, one state eschewed legal measures to instead rely on non-binding recommendations and decentralised administration (Sweden). Likewise there was variation in respect of whether states that declared formal emergencies reported derogations or limitations to the relevant international institutions (Colombia) or failed to do so (Hungary). The decision of whether or not to invoke emergency provisions, even where it could be justified as the more appropriate legal basis for the measures subsequently adopted by governments, often appeared to be primarily determined by political choice informed by wider socio-historical context – for example, negative historical associations with the abuse of power during a previous emergency (India, South Africa).

The *consequences* of such choices in terms of protecting democratic accountability and the rule of law also present a mixed picture: the declaration of a state of emergency or the use of emergency powers was not necessarily an indicator of abusive practices where it was accompanied by robust democratic accountability (New Zealand, Taiwan), and nor was rejection of emergency measures in favour of ordinary legislation or other non-emergency measures definitive proof of good governance where it opened the door to unchecked executive discretion (India, Turkey).

By the same token, pre-COVID-19 estimations of states' *preparedness* for a health emergency proved to be fundamentally mistaken. The 2019 Global Health Security Index ranked the United States and the United Kingdom first and second globally for their 'pandemic preparedness',[1] yet they were manifestly exposed as being ill-prepared; by the same token, some states (such as Rwanda, ranked 117th[2]) outperformed expectations. This comparison also indicates the unreliability of a state's income as a predictor of public health outcomes, with prior experience of confronting a pandemic, deployment of technology, community mobilisation, and

1 NTI and Johns Hopkins Center for Health Security, *2019 Global Health Security Index* (October 2019) 20 https://www.ghsindex.org/wp-content/uploads/2020/04/2019-Global-Health-Security-Index.pdf accessed 15 January 2022.

2 ibid 26.

trust in public health messaging being crucial factors in Rwanda's relative success (along with that of states such as Singapore and Taiwan). A lesson for the future, then, is the need to review how pandemic preparedness is measured, particularly where predictions are then the focus for investment and development: it is not only health security indicators that matter, but also indicators relating to good governance and public trust, for these have proved inseparable during the COVID-19 pandemic.

A further lesson is the need to understand the divergence between laws on paper, and laws as they were applied in practice during the COVID-19 crisis. This volume is replete with instances that demonstrate the need to design laws to confront infectious disease with appropriate safeguards to ensure conformity with the principles of legality, legal certainty, accountability, prevention of the misuse of power, access to justice and equality before the law. Yet attention must also be paid to the environment in which law is applied and the health of the institutions that oversee its enforcement. Arbitrariness, corruption, abuses of power, sluggish bureaucracies, misguided thinking and sheer complacency flourish where parliaments are suspended, side-lined or abdicate their duties of oversight (Australia, Egypt, France, Hungary, India, Iran, Kenya, Malaysia, Pakistan, the Philippines, Thailand, Turkey); judiciaries are supine (Hungary, India, Iran, Malaysia, the Philippines, Thailand, Turkey); watchdog bodies are hobbled (Colombia); or civil society mobilisation is suppressed (Colombia, the Philippines, Turkey). Such negative externalities not only correlate with a poor response to pandemic emergency, but also entrench perception of the weak capacity of these institutions beyond pandemic conditions. The positive inverse of this analysis is states whose democratic institutions rose to the challenge of the pandemic and ensured real-time oversight of restrictive measures, ensuring that they could be interrogated, fine-tuned and as a consequence enjoy greater public confidence (New Zealand, Taiwan).

Yet another insight emerging from this book is that states do not generally present a picture of either unalloyed success or rampant failure, especially when we look beyond the centralised institutions of the state towards regional and local governance and civil society. Three findings stand out from our contributors' analyses. First, in some countries where federal executives and bureaucracies were weak or ineffective in their response to the pandemic, regional or local governments, civil society organisations and grassroots communities were catalysed into implementing measures of containment and creating networks of support (Brazil, Kenya, the Philippines, South Africa). Civil society mobilisation, and the receptiveness of state institutions to such pressure, can not only improve the quality of governance and decision making, but also increase public compliance; take, for example, instances where 'track and trace' apps were modified in response to loudly-expressed privacy concerns by the public and civil society, thereby encouraging wider take-up (Singapore, Taiwan). Second, progress in terms of pandemic response was not linear, and not only because of regime changes (such as the dramatic shift from Trump to Biden): take, for example, Kenya, which introduced social protection measures early on, only to withdraw them without justification; or China, whose initial troubled response was supplanted by a more concerted (if draconian) mobilisation of resources. A temporal dimension must therefore be built into any analysis of a state's response. Third, even in states that performed poorly overall from a public health or rule of law perspective, elements of good practice were visible, frequently connected to innovation through technology: digital democracy practices and use of technology to enable people to access justice, education and other public services must be sustained as an enduring and positive consequence of the necessity of isolation in regimes of all types.

Evidently, then, we should not view either individual states or regime types as monolithic when assessing their performance during the pandemic or their preparedness for future emergencies. To do so is to blind ourselves to the lessons that emerge from the variation of experience documented in this volume. To assume that autocratising states will contain the virus more effectively than democracies that respect constitutional restraints on executive power is to ignore the evidence that to control a population is not necessarily to control disease (as Hungary has learned), just as initial control of infection will not forgive consequent complacency (as the Philippines, Malaysia and India demonstrated to devastating consequence). In the same vein, to understand the wide variations in health outcomes between more-or-less democratic states requires apprehension of the symbiosis between, on the one hand, health systems and, on the other hand, institutions that ensure good governance and protection of democracy, human rights and the rule of law.

Certainly, approaching the pandemic as a 'zero-sum' game, in which saving lives trumped respect for other rights and freedoms, proved misguided. States that embraced this approach (exemplified by the Thai prime minister's "health before rights" slogan) tended to sacrifice one to protect neither. Rather, the pandemic was a dramatic confirmation of what has long been an orthodoxy in human rights practice and scholarship – that the rights to life, health and other freedoms are indivisible and interdependent, and should be balanced, *especially* in the heat of pandemic decision-making, using the well-tested framework of legality, necessity and proportionality provided by international human rights treaties and national laws and constitutions. Empirical measures of human rights compliance in this volume add ballast to this observation, showing that strong (or weak) observance of rights in *any* category tended to correlate with a high (or low) performance across *all* categories.[3] In other words, upholding the rights to life and health, far from requiring states to ride roughshod over (say) freedom of expression or assembly, co-existed with protection of these rights and freedoms in terms of restrictions being properly justified and proportionate.

The corollary of this insight is that public health outcomes should not be the only measure of success (or failure) of a state's response to pandemic disease; the health of the institutions that guard democracy, human rights and the rule of law matter, too, for they will be integral to success or failure in recovery from this pandemic and preparation for future emergencies. Indeed, such preparation requires

3 See Scheinin, chapter 9.

nothing less than the conceptualisation of "public health and health care as part of the fabric of a democratic society",[4] with consequent concern for, inter alia, equality of access and meaningful involvement of communities.

3. Lessons about Preparing for Future Emergencies

Preparation for emergency is invariably informed by experience of the last: put another way, generals are always prepared to fight the last war. The SARS-CoV-2 virus was unique as a pathogen, although coronaviruses were not new to scientific study, which enabled faster identification of diagnostics, therapeutics and vaccines. The next pandemic could be different, and the next global crisis – whether environmental, security or health – will be different, too. As a consequence, we need new and nimble legal and constitutional models which can adapt to the modalities of different threats, without disregarding the essential values which provide them with a basis of legitimacy and rationality. One common reality across all forms of emergency is that the speed of response is a prerequisite for positive outcomes across public health, the economy, public institutions and, ultimately, trust in authority: but a rapid response to future emergencies will, in turn, rely on preparation and the reform of legal provisions, institutions and frameworks where they have been found to be deficient.

Below, we identify lessons in relation to legal reform; use of expertise; inequality; democratic rehabilitation; global and multilevel governance; and truth, rationality and trust.

3.1 Building the Ship in Safe Harbour

The task of review and reform of legal frameworks for emergency situations is a pressing one: to use a metaphor, the strongest ships are built in safe harbour and not in the midst of the storm. In legislation drafted during emergencies, we see a microcosm of the challenges to adherence to rule of law standards where ostensibly 'higher' demands for immediate action to save lives can lead to the sacrifice of procedural and substantive requirements of legal process, leading to legal uncertainty, lack of accountability and unrestricted discretion beyond the proper boundaries of legality. The rapidity with which emergency laws were introduced during the pandemic, providing for unprecedented discretionary powers which have sometimes lingered long on the statute books, frequently showed manifest disregard for the rule of law and democratic norms. The political justificatory rhetoric of exceptionality can ultimately infect the legal culture and law – and policy-making processes.

Where such provisions are extended until they become permanent fixtures of the law, countries risk the "permanence of the temporary"[5] and the 'emergency

4 Alicia Ely Yamin, 'A Wake-Up Call in Our Upside-Down World: Three Starting-Points for Advancing Health Rights and Social Justice in a Post-Pandemic Future' (2020) 12(2) Journal of Human Rights Practice 260, 262.

5 David Dyzenhaus, 'The Permanence of the Temporary: Can Emergency Powers be Normalized?' in Ronald J Daniels and others (eds), *The Security of Freedom* (University of Toronto Press 2001).

creep' of exceptional powers into ordinary modes of governance. The exceptionality of emergency situations will inevitably call for (new) legal provisions where they have not existed before, and the exigencies of a threat can necessitate measures which would not ordinarily be justified. However, emergency conditions do not negate the importance of the 'ordinary': laws made during emergency must be subject to well-established limitations in constitutional and international law – legality, necessity, proportionality and respect for human rights. Critically, they must also be temporary. Adherence to rule of law principles in this way provides a 'perimeter of legitimacy' to the measures.

When the time comes – after the storm – to consider reform of emergency frameworks and their use during emergency, action should be guided not only by interrogation of national response but also by global comparative experience, suitably adapted to local conditions, institutions, cultures and environments. A point of departure will be to examine why emergency frameworks were engaged (or not) and when. This will provide administrations with insights on decision-making and information flow, crisis management, and early identification mechanisms to isolate systemic risk; as well as the capacity of relevant legal frameworks to balance the power to take rapid action with substantive and procedural requirements of legal certainty and legality. In the ultimate reform of law, the focus should be not only on textual provisions but also on the *application* of the law, the *use* of powers, the *oversight* of its enforcement, and the *process* by which laws are made in each national context, with a premium on transparency and accountability.

3.2 Broadening the Range of Voices around the Policy Table

Pandemic preparedness is not only a matter of who makes critical decisions and when, but also who sits around the table to advise the decision-makers, and whose voices are missing. The pandemic revealed diverse approaches to the *types* of expertise harnessed by political decision makers. Where COVID-19 bred 'shadow' pandemics of educational deprivation, domestic violence, unemployment, poverty, isolation and mental health crises, further and broader expertise in both the sciences and social sciences is needed to inform not only immediate measures, but also longer-term strategies for recovery. The contributions to this volume suggest that experts in human rights, constitutional law or democratic governance were rarely among the epistemic communities, such as epidemiologists and economists, with a seat at national policy tables or exerting influence on public discourse (with exceptions, such as Germany and Finland). This realisation creates a dual onus – on those with expertise in law and governance to find ways to insert their voices into debates about post-pandemic reform, and on state institutions and policy-makers to spread their nets wider in respect of the forms of expertise and academic disciplines seen as indispensable to this endeavour.

3.3 Confronting the Unequal Burden of the Pandemic

Other voices that were deprioritised during COVID-19 were those of already marginalised populations: not only were they most negatively affected by the pandemic in terms of illness and death, but they were also most isolated from any protections that governments extended, and least able to affect change through democratic voice.[6] Chapter after chapter in this volume reveals the extent to which minority communities and those living on the social periphery fared disproportionately badly, paying with their lives and livelihoods for measures that aggravated pre-existing patterns of disadvantage and discrimination, or actively targeted them through, for example, punitive policing of COVID-19 restrictions or stigmatisation on the basis of characteristics such as race or religion. Further structural injustice is being perpetuated by the exclusion of certain populations, by unconscious design or neglect, from rollouts of COVID-19 vaccinations.

Evaluations of pandemic responses and preparations for future emergency must, as a starting point, recognise the direct and indirect discrimination which caused the grotesque distortion in the burden of the pandemic along lines of gender, race, ethnicity, disability, class and other socially constructed vulnerabilities, and quantify its effects through disaggregated data. On the strength of that analysis, governance structures at both national and international level must identify and dismantle structural barriers to health care, vaccines, social protection and access to justice.[7] This in turn will require the voices, knowledge and experiences of the most deeply affected populations to be amplified in the debate about post-pandemic recovery. This is not only normatively desirable but also of instrumental value, since community mobilisation, especially when informed by experience of past pandemics, has been shown to compensate for the frailties of state responses. Moreover, active political and democratic engagement across the most diverse range of society is essential to (re)build public trust in democratic institutions and their capacity to manage crisis.

3.4 Rehabilitating Democratic Institutions

A recurrent theme of this volume is the opportunity, forged by the scale and intensity of the calamity, for transformative thinking about what it means to govern, and to govern democratically.[8] The virus peeled back the accreted layers of convention to reveal not only injustices and dysfunctions but also the seeds of resilience and renewal. Remarkable accounts of creativity and solidarity at grassroots level abound, whether to give voice to protest, organise citizens' assemblies or initiate community-based media and alternative sources of public information. Governments, policymakers, jurists, scholars and citizens – all these constituencies have had to confront the challenges of very different and adapted modes of operation and day-to-day living. But the necessity of adaptation created the opportunity for re-making democratic governance. All must seize this chance before the relief of waning infection rates causes modes of governance that have been found so

6 See Al Saba and Gougsa, chapter 32.

7 See Singh, chapter 2.

8 See Daly, chapter 1.

desperately wanting to reassert themselves, and again fall short in response to the challenges of decades to come. The anaemic term 'new normal' does not capture the ambition required. The pandemic must not only shake us out of complacency but has also provided us with insights and tools to effect transformation.

Documented within this volume are experiments with technological innovations in the conduct of elections and parliamentary and court proceedings which could achieve permanent gains in their accessibility and inclusiveness. Live broadcast of parliamentary proceedings, virtual access to justice, networked communication across civil society and accessible lines of engagement between citizens and authorities capitalised on our increasingly digitised world. However, as a qualification, such innovation has to be supported by infrastructure and education: for example, where government services during the pandemic were *only* provided online, they were exclusionary and isolating for the digitally disenfranchised. The effective realisation of democratic innovation requires not only adaptation and adoption but also investment in, and equitable access to, digital technologies. Long-standing practices can also serve to support democratic renewal when applied with fresh commitment to achieving a dialogic conception of democratic accountability: for example, establishing specialised parliamentary committees and inquiries, and requiring mandated and regular reporting to substantiate official claims and evaluate the impact of law and policy.

Above all, democratic rehabilitation requires a reversal of the trend towards the marginalisation of parliaments and the passivity of courts, to the detriment of any effective separation of powers or accountability of government. A pandemic, we have learned, does not absolve these bodies of the responsibility of oversight, but heighten the need for it to be robust, independent and responsive to dynamic conditions.

3.5 *Effectively Engaging Levels of Governance from Global to Local*

Structural dysfunctions, and the division of power and authority across levels of governance, have also been exposed in the pandemic. From the point at which the World Health Organisation declared COVID-19 as a Public Health Emergency of International Concern on 30 January 2020, institutions of global governance have been under the spotlight in terms of their pandemic response. Criticism was levelled at the perceived failure of global governance in effectively tackling the crisis. Successes have been qualified: for example, where information flow based on 'open data' principles allowed for the shared identification of new strains and quicker development of therapeutics and vaccines, these have not necessarily resulted in equitable access to the fruits of this labour, which requires a rethink of the means to ensure good global data governance and stewardship.[9] Even as discussions are ongoing as to the possibility of a 'pandemic treaty' or other legal instrument against the backdrop of the identified deficiencies of the

9 See Staunton, chapter 24.

International Health Regulations (2005), further immediate steps can be advised. The World Health Organisation, and similar international organisations, should provide more concrete guidance on state obligations during a pandemic – including their human rights obligations. International human rights institutions might also revisit their procedures to encourage formal derogation during global public health emergencies (with their requirements of temporariness and proportionality) rather than relying on hard-to-monitor limitations clauses.[10] In negotiating any new international legal instrument, asymmetries in capacity must be reflected: to ensure legitimacy, collective investment and adaptability to local conditions, a democratised process involving wide representation and participation from varied constituencies, including civil society across countries of differing income and resource levels, must be present.

Focusing on global governance for future emergency response, however, does not accurately reflect lived experience in countries during the COVID-19 pandemic wherein most action was undertaken by national executives, largely to the exclusion of any international coordination or influence. Reflected, too, within the panoply of approaches is the division of power and responsibility between different levels of (national) government: federal, provincial, state, regional and local authorities. The pandemic frequently revealed conflict between the centre and the periphery, particularly where there were ideological divisions as to the degree of threat that the virus posed, or disagreement about the economic or political costs of restrictive measures (as evidenced in the fractious dissent in some US states and Pakistani provinces against federal executives). A breakdown in communication and information flow between levels of government (as, for example, between the central Westminster government and the devolved legislatures in the United Kingdom) has the effect of weakening coordination, just as an entirely centralised response loses the advantages of local adaptation and 'buy in'. Conversely, where (as in Sweden, and initially in China) administrative functions and regulatory capacity are highly decentralised, there are risks of creating a siloed mentality which does not take account of the innate interconnectedness of societies.

This volume reveals instances where indecisiveness and lack of coordination at federal level, or institutional incapacity to regulate regions, caused chaos and uncertainty, as it required local leaders to assume control without the benefit of any centralised or coordinated measures (as happened in Pakistan). However, sub-national governance can also provide an arena in which democratic recession at the centre can be resisted and reversed. These decentralised and even subversive trends are visible, for example, in the revival of 'free cities' in the face of the authoritarian drift in eastern Europe, or the coordinating action of local governments in the Philippines. A simple formula would be to advocate for sub-national authorities to have the capacity for local adaptation to enable investment, ownership and responsibility as close to the 'front line' as possible, but with necessary coordination at national level, and solidarity at global level to ensure that "knowledge and

10 As proposed by Emmons, chapter 30.

resources are shared equitably, and that recovery and resilience for all are perceived as humankind's shared responsibility".[11]

3.6 Building Trust Through Truth and Rationality in Public Discourse

Beyond institutional reform, the 'post-pandemic' period must see concerted efforts to reverse the tide of disinformation that poisons public discourse, disparages expertise, eschews evidence and propagates conspiratorial and discriminatory rhetoric. These lamentable practices have been at times officially sponsored, and at other times manipulated by insurgent groups such as 'anti-vaxxers'. Another much-needed aspect of democratic renewal, then, is to rehabilitate not only its institutional forms but also its epistemic basis – the very 'rules of the game' by which democratic politics is played. This requires that debate and disagreement across ideological, religious or other boundaries is conducted on a spectrum of reason and informed by evidence. It also requires that the exercise of power carries with it the expectation of reasoned public justification. This is the "culture of justification" espoused by Mureinik, who foresaw in post-apartheid South Africa a "community built on persuasion, not coercion", in which "leadership given by government rests on the cogency of the case offered in defence of its decisions, not the fear inspired by the force at its command".[12] The revival of such a culture is timely since both COVID-19 and earlier pandemics such as HIV-AIDS showed that coercion alone is not a sustainable means of ensuring compliance with the restrictive measures needed to suppress infection. The resort to criminal sanctions, punitive policing and stigmatisation as the primary means of enforcement (as in Kenya and the Philippines) suggested that no lessons had been learned about the value of social solidarity, community mobilisation, clear and accessible public communication and the formation of trust in combatting disease.

This volume suggests that trust was a precious yet elusive asset during the pandemic. Jasanoff and Hilgartner venture that it is in the realm of politics, rather than in technocratic arenas, that "trusting relations are built among citizens, between citizens and the state, and among states and international organisations".[13] Politicians and (later) judges must weigh the merit of developing scientific findings and sometimes conflicting expert advice. Some did so with admirable clarity and consistency (as in Finland, New Zealand, Rwanda and Taiwan). Yet our contributors point to numerous instances where science was politicised and partisanship trumped evidence to fatal effect (recall leaders such as Bolsonaro, Modi and Trump who flouted scientific consensus by holding 'superspreader' events, promoting quack cures and ridiculing mask-wearing mandates). Elsewhere, in

11 Jasanoff and Hilgartner, chapter 23, 292–293.

12 Etienne Mureinik, 'A Bridge to Where? Introducing the Interim Bill of Rights' (1994) 10(1) South African Journal on Human Rights 31, 32.

13 Jasanoff and Hilgartner, chapter 23, 293.

both authoritarian states (including China) and democratic states, there was no significant public controversy about the scientific evidence, in part due to prior experience of pandemics and consequent trust in the ability of state institutions to manage COVID-19.

Looking ahead, attention must be paid to the "principles of delegation and accountability" by which scientific expertise exerts political influence, and potential reform of the "institutional processes for integrating scientific and political consensus-building", since trust in health expertise has been shown to depend on trust in wider political authority.[14] A guiding principle here is transparency, for example in respect of the terms of reference and membership of scientific advisory bodies and the guidance they provide, together with a commitment by governments to respect their integrity and independence (South Africa, where experts who criticised the government's performance were removed from ministerial advisory committees, provides cautionary experience). Transparency and consensus-building are not merely normative desirable, but also instrumental in achieving public health outcomes, since those subject to onerous restrictions must be convinced that their sacrifices serve both the individual and collective good. Like the reform of democratic institutions, this task of (re)building public trust is urgent, and cannot wait for the next emergency to strike, for trust is a currency that is slowly earned and quickly squandered.

4. 'Post-Pandemic'

Trust in the 'post-pandemic' world must continue to be built on the basis of rational and well-informed analysis, and in this we must again pay tribute to the global community of scholars and advocates engaged in the promotion of democracy, human rights and the rule of law as essential components of post-COVID-19 recovery, among them the contributors to this volume. They shine the brightest light on the corrosive practices that must be eliminated and the gains that must be preserved. We hope readers in a post-pandemic future will be guided and inspired by their insights, for only in collective and critical reflection can we understand the lessons of our past and present, that we may better prepare for our future.

14 ibid, 294, 297.

INDEX

Note: Page numbers in *italics* indicate figures, **bold** indicate tables